Mandela: The Authorised Biography

ANTHONY SAMPSON had been ke [illegible] s since 1951 when, after leaving Ox [illegible] o become editor of the black maga [illegible] t Nelson Mandela that year in Sow [illegible] e Defiance Campaign against apart [illegible].

In 1956 Anthony Sampson pub [illegible] r-taining account of his four years as editor (*Drum: An African Adventure*) – and frequently revisited South Africa thereafter. Subsequently he wrote a book about the Treason Trials in 1958, and reported Mandela's own trial before he was sentenced to life imprisonment in 1964.

In London Sampson worked for the *Observer* for six years before publishing (in 1962) his groundbreaking, bestselling *Anatomy of Britain* (later updated four times, and read by Mandela in prison). He followed it with a succession of major books about international affairs, including *The Seven Sisters*, *The Arms Bazaar*, *Black and Gold* (an account of the relations between business and apartheid) and *Company Man*. Anthony Sampson died in 2004.

The Afterword

As political commentator, editor and foreign correspondent, John Battersby has covered the unfolding of South Africa's epic transition to democracy as correspondent for the *New York Times* and the *Christian Science Monitor* and as editor of the *Sunday Independent* in Johannesburg. Battersby collaborated with Anthony Sampson as friend, mentor and editor over two decades (1985 to 2005) and assisted Anthony's widow, Sally, in setting up the Anthony Sampson Foundation to encourage analytical journalism in South Africa. Since 2004 he has been engaged in advocacy work in the United Kingdom for Brand South Africa, an agency of the South African government. He is the co-author with award-winning American author and editor David Elliot Cohen of *Nelson Mandela: A Life in Photographs*.

From the reviews of *Mandela*:

'The central challenge any serious biographer of Nelson Mandela confronts is to track, dissect and explain how it was that he managed to reconcile a nation so bitterly divided by the perversions of apartheid; to bring stability where the scale of the injustice, and the potential for bloodshed, was biblical. Anthony Sampson's authorised biography of one of the century's great individuals, of South Africa's indispensable man, achieves just that. And he does so, at Mandela's express bidding, without stooping to hagiography. The triumph of *Mandela* is that it successfully demythologises the man without in any way undermining his heroic stature … Anthony Sampson's work will endure as a lasting monument to Mandela's imperishable greatness' JOHN CARLIN, *New York Times Book Review*

'Definitive … Sampson continually surprises with depth, nuance and freshness … It is the standard Mandela text, the comprehensive text, the biographical centrepiece about which all else, fundamental or ephemeral, will be arranged … [Sampson] has simply gone further than his predecessors, dug deeper, thought about the subject more, and viewed the life of his man through a wider lens … The treatment of the decline of the marriage to Winnie is exceptional: sensitive, straightforward and detailed'
Johannesburg Star

'Engrossing … Sampson was not just an inspired choice for the authorised biography; in a sense he was the only one … His writing has an Orwellian clarity and stylishness … He has had unparalleled access to private papers and to key interviewees … and has produced an absorbing, revealing study … At the end, we are left with the feeling that, insofar as it is possible to know any man by reading words on a page, we know Mandela with something approaching intimacy' JOHN HORGAN, *Irish Times*

'A magisterial, detailed and invaluable account of one of this century's greatest figures … it is hard to believe that a better biography will ever be written' JUSTIN CARTWRIGHT, *Sunday Telegraph*

'Measured, detailed without a moment of tedium, incisive in its perceptions and, at times, profoundly moving. It is worthy of its subject'
RONALD SEGAL, *Observer*

'This will be the last word on Mandela for years to come; it also becomes the central text in all future discussion of the momentous and peaceful transfer of power from white to black in South Africa ... it will be hard to improve upon this crowning conclusion to Sampson's long career as a loving and expert chronicler of South Africa'

J.D.F. JONES, *Evening Standard*

'Anthony Sampson's authorised biography is warmly to be welcomed, not least because it is more substantial and revealing than Mandela's bestselling autobiography ... This biography is a great leap forward in our understanding of a man who is both enigmatic and private ... Sampson has carried out his difficult commission with skill and sensitivity'

DENIS JUDD, *Independent*

'This is the book for which Anthony Sampson has been in training for half a century and which he has been incubating for some years now. He has the advantage of stamina, of intimacy with the subject, of access to the stable gossip and to a good deal of information from the horse's mouth ... This will for a long time be the definitive life'

MAURICE HAYES, *Sunday Independent* (Ireland)

'A great strength of Anthony Sampson's thoroughly researched book is that the author stands at an ideal distance from his imposing subject ... He has also had the credentials to talk very personally with many of Mandela's allies and rivals within the movement for African freedom'

ANGUS CALDER, *Scotland on Sunday*

'The task Sampson set himself was to penetrate the myth and write about the man rather than the icon ... In the process he has produced a lucid, often moving and always readable book ... The chapters on Mandela's twenty-seven years of imprisonment make compelling reading ... Sampson leaves us with an understanding of the man that does transcend the myth'

GILLIAN SLOVO, *Financial Times*

'The definitive political biography ... Sampson threads it all together into a rich tapestry, replete with anecdotes and colourful quotes from friends and enemies, prison warders and presidents. He has some valuable new insights on the importance of the prison years for Mandela, both as a human being and as a politician'

RICHARD DOWDEN, *Tablet*

'Masterly … Anyone wishing to understand the transition and South Africa's first five years of democratic rule should start here … a monumental piece of work which is likely to stand for many years as the definitive biography of Mandela'

SHULA MARKS, *Times Higher Education Supplement*

'A richly detailed political history, a generous portrait of a consummate politician, and a true profile in courage – a courage both unimaginably immense and stunningly rare' *Kirkus Reviews*

'Superb … It is an amazing story … Sampson was an inspired choice as authorised biographer' BRYAN ROSTRON, *The Oldie*

Also by Anthony Sampson

DRUM: A VENTURE INTO THE NEW AFRICA
THE TREASON CAGE
COMMONSENSE ABOUT AFRICA
ANATOMY OF BRITAIN
ANATOMY OF BRITAIN TODAY
MACMILLAN: A STUDY IN AMBIGUITY
THE NEW EUROPEANS
THE NEW ANATOMY OF BRITAIN
THE SOVEREIGN STATE
THE SEVEN SISTERS
THE ARMS BAZAAR
THE MONEY LENDERS
THE CHANGING ANATOMY OF BRITAIN
EMPIRES OF THE SKY
BLACK AND GOLD
THE MIDAS TOUCH
THE ESSENTIAL ANATOMY OF BRITAIN
THE OXFORD BOOK OF AGES *(with Sally Sampson)*
COMPANY MAN
THE SCHOLAR GYPSY
WHO RUNS THIS PLACE? THE ANATOMY OF BRITAIN IN THE 21ST CENTURY
THE ANATOMIST

MANDELA

The Authorised Biography

ANTHONY SAMPSON

Now with updated material by John Battersby

Harper
Press

Harper*Press*
An imprint of HarperCollins*Publishers*
77–85 Fulham Palace Road
Hammersmith, London W6 8JB

This Harper*Press* paperback edition published 2011

1

First published by Harper*Press* in 1999
Published in paperback in 2000,
reprinted 14 times

A catalogue record for this book is
available from the British Library

ISBN 978-0-00-743797-9

Set in PostScript Linotype Minion with Photina
and Castellar display by Rowland Phototypesetting Ltd,
Bury St Edmunds, Suffolk

Printed and bound in Great Britain by
Clays Ltd, St Ives plc

MIX
Paper from
responsible sources
FSC C007454

FSC is a non-profit international organisation established to promote the responsible management of the world's forests. Products carrying the FSC label are independently certified to assure customers that they come from forests that are managed to meet the social, economic and ecological needs of present and future generations, and other controlled sources.

Find out more about HarperCollins and the environment at
www.harpercollins.co.uk/green

CONTENTS

ILLUSTRATIONS

The plain thatched *rondavel* which was the home of the young Mandela from the age of nine. *(Photograph reproduced courtesy of the Mayibuye Centre/Link Picture Library)*

Chief Jongintaba Dalindyebo, Mandela's guardian for much of his youth.

The nineteen-year-old Mandela. *(Photograph reproduced courtesy of the Mayibuye Centre/Link Picture Library)*

In 1944 Mandela was married in Johannesburg to Evelyn Mase. *(Photograph reproduced courtesy of the Mayibuye Centre/Link Picture Library)*

Mandela in the offices of Mandela & Tambo. *(Photograph © Jürgen Schadeberg)*

Black Johannesburg in the 1950s was bursting with creative energy. *(Photograph © Jürgen Schadeberg)*

Mandela immersed in protests against the apartheid government, with Walter Sisulu, J.B. Marks and Ruth First. *(Photograph © Jürgen Schadeberg)*

In the Defiance Campaign of 1952 Mandela worked alongside both the conservative Dr Moroka and the communist Dr Dadoo. *(Photograph © Jürgen Schadeberg)*

Mandela sparred regularly with boxing champions like Jerry Moloi. *(Photograph by Bob Gosani for Drum Magazine. © Bailey's African History Archives/Link Picture Library)*

The accused in the Treason Trial which began in 1957.

Mandela's wedding to his second wife Winnie in 1958.

Winnie, Mandela and their second daughter Zindzi, photographed in 1961. *(Photograph © Alf Kumalo)*

Mandela at the Treason Trial in 1958. *(Photograph © Jürgen Schadeberg)*

Mandela burns his pass-book in the turmoil after the Sharpeville massacre in 1960. *(Photograph © IDAF/Sipa Press/Rex Features)*

Mandela meets the exiled Oliver Tambo at a conference in Ethiopia in 1962. *(Photograph reproduced courtesy of the Mayibuye Centre/Link Picture Library)*

At the military headquarters in Algeria, Mandela and Robert Resha met revolutionary leaders and received advice about guerrilla warfare.

Mandela in London in June 1962. *(Photograph by Mary Benson)*

The eight men sentenced to life imprisonment at the Rivonia trial in 1964. *(Photograph reproduced courtesy of the Mayibuye Centre/Link Picture Library)*

Mandela's mother came to Pretoria in 1964 for her son's trial, and watched him being sentenced to life imprisonment. Four years afterwards she visited him on Robben Island, and died a few weeks later. *(Photograph © Alf Kumalo)*

Prisoners, including Mandela, in the Robben Island courtyard in 1965. *(Photograph © Juhan Kuus/Sipa Press/Rex Features)*

Mandela and Sisulu on Robben Island. *(Photograph reproduced courtesy of the Mayibuye Centre/Link Picture Library)*

Kaiser Matanzima, Mandela's nephew and earlier his hero, visits Winnie in Soweto. *(Photograph © Alf Kumalo)*

Mandela in the garden on Robben Island in 1977 with the Namibian leader Toivo ja Toivo and Justice Mpanza. *(Photograph © Reuters/Popperfoto)*

Images of Mandela:

The handsome man-about-town with his glamorous young wife Winnie. *(Photograph reproduced courtesy of the Mayibuye Centre/Link Picture Library)*

The bearded 'Black Pimpernel'. *(Photograph reproduced courtesy of the Mayibuye Centre/Link Picture Library)*

The Xhosa prince appearing in tribal regalia for his trial in 1962.

The larger-than-life bust of Mandela on London's South Bank, unveiled by Oliver Tambo in 1985. *(Photograph © Jillian Edelstein/Link Picture Library)*

Mandela emerges from prison, hand-in-hand with Winnie. *(Photograph © Argus/I-Afrika/Link Picture Library)*

The first meeting between the ANC and the government in May 1990. *(Photograph © Benny Gool/PictureNET Africa/Link Picture Library)*

Mandela and de Klerk at the national peace conference in Johannesburg in September 1991, smiling … *(Photograph © Rodger Bosch/I-Afrika/Link Picture Library)*

… and glowering. *(Photograph © Rodger Bosch/I-Afrika/Link Picture Library)*

Zulu Chief Buthelezi refuses to shake hands with Mandela and de Klerk at the end of the conference. *(Photograph © Louise Gubb/I-Afrika/Link Picture Library)*

Mandela and the ninety-four-year-old widow of Hendrik Verwoerd. *(Photograph © Henner Frankenfeld/PictureNET Africa/Link Picture Library)*

Mandela visits Verwoerd's statue. *(Photograph © Reuters/Popperfoto)*

Mandela and Percy Yutar, who as prosecutor had helped to send him to jail for twenty-seven years. *(Photograph © Louise Gubb/I-Afrika/Link Picture Library)*

Mandela and P.W. Botha. *(Photograph © PA News)*

Mandela presents Springbok captain Francois Pienaar with the 1995 rugby World Cup. *(Photograph © PA News)*

Mandela and Winnie with lawyers Ismail Ayob and George Bizos at Winnie's 1991 trial for kidnapping Stompie Seipei. *(Photograph © Link Picture Library)*

Mandela takes President Clinton to see his old cell on Robben Island. *(Photograph © PA News)*

Mandela and the Queen during his 1996 state visit to Britain. *(Photograph © Louise Buller/Associated Press)*

Mandela with Diana, Princess of Wales. *(Photograph © PA News)*

Mandela with a group of his grandchildren. *(Photograph © Siphiwe Mhlambi/Sygma)*

Thabo Mbeki succeeds Mandela as President of the ANC in December 1997. *(Photograph © PA News)*

Mandela's eightieth birthday banquet in July 1998 also became the celebration of his wedding to Graca. *(Photograph © Sygma)*

Mandela is greeted by President-elect Jacob Zuma. *(Photograph © AFP/Getty Images)*

Mandela at the 2010 World Cup Final. *(Photograph © AFP/Getty Images)*

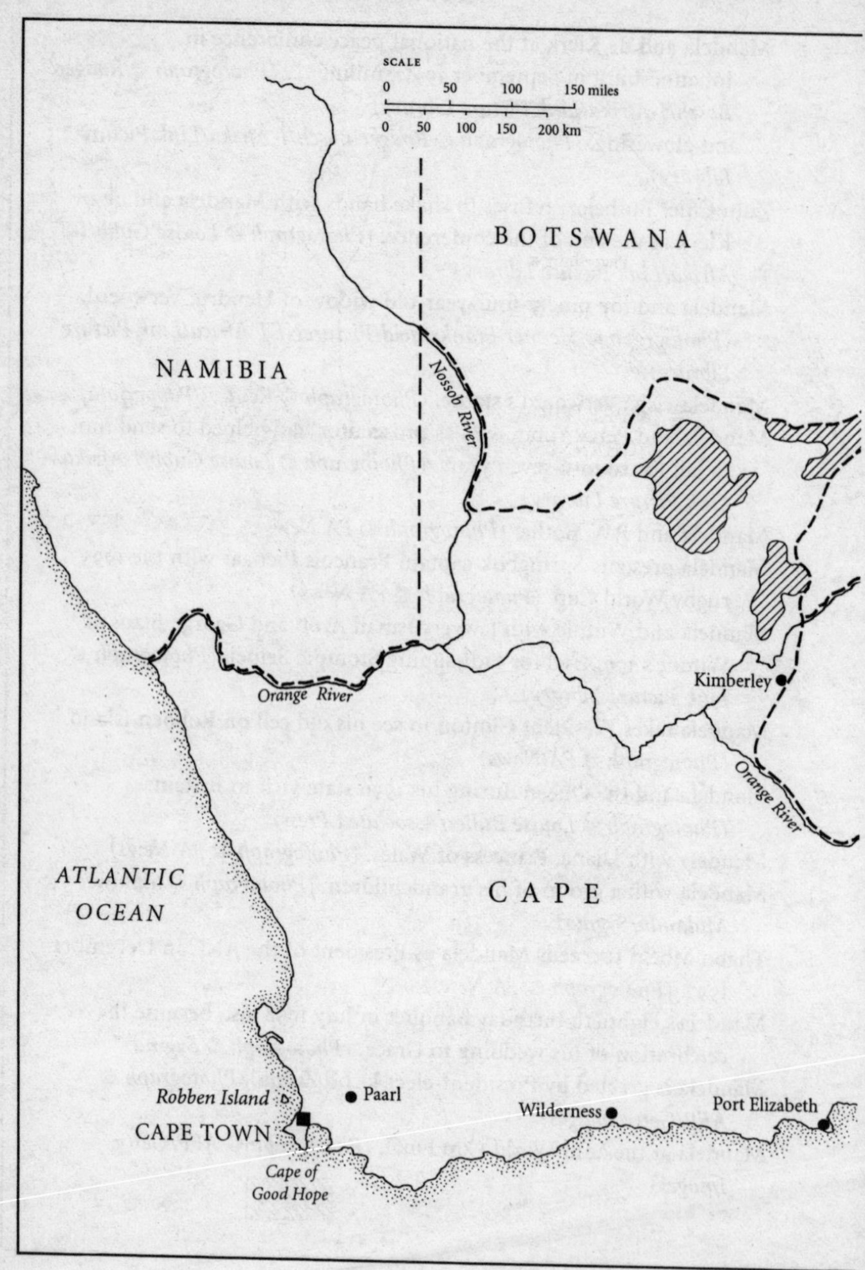
SCALE
0
50
100
150 miles
0
50
100
150
200 km
BOTSWANA
NAMIBIA
Nossob River
Orange River
Kimberley
Orange River
ATLANTIC
OCEAN
CAPE
Robben Island
Paarl
Wilderness
Port Elizabeth
CAPE TOWN
Cape of
Good Hope

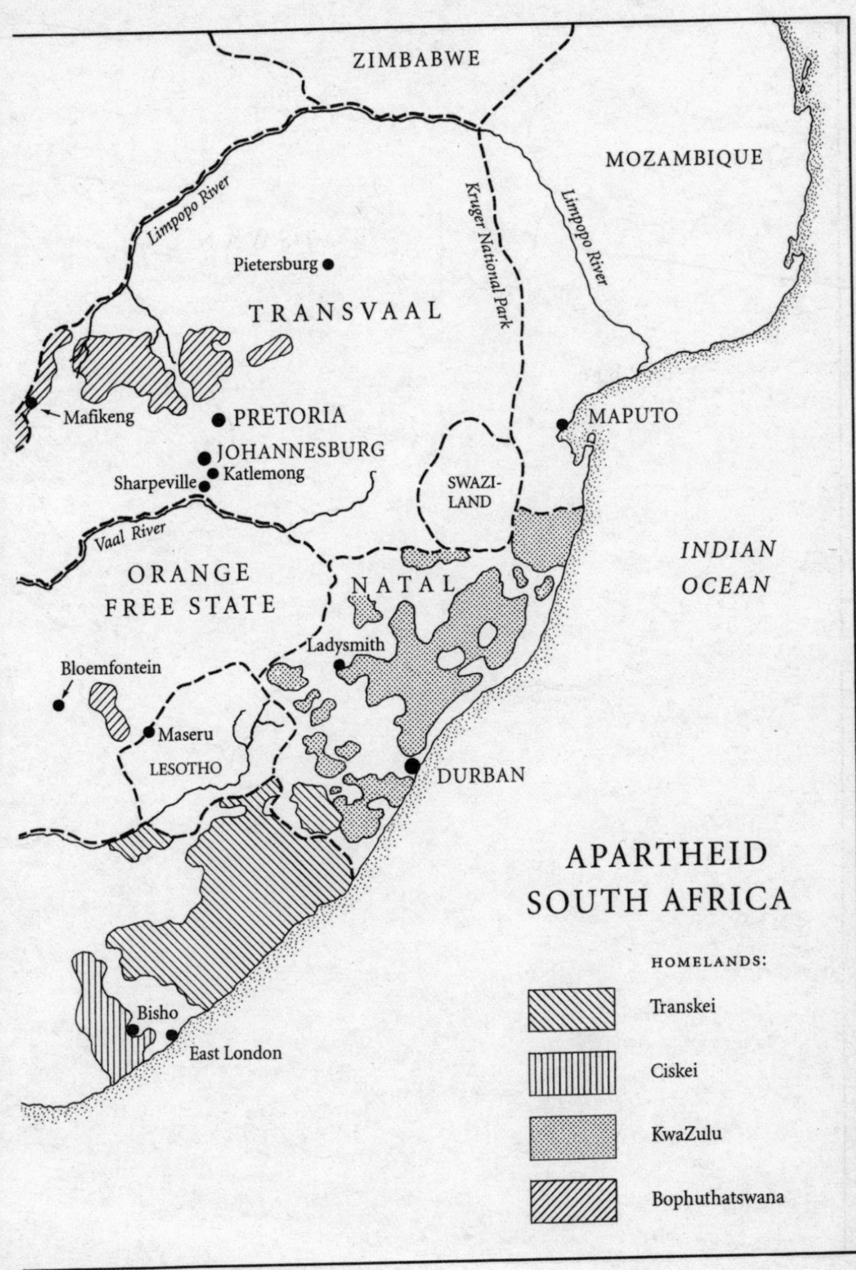
ZIMBABWE
MOZAMBIQUE
Limpopo River
Kruger National Park
Limpopo River
Pietersburg
TRANSVAAL
Mafikeng
PRETORIA
MAPUTO
JOHANNESBURG
Katlemong
Sharpeville
SWAZI-
LAND
Vaal River
INDIAN
OCEAN
ORANGE
FREE STATE
NATAL
Ladysmith
Bloemfontein
Maseru
LESOTHO
DURBAN
APARTHEID
SOUTH AFRICA
HOMELANDS:
Transkei
Bisho
East London
Ciskei
KwaZulu
Bophuthatswana

INTRODUCTION

I am conscious of both the unusual opportunity and the responsibility in undertaking this book. When I wrote to President Mandela in 1995 suggesting an authorised biography he invited me to breakfast in his house in Johannesburg, and told me he would like me to write it because of our long friendship – 'Provided,' he joked, 'that you don't mention that we first met in a shebeen.' He reminded me that he had read my book *Anatomy of Britain* when he was awaiting trial in 1962. He promised to discuss critical questions with me, to try to ensure that the facts were accurate, and to let me see relevant letters and documents. But he would leave me free to make my own judgements and criticisms: it was important, he said, for the movement to learn from mistakes; and, he insisted, 'I'm no angel.'

It had been my good luck to have first known Mandela in Johannesburg in 1951, and to have seen him at several decisive moments over the next decade before he went to prison. I first encountered him after I had come out to South Africa to edit the black magazine *Drum*, which opened all doors into the vibrant and exciting world of black writers, musicians and politicians in the Johannesburg in which Mandela moved, and gave me a front seat from which to observe the mounting black opposition to the apartheid government which had come to power in 1948. I attended the ANC conference which approved the Defiance Campaign of 1952; I watched Mandela organising the first volunteers, and mobilising resistance in 1954 to the destruction of Sophiatown, the multi-racial slum where I had spent many happy evenings. In 1957 I saw him frequently at the Treason Trial, about which I later wrote a book; and in 1960, as a correspondent of the *Observer*, I covered the Sharpeville crisis and interviewed Mandela in Soweto just after the massacre. My last, poignant sight of him was in 1964, when I was observing the Rivonia trial in Pretoria, which gave me a chance to see the final speech he was then preparing (see pp.192–3). As a journalist I could not see Mandela during his twenty-seven years in prison, but I revisited black South Africa and kept in touch with exiles in London and elsewhere. In the mid-1980s, when the conflict was escalating, I saw much of Oliver Tambo, the ANC President, in London, and arranged meetings for him with British businessmen. I also talked often to Winnie Mandela by telephone. I returned to Johannesburg for the crises of 1985 and 1986, preparing a book about black politics and business, *Black and Gold*, before the South African government in 1986 banned me from returning. My ban was temporarily lifted just in time for me to return before Mandela's release from jail in February 1990; later, I visited him twice a week in his Soweto house. Over the next four years I saw him many times, both in London – where he asked me to introduce him at fund-raising receptions – and in Johannesburg, to which I often returned, and where I watched the elections of April 1994.

Since beginning this book I have made several journeys through South Africa with my wife Sally, trying to piece together the jigsaw of Mandela's varied life, while immersing myself in the fast-changing contemporary scene. I have seen President Mandela in contrasted settings: in his offices and mansions in Pretoria and Cape Town, in his own house in Houghton, on Robben Island, at banquets and conferences, in Parliament in Cape Town, at the UN in New York or at state occasions in London. I have travelled to the Great Place where he was brought up in the Transkei, and to his new house in Qunu. I have talked to scores of his old friends and colleagues, but also to his former opponents, whether warders, officials or political leaders – including ex-President P.W. Botha in Wilderness, ex-President F.W. de Klerk in Cape Town, and the former Foreign Minister Pik Botha in the Transvaal.

Mandela's moving autobiography *Long Walk to Freedom*, published in 1994, has provided his own invaluable record of his political development; I have had generous advice from his collaborator Richard Stengel, whose recorded interviews with Mandela have also been useful. I have also been given access to the unpublished memoir which Mandela wrote in jail, and have seen the original manuscript in his own hand. But Mandela's own autobiography, published when he had first become President, with political discretion and modesty, leaves all the more scope for a many-sided picture which can describe him as others saw him, show how he interacted with friends and enemies, and put his life into a global context.

In writing this book I have tried to show the harsh realities of Mandela's long and adventurous life as they appeared to him and to his friends at the time, stripped of the gloss of mythology and romance; but also to trace how the glittering image of Mandela was magnified while he was in jail, acquiring its own power and influence across the world; and to show how the prisoner was able to relate the image to reality.

I have given special emphasis to the long years in prison, with the help of extensive interviews, unpublished letters and documents; for Mandela's prison story has unique value to a biographer, with its human intensity and tests of character, providing an intimate play rather than a wide-ranging pageant; and Mandela's relationships with his friends and warders became a universal drama, with a significance that transcended African politics. The prison years are often portrayed as a long hiatus in the midst of Mandela's political career; but I see them as the key to his development, transforming the headstrong activist into the reflective and self-disciplined world statesman.

I also try to put Mandela's life into a wider global context, with the help of his letters and hitherto unpublished diplomatic and intelligence sources. I trace how the Western world misunderstood and mishandled the gathering South African crisis in the 1960s and seventies, and was misled about Mandela and his friends through the obsessions and crusades of the Cold War; how he so nearly disappeared from the world's radar screens, and how governments and individuals contributed to his triumphant return. I have tried to trace the changing and contradictory perceptions of South Africa in the outside world, providing first dire predictions of an imminent bloodbath, then a model of negotiation and reconciliation, with Mandela at the centre.

In this ambitious task I owe an obvious huge debt to President Mandela himself, who has been generous with his precious time, not only by giving personal interviews, but by reading the draft typescripts. He has corrected points of fact and detail, while honouring the agreement not to interfere with my own judgements; and his lively comments have added rather than subtracted from the original draft. It has been a rare experience to have such exchanges with a major historical figure in his own lifetime, which I hope compensates for any of the limitations of a contemporary biographer.

I also owe debts to Mandela's close friends, some of whom have been friends of mine since the early fifties. Ahmed Kathrada, Mandela's colleague in jail for twenty-five years, has been my chief adviser and a major source throughout the enterprise, and has unlocked doors which would otherwise have remained closed; he has selflessly given long interviews and allowed me to see his valuable letters – which will soon be published. Walter Sisulu, whom I often interviewed in the fifties and sixties, has patiently given his time for long, reflective talks, adding his special insights into the political background and thinking over fifty years. Mac Maharaj has been through the drafts and has added his unique knowledge of events in and out of jail. Professor Jakes Gerwel, the Secretary of the Cabinet, has given me many ideas and perceptions about Mandela and his government. Nadine Gordimer, my oldest and most valued white South African friend, with whom I usually stayed in Johannesburg, has contributed her unique observations as a close friend of the President and as witness to many historical events. Frank Ferrari, the most distinguished American authority on South Africa, has shared many experiences with me and has added his own judgements. Dr Nthato Motlana, another veteran of the fifties, has been forthcoming with his own witty recollections and insights. Adelaide Tambo, the widow of Oliver Tambo, who has been a friend in both London and Johannesburg, has provided reminiscences and letters which throw new light on the friendship between the Mandelas and the Tambos. George Bizos, Mandela's chief lawyer whom I first met at the Rivonia trial and whom I have seen on every successive visit to South Africa, has been generous with his wisdom and vivid memories from the front line.

Old *Drum* colleagues, who have witnessed the extraordinary changes in South Africa over five decades, have provided their varied recollections and views. They include Jim Bailey, the former owner of *Drum*; Es'kia Mphahlele, the former literary editor; Jürgen Schadeberg, the pioneering photographer and picture editor, and Peter Magubane, his distinguished successor; Arthur Maimane, the versatile writer whom I first lured into journalism in 1951; Esme Matshikiza, widow of the brilliant composer and journalist Todd Matshikiza, together with their son John Matshikiza; and Sylvester Stein, my immediate successor as editor in 1955.

Two former biographers of Mandela, both lifelong friends of the President, have been wonderfully unselfish and forthcoming with advice and documents: Mary Benson, the veteran campaigner against apartheid in London, has had unique insights into the ANC and the Mandela family over forty years; while Fatima Meer, who has seen Mandela through many critical experiences since the fifties, has given me invaluable advice and precious documentation. My old friend Joe Menell generously allowed me to see transcripts of the extensive original interviews for his documentary film about Mandela. For more general advice on difficult problems of biography I am grateful to Michael Holroyd and Arthur Schlesinger.

Among the many new friends who have helped me I am especially grateful to Gail Gerhart, the uniquely well-informed editor of the five-volume history of black politics in South Africa, *From Protest to Challenge*, which is indispensable to any student of the subject. She has been unstinting in her advice and in sharing her sources, including unpublished documents and interviews. I am grateful to Iqbal Meer, President Mandela's London lawyer, both for making the arrangements for the book, and for very constructive suggestions. I have appreciated the help of Ismail Ayob, the President's long-standing attorney in Johannesburg. And I have learnt much from Guy Berger and his colleagues at Rhodes University, where I enjoyed a very productive stay.

I have had wonderful assistance from librarians and archivists in South Africa who have put previously unseen documents at my disposal. They include the Brenthurst Library, with its unique collection in Johannesburg; the Cullen Library at Witwatersrand University; the ANC archives in Shell House, Johannesburg and also at Fort Hare University; the valuable Cory Library at Rhodes University, Grahamstown; the Harry Oppenheimer Library at the University of Cape Town; the Mayibuye archive at the University of the Western Cape; and the admirable press cuttings of the Johannesburg *Star* and the *Cape Times*. I have also been given access to government archives which must remain more discreet. In London my researcher has used the libraries of the School of Oriental and African Studies and the Institute of Commonwealth Studies; while in Washington the National Security Archive has been wonderfully helpful.

My whole task has been made much easier by the energy and resourcefulness of my research assistant Dr James Sanders, who has been persistent in tracking down documents, checking sources, and finding new avenues of investigation which have unearthed remarkable new information from archives in London, Washington and Pretoria. His contribution has gone far beyond research, and I owe much to his creative and scholarly mind, which provided ideas, questions and solutions to difficult problems, and made the whole enterprise less lonely and more enjoyable.

Through the stressful process of editing and preparing the book for publication I have enjoyed marvellous support and cooperation from the team at HarperCollins. The first idea of the book came from Stuart Profitt, without whom it would not have happened; but after he left HarperCollins in 1998 it was strongly backed by the chairman Eddie Bell, by my long-suffering editors Richard Johnson and Robert Lacey, and by Helen Ellis the publicity director, all wonderfully committed to the project. I have also benefited from the encouragement and long experience of my American editor, Charles Elliott of Alfred A. Knopf. I am grateful to Jonathan Ball, my publisher in South Africa, for his help and enthusiasm. My indexer Douglas Matthews has, as with previous books, added his scholarship. As always I have been loyally supported by my agent Michael Sissons, who has now seen me through over twenty books. And I could not have got through the task without my assistant Carla Shimeld, who has once again remained efficient and unflappable in producing order out of chaos. Above all, my enjoyment and human understanding of the subject has been magnified by having my wife Sally with me through many of my travels and interviews.

I have been indebted to many people for corrections and clarifications, but I must take full responsibility for any surviving errors; and I will be grateful for any rectifications and suggestions from readers which I can incorporate in subsequent editions.

I would like to thank all the following people in South Africa who have generously contributed interviews and conversations with myself or my assistant James Sanders (marked with an asterisk):

Rok Ajulu, Neville Alexander, Charles Anson, Kader Asmal, Ismail Ayob, Beryl Baker, Fikile Bam, Niël Barnard, John Battersby, David Beresford, Guy Berger, Hyman Bernadt, George Bizos, Tony Bloom, Alex Boraine, Pieter Botha, Pik Botha, P.W. Botha, Lakhtar Brahimi, Christo Brand, Jules Browde, Gordon Bruce*, Brian Bunting, Mangosuthu Buthelezi, Amina Cachalia, Andrew Cahn, Luli Callinicos, Arthur Chaskalson, Frank Chikane, Colin Coleman, Keith Coleman, Jeremy Cronin, Eddie Daniels, Apollon Davidson, F.W. de Klerk, Ebbe Demmisse, Robin Denniston, Helena Dolny, John Dugard, Barend du Plessis, Tim du Plessis, Dick Endhoven, Ivan Fallon, Barry Feinberg, Ilse Fischer, Maeve Fort, Amina Frense, Phillippa Garson, Mark Gevisser, Angus Gibson, Frene Ginwala, Pippa Green, James Gregory, Louisa Gubb, Adrian Hadland, Anton Harber, Tony Heard, Rica Hodgson, Bantu Holomisa, Evelyn Holtzhausen, John Horak, Verna Hunt, Charlayne Hunter-Gault, Zubeida Jaffer, Joel Joffe, R.W. Johnson, Shaun Johnson, Pallo Jordan, Ronnie and Eleanor Kasrils, Mark Katzenellenbogen, Liza Key, Martin Kingston, Horst Kleinschmidt, Mavis Knipe, Wolfie Kodesh, Alf Kumalo, Terror

Lekota, Hugh Lewin, Tom Lodge, Raymond Louw, Enos Mabuza, Graca Machel, Winnie Madikizela-Mandela, Peter Magubane, Stryker Maguire, Arthur Maimane, Evelyn Mandela, Maki Mandela, Parks Mankahlana, Barbara Masekela, Nathaniel Masemola, Kaiser Matanzima, Don Mattera, Joe Matthews, Govan Mbeki, Thabo Mbeki, Iqbal Meer, Irene Menell, Roelf Meyer, Raymond Mhlaba, Abdul Minty, Joe Mogotsi, Ismail Mohammed, Popo Molefe, Eric Molobi, Ronnie Momoepa, Ruth Mompati, Murphy and Martha Morobe, Shaun Morrow, Mendi Msimang, Mary Mxadana, Beyers Naude, Joel Netshitenzhe, Lionel Ngakane, Carl Niehaus, Wiseman Nkhuhlu, Kaizer Nyatsumba, Andre Odendaal, Chloe O'Keefe, Marie Olivier, Dullah Omar, Harry Oppenheimer, Tony O'Reilly, Aziz Pahad, Essop Pahad, Sophie Pedder, Benjamin Pogrund, Cyril Ramaphosa, Narissa Ramdani, Mamphela Ramphele, Dolly Rathebe, Bryan Rostron, Anthony Rowell, John Rudd, Albie Sachs, Peter Saraf, Raks Seakhoa, Jeremy Seekings, Ronald Segal, Michael Seifert, Wally Serote, Tokyo Sexwale, Lazar Sidelsky, Mike Siluma, Albertina Sisulu, Elinor Sisulu, Zwelakhe Sisulu, Gillian Slovo, Mungo Soggott, Roger Southall, Allister Sparks, Tim Stapleton, Hendrik Steyn, John Sutherland, Helen Suzman, Tony Trew, Ben Turok, Desmond Tutu, Philip van Niekerk, Xolisa Vapi, Ben Verster, Esther Waugh, Enid Webster, Leon Wessels, General Johan Willemse, Moegsien Williams, Jacob Zuma.

And to the following in London and elsewhere abroad:

Heribert Adam, David Astor, Mary Benson, Rusty and Hilda Bernstein, Betty Boothroyd, Lord Camoys, Cheryl Carolus, Lady (Lynda) Chalker, John Colvin, Ethel de Keyser, David Dinkins, John Doubleday, Richard Dowden, Marcus Edwards, Eleanor Emery*, Sir Patrick Fairweather, Michael Gavshon, Dennis Goldberg, Denis Healey, Sir Edward Heath, Denis Herbstein, Eric Hobsbawm, George Houser*, Trevor Huddleston, Lord (Bob) Hughes, Paul and Adelaide Joseph, Glenys Kinnock, Brian Lapping, Colin Legum, Martin Leighton*, Freda Levson, Anthony Lewis, John Longrigg*, Trevor Macdonald, Sir Kit McMahon, Shula Marks, Jacques Moreillon, Lionel Morrison, Lady (Emma) Nicholson, Robert Oakeshott, Thomas Pakenham, Nad Pillay, Vella Pillay, Elaine Potter, Sir Charles Powell, Lord Renwick, Jon Snow, Lady (Mary) Soames, George Soros, Richard Stengel, John Taylor, Noreen Taylor, Michael Terry, Stanley Uys, Randolph Vigne, Per Wastberg, Brian Widlake*, Donald Woods, Ann Yates, Andrew Young, Michael Young.

In this revised paperback edition I have made some corrections and additions to the original text. I am grateful to all those correspondents who have taken the trouble to suggest changes.

ANTHONY SAMPSON
London, December 1999

PROLOGUE

The Last Hero

Westminster Hall in London, the ancient heart of the Houses of Parliament, is preparing to honour a visiting head of state, in a ceremony which happens only once or twice in a lifetime. The last such guest of honour was General de Gaulle in 1960; this time, in July 1996, it is President Nelson Mandela. The comparison is apt, for both were solitary, lost leaders who came to be seen as saviours of their country. But Mandela's transformation is much more surprising than de Gaulle's. In the past, many of the politicians in the audience had regarded him as their enemy, who should never be permitted to lead his country. Many Conservative Members of Parliament had condemned him as a terrorist; the former Prime Minister Lady Thatcher, who is sitting near the front, had said nine years before that anyone who thought the African National Congress was ever going to form the government of South Africa was 'living in cloud-cuckoo land'. Now cloud-cuckoo land has arrived in Westminster Hall. But the ceremonials in this medieval hall have legitimised many awkward shifts of loyalty over the centuries, whether from Richard II to Henry IV in 1400 or from Charles I to Oliver Cromwell in 1649. And now all recriminations are drowned in a fanfare of trumpets.

It is like a scene from grand opera, with Beefeaters lining the steps and helmeted guardsmen at the back of the hall. The Lord Chancellor, Lord Mackay of Clashfern, arrives in his robes of state. Then, at last, the tall, lean figure of Nelson Mandela appears and walks shakily down the grand staircase, holding the hand of the Speaker of the House, Betty Boothroyd: she says afterwards it was the most memorable five minutes of her life. The Labour peer sitting in front of me allows tears to flow down his cheek. The band of the Grenadier Guards plays '*Nkosi Sikelel' iAfrika*', for decades the hymn of South Africa's black revolutionaries. The Lord Chancellor makes a modest speech, recalling how this hall has witnessed the slow evolution of democracy, ever since the Magna Carta in 1215, and how Britons and South Africans share the democratic right to one person, one vote. Then he warmly introduces the former revolutionary, who now looks as benign as an old-fashioned English gentleman.

Mandela speaks slowly, with his usual formal emphasis. Although most guests cannot hear him through the echoing acoustics, it is a tough speech which does not please Lady Thatcher, as she says afterwards. He looks back two hundred years, to when Britain first colonised South Africa and seized the land of his forebears. He reminds his audience how the ANC first petitioned the British parliament eight decades ago, in protest against being left to the mercy of the white rulers of the new Union of South Africa. But now, he says, he comes as a friend of Britain, to the country of allies like William Wilberforce, Fenner Brockway, Archbishop Trevor Huddleston. He goes on to refer to the horrors of racism, whether in South Africa or in Nazi Germany – 'How did we allow these to happen?' – and the appalling massacres and miseries in other parts of Africa; but he ends by looking ahead to the closing of the circle, to Britain and South Africa joining hands to construct a humane Africa.

This is the historic Mandela: the last of the succession of revolutionary leaders in Asia and Africa who fought for their freedom, were imprisoned and reviled, and were eventually recognised as heads of state. But the Afrikaner nationalists were much more ruthless enemies, and he now shows more magnanimity than his predecessors, giving hope both to his own people and to others that they can bridge their own racial chasms. He has become a universal hero at the end of the twentieth century. In a time of vote-counters, spin-doctors and focus groups, he conjures up an earlier age of liberators, war leaders and revolutionaries. To conservative traditionalists he evokes memories of great men who personified their own country; to the liberal left, battered by lost causes, he brings new hope that righteous crusades can still prevail; his three decades in jail cut him off from the surge of materialism and consumerism that swept through the Western world.

As Mandela goes through the pompous routines of a state visit, he even brings new life to the British monarchy itself, under siege with its own troubles. Some of the audience go straight from Westminster Hall to the Dorchester Hotel, where he is giving a banquet for the Queen. He arrives with her, looking both more regal and more at ease than the monarch as he lopes between the guests. At the end of the lunch he gives another brief speech, reminding the Queen that he's just a country boy, thanking her for opening all doors to British society and for letting him walk in her garden early in the morning. The Queen's relaxation in his company is obvious as they talk. 'She's got a lot in common with him,' one courtier explains. 'You see, they've both spent a lot of time in prison.'

In the evening another Mandela is presented to the young generation: the showbiz idol and friend of pop stars. He is the guest of Prince Charles, together with most of the royal family, for a concert attended by five thousand people at the Albert Hall. Mandela has always praised musicians for their role in confronting racism, and for agitating for his release from jail; now they have gathered to pay him tribute, beginning with Phil Collins' Big Band and ending with a triumphant finale led by the South African trumpeter Hugh Masekela. The whole audience clap and sway. In the royal box Mandela jumps to his feet and begins jiving, jauntily swinging his arms. Prince Charles awkwardly begins to shuffle, the Queen makes some cautious claps, and even Prince Philip is seen to tilt. Beside them Mandela seems like a fantasy monarch: the man with rhythm who can swing and dance with his subjects.

The next morning there is another Mandela: the champion of the underdog, the people's president who can bring all the races together. With Prince Charles he makes a tour of the multi-racial south London suburb of Brixton, where he is greeted by a huge crowd of black and white Londoners. From there he goes on to Trafalgar Square, dominated on one side by South Africa House, the old fortress of apartheid which is now the symbol of liberation. The square is closed to traffic, and is packed solid with people wearing Mandela T-shirts and waving flags. As he walks slowly through the crowd children gaze in wonder, and reach out to touch him. When he appears on the balcony of South Africa House he seems more like a pope blessing the crowd than a politician: 'I would like to put each and every one of you in my pocket.' He talks about love, without embarrassment: 'I am not very nervous of love, for love is very inspiring.'

Why should an elderly African politician attract such unique affection – not just in Britain, but throughout Europe, America and Asia – at a time when politicians everywhere are more distrusted than ever before? What has happened, I cannot help wondering, to the stiff, proud young lawyer and revolutionary whom I first knew in Johannesburg in the fifties, who looked so suspiciously at the hostile white world and made fierce speeches denouncing the British imperialists? What has changed that young man's flashing smile into the welcoming grin which seems so genuinely warm?

From Trafalgar Square he goes on to the Dorchester, where I have the chance to talk to him briefly in private. He is in a euphoric mood, delighted by his welcome from the Queen and from the crowd in Brixton. He recalls how he first visited London in 1962 when he was on the run as a 'raw revolutionary', two months before he went to jail for twenty-seven years. I ask him why he seems so transformed. He laughs: 'Perhaps I was defensive then.' Now he seems totally at ease with everyone, including himself; but he makes it clear, as always, that he does not wish to talk about his own feelings.

It is not easy for a biographer to portray the Nelson Mandela behind the icon: it is rather like trying to make out someone's shape from the wrong side of the arc-lights. The myth is so powerful that it blurs the realities, turning everything into show business and attracting *Hello!* magazine as much as the *New York Times*. It is a myth which fascinates children as much as adults, the world's favourite fairy-tale: the prisoner released from the dark dungeon, the pauper who turns out to be a prince, the bogeyman who proves to be the wizard. Cynical politicians also wipe away tears in Mandela's presence, perhaps seeing him as a secular saint who makes their own profession seem noble, who rises above their failings. Some have warned me: 'I don't want to hear anything bad about him.'

But it is not realistic to portray Mandela as a saint, and he himself has never pretended to be one: 'I'm no angel.' No saint could have survived in the political jungle for fifty years, and achieved such a worldly transformation. Mandela has his share of human weaknesses, of stubbornness, pride, naïveté, impetuousness. And behind his moral authority and leadership, he has always been a consummate politician. 'I never know whether I'm dealing with a saint or with Machiavelli,' one of his closest colleagues has said. His achievement has been dependent on mastering politics in its broadest and longest sense, on understanding how to move and persuade people, to change their attitudes. He has always been determined, like Gandhi or Churchill, to lead from the front, through his example and presence; and he learnt early how to build up and understand his own image.

For all his international acclaim, Mandela remains very African: and in Africa he emerges even more clearly than elsewhere as the master of politics. A week after his visit to Britain he is giving a birthday party in the grounds of his official mansion in Pretoria for 'veterans of the struggle'. Coachloads of guests, including ancient grandmothers and grandfathers, converge on the huge marquee. Mandela appears at one end, towering above them, luminous in a brightly coloured loose shirt, while his bodyguards dart to and fro to cover his highly visible back. He works the room like any presidential candidate, revelling in the love from the crowd, spotting distant faces, remembering names, radiating goodwill and reaching out with his big boxer's hands. He fixes each guest with an intimate look, a personal smile, listening apparently intently – 'I see, I see' – leaving them glowing with pride and pleasure. He moves to the middle of the marquee to welcome his special guests, enfolding them in his bony embrace, including his cabinet and a few white friends like Helen Suzman and Nadine Gordimer. He sits between two friends of fifty years' standing, Walter Sisulu and Ahmed Kathrada. But he remains the arch-politician, showing little difference between his political and private self, relating to everyone in the same hearty style.

And he has his own agenda of nation-building, which he explains in an impromptu speech, without spectacles, with no journalists to report it. He has invited his guests, he says, because each of them has made some contribution to South Africa's peaceful transformation; but also to remind them where they came from: 'The history of liberation heroes shows that when they come into office they interact with powerful groups: they can easily forget that they've been put in power by the poorest of the poor. They often lose their common touch, and turn against their own people.' Here Mandela is playing his last political game, for the highest stakes: to hold together the disparate South African nation. 'I'm prepared to do anything,' he says later 'to bring the people of this country closer together.'

As the band strikes up and the real party begins, the old man at the top table surveys the scene. The musicians and singers include stars of the fifties like Dolly Rathebe and Thandi Klaasens, who conjure up memories of Mandela's youth in Johannesburg. The guests come from every stage of his long political career: country tribespeople who still see him as a traditional ruler; white and Indian communists who shared his struggle in the fifties and sixties; ex-prisoners from Robben Island who hacked limestone with him in the quarry; white businessmen who condemned him as a terrorist until the nineties, then welcomed him to their dinner parties. With each group he extended his political horizons, and he moves casually between them all, slipping easily from township slang to financial jargon. But in repose, he suddenly gives a glimpse of another Mandela, with a turned-down mouth and a weary gaze of infinite loneliness, as if the scene around him is only a show. And behind all his gregariousness he still maintains an impenetrable reserve, defending his private hinterland, which seems much deeper than that of other politicians.

A few days after the party, in his sombre presidential office in the Union Buildings in Pretoria, he reflects quietly about the hectic past two weeks. He happily remembers the warmth and enthusiasm of his welcome in Britain, but he becomes much more intimate when he goes on to talk about his twenty-seven years in jail. He recalls again how he came to realise in prison that the warders could be good or bad, like any other people. 'It was a tragedy to lose the best days of your life, but you learnt a lot. You had time to think – to stand away from yourself, to look at yourself from a distance, to see the contradictions in yourself.'

He still seems to keep his prison cell inside him, protecting him from the outside world, controlling his emotions, providing a philosopher's detachment. It was in jail that he developed the subtler art of politics: how to relate to all kinds of people, how to persuade and cajole, how to turn his warders into his dependants, and how eventually to become master in his own prison. He still likes to quote from W.E. Henley's Victorian poem 'Invictus': 'I am the master of my fate, I am the captain of my soul.'

In this book I try to penetrate the Mandela icon, to show the sometimes harsh realities of his long and adventurous journey, stripped of the gloss of mythology; and to discover how this most private man relates to this most public myth. I try to penetrate into the prison years, when for almost three decades he was hidden from the glare of public politics, and gained the detachment which steeled him for the ordeals ahead. And I try to trace the unchanging man behind all the Mandelas in his bewildering and wide-ranging career: the son of an African chief who retained many of his rural values while bestriding the global stage.

PART I

1918–1964

1

Country Boy

1918–1934

FEW PARTS of South Africa are more remote from city life than the Transkei, six hundred miles south of Johannesburg. It is one of the most beautiful but also one of the poorest regions of the country. The limitless vistas of rolling hills, pale green grass and round thatched huts, with herdboys and shepherds driving their flocks between them, present an almost Biblical vision of a timeless, idyllic, pastoral life. But the beauty is skin-deep: the land is desperately overpopulated, and the thin soil is so eroded that it can only sustain scattered groups of scrawny cattle or sheep and sporadic crops of maize.

It is here that Nelson Mandela was born and brought up, and here that he has built the house to which he retreats for Christmases and holidays, and where he intends to retire. It is a large red-brick bungalow with Spanish-style arches alongside the main road, the N2 from Durban to Cape Town, a few miles south of Umtata, Transkei's biggest town. It stands at the end of an avenue of cypresses, surrounded by a wall and a bushy garden which cuts it off from the open countryside. Mandela conceived the house during his last year in jail, and based its floor-plan on the warder's house in the prison compound where he was living. He chose the site, which looks over his home district of Qunu, in the belief that 'a man should die near where he was born'.

Mandela's actual birthplace is several miles south, in the small village of Mvezo on the banks of the winding Mbashe (Bashee) river, where his father was hereditary chief. (The family's group of huts, or *kraal*, is no longer there: in 1988 Mandela, then in jail, would ask a local lawyer to locate it, but he could find no trace.[1]) Rolihlahla Mandela was born in Mvezo on 18 July 1918 – at a time, he would later reflect, when the First World War was coming to an end, the Bolshevik revolution in Russia was being consolidated, and the newly-formed African National Congress sent a deputation to London to plead for the rights of black South Africans. The British Cape Colony, which included the 'native reserve' of the Transkei, had been absorbed into the Union of South Africa in 1910, and three years later the Native Land Act dispossessed hundreds of thousands of black farmers, many of whom trekked to the Transkei, the only large area where Africans could own land. The Transkei has produced more black leaders than any other region of South Africa, and it was with this history that they were brought up.

Rolihlahla's father, Hendry Mandela, suffered his own dispossession. The year after his son was born the local white magistrate summoned Hendry to answer a tribesman's complaint about an ox. Hendry refused to come, and was promptly charged with insubordination and deposed from the chieftainship, losing most of his cattle, land and income. The family moved from their ancestral *kraal* in Mvezo to the nearby village of Qunu, where the boy Mandela would spend his next few years. Although their fortunes had suddenly declined, they kept together without too much hardship. They shared food and simple pleasures with cousins and friends, and Mandela never felt alone: in later life he would look back warmly on that collective spirit and sense of shared responsibility, before Western influences began to introduce competition and individualism.

Hendry Mandela was a strict father, with a stubbornness which his son suspects he inherited. He was illiterate, pagan and polygamous; but he was tall and dignified, darker than his son, and with no sense of inferiority towards whites. He inhabited a self-contained rural world with its own established customs and rituals. He had four wives, of whom Mandela's mother, Nosekeni Fanny, was the third. Each had her own *kraal*, which was more or less self-sufficient, with its own fields, livestock and vegetables.[2] Hendry would move between the different *kraals* visiting his wives, who appear to have been on good terms with each other. He kept some home-brewed liquor in his hut, with a bottle of brandy in the cupboard which would last three or four months. He respected tribal customs: when a baby was born he slaughtered a goat and erected its horns in the house.[3]

Hendry never became a Christian, but he had some Christian friends, including the Reverend Tennyson Makiwane, a scholarly community leader who was part of the elite of the Transkei (his offspring were later to be controversial members of the ANC).[4] He was also close to the Mbekela brothers, George and Ben, who belonged to the separate tribal group called Amamfengu, or 'Fingoes'; this group remained apart from the Xhosa people, and were more influenced by missionaries and Western customs, many of them becoming teachers, clergymen or policemen. The Mbekela brothers converted Mandela's mother to Methodism, after which she began wearing Western dresses instead of Xhosa garb. She had her son baptised as a Methodist, and later the brothers persuaded both parents that Mandela should go to the local mission school – the first member of the family to do so.

Mandela's sisters Mabel and Leabie would recall with pleasure the simple country life of their childhood in Qunu, revolving around the three round huts or *rondavels* in their mother's *kraal* – one for sleeping, one for cooking, one for storing food – fenced off with poles. The *rondavels* were made by their mother from soil moulded into bricks; the simple chairs and cupboards were also made of soil, and the stove was a hole in the ground. There were no beds or tables, only mats. The roofs were made of grass held together with ropes.[5] They lived largely on maize, which was stored in holes (*izisele*) in the *kraals*. The boys spent the day herding the cattle, and the girls and women of the family prepared the food together in one of the houses, grinding the maize between stones, cooking it in black three-legged metal pots and mixing it with sour milk. The family would all take the main meal together in the evening, sitting on the ground eating from a single dish.

Mandela's father already had three sons by other wives, but they had already left home. As a boy, he had much more freedom than his sisters. He was very close to his mother, but would often stay with another of his father's wives, with whom he felt the same security and love as with Nosekeni Fanny. Throughout his life he would always feel most at ease with women – particularly with strong women who could provide rewarding friendships, which may be linked to his childhood experience. He thrived within his extended family of cousins, stepmothers and half-brothers and -sisters (Bantu languages have no words for stepsisters or stepmothers, so he called all his father's wives his 'mothers'). 'I had mothers who were very supportive and regarded me as their son,' he recalled. 'Not as their stepson or half-son, as you would say in the culture amongst whites. They were mothers in the proper sense of the word.' His happy experience as a son loved by four mothers made his childhood very secure, and he sometimes talks nostalgically about polygamy at that time, although he firmly rejects it in today's conditions: 'Quite inexcusable. It shows contempt for women, and it's something I discourage totally.'[6]

In his letters and memoirs Mandela often harks back to his life as a country boy. From his prison cell he wrote vividly about the splendour of the hills and streams, the pleasures of swimming in the pools, drinking milk straight from the cows' udders or eating maize roasted on the cob. Many world leaders, caught up in power-politics in the capitals, have played up their romantic rural roots, like Lloyd George revisiting his Welsh village or Lyndon Johnson longing for his Texas ranch. But President Mandela would be more insistent in calling himself a country boy; and with more reason, for the security and simplicity of his rural upbringing played a crucial part in forming his political confidence.

He was also fortified by his knowledge of his ancestors. His father was the grandson of Ngubengcuka, the great king of the Tembu people who died in 1832, before the British finally imposed their power on Tembuland, the southern part of the Transkei. The Tembu royal family, however poor and dependent they might seem to whites, retained a special grandeur in the Transkei, commanding the loyalty and respect of their people. Mandela was a minor royal, and he always stressed that he was never in the line of succession to the throne.[7] He was only one of scores of descendants of King Ngubengcuka, and he came from a junior line. But his father was a trusted friend and confidant of King Dalindyebo, who had succeeded to the Tembu throne, and later of his son King Jongilizwe. Hendry in fact was a kind of prime minister, and the boy Mandela commanded respect in his community.

His was a royal family, as they saw it, but under an occupying force, for since the time of Ngubengcuka their powers had been circumscribed: first by the British government, then after 1910 by the new Union of South Africa, and the Transkei monarchs were torn between their duties to their people and the demands of an alien power. However proud and respected the Tembu royals remained, they were always conscious that the new patricians, the British and the Afrikaners, had deprived them of their authority and wealth. When the young Mandela began to travel beyond his home district, he saw that the towns in the Eastern Cape – Port Shepstone, King William's Town, Port Elizabeth, Alice – were named after British, not Xhosa, heroes, and that the white men were the real overlords.

Many mission-educated children of Mandela's generation were named after British imperial heroes and heroines like Wellington, Kitchener, Adelaide or Victoria, and at the age of seven Mandela acquired a new first name, to precede Rolihlahla. 'From now on you will be Nelson,' said his teacher. His mother pronounced it 'Nelisile', while others would later call him 'Dalibunga', his circumcision name. His later city friends called him 'Nelson' or 'Nel', until he expressed a preference for his clan name, 'Madiba', which the whole nation was to adopt.

In 1927 Mandela, then aged nine, came closer to royalty. His father had been suffering from lung disease, and was staying in Mandela's mother's house. His friend Jongintaba, the Regent of the Tembu people, was visiting, and Mandela's sister Mabel overheard Hendry telling him: 'Sir, I leave my orphan to you to educate. I can see he is progressing and aims high. Teach him and he will respect you.' The Regent replied: 'I will take Rolihlahla and educate him.' Soon afterwards Hendry died. His body was carried on a sledge to his first wife's house, and a cow was slaughtered; but he was also given a Christian funeral conducted by the Mbekela brothers, and was buried in the local cemetery.[8]

Mandela was taken by his mother on a long journey by foot from Qunu to the 'Great Place' of Mqhekezweni. It was from here that the Regent presided over his people as acting king, since the heir apparent, Sabata, was too young to rule. Jongintaba, who was also head of the Madiba clan, was indebted to Mandela's father for recommending him as Regent, which may explain why he so readily agreed to adopt Mandela as if he were his own son. But the tradition of the extended family was much stronger in rural areas than in the towns, for which Mandela remained grateful. As he wrote from jail: 'it caters for all those who are descended from one ancestor and holds them together as one family'.[9]

The Great Place at Mqhekezweni hardly conforms to the European image of a royal palace. Even today it remains ruggedly inaccessible, and is difficult to reach by car. From the main road a rough, deeply-rutted dirt track twists across the landscape, down into dried-up riverbeds and up stony banks, passing isolated clusters of *rondavels* and huts and a deserted railway station. At last a small settlement appears: two plain houses facing a group of *rondavels*, with an overgrown garden between them, a school building and some huts beyond. From one house a fine-looking, naturally dignified man emerges and reveals himself as the local chief, the grandson of Jongintaba; he still presides over the local community. He points out the plain *rondavel* where President Mandela lived as a boy. A photograph on the wall of one of the houses shows the fine face of Jongintaba, with a trim moustache. Nearby is a solemn-looking young Mandela, alongside his smiling face on an election poster of 1994.

To the Western visitor today the Great Place may seem small and remote, but to the young Mandela in 1927 it was the centre of the world, and Mqhekezweni was a metropolis compared to the huts of Qunu. It was here that Mandela spent his most formative years and gained the impressions of kingship which were to influence his whole life. He would never forget the moment when he first saw the Regent arriving in a spectacular motor car, welcomed by his people with shouts of '*Aaah! Jongintaba!*' (The scene would be re-enacted seventy years later when President Mandela was hailed by cries of '*Aaah! Dalibunga!*') Mqhekezweni was more prosperous then, and almost self-sufficient; its chief was then also regent, attracting tribesmen from all over Tembuland to consult him.

The nine-year-old boy arrived with only a tin trunk, wearing an old shirt and khaki shorts roughly cut from his father's old riding breeches, with a piece of string as a belt. His cousin Ntombizodwa, four years older, remembered him as shy, lonely and quite silent, but he was immediately welcomed by Jongintaba and his wife No-England.[10] Mandela shared with their son Justice a small whitewashed *rondavel* containing two beds, a table and an oil lamp. He was treated as one of the family, together with Jongintaba's daughter Nomafu, and later with Nxeko, the elder brother of Sabata, the heir to the kingdom. He saw himself as a member of a royal family, with a much grander style of life than that of Qunu; but he did not altogether belong to it – which may have spurred his ambition.

The Regent, Jongintaba, otherwise known as David Dalindyebo, became Mandela's new father-figure. He was a handsome man, always very well-dressed; Mandela lovingly pressed his trousers, inspiring his lifelong respect for clothes. Jongintaba was a committed Methodist – though he enjoyed his drink – and prayed every day at the nearby church run by his relative the Reverend Matyolo. His son Justice, four years Mandela's elder, was to be his role model for the next decade, the ideal of worldly prowess and elegance, as sportsman, dandy and ladies' man. Justice was an all-rounder, excelling in team sports like cricket, soccer and rugby. Mandela, less well co-ordinated, made his mark in more rugged and individual sports like boxing and long-distance running. A photograph shows Justice as bright-eyed, confident and combative, while the young Mandela was less assertive, and strove to acquire Justice's assurance. Justice was after all the heir to the chieftaincy, while Mandela depended on the Regent's favours.

Mandela loved the country pleasures at Mqhekezweni, which were more numerous in those days than they are now, and included riding horses and dancing to the tribal songs of Xhosa girls (how different, he reflected in jail, from his later delight in Miriam Makeba, Eartha Kitt or Margot Fonteyn). But Mandela was also more serious and harder-working than the other boys. He thrived at the local mission school, where he began to learn English from *Chambers' English Reader*, writing on a slate and speaking the words carefully, with a slow formality and the local accent which never left him.

Whites were hardly visible at Mqhekezweni, except for occasional passers-by. Mandela's sister Mabel remembers being impressed when he and his schoolfriends met a white man who needed help because his motorbike had broken down, and Mandela was able to speak to him in English.[11] But Mabel could also be quite frightened of Mandela: 'He didn't like to be provoked. If you provoked him he would tell you directly . . . He had no time to fool around. We could see he had leadership qualities.'[12]

A crucial part of Mandela's education lay in observing the Regent. He was fascinated by Jongintaba's exercise of his kingship at the periodic tribal meetings, to which Tembu people would travel scores of miles on foot or on horseback. Mandela loved to watch the tribesmen, whether labourers or landowners, as they complained candidly and often fiercely to the Regent, who listened for hours impassively and silently, until finally at sunset he tried to produce a consensus from the contrasting views. Later, in jail, Mandela would reflect:

> One of the marks of a great chief is the ability to keep together all sections of his people, the traditionalists and reformers, conservatives and liberals, and on major questions there are sometimes sharp differences of opinion. The Mqhekezweni court was particularly strong, and the Regent was able to carry the whole community because the court was representative of all shades of opinion.[13]

As President, Mandela would seek to reach the same kind of consensus in cabinet; and he would always remember Jongintaba's advice that a leader should be like a shepherd, directing his flock from behind by skilful persuasion: 'If one or two animals stray, you go out and draw them back to the flock,' he would say. 'That's an important lesson in politics.'[14]

Mandela was brought up with the African notion of human brotherhood, or '*ubuntu*', which described a quality of mutual responsibility and compassion. He often quoted the proverb '*Umuntu ngumuntu ngabantu*,' which he would translate as 'A person is a person because of other people,' or 'You can do nothing if you don't get the support of other people.' This was a concept common to other rural communities around the world, but Africans would define it more sharply as a contrast to the individualism and restlessness of whites, and over the following decades *ubuntu* would loom large in black politics. As Archbishop Tutu defined it in 1986: 'It refers to gentleness, to compassion, to hospitality, to openness to others, to vulnerability, to be available to others and to know that you are bound up with them in the bundle of life.'[15]

Mandela regarded *ubuntu* as part of the general philosophy of serving one's fellow men. From his adolescence, he recalled, he was viewed as being unusually ready to see the best in others. To him this was a natural inheritance: 'People like ourselves brought up in a rural atmosphere get used to interacting with people at an early age.' But he conceded that, 'It may be a combination of instinct and deliberate planning.' In any case, it was to become a prevailing principle throughout his political career: 'People are human beings, produced by the society in which they live. You encourage people by seeing good in them.'[16]

Mandela's admiration for tribal traditions and democracy was reinforced by the Xhosa history that he picked up from visiting old chiefs and headmen. Many of them were illiterate, but they were masters of the oral tradition, declaiming the epics of past battles like Homeric bards. The most vivid story-teller, Chief Joyi, like Mandela a descendant of the great King Ngubengcuka, described how the unity and peace of the Xhosa people had been broken by the coming of the white men, who had divided them, dispossessed them and undermined their *ubuntu*.[17] Mandela would often look back to this idealised picture of African tribal society. He described it in a long speech in 1962, shortly before he began his prison sentence:

> Then our people lived peacefully, under the democratic rule of their kings and their *amapakati*, and moved freely and confidently up and down the country without let or hindrance. Then the

> country was ours, in our own name and right. We occupied the land, the forests, the rivers; we extracted the mineral wealth below the soil and all the riches of this beautiful country. We set up and operated our own government, we controlled our own armies and we organised our own trade and commerce.

It was, in his eyes, a golden age without classes, exploitation or inequality, in which the tribal council was a model of democracy:

> The council was so completely democratic that all members of the tribe could participate in its deliberations. Chief and subject, warrior and medicine man, all took part and endeavoured to influence its decisions. It was so weighty and influential a body that no step of any importance could ever be taken by the tribe without reference to it.[18]

The history of the Xhosas was very much alive when Mandela was a child, and old men could remember the time when they were still undefeated. The pride and autonomy of the Transkei and its Xhosa-speaking tribes – the Tembus, the Pondos, the Fingoes and the Xhosas themselves – had survived despite the humiliations of conquest and subjection over the previous century. Some Xhosas had intermarried with other peoples, including the Khoikhoi (called 'Hottentots' by white settlers), which helped to give a wide variety to their physical features: Mandela's own distinctive face, with his narrow eyes and strong cheekbones, has sometimes been explained by Khoikhoi blood.[19] But the Xhosas retained their distinctive culture and language. Many white colonists who first encountered them in the late eighteenth century were impressed by their physique, their light skin and sensitive faces, and their democratic system of debate and government: 'They are equal to any English lawyers in discussing questions which relate to their own laws and customs,' wrote the missionary William Holden in 1866. In the 1830s the British Commander Harry Smith called the Xhosa King Hintsa 'the very image of poor dear George IV'.[20] But, over the course of a hundred years and nine Xhosa wars, the British forces moving east from the Cape gradually deprived the Xhosas of their independence and their land. By 1835 Harry Smith had crossed the river Kei to begin the subjugation of the Transkei. By 1848 he had imposed his own English system on the Xhosa chiefs, informing them that their land 'shall be divided into counties, towns and villages, bearing English names. You shall all learn to speak English at the schools which I shall establish for you . . . You may no longer be naked and wicked barbarians which you will ever be unless you labour and become industrious.'[21] In the eighth Xhosa war in 1850 the British Army – after setbacks which strained it to its limit and atrocities committed by both sides – drove the Xhosa chiefs out of their mountain fastnesses and firmly occupied 'British Kaffraria', later called the Ciskei. The Tembu chiefs who ruled the southern part of the Transkei had been relatively unscathed by the earlier wars, but now they were subjugated and sent to the terrible prison on Robben Island, just off the coast from Cape Town, which became notorious in Xhosa folklore.

After this humiliation and impoverishment, in 1856 the Xhosas accomplished their own self-destruction. A young prophetess, Nongqawuse, told them to kill all their cattle and to prepare for a resurrection. As a result, over half the population of the Ciskei starved to death. By the end of the ninth Xhosa war in 1878 the two chief houses of the Xhosa people, the Ngqika and the Gcaleka, had been subjugated and were forced into a new exodus across the Kei. Successive leaders were sent to Robben Island, in keeping with the order of Sir George Grey, the Governor of the Cape, 'for the submission of every chief of consequence; or his disgrace if he were obdurate'.[22]

It was not till 1894 that Pondoland, in the northern part of the Transkei, came under the Cape administration. But after the Union of South Africa came into being in 1910, the Xhosas faced growing controls by white magistrates. The whites, as Mandela came to see it, captured the institution of the chieftaincy, and 'used it to suppress the aspirations of their own tribesmen. So they almost destroyed the chieftaincy.'[23]

In the later nineteenth century the Zulus, the other major tribal power to the north, became more famous among whites and foreigners as ruthless fighters than the Xhosas, particularly the Zulu warrior-king Shaka, who had set out to conquer and unify all the southern tribes in the 1820s. The Zulus attracted the admiration of many British churchmen, including the dissident Bishop John William Colenso of Natal; but they acquired unique military fame in January 1879 when the British provoked a war with Shaka's successor Cetewayo, whose army completely destroyed a British force of 1,200 at the battle of Isandhlwana. When the British sent out reinforcements they included the Prince Imperial, son of Louis Napoleon, who was ambushed and speared to death by Zulu assegais.

('A very remarkable people the Zulus,' said Disraeli. 'They defeat our generals, they convert our bishops, they have settled the fate of a great European dynasty.'[24]) The humiliation of Isandhlwana was finally avenged in July when the British crushed Cetewayo at the battle of Ulundi and subjugated the Zulus; but their reputation for fighting spirit remained.

The Xhosa chiefs appeared less martial and intransigent than the Zulus, and after the Xhosa wars they seemed defeated and demoralised – sometimes with the help of alcohol. But out of the desolation of the Xhosa wars another tradition was growing up, that of mission schools and Christian culture, which gradually produced a new Xhosa elite of disciplined, well-educated young men and women. While embracing Western ideas, they still aspired to restore the rights and dignity of their own people. The British liberal tradition was reasserting itself in the Cape, with the expansion of the mission stations and the introduction of a qualified vote for blacks. Educated young Xhosas were exploiting the aptitude for legal argument, analysis and debate which early white visitors had observed. It was a route that would in time lead some of them into the political campaigns of the black opposition in the 1960s – sometimes called the tenth Xhosa war – and, like their predecessors, to Robben Island; but they would win their battle, and not through military might, but through their skills in argument and reasoning.

Like other conquered peoples such as the Scots or the American Indians, the Xhosas retained their own version of history which, being largely oral, was easily ignored by the outside world. 'The European insisted that we accept his version of the past,' said Z.K. Matthews, the African professor who would teach Mandela. But 'it was utterly impossible to accept his judgements on the actions and behaviour of Africans, of our own grandfathers in our own lands'.[25] Mandela, despite all his Western education, would always champion oral historians, and would continue to be inspired by the spoken stories of the Xhosas which he had heard from his elders: 'I knew that our society had produced black heroes and this filled me with pride: I did not know how to channel it, but I carried this raw material with me when I went to college.'[26] While most white historians regarded the Xhosa rebellions as firmly placed in the past, overlaid by the relentless logic of Western conquest and technology, Mandela, like other educated Xhosas, saw the white occupation as a recent interlude, and would never forget that his great-grandfather ruled a whole region a century before he was born.

2

Mission Boy

1934–1940

IN 1934, when he was sixteen, Mandela went with twenty-five other Tembu boys, led by the Regent's son Justice, to an isolated valley on the banks of the Bashee river, the traditional setting for the circumcision of future Tembu kings. No rural Xhosa could take office without this ritual. Mandela would vividly remember the ceremony which marked the coming of manhood: the days spent beforehand with the other boys in the 'seclusion lodges'; singing and dancing with local women on the night before the ceremony; bathing in the river at dawn; parading in blankets before the elders and the Regent himself, who watched the boys to see that they behaved with courage.

The old circumcisor (*incibi*) appeared with his assegai, and when their turn came the boys had to cry out 'I am a man!'[1] Mandela was tense and anxious, and when the assegai cut off his foreskin he remembered it as feeling like molten lead flowing through his veins. He briefly forgot his words as he pressed his head into the grass, before he too shouted out, 'I am a man!' But he was conscious that he was not naturally brave: 'I was not as forthright and strong as the other boys.'[2]

After the ceremony was over, when they had buried their foreskins, covered their faces in white ochre and then washed it off in the river, Mandela was proud of his new status as a man, with a new name – Dalibunga, meaning the founder of the council – who could walk tall and face the challenges of life. He still felt himself to be part of a proud tribe, and was shocked when Chief Meligqili told the boys that they would never really be men because they were a conquered people who were slaves in their own country.[3] It was not until ten years later that Mandela would recognise that chief as the forerunner of brave politicians like Alfred Xuma and Yusuf Dadoo, James Phillips and Michael Harmel. In the meantime he would take great pride in his circumcised manliness and the superiority it implied; at university he was shocked to learn that one of his friends had not been circumcised. Only when he later became immersed in politics in Johannesburg did he, as he put it, 'crawl out of the prejudice of my youth and accept all people as equals'.[4]

Mandela soon had to make a more fundamental social transition – into the midst of a rigorous missionary schooling. The Regent was determined to have him properly educated, as a prospective counsellor to Sabata, the future king, so he sent him to board at the great Methodist institution of Clarkebury, across the Bashee river, which had educated both the Regent and his son Justice, and would educate Sabata. For the Tembu royal family Clarkebury had a special resonance: it was founded in 1825, when King Ngubengcuka, Mandela's great-grandfather, had met the pioneering Methodist William Shaw and promised to give him land to set up a mission.[5] The station was duly founded by the Reverend Richard Haddy, some miles from the king's Great Place, and named in honour of a distinguished British theologian, Dr Adam Clarke.

The Methodists were the most adventurous and influential of the missionaries who had penetrated the Eastern Cape at the same time as the British armies – sometimes in league with them, sometimes at odds. To many Xhosa patriots missionaries were essentially the agents of British governments, who used them to divide and disarm the rival chiefs: the Trotskyist writer 'Nosipho Majeke' wrote in 1952 that the Wesleyan missions were 'ready at all times to co-operate with the Government', and were able to surround the great King Hintsa, turning other chiefs against him.[6] But the mission teachers were frequently in opposition to white administrations, and played an independent role in the development of the Xhosa people. By 1935 the mission schools throughout South Africa registered 342,181 African pupils, and as the historian Leonard Thompson records, they 'reached into every African reserve community'.[7]

Mandela would retain a respect for the missionary tradition, while criticising its paternalism and links with imperialism. 'Britain exercised a tremendous influence on our generation, at least,' he has said, 'because it was British liberals, missionaries, who started education in this country.'[8] Sixty years after his schooling, in a speech at Oxford University, he explained: 'Until very recently the government of our country took no interest whatsoever in the education of blacks. Religious institutions built schools, equipped them, employed teachers and paid them salaries;

therefore religion is in our blood. Without missionary institutions there would have been no Robert Mugabe, no Seretse Khama, no Oliver Tambo.'[9] In jail he would argue with Trotskyists who quoted Majeke's attacks on the missionaries, and would welcome priests who brought encouragement and news from outside.[10] And he would write to some of his old mission teachers, to reminisce and to thank them. In prison he became more aware of the political influence of both the chieftaincy and the missions: 'I have always considered it dangerous to underestimate the influence of both institutions amongst the people,' he wrote. 'And for this reason I have repeatedly urged caution in dealing with them.'[11]

By the time of Mandela's matriculation in 1934, Clarkebury had become the biggest educational centre in Tembuland, with a proud tradition of teaching, mainly by British missionaries. It had expanded into an imposing group of solid stone buildings, including a teacher-training college, a secondary school and training shops for practical courses, with boys' and girls' hostels, sports fields and tennis courts – a self-contained settlement dominating an isolated hillside in the Engcobo district, with its own busy community. Its past achievement would look all the more remarkable after the coming of Bantu Education in 1953, when it lost its funds and became a ruined shell, with only a small school and a Methodist chapel to maintain its continuity. Today it presents a tragic vista of crumbling buildings, collapsed roofs and gutted schoolrooms, burnt down by pupils rioting against the Transkei Bantustan government. There are still memorials of its past glory, including a plaque commemorating the Dalindyebo Mission School built in 1929. And some of the buildings are being restored, to provide a revived school: the rector explains that it will train Xhosas in how to create jobs, rather than to seek them, and that Mandela inspires local people to realise that small communities can produce great leaders. Mandela still revisits Clarkebury, talks and writes about it with warmth, and chose it as the location from which to launch a new version of his autobiography.[12]

In 1934 Clarkebury was near the peak of its achievement. It was run by a formidable pedagogue, the Reverend Cecil Harris, who was closely involved with the local Xhosa communities and their chiefs. The Regent warned Mandela to treat Harris with suitable respect as 'a Tembu at heart', and Mandela shook his hand with awe – the first white hand he had ever shaken. Harris ruled Clarkebury with an iron hand, more like a field commander than a school head.[13] He had an aristocratic style, and walked like a soldier, which he had been in the First World War. 'He was very stern dealing with the students,' Mandela recalled; 'severe with no levity.'[14] But Mandela also saw a much more human and friendly side of Harris and his wife when he worked in their garden. Years later, while in jail, he traced the address of the Harrises' daughter Mavis Knipe, who had been a child when he was at Clarkebury. She was 'flabbergasted' to receive a letter from the famous prisoner.[15] Mandela reminded her how her mother would often bring him 'a buttered scone or bread with jam, which to a boy of sixteen was like a royal feast', and asked her for information about the Dalindyebo family: 'At our age one becomes deeply interested in facts and events which as youths we brushed aside as uninteresting.'[16]

Mandela was expecting the other pupils to treat him with respect, as a royal whose great-grandfather had founded the school. Instead he was mocked by one girl pupil for his country-boy's accent, his slowness in class and for walking in his brand-new boots 'like a horse in spurs'.[17] He found himself in a community which respected merit and intelligence more than hereditary status. But after the first shock he held his own, and with the benefit of his retentive memory he passed the Junior Certificate in two years. He also made some lasting friends, including Honourbrook Bala, later a prosperous doctor who joined the opposition in the Transkei and corresponded with Mandela in jail; Arthur Damane, who became a journalist on the radical paper the *Guardian* and was in jail with Mandela in Pretoria in 1960; Sidney Sidyiyo, the son of a teacher at Clarkebury who became a prominent musician; and Reuben Mfecane, who became a trades unionist in Port Elizabeth and, like Mandela, ended up on Robben Island.[18]

Mandela was occasionally critical of the hierarchy at Clarkebury, and particularly of the food, which was minimal and at times almost inedible. But his first *alma mater* opened his eyes to the value of scientific knowledge, and introduced him to a much wider world than Tembuland, including as it did students from Johannesburg and beyond of both sexes – for unlike British public schools Clarkebury was co-educational. Even so, he still saw himself as a Tembu at heart, destined to advise his royal family, and continued to believe that 'My roots were my destiny.'[19]

After two years at Clarkebury Mandela was sent further away to Healdtown, a bigger Methodist institution, again following in the footsteps of Justice, the Regent's son. Healdtown was almost as remote as

Clarkebury: to reach it students had to walk ten miles from Fort Beaufort along a dirt road which wound through the valley, crossing and recrossing the stream, until it reached a cluster of fine Victorian buildings with red corrugated roofs, looking over a ravine. Today, like Clarkebury, the school is largely ruined. The handsome central block, with its picturesque clock-tower, has been restored and, sponsored by Coca-Cola, revived as the comprehensive high school; but most of the schoolrooms and houses are empty shells with smashed windows, rusty roofs and overgrown gardens, occupied by nothing but the ghosts of the old community on the hillside.

Healdtown, thirty years younger than Clarkebury, had an even more resonant history. It was established in 1855, after Sir Harry Smith had subjugated the surrounding Xhosa tribes, in the midst of the battle-areas. It was well placed as a British outpost, below the great escarpment of the Amatola hills where the defeated Xhosa had taken refuge, and surrounded by old military frontier-posts – Fort Beaufort, Fort Hare, Fort Brown. It was strictly Methodist, named after James Heald, a prominent Wesleyan Methodist British Member of Parliament, but it was also intended to serve as a practical experiment in training Fingo Christians in crafts and industry. That first experiment failed, but the college widened its scope and intake to become a teacher-training college and an important secondary school. By the 1930s it had over eight hundred boarders.[20] It was close to other great missionary educational centres such as Lovedale, St Matthew's and Fort Hare, and together they comprised the greatest concentration of well-educated black students in Southern Africa.

Healdtown, like Clarkebury, offered an uncompromising British education with few concessions to Xhosa culture. The missionary and imperialist traditions often converged, particularly on Sundays, when the schoolboys and girls, in separate ranks, marched to church in their white shirts, black blazers and maroon-and-gold ties. The Union Jack was hoisted and they all sang 'God Save the King' and '*Nkosi Sikelel' iAfrika*', accompanied by the school brass band and watched by admiring visitors who came from far and wide.[21] The school governor since 1927 had been the Reverend Arthur Wellington – whom Mandela would always enjoy mimicking – a diehard English patriot who boasted of his descent from the victor of Waterloo. Wellington inculcated British history and literature in his students, assisted by a mainly English staff, and publicised the school by inviting eminent Britons to visit it, among them Lord Clarendon, the Governor-General of South Africa, who shortly before Mandela's arrival had laid the foundation stones for the new dormitories and dining hall.[22] Wellington was a hard-driving autocrat – though he protested that he was naturally lazy – who claimed to run the largest educational institution south of the Sahara (Lovedale was in fact bigger).[23] He banned alcohol at Healdtown. His staff called him 'the Duke', and regarded him as a missionary-statesman. Under Wellington, wrote Jack Dugard, who ran the teacher-training school after 1932, 'within a short time the once rather dowdy mission was transformed into an attractive education centre'.[24]

The Methodism of Healdtown and Clarkebury did not make a deep religious impact on Mandela. He would never be a true believer, although many of his later friends, including his present wife, were educated by Methodists. But he would always be influenced by the schools' puritanical atmosphere, the strict discipline and mental training, the Wesleyan emphasis on paring down ideas to their bare essentials, avoiding frills and distractions. He would always disapprove of heavy drinking or swearing; and the self-reliance in these boarding-school surroundings would add to his fortitude.

Mandela was immersed not just in Methodism, but in British history and geography. 'As a teenager in the countryside I knew about London and Glasgow as much as I knew about Cape Town and Johannesburg,' he would recall from jail fifty years later, writing to the Provost of Glasgow and mentioning Scots patriots like William Wallace, Robert the Bruce and the Earl of Argyll.[25] But he was resistant to becoming a 'black Englishman', and took great pride in his own Xhosa culture, encouraged by his history teacher, the much-liked Weaver Newana, who added his own oral history to the accounts of the Xhosa wars already familiar to the boy. Mandela won the prize for the best Xhosa essay in 1938; and he was thrilled when the famous Xhosa poet Krune Mkwayi visited the college, appearing in a *kaross* of hide, with two spears, to recite his dramatic poems in praise of the Xhosas.

Mandela made close friendships with several Xhosa boys who subsequently joined the ANC, including Jimmy Njongwe, with whom he later 'starved and suffered in Johannesburg', and who became a doctor and later a key organiser of the Defiance Campaign.[26] He also made friends outside his tribe among Sotho-speakers like Zachariah Molete, who later befriended him in Alexandra township in Johannesburg, and the zoology teacher Frank Lebentlele.[27] Mandela was much impressed by another Sotho-speaker, his housemaster the Reverend Seth Mokitimi, who later became the first black president of the Methodist Church; Mokitimi pushed through reforms to give students more freedom and better food.[28]

The white teachers at Healdtown kept aloof from the black teachers, eating separately: one even had to resign after other teachers complained that he was fraternising with blacks. 'What a racist place Healdtown was and continued to be!' wrote Phyllis Ntantala, who was a student till 1935, and whose son Pallo Jordan would later join Mandela's cabinet.[29] A few of the younger white teachers, though, were beginning to make friends with black colleagues and some students.[30] Like Clarkebury, the school was co-educational, but girls and boys were strictly separated outside the schoolrooms, and could be expelled for talking to each other. By 1935, however, the Reverend Mokitimi had instituted mixed dinners every Sunday, where girls and boys sat together wearing their best clothes. The more sophisticated and prosperous students loved to show off: as Phyllis Ntantala wrote, 'They went to those dinners dressed to kill.'[31] But for those from simpler homes the European etiquette of knives and forks was a strain. Mandela recalled: 'We left the table hungry and depressed.'[32]

The Duke and his white staff had little sense that they were educating future black leaders. They were exasperated by the students' periodic protests and strikes, usually starting over the poor food, but which they suspected were really based on conflicts between tribes, or between town and country. In 1936 there were more serious political protests when the government's new 'Hertzog Bills' removed blacks from the common voters' roll and abolished the title deeds of the local Fingo people, who were in turn disillusioned by the failure of the missionary staff to defend their interests.[33] But Mandela was only vaguely aware of black politics. At Healdtown he first heard about the African National Congress, which was set up in 1912; the Tembu king had paid thirty cattle to enrol his own tribe in it. Yet to Mandela 'it was something vague located in the distant past'.[34] The mission teachers were inclined to ascribe any political protests to 'agitators' stirred up by communism, and most saw themselves as educating a small elite who were quite different from ordinary blacks: as one envious government official explained to them, they were dealing with the layer of fertile soil on top, while he dealt with the hard rock which was impervious to change.[35]

Mandela was still torn between the two aspects of the British presence in South Africa: the brutal military subjugation of the Xhosas and the enlightened influence of liberal English education. This contradiction had been summed up in a poem, 'The Prince of Britain', by Mandela's favourite poet Mkwayi, written to celebrate the visit of the Prince of Wales to the Ciskei in 1925:

> You sent us the truth, denied us the truth;
> You sent us the life, deprived us of life;
> You sent us the light, we sit in the dark,
> Shivering, benighted in the bright noonday sun.[36]

Mandela graduated from Healdtown in 1938, and the next year went on to the university at Fort Hare, a few miles from Healdtown and a mile from the great missionary school of Lovedale, to which it was linked. The Regent bought him a three-piece suit: 'We thought there could never be anyone smarter than him at Fort Hare,' said Mandela's cousin Ntombizodwa.[37]

The 'South African Native College' at Fort Hare was a tiny black university, the only one in South Africa, but it was destined to be a seedbed of the revolution that followed. In 1939 it was only twenty-three years old, having been set up, surprisingly, in the midst of the First World War, and opened by the Prime Minister Louis Botha himself. The first principal, Alexander Kerr, suspected that Botha had regarded it as a sop, a gesture to the blacks in wartime, when the whites feared 'native trouble'. But after white governments hardened their attitudes to blacks in the 1920s, the anomaly of its existence was even more remarkable.[38] The later Prime Minister General Jan Smuts worried little about its revolutionary potential; he viewed Fort Hare in the context of his policy of trusteeship. When he addressed the university's graduates in 1938, the year before Mandela arrived, he argued: 'The Europeans have come here as the bearers of the higher culture. They have been in some sense a missionary race, but if salvation is ever to come to the native peoples of South Africa it will finally have to come from themselves.'[39]

The university's start had been very modest, with twenty students preparing for matriculation (the first four candidates all failed).[40] When Mandela arrived there were still fewer than two hundred students (of whom sixty-seven were Xhosa-speaking), including ten Indians and sixteen Coloureds.[41] But the influence of Fort Hare already went far beyond its student numbers. Supported by the surrounding schools, it had become the focus for the intellectual elite of black South Africans. Its student body was both aristocratic and meritocratic, bringing together royal and mission families. It had been founded not only by white missionaries but by black educationalists from pioneering mission families, including the Jabavus, the Makiwanes and the Bokwes, all of whom were linked by marriage. The great teacher John Tengo Jabavu, editor of the black newspaper *Imvo*, was a promoter of Fort Hare: his son 'Jili' was its first black professor, and married the daughter of the Reverend Tennyson Makiwane. Jili Jabavu was later joined as professor by Z.K. Matthews, the son of a Kimberley miner, who had become the first graduate of Fort Hare; he called himself 'a new specimen in the zoo of African mankind'.[42] Matthews in turn married Frieda Bokwe, the sister of his college friend Rosebery Bokwe, from another prominent mission family.

This small elite was all the better educated because Fort Hare had admitted women students from the beginning. The principal had objected, but the African members declared that 'there was little point in educating their young men if their future wives were unable to offer them the companionship and community of interest which only an educated woman could give'.[43] By the late thirties, when Mandela arrived, Fort Hare still had only a handful of women students, housed in a separate hostel in an old farmhouse. They were correspondingly in demand, and were often cleverer than the men – which came as a shock to Mandela. But he was aware of the strong women among his Xhosa forebears, including the mother of the Mandela who founded his clan. 'Women have been monarchs and leaders,' he explained later, 'in some of the most difficult times in our history.'[44]

Generations of students from Fort Hare and Lovedale, many connected with the chiefly families of the Transkei, would develop formidable family networks, often with strong Christian values, self-disciplined and frequently teetotal, reminiscent of early Victorian British networks like the Clapham Sect. Jili Jabavu's daughter Noni, who spent some years in Britain, described her own extended family's 'all-embracing net' as spreading out from Fort Hare and Lovedale, reminding her of the English old school ties.[45] That network was to be tragically torn apart during the apartheid years by political persecution and exile. But the black professional middle class with its missionary influence would never be destroyed or bypassed, as it was in other parts of Africa like Ghana or Uganda; and some of its offspring – including Pallo Jordan, the son of Phyllis Ntantala and A.C. Jordan, and Stella Sigcau, daughter of the King of East Pondoland – would join Nelson Mandela's government in 1994.

Mandela was never at the heart of this intellectual elite, but it included many of his friends and relations. And he always respected Z.K. Matthews, with whom he had family links. The big, square-jawed professor, who taught generations of black students at Fort Hare, infuriated many rebels with his political moderation, but usually came to influence them with his powers of reasoning and quiet argument. Mandela was to admire Matthews still more after he originated the ANC's Freedom Charter in the fifties. 'There are some people inside and outside the movement who are critical of his cautious attitude,' he wrote to Matthews's widow after he died in 1970, 'but I am not sure now whether they were not wild.'

The Fort Hare which Mandela joined in 1939 was a small, compact institution with a quadrangle of simple Italianate buildings surrounded by student hostels. It was still dominated by its first principal, Alexander Kerr, a strict and austere Scot who avoided public controversy but was dedicated to the advancement and academic standards of the university, without colour prejudice: 'He dealt with every student as he was,' said Z.K. Matthews, 'and colour did not enter the relationship.' Kerr was a passionate teacher of the English language, imbuing his students with a love of its literature – above all of Shakespeare, which he taught with a vividness which made him seem totally relevant to contemporary Africa.[46] Mandela would always remember verses from Tennyson's 'In Memoriam', which Kerr declaimed in his Scots accent:

> Strong Son of God, immortal Love,
> Whom we, that have not seen thy face,
> By faith, and faith alone, embrace,
> Believing where we cannot prove . . .[47]

The rigorous but liberal scholarship of Kerr and the two African professors Jabavu and Matthews fortified the students throughout their later revolutionary phases. As well as its Coloured and Indian students Fort Hare included a few local whites, but it was dominated by Africans. A young African-American academic, Ralph Bunche – later Under-Secretary General of the United Nations and a Nobel Prize-winner – visited Fort Hare in 1938, and declared that 'the good native student is the equal of any Indian or Coloured student.'[48]

Mandela was proud to be at Fort Hare, and the Regent was glad to have a member of his clan at the famous college. The teachers told their students that they would become the leaders of their people, and when Mandela arrived as a fresher of twenty-one he was daunted by the sophistication and confidence of his seniors. His friend Justice had stayed behind at Healdtown, but Mandela now found a new ally and idol in Kaiser Matanzima, his nephew from the Tembu royal family. Like Mandela, Kaiser (or K.D., as he was called) was descended from King Ngubengcuka, but through the senior line, the 'Great House', and he was destined to be a king or paramount chief. Technically he was Mandela's nephew, but he was older and more confident as both leader and scholar: he would be the first chief to take a degree.[49] He became Mandela's mentor, encouraging him in his future role as royal counsellor. In later years the two cousins were to become political opponents, but at Fort Hare they were best friends. They both lived in the Methodist hostel, went to church together, played football, went dancing, and did not drink. They were both very tall, with courtly manners, fond of clothes and quite vain. 'The two of us were very handsome young men,' Kaiser would recall, 'and all the women wanted us.'[50] Even the tribal circumcision names by which they called each other, Dalibunga and Daliwonga, made them sound like twins. Sixty years later, from his Great Place in the Transkei, Kaiser looked back with gratitude on that youthful friendship: 'We were always together: when someone saw me alone, they would say, "Where's Nelson?" . . . We had warm hearts together.' Mandela even found Kaiser his wife, Agrineth, the daughter of Chief Sangoni, which was all the more important since Kaiser had forsworn polygamy.[51] And despite their later political differences, Mandela would never deny his earlier admiration of Matanzima: 'You probably will not believe it,' he wrote to Fatima Meer from prison in 1985, 'when I tell you he was once my idol.'[52]

Mandela, though less grand than K.D., was nevertheless also seen as a young prince; and royal families still had a special status even in the intellectual atmosphere of Fort Hare, which inspired both respect and resentment. 'Xhosa princes think the world belongs to them,' said Joe Matthews, the professor's son who would follow Mandela to Fort Hare. 'Some would kick tribesmen out of their way, thinking everyone else unimportant. Aristocrats can't believe you'll contradict them – as in Britain, like the women in Harrods who ignore everyone else and say loudly: "I'll have some of that."'[53] Mandela never displayed that arrogance, and always respected commoners like Oliver Tambo who were cleverer than him; but he became accustomed to people treating him like a prince.

Mandela blossomed at Fort Hare. He loved the university's beautiful setting on the banks of the Tyume river, below the Amatola Hills, and would later reminisce about the journey by the railway line curving along the hillside, and the magnificent landscape: 'the green bushes and singing streams after the summer rains, the open veldt and clean air'.[54] He excelled at cross-country running and boxing, and his heroes were sportsmen and athletes rather than intellectuals: later, from jail, he would ask about his rival in the mile races, 'Sosthenes' Mokgokong.[55] He enjoyed ballroom dancing and the drama society: he once played John Wilkes Booth, the assassin of Abraham Lincoln. And he made new friends from many backgrounds in this meeting-place for blacks from all over the country. 'You saw the tribes welding into a new nation,' remembered Noni Jabavu. 'You had only to listen to the exclamations and shouts. Their various English accents gave you a sense of the vast spread of South Africa.'[56]

Some of Mandela's friends were already active in politics: Paul Mahabane, who spent holidays with him, was the son of a former president of the ANC; Ntsu Mokhehle, a brilliant scientist, would become head of the Basutoland Congress Party; Nyathi Khongisa stirred up the students by attacking Prime Minister Smuts as a racialist and publicly hoping that Nazi Germany would defeat Britain, so that Africans could overthrow European domination; Lincoln Mkentane, from another prominent Transkei family, joined the ANC and was imprisoned; Oliver Tambo, an outstanding scholar in both science and the arts, was already a keen political debater.[57] But Mandela himself was not then politically aware. He was not close to Tambo, and was embarrassed by the rebelliousness of friends like Mahabane. His immediate ambition was to be a court interpreter, a much esteemed profession in the rural areas, which promised both influence and status: 'I could not resist the glitter of a civil service career.'[58] He studied interpreting at Fort Hare, together with law, native administration, politics and English. He saw a degree as his passport not to political leadership, but to a position in the community which would enable him to support his family.

Most of the other students were not very political either, and expected to become civil servants or, most often, teachers, which worried the university's Governing Council: 'It cannot be expected that the teaching profession will continue to absorb all grades,' the council reported in

1940.[59] There had been a time when Fort Hare was more revolutionary. In the early 1930s the young communist Eddie Roux had pitched a tent on the hill near the university, and given courses in Marxism-Leninism which fascinated African students including the young Govan Mbeki, while the black American Max Yergan taught Mbeki about dialectical materialism.[60] But by Mandela's time most students were preoccupied by their careers, and the Red Star had waned after Stalin made his pact with Hitler in August 1939. Soon after Mandela arrived at Fort Hare, Britain declared war on Germany, and Prime Minister Jan Smuts immediately announced that South Africa was entering the war on Britain's side. When Smuts came to talk to the students at Fort Hare they nearly all applauded him – including Mandela, who was relieved that Smuts's English accent was almost as poor as his own.[61] Mandela eagerly supported Britain's stand against Hitler, and would remain fascinated by Winston Churchill. Over fifty years later he would tell Churchill's daughter Mary Soames how he listened to his wartime broadcasts at Fort Hare, and recalled how Churchill had escaped from the Afrikaners during the Boer War.[62] But at twenty-two, Mandela remembered, 'Neither war nor politics were my concern.'[63]

Mandela seemed to have golden prospects as a future civil servant, but they were to be smashed by his rebelliousness. This did not concern politics, but a more immediate cause – the terrible food. The meals at Fort Hare were Spartan, and the African students felt all the more hard-done-by after they discovered that the white students at Rhodes University, which they visited for sporting contests and debates, were much better fed.[64] In his second year Mandela had been elected to the Students' Representative Council, but only a quarter of the eligible students had voted, the majority having boycotted the elections and demanded improvements in the college diet and more powers for the council. Mandela and the other five elected representatives resigned, and the shrewd principal Dr Kerr ordered new elections, to be held at dinner, when all the students would be present. But again only a quarter voted, electing the same six representatives. The other five agreed to stay on the council, but Mandela felt he could not ignore the views of the majority, and resigned again. He was encouraged in his stand by Kaiser Matanzima, who had previously been on the council.

Dr Kerr summoned Mandela, and warned him sympathetically but firmly that if he continued to resist he would be expelled. Mandela spent a sleepless night, torn between his ambition and his duty to his fellow-students: 'I was frightened,' he said later. 'I feared K.D. more than Dr Kerr.'[65] The next day he confirmed that he would not serve. Kerr gave him one last chance to think again, and told him to return to his studies. Believing that Kerr was infringing students' rights, Mandela refused, and was expelled. He went home to the Great Place, where the Regent, angry with him for throwing away his career, told him to apologise and go back to Fort Hare. But Mandela's stubbornness came to the fore. 'He was very obstinate,' said his cousin Ntombizodwa. 'He would never go back.'[66]

Soon the Regent dropped a bombshell which brought their relationship to a head. He believed he would not live much longer, and had arranged for both his son Justice and Mandela to marry and to settle down with their own families. Mandela was horrified: the girl chosen for him was rather fat and did not attract him, and he also knew she was in love with Justice: 'She was probably no more anxious to be burdened with me than I with her.'[67] It was the breaking point. Mandela knew he owed a great deal to the Regent, who had adopted him as his own child and had paid for his education, and who was now ill and in need of support. But he was determined to have his own freedom: he would secretly run away with Justice, to try his fortunes in Johannesburg.

'Life has its own way of forcing decisions on those who hesitate,' he wrote afterwards. This was his own choice, which put an abrupt end both to his tribal expectations and, it seemed, to his university career: 'Suddenly all my beautiful dreams crumbled and the prize that was so near my grasp vanished like snow in the summer sun.' But the decision had even greater repercussions than he realised at the time. If he had not defied Fort Hare's principal, he reflected four decades later from jail, 'perhaps I would have been safe from all the storms that have blown me from pillar to post over the last thirty years'. As it was, he was plunged into a much more dangerous sea; but it rapidly opened up much wider horizons, through which 'I could see the history and culture of my own people as part and parcel of the history and culture of the entire human race.'[68]

3

Big City

1941–1945

In April 1941, aged twenty-two, Mandela left the Great Place for Johannesburg with Justice. He was one of the thousands of rural blacks who arrived every year in the 'City of Gold', most of them in blankets or tattered clothes, hoping to find jobs as mineworkers, servants or labourers. They were a familiar sight to white Johannesburgers, commemorated in contemporary films and novels, from *Jim Comes to Jo-burg* to *Cry, the Beloved Country*.[1] Their arrival seemed an extreme example of the transition from rural poverty to metropolitan sophistication, typified by the recurring image of a bewildered tribesman gazing in wonder at the skyscrapers, fast cars and bright lights of the white man's city. But it was a misleading image: rural Africans from rooted homes could have a deeper sense of security and a clearer ambition in the city jungle than rootless urbanites who took its confusion for granted. And few whites realised that the country bumpkins included highly-educated, ambitious young people with proud traditions, who were to prove capable of overturning white supremacy within their lifetime.

Johannesburg was only fifty-five years old, but was already one of the major cities of Africa, with a confident centre including grand hotels and a stone cathedral, wealthy suburbs spreading to the north and sprawling black townships in the south-west. The Second World War was now creating a boom economy in South Africa, as in other industrial centres across the world: the cutback of imports stimulated local production, and created an urgent need for black labour to replace white workers, many of whom were fighting overseas. Between the censuses of 1936 and 1946 the black population in South Africa's cities increased by almost 50 per cent, from 1,142,000 to 1,689,000. When the rural tribal areas were devastated by droughts the flow into Johannesburg turned into a flood, and for two years the government abandoned influx control and its enforcement by pass laws. The inrush created chaotic new shanty-towns around the fringes of the city, but also new opportunities and hopes for ambitious young blacks – and new political aspirations encouraged by the war.

The South African government needed the support of blacks in wartime, and 120,000 Africans and Coloureds had been recruited by the armed forces as drivers, servants and guards. They were armed with spears, not guns, but felt themselves to be part of the fight against Nazism and racism. In the middle of the war the government even began to relax the traditional policy of segregation that confined blacks to their own townships, schools and buses. In a major speech in February 1942, Prime Minister Smuts described how the high white expectations of segregation had been sadly disappointed, as the rest of the world moved in the opposite direction: 'Isolation has gone and segregation has fallen on evil days too.' It was fruitless to attempt to resist the movement to the cities: 'You might as well try to sweep the oceans back with a broom.'

But the African migration into the cities was provoking Afrikaner nationalists, who felt threatened by black competition. They campaigned all the more fiercely against the 'black peril', and demanded a more extreme segregation, which they called 'apartheid' – literally 'separateness'. Smuts dared not make concessions to the blacks which would risk frightening white voters into the nationalists' camp. 'What will it profit this country,' he wrote to a friend in June 1943, 'if justice is done to the underdog and the whole caboodle then, including the underdog, is handed over to the Wreckers?'[2]

It was in the goldmines that Mandela and Justice first looked for work. The mines, which were at the centre of Johannesburg's economy, were strictly segregated, with enclosed compounds and hostels for the black workers who made up the vast majority of their labour force cut off from the rest of the city. The mining companies maintained close links with chiefs in the rural areas, who helped provide their cheap labour, and reproduced the tribal hierarchies and divisions within the mines in order to bolster discipline and allegiance. The Regent had written some months earlier to arrange a job for Justice as a clerk with Crown Mines, one of the oldest and biggest; and Justice persuaded the headman to give Mandela a humbler job as a mine policeman, with the prospect of a clerical job in three months.[3] For a short time Mandela worked as a nightwatchman, with a helmet, whistle and knobkerrie or club – the very picture of the loyal company employee – patrolling the entrance to the compound, which bore notices reading 'Natives Cross Here' (one was amended to 'Natives *Very* Cross Here').[4] At the time the mineworkers were seething with discontent about their conditions and wages – anger which later erupted in the mine strike of 1946.[5] Mandela kept aloof from the politics, but would always remain proud of having been a mineworker, as he would later tell the union.[6]

However important Mandela may have felt in Qunu, he was quite insignificant in Johannesburg, and he soon found himself in trouble for boasting that he had run away from home and deceived the Regent. He and Justice were ordered to return home, and fired from the mine. Mandela, who had no wish to return to the country, now had to find a job urgently. A cousin sent him to see a black estate agent, Walter Sisulu, who had an office – before Johannesburg was as strictly segregated as it later became – in the Berkeley Arcade in the city centre.

Sisulu was a short, energetic man of twenty-eight, with light skin, gap-teeth, spectacles and a habit of chewing his lip. He lacked great presence, but he had extraordinary inner confidence – 'super-confidence', he called it – and was to be the most important political influence in Mandela's life.[7] He had already shown unusual resilience. Like Mandela he came from a poor region of the Transkei – in his case the Engcobo district – but he lacked Mandela's status. His father was a white magistrate called Victor Dickinson, who had fallen in love with his mother in Engcobo, but had left her with two children.[8] Walter's mother talked respectfully about his father, but Walter realised that he had failed in his duty to his family.[9] Walter was brought up by his mother and his uncle, a headman, to be God-fearing and respectful towards whites. He enjoyed reading the Bible, and identified with underdogs like David and Moses, but he rebelled against the conservatism of his mission teachers and his family, who once warned him: 'I doubt if you'll be *allowed* to work for the white man.'

Sisulu left school at sixteen, became a cowherd and then tried his luck in Johannesburg. He worked for four months in a goldmine, hacking rock a mile underground, where he came to be enraged by the brutality of the system. After working in a kitchen in East London he returned to Johannesburg with a new interest in trade unionism. He stayed with his mother, who was now working as a washerwoman for white housewives, and was fired from a succession of factory jobs for insolence and disobedience. He took refuge from his humiliations by learning Xhosa history from a great-grandson of Hintsa, the great chieftain who had also inspired Mandela, but at the same time he broadened his outlook to embrace a wider African unity. After working for two years in a bank he had recently set up his estate agency with five black friends, which he hoped would make him independent of whites (it was to be taken over by a white firm two years later).[10]

Sisulu's white father, Victor Dickinson, was now a judge at the Supreme Court in Johannesburg; Sisulu would sometimes watch him there, incognito. He was also chairman of a building society, and when Sisulu's estate agency began experiencing difficulties he went to see him to ask for help. Sisulu did not reveal their relationship: he wanted to give his father a chance 'to recollect that he had a son like that', but he gave no sign of recognition. He was, Sisulu remembered, decent and warm, but did not offer him any help with money.[11] It was a poignant encounter, about which Sisulu still remains reticent. Did Dickinson ever know that his son was to be one of South Africa's greatest leaders?

Mandela was immediately impressed by Sisulu's mastery of city ways and his fast-talking English, and assumed that he must have had a university education. Sisulu, in turn, was impressed by Mandela's air of command. 'When he came into my office,' he recalled, 'I marked him at once as a man with great qualities, who was destined to play an important part.'[12] It was the beginning of a partnership which would be crucial to Mandela's political career. Mandela recognised Sisulu as his intellectual superior, a mentor with an analytical mind. He would never be his rival. He would be the kingmaker, never the king; the trainer, not the boxer. And he provided, by a happy chance, the first crucial rung in Mandela's city career. 'It was the most difficult time in my life,' Mandela wrote later.[13]

Mandela's real ambition was to be a lawyer, so Sisulu took him to see Lazar Sidelsky, of the firm of Witkin, Sidelsky & Eidelman, which had black clients as well as white. Sidelsky was a lively, bright-eyed young Jewish attorney who disapproved of politics but believed in treating blacks fairly, and had been shocked to see big law firms 'suck the blood out of their black clients'. He respected Sisulu, who brought him Africans who needed mortgages, remembering him as 'a cunning bloke, a bit of a blighter, but astute'. Sidelsky agreed to employ Mandela as an articled clerk, without charging a fee. He soon saw his potential: 'He was conscientious, never devious, tidy in person and in mind.' He took an interest in the young man, lent him £50 – a generous sum – and gave him an old suit, which he was to wear for five years. He urged Mandela to keep out of politics: 'You could serve your people better,' he told him, 'if you could prove that there's one black attorney who's honest and successful.'

Mandela never forgot that Sidelsky, as he has written, was 'the first white man who treated me as a human being', the man who 'trained me to serve our country'. A few years later, when Mandela was briefly prosperous and was driving an Oldsmobile, he noticed Sidelsky, who had fallen on hard times, waiting at a bus stop, and gave him a lift home. Sidelsky was puzzled that Mandela would go no further than the kitchen; and the next day Mandela sent him a cheque repaying the £50. Forty years later Sidelsky and his daughter visited Mandela in prison, and joked about his advice to keep out of politics: 'You didn't listen, and look where you ended up!'[14]

But politics were all around him. He shared an office with a young white lawyer named Nat Bregman, a cousin of Sidelsky, a 'light-hearted communist', as he later called himself. Bregman, a part-time stage comedian, enjoyed Mandela's company, finding him reserved but with a good sense of humour.[15] He took Mandela to communist lectures and to multi-racial parties where he met friendly white left-wingers, including the young communist writer Michael Harmel. Mandela was amazed by Harmel's combination of intelligence and simple living – he refused to wear a tie – and later he would become a close friend.

In the law office Sidelsky warned Mandela against a black communist, Gaur Radebe, who worked in the firm. A flamboyant, strongly-built man ten years older than Mandela, Radebe spoke five languages, and was helping to set up the new African Mineworkers' Union.[16] He did not conceal his militant views in the office. 'Keep away from Gaur,' said one colleague. 'He will poison your mind. Every day he sits on that desk planning a world revolution.' But Radebe befriended Mandela, and told his white bosses he was really a chief: 'You people came all the way from Europe, took our land and enslaved us. Look now, there you sit like a lord while my chief runs around on errands. One day we will catch all of you and dump you into the sea!' Mandela was dazzled by the coolness and confidence with which Radebe argued with whites.[17] Radebe urged him to join the communists, but Mandela was working too hard in the evenings for his law examinations. Twenty years later the two men had almost reversed their positions: Radebe, after being expelled from the Communist Party in 1942 for money-lending activities, joined the anti-communist Pan Africanist Congress, while Mandela defended the communists within the ANC.[18]

Mandela was now living in the midst of a black slum, lodging with a minister, the Reverend Mabutho, at 46 Eighth Avenue, Alexandra, a chaotic township six miles north of the city with no electricity, called 'the Dark City'. Alexandra was a jumble of brick houses and makeshift shacks overflowing with the wartime influx of workers from the countryside. It was insanitary and noisy with hungry dogs – a total contrast to the secluded white mansions beyond its fence. But Alexandra had a village vitality and a sense of community which they lacked. It was 'a cauldron of black aspirations and talent, and a mirror of black frustrations', wrote the activist Michael Dingake.[19] Alexandra mixed up the tribal Xhosas, Zulus and Sothos in the scramble for urban survival, and Mandela was surprised to find himself pursuing a Swazi girl. He became more interested in other tribes, learning about the Zulus' past glories from a property-owner called John Mngoma, who told him long stories about the heroism of the Zulu King Shaka and described events which never appeared in the whites' history books.[20]

In Alexandra, Mandela was among the poorest, sometimes having to walk twelve miles a day to save the bus-fare to and from the office in the centre of town. He remembers feeling humiliated when girls noticed his shabby clothes, and was envious of the more glamorous young 'Americans', the dandies in sharp suits with wide hats and flashy watches, often stolen, who attracted women; but he maintained his more staid English style.[21] He was helped by friends who lodged in the same house: later he felt guilty that 'not once did I think of returning their kindness'.[22]

Mandela soon found his feet as an urban African, able to fend for himself. He no longer needed the support of his father-figure the Regent, who was now very frail. The Regent visited him in late 1941, and did not reprove Mandela for his past disobedience; six months later, when the old man died, Mandela went to his funeral in the Transkei, and regretted that he had not been more grateful for the Regent's past kindness. He also wished he had taken the opportunity to ask him about white supremacy and the liberation movement.[23] By now he had outgrown his purely Xhosa perspectives, but he was still torn between his tribal obligations and the opportunities offered by the big city.

Mandela completed his BA degree through a correspondence course, but soon realised it was not the key to success: 'Hardly anything I had learned at university seemed relevant in my new environment.' He returned to Fort Hare to receive his degree, wearing a new suit bought with a loan from Sisulu. His nephew Kaiser Matanzima, now preparing to be a chief, urged him to return as a lawyer to the Transkei, but Mandela was becoming more interested in the national stage.

He soon moved out of Alexandra. To save money he lived for a short spell in the mining compound of Wenela (Witwatersrand Native Labour Association), which provided special quarters for visiting chiefs; there he met tribal dignitaries, including the Queen Regent of Basutoland. Then he moved to Orlando (now part of Soweto), a municipal suburb twelve miles outside Johannesburg which had been planned in 1930 as a model township for 'the better class of native'. Orlando stretched out across open farmland, overshadowed by the giant towers of a power station, a vista of two-roomed houses without floors or ceilings between bumpy dirt tracks. It was more hygienic but less intimate than Alexandra: Mandela liked to say that in Alexandra he had no house, but a home, while in Orlando he had a house without a home. But he was now close to Walter Sisulu, who lived with his mother in a house noisy with politics; and Orlando was destined to set the pace for all black South Africa.

Mandela still had to study – this time for a law degree. Early in 1943 he enrolled at the University of Witwatersrand, which stood, with its imposing columns, on a hill north of Johannesburg. 'Wits', unlike the Afrikaans universities, admitted a handful of black students to study alongside whites, though they could not use the sports fields, tennis courts or swimming pool. Some white lecturers strongly disapproved of black students, including Professor Hahlo, a German-Jewish lawyer who regarded law as a social science for which blacks and women lacked the mental discipline and experience.[24] But other law lecturers, like Julius Lewin and Rex Welsh, were generous liberals, and many of the white students had returned from the war with a hatred of racism. Among them were several communists, including Joe Slovo and his wife Ruth First, Tony O'Dowd and Harold Wolpe. Ruth First, who was later to be a close friend and colleague, remembered Mandela as 'good-looking, very proud, very dignified, very prickly, rather sensitive, perhaps even arrogant. But of course he was exposed to all the humiliations.'[25] Joe Slovo had the impression of 'a very proud, self-contained black man, who was very conscious of his blackness' and very sensitive to the perception that 'when you work with a white man, he dominates'.[26] Ismail Meer, who was Ruth's close friend, found Mandela 'fairly unsure of himself' and detached from student politics: 'He was the best-dressed student, and he was not going to get involved readily in the political activities at the campus. He was very cautious.'[27] Mandela 'had a friendly dignity about him', recalled another contemporary, Nathan Lochoff: 'a little shy, not assertive in any way'.

Mandela was to spend six years at Wits, from 1943 to 1949, without any great distinction. He had an excellent memory, but his studies had to be squeezed in between his job as an articled clerk and his political commitments. Professor Hahlo could be scathing: 'You call this an essay?' 'You know what I wish for him?' Mandela told one of his white friends, Jules Browde: 'That one day he has to write by paraffin light in Soweto.'[28] When he failed at the end of his course he applied to Professor Hahlo for permission to resit some papers, explaining that he often arrived home in Orlando after 8 p.m., 'feeling tired and hungry and unfit to concentrate on my studies . . . if I could have done my work under more suitable conditions, I would have produced better results.'[29] But Hahlo, strictly following the rules, turned down his application, and Mandela was eventually to leave Wits without his LlB degree. Despite his justifications, he still felt a sense of failure.[30]

At Wits Mandela suffered many humiliations. When he sat at a table in the law library, a white student moved away. When he went to a café with some white students, they were kept out because there was a 'kaffir' among them; one of them, Julius Wulfsohn, protested, but Mandela put his hand on his shoulder and simply said, 'Just leave it.'[31] When he went on a whites-only tram with two Indians the conductor called him their 'kaffir friend', and had them charged in court.[32] But he revealed no lasting grudges. Fifty years later, as President of the Republic, he invited the whole class of '46 to a reunion at Wits. 'I am what I am,' he told them, 'both as a result of people who respected me and helped me, and of those who did not respect me and treated me badly.'[33]

Back in Orlando, Mandela was seen as a man about town, and a ladies' man. ('I can't help it if the ladies take note of me,' he said later. 'I'm not going to protest.'[34]) He spent much of his time with Walter Sisulu and his mother 'Ma' in their small Orlando house. In 1944 Walter married Albertina Thethiwe, a young nurse from the Transkei who had been educated by Catholics. She soon became 'the backbone of the home', as Sisulu described her, strong enough to be both mother and politician, while providing a fixed base.[35] Albertina felt protective towards the handsome young country boy – 'You could see from the way he dressed that he was from the country' – and worried that gangsters in Alexandra, 'the Spoilers', would recruit him and exploit his aggression.[36]

But Mandela soon seemed to be settling down. In the warm atmosphere of the Sisulus' house he met Walter's young cousin Evelyn Mase, four years younger than him, who had also recently arrived from the Transkei, to become a nurse – the most respected profession for African women – and was working at the Johannesburg General Hospital with Albertina. Their neighbour Es'kia Mphahlele later described her as an unassuming girl, with lazy eyes and a subdued and coy smile.[37] Mandela was quickly attracted to Evelyn: after a few days they were going steady, and within months he proposed to her. They were married simply in 1944 at the Native Commissioner's Court, without church bells or a wedding feast. At first they lived in one room of the small Orlando house of Evelyn's brother Sam Mase, and later moved in with her brother-in-law Mgudlwa, a clerk in a mine.

'Everyone we knew said that we made a very good couple,' recalled Evelyn.[38] She was very house-proud, always busy polishing, gardening or cooking, and took good care of Mandela. 'She was a well-behaved, quiet lady, devoted to her family and husband,' Mandela said.[39] She was religious, from a more devout mission background than his. She did not see him as a politician, she recalls, but as a student.[40] Mandela's young sister Leabie, who came to stay with them, noticed that Evelyn 'didn't want to hear a thing about politics'.[41] But she was supportive of her ambitious husband. 'It was during his years with Evelyn that he grew and blossomed politically into the national figure he is today,' wrote Phyllis Ntantala, who was a friend of both.[42]

A year after the wedding Evelyn gave birth to their son Thembi. They moved briefly to 719 Orlando East, and soon afterwards to 8115 Orlando, one of hundreds of identical three-roomed 'matchbox' houses, with no electricity or inside lavatory. A stream of visitors, including Nelson's nephew Matanzima, came to stay in the little house, often sleeping on the floor. The next year Evelyn produced a daughter, Makaziwe, who died after nine months.

Evelyn was often helped by Nelson's mother, who came up from the

Transkei; the two women got on well. Mandela also helped with the shopping, bathing the babies, and even sometimes took over the cooking. 'Many wives envied Evelyn for her man who was dedicated to the family and bought food in town to take home,' recalled Oliver Tambo's wife Adelaide.[43] He was 'a highly organised person and very regular in his habits', said Evelyn. 'He was up at crack of dawn, jogged a few miles, had a light breakfast and was off for the day.'[44]

In four years in Johannesburg Mandela had come a long way from the quiet rural life of the Transkei. He had survived in the crowded townships, worked in a law office, studied at university and married. He had found his feet in a harsh and competitive environment. He still felt like a country boy confronting streetwise townsmen, fast-talking in English and Afrikaans. Yet his rural values and upbringing gave him an inner security, and he was conscious of being royal. 'Whatever he did he was thinking more of becoming a chief and an important person of the royal house,' said Sisulu. 'When he was getting into big politics he still had that in mind.'[45]

But Mandela was being drawn into the political fray, which would give a wider context and a purpose to his urban life. As a proud aristocrat he had come up against all the frustrations and humiliations of a black man in the white man's city, which had made him more aware of being one black man among millions. He was now having to see himself in a much harsher mirror; and soon he was to become an aspiring African nationalist, with an aggression and anger which it would take him a long time to control.

It was Mandela's militant office friend Gaur Radebe who first brought him into politics in Alexandra township. In August 1943 Radebe helped organise a spectacular boycott of the buses to the city – the third in three years – after the fares went up from fivepence to sixpence. Mandela joined the boycott and a march of 10,000 blacks, which left the buses empty for nine days until the fare was put back to its former rate. It was an encouraging lesson in the power of boycott.[46]

It was also Mandela's first close contact with the African National Congress, the main black political body, which was now reawakening from a long slumber. The ANC had been set up in 1912 by a Zulu lawyer, Dr Pixley ka Seme, in direct response to the creation of the Union of South Africa in 1910, which had brought together the Afrikaners and the British: a union, said Seme in his opening address, 'in which we have no voice in the making of the laws and no part in the administration'. The ANC's first President was Dr John Dube, a Zulu educationalist, and the Secretary was Sol Plaatje, an interpreter and writer from Kimberley, while Seme was made Treasurer.[47] As the ANC leaders watched their worst fears about white supremacy being borne out they organised delegations, demonstrations and protests, but they dreaded mass action or confrontation. The ANC was a staid, formal body with many members from royal families, represented in their own House of Chiefs – like the House of Lords – and Mandela came to see it as 'obsessed with imperialist forms of organisation'.[48] It was easily bought off by ineffectual government bodies: when Africans in the Cape Province were deprived of their vote in 1936, Congress leaders agreed to join the 'Natives' Representative Council', which was supposed to advise the government, though they soon discovered it was (as one of them, Paul Mosaka, called it) a 'toy telephone'.[49] By the late thirties the ANC had become dormant and disorganised, overshadowed in its protests by communists and Trotskyists, and discredited by putting its faith in easily-broken white promises.

In 1940 the ANC had elected a more effective President, Alfred Xuma, a small, busy doctor with a black American wife, who like Sisulu had begun as a herd-boy in Engcobo. He now lived in a comfortable house on the edge of Sophiatown, a multi-racial suburb of Johannesburg. Dr Xuma quickly pumped life into the moribund body. 'There was no membership to boast about, no records, and the treasury was empty,' as he described it.[50] He toured the country, reviving the branches, and took personal control over the Transvaal, whose overflowing black population provided many new recruits. He brought a new unity to the Congress, breaking down its tribal divisions and abolishing the House of Chiefs.[51] But it remained mainly middle-class and middle-aged, and while only Africans were admitted it had no popular following. Xuma was fussy about his dignity and proud of his respectable white friends, including government officials; and he dreaded the demagogy and militancy of the younger leaders who were now making themselves felt.

It was at Sisulu's house in Orlando in 1943 that Mandela first met the fiery young Zulu activist Anton Lembede, then only twenty-nine, who had just given up teaching to work in the law firm of Dr Seme, the co-founder of the ANC. Lembede, the son of a farm labourer, was a devout Catholic who, appalled by the moral degradation of the townships, had resolved that blacks must mobilise themselves without relying on whites or Indians. He believed the British were systematically working 'to discourage and eradicate all nationalistic tendencies among their alien subjects' and to co-opt the young black elite, making them their instruments. It was a charge to which Mandela felt himself vulnerable.[52]

Lembede had a strong populist touch: 'A pair of boots,' he said, 'is worth all the works of Shakespeare.'[53] But he was also an intellectual, steeped in English literature (including Shakespeare) and inspired by such black American leaders as Marcus Garvey and W.E.B. du Bois. 'My soul yearns for the glory of an Africa that is gone,' Lembede said, 'but I shall labour for the birth of a new Africa, free and great among the nations of the world.'[54] Mandela realised that Lembede was unscientific, verbose and sometimes irrelevant, but he admired the vigour of his rhetoric and his vision, which evoked past Xhosa heroes.[55]

Lembede became the leader of a small group of young blacks, including Sisulu and Mandela, who wanted to form a Youth League within the ANC. Their aim was to press the organisation towards mass action of the kind which had been so successful in the Alexandra bus boycott. While they supported the ANC, they resented Xuma's 'heavy hand'. They also felt challenged by the new African Democratic Party under Paul Mosaka which had just broken away from the Congress and, as they saw it, could 'prance around the country'.[56] They were encouraged by the Anglo-American idealism of the war against Hitler, particularly by the apparent radicalism of the Atlantic Charter, which Churchill and Roosevelt had signed in August 1941; this committed the signatories to 'respect the rights of all peoples to choose the form of government under which they will live'. Churchill soon afterwards began backtracking from the anti-colonial implications of the Charter, explaining to Leo Amery, the Secretary of State for India, that he did not mean the 'peoples' to include the natives of Nigeria or East Africa, let alone Arabs who might expel Jews from Palestine.[57] But Mandela and his friends took the Charter at its face value and admired Churchill for it; while Smuts appeared to support its application to Africa, particularly after the Japanese victories in the Pacific at the end of 1941, when he feared that Japan might invade Africa with support from blacks. (There was some reason for Smuts's fear: Walter Sisulu, among others, admired the Japanese as a successful coloured people, and declared himself 'happy when South Africa was threatened by the Japanese'.[58]) The ANC set up a committee under Professor Z.K. Matthews to interpret the Atlantic Charter. It produced a document called *Africans' Claims in South Africa*, which reasserted the right of all peoples to choose their government: the acid test of the Charter, it said, was its application to the African continent.[59]

Mandela was now, at twenty-five, committed to ANC politics, and in 1943 he joined a delegation led by Lembede to put the idea of the Youth League to Dr Xuma in the library of his Sophiatown house. It was a historic but spiky encounter. Mandela admired Xuma for having revived the ANC, and was impressed by his international friends like Tshekedi Khama of Bechuanaland, Hastings Banda of Nyasaland and King Sobhuza of Swaziland.[60] But he disliked Xuma's pompous English style, and his obsession with delegations and telegrams. Xuma, for his part, craved the support of young intellectuals, and was quite flattered by the visit of 'my Kindergarten boys', as he called them; but he warned them that the ANC was not ready for mass action.[61] Mandela, Sisulu and others nevertheless pressed ahead with a provisional committee, working away on a manifesto in the dingy Congress office in the Rosenberg Arcade in downtown Johannesburg.[62]

In April 1944 the Youth League was formally launched at the Bantu Men's Social Centre in Johannesburg, with Lembede as President and Sisulu, Tambo and Mandela on the executive committee. The stirring manifesto opened with Lembede's description of the difference between white and black perceptions:

> The white man regards the Universe as a gigantic machine hurtling through time and space to its final destruction; individuals in it are but tiny organisms with private lives that lead to private deaths . . .
>
> The African, on his side, regards the Universe as one composite whole; an organic entity, progressively driving towards greater harmony and unity whose individual parts exist merely as independent aspects of one whole . . .

The manifesto went on to reject any claim that the white man was helping to civilise the African, and to insist that the African 'now elects to determine his future by his own efforts'. It endorsed the ANC, with some reservations, and promised the support of the new Youth League as 'the brains-trust and power-house of the spirit of African nationalism'.

'The hour of youth has struck,' said a flyer issued by the provisional committee in September, which ended with the lines from *Julius Caesar*:

> The fault . . . is not in our stars,
> But in ourselves, that we are underlings.[63]

This was the first time, Mandela reckoned, that the idea of African nationalism had been set out in a clear fashion. But the policies were still uncertain. Did they really aim to drive the white man into the sea, as the radicals claimed? Eventually a more moderate view prevailed, shared by Mandela: that other racial groups were in South Africa to stay, but white supremacy must be abandoned.[64]

Another political organisation had also gained support from the convulsions of wartime. The Communist Party of South Africa, which Mandela first encountered at Wits, was now quite rapidly gaining popularity among Africans after twenty turbulent years. It had been formed in 1921, led by a small group of Jewish immigrants and British non-conformists, and operated under the strict rules of the Comintern in Moscow. South Africa, with its highly concentrated mining finance, interested many Marxist theorists, including Lenin, as a case-history of economic imperialism and monopoly capitalism; but on the ground many communist leaders became confused between class and race conflicts. At first the communists showed little interest in attracting black members or leaders: in 1922 they actually supported the all-white Labour Party in the mine strike, under the slogan 'Unite for a white South Africa'. The communists broke with the white Labour Party when it joined a cynical coalition with the Afrikaner nationalist government two years later; but in 1926 the Party alienated many white members when it accepted the new Comintern doctrine of a 'black republic'.

By the 1930s the communists were recruiting more black members, including two able young activists, J.B. Marks and Moses Kotane, who were trained at the Lenin Institute in Moscow and returned to help organise black unions. The communists had little appeal to the ANC, still influenced by traditional chiefs. In 1939, loyal to the pact between Hitler and Stalin, the Communist Party opposed the war. But after Russia was invaded by Hitler in June 1941 and became Britain's ally, the communists were more acceptable, and also more concerned with championing black rights. By 1945, helped by extra newsprint allocations, the circulation of the two South African communist-influenced papers the *Guardian* and *Inkululeko* had gone up to 67,000.[65]

Mandela had been impressed, through white friends like Nat Bregman and Michael Harmel, by the multi-racialism of the communists, who brought blacks into contact with whites on an equal footing. It was only the communists, Mandela wrote later, who 'were prepared to treat Africans as human beings and their equals; who were prepared to eat with us, talk with us, live with us and work with us. They were the only political group which was prepared to work with the Africans for the attainment of political rights and a stake in society.'[66] The ANC included many African communists in its ranks, and most members did not regard them as a threat. The ANC's Secretary-General from 1936 to 1949, the Reverend James Calata, believed that 'Communism had no influence worth worrying about.' He saw African national life as still built on a binding system, linking the individual to the family, to the clan, to the tribe: 'Communism, which is a purely materialistic system, cannot change the heart of the African towards it until that particular African feels that it is the only way out of oppression.'[67]

But the young nationalists of the ANC Youth League were very hostile to the communists, whom they saw as alien influences corrupting African nationalism, the 'vendors of the foreign method'.[68] Lembede fiercely attacked them, and broke up one communist meeting in Orlando with such a menacing tirade that *Inkululeko* commented: 'Hitler may lose the war in Europe but he has found a convert in S. Africa.'[69] Mandela (in spite of his communist friends) and Tambo shared Lembede's distrust, and the three put forward a motion that 'members of political organisations' should resign from the ANC. It was rejected by the national conference, but the Youth League's crusade against communists continued.

The conflict was part of a broader rivalry between nationalism and communism within liberation movements across Africa and Asia that would flare up after the Second World War. The nationalists could appeal to the historical pride of their people and offer them a new self-esteem; while the communists, backed by the victorious Soviet Union, could provide organisation and funds, and an intellectual critique of imperialism. But South Africa was a special ideological battlefield. The Africans had suffered domination and humiliations, which gave impetus to their nationalism; but the country's white minority was too large simply to be sent home, as was being urged elsewhere in Africa. 'They talked of independence,' said Govan Mbeki. 'We talked of freedom. There's a great difference.'[70] The Communist Party of South Africa was the only party which embraced all the races, and it was becoming more genuinely multi-racial than any other Communist Party.[71] It was between these magnetic poles of nationalism and communism that Mandela was now pulled.

4

Afrikaners v. *Africans*

1946–1949

THE HOPES OF MANDELA and his friends for a more benign post-war world were soon dashed: not by an apartheid regime, but by the United Party government of Jan Smuts, who had been Churchill's loyal ally in the war, and who was supported by South Africa's English-speaking businessmen. In 1946, only months after the final Allied victory over Japan, Smuts made two ruthless moves which pushed both Africans and Indians into greater militancy, and into working together.

The first was against a strike by the newly-formed African Mineworkers' Union, whose prime mover and first President was Mandela's friend Gaur Radebe. Radebe had been succeeded in 1942 by J.B. Marks, a robust African communist who had studied in Moscow and who led the strike of 70,000 black miners in August 1946, demanding more pay and better food and conditions. The mining companies, supported by the government, forced the workers back down the mines with bayonets, killing nine and wounding hundreds. Ten days later, fifty of the leaders were charged with fomenting a strike. Several were found guilty, and were fined or imprisoned.[1]

Most whites saw the crackdown as a necessary response to the communist menace, which was now re-emerging after the wartime truce. Smuts flew off to London, 'not unduly concerned', while the *Rand Daily Mail* attacked the 'wild speeches and absurd demands' of the union leaders, including 'J.B. Marx'.[2] The conservatives within the ANC, including Dr Xuma, blamed the communists for provoking a premature test of strength, but the Youth Leaguers criticised Xuma for not calling a general strike in sympathy.[3] The brutal suppression seemed to vindicate Lembede's warning that blacks could expect no mercy from the whites. Mandela was moved by the bravery and solidarity of the strikers – some of whom he knew – and he visited them with J.B. Marks. He discussed communism with Marks, and was struck by his humour and humility. Marks saw Mandela as a rabid nationalist, but thought he would outgrow that phase.[4]

The crushing of the mine strike made fools of the patient delegations of the ANC 'Old Guard', who had put their faith in Smuts. While the black miners were being bayoneted, the Natives' Representative Council was quietly debating black grievances with the government in Pretoria. Its members adjourned in protest, but did not actually boycott the Council. Smuts, however, realised that he had alienated 'moderate intellectuals of the Prof. Matthews type', and the next year he tried to placate a delegation of Council members headed by Matthews.[5] Smuts spoke in his usual paternal mode: 'This young child, South Africa, is growing up, and the old clothes do not fit the growing boy.' He deplored their 'sulking' attitude, and offered them 'a bone to chew' in the form of a bigger Council, all black and all elected, and legalised black unions, though not in the mines. Matthews was sceptical, and explained that the black people had lost confidence in the Council. Afterwards he told the press that the mountain had given birth to a mouse, and that the hungry masses needed more than a bone to chew.[6] But the Natives' Representative Council remained passive and ineffective (it would be abolished by the first Nationalist government).

Nelson Mandela was more lastingly influenced by Smuts's second harsh move, against the Indians in South Africa. The 300,000 Indians who had arrived in Natal since the 1860s, first as contract labourers, then as traders, had their own history of discrimination and protest. They had first learnt about peaceful protest in 1911 from Mohandas Gandhi, who devised his kind of passive resistance while he was working as a lawyer in South Africa, and had led thousands of Indians illegally from Natal into the Transvaal. Africans and Coloureds tried similar protests in 1919 and 1939, but without success. The Indians, some of whom had become prosperous merchants, kept themselves aloof from blacks, and hoped for better treatment after the war. But in 1946 the Smuts government introduced the Asiatic Land Tenure Bill, the 'Indian Ghetto Act', which banned the sale of any more land to Indians, while offering them the sop of white representatives in Parliament and an advisory board. It shook the Indians out of their complacency. For two years they sustained a passive-resistance campaign echoing Gandhi's of thirty-five years before, occupying land reserved for whites: two thousand protesters went to jail, including the campaign's two leaders, Dr 'Monty' Naicker and Dr Yusuf Dadoo.[7]

Mandela was coming closer to the Indians. He was impressed by their progress from speech-making and resolutions to mass action, in contrast to the inertia of the ANC. He was struck by the solidarity and sacrifice of the protesters, who included both militant and conservative Indians, and he admired both Naicker and Dadoo.[8] In Johannesburg he was now meeting many Indians, and found himself personally at ease with them. A flat in downtown Johannesburg, 13 Kholvad House, in Market Street, had become a crucial meeting-place between the races. There Mandela would meet Ismail Meer, Ruth First, Yusuf Cachalia and many other Indian and white communists in a relaxed atmosphere. He also spent much time at the home of Amina Pahad (whose two sons Aziz and Essop were later to join the Mandela government), where they would all eat curry and rice with their fingers. It reminded him of his childhood at Jongintaba's Great Place.[9] And after some early arguments he worked closely with Ahmed Kathrada, a young Indian communist who was to spend twenty-five years with him in prison.

Through his Indian friends Mandela became more interested in India itself, which was then on the verge of independence, and in the achievements of Gandhi and his disciple Jawaharlal Nehru. 'When we were starting the struggle we really had very little to go by from the leadership in our country,' he recalled, 'because their experiences were not reduced to writing, whereas people like Gandhi and Nehru had recorded their experiences. So we had to look up to them, and their influence was tremendous.' He was more influenced by Nehru, who was not a pacifist, than by Gandhi: 'When a Maharajah tried to stop him he would push him aside. He was that type of man, and we liked him because his conduct indicated how we should treat our own oppressors. Whereas Gandhi had a spirit of steel, but nevertheless it was shown in a very gentle and smooth way, and he would rather suffer in humility than retaliate.'[10]

The Indian passive resisters in South Africa in 1946 and 1947 taught Mandela and other African politicians an important lesson. Only a few non-Indians joined them (including the radical British monk Michael Scott), but they soon attracted support from the ANC. In 1947 the ANC president Dr Xuma joined with Naicker and Dadoo in the so-called 'Doctors' Pact', which promised co-operation between the ANC and the two Indian Congresses. Xuma reinforced the alliance by appearing at the first session of the United Nations in New York in company with an Indian representative, H.A. Naidoo, to protest against the 'Ghetto Act', thus initiating the UN's campaigns against racism. Mandela would come to see this pact as the origin of all the later collaborations between the races, and many young Indians were inspired by the prospect of racial co-operation.[11] 'It was this pact which gave me and my generation a sense of what it is to be South African,' said Kader Asmal, later Minister of Water Affairs in Mandela's government.[12]

But at the time, Mandela opposed closer political co-operation with Indians. He was convinced that only separate Congresses could effectively mobilise their masses, and was worried that the Indians or the Communist Party would take over or dominate the ANC for their own purposes, watering down the concept of African nationalism.[13] He still had a burning sense of the Africans' special suffering and identity, and he felt defensive, both personally and politically, in face of the more qualified and sophisticated Indians.

The two showdowns of 1946 both ended in defeat. The African Mineworkers' Union was effectively destroyed, not to be resurrected until the 1980s, and the Indians were increasingly restricted to their ghettos.[14] The setbacks left a deep mark on Mandela and other young black politicians. The Old Guard of delegations and petitions, epitomised by the Native Representative Council, was now discredited, and there were signs of a more courageous leadership emerging among the Indians and the communists.

The independence of India in August 1947 provided a powerful precedent for the struggle in South Africa, as in the rest of the continent, by showing how an established ruling power could be defeated by a unified and organised mass-movement. India's first Prime Minister, Nehru, had been urging Indians to co-operate with Africans in South Africa ever since 1927, and he would soon show himself a determined ally of both Congresses, making India the first country to impose sanctions against South Africa.[15] Mandela would always be grateful to Nehru for this. The influence of Indian communists would become an obsession for both the South African and the British governments, but Nehru, without being a communist, could provide a broader message for Mandela and others, to see beyond racial and local nationalism. 'Nationalism is good in its place,' Mandela would quote Nehru, 'but it is an unreliable friend and an unsafe historian. It blinds us to many happenings and sometimes distorts the truth, especially when it concerns us and our country.'[16]

The ANC Youth League in the meantime was moderating some of its nationalism. In July 1947 its firebrand founder Anton Lembede suddenly died, aged thirty-three, only a few hours after Mandela had been talking to him.[17] Mandela was appalled; but Lembede's successor Peter Mda proved a clearer political thinker and a greater influence (though Mandela would later find him too cautious).[18] Mda was a spellbinding talker, with a rich vocabulary, a small head and a huge laugh. The son of a Xhosa shoemaker, he had been educated by Catholics, and as a former teacher and lawyer he had both practical and intellectual training.[19]

Mandela himself became Secretary of the Youth League, responsible for political organisation and setting up branches.[20] With Mda he recruited more members beyond the Transvaal, in Natal and the Cape. He tried to infiltrate African schools, visiting St Peter's in Johannesburg, where Oliver Tambo had taught, in an attempt to address the students. But the headmaster, D.H. Darling (as he told Tambo afterwards) felt he could not allow the school to be used as a platform.[21] Mda had more success at Fort Hare, where he persuaded a young lecturer in anthropology, Godfrey Pitje, to start a branch of the Youth League, to 'soak them in our nationalistic outlook' and to work hand-in-hand with the executive in Johannesburg, 'of which the general secretary is N.R.D. Mandela Esq, BA, a law student'.[22] Pitje's professor, Z.K. Matthews, was sceptical of the 'armchair intellectualism' of the Youth League but did not prevent it from operating in Fort Hare. The university became the Youth League's most valuable seedbed, attracting a militant new generation of students that included Robert Sobukwe, Joe Matthews and T.T. Letlaka, into the ANC.[23]

Mda insisted that he was not against white men as such, only against white domination: but he warned that Africans could not expect whites to side with them 'at the time when the horizontal colour bar gave them a privileged way of life'.[24] He wrote a new manifesto for the Youth League, less rhetorical and more analytical than Lembede's, which Mandela approved. It defined African nationalism as 'the militant outlook of an oppressed people seeking a solid basis for waging a long, bitter and unrelenting struggle for its national freedom'. It warned Africans not to 'look up to Europeans either for inspiration or for help in their political struggle'. But it was more conciliatory about Indians, recognising that they were an oppressed group who 'had not come to South Africa as conquerors and exploiters, but as the exploited'.[25]

Mandela, in spite of his Indian friendships, was still worried that Indians would dominate the ANC in the Transvaal.[26] The tension came to a head after a 'Votes for All' campaign was launched in May 1948 at a 'People's Assembly' in Johannesburg, opened by Michael Scott, demanding universal suffrage. The Transvaal branch of the ANC was divided: Mandela complained that the People's Assembly had bypassed existing organisations, while Walter Sisulu insisted that Africans must find allies where they could.[27] Mandela and Tambo went to a meeting of the Indian Congress with Sisulu, and were so angry when he supported the Indians' arguments that they did not talk to him after the meeting, and departed in different directions.[28] But they were gradually becoming less suspicious of communist friends like J.B. Marks and Moses Kotane. 'If Moses represents the Party,' said Tambo, 'I don't think I will quarrel with it.'[29]

Mandela joined the Transvaal National Executive of the ANC in 1947, and became fiercely loyal to it. He was befriended by its President Constantine Ramohanoe, who taught him how to keep in touch with the grassroots.[30] But Ramohanoe wanted to cooperate with Indians and communists, a move which was opposed by the majority, including Mandela. When he defied them by making his own statement Mandela, seconded by Oliver Tambo, moved to depose him, which led to a stormy meeting and Ramohanoe's departure. 'Loyalty to an organisation,' Mandela would always maintain, 'takes precedence over loyalty to an individual.'[31] He maintained that stern rule over the next fifty years, as dissidents would learn to their cost. Having subjugated his own will to the movement, he was determined that others should do so too.

Mandela encountered many intellectuals who were fiercely critical of the ANC; particularly in Cape Town, where Trotskyists had formed the 'Unity Movement', which included many leading African and Coloured academics who insisted on total non-collaboration. In 1948 he visited Cape Town for the first time, staying for three months. He went up Table Mountain by the cable car, and gazed across at Robben Island.[32] He was invited to visit A.C. Jordan, a university lecturer prominent in the Unity Movement, who had written a book much admired by his Tembu friends, *Ingqumbo yemiNyanya* (The Wrath of the Ancestral Spirits), and was impressed by his intellect. With Jordan was Isaac Tabata, a founder and propagandist for the Unity Movement who talked brilliantly about South African history, but criticised Mandela with venom for joining the ANC:

'I am sure you did so simply because your father was a member.'[33] (In fact Mandela's father was only part of his tribe's collective membership.) Mandela was in some awe of Tabata: 'It was difficult for me to cope with his arguments . . . I didn't want to continue arguing with the fellow because he was demolishing me just like that.'[34] He was shocked that Tabata seemed more hostile to the ANC than to the government.[35] Afterwards Tabata wrote him a very long letter, warning him against the 'collaborators' of the ANC and pressing him to base his actions on principles, to 'swim against the stream'.[36] But Mandela thought the Trotskyists' insistence on non-collaboration was merely 'their pet excuse for doing nothing'. Cape Town left him more than ever convinced that only the ANC could mobilise his people to provide effective mass action.[37]

However disillusioned he was by the Smuts government, Mandela – like many of his friends – still placed some hope in the liberalism of the post-war transatlantic alliance, of the UN and of the Labour government in Britain. In April 1947 King George VI, with his Queen and the two young Princesses Elizabeth and Margaret, made a spectacular two-month state visit to South Africa which was intended to bolster the links between the two countries. But the British High Commissioner in South Africa, Sir Evelyn Baring, correctly warned London that Afrikaner nationalists would attack the visit as a symbol of the 'Empire bond which they had pledged themselves to break'.[38] The royal party spent thirty-five days touring the whole country in a special white train. Smuts – more of a hero to the British than to the South Africans – made the most of it, declaring a public holiday to celebrate the twenty-first birthday of Princess Elizabeth, later Queen, who would always look back on the tour warmly as her first experience of the Commonwealth. The celebrations were officially boycotted by the ANC, including the Youth League, which met at Mandela's house to discuss it.[39]

The King's contacts with Africans during the tour were strictly limited by the Smuts government. He was not allowed to shake black hands at official ceremonies, but crowds of black spectators cheered the royal visitors, and Dr Xuma, the President of the ANC, could not resist travelling to Zululand to see the King.[40] The left-wing *Guardian* in Cape Town was exasperated by the Africans' celebrations: 'If the pitch and tone of the people's struggles for freedom can be lowered by these spectacular feudal devices,' complained an editorial, 'it will be extremely difficult to recover the ground that has been lost.'[41] Mandela himself, with his own chiefly background, thought the British monarchy should be respected as a long-lasting institution, and noted the veneration which the Xhosa chiefs showed for George VI. One Xhosa poet described how the then Paramount Chief Velile Sandile 'pierced the ground' in front of the King. 'He was grovelling really,' Mandela recalled, 'but I can't blame him. I might have done the same.'[42]

Smuts was already losing much of his popularity with white South Africans, particularly Afrikaners, before the general election of May 1948. He had been careful not to alarm the white electorate by making concessions to blacks, but the Afrikaner National Party under Dr Daniel Malan, with its doctrine of apartheid and its warnings against the 'black peril' and the 'red menace', was gaining support as Africans became more visible in the cities. The ANC saw the white election as a choice between two evils, while Dr Xuma claimed that apartheid was nothing new, merely 'a natural and logical growth of the Union Native policy'.[43] Educated black Africans in Orlando despised the raw Afrikaners who made up most of Malan's supporters. 'We only knew Afrikaners as tram-drivers, ticket-collectors, policemen,' said Mandela's friend Esme Matshikiza. 'We thought they couldn't run the country. We didn't know that their leaders had studied in Nazi Germany.'[44]

In the election Dr Malan's National Party gained victory, in alliance with the smaller Afrikaner Party. Its majority was only eight, but this was enough for the country to be ruled for the first time by Afrikaner nationalists without more moderate English-speaking support. Smuts was humiliated, and when he died two years later he was venerated in the outside world as a statesman and war leader, but blamed in his own country for ignoring both Afrikaners and Africans – a warning to his successors that a statesman must not forget to remain a politician.

Malan's new government soon changed the whole character and perspective of the South African state. The Afrikaners, descendants of Calvinist Dutch settlers in the seventeenth century, had retained a very separate culture from the English-speakers, little influenced by subsequent European liberalism. Their oppression by British imperialists, culminating in the Boer War at the turn of the century, had forged a powerful nationalism, with its own religion and epics, and they nursed their grievances against the British. When the Union of South Africa was created in 1910 the British had hoped to retain an English-speaking majority, gradually softening the Afrikaners' resentment. But the numbers of

Afrikaners had multiplied, while their relative poverty and continuing experience as underdogs fuelled their nationalism. The Afrikaners (as British Prime Minister Harold Macmillan would tell them in 1960) were really the first of the African nationalists, with their own need to prove themselves and defend their culture; and they would inevitably come into conflict with black African nationalists who threatened their jobs and their supremacy.[45] As Mandela later looked back on forty years of rivalry: 'Perhaps history ordained that the people of our country should pay this high price because it bequeathed to us two nationalisms that dominate the history of twentieth-century South Africa . . . Because both nationalisms laid claim to the same piece of earth – our common home, South Africa – the contest between the two was bound to be brutal.'[46]

The new Afrikaner government did not conceal its intention to further separate the races and to build an Afrikaner state. 'For the first time since Union,' said Dr Malan, 'South Africa is our own.' Sir Evelyn Baring had few illusions: his despatches to London would compare Afrikaner nationalism to Nazism, and he came to dislike the Afrikaner ministers so much (his wife complained) that he could hardly keep the venom out of his voice.[47] But at first most British politicians and commentators were not seriously worried by the change in government. 'Dr Malan's majority is far too small,' wrote the *Economist*, 'to enable him to do anything drastic.'[48] The Labour government in London, beset by economic crises, needed South African uranium and was anxious not to offend the Malan government lest it take over the three British protectorates – Swaziland, Basutoland and Bechuanaland – on its borders.

Many Africans, including Oliver Tambo, actually welcomed the victory of Malan's party, an unambiguous enemy that would unite the blacks against it; but Mandela was 'stunned and dismayed'.[49] Twelve years later he would still explain the possibility that growing black pressure would gradually compel white governments to extend the vote, leading eventually to universal suffrage.[50] But now that prospect seemed much less likely. And, like nearly all black politicians, he seriously underestimated the Afrikaner determination to impose total segregation and to suppress black resistance, against the trend elsewhere in Africa and in America. Hardly anyone foresaw that over the next forty years successive National Party governments would pass laws which would ban the black leadership, imprison them or force them into exile.

In the face of this new threat, the Africans proved slow to unite. In

December 1948 the ANC held a joint meeting with its rival body the All-African Convention, which was dominated by Trotskyists, including Mandela's opponent Isaac Tabata. Dr Xuma called for blacks to 'speak with one voice'. J.B. Marks warned that 'the people are being crushed while we complacently quibble about technical difficulties'. Peter Mda insisted that the basis of unity must be African nationalism. But Tabata called for unity among all non-Europeans on the basis of total non-collaboration, which ANC delegates could not accept.[51] The meeting was inconclusive, and the arguments continued at another assembly four months later.

The need for unity emerged much more sharply with riots in Durban in January 1949, when enraged Zulus set on Indians and the police and military intervened, leaving 142 dead. Mandela heard from his Indian friends that whites had encouraged the riots by transporting Zulus to the scene.[52] The bloodshed, Mandela thought, put the 'Doctors' Pact' to the test, and he was impressed to see Dr Naicker playing a critical role in quickly restoring peace and promoting goodwill. 'The year 1949,' he wrote thirty years later, 'was an unforgettable experience for those who have given their lives to the promotion of inter-racial harmony.'[53] Dr Xuma blamed the riots on the government's divisive policies, and warned against 'the law of the jungle'. The black fury spread to the Johannesburg area, where some Indian and African leaders hoped the Congresses would jointly appeal for calm. Ahmed Kathrada went with a journalist, Henry Nxumalo, to Mandela's house in Orlando to try to persuade him to support a joint statement, but Mandela, still wary of the ANC being influenced by Indians, insisted that the ANC should act on its own.[54]

By mid-1949 Dr Malan's government was preparing to enforce apartheid with drastic laws: each person would be classified by race; the races would live in separate parts of the cities; and mixed marriages would be forbidden. The firebrands of the Youth League, including Mandela, felt challenged to respond. Their President Peter Mda advocated a 'Programme of Action' based on organising mass protests against the government. The Youth League was gaining more support in the ANC as a whole, and was losing patience with Xuma's caution. In November 1949, a few weeks before the ANC's annual conference, Mda went with Sisulu, Mandela and Tambo to see Xuma in Sophiatown. They argued that the ANC must adopt mass action and passive resistance like Gandhi's in India, or the Indians' in South Africa three years before. Xuma retorted that it was too early, that action would only provoke the government to crush the ANC. The Youth Leaguers warned him that if he did not support them they would vote against his presidency at the conference. Xuma replied angrily that they were young and arrogant, and showed them the door.[55]

Looking round for an alternative President, they first asked Professor Matthews, who thought they were naïve and immature, with their emotive rhetoric, and turned them down.[56] Then they made a rash choice, turning to Dr James Moroka, a dignified and relatively wealthy African doctor who had inherited a small estate in the Orange Free State, where a century before his great-grandfather Chief Moroka had welcomed the Afrikaner Voortrekkers – who then betrayed him. Moroka, a courteous gentleman, had, like Dr Xuma, many white friends and patients. He had been courageous in opposing the 'Hertzog Bills' in 1936, but he had since been attracted by the Trotskyists, and had become President of the ANC's rival the All-African Convention. Now, surprisingly, he told the Youth Leaguers that he supported their radical Programme of Action, and agreed to stand against Xuma even though he was not even a member of the ANC – which he kept calling the 'African National Council'.[57]

The ANC Youth League opened its own conference on 15 December 1949, just before the main ANC conference at Bloemfontein, with a humble prayer:

> Thou, Heavenly Father, art continuing to lift us up from the sinks of impurity and cesspools of ignorance. Thou art removing the veil of darkness from this race of the so-called 'Dark Africa'.[58]

The inner group of Youth Leaguers – headed by Mda, Sisulu, Mandela and Tambo – clearly emerged at the conference as 'the kingmakers', though Mandela could not attend. They had some differences: Mda remained a firm African nationalist, with Mandela closest to him. Sisulu was much more open to other racial groups, while Tambo remained diplomatic.[59] But they all demanded mass action.

The main ANC conference was eclipsed in the South African press by a much more melodramatic event: the opening by Prime Minister Malan of the vast Voortrekker Monument outside Pretoria, commemorating the sufferings of the Great Trek, before a crowd of 100,000 Afrikaners. 'The hour has come,' said Malan. 'A sunbeam from the heavens is striking down on the sarcophagus.'

Dr Xuma did his best to challenge this ceremony, with a speech in the market square of the Bloemfontein township in which he warned prophetically that the Voortrekker Monument would remind future generations of the racial strife between Europeans and Africans. The white press took little notice.

In his presidential address to the ANC conference Xuma tried to rally support, and emphasised that Africans were united against apartheid.[60] But he firmly rejected the Youth League's policy of boycotting apartheid institutions. His speech received meagre applause, and Diliza Mji, an outspoken young medical student in the Youth League, then moved a vote of non-confidence. 'A shock-wave went through the hall,' as Mji described it. 'Never in the history of the ANC had the President been criticised.'[61] The kingmakers then turned to Moroka, who had already pledged his support, and the conference elected him as President. Xuma remained on the executive until he resigned on 13 March 1950, complaining that the Youth League had betrayed him. But Sisulu, Mandela and Tambo wrote a forceful rebuttal in the *Bantu World*: 'We are as a nation entitled at any time to call upon any one of us to lead the struggle.'[62]

The ANC also elected a much more radical National Executive, including the Youth Leaguers Peter Mda, Oliver Tambo and Godfrey Pitje, the young activist from Fort Hare. Mandela himself was co-opted onto the National Executive two months later, to fill the place left by Xuma. More importantly, the Congress chose a new Secretary-General. The veteran clergyman James Calata stood down, finding the Programme of Action too radical, and in his place Walter Sisulu was elected by one vote.[63] Sisulu was the right man at the right time. Unlike Moroka, he was totally dedicated to the ANC and its new policy. As he recalled: 'Once they had decided to elect me my approach was: "I have nothing to live for except politics. So I cannot draw up a programme of action which I am not able to follow myself." That required me to be confident of the future, otherwise I would weaken somewhere. That confidence kept me in.'

Mandela had a narrower view than Sisulu. 'When I became Secretary-General my duty was to unite people,' Sisulu said later, 'whereas Nelson and Mda were still thinking in terms of projecting the Youth League.'[64] But Mandela thought the Programme of Action would transform the attitudes and methods of the Congress. 'The ANC was now going to rely not on a mere change of heart on the part of the authorities,' he explained later. 'It was going to exert pressure in order to compel the authorities to grant its demands.'[65] He was now at the heart of a new movement towards confrontation with the Afrikaner nationalists. As Frieda Matthews, the wife of the staid professor at Fort Hare, described it: 'People were excited, men and women, young and old. At last there was to be ACTION!'[66]

5

Nationalists v. Communists

1950–1951

THE AFRICAN TOWNSHIPS of Johannesburg were the key to political action. They were the magnet for most black South Africans, their opening to a new-found Westernised world of films, jazz, jiving and sport. Rural blacks, steeped in the Bible or Shakespeare by their mission teachers, were exposed here to wider influences and incentives which provoked an explosion of creative talent in music, writing and drama. Educated Africans took much more readily to city life than Afrikaners, whose culture was still rooted in the countryside. The cultural renaissance of this 'new African' would be compared to the Harlem renaissance in New York in the 1920s, displaying the same kind of passionate expression on the frontier between two cultures. But Johannesburg had the broader confidence of a black majority and a whole continent behind it.[1]

For the few whites who crossed the line, black Johannesburg in the fifties, with its all-night parties, shebeens (speakeasies) and jazz sessions, offered a total contrast to the formal social life of the smart northern suburbs, where white-gloved African servants served at elaborate dinner parties. Soweto had a bubbling vitality and originality which shines through the autobiographies of young black writers of the time like Can Themba, Nat Nakasa, Es'kia Mphahlele, Bloke Modisane, Casey Motsisi and Peter Abrahams, or the short stories of the young white novelist Nadine Gordimer.[2] Politicians and intellectuals were pressed together with factory workers, teachers and gangsters, all feeling themselves part of the Western post-war world which they knew through magazines, movies and advertisements. They were fascinated by the exploits of black American sporting heroes, pop stars or political campaigners, and inspired by the international idealism of the new United Nations and the 'Family of Man'. The Johannesburg jazz, fashions, dancing and quick-fire talk reflected the mix of Western and African idioms and rhythms with their own original style; musical compositions like the penny-whistle '*kwela-kwela*' or the song '*Wimoweh*' would become recurring hits in America and Britain.[3]

But this vibrant culture was almost totally ignored by white Johannesburg. The two races converged in the city centre every day as masters and servants, and separated every evening: the whites in their cars to the north, the blacks in their buses to the south, beyond the mine-dumps. The whites saw blacks only as domestics, labourers or tribal villagers, barely literate and dependent on white patronage; to allow them to assert their political power appeared irresponsible, if not dangerous. But behind the colour bar the squalid and overflowing townships beyond South Africa's city centres were bursting with energy and ambition. 'The truest optimism in South Africa is in the crowded, disease-ridden and crime-infested urban locations,' wrote the great South African historian C.W. de Kiewiet in 1956. 'They represent the black man's acceptance of the new life of the Western world, his willingness to endure a harsh schooling and an equal apprenticeship in its ways.'[4]

Urban Africans were predominantly conservative, fascinated by the West, much influenced by Christian Churches, and full of optimism for the future. 'It was a time of infinite hope and possibility,' wrote the young Zulu writer Lewis Nkosi, describing what he called 'the Fabulous Decade' of the fifties. 'It seemed not extravagant in the least to predict then that the Nationalist government would soon collapse.'[5] 'It was the best of times, the worst of times,' the writer Can Themba liked to quote from Dickens.[6]

It was only slowly that the blacks realised that they were being squeezed in a vice; that this would soon become simply the worst of times. Over the next few years the apartheid governments, backed by Western Cold Warriors, would pursue policies which seemed designed to press them towards revolutionary politics, and to look for friends among communists and in the East.

In black Johannesburg Nelson Mandela was both typical and exceptional. He moved with growing confidence among his contemporaries in Orlando West, the enclave of more prosperous blacks. He loved the world of music and dancing, and was close to township musical heroes like the Manhattan Brothers, Peter Rezant of the Merry Blackbirds, and the composer and writer Todd Matshikiza. He was beginning to earn money as a practising lawyer, and adopted the style of the township big-shot, driving his Oldsmobile and eating at the few downtown restaurants which admitted Africans – the Blue Lagoon, Moretsele's and later Kapitan's, the Oriental restaurant which still remains in Kort Street, and bought his provisions from a nearby delicatessen. Joe Matthews, the sophisticated son of the Fort Hare professor, was surprised to find a country boy from the Transkei with such exotic tastes.[7] Above all Mandela took great trouble with his clothes – like Chief Jongintaba, whose trousers he had pressed as a child. Mandela's friend George Bizos, who later defended him when he came to trial, once met him near the Rand Club in downtown Johannesburg, having a final fitting with the fashionable tailor Alfred Kahn (who also made suits for the millionaire tycoon Harry Oppenheimer). Bizos was amazed to see Kahn going down on one knee to take the black man's inside leg measurement. Ahmed Kathrada was so impressed by a blazer with a special African badge which Kahn had made for Mandela that he ordered one for himself, only to be appalled by the bill.[8]

Mandela had the confidence of a man-about-town, great presence and charm and a wide smile. But he kept his distance, as befitted an aristocrat rather than a commoner. Even Nthato Motlana, who became his doctor, found Mandela's style kingly, and felt he had to choose his words with care when he was with him.[9] Mandela sounded very different from the fast-talking 'city slickers' brought up in Johannesburg, and retained his formal style in both Xhosa and English. He often ate lunch at the Bantu Men's Social Centre, the teetotal meeting-place for respectable middle-class blacks; it had tennis courts, table tennis, concerts and dances, and American connections through Ray Phillips, the Congregationalist who ran the Jan Hofmeyr Social Centre upstairs.[10]

Mandela avoided the drinking sessions which distracted many of his contemporaries, and did not venture into rowdy shebeens like the Thirty-Nine Steps or Back o' the Moon. But I met him in 1951 at a favourite ANC drinking place – a printing shop in Commissioner Street in downtown Johannesburg. Its Falstaffian Coloured proprietor Andy Anderson would produce beer and brandy bottles from behind the presses after hours, and pick up scrawny fried chicken from a Chinese take-away, while ANC leaders discussed forthcoming leaflets and campaigns. Mandela remained sedate and dignified compared to his more expansive colleagues: he did not really approve, he explained later, of hard liquor.[11]

At six-foot-two Mandela was physically imposing, with a physique which he took care to maintain. He was a keen heavyweight boxer, sparring for ninety minutes on weekdays at the makeshift gym in Orlando where he trained from 1950 onwards. He lacked the speed and power to be a champion, but he relished the skills of boxing – dodging, retreating, dancing, circling – and saw the sport as a means of developing leadership and confidence. Boxers had become role-models of black achievement and power, in South Africa as in America. Joe Louis, the American heavyweight champion of the world from 1937 to 1949, had been Mandela's boyhood hero, and Sowetans took intense pride in their local champions like Jerry Moloi and Jake Tuli, who became flyweight champion of the British Empire. Mandela would often reminisce later about the great matches. He loved to recall the last fight of the heavyweight champion 'King Kong', who began by mocking his opponent Simon 'Greb' Mtimkulu. Greb waited till the third round, then 'hit with a left, an over-right and a bolo to the body. End of fight.'[12] Mandela saw boxing in political terms, as a contest which was essentially egalitarian and colour-blind, where Africans could triumph over discrimination. He sometimes depicted his political career in boxing terms: by 1955 he felt he was in 'the light heavyweight division'.[13] The showmanship and individualism of the fighter, together with his physical strength, contributed to Mandela's political style as a militant loner who understood the importance of performance.

But it was politics which was now his chief game. The Youth League was clamouring for action, and Mandela was preoccupied with how it could be achieved. He explained in the League's journal *African Lodestar* that the organisation must maintain dynamic contact with ordinary blacks: 'We have a powerful ideology capable of capturing the imaginations of the masses. Our duty is now to carry that ideology fully to them.'[14] But the ANC was still ill-equipped for grassroots organisation, and slow to react: a year after the conference of December 1949, Sisulu as Secretary-General reported that 'the masses are marching far ahead of the leadership.' He complained of 'general negligence of duty' by the organisation's officials, a lack of faith in the struggle and a lack of 'propaganda organs such as the press'. He insisted that 'if Congress is to be a force in the liberation of the African people in this country, then it must of necessity put its machinery in order.'[15]

The ANC still had very inadequate resources, and as an exclusively

African organisation it was wary of seeking help from other races; the Indian Congress was much more efficiently run, as were the communists. But the situation soon changed when the government determined to make the Communist Party illegal, with a bill which in 1950 became the Suppression of Communism Act. 'Statutory communism' was defined far more widely than as following Marxist policies: it effectively meant believing in equality between the races. The government was taking advantage of white fears of a worldwide communist conspiracy even before Senator Joseph McCarthy began his witch-hunt in America. The Act certainly succeeded in hampering the activities of some formidable enemies of the government, but it also soon brought many banned communists much closer to the ANC's young activists, including Mandela, and pressed them both towards joint action.

The ban was a clear threat to free speech, and in March 1950 the Johannesburg Communist Party collaborated with the Transvaal ANC and Indian Congress to organise a 'Defend Free Speech Convention' which attracted 10,000 people to Market Square. They also proposed a one-day strike on May Day, to protest against the banning of communist leaders. Sisulu had been quick to realise that a threat to the communists was a threat to all opposition forces, but Mandela and many other ANC members distrusted the communist initiative, which had overtaken their own planned demonstration. The *African Lodestar* attacked the exploitation of black workers by foreign ideologues, declaring: 'the exotic plant of communism cannot flourish on African soil'.[16] Joe Slovo, the young communist lawyer from Lithuania, spent hours arguing with Mandela about the party's plan for a strike, and saw Mandela trying to resolve his internal conflict 'between the emotional legacy left by the wounding experiences of racism, and the cold grey tactics of politics'.[17]

Mandela was still militantly anti-communist, and he and other Youth Leaguers heckled communist meetings intended to prepare for May Day, which were sometimes broken up. In Newclare, a Johannesburg suburb, Mandela physically dragged the Indian leader Yusuf Cachalia from the platform.[18] 'You couldn't miss him, because he was so tall,' recalled Rusty Bernstein, a communist architect who first encountered Mandela there. He remembered that Mandela 'appeared to be heckler and disrupter-in-chief . . . He stood out from the gaggle of jeering, heckling Youth Leaguers, partly by sheer physical presence but mainly by the calm authority he seemed to exercise over them.'[19]

Mandela could be a rough agitator. At one meeting the African communist J.B. Marks delivered a clear and logical speech describing how white supremacy could be overthrown, to frequent applause. Mandela, who had been instructed by his Youth League bosses to break up the meeting, arrogantly went up to Marks and insisted on addressing the crowd. 'There are two bulls in this *kraal*,' he declaimed. 'There is a black bull and a white bull. J.B. Marks says that the white bull must rule this *kraal*. I say that the black bull must rule. What do you say?' The same people who had been screaming for Marks a moment earlier now turned round and said, 'The black bull, the black bull!' Mandela enjoyed telling the story forty years later.[20]

The May Day protest was effective, despite the Youth League's opposition, with at least half the black workers in Johannesburg staying at home. That evening Mandela experienced a moment of truth. He was walking home in Orlando with Sisulu, watching a peaceful march of protesters under the full moon, when they spotted some policemen five hundred yards away. The police began firing towards them. Mounted officers galloped into the crowd, hitting out with batons. Mandela and Sisulu hid in a nurses' dormitory, where they could hear bullets hitting the walls. By the end of the night eighteen blacks had been killed in Orlando and three other townships on the Reef.[21] Mandela was outraged. 'That day was a turning point in my life,' he recalled, 'both in understanding through first-hand experience the ruthlessness of the police, and in being deeply impressed by the support African workers had given to the May Day call.'[22]

Mandela was now revealing a basic pragmatism which would make him a master of politics. He warned in *African Lodestar* that the Suppression of Communism Act was not in fact aimed at the Communist Party ('an insignificant party with no substantial following'), but at the ANC.[23] At a meeting of the Congresses he advocated joint action, and was supported by Tambo. A joint committee soon proposed a 'Day of Mourning' with a stay-at-home strike on 26 June, in protest against both the shootings and the new Act.[24] Sisulu asked Mandela to organise the small, hectic ANC office in Johannesburg, where African, Indian and white leaders were coming and going. Mandela was now in the big time, a key figure in a major national protest, working alongside activists of other races.

The Day of Mourning proved an anti-climax, and the response was very poor in the Transvaal. The *Rand Daily Mail* called the event '95 percent a flop'.[25] Mandela, looking back, reflected that: 'A political strike is always riskier than an economic one.'[26] And some colleagues criticised the unnecessary loss of life. The black writer Bloke Modisane, then in the Youth League, vividly described the horrors of the police reprisals in Sophiatown: 'The rifles and the sten guns were crackling death, spitting at anything which moved – anything black.' Modisane condemned the protest as 'another of those political adventurisms . . . If a man is asked to die he deserves the decency of an explanation.'[27]

The Suppression of Communism Act was pushed through Parliament with the support of the English-speaking United Party opposition. But the Communist Party of South Africa was never the formidable organisation that the government had portrayed. The Central Committee of the Party in Cape Town voted to dissolve, with only two dissenters.[28] In Johannesburg, where the Party was strongest, members met in a downtown house opposite Yusuf Dadoo's surgery. They were astonished to hear Moses Kotane announce the decision that had been taken in Cape Town. 'Many of us were stunned,' said Joe Slovo.[29] 'No one believed it,' said Rusty Bernstein. 'We were convinced it was not the real story.'[30] Over the next months they waited for secret instructions, but none came. Gradually they formed separate small groups, which cautiously came together. It seemed a long way from the long hand of Moscow and the Comintern.

Was the ban a blessing in disguise for the communists? 'In the hour of dissolution,' wrote the Party's historians Jack and Ray Simons, 'the class struggle had merged with the struggle for national liberation.'[31] The Act, Brian Bunting claimed forty-five years later, 'did more than anything to bring the ANC closer to the communists: it transformed it from a hole-in-corner body to a national organisation'.[32] Certainly the communists had to rethink their attitudes to the ANC, which they had previously tended to regard as irrelevant and petit-bourgeois. The Youth League, said Rusty Bernstein, endowed the Party with 'an understanding of race and nationalism which communists did not have in other countries . . . The unique gift the Party brought to the struggle was its multi-racialism and internationalism.'[33]

In 1950 Mandela, who still had his doubts about Indians and communists, had been elected President of the Youth League in succession to Peter Mda, who had resigned after suffering from heart trouble and gastric ulcers.[34] He still maintained in discussions with Sisulu that Africans would resent co-operating with Indian shopkeepers and merchants, whom they saw as their exploiters. When the ANC's Executive Committee met in June 1951 he argued again for Africans going it alone, against the majority of the committee.

But privately he was changing his views. In June 1951 he drove down to Natal in a battered Volkswagen with two other Youth Leaguers, Joe Matthews and Diliza Mji. On the way they argued against collaborating with banned communists. To their amazement Mandela tore into what he called their emotional, nationalist attitudes, and told them to look at the real achievements of the South African communists, many of whom had identified with blacks and had sacrificed everything for their cause. 'I think that conversation altered the whole outlook within the Youth League towards the South African Communist Party,' said Matthews much later.[35]

Mandela had been attracted to the communists more by their personal commitment and practical planning than their ideology. 'When I met communists like Ismail Meer and J.N. Singh at university they never talked about ideas, but about political programmes,' he told me later. 'You relate to people as they relate to you. I was impressed that a man like Dadoo, a doctor from Edinburgh, was living simply, wearing a khaki shirt, big boots and an army overcoat.'[36]

But Mandela was also beginning to think more seriously about political theory. He did not see himself as an intellectual like Tambo, or even Sisulu, but he was reading voraciously, with a concentration which amazed his friends, marking passages, taking notes, making comparisons. For his BA degree he had majored in Politics and Native Administration, and he read many Western philosophers including Harold Laski, Bertrand Russell and Bernard Shaw, as well as South African liberals like Edgar Brookes and Julius Lewin and the publications of the Institute of Race Relations, in Johannesburg, which he found indispensable. He also looked for more practical accounts of liberation struggles, reading the works of black nationalists like Nnamdi Azikiwe of Nigeria, Kwame Nkrumah of Ghana and George Padmore of Jamaica; and after the Indian passive resistance campaign he had read Gandhi and Nehru.

Mandela found that Marxist writings gave him a wider perspective. He did not get far with *Das Kapital* or *The Selected Works of Marx and Engels*, but he was impressed by *The Communist Manifesto* and by the biographies of South African Marxists like Sidney Bunting and Bill Andrews. He was struck by the Soviet Union's support for liberation movements throughout the world, and by the relentless logic of dialectical materialism, which he felt sweeping away the superstitions and inherited beliefs of his childhood, like 'a powerful searchlight on a dark night, which enables the traveller to see all round, to detect danger spots and the way forward'. He experienced some pangs at abandoning the Christian beliefs that had fortified his childhood, such as the story of St Peter three times denying Christ. But, he was later to reflect in jail, the true saints in the fight against cruelty and war were not necessarily those who had mastered the scriptures, or who wore clerical robes.[37]

Mandela was certainly no saint himself, and he would never have a strong religious faith. But he was beginning to show himself a more far-sighted politician than most of his contemporaries. He had already learnt to restrain his cruder nationalist instincts, to be guided more by his head than his heart, and to widen his view of the struggle. He accepted that the ANC needed allies, and the Indians and communists were the only allies available. He now seized the opportunity to join them in the first major passive resistance campaign in the ANC's history.

6

Defiance

1952

IN DECEMBER 1951 the ANC held its thirty-fifth annual congress in the black township outside the hot, sleepy Afrikaner stronghold of Bloemfontein. The event would prove to be a historic turning point, but it was hardly noticed by the whites or the world at the time.

The conference began two hours late, with three hundred delegates trooping into the baking-hot hall. A press table was improvised for the five journalists present, who included Ruth First from the left-wing *New Age*, two local reporters from the Bloemfontein *Friend*, and Henry Nxumalo and myself from *Drum* magazine. Many of the delegates resisted having their photographs taken. On the platform was the courteous, conservative ANC President Dr Moroka, and close by him was a small, ascetic figure with a wizened face. This was Manilal Gandhi, the son of the Mahatma, who lived in his father's old settlement in Natal and saw himself as the keeper of the pure spirit of passive resistance. Both Moroka and Gandhi seemed a world away from the firebrands of the Youth League, including the proud thirty-three-year-old Nelson Mandela.

The three-day meeting seemed long-winded and inconsequential. Then, on the last day, the General Secretary Walter Sisulu produced his report on a joint programme of passive resistance, or 'civil disobedience', aimed at deliberately defying the Nationalist government's racial laws and inviting imprisonment. The plan was partly based on the Indian campaign in Durban in 1946. The ANC would ask the government to repeal 'six unjust laws': those imposing passes and limiting stock, the Group Areas Act, the Voters' Representation Act, the Suppression of Communism Act and the Bantu Authorities Act. If it refused, they would embark on their 'Defiance Campaign'.[1] Dr Moroka supported the plan with a surprisingly eloquent speech, multiplied by interpreters, affirming that the ANC was prepared to work with Europeans, Indians and Coloureds, provided they were on equal terms.[2]

Mandela had now finally committed himself to co-operation with decisive pragmatism. At the conference he had begun by insisting again that the ANC should go it alone, without the Indians, but he soon sensed that the majority was in favour of co-operation, and in his speech as President of the Youth League he turned right round with apparent conviction, as if he had never believed otherwise.[3] He called for a non-European front against fascism, which, he explained, was being smuggled into South Africa behind a screen of fear of communism. Africans must be the spearhead of the organised struggle, but with Indians and Coloureds as their determined allies.[4]

The Indian influence was evident in the idea of passive resistance, but there was much argument about its nature. Manilal Gandhi protested that Congress leaders did not have 'the spirit of true sacrifice', and insisted that passive resistance was more a process of moral purification than a political weapon.[5] His worry was shared by older South African Indians who had been influenced by the Mahatma. The saintly veteran Nana Sita, who had helped to instigate the Durban campaign in 1946, had met Gandhi as a child in Pretoria. Yusuf Cachalia and his brother Maulvi had been attracted to Gandhi's methods while living in India. But most communist leaders were critical of the Mahatma's lack of concern for the African cause while he was in South Africa. Gandhi had shown little evidence, wrote Joe Slovo, of having 'absorbed the ancient lesson that freedom is indivisible'.[6] The communists saw passive resistance purely as a means of mobilising the masses rather than as a 'soul-force'.[7] And some Youth Leaguers regarded the campaign as altogether too non-violent: 'The Defiance Campaign was anti-revolutionary,' Peter Mda said later, 'in the sense that it was "passive" resistance: you couldn't hit back.'[8]

Mandela was more pragmatic. He certainly lacked Gandhi's asceticism: 'Some Indians said he was like Gandhi,' said his friend Fatima Meer. 'I told them, "Gandhi took off his clothes. Nelson *loves* his clothes."'[9] Mandela admired Gandhi as 'one of the pioneers of South Africa's liberation movement', and had been deeply shocked when he was assassinated in February 1948; but he did not share his purist view of the struggle: 'I saw non-violence on the Gandhian model not as an inviolable principle,' he said later, 'but as a tactic to be used as the situation demanded.'[10]

His expectations for the Defiance Campaign were certainly high: he believed it would be so effective that it would lead to the ANC being 'in a position of either getting the government to capitulate or to get them thrown out by the voters'.[11] But he also, like the communists, saw the action as a means of educating the masses, and the beginning of a much harsher confrontation. He did not harbour any illusions, Joe Slovo reckoned, about 'converting the ruling class without a tough revolutionary struggle'.[12]

The plans went rapidly ahead in January 1952, in a spurt of activity very different from the ANC's usual leisurely style. Mandela joined a committee of four, with Z.K. Matthews, Ismail Meer and J.N. Singh, which drafted a letter to the Prime Minister, Dr Malan, demanding the repeal of the six unjust laws.[13] Mandela drove down to the Orange Free State with the document for Dr Moroka to sign. When the Prime Minister's Secretary received the letter he replied that the differences between the races were 'permanent, not man-made', and that the new laws were not oppressive and degrading, but protective.[14] Moroka and Sisulu reiterated their demands, while promising 'to conduct the campaign in a peaceful manner'.[15]

Mandela was soon looking more like a future leader of his people. On 31 May 1952 the ANC executive met in Port Elizabeth and announced that the campaign would begin on 26 June. A banquet was held to say goodbye to Professor Matthews, who was leaving to spend a year in America, and Matthews's son Joe recalls Mandela saying that he (Mandela) would be the first black President of South Africa.[16] He was clearly putting himself in the forefront of the ANC's organisation, offering to take the key position of Volunteer-in-Chief for the campaign, responsible for national recruitment, which would give him high visibility, in a quasi-military role, across the country.

On the 'Day of the Volunteers', four days before the campaign began, Mandela drove down to Durban to be the main speaker to a crowd of 10,000, by far the biggest audience he had ever addressed. It was not a populist speech – he would never develop the emotional rhetoric of some of his contemporaries like Robert Sobukwe or Gaur Radebe – but he found it an exhilarating experience, and received prolonged applause. He told his listeners they were making history; this would be the most powerful action ever undertaken by the oppressed masses, and with the races working together: 'We can now say unity between the non-European people in this country has become a living reality.'[17]

On 26 June, when the Defiance Campaign was launched, Mandela set out for Boksburg, a mining town near Johannesburg, with Yusuf Cachalia and Walter Sisulu, after being delayed by a long conversation with the local white magistrate, whom he knew. The man spoke to him courteously, which Mandela suspected was 'not unrelated to the fact that we were acting from a position of strength'.[18] In Boksburg fifty-two volunteers gathered outside the big gates of the African township, then walked in without the permits required for entry, led by Nana Sita in his white Gandhi cap and surrounded by hundreds of supporters. They wore the ANC colours on their arms – black for the people, green for the land, yellow for the country's gold – and held up their thumbs in the Congress salute, singing the hopeful song 'Open the door, Malan, we are knocking'. Mandela looked on calmly, aloof but highly visible, with a military dignity. His manner seemed to symbolise his relationship to the struggle: the proud loner who was at the same time totally committed. The police, who had been waiting, arrested the volunteers, bundled them into a troop carrier and drove them to the cells.

Mandela would soon have his own first taste of jail. On the same evening the ANC held a meeting at the Garment Workers' Hall in Johannesburg. An 11 p.m. curfew was in force, and when a procession of Africans marched out into the street the police were waiting for them, standing shoulder to shoulder, peering beneath their helmets at the meek-looking blacks and ready to pack them into police trucks. Mandela and Yusuf Cachalia were there as observers, but the police insisted on arresting them, too. So Mandela spent two nights in the jail at Marshall Square, squashed in with his fellow-protesters. He was appalled by the conditions, and would never forget how one of the prisoners was pushed down the steps, broke his ankle, and spent the night writhing in pain.[19] He also soon realised that two of his fellow-prisoners were informers planted by the police.

The first day set the pattern for the Defiance Campaign. Over the next five months 8,000 people all over the country went to jail for one to three weeks for marching into townships, whites-only railway entrances or carriages, or for being out after curfew, always peacefully. The national organisation was Mandela's achievement: before and during the campaign he travelled through the Transvaal, Natal and the Cape, recruiting and explaining, sometimes from house to house, with little publicity from the white-owned newspapers and radio. He learnt at first hand about the problems of reconciling hot-headed local activists to centralised discipline: 'It is no use to take an action to which the masses are opposed,' he realised, 'for it will then be impossible to enforce.'[20] Significantly, the campaign's most striking success was not in the Johannesburg area, where the communists had been strongest, but in the Eastern Cape, which provided half the volunteers: the conditions in factories in Port Elizabeth had generated a surge of discontent.[21]

Mandela seemed full of optimism, as he showed in an article for the August 1952 issue of *Drum* magazine:

> Though it takes us years, we are prepared to continue the Campaign until the six unjust laws we have chosen for the present phase are done away with. Even then we shall not stop. The struggle for the freedom and national independence of the non-European people shall continue as the National Planning Council sees fit.[22]

The campaign gave blacks a new sense of confidence in their own strength; and it was also succeeding, as Mandela noted, in removing the stigma from having served a jail sentence. 'From the Defiance Campaign onward,' he wrote later, 'going to prison became a badge of honour among Africans.' But the government, having been caught off guard, was soon preparing reprisals, with the support of the main white opposition. The United Party, which represented most English-speaking voters, sent two Members of Parliament to ask the ANC to abandon the campaign and to support them in the forthcoming elections.[23] The ANC asked them to promise to repeal the pass laws if they returned to power, and when they refused to do this the talks broke down.[24] Two liberal leaders, Senator William Ballinger and J.D. Rheinallt Jones, warned Mandela and others that the Defiance Campaign would alienate white support; and the liberal Institute of Race Relations also complained. As Mandela recalled, 'They came to us and said: "Gentlemen, we don't think this is the best way of expressing your grievances. Please withdraw it." And when we refused they attacked us.' But Mandela was pleasantly surprised by the liberal white press: the *Rand Daily Mail*, he noted, gave the campaign as much publicity as did the left-wing weekly *New Age* (formerly the *Guardian*).[25]

The Defiance Campaign gave the government an excuse to impose much fiercer laws; and it had fewer inhibitions than the British did when faced by Gandhi's passive resistance in India. Mandela and his colleagues were taken by surprise. One young black politician, Naboth Mokgatle, warned a meeting of Youth Leaguers, including Mandela, that 'Their actions were like throwing things into a machine, then allowing the owner to dismantle it, clean it, sharpen it and put it together again before throwing in another thing. My advice was in vain.'[26]

In July the police had raided the homes and offices of African and Indian leaders, collecting piles of documents. They were still relatively amateurish, and even quite friendly: when they searched the offices of the Transvaal Indian Congress, Amina Cachalia, the wife of Yusuf, brought them tea and sandwiches and led them to unimportant documents while Ahmed Kathrada was removing crucial evidence from other shelves.[27] Mandela would reminisce with some warmth about the police chatting with him in Xhosa over tea. But the raids were the prelude to more serious moves. On 30 July Mandela was handed a warrant for his arrest on a charge of violating the Suppression of Communism Act, and another twenty Defiance Campaign leaders were arrested throughout the country.[28]

The twenty-one leaders were freed on bail, and went on trial in September in a Johannesburg magistrates' court, before Judge Frans Rumpff. A loud multi-racial crowd converged on the courtroom. But the defendants' solidarity was spectacularly undermined by Dr Moroka, who had taken fright at the charges levelled against him and hired a separate attorney to plead his innocence. Mandela had attempted to dissuade him the day before the trial began, but Moroka complained about not having been consulted and about the association with communists – though he had not objected to this in the past. When he came before Judge Rumpff he stated that he did not believe in equality between black and white. He then began pointing out the communists among the other defendants – including Sisulu and Dadoo – until the judge stopped him.[29]

To Mandela, Moroka's defection was a 'severe blow', and was hard to forgive: 'He had committed the cardinal sin of putting his own interests ahead of those of the organisation and the people.' But he was also aware of Moroka's past courage, and that as a rich man he had much more to lose than poorer campaigners, and had many Afrikaner friends. Mandela forgave him later, as he was to forgive so many who betrayed him; he wrote warmly about Moroka in the autobiography written in jail, and later asked him to be godfather of his daughter Zeni's first child.[30] But others were less forgiving.

Judge Rumpff impressed Mandela with his fair-mindedness. Predictably, he found the leaders guilty, but the sentence – nine months' imprisonment with hard labour, suspended for two years – was relatively lenient. And he stressed that they were guilty of 'statutory communism', which, he admitted, had 'nothing to do with communism as it is commonly known'.[31]

The government's definition of communism was palpably perverse, but it helped gain support from anti-communists elsewhere, particularly in America, where the Cold War was hotting up. In 1952 Mandela had a glimpse of the ardour of the Cold Warriors when he encountered the black American political figure Dr Max Yergan, who visited South Africa in the midst of the Defiance Campaign. Yergan had earlier spent many years in the Eastern Cape, converting a number of young blacks, including Govan Mbeki, to communism.[32] But after returning to America he had become fiercely anti-communist, as he now revealed. In Johannesburg he addressed a meeting at the Bantu Men's Social Centre, attended by black politicians and luminaries including Mandela. Yergan concluded, Mandela later recalled, with 'a concentrated attack on communism, and drew prolonged ovation from that elitist audience'. But then Barney Ngakane, Mandela's friend and neighbour in Orlando, counter-attacked, pointing out Yergan's deafening silence about the Defiance Campaign and about the pernicious influence of American business interests. As Mandela described it: 'He challenged the guest speaker to speak about the giant American cartels, trusts and multi-national corporations that were causing so much misery and hardship throughout the world, and he foiled Yergan's attempt to drag us into the Cold War.'[33]

By the time of Mandela and the other leaders' arrests at the end of July, the government was determined to stamp out the Defiance Campaign, which had reached a stage, Mandela thought, 'where it had to be suppressed by the government or it would impose its own policies on the country'.[34] The government's chief weapon was to ban the campaign's leaders from holding positions in the ANC or from attending meetings. In May the communist J.B. Marks had been banned as President of the Transvaal ANC, and had recommended Mandela as his successor. Mandela was opposed by a nationalist demagogue named Seperepere Marupeng, a leader of a militant group called Bafabegiya ('those who die dancing'). Mandela, with his reputation as a ladies' man, was taken aback when one of the militants, a beautiful young woman, asked: 'How can I criticise Mandela when he has left his hat in my house?'[35] But in October he was overwhelmingly elected to the key position. His triumph was short-lived: in December, along with fifty-one other ANC leaders, he was banned for six months from attending any meeting or from talking to more than one person at a time, and was forbidden to leave Johannesburg without permission. His public position in the ANC hierarchy was now illegal; but his status was reinforced as an individual leader and man of action.

The Defiance Campaign was now petering out. In October it faced another setback when an outbreak of riots in Port Elizabeth and East London (and later in Kimberley) led to the deaths of several innocent people, including a nun. The ANC hastened to offer sympathy to the families, both black and white, who had suffered from 'this unfortunate, reckless, ill-considered return to jungle law', and charged the government with deliberately sending out agents provocateurs (which could never be proved). But the riots damaged the protesters' non-violent image, and gave the government new justification for bannings.[36]

By December the Public Safety Act and the Criminal Laws Amendment Act provided fiercer penalties against deliberate law-breaking, punishable by up to three years in jail and flogging. Again the ANC was taken by surprise. 'We had never visualised such drastic penalties,' Mandela admitted later.[37] 'The tide of defiance was bound to recede,' as he reported the next year, 'and we were forced to pause and take stock of the new situation.'[38]

For a brief time the campaign seemed to be drawing broader support. In early December a young ex-colonial officer, Patrick Duncan, the son of a former Governor-General of South Africa, entered the fray. Duncan was a courageous idealist, with the boyish zeal of a John Buchan hero, passionately anti-communist but also an admirer of Gandhi. Mandela and Yusuf Cachalia persuaded him to join the campaign, to show other whites the way. 'Pat's offer came as a gift from heaven,' Cachalia said. 'It stopped the campaign becoming racial.'[39] Duncan, together with Manilal Gandhi (whom he had persuaded to join him) and a few other whites entered Germiston township near Johannesburg without permits, and were arrested. In the blaze of publicity that followed many blacks were moved by Duncan's courage, and when he was eventually sent to jail, Mandela, Cachalia and Dadoo came to wish him good luck. But Duncan was not joined by other whites, as they had hoped, and he proved an awkward ally. In the courtroom he pleaded not guilty, then unsuccessfully appealed against his guilty verdict, but never served his full six-week sentence. After his release he became worried about communist influence within the ANC. He later joined the new Liberal Party, and then the Pan Africanist Congress, which became the ANC's most serious rival.[40] But Mandela would always remember his bravery with respect.

By the end of 1952 the Defiance Campaign was over. It had been a six-months' wonder. Politicians and historians continue to argue over its success or failure. Mandela admitted it never spread much beyond the cities and larger towns, except in the Eastern Cape.[41] But he claimed it as an 'outstanding success' which had boosted the ANC's membership – from 4,000 to 16,000 in the Transvaal, while in the Cape it reached 60,000.[42] The ANC had shown an ability for national organisation which few observers had suspected, and for which Mandela could take much credit. This gave him an important psychological boost, freeing him, as he wrote later, 'from any lingering doubt or inferiority I might still have felt . . . I could walk upright like a man, and look everyone in the eye with the dignity that comes from not having succumbed to oppression and fear.'[43]

The Defiance Campaign also drastically changed the character of the ANC, scaring off the more timid, conservative leaders like Dr Moroka, who was ousted. The young 'kingmakers', who included Mandela, looked for a more steadfast President, and found one in Albert Luthuli, a Zulu chief of fifty-three. Luthuli was a large, avuncular figure with slow speech and a generous smile. A former teacher and Methodist preacher based at the mission station of Groutville in Natal, he appeared to be thoroughly conservative. But he had progressed, as he said, 'along the line of softness to hardness'.[44] Luthuli became President of the Natal ANC in 1951, and had supported the Defiance Campaign despite pressure from the government, which sacked him from his chieftaincy. He responded with a moving Christian statement called 'The Road to Freedom is via the Cross'.[45]

Luthuli deeply respected Gandhi, and admired the moderation of the British Labour Party, but he was not afraid to work with communists. 'Extreme nationalism is a greater danger than communism, and a more real one,' he told me when he was elected as ANC President in December 1952.[46] Over the next fifteen years – the longest presidency in the ANC's history – he was often banned and confined to the area of his home in

Natal, and was sometimes seen as a mere figurehead. But Mandela would always regard him as his leader, and a hero of the struggle.

The Defiance Campaign came and went without making much dent on white South African attitudes or on opinion abroad, beyond some left-wing protests. The British diplomats in Pretoria watched events with scepticism, and depicted the Africans as the pawns of Indians and communists. 'The natives have only a rudimentary political organisation and no effective leaders,' said one despatch to London in May 1952. The diplomats' main fear was of 'civil war between the two white races', in which the natives might intervene.[47] The High Commissioner, Sir John Le Rougetel, was upset by the 'extravagance and scurrility' of American criticism of the apartheid government, and by a resolution of the Labour Party, then in opposition, which condemned it. He insisted that the British should 'leave the South Africans to fight their own battles' – particularly since the more liberal United Party was 'stiffening up'. Sir John accepted the views of the head of the South African Special Branch, Colonel du Plooy, that the ANC was being financed by the Indian Congress and that 'its leadership comes entirely from the communist leaders'; he passed on this 'intelligence' in a remarkably ill-informed despatch to London in November. The riots in Port Elizabeth he blamed partly on Indian communists who needed a spectacular event to revive the United Nations' interest in South Africa.[48]

Winston Churchill, who had recently returned to power in Britain as Conservative Prime Minister, had his own confident view, minuted on 16 October: 'Nothing could be more helpful to Dr Malan in his approaching elections than the Indians and Kaffirs forcing their way into compartments and waiting rooms reserved for whites. The overwhelming mass of the white population of South Africa would be opposed to this intrusion. So what the communists and Indian intriguers are doing is really to help Malan. They must be very stupid not to see this.'[49]

A few Western diplomats were more perceptive. The Canadian High Commissioner, T.W.L. MacDermot, reported to Ottawa in February 1953: 'The ANC is a great deal more than a political party. Representing as it does the great majority of articulate Africans in the Union, it is almost the parliament of a nation. A nation without a state, perhaps, but it is as a nation that the Africans increasingly think of themselves.'[50]

7

Lawyer and Revolutionary

1952–1954

To outward appearances, in his early thirties Nelson Mandela was leading a settled home life in the matchbox-house in Orlando. His wife Evelyn ran the home with a dedication that impressed many of their friends. 'Without Evelyn's encouragement and assurance that she would always be there to keep the home fires burning,' wrote Phyllis Ntantala later, 'he would not have made it.'[1] Always in the background, she cooked and cared for the spotless house, maintaining a simple lifestyle: when Mandela's English supporter Canon John Collins visited it in 1954, Mandela brought him a bowl of water to wash his hands in, and led him to the outside lavatory, a tumbledown shed containing a bucket. Collins was struck that Evelyn did not join them for lunch.[2]

But it was not a happy home, and was much less stable than the Sisulus' or the Tambos'. Evelyn disapproved of Mandela's political career, and he realised that her religion 'would not support political activity'.[3] When she had married him, she explained, she had thought he was a student, not a politician. Though she sometimes put on an ANC uniform, she said: 'I was just trying to please him.'[4] She was becoming more religious as her husband became more political: a dedicated Jehovah's Witness, she spent much of her time reading the Bible. Their friend the writer Es'kia Mphahlele believed Evelyn's religion was partly an escape from the political pressure, and felt that the Mandelas were incompatible: 'It could never work.'[5] Certainly the household was showing strain. Mandela's younger sister Leabie, who sometimes stayed in the house and saw him almost as a father, was very aware of the tension. Evelyn, she remembered, 'didn't want to hear a thing about politics'. Leabie could not understand why people were always hiding, or going away and coming back in the early morning: 'I would feel bitter because there was no happiness.'[6]

Outside the home, Mandela was being pulled in different directions, with contradictory careers. On the one hand he was practising as a lawyer, involved every day with all the ordered legal machinery of the state. On the other he was caught up in revolutionary politics, and was beginning to see violence as the inevitable outcome of the confrontation. His respect for the law proved the key to his survival, but it was severely tested. 'Little did he think,' said Mandela's white barrister friend George Bizos, 'that he would spend more time in the courts accused of capital and other crimes than representing others.'[7]

Mandela's legal career had progressed while he was carrying out all his political activities. After leaving Witkin, Sidelsky & Eidelman, he had worked for three white partnerships: first for Terblanche & Briggish, then for Helman & Michel, and then for H.M. Basner, a left-wing former Senator under whom he finally became a fully qualified attorney. In 1952 he established the first African law firm in the country together with Oliver Tambo, the Youth League colleague whom he had known since they were fellow students at Fort Hare.

It was to prove a historic partnership, more surprising than Mandela's political relationship with Sisulu. Tambo was also from the rural Transkei, and had tribal markings on his cheeks. Like Mandela he had had a polygamous father, and had been expelled from Fort Hare. In other ways he was Mandela's opposite: he was quiet, academic and religious, from a peasant family who did not expect others to do things for them. But Tambo had a clarity of mind which impressed both his teachers and his fellow students. He came to Johannesburg to teach mathematics at St Peter's School, where he politicised many boys, until Walter Sisulu persuaded him to become a lawyer. Mandela respected Tambo's maturity and reflective mind, and always listened to his advice.

The firm of Mandela & Tambo opened in August 1952 in a picturesque old building called Chancellor House, opposite the magistrates' courts in downtown Johannesburg and only a few blocks from the grand fortress of the Anglo-American Corporation, the centre of South African capitalism. 'MANDELA AND TAMBO' was painted in big letters on the windows – which offended conservative white lawyers. The offices were in the same building as the ANC headquarters run by Sisulu, and it was part of a dissidents' enclave of Indian-owned buildings, including Kapitan's restaurant and Kholvad House, the radical Indian meeting-place. The black occupants of Chancellor House were soon under threat from the Group Areas Act, which designated South Africa's city centres for whites only; but Mandela & Tambo stayed there illegally until 1961 – by which time they were under constant surveillance.[8]

The firm became the official attorneys for the ANC, and were much in demand from other black clients with a host of claims and complaints. 'We depended on Mandela & Tambo,' recalled Joe Mogotsi, who sang with the Manhattan Brothers, 'if we were arrested after giving a concert in town, without our passes.'[9] They had many rural clients. 'To reach our desks each morning,' Tambo recalled, 'Nelson and I ran the gauntlet of patient queues of people overflowing from the chairs in the waiting room into the corridors . . . Weekly we interviewed the delegations of grizzled, weather-worn peasants from the countryside who came to tell us how many generations their families had worked a little piece of land from which they were now being ejected . . . Every case in court, every visit to the prisons to interview clients, reminded us of the humiliation and suffering burning into our people.'[10]

They were soon assisted by Mendi Msimang, a young Zulu activist who had been helping Sisulu, and by Godfrey Pitje, a Youth Leaguer who had been best man at Tambo's wedding.[11] As a humble country boy, Pitje felt himself a commoner beside Mandela: 'It wasn't difficult to defer,' he said later. 'It was the natural thing, to the son of a chief.'[12] Mandela liked to show himself to be in command, but he could also listen to his staff. When he dictated letters to his efficient secretary Ruth Mompati – who became a close friend, and later Ambassador to Switzerland – she would sometimes suggest a correction which he would first ignore, but accept soon afterwards.[13]

The two partners' talents were complementary. Mandela spent much of his time in court, arguing in flamboyant style, or writing political speeches long into the evening. The quietly reflective Tambo stayed in the office doing much of the paperwork, sucking at a small unlit pipe. In the courtroom Tambo behaved calmly and unobtrusively, relying on his knowledge of the law. But Mandela cultivated an assertive, theatrical style with sweeping gestures. He made his presence felt as soon as he entered the court, which made magistrates and prosecutors complain that he was uppity.[14] Godfrey Pitje was amazed: 'All he needed was to turn around and look up and there was almost a flare-up round him.' But

Pitje was thrilled to hear Mandela treating racist magistrates with contempt, and to see him defying apartheid restrictions. Once when Mandela walked boldly through the 'whites only' entrance to a courtroom he was told by a young white clerk with a dark complexion: 'This is for whites.' Mandela replied: 'Then what are you doing here?'[15]

Mandela often defended clients in the rural Transvaal, where crowds would gather to see this legendary black lawyer, without necessarily understanding the law. When he achieved the acquittal of one client who had been charged with witchcraft, some spectators, he suspected, ascribed the outcome to the power of magic, rather than to the law.[16] He often briefed liberal white barristers like George Bizos to plead important cases; they would bewilder the local Judicial Officer by calling black witnesses 'Mr' or 'Mrs', rather than 'Jim' or 'Martha'.

Mandela and Tambo often found themselves fighting a losing battle against the new 'tribal authorities', who were gradually extending the powers of government and imposing prosecutions and fines. But as the rural blacks became more politicised and met more workers in the cities, they were becoming more aware of their legal rights. The government banned meetings of more than ten people, and when the police dispersed or arrested the spectators, they would shout to their relatives: 'Phone Mandela & Tambo!'[17]

Mandela became suspect among many white lawyers after receiving his suspended sentence for helping to organise the Defiance Campaign, and in 1954 the Law Society demanded his removal from the roll of attorneys. In a historic case he was defended by two respected white lawyers, Walter Pollak QC and Blen Franklin, who argued that Mandela had a right to fight for his political beliefs under the rule of law. The presiding Judge Ramsbottom upheld their argument and ordered the Law Society to pay costs. Mandela was heartened by the number of barristers, including Afrikaner nationalists, who came to his support: 'Even in racist South Africa professional solidarity can sometimes transcend colour.'[18] Forty years later, when he addressed the Law Society, he reminded them: 'Here I am with my name still on the roll.'[19] But his professional scope was soon restricted by the bans placed on him as a political activist. When he applied for permission to appear in a case in Pretoria in 1955, the Police Commissioner informed the Minister of Justice: 'Mandela cannot be trusted, and visits by him to Pretoria and Vereeniging must be treated with suspicion.'[20]

As Mandela became more prominent politically, he attracted still more resentment. In November 1955 he was defending a black client before a testy Afrikaner magistrate named Willem Dormehl, who immediately asked Mandela to produce his attorney's certificate; he could not, and Dormehl adjourned the case. When Mandela later brought the certificate and began his defence, Dormehl kept interrupting his 'irrelevant questions' with shouts of 'Hey, you,' finally saying 'Hey, you, sit down.' Mandela insisted that all the magistrate's remarks be recorded, and finally stated that he could not defend his client under these circumstances. The case was remanded. A furious Mandela went to see George Bizos, who advised him to petition the Supreme Court. The case came in front of Judge Quartus de Wet – later to sentence Mandela to life imprisonment – who was outraged by Dormehl's behaviour, saying: 'Everyone knows that Mandela is an attorney.' De Wet ordered the magistrate to remove himself from the case, and complained: 'This is the sort of thing that brings the administration of justice into disrepute in our country.'[21]

'The law was used in South Africa,' Mandela would explain as President forty years later, 'not as an instrument to afford the citizen protection, but rather as the chief means of his subjection. As a young law student, it was one of my ambitions to try to use my professional training to help tilt the balance just a wee bit in favour of the citizen.'[22] He could occasionally be surprised by the fairness of judges, but at the same time he was aware of the limitations of the courts as the guardians of civil liberties. As he later wrote in jail: 'In our country where there are racial laws, and where all the judges and magistrates are white and reeking of the stale odour of racial prejudice, the operation of such principles is very limited.' He saw the government packing the courts with its own supporters, but he recognised that South Africa was still producing great judges, who might also be Afrikaner nationalists, but who could take a brave stand against the government. In jail he would recall with pleasure how the respected Judge Blackwell told the Chief of Security Police on the Rand: 'This country is not a police state yet!'[23]

Mandela would remain divided between his respect for the rule of law and his determination to overthrow a racist regime. Increasingly he was finding himself on the receiving end of the legal machinery, marked down as a dangerous politician and compelled to operate from the shadows. For most of the ten years from 1952 until he was jailed he was banned from holding any elected office and forbidden to make public speeches. He had no formal position with the ANC. He had to rely on his personality and his image; but it was an image which was beginning to shine brightly.

Mandela had a brief period of freedom when his six-month ban from attending meetings or leaving Johannesburg expired in June 1953, and he revelled in a journey through the Orange Free State to appear as a lawyer in court in the small *dorp* of Villiers. The open landscape gave him a sense of liberty: he even felt some affinity with the Afrikaner Boer War hero General de Wet, who had fought the British across that countryside.[24] But it was a false dawn: in Villiers he was served with a new ban, restricting him to Johannesburg again and requiring him to resign from all organisations, including the ANC, for two years. It was the beginning of his hunted life, as he recalled nine years later: 'I found myself restricted and isolated from my fellow-men, from people who think like me and believe like me. I found myself trailed by officers of the security branch of the police force wherever I went. In short, I found myself treated as a criminal, an unconvicted criminal.'[25]

Mandela knew that the bans could soon debilitate the ANC by restricting the leaders' contacts and activities, and encouraging 'the crippling evils of factionalism and regionalism'.[26] Anticipating the ANC being banned altogether, he worked out a plan by which the leaders could communicate secretly and quickly with each other and subordinates by means of an underground network of cells.[27] This was called the 'M-Plan' – rather than the Mandela Plan, which would have revealed that he was illegally participating in the ANC. The plan's main object was to inform, mobilise and recruit members, but it could also be used to build up labour unions without public meetings.[28] As Mandela urged the Transvaal Congress in September 1953: 'If you are not allowed to have your meetings publicly, then you must hold them over your machines in the factories, on the trams and buses as you travel home. You must have them in your villages and shanty towns. You must make every home, every shack and every mud structure where our people live, a branch of the trade union movement, and you must *never surrender*.'[29]

The M-Plan was implemented in the Eastern Cape, where the mood of defiance was strongest. This gratified Mandela, since it was largely organised by Africans, with little help from Indians or whites.[30] But there were many problems in other regions. Strong local leaders resented central control, lacked paid organisers to run the plan, and often did not believe the ANC would actually be banned. In December 1955 the National Executive reported that they had 'not yet succeeded in moving out of the domain of mass meetings and this type of agitation'.[31] It was not until 1961, after the ANC had been banned, that a modified version of the plan was implemented.[32]

Mandela's next open political challenge came in 1953, in the multi-racial township of Sophiatown, close to the white centre of Johannesburg. It was a 'black spot' which the government was determined to move out to the edge of Soweto. Sophiatown was an overcrowded slum district, with filthy backyards reeking of stale beer; but it was one of South Africa's most cosmopolitan areas, with an overwhelming vitality and its own harsh beauty, commemorated by poets, photographers and the black painter Gerard Sekoto. More importantly politically, it was the only part of Johannesburg where blacks could own freehold property – which the government could not tolerate. When black residents were forced to leave their homes in return for wretched compensation, Mandela denounced the compulsory removals as 'a calculated and cold-blooded swindle'.[33] The ANC had some strong supporters in Sophiatown, led by two fire-brands, Robert Resha and Peter Nthite, and including part-time *tsotsis*, or gangsters, and the National Executive felt impelled to resist the removals, while maintaining their policy of non-violence. It was a difficult challenge.

Soon after Mandela's ban expired in June 1953, he presided over a meeting in the Odin Cinema in Sophiatown, alongside the Indian leader Yusuf Cachalia – whom the police arrested on the platform. Mandela succeeded in calming the audience with the help of ANC songs, but he was becoming impatient with non-violent methods. Addressing an angry crowd in 'Freedom Square' soon afterwards, he was carried away by his own oratory, and told them to prepare before long to use violence. Pointing to the police who surrounded them, he sang an ANC song which included the words 'There are our enemies!' He was given a stern reprimand by the ANC's National Executive, which he accepted; but he felt in his heart that 'non-violence was not the answer'.[34]

The Sophiatown protests nevertheless continued peacefully, with hundreds of speeches by local leaders carefully avoiding violent rhetoric: 'The throwing of one small stone at the police,' an ANC report concluded afterwards, 'would have made Sophiatown a bloodbath.'[35] They were supported by a prominent and imposing English monk, Father Trevor

Huddleston, who presided over the church of Christ the King, which dominated Sophiatown, and the nearby mission school of St Peter's at Rosettenville. Huddleston was already the friend and mentor of Oliver Tambo, and had been moved by the Defiance Campaign to identify himself closely with the ANC's struggle. 'It has been the teaching of the Church through the centuries,' he had told a spellbound black audience at the Trades Hall in February 1953, 'that when government degenerates into tyranny ... laws cease to be binding on its subjects.' Huddleston was not worried by working alongside communists. 'I'm convinced that communism is not a serious danger in South Africa,' he told me.[36] He saw it as his Christian duty to protect his parish in Sophiatown, with all its humanity, which he loved.[37]

Mandela realised that Huddleston, like his white communist friends, completely identified with the people, and he was to become his lifelong friend and supporter. Huddleston found no difficulty, he said later, in discussing religion with Mandela, whom he saw as an agnostic, not an atheist: 'He accepts that God is a mystery, and accepts those whose life is structured in the belief in God ... He believes in the gift of free will, the freedom to choose – which goes deeper than a political belief.'[38]

The ANC continued to agitate against the destruction of Sophiatown with slogans like 'We Won't Move' and 'Over Our Dead Bodies'. Mandela soon realised that this was a serious mistake. 'A slogan is like a bullet,' he wrote later in jail: its effectiveness 'depends on matching the bore of the gun'.[39] But these bullets could not penetrate. The world's press had converged on the slum township with high expectations of a bloodbath, even a revolution. 'It was coming for sure, so we all believed,' wrote Don Mattera, a gang-leader and poet who lived in Sophiatown.[40] Mandela and Tambo came to the township every day to co-ordinate the leadership and to represent the dispossessed owners. But Mandela could offer no peaceful means to prevent the removals. 'At no time during the course of this campaign did we think we could beat the government,' he wrote later.[41]

The mood was still expectant when I visited Sophiatown on 9 February 1954, the day on which the removals were to take place. At dawn the township was echoing with the sound of the *tsotsis* hitting the telegraph poles – the battle-cry of Sophiatown. But the government had imposed a total ban on meetings, and 2,000 police were patrolling the streets in cars and heavy trucks; the trucks soon began loading up furniture and those tenants who were glad to leave. The ANC leaders looked on disconsolately; the crowds just stared. By the evening the police were looking bored and confident.[42]

Mandela had learnt a grim lesson – not to raise premature hopes of revolt: 'Sophiatown died not to the sound of gunfire but to the sound of rumbling trucks and sledgehammers.' He was convinced that in the future 'we had no alternative to armed and violent resistance', and he sometimes seemed to be impatient for a confrontation in which he could prove himself.[43] He was restrained by Sisulu, who was more exposed to the militant youth: 'They were coming to our meetings with only one idea,' he recalled: 'For me to utter revolution.'

Sisulu did not utter it, and he was further advised against violence from an unexpected quarter. In 1953 he was invited with the young ANC activist Duma Nokwe to a communist youth festival in Bucharest, Romania, on the initiative of Ahmed Kathrada. They bribed their way onto an Israeli El Al plane, and made their first contacts with European communists. Mandela had persuaded Sisulu that he ought to secretly visit China, in order to discuss whether it might supply the ANC with arms. Sisulu's Chinese hosts surprised him by warning against an armed struggle: 'Look, this is a dangerous route,' they told him. 'Don't come to this solution till you are ready for it. Once you are beaten you have no chance.'[44] Sisulu returned convinced by the advice, which Mandela accepted; but his unauthorised visit to China shocked conservative ANC leaders like Luthuli and Matthews, who demanded an apology. Mandela was still convinced that 'an armed struggle would be absolutely necessary', but he was to realise later that he had been precipitate, thinking like 'a hotheaded revolutionary.'[45]

Mandela was still something of a maverick, a loose cannon within the ANC, and his speeches had inflammatory touches which were to bring trouble from the government. In 1953 he wrote his first major speech as President of the Transvaal ANC. It was read out for him at the annual conference in September, since he was banned from attending. The speech proclaimed: 'Today the people speak the language of action; there is a mighty awakening among the men and women of our country.' He looked back on the glories of the Defiance Campaign, when 'the entire country was transformed into battle zones where the forces of liberation were locked up in immortal conflict against those of reaction and evil

. . . our flag flew in every battlefield.' (He later had to explain to judges that he was writing metaphorically.)[46]

The speech went on to link the South African struggle to others in Africa, where anti-imperialists were gathering momentum: 'The entire continent is seething with discontent and already there are powerful revolutionary eruptions in the Gold Coast, Nigeria, Tunisia, Kenya, the Rhodesias and South Africa.' He described how 'the massacre of the Kenyan people by Britain has aroused worldwide protest. Children are being burnt alive, women are raped, tortured, whipped and boiling water poured on their breasts to force confessions from them.' He ended with a quotation lifted from Nehru, which gave the speech its title, 'No Easy Walk to Freedom': 'You can see that there is no easy walk to freedom anywhere, and many of us will have to pass through the valley of the shadow of death again and again before we reach the mountaintops of our desires.'[47]

Mandela was more influenced by Nehru than he liked to admit: 'I used a lot of the writings of Nehru without acknowledging it, which was a silly thing to do,' he said forty-four years later. 'But when there is a paucity of views in you, you are inclined to do that.'[48] He was also becoming more attached to the rhetoric of Marxist anti-colonialism. A few months later, when his ban was again briefly lifted, he addressed the left-wing Peace Council with a blood-curdling attack on imperialist greed. 'In their mad lust for markets and profits these imperial powers will not hesitate to cut one another's throats, to break the peace, to drench millions of innocent people in blood and to bring misery and untold suffering to humanity.' He did not share, he explained, the bourgeois belief in continuous development: he foresaw a break in continuity, a 'leap from one stage to another'.

On 13 December 1953 Mandela spoke for an hour and a half at a big meeting in Soweto. His speech was recorded (luckily inaccurately) by a policeman, Detective-Sergeant Helberg, and was later used as evidence of treason. Mandela warned the huge crowd: 'We have to employ new methods in our struggle. It is no longer sufficient to speak from platforms. More work must be done behind the scenes, even underground.' He went on to tell them: 'You will not shed blood in vain. We will erect a monument for you next to Shaka.'[49]

His speeches were undoubtedly becoming more warlike, and Mandela the revolutionary was now openly competing with Mandela the lawyer.

But behind his showmanship, in the courts and on the platforms, there were still doubts about his seriousness as a leader. Like other combative politicians out of office, such as Theodore Roosevelt in the 1890s and Winston Churchill in the 1930s, he often seemed to be spoiling for a fight, without a real organisation or plan behind him.

8

The Meaning of Freedom

1953–1956

DESPITE MANDELA'S political evolution, he still retained his basic African nationalism: his pride in his people and their history, and his determination to regain their rights. But he sought allies wherever he could find them: from among white liberals, Indian Gandhi-ists and Christian priests. And his most effective and committed friends were the communists, who in 1953 had reformed themselves as the South African Communist Party – a name which stressed their home-grown, patriotic basis. Uniquely multi-racial, the SACP remained very different from other white parties, and from Communist Parties elsewhere, and it included some very unrevolutionary members. But because of Pretoria's special definition of 'statutory communism', devised against the background of the escalating Cold War, they could all be branded as dangerous revolutionaries who were taking over the ANC, thus scaring other potential supporters away.

The communist bogey would be portrayed more menacingly in the next stage of the ANC's crusade, the preparation of what would be called the 'Freedom Charter'. South African liberals and many Western sympathisers would depict the Charter as a typical communist ploy aimed at discreetly achieving influence through a popular front with carefully-orchestrated demonstrations, using ANC leaders as gullible pawns to endorse their propaganda. But that view was distorted by the magnifying glasses of the Cold War. The Charter's message was directed not against capitalists or Western democrats, but against narrow nationalists, both Afrikaner and African. For Mandela and most of his colleagues the Charter was a historic breakthrough. It committed the ANC to discarding racialism and to widening the basis of the struggle, and was to become its key manifesto for the next forty years.

The originator of the Freedom Charter was neither a communist nor a militant, but the conservative elder statesman of the ANC, Z.K. Matthews, Mandela's mentor at Fort Hare. Matthews had been forced to return to South Africa after a year in the United States in May 1953, when the government had refused to extend his passport. He came back in a more radical mood. He was now less admiring of the traditional black American hero Booker T. Washington than of his radical opponent Dr W.E.B. du Bois, the founder of the NAACP (National Association for the Advancement of Colored People).[1] When Matthews arrived at the airport the Special Branch took away books by authors including Arnold Toynbee, and also a photograph of Z.K.'s friend the singer, actor and communist Paul Robeson.[2]

Matthews found his people's prospects much deteriorated. The Nationalists' second election victory the year before was really greater than it appeared, he pointed out, because 'the opposition parties are but pale reflections of the government party as far as their colour policies are concerned'.[3] Over lunch with his sons at home, Matthews first discussed the idea of a gathering of all races to discuss the possibility of a multi-racial constitution.[4] Other groups took up the idea, and in August 1953 Matthews, as President of the Cape ANC, formally proposed it at their annual conference: 'I wonder whether the time has not come for the ANC to consider the question of convening a National Convention, A CONGRESS OF THE PEOPLE, representing all the people of this country irrespective of race or colour to draw up a FREEDOM CHARTER for the DEMOCRATIC SOUTH AFRICA OF THE FUTURE.'[5]

'Little did I realise when I uttered those words,' he recalled later, 'that I was laying the foundation of a charge of treason.'[6] It was ironic, Mandela commented in jail twenty years afterwards, that Matthews, who had been criticised as a fence-sitter, should have conceived the dynamic idea which became 'the vortex of our aspirations'.[7] Mandela welcomed the proposed convention as a public display of strength, and compared it to the founding of the ANC in 1912. It was all the more important since he suspected that the ANC might soon be banned altogether.[8]

The idea was endorsed at the next annual conference of the ANC in Queenstown in December 1953. It was much more confident and well-reported than the Bloemfontein conference two years earlier which had initiated the Defiance Campaign. There was clearly tension between Marxist speakers, who saw the struggle in class terms, and the Christian approach of the President, Albert Luthuli, who insisted: 'The urge and yearning for freedom springs from a sense of DIVINE DISCONTENT and so, having a divine origin, can never be permanently humanly gagged.'[9] Some of the nationalists wanted to expel Sisulu for collaborating with other races, but the majority of the delegates were convinced of the need to co-operate: Luthuli pointed to the dangerous example of narrow Afrikaner nationalism, and insisted that African nationalism be broader, democratic and progressive. The need for a Freedom Charter was agreed upon, and the conference instructed the executive to make immediate preparations for a Congress of the People, including a corps of national 'Freedom Volunteers'.

In March 1954 Sisulu and Mandela helped organise a meeting with some of the ANC's allies at Tongaat, close to Luthuli's home area, to which he was now restricted.[10] An eight-member National Action Council was set up to prepare for the Congress of the People. Only two of the council members (Luthuli and Sisulu) were from the ANC, which the nationalists were quick to depict as a sign of domination by outsiders. The other six included two from the South Africa Indian Congress, two from the newly-formed South African Coloured People's Organisation, and two from the new body of white ANC supporters, the Congress of Democrats, which was made up largely of communists, whose involvement brought new controversies and suspicions.

The SACP's Central Committee, which included Joe Slovo and Rusty Bernstein, threw itself into organising the Congress of the People, holding many secret meetings.[11] The more nationalist ANC members, the 'Africanists', were alarmed by the communist influence, but Mandela appreciated the hard work and total commitment of friends like Bram Fischer and Michael Harmel, who had been hounded and persecuted as much as the blacks, and who shared his goal of overthrowing white domination.[12] He no longer believed that communists were necessarily against the Church as he noted that many black communists were genuine Christians.[13] When Canon Collins came to Johannesburg from London in 1954, Mandela assured him that the ANC was not communist, though the government was driving it in that direction: 'There was little time left for there to be a possibility of real co-operation between black and white.'[14]

The ANC invited another newly-formed white organisation as well as the Congress of Democrats to co-sponsor the Congress of the People. The Liberal Party had been formed in the wake of the April 1953 general election – in which the Nationalists had increased their majority – to counter the forces of racism. Its leaders included respected academics and intellectuals including the novelist Alan Paton, and it would be helped by Harry Oppenheimer, the Chairman of the huge Anglo-American Corporation. The Liberals were totally opposed to apartheid, but they stopped well short of calling for universal franchise, and were hostile to the communists. 'Between communists and liberals,' wrote Paton later, 'there is a fundamental incompatibility.'[15]

Most Liberals remained aloof from the ANC and its communist friends, but some ANC leaders would make friends with individual members of the new party: President Luthuli was in touch, Mandela noted, with the most liberal Liberals, and welcomed the party as an ally against white supremacy. Mandela too had Liberal friends – notably Patrick Duncan, who had joined the Defiance Campaign – but he was critical of the Liberal Party. He was already foreseeing the need for violence, and thought the Liberals would get in his way. And he was impatient with the Liberals' refusal to support universal suffrage.

In June 1953 Mandela wrote an article entitled 'Searchlight on the Liberal Party'. It was published in a new monthly periodical, *Liberation*, which was edited by Michael Harmel, with Mandela himself on its editorial board. He attacked the Liberals' insistence on 'democratic and constitutional means' and their refusal to support 'one adult, one vote'. He saw them as part of the European ruling class which, he said, 'hates and fears the idea of a revolutionary democracy in South Africa just as much as the Malans and the Oppenheimers do'.[16] He predicted a clear parting of the ways between those who committed themselves to the revolutionary programme and those who did not, between the friends and the enemies of Congress. And he asked, as he would often ask again: 'Which side, gentlemen, are you on?'[17]

The Liberals replied through Professor Tom Price, who poured scorn on Mandela's 'rosy clichés born of the October Revolution' – an attack which, as the Liberal Party's historian Randolph Vigne lamented, 'served only to draw the battle lines between the Liberals and the new Congressites, black and white'. The Liberals at first welcomed the chance to co-sponsor the Congress of the People; but they soon became convinced that they were being lured into a 'popular front' whose decisions were taken in advance by communist elements. They believed, moreover, that the Congress would be 'a very minor affair', and decided to withdraw before it was held – to the later regret of many of their members: the historian David Everatt concluded that the decision was 'one of the most damaging the party ever took'.[18]

Preparations continued without the Liberals, but with much input from the white communists in the Congress of Democrats. Groups across the country held hundreds of meetings, submitting their own drafts and proposals which would be incorporated in a grand Freedom Charter to be put forward at the Congress. The response was certainly vigorous, welcoming very different concepts of freedom – including the freedom to have ten wives. As Joe Slovo later described it: 'Tens of thousands of scraps of paper came flooding in: a mixture of smooth writing-pad paper, torn pages from ink-blotched school exercise books, bits of cardboard, asymmetrical portions of brown and white paper bags, and even the unprinted margins of bits of newspaper.'[19]

Some suspected that this democratic outpouring was not quite as spontaneous as it looked. Sydney Kentridge, who was later to be Mandela's counsel, noticed that many of the demands were in the same handwriting, and suspected that a classic communist technique was secretly at work: to detach the masses from their previous leaders.[20] But the eventual Freedom Charter was very far from being a communist manifesto. Long after, Mandela remained convinced that 'it was a document born of the people. It was not something that was imposed from the top. And that is why it is still relevant even today.'[21] He was impressed by 'how far ahead of the politicians the masses were, in several respects'. The people realised that political power was essential, but also that it would be meaningless without economic power. He was struck too by their lack of extreme nationalism, and their acceptance of the principle that South Africa belonged to all its people.[22]

Behind the scenes, Mandela worked very closely with Walter Sisulu, who was now being pursued by the police. Z.K. Matthews told the Cape ANC in June that Sisulu was operating behind the 'iron curtain' of the Transkei as a Scarlet Pimpernel (before Mandela inherited the title): 'They sought him here, they sought him there, they sought him everywhere.'[23] The police soon caught up with him in his house in Orlando in July 1954. I happened to be with him. He was talking with his usual analytical detachment about bannings and detentions, when two Afrikaner detectives walked in. They were surprisingly friendly: 'Ah, we've found you at last: two letters from the Minister of Justice for you!' 'I've been expecting you,' Sisulu answered. 'Only two? It won't make any difference, you know. The struggle will go on!' The detective smiled: 'Cheerio then – *Afrika!*'[24]

The next day Sisulu was arrested, and was later sentenced to three months' imprisonment for having attended a gathering of five people. But he remained the moving force behind the African National Congress. In August 1954 he recalled how five years earlier he had promised that, as Secretary of the ANC, 'I shall be entirely at your disposal.' He described how crippling bans had already removed most members of the National Executive, including Mandela, but insisted that the movement was growing in strength: 'The government has already been shaken, the time has passed when they could rule the country as if we, the people, did not exist.'[25] In fact Sisulu was still regarded by his colleagues as Secretary of the ANC, with Mandela as his close partner.

The first draft of the Freedom Charter was created by the communist architect Rusty Bernstein, who rather casually added a rhetorical beginning and ending – which he later thought overblown.[26] In early June it was passed on to a small planning group, including Mandela, who made a few changes. The Charter's meaning was to become a battleground for the next thirty-five years while it remained pickled in history, its authors jailed or exiled. It was frequently condemned as a Marxist document, with its bold promise: 'The mineral wealth beneath the soil, the banks and monopoly industry shall be transferred to the ownership of the people as a whole.' But in fact it was carefully designed to be all things to all men: Mandela saw it as having been welded from the demands of the masses, arising out of their daily lives.[27] It proclaimed principles rather than policies, in a declamatory style like a political psalm. Michael Harmel, the Marxist historian of the SACP, claimed with some reason that it 'stems from the tradition of the proclamation of rights of the French and American revolutions and echoed in the UN Declaration of Human Rights'.[28]

The Freedom Charter opened with the words:

> We, the people of South Africa, declare for all our country and the world to know:
>
> That South Africa belongs to all who live in it, black and white, and that no government can justly claim authority unless it is based on the will of the people.[29]

The Congress of the People was fixed for 26 June 1955 (now established as the annual 'Freedom Day'). It was held on a private sports field in Kliptown, near Soweto. Three thousand delegates converged from all over the country on the cheerful scene, which looked more like a Derby Day than a militant demonstration. They included wizened black countrymen and office-workers with bright American ties, smooth Indian lawyers with their wives in saris, and swaying black grandmothers in wide skirts in the ANC colours.[30] There was a clear communist influence, with stalls distributing left-wing pamphlets and a fraternal message from Chou En-lai in Beijing. But the meeting itself had the leisurely, casual character of traditional Congress meetings, with Christian elements including Father Huddleston, who was given a special ANC honour.

Mandela, like most of the organisers, was banned from the meeting and could only watch it from afar. He had driven to Kliptown with Sisulu, and moved round the edge of the crowd in a thin disguise, standing for a time next to a bearded man from the Transkei, marvelling at the people's dedication.[31] It seemed surprising that the Kliptown meeting was not itself banned; the reason for this soon became clear.

Mandela watched the Congress follow its slow course. On the first day the Freedom Charter was recited in three languages, and was approved with shouts of '*Afrika!*' from the crowd. On the second day each section of the Charter was acclaimed in turn, until they reached the words 'there shall be peace and friendship'. At that point the meeting was suddenly disrupted by detectives and policemen armed with sten guns bursting into the crowd. An Afrikaner officer took the microphone and announced that they were investigating high treason, and were searching for subversive documents. The police took down the name of every spectator before they were allowed to leave, trooping away peacefully while a band with a dented tuba and broken drums played African songs. Mandela was tempted to join them, but thought better of it, and drove back to Johannesburg for an emergency meeting of the ANC leadership. It was gratifying that the police had recognised the importance of the Congress, but Mandela knew that the raid 'signalled a harsh new turn'.[32]

The Freedom Charter soon acquired an independent momentum. It had not been completely endorsed at the Congress of the People, so its status was uncertain: as Rusty Bernstein saw it, the Charter had 'drifted out of the Congresses' control – and for lack of foresight had taken on a free-floating life of its own'.[33] The white newspapers prominently reported the meeting and the police intervention, while not printing the Charter itself. But the text of the Charter soon reverberated within the ANC, and was challenged by formidable critics.[34]

In December 1955 the annual conference of the ANC debated the Charter in a stormy atmosphere, while most of its architects were banned from attending. The National Executive complained that many ANC branches 'showed a complete lack of activity, as if some of them regretted the birth of this great and noble idea'.[35] Luthuli himself was uneasy, as he told his Congress colleague Arthur Letele, about 'certain new trends or cliques in Congress', but he commended the Charter, and advocated an 'all-inclusive African nationalism' which embraced all South Africans. Many nationalists, who now called themselves 'Africanists', resisted co-operation with other races. The former ANC President Alfred Xuma wrote a letter complaining about 'certain tendencies' within Congress, which he believed had 'lost its identity as a National Liberation Movement with a policy of its own and distinct African leadership'. Mandela's former mentor Peter Mda reasserted the original nationalism of the Youth League in an article in his journal the *Africanist*: 'From our inception we saw the burning need of ridding the ANC of foreign domination.' He proclaimed: 'NO WHITE MAN HAS EVER IMPRESSED US.'[36]

The annual conference eventually put off endorsing the Freedom Charter until a special conference in Orlando in April 1956. There it provoked a new storm. The Africanists complained that the conference had been packed by the 'Charterists', and attacked the idea that the land belonged to everyone, implicit in the phrase 'South Africa belongs to all who live in it', which suggested public ownership. Luthuli and the Natal branch had their own concerns about the economic clauses of the Charter, but they gave way in the cause of unity, not wanting to strengthen the hand of the Africanists.[37] Luthuli was resisting pressure to dissociate himself from left-wing allies: that year his eccentric white Californian friend Mary-Louise Hooper, who had been raising funds for the ANC in America, suggested to him that the ANC should change its official lawyers, Mandela & Tambo, because their left-wing reputation was putting off potential donors. Luthuli replied that while he did not like communists, 'it would not only be unwise but mean to forgo the services of any of our faithful and tried lawyers solely on the grounds of leftist leanings'.[38]

The Freedom Charter was eventually approved by the conference. It was a remarkable achievement, just when the Afrikaner government was imposing its exclusive racial power, for the ANC to adopt a manifesto which was above all anti-racial.[39] 'For the first time in the history of our country,' wrote Mandela a year later, 'the democratic forces irrespective of race, ideological conviction, party affiliation or religious belief have renounced and discarded racialism in all its ramifications.'[40] But the Charter was approved at the cost of fierce dissension, which would split the ANC apart two years later.

Nelson Mandela gave his own interpretation of the Freedom Charter, which would later become significant, in an important article in *Liberation* in June 1956, the first anniversary of the Congress of the People. It was not just his view: all the articles in *Liberation* were carefully edited by the magazine's whole board, and Mandela had been asked to 'correct the assumption that the Freedom Charter was the embryo of a socialist state'.[41] The article largely conformed to the Marxist interpretation of the Charter, which Mandela argued was a 'revolutionary document precisely because the changes it envisages cannot be won without breaking up the economic and political set-up of present South Africa'. And he underlined the need for public ownership: 'The Charter strikes a fatal blow at the financial and gold-mining monopolies that have for centuries plundered the country and condemned its people to servitude.'[42]

But in a crucial passage he welcomed the opportunity that would be created for free enterprise to expand: 'The breaking up and democratisation of these monopolies will open up fresh fields for the development of a prosperous non-European bourgeois class. For the first time in the history of this country the non-European bourgeoisie will have the opportunity to own in their own name and right mills and factories, and trade and private enterprise will boom and flourish as never before.'[43]

For decades these two sentences would reverberate through subsequent trials and angry debates on Robben Island. They were omitted – as Trotskyists noted with relish – from the *Liberation* article when it appeared in Mandela's published speeches and writings, edited by Ruth First in London and several times reprinted.[44] But Mandela continued to state his belief that under the ANC private enterprise would 'flourish as never before' – which would have a very practical significance forty years later.

* * *

The arguments about future economic systems were beginning to be overshadowed by the more immediate activities of the Afrikaner government. By the mid-fifties the Nationalists were extending their policy of apartheid much more rapidly and thoroughly than Mandela and his colleagues had first anticipated. In 1954, at the age of eighty, Dr Malan retired, to be succeeded as Prime Minister by Hans Strijdom, a cruder advocate of white domination, with little intellectual subtlety. But a much more ambitious concept of 'grand apartheid' was being prepared by Dr Hendrik Verwoerd, the Minister of Native Affairs, who would become Prime Minister in 1958.

Verwoerd, with his innocent face and gentle voice, was a visionary who had no doubts about the moral rightness of his plan to completely separate blacks from whites, a plan which attracted Afrikaner intellectuals and others as the ultimate solution to the problem of race relations. But it could be achieved only by a programme of drastic social engineering and mass removals which was closer to the actions of communist governments in Eastern Europe than to any free-enterprise model in the West. While Afrikaner governments were representing themselves as champions of free enterprise, they were embarking on unprecedented state intervention which constantly impinged on the daily lives of Africans. The new black townships, with their thousands of identical houses unrelieved by shops or businesses, looked like caricatures of socialist housing for the *lumpenproletariat*.

Mandela spent much time analysing and criticising 'Verwoerd's Grim Plot', as he called it.[45] He regarded Verwoerd as following the broad ideas of Hitler's national socialism and racial principles, through which he had planned to rule Germany's African colonies. 'Fascism has become a living reality in our country,' Mandela wrote in June 1957, 'and its defeat has become the principal task of the entire people of South Africa.'[46] But Verwoerd had reason to believe that he could gain support from tribal leaders, by encouraging their rivalries and differences. He had a special opportunity to do this in the rural areas, where the chiefs were jealous of their territorial influence and privileges. Only a few chiefs, like Albert Luthuli, were prepared to resign their chieftainship rather than serve an alien power. As in wartime Europe, it required great courage to resist the temptation to collaborate with an all-powerful regime.

Mandela now saw himself as belonging firmly to Johannesburg, which had forged his mature attitudes and politics. But he still kept his links with the countryside, and his royal ancestry and upbringing had given him a deeper sense of involvement with his home territory than most of his colleagues. 'Fourteen years of crammed life in South Africa's largest city,' he wrote later, 'had not killed the peasant in me.' In September 1955 his travel ban had again expired, and he decided to revisit the Transkei.

Driving through Natal, he again enjoyed the wild, open landscape and his closeness to nature, with a relish which comes through in his writings. He recalled the land's historical associations, and reflected on the old battles for territory: first between Zulus and British, then between Afrikaners and British. 'Was it the same Afrikaner who fought so tenaciously for his own freedom,' he wondered, 'who had now become such a tyrant, and was persecuting us?'[47] In Durban he stayed with his Indian friends Ismail and Fatima Meer, and visited the banned Luthuli in Groutville. Arriving home in the Transkei he saw his mother again, with a mixture of nostalgia and guilt. He had invited her to come and stay with him in Johannesburg, but she had chosen to continue living alone, twenty miles from a doctor, still a simple peasant woman ploughing the fields and surviving in the rugged conditions.[48] In jail he would always have an uneasy conscience about her: but she had encouraged him to fight for his beliefs, and he reassured himself that his struggle was giving his people a new meaning to life.[49]

His main purpose in visiting the Transkei was political. The government was now determined to extend apartheid by means of the new Bantu Authorities Act, which would promote the chiefs locally while subordinating them to their white rulers in Pretoria. The Transkei was to be the showpiece. The Bunga, the council of Transkei chiefs, had rejected the new Act in 1952, but the government had lured them with greater juridical and financial powers, and in 1955 the Bunga voted to accept it. Mandela was upset, but realistic: with his own chiefly background he clearly understood the temptation to collaborate. In July 1955 he wrote a well-argued article for *Fighting Talk* called 'Bluffing the Bunga into Apartheid'. He pointed out how every chief and headman would now be paid by the government, and fired if they defied it, as Chief Luthuli had been fired in 1952. It was 'part of a deliberate bluff' to deceive the credulous tribal leaders into believing that they had a voice in their own government. But he recognised the weakness of ANC propaganda in the face of the chiefs' influence over their people, and urged the ANC to reconsider its decision to boycott the forthcoming Transkei elections: 'Should these bodies not be used as platforms to expose the policies of the Nationalist government, and to win the people over to the liberation movement?'[50]

Mandela saw the conflict in very personal terms. Kaiser Matanzima, his nephew and one-time hero at Fort Hare, was now an influential chief in the territory of Western Tembuland, and he had helped to persuade the Bunga to accept the new Act. The two men, both born to rule, both confident lawyers, had much in common, and they would always maintain a family intimacy. But they now had very different loyalties, and found themselves on opposite sides in the classic debate between collaborator and resister. Mandela no longer believed in the hereditary principle which had benefited Matanzima, while Matanzima saw Mandela as now being a Johannesburger, 'far away from his home people'.

During his visit to the Transkei Mandela argued with Matanzima through the night, carefully avoiding theoretical 'isms'. He warned him that the government aimed to divide and rule the black people, and claimed that resistance would avoid future massacres. Matanzima replied that the chiefs would be strengthened by the apartheid system, and that multi-racial policies would increase racial friction, leading to bloodshed and bitterness. He saw himself as being in the thick of battle. 'My attitude was one of reconciliation with the Afrikaners,' Matanzima recalled forty years later. 'Black and white must meet together in the Transkei.'[51] Mandela was distressed by the deadlock. 'I would have loved to fight side by side with him,' he wrote later in jail, 'and share with him the laurels of victory.' But by then Matanzima was firmly allied with the ANC's enemies.

Mandela continued his tour of the country. He drove on to Port Elizabeth, where he first met Govan Mbeki, the Marxist activist who was organising the ANC in the Eastern Cape. Then he visited the campaigning Englishman Christopher Gell, who lived in an iron lung – from which he dictated shrewd advice to the ANC and sharp critiques of apartheid for the newsletter *Africa X-Ray Report*. Mandela never forgot this unusual ally: when Gell died the ANC organised his funeral, with more blacks than whites among the mourners.

Mandela went on to Cape Town, enchanted by the famous Garden Route, stopping near Clarkson to appreciate both the glorious view and the opportunities for guerrilla fighters to hide in the forests: 'My head was full of dangerous ideas.' In Cape Town he did not see the Trotskyists with whom he had argued seven years earlier, but moved between communists and clergy. He visited the offices of *New Age* to find the police searching them and seizing papers: an omen of trouble to come. He stayed for two weeks in the black township of Langa with Methodist ANC activists, driving round the Cape to organise branches (though resting on Sundays). Before he left the Methodists knelt and prayed for his safe journey home.

Mandela returned to his family in Orlando feeling refreshed and reactivated, and much better informed about rural realities. He warned his colleagues that the ANC was very weak in the Transkei, faced by conservative chiefs and strong security police, and urged a 'boycott from within'. The argument was urgent, as the government pressed ahead with 'grand apartheid'. A government commission, headed by Professor F.R. Tomlinson and including no blacks, had outlined an ambitious scheme to invest in separate homelands, or 'Bantustans', in which Africans would 'develop along their own lines', with their own administration and industries. The government accepted much of it, while rejecting its more liberal proposals, and prepared to cut up South Africa into separate Bantustans: the Transkei would be the first. Mandela warned that the Bantustans would have no real scope for developing their own policies, while providing reserves of cheap labour for white employers.[52]

Apartheid plans were stretching out everywhere, and the government was also determined to enforce complete segregation in schools. The Bantu Education Act of April 1953 gave Pretoria control over all the mission schools, in order to enforce the principle (in Verwoerd's famous words) that: 'There is no place for the Bantu in the European community above the level of certain forms of labour.' As Verwoerd told Parliament: 'Racial relations cannot improve if the wrong type of education is given to Natives. They cannot improve if the result of Native education is the creation of frustrated people who, as a result of the education they received, have expectations in life which circumstances in South Africa do not allow to be fulfilled immediately.'[53]

Mandela was just such a frustrated native. For all his past complaints about the missionaries' imperialism, he was always appreciative of his teachers – and he would become more grateful to them later. He was saddened when the Methodists agreed to hand over their schools to the government: 'Verwoerd must have danced.'[54] Most Anglican schools were likewise handed over, but the Roman Catholics kept their schools going without the help of the state.[55] Mandela feared that the new tribal education system, on top of the territorial segregation, would further undermine the national unity of the ANC: 'The African people are being broken up into small tribal units, isolated one from the other, in order to prevent the rise of national consciousness amongst them and to foster a narrow and insulated tribal outlook.'[56]

The Bantu Education Act brought to a head the thorny question of apartheid schools. Mandela was more realistic than most of the National Executive of the ANC, who wanted a permanent boycott. He warned that they would not be able to sustain it, and could not provide an effective alternative: they should not promise what they could not deliver. He was overruled, and the ANC called for children to stay away, and tried to create schools of its own. But the ANC schools were harassed by the police, and parents became desperate for some kind of education. The ANC was compelled to give up the boycott. Historians would judge its mistake harshly: 'Of all campaigns conducted by the ANC,' wrote Frank Welsh in 1998, 'that against Bantu education was the most poorly-planned, the most confused and, for Africans generally, the most confusing.'[57] Mandela's warning had been vindicated. 'It was a heavy responsibility,' he wrote, 'to choose between two evils: fighting to the bitter end, even if all the children were turned into the streets, and a compromise which at least would keep them in the classroom.'[58]

Apartheid in schools was soon followed by apartheid in universities, as the government forced higher education into the same mould. The Extension of University Education Act of 1959 would remove the independence of Mandela's old academies, Fort Hare and Wits, and impose strict segregation. It would kick away the ladder by which he and his friends had reached a wider world, and break black students' contacts with other races, which threatened the government's system. 'The friendship and interracial harmony,' Mandela wrote in *Liberation* in 1957, 'constitute a direct threat to the entire policy of apartheid and *baasskap* [white domination].'[59]

Mandela watched the avenues of his hopeful youth closing behind him. The schools and universities were being cut off from the wider influences of English liberal culture which had forged his own attitudes. The government was showing the full ruthlessness of its policies, while dividing his people to frustrate their opposition. Mandela still believed the new structures should be resisted from within; but he had to wait twenty years to be proved right, by the schoolchildren of Soweto. In the meantime his old schools had been first cut back, then devastated, by apartheid: when Jack Dugard, the former principal of the teacher-training school at Healdtown, returned there in 1976 he found that all but one of the staff were Afrikaners, obsessed by their own personal safety, while the classrooms had been wrecked by fires. He asked: 'How could education progress in such an atmosphere?'[60]

Keeping in touch with his rural roots gave Mandela a special perspective. In February 1956 he made another brief trip to the Transkei with Sisulu, to buy a plot of land in Umtata, following his principle that a man should own land near his birthplace.[61] Soon after returning to Johannesburg he was banned for the third time, preventing him from leaving the city for another five years. He judged that 'The police thought they had given me enough rope to run around.' But he was now more defiant, and contemptuous of bans. 'I was determined,' he wrote in jail, 'that my involvement in the struggle, and the scope of my political activities, would be determined by nobody else but myself.'[62] His bans had compelled him to become more self-reliant, more detached from any party machine. But at the same time the government's oppression was forcing the ANC and its allies closer together.

Mandela was set on a clear collision course with the government, which was watching him carefully. After being served with his bans he wrote to the Minister of Justice on 13 April asking him for his reasons. Three months later he received a long reply (still retained in the Department's archives) stating that he had vilified the whites and incited blacks to disobey laws and establish a black government, and reminding him of inflammatory speeches he had made over the previous six years. On 22 June 1950 he had said: 'It is about three hundred years since the Europeans came to this country. Heroes and beauties of Africa died. Our country was taken away and slavery came up.' 'This is the organisation,' he had said of the ANC on 22 March 1952, 'which will be the future government of this country.' 'If everybody stood together and remained together,' he said on 7 November 1952, 'there would come a time when we would repay the blood of those killed.' 'We are in a better position against the Afrikaner people than they were when they fought the British imperialists,' he said on 7 March 1954. 'I know as sure as the sun will rise in the east tomorrow that a major clash will come and all forces of reaction will collapse against the forces of liberation.'[63]

He was right about the clash, but wrong about the collapse.

9

Treason and Winnie

1956–1957

EVER SINCE the Congress of the People in June 1955, and the subsequent raids, the government had threatened mass arrests and charges. In April 1956 the Minister of Justice, C.R. Swart, told Parliament that the police were investigating a serious case of high treason, and that about two hundred people would eventually be arrested. But ANC officials were inclined to dismiss the urgency. In November 1956 the President of the Transvaal ANC, E.P. Moretsele, told his conference: 'The whole affair is an election stunt to win them votes. In all probability the Nationalists will carry out their threat, but they are in no hurry to do so, for the election takes place two years from now.'[1]

There was some hurry. A month later, early in the morning of 5 December 1956, Mandela was awakened by loud knocking, and found three white policemen at the door with warrants to search the house and to arrest him on a charge of high treason. Over the next ten days another 155 leaders of all races within the Congress alliance were arrested on the same charge.

Mandela was not altogether surprised, but he was not prepared for a marathon trial which would cripple his political activity and his law practice for five years. Most of the prominent participants of the Congress of the People were now in jail – with some important exceptions, including Dr Dadoo, Yusuf Cachalia, J.B. Marks and Govan Mbeki. Trevor Huddleston, the monk who had been honoured at the Congress and who would have given the accused a special Christian respectability, had been recalled to Britain by his superior. The Liberals, having stayed away from the Congress, were also not included in the arrests, and as a result nearly all the whites at the trial were communists, which gave credence to the government's allegations of a Marxist conspiracy – and also gave the communists a new prestige among Africans as fellow martyrs who shared their sacrifices for the cause.

The mass arrests marked the end of the 'phoney war'. On the night before they took place, the black Johannesburg writer and journalist Can Themba was, as he put it, 'doing my routine round-up of the shebeens with my news nose stuck out'. In one he came upon a drunken gathering which included three prominent ANC activists, Robert Resha, Tennyson Makiwane and Lionel Morrison, who were accusing a fellow boozer of leading a dissolute life. They decided to hold a mock-trial, with Resha as defence counsel and Makiwane as prosecutor. Themba joined in as the magistrate, and after lively pleadings found the accused guilty. The next morning all three of the activists were arrested for high treason. When Themba described the shebeen scene in the next issue of *Drum*, which appeared while the suspects were preparing their defence, Mandela was furious with him for showing his Congress colleagues in such a frivolous light.[2]

There was nothing frivolous about the arrests. Mandela had joked with his arresting officer Detective-Constable Rousseau, but the policeman had warned him, 'You are playing with fire;' Mandela had replied, 'Playing with fire is my game.'[3] The police were determined to humiliate the prisoners, who were eventually all collected together in 'The Fort', the legendary prison on the hill looking over Johannesburg. All of them, including venerable dignitaries like Luthuli, Z.K. Matthews and James Calata, were ordered to strip naked in the outdoor quadrangle, where they waited for an hour for a white doctor to question them, shyly not looking at each other, revealing their bellies and trying to cover their private parts. Mandela, conscious of his own fine physique, remembered the proverb that 'Clothes make the man', and reflected that if a fine body was thought essential to leadership, few of the prisoners would qualify: 'Only a handful had the symmetrical build of Shaka or Moshoeshoe in their younger days.' His Natal colleague Masabalala (Martin) Yengwa draped himself in a blanket and recited a traditional Zulu praise-song honouring Shaka. The other prisoners listened in delight, and the staid Chief Luthuli exclaimed in Zulu, 'That *is* Shaka!' and began to chant and to join in the dance with the others – though most were in fact not Zulus. 'We were all nationalists,' Mandela reflected, 'bound together by love of our history.'[4]

The prisoners soon found compensations for their detention. Like most of the others, Mandela had long been banned from meetings and travel, and now he had a rare opportunity to exchange views with friends from other cities. The prisoners soon organised lectures about the current crisis and the history of the ANC. In themselves they comprised a living history of Congress, with veterans like Calata and Matthews alongside young activists from Sophiatown such as Robert Resha and Peter Ntithe, and members of old ANC families like Tennyson Makiwane.[5]

After two weeks in the Fort, the prisoners were taken to the temporary courtroom which had been prepared for the trial. The old Drill Hall in the centre of Johannesburg was a forbidding military relic, with a corrugated-iron roof half-lined with hessian and a quaint gabled façade overlooking a parade ground. Mandela and the other prisoners were driven there in police vans escorted by troop-carriers; crowds of sympathisers were waiting for them outside the hall, and others inside watched them emerge into the improvised courtroom. Can Themba described the scene: 'The accused came up in batches of twenty, some of them cheerful, some sullen, some frightened, some bewildered, some consumed in high wrath . . . When Nelson Mandela, attorney, came up he hunched his shoulders and seemed to glower with suppressed anger.'[6]

The magistrate was F.C.A. Wessel, an elegant, silver-haired Afrikaner from Bloemfontein. He began speaking, but it soon became clear that his words were inaudible without loudspeakers; the hearings were adjourned until the next day. When the prisoners returned they were put inside a huge wire cage built in the courtroom; the defence lawyers immediately objected, and the cage was eventually dismantled.

At last the chief prosecutor began reading the 18,000-word indictment. The charge of high treason was based on speeches and statements made by the accused over the previous four years, beginning in October 1952, when the Defiance Campaign was at its peak, and continuing through the Sophiatown protests, the Congress of the People and the Freedom Charter, which formed the main basis of the charge. The prosecution argued that the accused conspired to overthrow the government by violence and to replace it with a communist state; but they had to prove the violent intentions.

Mandela reflected how often treason had recurred throughout South Africa's short history. In both world wars some Afrikaners had rebelled against war with Germany, taking up arms on the enemy's side, and had been tried for treason. The Afrikaners in office had been reluctant to execute their own people, and when Dr Malan's government came to power it had released all those convicted of treason during the Second World War, most notably the notorious Nazi Robey Leibbrandt. But Mandela knew that the Nationalists would be much harsher towards their black enemies. He did not think the government genuinely believed that the accused were guilty of treason: the Freedom Charter, after all, enunciated principles which were accepted throughout the civilised world. He thought the whole trial was a frame-up, and that the government merely intended to put the Congress leaders out of action for several years.[7]

He soon realised that the trial would be much more prolonged than he had expected. On the fourth day the 156 prisoners were released on bail of £25 for blacks, £250 for whites ('Even treason was not colour-blind,' Mandela commented), the money being guaranteed by supporters.[8] The court adjourned until January 1957, and the accused were allowed to return to their homes. But it was clear that their lives would be disrupted for a long time to come.

The preliminary hearings, which began in January 1957, were intended only to establish whether there was a sufficient case to go for trial before the Supreme Court: but this process was to stretch over nine months and three million words, before any of the accused had even been examined or cross-examined. After the initial high drama of the arrests, the hearings soon settled down to an eerie combination of tedium, humour and menace. Day after day through the sweltering summer the ritual continued under the tin roof. Each morning Wessel, the courteous magistrate, would enter, lightly touching the corner of his desk as he passed, and the tousle-haired prosecutor Van Niekerk – Joe Slovo called him 'Li'l Abner' – would resume his indictment in a monotone.[9] Most of the accused managed to maintain their sense of humour. When Kathrada passed a strip cartoon about Andy Capp – the cloth-capped male chauvinist in the London *Daily Mirror* – to one of the comrades he replied that he couldn't see its relevance to Marxism-Leninism; Kathrada suggested it might help people to understand the *lumpenproletariat*.[10]

The trial soon dropped out of the headlines, and white Johannesburgers forgot about the supposed threat to their survival which was being examined in their midst. Watching it day after day, I had to keep reminding myself of the trial's real significance as a succession of Afrikaner and black policemen revealed their incompetence and ignorance. The chief defence lawyer Vernon Berrangé, a former racing driver and fighter-pilot, was a sharp and theatrical questioner who shot down much of the evidence presented by barely literate detectives and spies. Writing from prison, Mandela recalled that he had been nicknamed 'Isangoma' (diviner) by the accused.[11] Berrangé achieved his greatest coup when he cross-examined the state's 'expert witness' on communism, Professor Murray, and quoted a passage which Murray condemned as 'communism straight from the shoulder'. It turned out to have been written by Murray himself.

The farcical nature of much of the evidence concealed the trial's real danger: 'These proceedings are not as funny as they may seem,' the magistrate warned the giggling suspects at one point.[12] Mandela was worried by the frivolity of some of the young accused: when Lionel Morrison and others put up an umbrella to protect themselves from the leaking roof, he reproved them sternly.[13] He was well aware of the high stakes, and knew that the humiliations of the police would only harden the government's determination to put the ANC out of action.

Mandela took heart from a bus boycott in Alexandra, which began a week after the treason arrests – fourteen years after the boycott which had so impressed him when he had lived in Alexandra in 1943. Once again, black commuters walked twelve miles a day rather than pay an extra penny on the buses. The ANC, as Luthuli admitted, had no part in organising the boycott; it could only claim that it 'helped create a climate of resistance in which such action could take place'.[14] But the boycott threw up new local organisers outside the courtroom, including two ANC activists, Thomas Nkobi and Alfred Nzo, who later became prominent leaders. Eventually the government had to give way to the boycotters by passing a special bill requiring employers to subsidise the bus fare. It was the first Act of Parliament in the forty-seven years of the Union to have been passed as a result of African pressure, and it reminded Mandela that boycott could be a powerful instrument, but as a tactic, not a fixed strategy: 'The boycott is in no way a matter of principle,' he wrote in *Liberation* the next year, 'but a tactical weapon.'[15]

Mandela kept a lower profile in the courtroom than Luthuli, Matthews or Sisulu: he never featured in the coverage of the left-wing paper *New Age*, the main chronicler of the trial.* His tall figure, immacu-

* When I was writing a book about the trial, *The Treason Cage*, I included profiles of Luthuli, Sisulu and Tambo, but not Mandela; I thought he was too detached to be a future leader, and would be less forthcoming.

lately dressed, carrying a briefcase and talking with slow deliberation, always seemed aloof from the rest. He still had some of the style of a proud chief who had been caught up with a slightly louche urban crowd. Mandela's later biographer Mary Benson, who worked with him on the Treason Trial Defence Fund, saw him then as a rather slick young man, and 'did not take him very seriously'.[16] But the defence lawyers noticed that he had a quiet authority over his fellows, who often sought out his legal advice; and his own testimony would reveal how deeply he had considered his commitment to the cause.[17]

Z.K. Matthews, with his rigorous legal mind, listened to the trial with growing contempt: 'These chaps seem to think that I am the mastermind of the ANC campaign, with everyone else doing what I want,' he wrote to his wife Frieda. 'How wrong they are!' He watched the semi-literate police presenting their incoherent evidence in muddled English and producing supposedly incriminating documents like a 1956 calendar or a notice saying 'Soup with Meat'. He saw how the Afrikaner hatred of blacks was linked to their resentment of English disdain: 'It is amazing how deeply the Afrikaners resent the superior attitude of the English. They are making us suffer too because they think we have sold our souls to the English.' But he worried that in ten years' time 'the hatred of the African for the European will be worse than the hatred of the white man for the black'.[18]

The long Treason Trial brought the various racial groups inside the courtroom much closer together. 'I doubt whether we could have devised so effective a method of ensuring cohesion in resistance and of enlarging its embrace,' said Luthuli.[19] 'We didn't realise we had so much in common,' said Paul Joseph, an Indian ex-factory worker from a humble background who became a friend of Mandela. 'The trial created a cohesion which didn't exist before.'[20] The Africans found themselves pressed together with whites, Indians and Coloureds in roughly the same proportion as the population of the country. It was just the kind of multiracial partnership many of them had been advocating. Whatever propaganda motives had led the government to bring the accused to trial, they could now spread their own counter-propaganda that this was a united, genuinely non-racial movement.

During the daily lunch-hour the accused shared their sandwiches and devised recreations, including the 'Drill Hall Choir', and discussed their arguments and problems. When they went home in the evenings they were made to feel like heroes rather than traitors, with free drinks in shebeens and parties given by white and Indian well-wishers, which extended their contacts and friendships among the other races. Bram Fischer and his wife gave dinners for black leaders, including Luthuli and Mandela, where they met his lawyer friends; Joe Slovo and Ruth First held parties at which Africans, Indians and whites drank, jived and embraced, apparently oblivious of colour. They joked about being hanged for treason, and seemed unconcerned about spies, even welcoming the local CIA agent Millard Shirley, an engaging and gregarious American who was ostensibly writing a book ('My Mother was a Missionary') but was always turning up at ANC functions.[21] But the courage of the 'traitors' was real enough. Some of the accused may have been careless or histrionic – 'peacocking', as Africans called it – but the courage and the danger were real enough. In jail later, Mandela remembered one of the defendants' white liberal benefactors, Ellen Hellman, the Chairman of the Institute of Race Relations, arriving in the courtroom to discuss fund-raising. He began to compliment her on her elegant outfit, but she cut him short: 'Mr Mandela, just tell me in simple terms, what do you want, what do you want?'[22]

There was also some interest from liberal South African businessmen. Luthuli and a few others, not including Mandela, were invited to meet Harry Oppenheimer of the Anglo-American Corporation. He politely told them that their demands for universal suffrage were too extreme, and that boycotts put off white support. They replied that they could not conceal their real demands, however unpleasant they might seem to whites.[23] Oppenheimer discreetly gave £40,000 to the Treason Trial Defence Fund.[24]

Practical help from abroad was received from British and other well-wishers through the Defence Fund, which was launched by Canon Collins in London and Bishop Reeves in Johannesburg to cover legal and other costs. It was administered first by Hilary Flegg, then by Mary Benson, then by Freda Levson, with all of whom Mandela became friends.[25] Mandela was also heartened by the appearance as observers of many Western jurists, including Gerald Gardiner, the British barrister who later became Lord Chancellor, and by American solidarity, including a visit from George Houser of the American Committee for Africa, and gifts from Sammy Davis Junior.[26]

But British and American diplomats in Pretoria continued to avoid meetings with the black opposition, lest they offend the Afrikaner government. Ambassador Byroade invited only whites to the US Embassy's Independence Day party in July 1957, in contrast to the Soviet Consul-General's open hospitality.[27] Successive British Ambassadors invited no blacks to their Queen's Birthday parties, and made no direct contact with any ANC leaders: their diplomats relied on quoting journalists in their despatches, which made no reference to Mandela.[28] In London, South Africa had been under the Dominions Office, which had a cosy family relationship with the white Commonwealth who had been allies in the Second World War, and was more concerned with keeping lines open to Afrikaner nationalists than with African troublemakers; while the Conservative Prime Minister Harold Macmillan was not yet grappling with the problems of Africa.[29]

All through the Treason Trial Mandela had been existing in a strange limbo, between normality and danger; but his life had been further disrupted by a thrilling romance. When the trial began he had been leading a bachelor existence. His marriage with Evelyn had fallen apart, with recriminations on both sides. Evelyn would recall with some bitterness how Mandela would spend nights away without explanation, and claimed that he once nearly throttled her – a charge which Mandela emphatically denies.[30] She was more alienated as her husband became more political. After he was first arrested for treason, he returned home from prison on bail to find Evelyn departed and the house emptied, even of its curtains. Mandela had to try to reassure his two children, Makgatho and Makaziwe (Maki), who were deeply upset.[31]

Mandela's friends speculated whether he would remarry, and he was often seen with eligible women. One of his female companions was Ruth Mompati, the resourceful secretary in his law office. Another was Lilian Ngoyi, the vivacious and forceful leader of the ANC Women's League, who was one of his fellow-accused in the Treason Trial. Helen Joseph, who was close to both of them, thought how effective they would be as man and wife.[32]

But it was not an experienced politician who was to capture Mandela, nor any of the other women he and Evelyn had quarrelled over, but a newcomer, a beautiful young social worker of twenty-two, sixteen years younger than Mandela.[33] Winnie Nomzamo Madikizela came from Bizana in Pondoland, part of the Transkei, where her father Columbus Madikizela was a headmaster. (It was also the home area of her hero, Tambo: 'I was actually made by Oliver Tambo,' she says now.[34]) Winnie's clan, the Ngutyana, was one of the most powerful in Pondoland. Her great-grandfather Madikizela had been a fierce chieftain in Natal until he fled from Shaka's Zulu army to settle near Bizana. Her grandfather Chief Mazingi, a prosperous trader with twenty-nine wives, was converted to Methodism. Her mother, who was thought to have white blood, was passionately religious, and had nine children before she died when Winnie was aged nine, after which her father raised her strictly as a Methodist. He remained awesomely aloof, leaving Winnie's two strong grandmothers to influence her most. Her father's mother Makhulu taught her the ways of her ancestors, while her mother's mother, 'Granny', was a staunch Methodist who made her own Western-style dresses. 'She derived from Makhulu her imperious authority,' said Winnie's lifelong friend Fatima Meer, 'and from Granny her love for smart clothes and an obsession with cleanliness.'[35]

Winnie as a child had been strong-willed, rebellious and sometimes violent. Once she made a knuckleduster with a tin and a nail with which she hit her sister in the mouth: the wound had to be sewn up by the doctor. Winnie never forgot the thrashing her mother gave her for it. 'It was survival of the fittest,' she explained later. 'I had to fight my brothers and sisters; I never had clothes of my own. There used to be a lot of physical fights. Looking back, I got quite ashamed when I was older.'[36] She excelled at school, and kept clear of politics: when her schoolfriends rebelled in sympathy with the Defiance Campaign, she stuck to her studies.[37]

In 1953 Winnie came up to Johannesburg to become a social worker, living at the Helping Hand hostel in Jeppe Street and studying at the Jan Hofmeyr School of Social Work, above the Bantu Men's Social Centre. She went around with two other attractive young students, Marcia Pumla Finca and Harriet Khongisa, together with Ellen Kuzwayo, an older student who later became a writer, who tried to protect them from predatory men.[38] Winnie was a bright student, and two years later she became the first black social worker at Baragwanath Hospital. She was sociable, spirited, fascinated by clothes and by shoes (which she did not wear until she went to secondary school). 'I had to become a smart city girl, acquire glamour,' she explained much later, 'before I could begin to be processed into a personality.'[39]

In Johannesburg Winnie went to a few meetings of the Trotskyist

Unity Movement, to which her brother belonged, but stayed aloof from politics. One day when she visited a law-court with a friend she saw the towering figure of Mandela coming in to conduct a case, as the crowd whispered his name. Soon afterwards she was introduced to him at a delicatessen by Adelaide Tsukudu, a nurse at Baragwanath Hospital who was soon to marry Oliver Tambo. 'I didn't play Cupid,' Adelaide insists, 'and Winnie didn't break up the marriage; it was already crumbling.'[40] Mandela was obviously fascinated by Winnie, and kept looking at her. The next day he invited her to lunch, on the pretext of asking her to help raise money for the Treason Trial Defence Fund. His friend Joe Matthews picked her up, and they lunched at Azad's Indian restaurant.[41]

Mandela spent as much time as possible with Winnie, between the Drill Hall and his law office: 'I was both courting her and politicising her,' he remembered.[42] He was able to wrest her away from a rival, who turned out to be none other than his opponent and nephew Kaiser Matanzima, and he introduced her to his political friends, including Indians and whites. In the midst of the treason ordeals, they were not sure what to make of this innocent-looking twenty-two-year-old, with her lively talk, her fascination with clothes and her big, soulful eyes, who seemed to belong to a quite different world. 'She was very glamorous but terribly shy,' said Paul Joseph's wife Adelaide. 'She was very innocent and naïve,' remembered Yusuf Cachalia's wife Amina. Mandela took Winnie to Rusty Bernstein's house on Sundays, where she would sit in the Bernsteins' daughter's bedroom reading fashion magazines. 'She was right outside the political circle,' said Bernstein, 'but Nelson didn't worry about that.'[43] Winnie embraced Mandela's political friends as her own: she stayed with Ismail and Fatima Meer in Durban, idolised Lilian Ngoyi, regarded Helen Joseph as a mother, and saw Tambo as a father-figure.[44] She was awed by Mandela's air of authority as a hereditary chief 'who would not listen to a woman . . . The way he walks, the way he carries himself he is in fact paramount chief.'

Mandela never formally proposed, but Winnie found herself swept into matrimony. Her family worried about the risks. 'My father was totally against the marriage,' she says now. 'My sisters literally cried, and they begged me not to marry such an older man.' They warned her that Mandela would end up in prison, and that she would be 'just an instrument' to keep the house going and to visit him.[45]

But they were in love. Mandela had now divorced Evelyn, and in

June 1958 he and Winnie were married, a year after they had met. Mandela was allowed a six-day relief from his bans to travel down to the Transkei for the wedding celebrations, first at the ancestral home of the Madikizelas, then at Bizana town hall, accompanied by friends including Ruth Mompati and the white communist Michael Harmel. In his speech Winnie's father warned her that Mandela was already married to the struggle, and that if she wanted to be happy with her in-laws she must do what they did: 'If your man is a wizard, you must become a witch.'[46] Mandela would lovingly call her a witch in his letters.

Mandela returned to the constraints of the Treason Trial, and his beautiful young wife provided an exotic contrast to the sombre tedium and commitment of the courtroom. His dramatic appearances with Winnie, both with wide smiles, seemed to belong to showbiz rather than to politics, and his image acquired a new dimension: not just the lawyer and revolutionary, but the lover with the adoring partner. They were visibly fascinated with each other, with a sense of drama which was heightened, as in a wartime romance, by the obstacles and dangers they faced. Through his long years in jail Mandela would relish the times they could snatch together, and would recall their former life: 'Do you remember the wonderful dish you used to prepare for supper? The spaghetti and simple mince from some humble township butchery! As I entered the house from the gym in the evening that flavour would hit me full flush in the tongue.'[47]

But his marriage to a passionate girl, with her own demands, and with all the complications of three alienated stepchildren, did not provide the kind of stable home base which many of his political friends took for granted. Walter Sisulu still had Albertina as his 'backbone', subsidising his own meagre pay and sharing all his political commitment: 'I could rely on her, and there was no complaining . . . she had mastered the situation in an amazing way, and that gave me wonderful courage.'[48] Mandela's life with Winnie was more exciting, but more distracting, less predictable; while she was soon aware of how much politics dominated his life: 'He did not even pretend that I would have some special claim to his time,' she remembered. 'There never was any kind of life I can recall as family life, a young bride's life where you sit with your husband. You just couldn't tear Nelson from the people: the struggle, the nation came first.'[49]

Winnie very soon developed her own political ambition and instinct.

'I discovered only too soon how quickly I would lose my identity because of his overpowering personality – you just fizzled into being his appendage, with no name and no individuality except Mandela's . . . I vowed that none of this should apply to me.'[50] Her older friend Ellen Kuzwayo observed that she was drifting away from routine social work.[51] She began to attend meetings where her white friends Helen Joseph and Hilda Bernstein taught black women about public speaking; but she soon burst out: 'I don't think we need to be taught how to speak. From our suffering we can just tell people how we feel.' She began to find her own voice, with an expressiveness and empathy which amazed her teachers. And she began campaigning with a powerful populist instinct, bypassing the more conventional speeches of the ANC leaders. 'She wasn't bothered about being in the limelight,' said her Indian friend Adelaide Joseph. 'She wanted to be there with ordinary people.'[52]

Winnie was soon drawn into the women's struggle, which had been gathering momentum in the wake of the Defiance Campaign. It showed its strength when the government determined to make women carry the hated pass-books which controlled Africans' movements, which until then had applied only to men. The ANC formed the Federation of South African Women, affiliated to its Women's League, which by August 1956 organised a march of 20,000 women to the Union Buildings in Pretoria to deliver a petition to the Prime Minister, Hans Strijdom. The marchers arrived singing their militant anthem: 'Strijdom you have tampered with women. You have struck a rock.'[53] Winnie joined the Orlando branch of the Women's League, and was soon making her mark.

'I've married trouble!' Mandela told his lawyer friend George Bizos one day. Winnie, it turned out, had been charged with inciting other women against carrying passes. When asked to show her own, she had shouted that she would never carry one, and when a policeman came to her house with a summons she had assaulted him. 'Have you married a wife or a fellow-agitator?' Bizos asked Mandela. Winnie later explained that the policeman had entered her bedroom, where she was dressing to be taken to prison. She had ordered him out, he had grabbed her, and she pushed her elbow into his chin so that he fell on the floor. He then charged her with assault. Bizos took on the case, and she gave her evidence with a confidence and clarity which amazed the Afrikaner magistrate, who let her off.[54]

Four months after their marriage, in October 1958, already pregnant,

Winnie shocked Mandela by announcing that she would join a mass protest in Johannesburg, and ignored his efforts to dissuade her. She was arrested and jailed together with a thousand other women, keeping up their spirits in prison and making friends with two Afrikaner wardresses. Mandela arranged bail for her, along with others. Winnie had embarked on her own passionate political crusade. Later, Mandela would reprove himself for having been too preoccupied with his own problems to give her support and advice in the face of all her frustrations. As he wrote to her: 'I then led a life where I'd hardly had enough time even to think.'[55]

Some of Mandela's old friends could never understand why he had chosen Winnie: they thought his leadership was being distracted by this aggressive 'new woman', who came from outside any ANC tradition, and that he had married too much trouble.[56] Yet there was clearly political as much as sexual electricity between the couple, as between the Peróns in Argentina or, later, the Clintons in America. Winnie's impetuous assertiveness and crowd-pleasing oratory complemented Mandela's more reserved campaigning, like a wilder descant to his steady bass. At social occasions, with their charisma and their sharp clothes, they were a model public couple of the late fifties, bringing an aura of American glamour to their politics as they entered a dance-hall, with the spotlight shining on them. Winnie was soon developing her own sense of theatre, and would soon appear as an Amazon of the revolution.

10

Dazzling Contender

1957–1959

WHILE THE TREASON TRIAL droned on, Mandela was caught up in the biggest political crisis in the forty-five years of the ANC's existence. It was ultimately to split the organisation apart, and to threaten Mandela's own position even more seriously than he realised at the time. Ever since the Congress of the People the ANC had been under attack from the exclusive African nationalists, or 'Africanists', who opposed the Freedom Charter, with its assumption that the land belonged to everyone, and who called for Africans to take militant action and to stop cooperating with communists or other races. The Treason Trial had given lustre and nationwide recognition to the ANC leaders, but it had also focused attention on their collaboration with Indians and whites, which further antagonised the Africanists.

Mandela was well-placed to understand the impatience and resentments of the Africanists, for they had something in common with his Youth Leaguers a decade earlier, and included some of his old allies. In different circumstances he could have been their leader, but now that he was committed to a broader multi-racial nationalism in alliance with the communists he regarded the rebels as a clear threat to the ANC's unity, which he saw as crucial to the struggle. He was the more exasperated because they were taking advantage of the Treason Trial to gain support from the grassroots. The two sides were depicted in straightforward ideological colours: nationalists versus communists, exclusive versus inclusive. There were in fact many overlaps and blurs, but behind the confrontation lay long-standing personal resentments and cross-currents which became clearer in retrospect, and which eventually made reconciliation impossible.

* * *

The Treason Trial continued to embroil Mandela and his fellow-accused in endless legal argument. Although the government showed no signs of giving up its case, in December 1957, after almost a year of preliminary hearings, the prosecutor dropped the charges against sixty-one of the accused – including, surprisingly, Luthuli and Tambo. Mandela, with his record of militant speeches, was among the remaining ninety-five. The defence applied for the whole case to be discharged, but instead a new prosecutor was appointed: the former Minister of Justice Oswald Pirow, a militant anti-communist who had been an avowed Nazi supporter during the war, and who now claimed that new evidence had emerged of a dangerous conspiracy which meant that the country was living on the edge of a volcano.

When the magistrate, Mr Wessel, concluded that there was enough evidence of treason for the case to go to the Transvaal Supreme Court in Pretoria, Mandela realised that he had become too confident that the whole trial would collapse, and that he and his fellow-defendants might yet be sent to jail.[1] Behind all the absurdities of the trial – the long-winded prosecutor, the incompetent detectives and the ridiculous definitions of communism – there still lay the government's original purpose: to put the accused out of action, and to convict them through existing legislation.

The ANC leaders' preoccupation with the day-to-day proceedings in the courtroom played havoc with their organisation, giving more opportunities to their opponents, who were not on trial. The leaders tried to rally supporters with a 'We Stand by our Leaders' campaign, but they had no opportunity for speech-making or canvassing. The Africanists, who were closer to the ground, accused the leaders of being high-handed and undemocratic, treating the membership like 'voting cattle'.[2]

The Africanists' strongest base was in Mandela's home territory of Soweto, where they were led by an impetuous populist, Potlako Kitchener Leballo. Mandela, who was his attorney, thought of Leballo as a wild-card, undeniably brave, but immature, like many of his followers.[3] He had worked for the United States Information Service office in Johannesburg under the American David Dubois, where he was allowed to duplicate his leaflets.[4] Joe Slovo claimed that the Pan Africanist Congress, which emerged in 1959 as the party of the Africanists, was founded at a meeting in the USIS offices.[5] Leballo's American links encouraged allegations that the CIA was backing the Africanists, which were never substantiated.

From Leballo's house in Soweto came the journal the *Africanist*, burning with diatribes and vituperation against the ANC's leftist leadership. The Africanists, like nationalists everywhere, had more scope for emotive language than the multi-racialists; their invective against 'aliens', 'Eastern functionaries' and 'vendors of the foreign method' was much livelier than the clichés of anti-colonialism and Marxism which Mandela and his colleagues favoured, and made better copy for the white journalists who did much to publicise them. And their spokesmen were also more colourful and picturesque. Josias Madzunya, the Africanist ANC Chairman in Alexandra, was a former peddler who wore a long overcoat in the hottest weather and who could be relied on for firebrand speeches. Peter Raboroko, their spokesman on education, was a brilliant talker who became a witty polemical journalist. Zeph Mothopeng, a dedicated teacher before he was fired for opposing Bantu Education, was an intellectual who at first sounded aridly theoretical, but who proved to be a fearless campaigner and was to be imprisoned on Robben Island.

The Africanists, including some of the old Youth Leaguers, attacked Mandela and his allies for becoming closer to the whites and the communists, and away from their own people. And Mandela was certainly now moving in different circles. 'He was not shy to admit that he had shifted ground,' said his law clerk Godfrey Pitje. '"Look, chaps, you can't blame me for this," Mandela would say in the office. "I'm beginning to look at things differently."'[6]

The Africanists saw Mandela's group being seduced by the charms of white communists like the Slovos in their comfortable suburbs, while they were men of the people who drank at the shebeens in the townships. Peter Raboroko, who had been at school with Tambo, described later how Mandela and his friends were 'catapulted from the atmosphere of African society into this . . . To be on a first-name basis with white women, and this type of thing, it just became so very glittering for them.' When Mandela denounced Raboroko as a 'shebeen intellectual', he took it as a compliment: 'My political reputation is going to be in rags and tatters,' he retorted, 'when people learn I was seen walking with you.' When Raboroko talked about the masses, Mandela said, 'You mean the shebeens?' 'Oh yes,' replied Raboroko. 'By the way, I'm not as fortunate as you – you have your drinks in posh houses in Lower Houghton and Parktown. I have to be content to be drinking with the people in shebeens!'[7] In fact Mandela spent most of his evenings working, and still avoided liquor. 'Now and again I went to a shebeen out of curiosity,' he said later, 'but even now I don't know what happens in a nightclub.'[8]

The Africanists were simmering with resentment against the ANC leadership in Mandela's own neighbourhood of Orlando, and the tension came to a head at a special conference of the Transvaal ANC in Orlando in February 1958. Leballo led the attack against the provincial executive, which was weakened by the absence of banned leaders like Mandela and Sisulu. The meeting broke up in disorder, and the ANC National Executive had to use emergency powers to take over the Transvaal branch. Two months later the national ANC faced humiliation when it tried to mount a stay-at-home protest against the whites-only general election in April 1958. The move, opposed by the Africanists, was a fiasco: Duma Nokwe, the Assistant Secretary of the ANC, called it 'bitterly disappointing, humiliating and exceedingly depressing'.[9] The ANC leaders could not tolerate the Africanists' open defiance, and at a secret meeting they expelled Leballo from the organisation.

The final break came in November 1958, when the Transvaal ANC summoned a crisis conference. It was opened by Luthuli, who again warned against reacting to the Afrikaners with 'a dangerously narrow African nationalism'. The Africanists regarded Mandela and Tambo as among their prime enemies. Tambo, still Secretary of the ANC, tried to calm the rival factions as they wrangled over credentials and delegates, with Africanist thugs confronting loyalist thugs. To avoid defeat in a vote the Africanists retreated from the hall, sending a letter to the leadership proclaiming that they had broken away to become 'the custodians of the ANC policy as it was formulated in 1912'.[10]

Could the split have been avoided? A potential mediator had been Ntatho Motlana, Mandela's family doctor, an impish, fast-talking man who had worked with him in the Youth League and the Defiance Campaign. Motlana was a rare phenomenon in Orlando: an entrepreneur who believed in capitalism: 'A sharp businessman,' Mandela recalled. 'Right from the beginning he was very shrewd.'[11] Motlana was suspicious of white communists, and was friendly with the Africanist Robert Sobukwe, who was his patient and who held meetings in his surgery; but he was against a split, and thought breakaways were setting back liberation struggles all over Africa: 'I told them not to run away from the whites – to stay in the ANC and fight them from there.'[12]

Motlana warned Mandela that the Youth Leaguers were complaining about communist influences, and threatening to leave the ANC, but

Mandela reassured him: 'Don't worry, Ntatho. The ANC is going to rule the country.'[13] Looking back later, Mandela felt the ANC had been too quick to reject the Africanists: 'There were cases where I think we could have exercised more tolerance and patience . . . We expelled too many people.' But he saw the split as probably inevitable in the wake of the Freedom Charter: 'I don't think we could have avoided it.'[14]

Mandela now parted ways with some of his oldest political friends, including his early mentor Gaur Radebe, now fiercely anti-communist. Peter Mda, his inspiration in the Youth League, remained an Africanist, and was convinced that Mandela was a secret Communist Party member, but still felt for him 'a friendship of the heart if not of the head'.[15] Mandela was less warm in remembering Mda: 'I never had any meaningful contact with him whatsoever as a public figure,' he wrote from jail. 'I have formed the picture of a man who has stuffed his bones with a lot of marrow, a thinker with a tongue that can both bite and soothe.' He saw Mda as being as different from himself as war from peace: 'Mda was a young man concentrating on the former and I drawing attention respectfully to the latter.'[16]

In April 1959 the Africanists formed their own party, the Pan Africanist Congress (PAC), at a national conference in Orlando. The conference was held on the national holiday celebrating the first permanent white settlement in South Africa by Jan van Riebeck of the Dutch East India Company in 1652 – which gave the PAC a cue to protest against 'the Act of Aggression against the Sons and Daughters of Afrika, by which the African people were dispossessed of their land, and subjected to white domination'.[17] The PAC liked to compare themselves to African nationalists in other parts of the continent, who were now confidently moving towards independence, and the new 'African Personality' proclaimed by Kwame Nkrumah of Ghana was certainly more in tune with the PAC's rhetoric than with the multi-racialism of the ANC.

As their President the PAC delegates did not choose a fiery demagogue like Madzunya or Leballo, but the much more reflective Robert Sobukwe, a lecturer in African languages at Witwatersrand University. At thirty-five, Sobukwe was six years younger than Mandela, and like him tall, handsome and physically strong; but he was from a humbler origin, and combined his intellectual grasp with a peasant's simplicity. Sobukwe was brought up in the Karoo, the half-desert region of the Cape, the son of a shop-worker. He was taken up by the Methodists and went to Healdtown school and Fort Hare, where he was much more academically successful than Mandela. He became a militant Youth Leaguer, fiercely attacking the missionaries and invoking the growing power of Africa: 'Even as the dying so-called Roman civilisation received new life from the barbarians, so also will the decaying so-called Western civilisation find a new and purer life from Africa.'

In 1949 Sobukwe became Secretary of the Youth League, enthusiastically supporting the Programme of Action of Mandela and his friends. For a few years he was preoccupied with teaching and cultural interests (including translating *Macbeth* into Zulu), but just before the Congress of the People, shocked by what he saw as the growing influence of communists and non-Africans, he was drawn back into ANC politics.[18] Whites, he believed, could never fully identify with the black cause because 'a group in a privileged position never voluntarily relinquishes that position.'[19] Like other Africanists he complained about the multi-racial activities of the ANC leaders, whom he accused of 'dancing with white women in the Johannesburg interracial parties instead of getting down to the job of freeing Africa from white domination'.[20]

The emergence of the PAC, headed by an eloquent, intellectual anti-communist, was welcomed by conservatives in Europe and America as providing a promising alternative to the ANC. Mandela thought the US State Department 'hailed its birth as a dagger in the heart of the African left'.[21] British diplomats were unsure which was the greater danger to the West, communism or racialism; the British High Commission had praised Luthuli's 'staunch and comparatively moderate stance' on racial tolerance.[22] But the British acquired an exaggerated respect for the PAC, influenced by the South African Police. On 17 August the Police Commissioner gave a long report to the British High Commission explaining that 'the Africanists look upon their own organisation as being but one of a number of similar organisations throughout the African continent, all dedicated to the task of freeing the African from "imperialism" and "white domination" and the eventual establishment of a so-called United States of Africa.'[23] Meanwhile, both the British and the Americans still saw the apartheid government as ultimately an ally against global communism. As the State Department's African expert Joseph Satterthwaite said in October 1958: 'When the chips are down, they're such very loyal friends.'[24]

Mandela still hoped that the two factions of the ANC could be reunited. He had been Sobukwe's attorney as well as Leballo's: he respected Sobukwe's sense of honour, and regarded him as 'a dazzling orator and incisive thinker'.[25] But Mandela was impatient with the immaturity of Sobukwe's crude black nationalism – which he himself had abandoned a decade ago – and the Africanist bandwagon of politicians settling old scores. He was especially worried by Sobukwe's intolerance of the rights of minorities, which was summed up in the Africanist manifesto: 'The African people will not tolerate the existence of other national groups within the confines of one nation.' Mandela would always argue that tribal and ethnic minorities – whites included – must have their rights guaranteed. Sobukwe, he thought, was evading the issue.[26]

But Mandela underestimated the threat that Sobukwe represented to the ANC, and the appeal of the PAC's nationalism to young black intellectuals. He was now facing his first serious political challenge; and looking back forty years later, he would recognise Sobukwe as his most formidable rival.[27]

When the Treason Trial resumed it was moved to the Afrikaner stronghold of Pretoria, an hour's drive from Johannesburg, where the ANC's support was much weaker, and the white population more hostile. Three judges presided in the ornate courtroom – a converted Jewish synagogue – led by the same Justice Rumpff who had already tried many of the accused during the Defiance Campaign. Mandela respected Rumpff, but thought he wanted a conviction: 'He wanted to send us to jail, but he was too brilliant a judge to commit a disgrace.'[28]

The defence team still included Vernon Berrangé, 'the human lie-detector', but it was now augmented by two very senior lawyers, Israel Maisels and Bram Fischer. Fischer, who became one of Mandela's closest friends, was already a hero to the ANC. He was a true Afrikaner, the son of a Judge-President of the Orange Free State, with the chubby red face and open style of a farmer. He had begun as an Afrikaner nationalist, but after studying at Oxford and visiting the Soviet Union he joined the Communist Party, and was influenced by J.B. Marks, Moses Kotane and Yusuf Dadoo. Mandela was deeply impressed by Fischer's stoic self-sacrifice and commitment: 'We embraced each other as brothers.'[29] Fischer devoted all his energies to organising both a political and a legal defence, and his skills attracted many of the accused to the law.

The trial stopped and started, with intricate wrangles. In August 1958 Berrangé embarked on a long legal argument questioning the vaguely-worded indictment. In October the prosecution suddenly withdrew their charges altogether; but a month later they returned with a more precise indictment, which left out sixty-one of the accused to be tried later, and was directed against only thirty people who were thought to be guilty of particularly revolutionary or violent incitement. Mandela was among them.

The trial was due to start again in Pretoria in February 1959. The night before, Mandela went to the first night of the black musical *King Kong*, composed by his friend Todd Matshikiza, which told the story of the black heavyweight boxer from Sophiatown whom Mandela had known, and who murdered his girlfriend. The premiere was held in the main hall of Wits University, the only auditorium in Johannesburg which would admit blacks and whites together (though segregated by rows). The show, which was later taken to London, expressed all the creative energy of the black townships, with an exuberant cast including Mandela's friend Nathan Mdledle of the Manhattan Brothers, who played King Kong. Mandela was thrilled by the performance, and afterwards he embraced Todd Matshikiza and his wife Esme. He was particularly moved, he said, by the song 'Sad Times, Bad Times', with its refrain 'What have these men done that they should be destroyed?', which reminded him of the trial beginning the next day.[30]

The trial resumed, was adjourned, and then started again, making Mandela's life still more unpredictable, and his work in his law practice more difficult. The activities of most of the ANC leaders were circumscribed, either by the trial or by bans. The President, Luthuli, was no longer on trial, but in June 1959 he was confined again for a further five years to his home district in Natal. Luthuli now had a high international profile. The British diplomat Eleanor Emery told London that the ban had removed 'the most stable and moderate of the ANC leaders', and predicted that it would lead to more extremism, and perhaps to a general banning of the whole ANC.[31] The *New York Times* published a profile of Luthuli, saying that the South African government had chosen 'a worthy foe', and the new American Ambassador Philip Crowe – much more sophisticated than his predecessors – went to visit Luthuli in Groutville three months after he was banned.[32] But Western diplomats continued to steer clear of the more militant ANC leaders like Mandela.

Mandela was under still greater pressure in the trial, but he remained very active behind the scenes. He could see Tambo nearly every day in their law offices, and was closely in touch with Sisulu both in the courtroom and in Orlando. Sisulu remained very influential. 'I was still looked upon by everybody as Secretary-General,' he explained later, 'because I was doing the work, although it was Oliver Tambo or Duma Nokwe who was formally Secretary-General. I was having a discussion with Nelson, I think, daily.'[33]

But the ANC had remained disorganised through the 1950s. As a 'banned leader' described it in *Liberation* with devastating candour in 1955:

> There exists great inefficiency at varying levels of Congress leadership: the inability to understand simple local situations, inefficiency in attending to the simple things, such as small complaints, replying to letters, visiting of branches. There is complete lack of confidence of one another, lack of teamwork in committees, individualism and the lust for power. The result is sabotage of Congress decisions and directives, gossip and unprincipled criticisms.[34]

Mandela was aware of the incompetence, but was touchy about criticism of the ANC, particularly from whites. The reporter Martin Leighton wrote an article in the *Rand Daily Mail* which described how the ANC did not have a real organisation, with no files or membership lists, while its officials were cringing compared to Africans in bordering countries. Mandela was furious, and when Leighton called on him he said he felt like choking him; but not, he reflected later, because the article was false: 'The criticism which hurts me is the criticism which is correct.'[35]

The ANC's Transvaal branch was both the most important and one of the most incompetent. 'There is no awareness of the need to be alert and vigilant in branch activities,' the Transvaal executive had complained in November 1956. 'There is a great deal of sluggishness and inefficiency in our style of work.' The more leaders were banned, the more urgent the problem became: in December 1958 the National Executive reported that 'our aim should be to make the Congress a body that can survive any attack or onslaught made upon it, however severe.' They advocated an immediate efficiency campaign. But a year later the new Secretary-General, Duma Nokwe, who had succeeded Tambo, was lamenting that the problems of organisation 'have now become hardy annuals'. He warned that 'the idea that a huge organisation like ours with all the duties and responsibilities that fall to it, can be run on a part-time basis, is ridiculous.'[36] He wanted the M-Plan – the emergency resistance network which Mandela had originated eight years earlier – put into action without further delay, to 'withstand and defeat the savage onslaught'. But there was little improvement in the ANC's defences while the security police did not appear a ruthless enemy. When two Afrikaner policemen who spoke Xhosa well visited the ANC offices, Mandela recalled, tea would be made for them and they would be given 'chairs to sit down so they could take their notes, because they were so polite'.[37]

After the formation of the PAC in April 1959 the ANC was forced to take a more militant stance. It placed much hope in economic boycotts, which it saw as a major political weapon, with unlimited possibilities.[38] To boycott products from pro-apartheid companies or shops seemed the answer to the bans on other protests: 'Don't say anything, just don't buy.'[39] Luthuli wanted to put pressure on vulnerable companies, to 'hit them in the stomach', as Mandela put it.[40] In May 1959, encouraged by a partial boycott of Rembrandt cigarettes, which was controlled by the Afrikaner nationalist tobacco-king Anton Rupert, the ANC announced a boycott of potatoes in protest against the inhuman treatment of farm workers. At first this had some success, and Mandela saw it as the start of a new mood of resistance.[41]

Mandela was warning about the ruthlessness of the new government of Dr Hendrik Verwoerd, who had become Prime Minister in September 1958, following Strijdom's death. But he was confident that Verwoerd's regime, with its 'grim programme of mass evictions, political persecution and police terror', would not last long: 'It is the last desperate gamble of a hated and doomed fascist autocracy – which, fortunately, is soon due to make its exit from the stage of history.'[42]

The ANC was under growing pressure to take mass action to defy the pass laws by making a bonfire of the hated pass-books, which were seen as the main instrument of black oppression. In theory this could have made the whole system unworkable, but the ANC was very conscious of the failure of past campaigns. At the annual conference in December 1958 the National Executive reported that resistance to passes was mounting, but they were still cautious: 'To hope that by striking one blow we would defeat the system would result in disillusionment. On the other hand we cannot sit until everybody is ready to enter the battlefield . . . the struggle for the repeal of pass laws has begun; there is no going back but "forward ever".'[43]

Duma Nokwe, the new ANC Secretary-General, was a compact, lively graduate of Wits who had become the first black barrister in South Africa. He was a protégé of Tambo, who had taught him at St Peter's school, and a boxer, with a pugilist's aggression which Tambo often had to restrain.[44] He was forged by the Defiance Campaign and the Treason Trials, and he became a committed communist while enjoying good living and drink. As Secretary-General he was determined to reorganise the ANC, and working closely with Sisulu, Mandela and Tambo, he prepared a detailed plan for approval at the ANC's annual conference in December 1959. It proposed first an extension of the economic boycott, and then the launch of an anti-pass campaign, planned to begin on 31 March 1960 – the anniversary of the first serious demonstration against the pass laws in 1919 – and culminating in a bonfire of passes on 26 June.

But the ANC's thunder was being stolen by the PAC, who were impatient for immediate action. A week after the ANC's 1959 conference, the PAC executive reported to their first national conference. Their main proposal was oddly moderate: a 'status campaign' to insist on Africans receiving courteous treatment in shops or workplaces, so that they could assert their own personalities and 'exorcise this slave mentality'.[45] This was quickly overtaken by Sobukwe, who put forward his own campaign to defy the pass laws. It was a half-baked proposal, with no realistic assessment of the risks involved, but it was rapidly and unanimously approved. The PAC, said Sobukwe, would now 'cross its historical Rubicon'.[46]

The ANC leaders believed the PAC were playing the role of spoilers, trying to undermine and outbid their own initiatives. 'What the PAC had embarked upon,' wrote Joe Slovo, 'was an ill-organised, second-class version of the 1952 Defiance Campaign.'[47] Mandela was frustrated to watch his rival Sobukwe, the 'dazzling orator and incisive thinker', playing the demagogue and ignoring the historical warnings of failure. But the ANC could not afford to ignore the popular excitement Sobukwe had released. Four months later his rash plan was to prove the catalyst which transformed the whole South African scene, and impelled Mandela into a far more militant revolutionary role.

11

The Revolution that Wasn't

1960

THE PROMISE of independence in other African countries had brought new optimism to the ANC as well as to the PAC. 'The people of Africa are astir,' wrote Mandela in *Liberation* in March 1958, in a fierce attack on 'American imperialism'. 'The future of this continent lies not in the hands of the discredited regimes that have allied themselves with American imperialism. It is in the hands of the common people functioning in their mass movements.'[1]

'During the past year there has been an unprecedented upsurge in Africa,' said the ANC report in December 1959. 'Self-government has become the cry of the peoples throughout the length and breadth of the continent.'[2] '*Afrika!*' had become a rallying cry, and babies were being christened Kwame or Jomo, after Nkrumah and Kenyatta. White domination in South Africa was now looking still more out of step with the rest of the continent, and more vulnerable. 1960 was proclaimed beforehand by journalists and diplomats as the 'Year of Africa'. A succession of British and French colonies were due to become independent, and the ex-imperial powers were now wooing their new leaders to maintain their trade links and join the Cold War against communism.

In Britain, the Conservative Prime Minister Harold Macmillan was becoming aware of the importance of black Africa – which he compared to a lazy hippo which had been suddenly prodded into action.[3] He was concerned about the intransigent white settlers in Central Africa and the political costs of British links with the apartheid government in South Africa. After his election triumph in October 1959 he planned a tour of Africa, culminating in Cape Town.

South African black leaders and liberals feared that Macmillan would be condoning apartheid, and four of them – Albert Luthuli, Alan Paton,

Monty Naicker and Jordan Ngubane – signed an open letter to Macmillan before he set off. Published in the London *Observer*, then known as 'the black man's friend', it warned Macmillan that apartheid was evil and unjust, and pleaded with him not to say 'one single word that could be construed to be in praise of it'.[4] Macmillan privately agreed with every word of the letter, and took it seriously enough to ask his officials whether they thought its signatories would be satisfied with the speech he was already preparing for South Africa.[5]

Macmillan began his tour in Ghana, where he praised the Prime Minister Kwame Nkrumah, and first mentioned the 'wind of change' (though no journalist noticed). He continued via Nigeria, the Rhodesias and Nyasaland to South Africa. In Cape Town he stayed with Dr Verwoerd, and soon realised his full intransigence: 'Nothing one could say or put forward would have the smallest effect upon the views of this determined man.'[6] Macmillan was appalled by the foolishness, as he told his press secretary Harold Evans, of 'elevating segregation into a doctrine': 'If they didn't make an ideology of it they would almost certainly succeed in getting the results they seek with a minimum of concession. Economic differences between black and white would alone be sufficient to achieve practical separation. Of course, they would have to accept the really talented African.'[7]

On his way through Africa Macmillan kept revising the speech he would deliver in Cape Town, and it was repeatedly redrafted by his officials, including two rarefied mandarins in his entourage: the polymath David Hunt from the Commonwealth Office, and the dapper High Commissioner Sir John Maud ('With Maud,' said a South African wit, 'you have to take the smooth with the smooth'). Macmillan was so nervous just before he went into Parliament in Cape Town that he had to go to the lavatory to be sick. It was a masterly speech, with a style and historical sweep which at first disarmed the Afrikaner MPs. He praised their nationalism as the first of the African nationalisms, before spelling out that 'there are some aspects of your policies which make it impossible' for Britain to support South Africa in the Commonwealth.[8] It was not until the British press had underlined the speech's true meaning that the message struck home. As *Die Burger*, the leading Afrikaans paper, put it: 'Britain could no longer afford to be seen in our company when certain of our affairs are broached.'[9]

Macmillan had asked to meet the leading black politicians, but his programme was tightly controlled by Verwoerd's government, and the High Commission, as we have seen, knew little about African leaders like Mandela. At the whites-only garden party given by Sir John Maud, Patrick Duncan urged Macmillan to see the black leaders, but found him suddenly deaf.[10]

Eventually Macmillan decided that his Cape Town speech had made such an impact that he would be forgiven if the meeting with the ANC leadership never came off.[11] Albert Luthuli would have told Macmillan, he said afterwards, that Africans would be better off if South Africa were outside the Commonwealth: 'Britain would have more influence, and the Afrikaners would be more isolated.' But he was pleasantly surprised by Macmillan's speech: 'It gave the African people some inspiration and hope.'[12]

Mandela too thought it was 'a terrific speech'. Despite his distrust of British imperialism, he would never forget Macmillan's courage in the lions' den, warning a 'stubborn and race-blinded white oligarchy' about the wind of change. Thirty-six years later in Westminster Hall, Mandela would partly model his own speech on Macmillan's, with the same historical sweep; and he would recall a cartoon in a South African paper showing Macmillan after the speech, with the caption from *Julius Caesar*:

> O! pardon me, thou bleeding piece of earth,
> That I am meek and gentle with these butchers.[13]

Macmillan's 'wind of change' soon proved an understatement: only six weeks later he had to explain that he had not meant 'a howling tempest which would blow away the whole of the new developing civilisation. We must, at all costs, avoid that.'[14] Even while he was touring Africa the Belgian government was deciding, with minimal preparation, to give independence four months later to the Congo – which would rapidly disintegrate into civil war and chaos, introducing the Cold War into the heart of the continent and spreading fear through white South Africa. The headlong pace of the imperial retreat encouraged the PAC to promise to overthrow white domination in South Africa by 1963. Mandela was exasperated by their assumption that the Afrikaners would give up power as easily as the colonial powers had. 'The PAC did not appear to have any plans to prepare the people for that historic moment,' he wrote later from jail. They assumed it would be achieved 'merely by going to jail and waiting there for the Nats to fall on their own'.[15]

The two rival Congresses were now bitterly divided – like so many rival liberation movements in Africa – criticising each other as much as their common enemy. While the ANC was preparing for its demonstration against pass laws on 31 March 1960, Sobukwe and the PAC were pushing ahead with their own anti-pass campaign, with much less planning. Sobukwe believed that bold, spontaneous leadership would automatically mobilise the masses, and on 18 March he abruptly announced that in three days' time – ten days before the ANC's planned demonstration, 'In every city, town and village, the men must leave their passes at home,' and surrender themselves at police stations for arrest, pledging themselves to 'No bail, no defence, no fine.' He belatedly invited the ANC to join them, but Nokwe predictably declined, saying that the plan had 'no reasonable prospects of success'.[16] Mandela was equally sceptical: he thought that the PAC was merely a 'leadership in search of followers', and was pre-empting the ANC's own plans with blatant opportunism.[17]

On 21 March Sobukwe and about 150 others surrendered themselves without passes at Orlando police station – where the PAC's following was weak, as it was in most of South Africa. But it was much stronger in the black townships of Cape Town and in Sharpeville, outside Vereeniging in the Transvaal, where the ANC had long been poorly organised.[18] In Cape Town 1,500 people offered themselves for arrest, while huge crowds gathered in protest until the police dispersed them, killing two. In Sharpeville a crowd of about 10,000 surrounded the police station, unnerving the police, who opened fire and shot sixty-seven people dead.

The Sharpeville massacre, like no previous South African confrontation, immediately reverberated round the world. In Washington, President Eisenhower, facing his own racial problems in election year, said he would not sit in judgement on 'a difficult social and political problem 6,000 miles away'. But the State Department unprecedentedly criticised Pretoria, and hoped that black South Africans would be able to 'obtain redress for legitimate grievances by peaceful means'.[19] At the United Nations the Security Council blamed the government for the shootings, with Britain and France abstaining.[20] In South Africa the stock market collapsed, and whites queued to buy guns or to apply to emigrate.

The black political scene was transformed overnight. Sobukwe and the PAC had received a huge boost. It was, Mandela thought later, 'not so much because of what they were saying, which was quite immature.

It was because of the massacre.'[21] But the surge of mass anger seemed at first to vindicate Sobukwe's belief in spontaneous action. The PAC's nationalist rhetoric caught the black imagination more vividly than the ANC's more cautious statements: 'Sobukwe's got a bang, man,' as one African journalist put it. 'He's down to earth, down, down, down.' Many blacks were openly singing the PAC anthem:

> We the black people
> Are crying out for our land
> Which was taken by crooks.
> They should leave it alone.[22]

Mandela accepted that the PAC leaders had shown courage, and he quickly realised that the ANC 'had to make rapid adjustments'.[23] After Sharpeville he spent the whole night secretly discussing how to respond with Sisulu, Nokwe and Slovo. They decided that the ANC leaders, beginning with their President Albert Luthuli, should publicly burn their pass-books. They would also call for a Day of Mourning, when workers would stay at home in protest against the massacre. They formed a sub-committee working from Slovo's house to prepare the strike, while Nokwe went to Pretoria to arrange for Luthuli to burn his pass.[24] Many communists, including Rusty Bernstein, had serious doubts about pass-burning, which they feared could lead to evictions, sackings and banishment; but the ANC had decided, and the communists tried to help.[25]

For ten days after Sharpeville the iron structure of apartheid seemed to be crumbling. On 26 March Luthuli was photographed holding the charred remains of his pass-book; two days later the great majority of black workers obeyed the ANC's call for a stay-at-home, while Mandela and Nokwe burnt their passes in front of cameras and journalists, and a few hundred others followed their example. 'Only a truly mass organisation could co-ordinate such activities,' Mandela reflected.[26] Most remarkably, the government appeared paralysed; on 25 March the Commissioner of Police had announced that he was suspending arrests for not carrying passes.

The ANC now seemed to be calling the shots. When I talked to Mandela in Orlando on 29 March he was dismissive of the PAC's reliance on spontaneous response: 'You've got to have the machinery, the organisation.' He was touchy about the PAC's role in originating the protest, insisting that the ANC's potato boycott had been a crucial prelude to the pass-burning, and sounded confident that the ANC initiative would succeed. With him was Duma Nokwe, his short body slumped in a huge armchair, who was jubilant that a thousand pass-books had already been burnt: 'We never dreamt it would happen so soon. We'll have them roasted. The country is now in a pre-rev . . .' – he stopped himself from saying 'revolutionary' – 'in the state before major changes take place.'[27]

Was it a revolution? It was certainly one of those brief interims in a nation's history when it seemed that anything could happen. In the shebeens there was sudden exuberance: 'There's a crack in the white wall'; 'The police are so polite, it hurts: one cop even called me *meneer* [mister]'; 'They've thickened our skins so much, we can't feel the pricks any longer.' Even the state-owned broadcasting system played an old revolutionary signature tune, smuggled into the studio by a militant black employee: 'Wake up, my people. Be united. The fault is with us. All nations keep us under their feet.'[28]

By 30 March the initiative was passing back to the PAC in Cape Town, their stronghold. A general strike had paralysed the city, and the police began brutally attacking the townships to break it. The black workers responded with an apparently spontaneous march of 30,000 people on the city centre, led by a twenty-three-year-old student in short trousers, Philip Kgosana, who had modelled himself on Sobukwe. When they reached the city he seemed for an hour to hold the country's future in his hand: but he was tricked into dispersing the crowd by the promise of a meeting with the Minister of Justice. Instead he was arrested and detained for nine months.[29] Historians continue to argue whether the march could have precipitated a revolution: certainly without the deception of the crowd the police might well have caused a far worse massacre than Sharpeville, which would have provoked a much more dangerous black explosion.[30]

As it was, the government quickly took advantage of the situation, declaring a state of emergency on the same day and detaining over 2,000 people. Mandela had been secretly tipped off beforehand by a friend in the security police, and had alerted colleagues including Ahmed Kathrada, who in turn told Bernstein, who warned his communist friends not to sleep at home.[31] It was decided that a few activists – including Harmel, Kotane and Dadoo – should disappear underground, while Mandela and the rest would submit to arrest.[32]

Mandela was arrested and taken to Newlands jail, near Sophiatown, where he spent the night in appalling conditions, which he described the next day to Helen Joseph, who had been imprisoned separately: 'Fifty detainees had been locked up for the rest of the night, after their arrest at one o'clock in the morning, in a yard open to the sky and lit by one electric bulb. It was so small they could only stand and were given neither food nor blankets. In the morning they were taken to a cell, about eighteen feet square, with sanitation only from a drainage hole in the floor, flushed at the whim of the policeman in charge. Food, even drinking water, came only at three o'clock in the afternoon, twelve hours after the men had been brought to the cells.'[33]

The government was now moving rapidly to prevent further protest. On 8 April, with the support of the opposition United Party, it pushed through a new Unlawful Organisations Bill by which, after forty-eight years, the ANC was finally made illegal, together with the PAC. They would remain so for the next thirty years. The black townships were in political confusion, as no one knew who was in prison and who had escaped. The crisis atmosphere was intensified on 9 April, when Dr Verwoerd was shot and wounded by a white farmer named David Pratt at an agricultural show in Johannesburg.

For a few days South Africa remained in a political limbo, with Verwoerd out of action and his cabinet bewildered. One Minister, Paul Sauer, made a speech on 19 April stating that Sharpeville had closed the old book of South African history, and that the country must reconsider its race relations 'seriously and honestly'.[34] But this conciliatory mood soon passed. Verwoerd recovered rapidly and took charge, more intransigent than ever. The police enforced their powers still more brutally. The heroic bonfire of pass-books petered out as people remembered that without a pass they could not draw a pension or post office savings, or apply for a house. They began queuing up to replace the passes they had burnt.

Already by the end of April, a month after Sharpeville, the talk of imminent revolution looked wildly premature. 'This isn't it,' said the journalist Can Themba. 'The guys have been talking about the wind of change becoming a hurricane: it never seemed to occur to them that it might be only a breeze.'[35] The relaxation of the pass laws had proved purely tactical, intended to prepare for a much more systematic clamp-down. Pretoria showed no signs of yielding to pressure from Macmillan or any other Western leader; and the government was soon making plans to train the police, with help from abroad, in much more efficient and ruthless methods of surveillance and torture.

The aftermath of Sharpeville had revealed the lack of realism in both the ANC and the PAC. There were few parallels between South Africa and the rest of the continent, where the colonial governments were reluctant rulers and the liberation movements faced much easier rides to freedom. The struggle of black South Africans against the Afrikaners would clearly be much tougher than victories further north.

In this extraordinary atmosphere the three judges in Pretoria had resumed the Treason Trial, calmly listening to the evidence about events of five years before. Each day, the thirty accused were brought into the courtroom from prison. Mandela was eventually allowed out at weekends to visit the offices of Mandela & Tambo, whose practice had been undermined by the trials. He was escorted by a sympathetic Afrikaner policeman, Sergeant Kruger, who trusted him not to escape. But during the week he had to spend the nights in prison and the days in court, facing the most crucial stage of the Treason Trial.[36] The government had now given the trial an added significance, as an alternative to an inquiry into the causes of the Sharpeville massacre, which the opposition was demanding. As Dr Verwoerd said on 20 May: 'The trial itself has in part the character of an inquiry into the causes of disturbances.'[37]

The defence lawyers, headed by Bram Fischer, were indignant about the constraints imposed by the state of emergency, and maintained that justice could not be ensured in such abnormal conditions, with their clients in prison and often unavailable for consulting. They proposed a bold strategy, which Mandela approved: they would withdraw from the case until the emergency was over, leaving the thirty accused to defend themselves. It was a controversial manoeuvre, but it would give the defendants a chance to demonstrate their intelligence to the judges, and to address them directly. The prisoners' long legal discussions in jail often surprised their warders: when Mandela visited Helen Joseph to discuss the proceedings he noticed that some of the female warders became fascinated by the arguments, and by the prisoners' political commitment. The withdrawal of the defence team laid a special responsibility on Mandela and Duma Nokwe, the only two lawyers among the thirty. They now had to help the others prepare their cases, but some of them complained about the lack of proper representation. Mandela assured them that they were making a strong moral argument.[38]

In August 1960, after five months of restrictions, the state of emergency was lifted and the lawyers returned to the courtroom. It was now Mandela's turn to give evidence – which he welcomed all the more since he had been banned from speaking anywhere else. The young barrister Sydney Kentridge was assigned to Mandela's defence, to prepare him for the witness box and conduct his examination. Kentridge's unassuming style concealed a relentless rationality; it would take him to the top of his profession in both South Africa and Britain, and he would become famous when he extracted the full horrors of Steve Biko's torture and death from police witnesses at the inquest. In the Treason Trial courtroom, Kentridge was soon full of admiration for Mandela. 'It was then that I first realised,' he recalls, 'that he was a natural leader of men. He was firm, courteous, always based on thought and reason. His real political intellect emerged from his answers to questions. He had no hidden agenda, which became clear in his evidence, under heavy cross-examination.'[39]

Certainly Mandela's testimony revealed a more thoughtful politician than had emerged before. Under all the pressure of his examination and the stormy political crisis, he rose to the challenge with total control. In his own statement he carefully explained his political development and philosophy, while stressing that it was not necessarily the philosophy of Congress. It was, he thought, the strongest speech he had ever made.[40] He described his earlier belief in African nationalism and his conversion to multi-racialism. He reasserted his emphasis on non-violence, and rejected the concept of revolution in the sense of 'mighty leaps'. He explained how he had visualised the ANC achieving universal franchise through gradual concessions of qualified voting, leading eventually to a people's democracy. He himself favoured, he said, a classless society, such as he believed existed in Hungary, China or Russia, but he conceded that for a long time Africans would have different classes – workers, peasants, shopkeepers and intellectuals. He was emphatically opposed to imperialism: 'Insofar as I have had experiences of imperialism personally, there seems to be very, very little to say for it . . . It has gone all over the world, subjugating people and exploiting them, bringing death and destruction to millions of people.' He was also opposed to capitalism, but claimed not to know whether it was linked to imperialism. He insisted that the ANC had taken no view on capitalism, and that the terms of the Freedom Charter, apart from breaking up the mining monopolies, would leave capitalism 'absolutely intact'.

He believed that the South African government was moving towards fascism, which could be expressed in the Xhosa phrase '*indlovu ayipatwa*' – 'an elephant that cannot be touched'. The ANC could expect to come up against more ruthless responses: 'The government will not hesitate to massacre hundreds of Africans.' But Mandela still seemed optimistic – even after Sharpeville – that 'The nationalist government is much weaker than when we began.' He was hopeful that the government would be brought to realise that its policies were futile, by internal and external pressures: 'Countries which used to support the racial policies of South Africa have turned against them.'[41]

Helen Joseph, who had already nervously testified, was inspired by Mandela's calm confidence. He was only rarely moved to anger, she noticed, for example when Judge Rumpff suggested that giving votes to uneducated people was like giving them to children: 'Isn't it on much the same basis,' asked Rumpff, 'if you have children who know nothing and people who know nothing?' Mandela was quietly furious, all the more so since his own father was illiterate, and two elderly men among the accused had never been to school.[42] He also faced problems when confronted with some documents and speeches by more militant colleagues. What about Robert Resha's statement to volunteers that if they were asked to murder, they should murder, murder? That was an 'unhappy example', said Mandela: 'He was merely dealing purely with the question of discipline.' What about his fellow-accused Thembile Ndimba, who had said: 'If instructions are given to volunteers to kill, they must kill'? It was, Mandela admitted, 'an unfortunate way of illustrating discipline', but was not ANC policy. When shown a reference to the 'seizure of power' from 1951, he responded: 'I don't read any force or violence in this phrase.' Asked about lectures prepared by Rusty Bernstein which had a clear Marxist message, he said: 'Unfortunately the manner in which they were handled may have given the impression that they carried some authority from the ANC.'

But Mandela was able to show that neither he nor the other ANC leaders had advocated violence at any time in the previous decade, and that while he refused to criticise the communists, he was not committed to the Party.

KENTRIDGE: Did you become a communist?
MANDELA: Well, I don't know if I did become a communist.

> If by communist you mean a member of the Communist Party and a person who believes in the theory of Marx, Engels, Lenin and Stalin and who adheres strictly to the discipline of the Party, I did not become a communist.[43]

When Kentridge privately asked him why he didn't attack Stalin after he was denounced by Khrushchev in 1956, he replied: 'It was not our political function. What Stalin did was not against us.' Kentridge reckoned that Mandela saw communists as his enemies' enemies, and therefore his friends; but after much contact with him, he was certain that he was not a Stalinist or a member of the Communist Party.[44]

Some of Mandela's colleagues would later insist that at this time he was indistinguishable from the communists, or was even a secret member of the Communist Party. 'He was very close,' said Ben Turok, who was a member of the Central Committee. 'If he wasn't in the Party, that was tactical.'[45] Rusty Bernstein said simply, 'By the sixties I found it hard to tell who was in the Party and who was not.'[46] The government would continue to charge that Mandela was a Party member, which anti-communists abroad would eagerly take up. Even in 1966, after four years on Robben Island, he would be informed by the Department of Justice that he was being listed as a member of the Party. He wrote back to 'emphatically deny that I was a member of the CPSA since 1960 or at any other time', and asked to see affidavits and details of any communist conferences that he had attended. Four months later the Department informed him that they had decided not to put him on the list 'at this stage'.[47] In fact, as his communist friend Ismail Meer said later, 'Nelson was never, never, in the closest scrutiny of a well-organised security system, found to be a member of the Communist Party.'[48]

The peculiar South African obsession with communism in any case distorted the question. Many South African communists and their sympathisers, like Mandela, were pragmatic in their support: Mandela would later suggest that he was using the communists more than they used him.[49] Subsequent events would show how little he was committed to their basic dogma. But in the early sixties, the more ruthlessly the apartheid government became, the more courageous and admirable the communists appeared – like the French communists in the wartime resistance against the Nazis.

Certainly the banning of the ANC pressed it closer towards the

Communist Party, forcing them together underground. After the state of emergency was lifted in August and most of the prisoners were released, the ANC leaders were able to meet secretly to work out how to operate as a banned organisation. Mandela realised that the ban necessitated a drastic reorganisation of the ANC to trim down the whole structure, dissolving the Youth League and the Women's League and concentrating on a small inner group. 'Politics for any active member became highly dangerous,' he wrote from jail, 'and a form of activity reserved only for the hard core.'[50] Operating in a climate of illegality, he recognised the need for a quite new psychological approach.[51] When the Communist Party had been banned in 1950, he had warned that the government was aiming at the ANC as much as the communists: now the enemy was using exactly the same weapon against both.[52]

For all the earlier warnings and Mandela's proposals for the M-Plan, the ban took the ANC, like the PAC, by surprise. 'Mere survival in the face of the police onslaughts,' wrote the historians Tom Karis and Gwen Carter, 'had become as much as either Congress could hope for.' Immediately after the state of emergency was lifted the ANC set up an Emergency Committee, which would continue to operate until the organisation was legal again, and it published a statement refusing to submit to the ban.[53] But with 2,000 people detained, the ANC was severely restricted.

The Communist Party, having already been banned for ten years, was more accustomed to underground work, and some key activists, including Mandela's friends Moses Kotane and Michael Harmel, were now in hiding. In the midst of the emergency Kotane and a few others had let it be known that the Party was back in business; and they were still able to issue some propaganda through their clandestine journal, the *African Communist*, which was first published in October 1959. This 'emergence' of the Party was criticised by many members who had not been consulted, but in fact (according to Bernstein) it simplified relations with the ANC, and dispelled fears of hidden agendas.[54] The ANC was still poorly organised for underground existence, with only fragments of the M-Plan able to provide street-level organisation. They needed the communists to help them to work undercover.

The ANC executive had taken one precaution which proved crucial: in June 1959 they had decided that in the event of a crisis Oliver Tambo should immediately leave the country through Bechuanaland, and set up an office in Ghana. Six days after Sharpeville, on 27 March 1960, Tambo left a Johannesburg suburb, seen off by friends including Ahmed Kathrada, to be driven across the border by Ronald Segal, editor of *Africa South*. He eventually made his way via Dar-es-Salaam to London.[55] Over the next thirty years Tambo's statesmanship, and the mutual trust between him and Mandela in jail, was to be the basis of the ANC's survival. At the time Mandela did not realise how vital the external wing of the organisation would become.[56]

Mandela was now much more on his own, separated from the partner whose judgement had always been so valuable to him. He was left with the bleak task of winding up the law practice of Mandela & Tambo. He continued to practise on his own, working from Kathrada's flat, 13 Kholvad House, where clients kept arriving until the long-suffering Kathrada, confined to the kitchen, began to protest.[57] Soon afterwards Mandela went underground, and had to abandon his law practice for ever.

1960 continued to be a year of crisis. In October the government held the all-white referendum Verwoerd had promised on the question of whether South Africa should become a republic. It was agreed by a surprisingly narrow majority – 850,000 votes to 775,000 – but it needed only a simple majority. Mandela did not feel strongly about the country becoming a republic. He thought it would not add 'even a fraction of an ounce' to South Africa's sovereignty, and saw it as merely an emotional question for Afrikaner nationalists, who looked back nostalgically to their old 'semi-feudal' republics in the nineteenth century, before the British undermined them. And he hoped that a republic, by removing their grievance, would 'loosen the rivets' which held Afrikaner intellectuals together. But he could not accept a referendum in which only whites could vote.

Despite the government's show of strength after Sharpeville, Mandela was determined to go ahead with yet another peaceful protest, a strike or 'stay-at-home'. He still, like most of the ANC leaders, retained a surprising optimism. He may have talked about South Africa moving towards fascism and becoming a police state, but he and his colleagues were almost totally unprepared for it when it came.[58] 'It is difficult to appreciate,' wrote Karis and Carter, 'the extent to which African leaders and other radical opponents of the government felt that the trend of events was in their favour.'[59]

12

Violence

1961

BY THE END OF 1960 Mandela's wide-ranging life in Johannesburg was rapidly narrowing. His law practice had collapsed, many friends were in exile, and the social network of Orlando had virtually dissolved. His family, he reckoned, was financially ruined.[1] His home life with Winnie was constantly interrupted by political tasks: when she gave birth to their second daughter, Zindzi, at the end of the year, he arrived home too late to be with her. 'I rarely sat down with him as a husband,' Winnie claims now. 'The honest truth of God is that I didn't know him at all.'[2]

Mandela's political life was already moving half-underground, and he was presenting a more subterranean image: no longer the youthful, clean-shaven face and the hair parted in the middle, but a rough moustache and a short black beard, so that his narrow eyes seemed to be peering out of the undergrowth.

He was nevertheless making another attempt at peaceful organisation with other parties. In December 1960 a group of thirty-six African leaders met at a Consultative Conference in Orlando and committed themselves to hold an 'All-In African Conference' which would in turn call for a National Convention of all races. It seemed oddly unrealistic in the light of the government's ruthless response at Sharpeville. It showed, argued the political scientist Tom Lodge later, 'just how intellectually unprepared the leadership of the Congress alliance was in 1961 to embark on a revolutionary struggle'.[3] But the Marxist Michael Harmel argued that it was 'essentially a demand for revolution'.[4]

The police raided the meeting in Orlando and confiscated all the papers, but the plans went ahead through a committee with Mandela as Secretary. Mandela and Sisulu, in between the last stages of the Treason

Trial, travelled around the country secretly to make preparations for the conference, even nipping over to Basutoland, where several ANC activists, including Joe Matthews, had gone into exile. At first they worked together with some Liberals, and also with the PAC, encouraged by the formation of a 'United Front' of the ANC and PAC abroad. But the collaboration soon broke up: the Liberals accused the ANC and communists of taking control, while the PAC decided they should crush the conference, partly because they suspected that 'plans were afoot to build up Mandela as a hero in opposition to Sobukwe'.[5] So Mandela and the ANC went ahead with support only from the communists. Their collaboration was becoming stronger, in a close-knit group who could trust each other.

The government was watching closely, and five days before the conference the police arrested ten of the organisers and served a warrant on Duma Nokwe. But the committee still managed to distribute leaflets with a 'Call to the African People of South Africa' to prepare for the 'All-In African Conference', to be held near Pietermaritzburg in Natal, on 22 March.

Mandela needed funds to arrange transport to the conference, and boldly asked to see Harry Oppenheimer, the Chairman of the Anglo-American Corporation. Oppenheimer was the first and only businessman Mandela would meet before he was jailed. Mandela had been influenced by labour movements, he explained later, 'at a time of utmost hostility to businessmen'. Oppenheimer received him very politely, as he received nearly everyone: 'When we came to his office,' Mandela recalled, 'he got up as if we were the president or the prime minister of a country.' Mandela asked for a particular sum: 'In terms of today it was peanuts.' Oppenheimer said it was a lot of money, and asked how it would benefit him. He asked questions about the ANC, and appeared to underestimate its strength. 'How do I know,' he asked Mandela, 'that after giving you assistance you will not be eliminated by the PAC?'[6] 'Mandela addressed me boldly like a meeting, with formal phrases,' Oppenheimer recalled later. 'I was ignorant about the ANC, but impressed by his sense of power.'[7] Mandela did not get his money.

On 22 March the Maritzburg Conference, as it was called, mustered a remarkable show of support for the ANC a year after it had been banned. There were 1,400 delegates from 145 different groups from all over South Africa, including the Southern Transvaal Football Association and the Apostolic Church in Zion. But the ANC clearly dominated, with their slogans, speakers and songs, including 'Spread the Gospel of Chief Luthuli'. The *New York Times* called the event 'the biggest political meeting of Africans ever held in South Africa', and the *Rand Daily Mail* gave it a big headline: 'AFRICANS INSIST ON A NATIONAL PARLEY'.[8]

By an apparent coincidence, Mandela's ban had expired just before the meeting – which the police seemed not to have noticed – and the Treason Trial had adjourned for a week. So Mandela was able to pop up like a jack-in-a-box, in his beard and a three-piece suit, to provide a dramatic climax to the conference and to make his first public speech since 1952.[9] The audience was thrilled, their fists punching the air like pistons as they shouted the new slogan '*Amandla! Ngawethu!*' ('Power to the People') – which was taking over from the less militant song '*Mayibuye*' ('Come Back Africa').[10] Mandela appealed again for African unity: 'Africans must feel, act and speak in one voice . . . We should emerge from this conference with fullest preparations for a fully represented multi-racial national convention.'[11]

The journalists present gave widely varying assessments of Mandela's impact. *New Age* wrote that 'every sentence was either cheered or greeted with cries of "shame".' Andrew Wilson of the *Observer* reported 'tumultuous applause'.[12] 'I was aware,' Wilson recalled later, 'that he was the chap on whom everyone was focusing their hopes for the future.'[13] Benjamin Pogrund in *Contact* described Mandela, 'bearded in the new nationalist fashion', as 'the star of the show'.[14] He nevertheless thought that the communists had exaggerated the impact of the speech, and that Mandela spoke dully, with poor delivery.[15] But the panache of his emergence from hiding gave his image a new magic. It was at Maritzburg, reckoned his communist friend Dennis Goldberg, that 'the sheer romanticism of the underground activity, appearing at a conference, made him a leader'.[16]

Mandela himself was reassured by the fortitude of ordinary country people: he proudly watched one elderly man in an old jacket, khaki shirt and riding breeches speaking about his campaign against the Bantu Authorities and saying, 'I will go away from here refreshed and full of confidence.' And Mandela was sure that the delegates were prepared for 'a stubborn and prolonged struggle, involving masses of the people from town and country'.[17]

The conference called on the government to summon a National Convention: if they refused, the ANC would organise multi-racial stay-at-home protests beginning on 31 May – the day on which South Africa was due to become a republic – for which Mandela would be the chief organiser (while strikes at the workplace were illegal, stay-at-homes were not). Mandela disappeared from the hall, which was riddled with security police, as suddenly as he had appeared. He was not to appear on a public platform in South Africa again for twenty-nine years.

Mandela returned to Pretoria for the Treason Trial, which still had several weeks to go before the final judgement was delivered. But on 29 March Judge Rumpff interrupted the trial and announced that the three judges had reached a unanimous verdict of not guilty: 'It is impossible for this court to come to the conclusion that the ANC had acquired or adopted a policy to overthrow the state by violence.' The judges agreed that the prosecution had failed to prove that either the ANC or the Freedom Charter were communist, and they singled out Mandela's June 1956 article for *Liberation*, which foresaw 'a non-European bourgeois advance under the Freedom Charter'.[18]

The thirty accused celebrated the verdict with a show of rapture. A cine-camera smuggled into the courtroom snatched blurred scenes of the accused lifting their defence lawyers onto their shoulders, and of a smiling Mandela in a smart checked suit edging his way through the crowd. Mandela was impressed, he said afterwards, that the judges had risen above their prejudices to produce a fair decision, and he was again struck that surprising people could reveal a streak of goodness. But it was a surreal rejoicing, in the midst of bans and oppression. Mandela knew that the government would not recognise the ANC's legitimate grievances, and would soon become much more ruthless, devising new laws that would bypass the courts.[19]

He had already decided that he must disappear underground. Winnie had noticed that he had been meditating silently for some weeks, not listening to her.[20] Walter Sisulu had been convinced that the ANC must have a single leader underground who could be much more active than Luthuli, now banned in Natal; and that it must be Mandela. Sisulu clearly foresaw the need for a martyr: 'When we decided that he should go underground I knew that he was now stepping into a position of leadership . . . We had got the leadership outside but we must have a leader in jail.'[21]

Just before the treason verdict, Mandela had arrived at the Orlando house with Sisulu, Nokwe and Joe Modise, and told Winnie: 'Darling, just pack some of my clothes in a suitcase with my toiletries. I will be going away for a long time.' She packed tearfully, asked the gods of Africa to take care of him, and appealed to him to sometimes spare some minutes for his family: 'He scolded me for reminding him of his duties.'[22]

Mandela's colleagues had decided that he should remain in hiding, to organise the protest planned for 31 May. But he still had to avoid arrest, while he simultaneously needed to publicise the strike as widely as possible. It was, paradoxically, from underground that he became chief spokesman for his people. He was to become more famous in the shadows than he had ever been in broad daylight.

Mandela still needed to persuade white liberals and well-wishers to support the ANC, and to counter the PAC's propaganda. For two months he kept popping up from hiding to talk to white editors, attempting to allay their worries, particularly about communist influence in the ANC. In Johannesburg he argued with Laurence Gandar, the sympathetic and self-effacing editor of the *Rand Daily Mail*. In Port Elizabeth he visited John Sutherland, the quiet, liberal editor of the *Evening Post* – who was concerned for Mandela's safety, since the paper's offices were opposite the police station. Mandela thanked Sutherland warmly for his past support before quickly rejoining Govan Mbeki, who was waiting outside; he was delighted when the *Post* splashed the stay-at-home campaign. In Cape Town he talked for two hours with Victor Norton, the experienced editor of the *Cape Times*. Norton, who had met many world leaders, afterwards told his political editor Tony Delius that he'd never met a more impressive man than Mandela.[23] He also told the British High Commission about his remarkable visitor: few white South Africans, he said to the British diplomat Peter Foster, 'had any idea of the calibre of the Africans with whom they would have to deal'. Norton virtually despaired of the whites' keeping the initiative in their hands for much longer, but nothing about Mandela or his planned strike appeared in the *Cape Times*.[24]

In Johannesburg Mandela saw his old ally from the Defiance Campaign Patrick Duncan, now editor of the fortnightly magazine *Contact*, who was fiercely criticising the banned ANC leaders for their communist influence and projected stay-at-homes. Finally Mandela said, 'Do you think I'm so stupid that I can't run an organisation without being influenced by people we've associated with?'[25] But at a second meeting in Cape Town, according to Randolph Vigne, who was present, the two men talked like old friends who never had any rows. This time Duncan admitted that the Treason Trial had clearly shown that the ANC was not communist, and promised to correct his past reports and to support the National Convention – which he did with a bold turnabout in the next issue of *Contact*.[26] He later told Peter Foster that he was impressed by Mandela's intelligence and confidence – though he 'made little secret of his left-wing sympathies'.[27]

The communist influence was still perplexing foreign diplomats. 'I must confess that we have very little idea of what the South African communists are up to,' Foster wrote to London in January 1961, adding that the government 'do not pass on much detailed information to us (if they possess it)'.[28] Later he blamed the government for banning moderates like Luthuli, thus putting a premium on the conspiratorial activities of militant 'neo-communists'. He reported that 'Mandela, though less certainly a communist than Nokwe, belongs to the group of highly intelligent younger leaders of the ANC who now appear to be in effective control.'[29]

The British government was now rethinking its relations with South Africa, which left the Commonwealth in March 1961. After the vote for a republic, Verwoerd had applied to remain within the Commonwealth, and Macmillan had tried hard to persuade the new black members and Canada – whose Prime Minister John Diefenbaker was especially hostile to apartheid – to allow South Africa to stay. But Verwoerd still refused to accept a black High Commissioner in Pretoria, which proved the last straw, and in the end he withdrew his application. Macmillan was devastated and depressed. 'The wind of change has blown us away, for the time,' he wrote to Sir John Maud, 'but peace will come one day, although perhaps after much sorrow and tribulation.'[30] But Oliver Tambo in London regarded white South Africa's exclusion as a victory; and he would later maintain that black South Africans had never left the Commonwealth.[31]

Mandela continued to place hope in pressure from the Commonwealth, influenced by its new Asian and African members; and he had been encouraged by the opposition to apartheid, particularly by Diefenbaker. The British Embassy, as it now became, felt somewhat less obliged to placate the apartheid government now that South Africa was outside the family atmosphere of the Commonwealth. By June the Ambassador Sir John Maud was proposing that the Embassy should 'reinsure' against the possibility of a future black government by making discreet contacts with black politicians – though these contacts did not amount to much.[32] The British government also decided to use its intelligence services to make every effort to penetrate the white citadel in Pretoria, which they knew would be difficult and delicate. So it proved: four years later a senior agent of MI6, acting as an Embassy official, was 'severely interrogated' about his contacts with the white opposition, and was soon afterwards 'PNG'd' – declared *persona non grata*. But MI6 decided that making links with black opposition leaders would be too risky, and could get them tortured or killed.[33]

Mandela was now concentrating on the three-day stay-at-home strike scheduled to begin on 31 May. His Action Committee wrote to Dr Verwoerd explaining the call for a National Convention. Verwoerd later told Parliament: 'A letter has been received, signed by N.R. Mandela, in arrogant terms, to which no reply has been given.'[34] Mandela also wrote to Sir de Villiers Graaff, the leader of the United Party, who had voted for the ANC to be banned in 1960. He warned Graaff that South Africans must choose between 'talk it out or shoot it out', and asked him: 'But where, sir, does the United Party stand? . . . If the country's leading statesmen fail to lead at this moment, then the worst is inevitable.' Graaff evidently took no notice: he made no mention of Mandela in his memoirs, published thirty years later.[35]

A month before Republic Day, Mandela went to Durban to discuss the protest with the banned ANC executive and their allies. Some delegates argued strongly that a stay-at-home was now quite inadequate in the face of the people's anger and the state's violence, and favoured a general strike. The run-up to Republic Day would clearly be a testing time for ANC discipline. Luthuli warned the *New York Times* that violence could easily be provoked: 'The police sometimes act in a manner that gives the impression they want to shoot the people.'[36] Mandela, who had been touring the country, was very conscious of the people's impatience, particularly since they had been provoked by the PAC. He had heard many complaints within the ANC that it was not politically correct to stress non-violence when the enemy was 'relying on naked force'.[37] The far left was much more critical: 'We thought this was an impossible demand to make on the workers,' said the Marxist historian Baruch Hirson, who was later to be sentenced to nine years in jail for sabotage.[38]

But Mandela kept emphasising the importance of non-violence in dramatic messages from hiding. Ten days before Republic Day he rang up the Johannesburg *Sunday Express* from a coin box: 'We emphatically deny reports that violence will take place or that the three-day stay-away will be extended.'[39] His campaign was gaining him brief support from English-speaking editors who were themselves opposed to an Afrikaner republic.[40] On 12 May the Johannesburg *Star* profiled Mandela for the first time, alongside a bright, smiling photograph: he had 'assumed the mantle of official spokesman for the Native people', though he stressed that 'native leadership is a collective leadership'.[41] He was also beginning to feature in British papers: as 'a large lawyer, untravelled but enormously well read, slow speaking, nattily dressed', in the *Manchester Guardian* of 27 May; and as a 'big handsome bearded man with a deep resonant voice' two days later.[42]

Meanwhile, the government was preparing an alarming show of strength, mustering its defence forces, cancelling leave and making mass arrests. On the morning of the strike Saracen tanks patrolled the townships, helicopters hovered overhead, and troops were posted at crossroads. It was, Mandela reckoned, 'the greatest peacetime force in South Africa's history'. The PAC, to the fury of the ANC, was helping the government by calling on everyone to go to work.[43] And the English-language press were now more anxious. Two days before the strike the *Star* reported: 'Next Monday promises to be as nearly normal in Johannesburg as any other Monday.'[44] Mandela thought the press and radio 'played a thoroughly shameful role', publicising every warning against the strike beforehand, and playing down its successes on the first day.[45] The *Rand Daily Mail* rushed out a special edition with the headline 'MOST GO TO WORK: ALL QUIET'. When Mandela rang his friend on the *Mail*, Benjamin Pogrund, Pogrund began apologising for the sub-editing of the article, until Mandela interrupted: 'It's all right, Benjie. I know it wasn't your fault.' In fact, as Pogrund looked back on it, 'The headline and the report was fatally flawed, the result of rushed and sloppy journalism.'[46]

Mandela and his secret Action Committee were in hiding and unable to watch the strike for themselves, which made them all the more sensitive to the press headlines they saw. They made the agonising judgement to call off the strike after the first day. 'It was a courageous decision,' wrote Rusty Bernstein, 'but left a deep depression in the movement.'[47]

In fact the strike, and the boycott of trains and buses, had been more successful than the ANC realised, and state evidence at the Rivonia trial three years later would reveal its effectiveness. The political scientist Tom

Lodge reckoned afterwards that 'there was a surprisingly widespread degree of participation.'[48] But at the time Dr Verwoerd could convincingly proclaim the calling off of the strike as a victory, which made Mandela deeply aware of the power of the media. It was a lesson he would never forget.

Some liberal whites welcomed the defeat of the strike as providing an opportunity for conciliation. 'The best use which opposition forces can make of this breathing space,' wrote Allister Sparks in the *Rand Daily Mail*, 'is to start organising a multi-racial National Convention without delay.'[49] But most whites now felt able to ignore the black threat.

Mandela was now convinced that peaceful protest policies had reached a dead end, and recognised that he must move into a new stage of his struggle. On the day of the strike Ruth First had arranged for a British reporter, Brian Widlake of Independent Television News, to interview him on television for the first time – and, as it turned out, the last time for nearly thirty years. Widlake was taken to the house near Zoo Lake of Professor Julius Lewin of Witwatersrand University. Mandela was filmed – with a brick wall behind him, which was thought an appropriate symbol – for twenty minutes, of which three were transmitted.[50] The atmosphere was tense, and Mandela's television debut was not inspiring – 'He appeared glum, weary and patently depressed,' Rusty Bernstein reckoned.[51] It did not cause much of a stir in Britain, but what Mandela said was to be crucial to South Africa's future. 'If the government reaction is to crush by naked force our non-violent demonstrations,' he declared, 'we will have to seriously reconsider our tactics. In my mind, we are closing a chapter on this question of non-violent policy.'[52] The ANC executive later criticised Mandela for defying their policy on non-violence, but he believed that 'sometimes one must go public with an idea to push a reluctant organisation in the direction you want to go.'[53]

Over the next few days Mandela kept popping up from hiding to act as the ANC's chief spokesman. But journalists were not excited by his stiff style. Ruth First – his usual go-between – took Stanley Uys of the Johannesburg *Sunday Times* to see Mandela in Hillbrow for a half-hour interview. Uys found him very tense, and when they met again thirty years later Mandela reminded him: 'You weren't impressed.'[54] Ruth First also took Patrick O'Donovan from the *Observer* and Robert Oakeshott from the *Financial Times*, together with Mary Benson, to a flat in the white suburb of Yeoville, where they found Mandela wearing a striped sports shirt and grey trousers. Benson was struck by his relaxed air and his laughter, but Oakeshott thought his formal rhetoric fell short of the occasion. Mandela claimed that the strike had been a tremendous success, and that non-violence was the only realistic policy against a highly industrialised state, while denying that it was a policy of moderation: 'Our feeling against imperialism is intense. I detest it!' But as they left he again said that he thought 'we are closing a chapter on this question of a non-violent policy.'[55] O'Donovan wrote in the *Observer* on 4 June that the ANC's recent tactics had 'served only to hand the government a well-publicised triumph'.[56] It was only at this time – on 7 June – that the Foreign Office in London at last opened a file on Mandela.[57]

In fact Mandela had been discussing abandoning non-violence with his colleagues since early 1960, when the government had ruthlessly suppressed the pass-burning campaigns. So long as the Treason Trial was continuing all the accused had to insist publicly that they supported non-violence as a principle, but many of them, including Mandela, had begun to see it as a tactic which might have to be abandoned.[58] Mandela was always more impatient of non-violence than Sisulu or Tambo, as he had shown in Sophiatown in 1953. But now ordinary people were overtaking him with an impatience that, as a politician responding to public opinion, he could not ignore.

Across much of the political spectrum there was a clamour for violent action, often wild and desperate, like the attacks of anarchists and assassins in Russia in the late nineteenth century. In Pondoland, Tambo's home area in the Eastern Cape, a peasant movement called Intaba ('the mountain') had taken over whole areas through guerrilla tactics before they were crushed by the government: Govan Mbeki, who met their leaders in the forests, now insisted that ANC must have a strategy 'that would mobilise both city and country dwellers'.[59] The PAC was soon to produce a terrorist offshoot in the Cape called Poqo ('alone'), which assassinated whites in reprisal for brutal oppression. A few liberals and leftists organised the African Resistance Movement (ARM), which aimed to blow up buildings. The Communist Party was forming its own semi-military units to cut power lines. Even members of the Unity Movement in the Cape were preparing their own sabotage movement, called the Yu Chi Chan Club after Mao's term for guerrilla warfare. As one of them, Neville Alexander, later wrote: 'All of us, regardless of political organisations or tendency, we were all pushed, willy-nilly, across this great divide, towards the armed struggle, from a non-violent background, totally unprepared.'[60]

Mandela and the ANC would often be criticised for the rashness and amateurishness of their armed struggle, but they felt compelled to move quickly, both to catch up with the mood of the people and to forestall the alternative of uncontrollable atrocities. 'Violence would begin whether we initiated it or not,' Mandela wrote afterwards. 'If we did not take the lead now, we would soon be latecomers and followers in a movement we did not control.'[61]

The ANC and the Communist Party were already talking about violence, as Rusty Bernstein recalls, in an unstructured way, without formal meetings.[62] 'At the moment when you're considering a new road,' said Joe Slovo, 'it doesn't come in one flash with everyone simultaneously realising it. It's a process – with Mandela playing a very important part in the process.'[63] The communists were more ready to advocate violence than the ANC, which under its President Albert Luthuli had been committed to non-violence; and the government liked to equate violence with communism. But the arguments crossed party lines, and many of the communist leaders were concerned to restrain black militancy.[64]

A month after Republic Day, Mandela put forward to the ANC working committee his historic proposal: that the ANC must abandon non-violence and form its own military wing. He argued persuasively, quoting the African proverb, 'The attacks of the wild beast cannot be averted with only bare hands'. To his surprise he was opposed by Moses Kotane, the veteran black communist who was close to Luthuli. Kotane still saw scope for non-violent methods, and warned that violence would provoke massacres. Sisulu privately agreed with Mandela that there was no alternative to violence, but kept quiet, and later arranged for Mandela to talk privately with Kotane, whom he persuaded to accept the armed struggle.

The crucial argument was then taken up in Stanger, in Natal, at two dramatic meetings presided over by Luthuli, who immediately made clear his Christian concerns about the move to violence. He nevertheless reluctantly agreed that there should be a military campaign with its own autonomous leadership, which would be separate from the ANC, though ultimately responsible to it. The second meeting, at which the ANC met with its Indian, white and Coloured allies, went on through the night. Mandela's plan for a military wing was opposed by many Indians, several of whom were still influenced by Gandhi. J.N. Singh, one of Mandela's oldest friends, restated his belief that it was not non-violence that had failed them, but 'we have failed non-violence'.[65] Other friends, including Monty Naicker and Yusuf Cachalia, prophetically warned that violent tactics would undermine the more pressing task of political organisation. Mandela would admit later that the ANC did make precisely that mistake: they drained the political organisations of enthusiastic and experienced men, concentrated their attention on the new organisation, and neglected the 'normal but vital task of pure political organisation'.[66]

Many younger Indians had rejected passive resistance, and Mandela and Sisulu were also supported by white communists, including Slovo and Bernstein. 'They had a sober approach,' Sisulu said later. 'You could reason everything, and they did not have a mechanical Party approach: they relied on people.'[67] The Party certainly played a major role in creating the military force, but the idea did not come from Moscow. 'It was presented as a fact,' said the Russian expert on Africa Apollon Davidson. 'Moscow was sometimes more moderate than the groups it supported, in Palestine, Algeria or South Africa.'[68] And the ANC had growing control over the military wing. After 1963, according to Slovo, it was almost exclusively directed by ANC exiles, while 'the Party involvement was negligible'.

By early morning the Congresses had agreed that Mandela should form a new military organisation, which came to be called Umkhonto we Sizwe (MK), or 'Spear of the Nation'. He could recruit his own staff, and MK would be kept quite distinct from the ANC, to avoid threatening the ANC's legal status (though within eighteen months the link between MK and the ANC became generally known when the ANC firebrand Robert Resha publicly proclaimed it).[69] It was the historic dawn of the new phase of struggle.

Luthuli remained ambivalent. He was worried about a violent struggle, but he was not a pacifist. Mandela would always remember him saying at Stanger: 'If anybody thinks I am a pacifist, let him go and take my chickens; he will know how wrong he is.' Luthuli would later complain that he had not been properly consulted, but he had deliberately kept his distance.[70] He never endorsed the decision, while he did not attack it. 'Despite his deep Christian commitment to non-violence,' wrote Slovo afterwards, 'he never forbade or condemned the new path, blaming it on the regime's intransigence rather than on those who created MK.'

But Mandela was now totally committed to the armed struggle as commander-in-chief of MK, and he threw himself into his new military role with enthusiasm. He was becoming a soldier overnight, like the Afrikaner guerrillas in the Boer War such as Jan Smuts or Deneys Reitz, about whom he had read much. It marked a complete break with ANC tradition: 'The decision that Mandela should become a fugitive, and henceforth live the life of a professional revolutionary,' as Slovo wrote later, 'was a major watershed in our history. It pointed the way to a qualitatively different style of clandestine work and set the scene for the complete break with pacifism or "legalism" which was made soon afterwards.'[71]

'We plan to make government impossible,' said Mandela in a press statement issued from hiding on 26 June, now proclaimed as 'Freedom Day'. He did not explain how this would be done, but warned that there would be 'other forms of mass pressure to force the race maniacs who govern our beloved country to make way for a democratic government of the people, by the people and for the people'. There was a warrant out for his arrest but he would not surrender himself, because in the present conditions 'to seek for cheap martyrdom by handing myself to the police is naïve and criminal'. 'I have chosen this latter course,' he continued, 'which is more difficult and which entails more risk and hardship than sitting in jail. I have had to separate myself from my dear wife and children, from my mother and sisters, to live as an outlaw in my own land. I have had to close my business, to abandon my profession, and live in poverty and misery.'[72] As he put it a year later, he had to 'say goodbye to the good old days when, at the end of a strenuous day at an office, I could look forward to joining my family at the dinner-table, and instead to take up the life of a man hunted continuously by the police'.[73]

For the first few weeks he hid in the homes of several Indian families in Johannesburg, emerging for secret meetings with the ANC executive, including Kathrada, Duma Nokwe, Alfred Nzo and Harold Wolpe, most of whom were forbidden to meet with more than two people. A small group was responsible for finding safe houses, among them Kathrada, who found the Indian hosts, and Wolfie Kodesh, an ebullient white journalist on *New Age*.

It was a precarious existence. One night Kodesh found a flat near his home in Yeoville which was temporarily vacant. Ten members of the executive converged there, including Mandela, in his favourite disguise as a chauffeur. But when Sisulu arrived Kodesh noticed two old people in the corridor looking closely at him, and overheard one of them say, 'Go phone up.' Kodesh quickly warned them all to disperse, but as they did not know where to hide Mandela, Kodesh suggested his own flat at 52 Webb Street. 'The police would never have thought that a black man would be in a white area like that,' said Kodesh, 'where he'd stick out like a sore thumb.' Mandela stayed there for two months, the tall, athletic commander and the stocky journalist an odd duo. As Kodesh remembers Mandela's first night: 'He insisted on sleeping on the camp-bed, against my protests. I was woken up at 4.30 a.m. by the creaking camp-bed, to find him getting dressed in longjohns and a tracksuit. He explained he was going out for a run, but I refused to give him the key, so he ran on the spot for an hour. He repeated it every morning, and later I joined in, gradually improving until I was running with him for the whole hour.'

It was dangerous for Mandela to go out, so he began to read voraciously, from books Kodesh had on his shelves or which Kathrada brought him from the public library. Kodesh told him that Clausewitz was to war what Shakespeare was to literature, so Mandela devoured Clausewitz's classic *On War*. 'I never saw a chap concentrate as he did,' said Kodesh; 'underlining, taking notes, as if it was for a legal examination.'[74] Mandela read widely, including the Afrikaner poet Ingrid Jonker (whom he was to quote in his inauguration speech forty years later). But his overriding interest was in books about liberation struggles: Mao Tse-tung and Edgar Snow on China, Menachem Begin on Israel, Louis Taruc's *Born of the People*, about the guerrilla uprising in the Philippines, and Deneys Reitz's classic about the Boer War, *Commando*.[75] He read carefully and attentively, as Mac Maharaj, who had found some of the books for him in London, discovered when they were later imprisoned together on Robben Island.

It was a time when many revolutionaries around the world appeared to be triumphant – Mao in China, Ben Bella in Algeria, Castro in Cuba. Mandela studied the rebellions throughout Africa – in Ethiopia, Kenya, the Cameroons, and particularly in Algeria, which the ANC saw as a parallel to their own struggle. But it was the Cuban revolution which most inspired him and many of his colleagues. It was a dangerous model, a freak victory, but they were fired by the story of how Castro and Che Guevara, with only ten other survivors from their ship the *Granma*, had mustered a guerrilla army of 10,000 in eighteen months, and had marched on Havana in January 1959.[76] Mandela was especially interested in the account by Blas Roca, the Secretary of the Cuban Communist Party, which described how it was Castro, not the Party, who had realised that the moment of revolution had come. He would never lose his admiration for Castro.

Mandela found it hard to adjust to his solitary life in Wolfie Kodesh's flat. 'I suddenly found that I had too much privacy,' he recalled from jail, 'and really missed the family, company and the gym where I could completely relax. It required a lot of discipline to keep the routine demanded by my new style of life.'[77] Particularly he missed Winnie, and Kodesh noticed that when Mandela talked about her and the children he dropped his military style, and had tears in his eyes. Kodesh helped to arrange several visits by Winnie, which were always tricky, as her house in Soweto was under constant watch from a nearby hill. She had to be driven by circuitous routes, changing cars on the way, exactly timed: if the car was late, the visit would be aborted. Sometimes she and Mandela would meet in a safe house elsewhere. They could always find friends of the movement who would take the risk, but they agreed never to cause them anxiety. Once they met at a house in Parktown owned by a sympathetic but nervous white editor. When he came into the room nervously rattling the drink-glasses on their tray, Kodesh quickly mentioned another appointment, and took Mandela away.

Kodesh worried more about Mandela's safety as the newspapers began publicising his disappearance, dubbing him 'the Black Pimpernel'. 'All the police have photos of the Black Pimpernel,' he warned him. 'Aren't you afraid of being caught?' Mandela replied: 'I don't think about it, I concentrate on my work.'[78] But two things happened to alarm them. Once Mandela overheard some domestic workers talking about the sour milk which he had left on the windowsill. This was an African delicacy, which they realised meant that there was a black man living in the white building.[79] Finally, Kodesh went one day to see the Zulu cleaner living at the top of the building, who had been told that the black stranger was a student who was waiting for a bursary to go overseas. On the man's bed he spotted a newspaper clipping. It was an 'article about the Black Pimpernel, with pictures of Nelson – though without a beard. I thought, "This is bad, he knows who I'm looking after." I said to Nelson: "Pack up, you're off, he's seen all the pictures."' Kodesh took Mandela to a house in the Johannesburg suburb of Norwood owned by a friendly doctor, where he stayed in the servants' quarters, pretending to be the gardener.[80]

Mandela had been recruiting a small group of experts to embark on MK's campaign of sabotage. The Communist Party already had its own group of specialists for its sabotage plans, but it was clear that the two groups needed each other, and they eventually merged. Mandela would always rightly insist that MK was founded by Africans, but it needed expertise and tactical skills which the ANC alone could not provide.[81] He recruited Joe Slovo, whom he trusted and admired, to serve on the High Command. 'The word "surrender" was not in his vocabulary,' Mandela said later. 'He was daring through and through.'[82] Slovo in turn praised Mandela in his own terms: 'My affection and admiration for him grew. There was nothing flabby or condescending about Nelson. Ideologically he had taken giant strides since we confronted one another in the corridors of the university during the early 1950s on the role of the Party in the struggle. His keen intelligence taught him to grasp the class basis of national oppression. But the hurt of a life whose every waking moment was dominated by white arrogance left scars.'

Slovo brought in a small group of communist experts, including Jack Hodgson and Wolfie Kodesh, who knew about explosives from their experience in North Africa during the Second World War, and Arthur Goldreich, who had fought the British in Palestine in the late 1940s. Their expertise, it turned out, was amazingly amateurish. 'Among the lot of us we did not have a single pistol,' wrote Slovo afterwards. 'Our knowledge of the techniques for this early stage of the struggle was extremely rudimentary.'[83] They practised their skills very rashly. One morning, when Kodesh went out to a brickworks outside Johannesburg to experiment with bombs with Jack Hodgson, Mandela insisted on coming along. At the brickworks Kodesh saw a black man who clearly recognised him, and wanted to abort the exercise. But Mandela went to talk to the man, then came back and told them to carry on. The bomb duly exploded, producing a cloud of topsoil, like a miniature atom bomb. As they drove away Mandela was ecstatic, said Kodesh, congratulating them all.[84]

It was in October 1961 that Mandela found a new hiding place at Lilliesleaf Farm, an isolated house with some huts in Rivonia, then a semi-rural suburb of market gardens and bungalows outside the municipal limits of Johannesburg. The farm had been secretly bought by the Communist Party, which disguised its ownership through Arthur Goldreich, who settled there with his family to establish a respectable front with a lifestyle that included horse-riding on Saturdays. It appeared in safe hands for Mandela when his friend Michael Harmel drove him out there, and was, he later testified in court, 'an ideal place for the man who lived the life of an outlaw. Up to that time I had been compelled to live indoors during the daytime and could only venture out under cover of darkness. But at Lilliesleaf I could live differently, and work far more efficiently.'[85] He felt happy at Lilliesleaf, he wrote later from jail, because 'the whole place reminded me of the happiest days of my life, my days of childhood.'[86] Lilliesleaf served as a safe house for members of the Communist Party as well as for Mandela, although only he and the Goldreich family were actually living there: he took over a small room in the outbuildings, and was known as David Motsamayi. The farm was not, he told the court later, the actual headquarters of either MK or the ANC; but Rusty Bernstein, who often visited, worried that it appeared to be turning into MK's semi-permanent headquarters.[87]

From Lilliesleaf, Mandela frequently left in the evenings in disguise to meet ANC leaders and others. Sometimes he would be in mechanics' overalls, sometimes as a nightwatchman in a long grey overcoat and big earrings, once even as a priest leading a fake funeral procession of disguised activists. He enjoyed the sense of theatre: in October a group of Indian activists assembled in a house in Fordsburg, and a man in dirty Caltex service station overalls walked in. It was not until he said, 'Sit down, comrades,' that they recognised Mandela.[88] Ahmed Kathrada was one of a small group deputed to make sure Mandela appeared as a 'new man'. They persuaded him to abandon his stylish clothes, but he still had his vanity: they could not get him to shave off his beard, which had become part of his revolutionary style.[89]

Many of Mandela's friends were worried about his lack of precautions. 'He was probably the most wanted man in the country at the time, and was taking great risks,' wrote Bernstein. 'But that was his style. He was one who led from the front. He never asked anyone to take a risk which he was not prepared to take first for himself.' Bernstein worried that there was an expanding circle of aides, drivers and visitors who knew about Mandela's hiding place at Lilliesleaf, and that the responsibility for security was dangerously divided between the Communist Party and Mandela himself: 'We were slow to realise the dangers in what was happening,' Bernstein recalled.[90]

Winnie visited Mandela several times at Lillisleaf, bringing him vegetables, and would then go on to see their Indian friends Paul and Adelaide

Joseph. 'I used to see the car was full of mud, clearly from a farming area,' said Paul. 'We knew that our house was under constant observation. They were all terribly careless. But it was the early days of the underground movement, with a certain amount of romanticism.' One day the Josephs were surprised when they were driven by Walter Sisulu to a small room in Fordsburg, near central Johannesburg. 'We walked in to find Nelson there. He gave us hugs, talked about family matters, and after a while said, "I'm glad I've seen you." That was that.' Years later they learnt that Mandela had been upset by a false story that their marriage was breaking up, and wanted to help.[91]

Underground life was a strain for many of the conspirators. 'I truly believe that people underground come to believe themselves invulnerable,' said Dennis Goldberg, who was working secretly in Cape Town. 'Eventually the stress becomes so great that they make mistakes subconsciously to put an end to it . . . It's like coming out of the cold.' Goldberg saw Mandela's 'Pimpernel phase' as inherently unstable: 'There's a downside to being the romantic leader: it makes you take more and more risks, because you must maintain that publicity, and when you're underground you're caught between disappearing into a hole in the ground and pulling in the lid, because you're then safe; and emerging to do more and more daring operations.'[92]

While he was in hiding Mandela travelled throughout South Africa, without much concern. Once when he drove down to Durban to stay with the Meers, Fatima was shocked to receive a phone call from a friend who asked: 'Has Nelson arrived?' When he stayed for two weeks on a sugar farm at Tongaat, near Luthuli's house, he pretended to be an agricultural demonstrator, until a farm worker asked him, 'What does Luthuli want?'[93] But he was determined to keep in touch with ordinary people, and was buoyed up by their support. In mid-November Mary Benson was invited to meet him outside Johannesburg. He was wearing his chauffeur's white coat, and had just toured Natal and the Cape. 'You can't comprehend,' he told her, 'unless you stay right there *with* the people.' She recalled how he joked about a recent narrow escape, reminisced about old times, then gave her a lift back to her sister's flat, driving an erratic old car which kept spluttering to a halt.[94]

While the MK command was plotting sabotage, white South Africans felt little sense of danger after the suppression of the stay-at-home strike. The ruling National Party had gained support from white voters by promising tougher measures against agitators. In October 1961 there had been a first shock of sabotage, when an electric pylon was cut and a government office burnt down; it turned out to be the work of the National Committee of Liberation (NCL), a group of liberals and leftists which later developed into the African Resistance Movement (ARM).[95] MK publicly dissociated itself from these saboteurs, whom they thought 'temperamentally inclined towards deeds of derring-do'; but privately they agreed to co-ordinate their actions.[96] The sabotage only increased the solidarity of most whites, and in the election soon afterwards the Nationalists achieved their biggest victory, with the electorate for the first time giving them a clear majority.[97]

16 December was Dingane's Day, which commemorated the Afrikaners' massacre of Zulus in 1838 but which had now become a focus for African protests. And it was then that MK performed its first acts of sabotage, with explosions in Johannesburg, Port Elizabeth and Durban. They caused a national furore, though the saboteurs had not been very efficient: one of them, Petrus Molife, was killed, and another had his arm blown off. Joe Slovo tried to blow up the Drill Hall in Johannesburg, but had to retreat after being discovered by an army sergeant.[98] But MK saboteurs succeeded in attacking government offices and an electrical transformer.

On the previous night ANC volunteers had scattered leaflets and stuck up posters proclaiming the founding of MK and explaining the need for new methods alongside the traditional organisations: 'The time comes in the life of any nation when there remain only two choices: submit or fight.' MK, they said, hoped to bring the government to its senses 'before matters reach the desperate stage of civil war'.[99] The police tore down most of the posters by morning, so few people got the message. 'Contrary to our intentions,' wrote one conspirator afterwards, 'the sabotage created only a ripple of concern in the government or the country at large.'[100] But Mandela and his colleagues were at first buoyant, believing that white South Africans would now realise that they were sitting on top of a volcano, and that the ANC had a 'powerful spear that would take the struggle to the heart of white power'.[101] 'We were elated by our initial successes,' Mandela wrote later from jail, 'and even those who had first doubted the wisdom of the new line were also swept away by the tide of excitement.'[102]

The timing of the explosions proved embarrassing to the ANC, as

Mandela admitted; only six days before, its President Albert Luthuli had been awarded the Nobel Peace Prize in Oslo. But they had made sure that Luthuli was safely back home before the sabotage took place, and the ANC was not publicly linked to MK. Luthuli continued to worry about the turn to violence. He had told a Canadian diplomat two months earlier that younger ANC members were thinking of violence, but that it would in his opinion be 'suicidal folly' to try to overthrow the government by force.[103]

Luthuli's Nobel Prize gave a formidable international endorsement to the ANC's struggle, and Mandela had been 'enormously pleased' when he heard the news of the award on the radio at Rivonia.[104] But the British Foreign Office remained wary of contact with Luthuli. When he stopped off in London on his way to Norway, an official advised that a meeting 'would be taken greatly amiss by the South African government and it would do nothing to enhance Chief Luthuli's cause in South Africa'.[105]

In fact there was no immediate contradiction between MK's explosions and the peaceful pressures still being applied by the ANC. The high command of MK remained optimistic that successive acts of sabotage would serve as 'a shot across the bows' to bring white South Africa to its senses.[106] But soon after the first explosions MK was thinking less about sabotage and more about guerrilla warfare. 'There was no formal decision,' said Bernstein, who was involved. 'It was something that seemed to develop spontaneously from the idea that sabotage would somehow lead to a "next phase".'[107] The high command began arranging for key leaders to go abroad for training, followed by young volunteers.

Mandela was now commander-in-chief of a burgeoning fighting force. He had the authority and prestige of a revolutionary leader taking on an unpopular military regime, in an age of revolutions when the forces of oppression seemed in retreat throughout Africa. All his previous roles – the boxer, the man-about-town, the lawyer, the family man – had been left behind by the new role of guerrilla leader underground. It was a surprising and unprepared translation, from many-sided politician to dedicated soldier. Mandela was to be a short-lived and amateurish soldier compared to Cuban or Chinese revolutionaries. He remained above all the politician who saw the need for symbolic gestures to lead his people to a new style of confrontation.

13

Last Fling

1962

BLACK AFRICA was now looming larger on the map, promising a new impact on the world, and powerful support for fellow-Africans in the south. In early 1962, after the first explosions of sabotage, the ANC executive decided that they must seek help from the rest of the continent to provide money and military training. They told Mandela to make the connections, and to speak at an African summit meeting in Ethiopia in February to explain the ANC's crusade. At the age of forty-three, Mandela had never been outside Southern Africa, and he agreed with gusto. But his African journey, as is revealed in his private diary, proved much more difficult and full of setbacks than he and his colleagues had expected.

It was a heady time to be travelling through the continent. Newly-independent states were rapidly emerging, full of ambitions for a pan-African role in the world. Their ex-imperial masters were offering them aid and friendship to keep them in the Western camp, while the Soviet Union and China were competing to lure them eastward. The Americans, under President Kennedy, were becoming more seriously interested. They worried that in Africa the Cold War would turn into a racial war, and that African states would rally against what they called the 'White Redoubt' – South Africa, Angola, Mozambique and the Central African Federation. In July 1962 a secret report was sent to Kennedy's key policy-makers, including Richard Helms at the CIA, recommending that the President should pay an early visit to Africa. It warned that the White Redoubt was 'antithetical to American history and political theory', and that the 'Communist Bloc will continue to fish in troubled African waters'. Black South Africans were seen as crucial but unpredictable players: 'Their leaders are flirting with violence and, in some cases, with communism.'[1]

Mandela would find his own view of Africa suddenly opening up, before it was closed off to him. Before leaving he went down to Natal to see the ANC President Luthuli, whom he found in high spirits. Luthuli approved of Mandela's trip, and asked to be consulted about the ANC's new operations. Mandela then spent two days in Johannesburg, where he saw old friends including Walter Sisulu and Duma Nokwe. He was angered when an Indian colleague did not turn up for a meeting because he was 'boozing'. Later in Bechuanaland he was angrier still when another colleague was arrested for drunken driving: 'An act of amazing irresponsibility and a betrayal,' he told his diary.[2] But he remained exhilarated about his trip.

On 10 January 1962 he said goodbye to Winnie and was driven across the border to Bechuanaland (now Botswana), which was then still a British protectorate. He fell in love with the country at first sight, he wrote later: he saw a wilder Africa, including a lioness crossing the road.[3] After the jungle of Johannesburg, he reflected, he was 'in another cosmopolitan centre where the survival of the fittest was the supreme law and where the tangled vegetation concealed all kinds of danger'.[4]

Bechuanaland was much used as an escape route for black activists, to whom the British authorities appeared tolerant; and they seemed happy to harbour Mandela, for whom (they noted) 'South African police have been searching for some months'. But the High Commission was watching him closely. It reported to London that he arrived in the border town of Lobatse on 12 January, and that he was 'known to possess funds estimated £600'.[5]

Mandela had 'the shock of his life' in Lobatse when he discovered that the immigration officer was also the security chief. He was suspicious when the man recognised him and offered him a safe house to avoid being kidnapped by the South African police, but was reassured when he found that he had also helped Oliver Tambo two years before.[6] There was good reason to be wary: British intelligence had reported several clandestine visits by the South African Special Branch since April 1960, including some 'political refugees' who were actually South African agents.[7] The local police also recruited many Afrikaners and commonly shared information with the South Africans, according to John Longrigg of the British Embassy in Pretoria.[8]

From Bechuanaland Mandela was flown with his friend Joe Matthews in a charter plane to Dar-es-Salaam in Tanzania. British intelligence was closely following Matthews, who was now based in Basutoland, and who they thought was 'probably a communist ideologist using the ANC as a front'; but they did not know who chartered the plane.[9] On the way it narrowly missed hitting a mountain – an experience which tested Mandela's self-control to the limit, and (he noted) stopped even Joe Matthews from talking.[10]

In Dar-es-Salaam Mandela was highly visible. He was received by a surprised Frene Ginwala, the ANC representative who acted as travel agent for escaping comrades. She had been told by Tambo that Mandela would arrive in a suit, and that he should be 'buried' – or concealed – among the Tanzanians. Instead he was wearing a Basuto hat, a safari suit and high mosquito boots: 'And I'm supposed to bury you!' Ginwala exclaimed.[11]

Mandela flourished in Tanzania, which had become independent the previous month. He was delighted by President Julius Nyerere's style as a man of the people, with his small car and modest house; and he inspected with some envy the three-storey headquarters of Nyerere's Tanganyika African National Union (TANU) party, with its staff of full-time officials. But he was distressed when Nyerere advised him to postpone the armed struggle and to collaborate with Sobukwe and the PAC, and he argued against Nyerere's belief that socialism was indigenous to Africa. Significantly, he did not share Nyerere's view of Africans as a pastoral, nomadic people with no class divisions: long before the arrival of the white men, Mandela insisted, Africans had developed mining and metallurgy, which had provided a social surplus and financed monuments from the Nile to Zimbabwe.[12]

From Tanzania Mandela flew briefly to West Africa, where he met up with Tambo, now bearded and with longer hair, who had been organising ANC offices in Ghana.[13] He then flew to Ethiopia for the Pan-African Freedom Conference in Addis Ababa. It was organised by the Emperor Haile Selassie, the legendary ruler who had inspired Mandela as a boy of seventeen when he first heard how he stood firm against Mussolini's invading forces. Selassie was neither a socialist nor a democrat, but he ruled over the one African nation that had always been independent, and was now shrewdly encouraging and advising the leaders of the other new nations. 'This was the country ruled by Africans, even if it had no democratic institutions,' wrote Mandela. 'Every structure I saw round there was the result of African initiative and skills.' Mandela was struck by the formal dignity of the tiny monarch in his uniform as he listened stiff as a log and bowed to the audience with a tilt of the head; and he was amazed to see American military advisers receiving medals and bowing like anyone else.[14]

Mandela made a dramatic entry to the conference, where he abandoned his alias as 'David' and delivered a speech which he had carefully prepared with advice from Tambo and Robert Resha. Mandela described the brutal oppression of black South Africans in 'a land ruled by the gun'. He thanked other African states for pressing for boycotts and sanctions, but insisted that his people should not look for their salvation beyond their borders: 'The centre and cornerstone of the struggle for freedom and democracy in South Africa lies inside South Africa itself.' He described the people's growing militancy and the vulnerability of the government – 'uneasy lies the head which wears the crown' – and the future for the campaign of sabotage which had begun the previous month: 'Hard and swift blows should be delivered with the full weight of the masses of the people.' But he had not entirely abandoned non-violent protest: 'The days of civil disobedience, of strikes, and mass demonstrations are not over, and we will resort to them over and over again.'[15] He would slip back into South Africa as soon as possible: the last ten months underground had been 'the most inspiring period of my life', he told the Johannesburg *Star*. 'Everywhere I have been inspired by the warm affection . . . and by the amount of confidence I have found among the African masses.'[16]

It was the most important speech of Mandela's career so far, but it was barely reported in South Africa. In London the *Observer* reported that he had given 'a grave warning that the situation in South Africa was explosive'; in an interview in the *Manchester Guardian* he disclaimed any connection with MK, but said that he thought it had raised the morale of the people, and had strengthened other forms of protest: 'This organisation can hit back in reprisal for attacks on innocent people by the government.'[17] In fact Mandela's speech had clearly implied the link between the ANC and MK; and it was soon spelt out emphatically by Robert Resha in exile, exasperating ANC leaders at home who wanted the legal distinction between the two organisations to be preserved.[18]

Mandela was worried about the tensions between African leaders, particularly the hostility towards Arab 'fraternal delegates'. The East and Central Africans were refusing to admit North Africans to their organisation PAFMECA (Pan-African Freedom Movement for East and Central Africa) – including the Algerians, who were just concluding their war against France. When Mandela protested, one delegate barked at him: 'In North Africa you have Africans who are not Africans.' Tambo passed him a note saying 'Shut Up!', but Mandela soon succeeded in getting the North Africans admitted, earning their gratitude. He also helped to create links between black South Africans and the North. PAFMECA was extended to include South Africa, and was renamed PAFMECSA: a year later it would be further extended to West and North Africa to become the Organisation of African Unity (OAU).

Mandela was still more worried by the perception of disunity in black South Africa, and by the impact of the ANC's rivals the PAC. His speech at the conference had been preceded by a more high-flown speaker, Peter Molotsi of the PAC, who had talked about 'the glory that was Africa' and the splendours of the ancient civilisation of Azania, the name the PAC gave to South Africa.[19] Mandela was surprised to find his old friend Michael Scott, who had once joined the squatters in Soweto, at the conference, apparently with the PAC; but he did not seem to be on very good terms with the PAC delegation, so Mandela kept him company and introduced him to black leaders.[20] The PAC had been spreading malicious stories against the ANC in the African states, calling it 'a Xhosa tribal army', and 'riddled with white communists'. Mandela was trying to show a united front, and to avoid antagonising the PAC. He talked with Philip Kgosana, the young PAC hero of the march to Cape Town in 1960, at a meeting of university students but failed to persuade him to join him.[21]

Mandela soon realised that the ANC's alliance with whites and Indians put them out of step with the black nationalism in the rest of the continent. The PAC's militancy had caught the imagination of Africa, as the ANC had not. Reports reached the ANC executive in Johannesburg that Mandela was having 'a rough ride' in Addis. To their dismay they realised that the PAC had gained more support abroad than they had thought. 'Their [the PAC's] credentials in Africa,' wrote Bernstein, 'were not in response to their paltry political record at home but to their radical rhetoric. They identified themselves with that popular African theme of "negritude", and turned it into a weapon against the multi-racial ANC programme.'[22]

Mandela now displayed his political pragmatism and sensitivity. In an important report for the ANC he described 'the widespread anti-colonial

This plain thatched *rondavel*, which still stands at the Great Place of Mqhekezweni, was the home of the young Mandela from the age of nine. It was in a remote part of the Transkei, scarcely touched by white intruders, but for Mandela it was the centre of the world.

Chief Jongintaba Dalindyebo, the acting regent of the Tembu people in the Transkei, was Mandela's guardian for much of his youth, and his model for benign authority and chiefly style.

ABOVE The nineteen-year-old Mandela was still a 'country boy' whose aspirations remained in the Transkei: he was conscious of his aristocratic background, not much interested in politics, and, like his guardian, very clothes-conscious.

ABOVE RIGHT In 1944 Mandela was married in Johannesburg to Evelyn Mase, a nurse from the Transkei who was a cousin of his close friend Walter Sisulu. She was not at all political, and was increasingly religious, becoming a Jehovah's Witness.

RIGHT From 1952 the law firm of Mandela & Tambo inhabited a picturesque old building which still stands in downtown Johannesburg. It became the focus for black people's rights and political activism. Tambo was the backroom lawyer, Mandela the more flamboyant pleader in court.

Black Johannesburg in the 1950s was bursting with creative energy, whether in music, writing, sport or dancing . . .

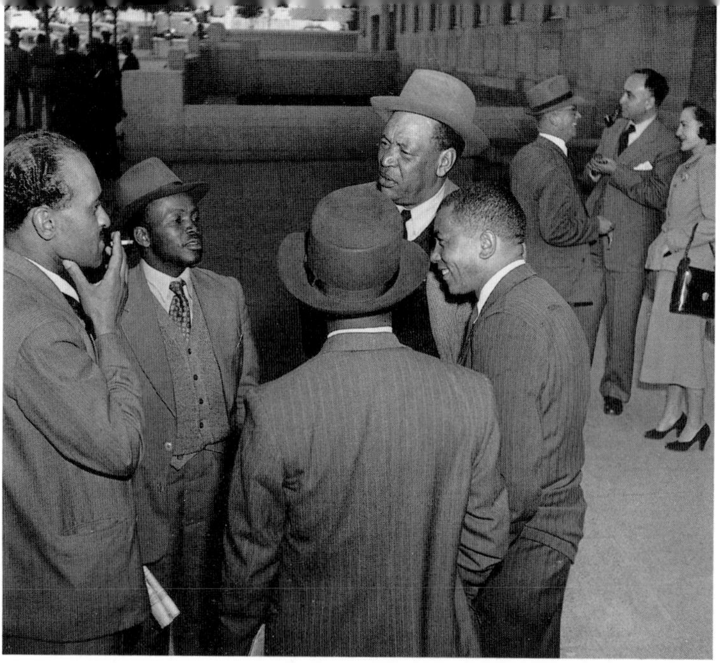

© Jürgen Schadeberg

. . . but Mandela was now immersed in protests against the apartheid government, with colleagues (*above*) like Walter Sisulu (*right foreground*), J.B. Marks (*centre, with hat*) and Ruth First (*right background*). In the Defiance Campaign of 1952 (*below*) he worked alongside both the conservative Dr Moroka (*left*) and the communist Dr Dadoo (*right*).

© Jürgen Schadeberg

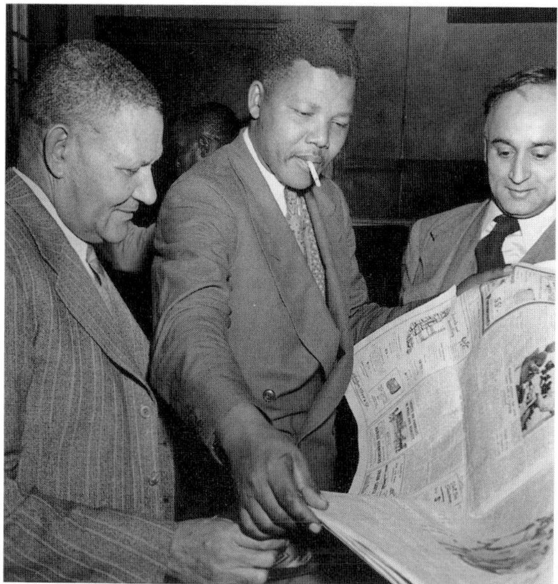

Mandela sparred regularly with boxing champions like Jerry Moloi; not just to keep fit, but as training in self-discipline and control, which had its own relevance to political leadership.

The accused in the Treason Trial which began in 1957, shown in this montage, came from all races, and were brought closer by the ordeal. They included most prominent African politicians, including Sisulu (*top row, third from right*), Duma Nokwe (*second row from top, smiling, in the centre*) and Mandela (*centre*). Among the many white accused were Rusty Bernstein (*front row, third from left*) and Helen Joseph (*second row, left*).

Mandela's wedding to his second wife Winnie in 1958 was attended by a few close friends, including the communist writer Michael Harmel (*left*) and Ruth Mompati (*next to Mandela*), Mandela's secretary who later became Ambassador to Switzerland.

LEFT Winnie, Mandela and their second daughter, Zindzi, photographed in 1961.

RIGHT Mandela at the Treason Trial in 1958 had a short-lived triumph when the prosecution briefly withdrew its indictment. He was known as the best-dressed man in the trial; but his close colleagues saw him as an increasingly serious leader and thinker.

OVERLEAF When Mandela burnt his pass-book in the turmoil after the Sharpeville massacre in 1960, he hoped to be initiating a mass pass-burning campaign. But the government soon clamped down on all protests, and banned the African National Congress for thirty years.

feeling and strong opposition to anything resembling partnership between white and black'. The ANC was widely seen as 'a communist-dominated organisation', while the PAC had started off with tremendous advantages because of its ideology, and had 'skilfully exploited opposition to whites and partnership'. Mandela was worried that Luthuli's Nobel Prize 'created the impression that Luthuli had been bought by the whites', and that his autobiography *Let My People Go*, which had been partly ghosted by the white priest Father Charles Hooper, and praised by Alan Paton, also made him appear 'a stooge of whites'. The ANC, Mandela reckoned, had helped to perpetuate the impression of excessive white influence by co-operating with whites at the top, but not among the masses: 'All these things have made it appear that the PAC is the only hope for African people. It must be remembered that the mere allegation that you are a stooge is of itself so demagogic that it must automatically discredit the ANC. The nature of the accusation we make against the PAC makes them some sort of heroes. It does not discredit any African politician in Africa to be called a racialist or anti-white.'[23] Mandela was not calling for a return to an earlier black African glory, but for a new kind of multi-racial society which had no parallel elsewhere in Africa. And for the first time he was coming up against the full force of African nationalism and anti-communism.

Through the rest of his tour Mandela would take care to explain the PAC's achievements and policies as well as the ANC's, so that the Africans would not be surprised when they encountered the PAC later. The Tunisian Minister of Defence even complained, 'If all that you say about Sobukwe is true, then what are you doing here?'[24] Mandela consistently found it hard to justify the ANC's multi-racialism to African leaders accustomed to a more straightforward struggle against white imperialists. And he thought the ANC had been too slow to counter the PAC's anti-communist propaganda: 'Our own chaps have been somewhat timid about attacking them . . . We have to do a lot of work indeed before we can say we have nailed them . . . There are many who say they may be naïve but they are the only organisation in South Africa that is in step with the rest of Africa.'[25]

The rest of his tour of Africa confirmed his worries. In Cairo, Egyptian officials complained that the left-wing Johannesburg weekly *New Age* had criticised President Nasser for attacking the communists. Mandela assured them that *New Age* did not necessarily represent the ANC's policy, and promised to take up the question when he returned.[26] He flew on to Tunis, where President Bourguiba offered him training and £5,000 for weapons; and then to Morocco, the centre for African liberation movements, including Mozambicans, Angolans and, most important, Algerians.

The Algerian war with France had just ended after eight years of mounting conflict and half a million deaths. It provided a terrifying warning of South Africa's possible fate, with its own rebel army confronting still more entrenched and well-armed white settlers. Mandela was welcomed by Dr Mustafai, the head of the Algerian mission in Morocco, who wisely explained that guerrilla fighters needed a strong military base outside the country, and offices abroad to mobilise international diplomatic support.[27]

At Oujda, close to the Algerian border, Mandela watched guerrilla fighters parading in honour of their returned leader Ahmed Ben Bella, just released from his island prison and soon to become the first President of independent Algeria. In a short speech Ben Bella explained that freedom for the Algerians was meaningless so long as Africa was under the claws of imperialism.[28] Mandela was thrilled by the crowds: 'Enthusiasm simply bewildering,' he noted in his diary.[29] With Ben Bella he watched 'an army that had been born in the fire of actual battle', which impressed him much more than the formal military procession in Ethiopia. 'I felt sure then, as I do now,' he wrote from jail fourteen years later, 'that once our units, operating from a friendly territory, set their foot on our soil, they would grow in numbers and striking-power so rapidly that Verwoerd would be plagued by all the problems which once tormented Chiang Kai-shek, Ngo Diem, De Gaulle, Batista and the British.'[30] He remained much influenced by the Algerian revolutionaries and by the advice of the Algerian military commander Houari Boumedienne (who in 1965 would replace Ben Bella following a coup); after talking with him, he told Neville Alexander later in jail, he realised there was no point in trying to overthrow the apartheid regime: the ANC had to force them to the negotiating table – an argument which to the Trotskyist Alexander was 'a red rag to a bull'.[31]

From Morocco Mandela made flying visits to the new black states of West Africa. In Mali the Defence Minister Madeira Keita warned him against 'precipitate action that might be disastrous'. In Senegal he was welcomed by President Léopold Senghor. He was also received by Sir

Milton Margai, the Prime Minister of Sierra Leone, and President Tubman of Liberia. His most frustrating visit was his return to Ghana, where he met up again with Tambo and tried to see President Kwame Nkrumah, in the hope that he could counter the PAC's powerful hold. They had encouragement from some Ministers, but the Foreign Minister Ako Ajei lectured them that the ANC was a tribal organisation, and said they could not see the President. Mandela realised that Nkrumah had not been told the truth about the ANC, and had to be content with handing in a memorandum. The Ghanaians did not even pay his hotel bill. But he had time to relax, and spent several evenings with Hilary Flegg, who had run the Treason Trial Defence Fund in Johannesburg.[32]

From Ghana Mandela flew to London for a ten-day visit. He had a travel permit from Tanganyika, but had a tense time with an immigration officer who asked him the purpose of his visit. Mandela said he was writing a book on the evolution of political thought in Africa, and wanted to visit museums and libraries. He soon realised that the officer knew better, and was aware that he was connected with Tambo (who was in another queue), but he was eventually waved through.

In London Mandela did not try to see anyone in Macmillan's government: 'I was a raw revolutionary,' he explained later.[33] His first purpose was to talk further with Tambo, whose wife Adelaide had written to Mandela warning that Tambo's asthma was worsening from the strain of overwork, and had prevented him from going to the UN in New York. Tambo had already been cold-shouldered by the Foreign Office in London, who were worried by the ANC's communist links, and were paying more attention to the PAC.[34] Later the ANC responded by sending out Robert Resha, the firebrand from Sophiatown, who (as Sisulu reckoned) 'spoke the PAC's language'.[35] Tambo was very encouraged by Mandela's vigour and total commitment to the struggle. 'However dangerous the situation, he always rose to it,' Adelaide Tambo recalled, 'as if he knew he had to keep up the people's spirit.'[36]

Mandela also took up his own British connections. Mary Benson had arranged to give dinner to Tambo in her small flat in St John's Wood; but to her amazement he arrived with Mandela, wearing an immaculate suit, who paced up and down the squeaking floorboards talking excitedly until 1.30 a.m., about the sense of freedom in his African tour. She wrote in her diary: 'N Gorgeous.'[37] She arranged for him to meet the Labour politician Denis Healey, a friend from her army days in Egypt, whom

Mandela found very helpful. 'He told me he had a background at university of having been a Marxist,' Mandela recalled, 'so he didn't have to fear to talk to me: I accept politics.'[38]

Tambo arranged to visit David Astor, the editor of the *Observer*, who was with Michael Scott and Colin Legum, the paper's African expert. Mandela entered the room already talking in a loud, cheery voice: 'I've come to thank you for all your paper has done for our people' – though he had in fact been worried by the *Observer*'s favourable reports on the PAC.[39] Mandela noted afterwards in his diary: 'Discussions are most cordial and each expresses flattering and inspiring comments.'[40] Astor was struck by Mandela's tremendous presence and confidence in representing his people, and arranged for him to meet the Labour and Liberal leaders Hugh Gaitskell and Jo Grimond (who apparently had never heard of him). Astor advised him to base himself in Washington rather than return to South Africa and be caught; but Mandela insisted that he must be among his people.[41] He explained to Colin Legum that he would extend the ANC's campaign to every possible front, including churchmen and liberals, but that the armed struggle was the priority: he was not looking forward to discussing it with Luthuli on his return.[42]

Mandela had some time in London for sightseeing and relaxation: Mary Benson showed him Parliament and Westminster Abbey – where he posed for photographs – with Freda Levson (who had run the Treason Defence Trial Fund for a time) and her husband Leon, with whom he lunched in Chelsea.[43] And he paid a surprise visit on his old Orlando friend Todd Matshikiza, the composer of *King Kong*, who was now living in exile in a small flat in Primrose Hill with his wife Esme. They were sitting there at midnight when Tambo arrived, bringing Mandela with him. Mandela looked thoroughly relaxed, while Tambo seemed tense. 'I'll never forget his vision that night,' Esme recalled. 'I really felt he was divinely inspired, completely unmaterialistic. With his great big vision he didn't even see the rumpled bed.' He described how the South African police were determined to catch him. 'Then why go back?' asked Esme. 'You should stay here.' He replied: 'A leader stays with his people.'[44] In the face of all the dangers, he was bent on defying the enemy at home, in spite of the likelihood of arrest. He seemed ready for martyrdom.

In London Mandela appeared very much his own boss, very confident of his personal authority, and determined to shift the ANC towards a more African position. His most painful encounter was with Yusuf Dadoo, his old communist friend who was now based in London. He saw him with the economist Vella Pillay, who had become a key link between the communists inside and outside South Africa. Mandela and Tambo had listened to complaints throughout Africa about how the ANC did not look African when they were represented abroad by white or Indian communists. Mandela now told Dadoo and Pillay that the ANC must show itself as an independent force, and be represented only by Africans at international conferences. 'It was very difficult, very tense,' Pillay recalled: 'Mandela was hard, and seemed not to be listening to us. His speeches in Africa had become more like the PAC's. But perhaps it was a necessary phase.'[45] Dadoo protested that Mandela was changing ANC policy, but Mandela insisted it was a change of image only. The ANC had to appear genuinely African: it had got 'lost in a nebulous organisation representing everybody'.[46]

Mandela returned to Ethiopia in June for a much more systematic assignment: to begin a six-month course in military training to prepare him as the leader of MK. On a hill outside Addis Ababa he handled an automatic rifle and pistol for the first time. On 29 June he recorded in his diary: 'First lesson in demolition.'[47] He fired mortars, made bombs, went on fatigue marches through forests and learnt about guerrilla fighting, enjoying the physical challenge and the military discipline. In retrospect, Mandela's attempted sudden transformation into a guerrilla commander seems romantic and unrealistic in the face of the modern, well-organised South African army. But it was in tune with the heady revolutionary atmosphere of Africa in the early sixties.

Back in South Africa the government was becoming more determined to stamp out black opposition, and to track down Mandela. Winnie complained that the police searched or visited her house nearly every day over the first three weeks in June, asking where Mandela was.[48] In July Parliament passed the Sabotage Bill, which allowed the courts to impose the death penalty on saboteurs for quite minor acts of destruction. The police were becoming much more efficient, wasting less time on liquor-raids or pass-raids. 'The people are facing an outright military build-up,' Sisulu told me in early July. 'They must prepare themselves for self-defence. The talk of non-violence is an anachronism.' The PAC was promising an early revolt, with a major campaign the next year: 'We told the people to expect action in 1960, and they got it,' their later President Zeph Mothopeng told me in Soweto. 'Now we tell them to expect it in

1963.'[49] The high command of the MK were also impatient for bolder action, and from their hide-out in Rivonia they were pushing ahead with much more ambitious plans. They urgently needed Mandela back in South Africa, and in mid-July he received a telegram telling him to return immediately to resume command.

He left Ethiopia with the gift of a modern pistol and two hundred rounds, and flew back via Khartoum and Dar-es-Salaam, where he was excited to find twenty MK recruits on the way from South Africa to Ethiopia for training.[50] When he arrived in Bechuanaland the British magistrate warned him that the South African police knew of his impending return. Kathrada and Sisulu had been there two weeks earlier to make arrangements, and he was met by Cecil Williams, a white communist theatre director who had driven up from Johannesburg in his new Austin Westminster car to collect him.[51] They drove through the night, across the open border, with Mandela still in the khaki uniform he had worn for his training in Ethiopia. They arrived at Lilliesleaf Farm in Rivonia at dawn on 24 July, where Mandela stayed in the thatched house.

The next day Winnie and the children came to see him for a brief reunion. She left filled with foreboding. That evening most of the ANC's working committee arrived at Lilliesleaf, including Sisulu, Kotane, Mbeki, Marks, Nokwe and Dan Thloome, another ANC activist, for a crucial discussion on strategy. Mandela reported on the military and financial support he had been offered by African leaders, and described their concerns about the ANC's links with Indians and whites. He advocated reorganising the Congress alliance to give the ANC a clearer leadership, as he and Tambo had agreed in London. Sisulu agreed that their tactics should be adjusted, but cautioned: 'We must bear in mind the sensitivity of other minority groups.' Nokwe responded vigorously: 'We are the prisoners of our own sins. We allowed ourselves to drift. I think co-operation has been carried too far.' Mandela said: 'What we lack is initiative. We should change our attitudes and exert ourselves. Our friends must understand that it is the ANC that is to pilot the struggle.'[52]

Mandela wanted to go immediately to Natal to report on the problem to Luthuli, particularly since the PAC was spreading rumours that Mandela had become an Africanist, and had joined the PAC. Kathrada, Mbeki and others wanted to delay the visit until they were sure it was safe, but they were overruled.[53] So the following night Mandela left Lilliesleaf for Durban with Cecil Williams, pretending to be Williams's chauffeur. They were rashly using the same conspicuous new car in which Williams had met him in Bechuanaland, and Mandela was carrying his pistol.

In Durban he saw Ismail and Fatima Meer, and met Monty Naicker of the Indian Congress. He tried to persuade them that the ANC must move to the forefront. He told Fatima how one African leader, hearing that the Freedom Charter was written by whites, had torn it down from the wall.[54] But the Indians were unconvinced. He then drove to Groutville to make his case to Luthuli. The ANC President objected to weakening the organisation's non-racial front at the behest of foreign leaders. Mandela argued that the situation was serious: they must ensure that the black states did not switch their support to the PAC. But Luthuli wanted to discuss it further with friends.[55]

Mandela then arranged to meet the MK saboteurs of the regional command in a safe house in Durban. He appeared dramatically in his new military style, with beard and khaki shirt and trousers, and greeted them in Arab style: 'Salaam.' Ronnie Kasrils, one of the saboteurs, thought he looked every inch a commander, but quite tense and solemn: he never smiled.[56] Billy Nair, another of the group, was much impressed by Mandela's authority on military questions: 'It was exhilarating – a wonderful experience.'[57] Even Bruno Mtolo, who was later to betray Mandela as a state witness, was impressed: 'He did not have to show off to prove that he was a leader; it was perfectly clear to anyone that he was. He was honest about everything which had to be done, and wanted it to be done in a simple way.'[58] Later in the evening Mandela unwisely joined a large party at the house of G.R. Naidoo, the hospitable photo-journalist from *Drum*, which included many unfamiliar guests. Mandela, still in khaki, seemed unconcerned, but his friends worried. He seemed almost to be courting arrest.

The next afternoon, Sunday 5 August, Mandela, in his white chauffeur's coat, set off back to Johannesburg with Cecil Williams, discussing sabotage on the way. Soon after they passed Howick, beyond Pietermaritzburg, they were overtaken by a police car, with two other cars closing in behind, and flagged down. Mandela hastily hid his gun and his notebook between the front seats. He was questioned by a police sergeant, who knew quite well who he was talking to. Mandela briefly considered jumping out onto the embankment and trying to make good his escape, but he did not know the terrain. The police drove him and Williams to Pietermaritzburg, and locked them in separate cells.[59] Mandela knew this was the end of his time underground, only seventeen months after he had made his climactic speech in the same town. (Thirty years later, as President, he came back to receive the Freedom of Howick. He remarked that revisiting the scene of his arrest made him feel a little impatient to be given the Freedom.)[60]

Who had tipped off the police? The question has still not gone away. The police, after suppressing the news of Mandela's arrest for two days, spread disinformation about their coup. On 8 August the *Rand Daily Mail* described how a squad had closed in on a house where Mandela was hiding. Four days later the Johannesburg *Sunday Times* wrote: 'Mandela was betrayed: Reds are suspected', and reported a 'fantastic story of intrigue and double-crossing'.[61] Joe Slovo detected 'the smell of some Judas in our ranks whose identity could not be pinpointed', but there were also foreign suspects.[62] Twenty-four years later the *New York Times* reported that a retired agent had boasted that the CIA had provided South African intelligence with the full details of Mandela's movements.[63] This is credible: the Americans needed Pretoria's military co-operation and South African uranium, and could offer efficient intelligence in return. But the claim cannot be substantiated. The South Africans could have tracked Mandela through Afrikaner employees in the Bechuanaland police. They could have seen Cecil Williams's conspicuous car when it picked him up in Bechuanaland, and when it drove on to Rivonia and Durban.[64] Whoever provided the information, Mandela had been careless in Durban, and had left too many clues. He himself showed no interest in finding the culprit afterwards: 'I've never seen any reliable evidence as to the truth of it.'[65]

After a brief period of denial, Mandela faced up to his predicament. He was driven to Johannesburg and held in a police station. Sisulu was in another cell, and he briefed him about his arrest. The next day he appeared in the magistrates' court, where he appeared in a Xhosa leopardskin *kaross*, 'literally carrying on my back the history, culture and heritage of my people'. He was encouraged to notice the evident discomfort of the magistrate and the lawyers: 'Mandela stared at the magistrate, who was transfixed like a mongoose looking at a snake,' said Wolfie Kodesh, who was watching. 'It took the magistrate two minutes to get his strength back.'[66]

It was a moment of truth for Mandela, who sensed that he was acquiring a new moral power: 'I was the symbol of justice in the court of the oppressor, the representative of the great ideals of freedom, fairness and democracy in a society that dishonoured those virtues.'[67] To make the most of his authority he decided to defend himself, using Joe Slovo only as his legal adviser. He was formally charged with incitement to strike and with leaving the country without a passport – he was relieved not to be charged with sabotage. The hearing was later set for October.

Awaiting trial in the Fort, Mandela maintained an apparent optimism. He asked the clergyman Arthur Blaxall, who visited him three times, for some Afrikaans grammar books, and seemed to appreciate Blaxall ending his visits with a prayer.[68] When he heard that his old English friend Helen Joseph had been put under house arrest – the first person to face this demoralising ordeal – he wrote to her condemning 'the cruel and cowardly order', but was confident that her courage would not fail her, as 'all signs point unmistakably to the early defeat of all regimes based on force and violence'.[69]

While awaiting trial Mandela was allowed to write letters and to read books; he was already starting a new programme of education which would continue off and on for the next three decades. With the help of books supplied by David Astor he began studying by correspondence for an LL.B. degree at London University, which would enable him to practise as a barrister. Astor also managed to send him political books via the British Ambassador Sir John Maud, who assured the Commissioner of Prisons, Victor Verster, that they were not pro-communist and would 'occupy Mandela's mind with a Western alternative'. The first six books included *A Short History of Africa* by Roland Oliver and J.D. Fage, *A History of Europe* by H.A.L. Fisher, and *Anatomy of Britain* by Anthony Sampson. Mandela wrote back very courteously to 'Sir John Maud, GCB, CBE' – his first contact with a British diplomat – thanking the anonymous friend for the valuable present.[70] Maud's colleague Lord Dunrossil, who had always been wary of the ANC, later reported to the Foreign Office that 'in the long run we may get some good will from Mandela for having helped him.'[71]

Mandela's arrest hardly came as a total surprise to the ANC, and he himself had clearly half-expected it since his return from abroad. But the speed of it came as a shock. 'This has been a grave blow at a wrong time,' Winnie wrote to her friend Adelaide Tambo in London in September. 'We knew it had to come, but it's come a little early.' Winnie was encouraged by the support for Mandela in London: 'Every day we greedily page through our papers to see what next you're doing.' She realised that Nelson might be in jail for some years, and was being urged by Bram Fischer and others to leave the country to study abroad, which she was resisting.[72] Some of her friends were already worried by Winnie's ill-advised friendships, and wanted her out of the way.[73]

While Mandela was in the Fort, the underground ANC scattered leaflets saying 'Mandela is in Prison: The People are in Chains', and calling for a mass meeting before he appeared for his trial. The leaflets promoted the new image of Mandela as the uncompromising outlaw, the lone fighter who symbolised the unity of the people: 'Nelson Rolihlahla Mandela is the fighting underground leader of the freedom struggle. He shows the way to freedom in the way of sacrifice, daring, courage, new methods of political struggle.'[74] As the *African Communist* hailed him in October 1962:

> The leader of a new type emerged in South Africa – the leader who would neither surrender tamely to Verwoerd terrorism, nor submit to arrest nor flee the country, but chose instead the life of an outlaw, living in the struggle, hunted, underground and yet in the midst of his people. Mandela's rise to prominence in South Africa has been by way of united struggle of the people – unity of all Africans, unity of all national groups, unity of communists and non-communists in the fight for freedom. His life has been lived in that atmosphere.[75]

Joe Slovo and other colleagues devised two different plans to get Mandela out of the Fort: the first involved escaping through the courtroom with a copied key, disguised in a wig and false beard; the second meant bribing the colonel in command of the prison, who had offered to allow him to escape in return for £6,000. But just before Mandela was due to appear in court the trial was shifted to Pretoria, rendering the plans useless.[76] In the Pretoria jail Mandela briefly met up again with Sisulu, who had been sentenced to six years' imprisonment for incitement to strike. With Mandela's support he applied for bail while waiting for his appeal, then jumped bail to continue to plot sabotage. Mandela himself did not ask for bail: his policy was to personify defiance.

He was now playing a more flamboyant role, using the magistrates' court as his theatre. At the opening of his trial on 22 October 1962 he began with supreme defiance, explaining that he would conduct his own defence and asking for the magistrate's recusal because of the impossibility of a fair trial: he was 'facing a white magistrate, confined by a white prosecutor, escorted by white orderlies'.[77] He did not try to dispute the evidence of the hundred or so witnesses who testified to his incitement and his departure from the country without a passport.

Lord Dunrossil, observing the trial for the British Embassy, noted that Mandela was 'clearly out of practice as a lawyer', and sometimes had to be helped by the prosecutor in his cross-examination.[78] But when Verwoerd's secretary, Mr Barnard, testified about Mandela's letter to the Prime Minister eighteen months earlier demanding a national convention, Mandela cross-examined him vigorously, claiming that it was improper of Verwoerd not to reply to a letter which raised such crucial issues. Barnard argued that Mandela's letter was aggressive and discourteous, and not calculated to obtain Verwoerd's friendly co-operation. Mandela dismissed this, but fourteen years later in jail he wrote that 'there might be some merit in his claim'.

When Mandela had finished his argument, the prosecutor, Mr Bosch, approached him privately and told him: 'For the first time in my career, I despise what I am doing. It hurts me that I should be asking the court to send you to prison.' Mandela shook hands, and assured him that he would always remember his words. But he had his own surprise waiting. He had told the magistrate that he would call the same number of witnesses as the prosecution, but in fact he had prepared none, knowing he was guilty of the charge. Instead he had prepared an eloquent 'plea in mitigation', which was really an hour-long political speech.

That morning the courtroom was surrounded by police, and packed with Africans including Winnie in Pondo tribal dress. Mandela walked in, raising his fist and shouting '*Amandla!*', which received a loud response of '*Ngawethu!*' His speech was a personal justification for defying the law, beginning with his own political development. He began by describing the democratic, peaceful life of the tribal society about which he had been told as a child, with 'no classes, no rich or poor and no exploitation of man by man'. He conceded that 'there was much in such a society that was primitive and insecure', but said it 'contained the seeds of revolutionary democracy in which none will be held in slavery or servitude'. The first draft of the speech had continued: 'My colleagues and I fight for such a society in our country,' but he amended this to the more cautious: 'This is the history which, even today, inspires me and my colleagues in our political struggle.' He then discussed the conflict between conscience and the law, quoting the British philosopher Bertrand Russell, who was sentenced to jail for protesting against nuclear weapons, and recalling how peaceful demonstrations in South Africa had been met by the government's violence. He concluded uncompromisingly: 'Posterity will pronounce that I was innocent and that the criminals that should have been brought before this court are the members of the government.'[79] It was a defiant political manifesto, and has since often been quoted by historians; but at the time it was carefully censored by the South African press. The Minister of Justice, John Vorster, had warned that speeches by banned people in court should not allow them 'to create a forum', and the Johannesburg *Star* consequently omitted Mandela's boldest statements.

On 7 November 1962 the magistrate delivered his sentence: three years' imprisonment for incitement, plus two years for leaving the country without a passport. The total of five years was the heaviest penalty yet given in South Africa, Mandela noted, for a political offence. But it was not unprecedented in Africa: eight years earlier the Kenyan leader Jomo Kenyatta had been sentenced to seven years (by a judge who had been bribed by the Governor Sir Evelyn Baring); he was now set to become the first Prime Minister of independent Kenya.[80] Mandela took some consolation from noting that he was sentenced on the anniversary of the birth of the first socialist state in Russia, which had supported liberation movements across the world, and that his trial had coincided with the crisis over Cuba, where Castro had confronted Kennedy with Soviet missiles. Above all he was encouraged that the General Assembly of the United Nations, just before his sentence, had voted for the first time to impose sanctions against South Africa.[81]

But Western governments remained deeply ambivalent in their attitudes to Mandela and the black opposition, and the archives in London and Washington provide a case history of the limitations of diplomats in the face of a dangerous but valuable foreign government. Since South Africa had left the Commonwealth, the British had been concerned that they might be backing the wrong horse – white rather than black. In June 1962, while Mandela was on the run, the Ambassador Sir John Maud had visited London for talks with Foreign Office officials. He himself found Verwoerd 'amiably repulsive', but he believed that Verwoerd saw

Britain as South Africa's only firm friend, and advocated a 'double game': being 'forthcoming and amiable' to Pretoria in order to protect British interests, while recognising that the continuing power of the Nationalist government was not in Britain's interest. Maud's policy of 'reinsurance' (discreet contacts with black politicians) had had little effect: in London the officials noted that no non-whites had been invited to the Embassy's Queen's Birthday party the year before. Maud explained implausibly that 'there were not many suitable non-Europeans in the Cape Town area', promised 'a more multi-racial flavour' at the next party, and made a tentative start by entertaining a mixed group of Girl Guides.[82] The South African government was watching closely: when Maud did give a multi-racial party in June 1963 he was berated for half an hour by Dr Verwoerd in his farewell interview.[83]

Maud claimed that American diplomats were more cautious than the British about developing black contacts, but in fact they had been more adventurous for some time, as they were in other parts of the world.[84] Back in January 1959 the American First Secretary in Cape Town, Paul Eckel, had told the British that he entertained many blacks in his home, and that the US Information Office in Johannesburg had a unique multi-racial reading-room (he did not mention its connection, through its copying machine, with the PAC). The American administration under Kennedy was becoming more concerned about the dangers of apartheid, and was seriously considering sanctions, to the dismay of the British; and the State Department was urging more contacts with Africans in case a black revolution was coming.[85] By 1963 the US Embassy was announcing with a fanfare a multi-racial Independence Day party for 4 July – the British Embassy in Washington said this had been arranged with 'half an eye on their own domestic racial problems'.[86]

The US Ambassador Joseph Satterthwaite – previously in charge of African policy in Washington – had been closely watching Mandela's relationship with the communists. In December 1962 he told the State Department about Mandela's visit to Durban immediately before his arrest, during which he had distanced the ANC from its white and Indian allies. 'The rank and file of the ANC,' Satterthwaite reported, without giving any evidence for his claim, 'did not know that this new tactic had been directed by the SACP and thought instead that Mandela was moving away from the white communist domination of the Congress Alliance.'[87] In fact his Embassy had no direct contact with Mandela.

The British were always more nervous of offending Pretoria, but in November 1962, after Mandela had been sentenced, they took a 'calculated risk' – as the Embassy reported to London – by allowing an enterprising junior diplomat, Marcus Edwards (now a judge), to meet political young blacks. He went drinking with some PAC journalists, including David Sibeko, a future leader who was to be murdered. They assured him that they were not 'a bunch of black Nats', and said the PAC would soon spring into action. A week later Edwards reported meeting more PAC members, who were rowdy, joking and shouting, but revealed their 'seriousness and extremism'. All of them, he reported, wanted 'one man, one vote, one party'.[88]

Another, unnamed, British diplomat made discreet contact with the ANC through Joe Matthews in Basutoland. Matthews explained that Mandela's commitment to violence had added to his prestige outside South Africa, and that (pointing to his own Mandela buttonhole) his arrest provided the ANC with a martyr. He and his ANC colleagues, he said, felt no sympathy for pan-Africanism, and despised the strident, ill-educated ministers in black Africa. As for the SA Communist Party, Matthews (although he was a leading member) said it had failed to become a mass movement because blacks found it alien, and could not swallow it emotionally. It was hard to believe, the diplomat concluded, that Matthews was a 'dyed-in-the-wool Moscow man'.[89]

The Foreign Office in London, relishing these titbits, pressed for more information about the black opposition.[90] But the Embassy resisted taking any more 'calculated risks', which it felt would encourage 'indiscreet blacks to boast about their contacts with the British'. 'The South African government can be expected to object violently,' wrote the diplomat Hilary Young, 'if it finds that members of the Ambassador's staff are in touch with proscribed organisations such as the PAC and the ANC whose acknowledged aim is to overthrow the present government.' Young concluded: 'There is an essential conflict between our short-term objective of maintaining friendly relations with the present government and our long-term objective of developing friendly relations with those people who may succeed them.'[91] In fact the long term was largely forgotten, and the British government made no contact with the major black leaders before they went to jail. 'I can't remember going to the British or American Embassy,' Mandela told me after he became President: 'I don't think they knew I existed.'[92]

Mandela's brief career as guerrilla leader and African statesman had ended as quickly as it began, without his receiving any very visible military reinforcements or diplomatic support from the West. He would often be criticised later for his amateurism, his play-acting and his inability to organise a serious military force; and he would accept some of the criticism. But the only way to present a serious threat to white South Africa would have been through a campaign of urban terrorism, as in Algeria, which would have caused horrendous reprisals and loss of life, which he and MK could not contemplate. He never imagined that the armed struggle would in itself, without sanctions or other pressures, have compelled white South Africa to change its policies. But his projection of himself as the militant and now martyred leader had a clear political message: it established him as the lost leader who had defied the system, 'hunted, underground and yet in the midst of his people'.

14

Crime and Punishment

1963–1964

MANDELA DISAPPEARED from public sight into jail leaving vivid images behind him: the Black Pimpernel who had evaded the police; the military commander who championed the people's struggle; the tribal leader in full regalia proclaiming his African identity. He did not need television – which the government would not allow into South Africa until 1976 – to capture people's imagination. From prison he could become, as Nehru described Gandhi, 'a symbolic expression of the confused desires of the people'.[1] His leadership depended on personal example rather than organisation. He had no official position in the ANC, the armed struggle which he commanded was still in its infancy, and he was now cut off from everyone. But he expected to re-emerge in five years at the most. He had no idea that he would be in jail for more than a quarter of a century.

Mandela began his sentence in Pretoria prison, which he already knew well, but his conditions were now harsher. He was no longer permitted to read books, and was allowed very few visitors. His sense of dignity was outraged by having to wear short trousers, and when he complained he was given the alternative of solitary confinement. He suffered it for a few weeks, tormented by lonely recriminations, until he decided he preferred companionship to trousers, and was allowed to join other political prisoners during the day.[2]

Among them was his old PAC rival Robert Sobukwe, who had been in jail since Sharpeville, and who had found himself eclipsed by Mandela's heroic image. They sometimes sat next to each other, sewing filthy mailbags infested with vermin. They got on well, calling each other by their clan names 'Madiba' and 'Hlathi', and arguing about everything, including whether Shaw was a better playwright than Shakespeare.[3] Mandela criticised Sobukwe for having called for 'Freedom in 1963', which could not possibly have been achieved, and for underestimating the Afrikaners. When some warplanes roared overhead he reminded Sobukwe of their military might. He urged him to read Deneys Reitz's Boer War classic *Commando* in order to understand their capacity for endurance. He was impressed by Sobukwe's reasoning powers, but found him often irritable, and surprisingly subservient to the warders. Sobukwe at first refused to join Mandela in protesting against their conditions, which he argued would amount to acknowledging the state's right to imprison them, but eventually he agreed to make a joint complaint. Sobukwe at that time was regarded as more dangerous than Mandela: when his sentence expired in 1963 he was immediately detained under a special law, known as the 'Sobukwe clause', and kept on Robben Island for a further six years, completely isolated from other prisoners – an ordeal which helped to unhinge him.*[4]

After six months in Pretoria Mandela was abruptly told to pack, because he was being transferred to Robben Island. He was handcuffed to three other political prisoners, herded into a windowless van containing only a bucket, and driven through the night to Cape Town. They were escorted, still handcuffed, to an old boat where they had to stand in the hold, below a porthole through which the warders urinated on them. In a few hours they arrived on the legendary prison island, South Africa's equivalent to Alcatraz.

Robben Island lies only eight miles from the mainland, separated from it by a cold, rough sea which prevents escape. It is two miles long, with some beautiful coastline and sandy beaches, full of wild birds, including small penguins. There are some pretty buildings on its village street, including a church and a schoolhouse. Today the island is a popular tourist attraction. But it had few charms for the political prisoners in their separate enclave, surrounded by maximum security.

Mandela, with his knowledge of Transkei history, was aware that the island had been a prison for Xhosa generals captured by the British in the nineteenth century. The continuity was powerful, and he would frequently refer to such predecessors as Makanna the Left-Handed, who

* When I visited Sobukwe in 1978 while he was under house arrest in Kimberley, I found him tolerant and perceptive about South African politics, but also paranoid, convinced that his body had been bugged by the police.

had died on the island after nearly defeating the British at Grahamstown in 1819. Since then it had been a leper colony and a lunatic asylum before becoming a military reserve in 1936. After Sharpeville it had been re-established as a prison, to hold the waves of political prisoners from different movements, as well as common criminals.[5] From 1962 it had come under a more brutal regime designed to humiliate and demoralise the prisoners; and two sadistic warders, the Kleynhans brothers, had earned a particular reputation for assault. In the two years from 1962 to 1964, according to a report by the academic Neville Alexander, who was imprisoned on Robben Island in 1962, there were weekly, often daily, brutal assaults on political prisoners.[6]

This time Mandela would stay only a few weeks on the island, but long enough to make his mark, and to establish the principle he was to follow throughout his prison years: that the behaviour of the warders was determined by a prisoner's attitude to them. He would often recall his first encounter with one of the Kleynhans brothers, who shouted, 'Here I am your boss!' and told him and the other three prisoners to jog to the cells, as if they were cattle. Mandela insisted on walking in front, deliberately slowing the pace, while Kleynhans yelled, 'We will kill you!'

When they reached their cell, which was flooded with water, two more officers appeared, one of whom shouted at the humblest prisoner that his hair was too long. Mandela intervened, saying: 'Look here, the length of our hair is determined by the regulations.' When the officer approached as if to strike him, Mandela was scared, but managed to say with characteristic bravado: 'If you so much as lay a hand on me, I will take you to the highest court in the land. And when I finish with you, you will be as poor as a church mouse.' The officer continued to threaten him, but Mandela became bolder when he saw that he was shaking.[7] The senior of the two officers – who turned out to be the head of the prison – quietly left the cell, after which his junior soon followed.

Later the four prisoners were taken to a more spacious cell, where after supper Mandela heard a tapping at the window, and a whisper of 'Nelson, come here.' It was a Coloured warder, who brought news from Winnie and offered to bring him tobacco and sandwiches, which he did almost every night. It reassured Mandela that even on the dreaded Robben Island, the warders could vary as much as other human beings.[8]

After a few weeks on the island he was told to pack his belongings again, and was taken back to solitary confinement in Pretoria. There was no explanation, while the government told the press, quite untruthfully, that he had been moved to protect him from being attacked by PAC prisoners.[9] It did not take long for him to learn the real reason.

Early in July Mandela heard that one of the ANC's lawyers, Harold Wolpe, had been detained; then in the prison corridor he was greeted by Thomas Mashefane, who had been the foreman at Lilliesleaf Farm. Several days later, in the prison office, he found himself face to face with the ANC leaders who had been hiding in Rivonia. During Mandela's eight months of incarceration Verwoerd's government had begun cracking down much more effectively on the black opposition, particularly after the secret terrorist offspring of the PAC, Poqo, had begun assassinating whites, first in the Transkei and then in Paarl, near Cape Town. On 1 May 1963 the government rushed through its most drastic legislation yet, again supported by the United Party. It included the notorious 'ninety-day law' which enabled the police to hold anyone for three months incommunicado without trial, thus giving the security police virtually free hands for interrogation and torture.[10] Ten days later the first arrests were made under the law. These were aimed not so much at Poqo as at discovering the whereabouts of the ANC leaders in hiding – including Sisulu, Kathrada and Govan Mbeki, who had all broken their house arrests and disappeared. 'We had not anticipated where and how they would start,' said Hilda Bernstein, whose husband Rusty was soon detained, 'and in that we showed our ignorance.'[11]

The ANC leaders and their allies were still moving in and out of Rivonia in disguise, discussing plans for sabotage and guerrilla warfare which would be launched with the help of selected MK recruits who had already been smuggled out of the country to be trained in Algeria, Ethiopia or the Soviet Union.[12] The high command of MK remained defiant, and on 26 June Sisulu made the first broadcast on Radio Freedom from a secret hideout, promising listeners that he would remain underground in South Africa – thus challenging the police to track him down.

Bruno Mtolo, the saboteur from Durban who was soon to betray his colleagues, described how he once saw the leaders assembled in the thatched house on Lilliesleaf Farm: Sisulu, with a trimmed moustache, wearing a green pullover and jeans, busy drafting a leaflet on a typewriter; Kathrada in sports shirt and sandals, with his ginger hair; Govan Mbeki in a workman's blue overalls.[13] They were preparing a highly ambitious plan called 'Operation Mayibuye', which had been drafted by Joe Slovo and Govan Mbeki. The document began: 'The white state has thrown overboard every pretence of rule by democratic process. Armed to the teeth it has presented the people with only one choice, and that is its overthrow by force and violence.'[14] It went on to propose establishing guerrilla warfare groups throughout South Africa, to be eventually supported by an armed invasion including foreign troops landed by submarines and aircraft.

It was a reckless and unrealistic scheme. Its main proponents in the MK high command were Mbeki, Slovo and Arthur Goldreich. Sisulu and others had strong reservations, and the plan was still being argued over in July. Luthuli, while still recognised as the ANC President, was confined to his home district in Natal, and was out of touch with both the Rivonia group and the ANC abroad: 'He is just not kept informed at all directly about activities outside,' Winnie Mandela wrote to Adelaide Tambo in London after visiting Luthuli. 'This is one of the greatest worries he is having.'[15] But some of the high command of MK were impatient for action, particularly after learning via Mandela of offers of foreign military training. Joe Slovo impulsively wanted to take the plan to Dar-es-Salaam to discuss it with Oliver Tambo and the ANC in exile; his colleagues consented, on the understanding that the document's final form was not yet agreed.[16] But by the time Slovo arrived in Tanzania the whole plot had been uncovered, in all its rashness. 'We had a completely euphoric view of what black independent Africa could do and not do,' Slovo admitted later. The plan 'probably was more than unrealistic'.[17]

By early July 1963 the police interrogations were already yielding information. One of the many people being held – the ANC still does not know who – revealed that Sisulu and his friends sometimes hid in Rivonia, then another gave more precise details of the farm. The bright young investigating officer, Lieutenant Van Wyk, located Lilliesleaf Farm. On 11 July a dry-cleaner's van arrived, and a mass of policemen and dogs rushed out to surround the farm buildings. Sisulu, Mbeki and Kathrada jumped out of a back window, but were quickly caught with the rest. The police collected hundreds of documents, including papers about Operation Mayibuye, and picked up another saboteur, Denis Goldberg, in the main house.[18]

This was the news that Mandela heard from his colleagues in Pretoria jail. He himself had not been at Rivonia since the previous year, just before his arrest, so he could not have authorised Operation Mayibuye.

But he had been the commander of MK, and had left scores of documents in his own handwriting at Lilliesleaf – like so many other revolutionaries, he felt compelled to record his thoughts. He had asked Joe Slovo via Sisulu to destroy these papers, but they were still there, waiting to incriminate him.[19] He was bound to be a chief target of any prosecution, and under the Sabotage Bill of July 1962, he could face the death penalty. Mandela became the First Accused.

The imprisoned leaders all realised that this trial would be more serious and more historic than the Treason Trials, whose basic charge had been flawed. The Rivonia conspirators were clearly guilty of planning sabotage, if not guerrilla warfare, and knew that they had to assemble the best possible defence team. Mandela looked once again to Bram Fischer to lead them, with his combination of legal mastery and commitment: in fact Fischer himself had been in and out of Rivonia, as Mandela and the other accused knew, though the public did not. During the trial he was already planning his own disappearance into the underground.

As a lawyer, Fischer maintained his professional calm. He was shocked by the naïveté and rashness of Operation Mayibuye – 'an entirely unrealistic brainchild of some youthful and adventurous imagination', he called it later during his own trial – but he was determined to give the conspirators the best possible defence, and assembled an even more formidable group of lawyers than before, all of whom would become close colleagues of Mandela. They included Vernon Berrangé, the 'diviner', whom Fischer persuaded to return from London; and a brilliant young barrister, Arthur Chaskalson, who though not at all communist admired Fischer and offered his services. Chaskalson in turn brought in a university friend, Joel Joffe, who had been planning to emigrate to Australia.[20] Joffe, a thin, self-effacing man with a long face, agreed to become the chief attorney, 'the general behind the scenes', as Mandela and the others called him. Another recruit was to become Mandela's special confidant. George Bizos, a big, bushy-haired Greek with an earthy peasant style, had emigrated from Greece as a boy to escape the Nazis. He had first met Mandela at Wits University, and had come to specialise in political trials, in which he gained Fischer's trust.

Joel Joffe had already met Mandela on social occasions, where Mandela looked fifteen years younger than he really was. Now, in his prison garb of short trousers and khaki shirt, Joffe found him 'thin and miserably underweight'. His face was 'hollow-cheeked, a sickly pale yellowish colour.

The skin hung in bags under his eyes.' But Joffe found him still easy-going, jovial and confident, and his morale appeared higher than ever.[21] 'It was almost unnatural,' said George Bizos, 'that he was at peace with himself.'[22] Mandela was still kept separately, as a convicted prisoner, the lowest of the low. He already, as he put it, 'lived in a pervading atmosphere of the death sentence: one head warder came into his cell at night and woke him, to say, 'You are going to sleep for a long, long time.'[23] When Mandela eventually met with his lawyers, Fischer warned him that the prosecution would ask for death sentences. As Mandela said: 'We lived in the shadow of the gallows.'[24]

The trial opened in Pretoria in October 1963 in a frenzy of public excitement whipped up by the newspapers, which told of revolutionary conspiracies leaked by the police. The Supreme Court, the 'Palace of Justice', was surrounded inside and out by uniformed and plain-clothes police, taking careful note of the identities of spectators.

When Mandela appeared in the courtroom from the cells below, some old friends were shocked by how much thinner and paler he had become. 'Have they so easily reduced this proud and sophisticated man,' wondered Hilda Bernstein, 'to the dress and status of the African tolerable to whites – to a "boy"?'[25] But then he flashed his smile, clenched his right fist and boomed '*Amandla!*', to which the blacks in the audience shouted '*Ngawethu!*' – causing panic among the army of security police.[26]

The judge was a respected and rigorous Afrikaner, Quartus de Wet, but the prosecutor, Percy Yutar, a small man with a grandiose, theatrical style, was a right-wing Jewish lawyer, close to the government, who relished confronting Jewish and black enemies. He would later claim that he refused to charge Mandela with high treason: 'I exercised my discretion and charged him only with sabotage.'[27] But he was a merciless prosecutor.

The defence team was convinced from the beginning that, as Joel Joffe put it, 'The heart and kernel of this case was not in this courtroom but in the world outside.'[28] Western governments were certainly watching the trial intently. They were now more aware of Mandela's leadership, and concerned about the possible consequences of a death sentence; but they continued to be constrained by their diplomatic links and investments. The British government was the most likely to influence Verwoerd's government, but was also the most fearful of offending it.

Sir John Maud, the smooth British Ambassador, wrote in his valedictory despatch in April 1963 that he was worried that the well-disciplined

ANC was being outbid by the more primitive and violent PAC. He thought the black resistance, with help from new African nations, would probably develop eventually into 'an organised guerrilla movement backed by the majority of world opinion'. He warned London that 'it will become increasingly difficult to continue treating South Africa as half-ally and half-untouchable at the same time,' and suggested, with prescience, that 'Christianity was a much more serious threat than communism to white supremacy'. But he remained non-committal, concluding: 'We shall need frequently and critically to reconsider where our balance of interest lies.'[29]

The new Ambassador, Sir Hugh Stephenson, was more conservative and ineffectual than Maud. The Foreign Secretary, Lord Home, warned him beforehand not to risk damaging Britain's economic and defence interests, but advised him never to appear to condone apartheid, which would prejudice relations with Africa and the UN. Home advised him to take into account the possibility that South Africa would pass into the hands of African nationalists 'within the foreseeable future', and commended Maud's policy of 'reinsurance' through 'discreet personal contacts with the non-European intelligentsia'.[30] But Sir Hugh was not a man for bold initiatives: a former Indian civil servant who was fond of gin, he never really grasped the realities of Africa, and confused Cape Town with Cairo, and Bechuanaland with Baluchistan. He dreaded offending Afrikaners. Before he presented his credentials to the State President he was reluctantly persuaded to make reference to 'points of view on which my government differs profoundly from yours', but when the South African Foreign Ministry objected, he removed the words.[31]

After the preliminary Rivonia trial had begun, the UN General Assembly passed on 11 October a sensational Resolution 1881, by which every nation except South Africa called for the release of political prisoners.[32] 'They daren't hang them after this!' Fischer told Bizos.[33] But the British Embassy was still reluctant to exert any pressure. The Foreign Office advised Sir Hugh Stephenson to warn Pretoria about the strength of British public opinion. Sir Hugh, after some resistance, eventually did tell the Foreign Minister, Dr Muller, about Britain's concern, while stressing to London that he 'always had my doubts about the value of such approaches'. He also quoted John Arnold, the British barrister representing the International Commission of Jurists at the trial, telling him that the principal accused were 'either communists or heavily communist-influenced', and 'as guilty as hell'.[34] He did not mention Arnold's serious reservations about the trial.[35]

The prosecutor, Percy Yutar, had botched the first indictment, which the judge impatiently quashed, and it was not until 3 December that the full trial began in Pretoria. Mandela remained defiant. When asked how he would plead, he replied simply: 'It is not I, but the government, that should be in the dock. I plead not guilty.'[36] Yutar, with bravura, then presented the revised indictment, which included the sensational central charge:

> The accused deliberately and maliciously plotted and engineered the commission of acts of violence and destruction throughout the country, directed against the offices and homes of municipal officials as well as against all lines and manner of communications. The planned purpose thereof was to bring about in the Republic of South Africa chaos, disorder and turmoil which would be aggravated, according to their plan, by the operation of thousands of trained guerrilla warfare units deployed throughout the country at various vantage points.

He concluded dramatically: '[They] had so planned their campaign that the present year – 1963 – was to be the year of their liberation from the so-called yoke of the white man's domination.' As Yutar unfolded the details of the charges, the defence team was enveloped in gloom: 'Was there any hope whatever,' Joffe wondered, 'that any of the accused would escape the death sentence?'[37] Yutar called a succession of witnesses, many of whom had been broken by interrogation, who fairly accurately described the movements of Mandela and others. Worse still, Yutar could refer to hundreds of documents picked up by the police at Lilliesleaf and elsewhere, which gave details of the ANC's secret operations. The defence lawyers soon came to dread the proliferation of handwritten notes, with 'some thoughts on' various subjects, which the accused had felt impelled to preserve. Govan Mbeki, who acted as co-ordinator at Rivonia, and told the others to burn their secret notes, had kept his own.[38] One secret directive about leafleting an anti-pass campaign was headed 'STRICTLY CONFIDENTIAL', and ended with the instruction: 'This document should not fall into wrong hands. Study and understand it. Then destroy it in the presence of, at least, two other comrades.' It was still there, for the police to pick up.

The cache of documents gave a vivid insight into the limitations of the banned ANC. 'Ort' (Oliver Tambo) exchanged messages in simplistic code with 'Thunder' (Duma Nokwe – Duma means 'thunder' or 'be famous' in Xhosa). They discussed plans to airlift freedom fighters – referred to as 'parcels' or 'matric students' – out of Botswana; but the writers became confused by the code words, and were frustrated by incompetence on the ground. One message from Lusaka reported: 'Of nineteen parcels you sent me twelve confiscated by excise, seven captured.' There was frequent confusion about money: 'We have received moneys from certain countries. Could you please let us know which countries have been helpful so far since the return home of Madiba [Mandela].'[39] The Rivonia documents showed a huge gap between the concept of the armed struggle and its execution, and the lack of what Lenin called 'decisions verified'.

Some of the most damaging documents were in Mandela's handwriting. 'He kept every bit of incriminating paper at Rivonia,' recalled George Bizos. 'It was a tremendous mistake. They gave it to the prosecution on a plate. He never suggested it was the fault of anyone else. He was very magnanimous.'[40] But the documents also give a fascinating picture of Mandela's thinking. There were his handwritten plans to escape from Pretoria jail, showing a dotted line from his cell through the exercise yard: 'I need not mention the disastrous effects politically of any abortive attempt.' There were notes about other revolutionary movements, and the techniques of guerrilla fighting: 'Guerrillas never wage professional warfare and they do not fight decisive battles.' There were quotations from a book about Irgun, the Israeli terrorist group: 'The world does not pity the slaughtered. It only respects those who fight . . . Capacity for sacrifice is the measure of revolt and the father of victory . . . A fighting underground is a veritable state in miniature.' There were notes about the Philippine revolutionary army Hukbalahap: 'People had to be convinced that their destiny was in their own hands.'

There were also more general quotations about politics and leadership, including some from a biography of the brilliant Boer War guerrilla leader General Christiaan de Wet: 'I would rather stand among my own people on a manure heap, than live in a palace among strangers.' There were extracts from a biography of General J.M. Hertzog by Oswald Pirow: 'Hertzog has become too much of a statesman and too little of a politician.' There were notes about Frederick the Great: 'He had in his army two mules who had been through forty campaigns, but they were still mules.' There were titbits from Field Marshal Montgomery: 'Total war demands total fitness'; and even from President Truman: 'A leader is a man who has the ability to get other people to do what they don't want to do, and like it.'

But the most apparently incriminating notes were sixty-two pages on a writing pad about communism, in Mandela's handwriting. They were in four parts, including one on Stalin's *The Foundation of Leninism*. The most embarrassing was the first part, mostly based on a pamphlet by the Chinese communist Liu Shao-chi on 'How to be a Good Communist', but including Mandela's comment: 'Under a CP government South Africa will become a land of milk and honey . . . There will be no unemployment, starvation and disease.'[41] It was very awkward for the defence lawyers, but Mandela explained it by recalling that he was merely paraphrasing the Chinese document, as part of an argument to show how turgid Marxist writing could be.[42] Rusty Bernstein later confirmed that he had lent Mandela the pamphlet, together with many others.[43] And Mandela's copious notes from Rivonia showed him as a tireless copier of documents from all kinds of sources.

The prosecution's star witness was publicly referred to only as 'Mr X', but was in fact Bruno Mtolo, the shrewd saboteur who had been at Mandela's meeting in Durban shortly before his arrest, and who had visited Rivonia. He had now turned state's evidence. 'I could not believe my eyes when I saw him take the witness stand,' wrote Mandela afterwards.[44] Mtolo, who had an excellent memory, was the first witness to directly connect Mandela with MK, by giving his account of what Mandela had told the saboteurs at their meeting in Durban: how African leaders had promised him military training and funds, how the campaign in South Africa would extend to guerrilla warfare, and how communists should conceal their true beliefs because they were unpopular in Africa. Mtolo insisted that the ANC was completely dominated by communists.[45]

It was devastating testimony. 'Once my notes were handed in I realised that the state would be able to secure a conviction against me,' Mandela wrote in jail. 'The evidence of Mtolo made this a certainty.'[46] Mandela would not deny his leadership of MK, nor his talk with the saboteurs in Durban: he would only deny that the communists had concealed their beliefs. The defence lawyers warned him that his admissions could cost him his life, but Mandela told them that he must accept responsibility for his leadership; and he wanted the truth to come out. He had, he said, to 'explain to the country and the world where Umkhonto we Sizwe stood, and why; to clarify its aims and policy, to reveal the true facts from the half-truths and distortions of the state case. If in doing this his life should be at stake, so be it.' He was now clearly determined to represent the struggle in his own person.

It was a tough position for his lawyers to defend. When Berrangé cross-examined Mtolo he was able to knock some holes in his evidence – for example pointing out that in Durban Mandela had said that communists who went abroad for MK should not try to advance the Party's cause or make communist propaganda, which would discredit MK. But the judge still seemed impressed by Mtolo, and in the meantime, as Joel Joffe commented: 'Our chief accused, Nelson Mandela, had admitted the main burden of the charge.'

The discussions between the accused and their lawyers were crucial, but were constrained by the conditions. The prison commander had built a special room, where the accused were lined up in front of a grating, facing their lawyers, seated on high stools like customers at a milk bar: when the lawyers first arrived, Mandela stood up smiling, and said: 'What will it be today, gentlemen? Chocolate or ice-cream soda?'[47] The lawyers got to know the accused intimately, and to feel the full strength of Mandela's personality. George Bizos was amazed at how he refused to be intimidated by the warders: one day he complained to the commanding officer about the rickety desk on which he had to write notes for his lawyers. Aucamp let fly: 'You're no longer an attorney, you're a prisoner! . . . You can't give orders.' Mandela coolly replied, 'Have you finished, Colonel? Then I will return to my work with the lawyers.' The next day, a marvellous table arrived.[48]

Joel Joffe reckoned that Mandela and Sisulu were the most at risk, with a fifty-fifty chance of hanging. But he found that Mandela's courage never wavered: 'It was quite different from courage in the field of battle, when you can be brave without thinking.' In Joffe's opinion, 'Nelson Mandela emerged quite naturally as the leader. He has, in my view, all the attributes of a leader – the engaging personality, the ability, the stature, the calm, the diplomacy, the tact and the conviction. When I first met him, I found him attractive and interesting. By the time the case finished I regarded him as a really great man. I began to notice how his personality and stature impressed itself not just on the group of the accused, but on the prison and the prison staff themselves.'

The principal accused had already admitted their involvement in sabotage and the planning of MK, and were determined to make a political justification for it. But the most serious charge – which the prosecutor, Percy Yutar, called 'the cornerstone of the state case' – was that they had approved Operation Mayibuye, which called for a nationwide guerrilla war assisted by foreign troops and arms. Mandela and Sisulu explained to the defence lawyers that the ANC had not yet approved the plan at the time of the police raid on Rivonia, though it might have become necessary if all other means failed. But Govan Mbeki, the oldest and most dogmatic of the accused, insisted that Operation Mayibuye provided the basis of all MK activities, and had been approved by the ANC as well as MK. His insistence could have sent him and his friends to the gallows. 'If it was proved that they had embarked on an armed revolution,' said Joffe afterwards, 'it would have been difficult under the Sabotage Act for the judge not to sentence them to death.'

But Mandela was now preoccupied with his political argument. He was determined, as in his previous trial, to make a final speech about his political ideals, which he could only do through a statement from the dock. This could not be cross-examined, and would therefore carry less weight with the judge. But he did not want to appear under cross-examination to be going back on his basic convictions – like the movie mogul Sam Goldwyn (he suggested) saying, 'These are my principles, gentlemen; but if you don't like them, I've got others.'[49] Mandela spent many evenings in his cell working on the speech with the help of his colleagues, lawyers and others. He was influenced by earlier great revolutionary speeches, such as Castro's 'History will absolve me,' and particularly wanted to make a powerful impact overseas.[50] He produced an eloquent statement in his own hand which clearly explained his political development. But the lawyers were worried by its defiant candour, which might provoke the judge to hang Mandela – particularly as it ended with the words: 'it is an ideal for which I am prepared to die'.* Mandela refused to leave them out, but eventually agreed to insert the words: 'if needs be'.[52]

* I had an insight into the speech when I visited the courtroom, reporting the trial for the *Observer*: as Mandela came up from the cells below he smiled at me and I involuntarily gave the clenched-fist salute in response, which alarmed the surrounding police: I was taken out for questioning before being allowed back. At the end of the day I was asked by Mandela

The defence case began with Mandela's long speech from the dock, which could not be interrupted, to the dismay of Yutar, who had been preparing for days to cross-examine him. For four hours Mandela explained his beliefs and political ideas, retracing his tribal background and early nationalism, and his conversion to multi-racialism. He admitted that he was the leader of MK and had planned sabotage; but he insisted again that non-violence had proved powerless to prevent the country from drifting into civil war. Sabotage, he claimed, offered the best hope for future race relations.

He compared his co-operation with communists to Churchill's co-operation with Stalin; but he also gave a more personal explanation, recalling how communists were the only political group who were prepared to treat Africans as human beings and equals. He admitted he had been influenced by Marxist thought, but denied that he was a communist, and praised the British and American parliamentary systems, which the communists regarded as reactionary. He stressed the Africans' lack of human dignity and rights, and the destruction of black family life, which was breaking down moral standards and fomenting violence: 'Africans want a just share in the whole of South Africa; they want security and a stake in society.' The ANC, he said, was engaged in 'a struggle for the right to live'.

He finished with his own apologia: 'During my lifetime I have dedicated myself to this struggle of the African people. I have fought against white domination, and I have fought against black domination. I have cherished the ideal of a democratic and free society in which all persons live together in harmony with equal opportunities.' He paused and looked at the judge: 'It is an ideal which I hope to live for and achieve.' Then, dropping his voice, he concluded: 'But if needs be, it is an ideal for which I am prepared to die.'[53] There was thirty seconds' silence, which seemed to Mandela like many minutes. To Joel Joffe it seemed like the silence after a play, before thunderous applause – but without the applause.[54]

The speech was the most effective of Mandela's whole political career. It identified him clearly as the leader not just of the ANC, but of the multi-racial opposition to apartheid. The anti-colonial clichés of his

through his lawyers to look through the draft of the speech he was preparing, and to advise about its impact on overseas opinion. I spent the evening going through it with the lawyers but I could suggest only minor changes, most of which were not accepted.[51]

earlier speeches had given way to a much more thoughtful and personal analysis. His words reverberated round the world, providing a manifesto for anti-apartheid campaigners everywhere. Some Western diplomats even began to change their view of Mandela as being dominated by communists. 'The reasons he sets out for collaboration with the communists are very difficult to answer,' commented John Wilson in the Foreign Office, while John Ure of the Information Research Department (used by MI6 to provide anti-communist propaganda) felt that Britain was losing ground with black South Africans as a price of its cautious policies: Mandela, he said, was 'going to be a popular figure over the whole continent whether we like it or not', and the secret service ('our friends') should take note of his admissions about collaborating with communists. Britain could make some propaganda from the message that 'Mandela and Co do not really like communism so they should be wary of playing along with it.'[55]

The accused had been buoyed up by the growing support from abroad, not only from many African countries but also, more to Mandela's surprise, from Britain. Halfway through the trial he had been elected President of the Students' Union of London University: 'an institution he had never attended', Joffe said, 'by people he did not know'.[56] The British government was now being pressed to intervene to prevent Mandela from being hanged. David Astor of the *Observer* wrote to the Foreign Secretary, R.A. Butler, to say that Mandela was 'one of the most impressive of all the African leaders'.[57] Butler was sympathetic, but worried that any British attempts at intervention might prove counterproductive.[58] Leon Brittan, the Chairman of the Conservative Bow Group, warned that a dead Mandela would become a martyr, making a solution to South Africa's problems even less likely.[59] A delegation from the anti-apartheid movement, including the Labour MP Barbara Castle and the future Lord Chancellor Lord Gardiner, visited the Foreign Office, but were told that any representations could damage Mandela's prospects.[60] On 7 May 1964 the Prime Minister, Alec Douglas-Home, offered to send a private message to Verwoerd about the trial. But Sir Hugh Stephenson recommended that 'no more pressure should be exerted', and contrary to some published reports there is no evidence that the message was sent.[61] When the South African Ambassador called on the Foreign Office that month he was told that the government was now under less pressure to take a stronger line against South Africa, though death sentences would bring the matter to a head again.[62] The British Embassy in Pretoria reported to London that Major-General Hendrik van den Bergh, the head of the South African Special Branch (who would later become head of the secret service BOSS), did not expect death sentences, and that Yutar would not ask for them.[63] But it was not until early June, a week before the verdict was delivered, that George Bizos was told by the inebriated British Consul-General Leslie Minford, who was thought to have intelligence links: 'George, there won't be a death sentence.'[64]

After Mandela's speech, Walter Sisulu had to face the more testing ordeal of cross-examination by Yutar. It had worried his lawyers beforehand, as they would not be able to help him, but they were aware that Sisulu, despite his lack of formal education, had a powerful intellect. 'He had an amazing knack of asking a simple question and demanding an answer,' said Bizos. 'The answer became self-evident, and was the solution to the problem.'[65] In the event Sisulu survived five days of questioning by Yutar, and many interjections from the judge, with coolness and shrewdness, and refused to incriminate any of the other conspirators. 'To sentence such a man to death,' thought Joffe, 'would not be easy for any judge.'[66]

Soon after Sisulu had given his evidence, his wife Albertina was invited by the British Consul, with a few other black guests, to the Queen's Birthday party in Johannesburg: when they arrived, five of the white catering staff walked out. The Rivonia prisoners were encouraged by the British invitation – the first to anyone openly associated with the ANC – but a Consulate spokesman explained that Albertina had been invited solely 'as a person well-known for her social work and charitable activities'.[67]

Sisulu was followed in the witness box by Kathrada and Raymond Mhlaba, two other Rivonia conspirators against whom the prosecutor's case was much weaker; then by Rusty Bernstein, against whom it was the weakest of all. Govan Mbeki came next; he was undeniably at the heart of the conspiracy, but did not defend Operation Mayibuye in court, and gave nothing away that was not already in evidence. He was followed by Denis Goldberg, Elias Motsoaledi and Andrew Mlangeni, also Rivonia conspirators. Then Percy Yutar delivered his final address – including extravagant accusations, some of which were punctured by the judge, but which still provided deadly ammunition – before Chaskalson and Fischer gave their final defence.

Judge Quartus de Wet adjourned for three weeks to consider his verdict, which he pronounced on 11 June. He accepted that the accused had not authorised Operation Mayibuye: 'It had not been proved that the plan had progressed beyond the preparation stage, and I adhere to this view.' But he judged that the ANC was a 'communist-dominated organisation', quoting Mandela's own account of the views of other African leaders. And he found all the accused, with the exception of Bernstein, guilty of sabotage.[68] Mandela was angry that Kathrada and Mhlaba had not also been acquitted, but he was not surprised by the verdict on himself. His only uncertainty was about the sentence, which would be delivered the next day. He was prepared for death, and thought of the words from Shakespeare's *Measure for Measure*:

> Be absolute for death; either death or life
> Shall thereby be the sweeter.[69]

If he was sentenced to death he had decided he would make a defiant statement, for which he wrote some very brief notes:

1 Statement from the dock.
2 I meant everything I said.
3 The blood of many patriots in this country has been shed for demanding treatment in conformity with civilised standards.
4 *
5 If I must die, let me declare for all to know that I will meet my fate like a man.[70]

Mandela, Mbeki and Sisulu had all decided early in the trial that whatever the sentence, they would not appeal for mercy: since this was a political trial, an appeal would be an anti-climax, and they wanted to convey the message, Mandela said, that 'no sacrifice was too great in the struggle for freedom'. He was convinced that the Appeal Court would not reverse the judgement anyway.[71] The defence lawyers were dismayed by the prisoners' refusal to appeal, and also stunned by their courage: 'The decision was politically unassailable,' Bram Fischer wrote to a young friend in exile, after describing the prisoners' discussion. 'I want you to know what incredibly brave men you and others will have to be to be their suc-

* Paragraph 4 consisted of five words which not even Mandela himself can now decipher or remember.

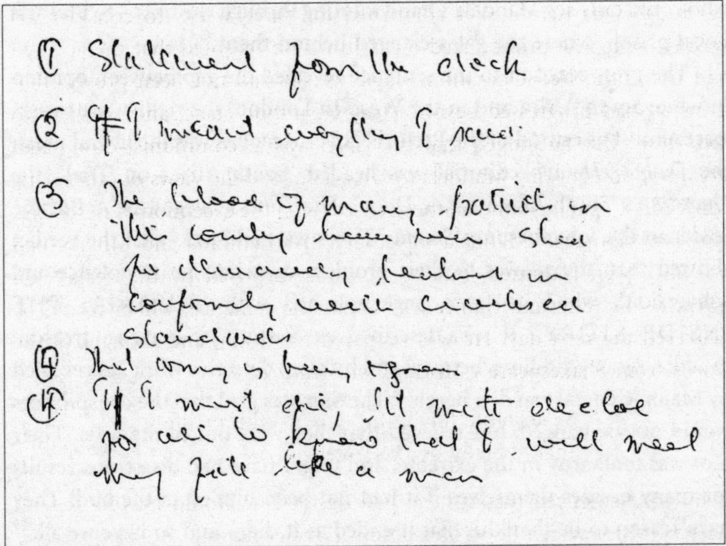

(1) Statement from the dock
(2) That I meant everything I said
(3) The blood of many patriots in this country have been shed for demanding treatment in conformity with civilised standards
(4) That army is beginning to grow
(4) If I must die, let me declare for all to know that I will meet my fate like a man

Mandela's notes for the statement he intended to make from the dock if he was sentenced to death.

cessors.'[72] But after the verdict the lawyers made a plea for mitigation, which was supported in court the next morning by the liberal novelist Alan Paton, who stressed the ANC leaders' sincerity and the importance of clemency for future peace, in spite of his worries about communism. 'I had no doubt that Bram Fischer was "using" me,' Paton wrote afterwards, 'and I had no objection to being used for a purpose of this kind.'[73]

When de Wet came to give sentence, Mandela was heartened to notice that 'it was not the accused in the dock who were visibly nervous but the judge himself.'[74] The judge said he had decided not to impose the supreme penalty – there was a gasp of relief in the courtroom – but that was the only leniency he could show. He then sentenced eight of them to life imprisonment. Mandela actually smiled; Sisulu was so relieved that he felt almost as if he'd been discharged.[75]

There was confusion in the courtroom as spectators rushed out with the news. Mandela could not even gesture to Winnie and his mother, the bent and bewildered figure beside her, before the police bore down on him and the other prisoners to take them to the cells below. After half an hour they were driven away in a police van – avoiding the crowd, who could only see Mandela's hand saluting through the bars – to Pretoria Local prison, where the gates clanged behind them.[76]

The press reaction to the sentence revealed the gap between opinion in white South Africa and in the West. In London, the right-wing papers were almost as critical of the Pretoria government as was the liberal press: the *Daily Telegraph* editorial was headed 'South Africa on Trial', the *Guardian*'s 'South Africa in the Dock', *The Times*'s 'Siege Law'.[77] But the leader in the Johannesburg *Sunday Times* warned blacks that the verdict showed that 'the answer to their problem does not lie in violence and subversion', while its front page splashed with 'RIVONIA: THE INSIDE STORY'. It was described as 'a story of intrigue, treason, muddle, money-fiddling, betrayal and brilliant detective work', as revealed by Major-General van den Bergh.[78] The *Star* was glad that the conspirators would not be hanged, but relieved that they were out of the way: 'Their plot was foolhardy in the extreme, and might have had disastrous results for many besides themselves if it had not been nipped in the bud. They have reason to be thankful that it ended as it did – and so have we all.'[79]

The British and American governments both considered bringing pressure on South Africa to reduce the sentences, but the American Ambassador agreed with Sir Hugh Stephenson, who thought that any intervention would 'produce the most strongly adverse reaction'.[80] The Foreign Office found the argument 'not wholly convincing', and looked for some American support. The Foreign Secretary Rab Butler wanted Stephenson to meet the South African Foreign Minister, Dr Muller, to 'express views in favour of abatement', but no such talk is recorded.[81]

In fact Mandela's refusal to appeal against the sentence helped let the diplomats off the hook, and the international attention soon subsided. The British Embassy was keen to resume friendly relations with Pretoria, who by July (the South Africans noted) were finding the Americans and the British more sympathetic towards them.[82] The British were now privately expecting that Mandela would eventually be released to play a useful role – like other 'prison graduates' elsewhere in Africa or in India. 'We can be very thankful that the judge did not give a death sentence,' Stephenson told Rab Butler in September, 'because it means that a leader of the calibre of Nelson Mandela, with his credentials enhanced by a term of imprisonment, should be available for the dialogue between black and white which must eventually take place in South Africa.' But Stephenson also warned that new black leaders would emerge, who would be 'unlikely to share the distaste for violence and the other civilised values that were a facet of Mr Mandela's speech'.[83]

It was ironic that Mandela was being praised as a possible saviour, worthy of Western support, by diplomats who had never tried to meet him, just when he was put completely out of their reach. Pretoria was confident that within a few years he would be out of sight and out of mind, the ANC forgotten and abandoned. Their expectations were soon close to being fulfilled.

Mandela went to jail with all the glory of a lost leader, in an aura of martyrdom. He could not, it was true, claim to be either a great military commander or a revolutionary mastermind. The ANC had been incapacitated by bans, and was frequently amateurish, as Rivonia had shown, while MK was a long way from being a disciplined fighting force. For the past decade Mandela's leadership had appeared not so much in a climb up an organised hierarchy as in successive images of the man of action, leading from the front: the chief of volunteer defiers; the militant speech-maker charged with treason; the bearded Black Pimpernel in hiding; the tribal patriot in full costume 'carrying Africa on his back'; the guerrilla commander in khaki fatigues, carrying a pistol. These images often seemed more theoretical than real, but the symbolism, the example, the clothes and performance were essential to his dramatic personification of his people, as they were to Churchill or to Gandhi. In his ability to reflect the people's mood and embody their aspirations, Mandela had become a master-politician of his time.

He had emerged from his two trials with more strength and depth than even some close friends had imagined possible. The earlier arrogance and aggression had subsided; the showmanship expressed in different roles had contracted into a single clear commitment; and no one could now doubt the extent of his sacrifice. His drive for leadership had met its challenge, and he seemed, as George Bizos noted, at peace with himself. The greater ordeal was still to come. For all his battlefields would now contract into a tiny stage, which would provide a much more intimate trial of character.

PART II

1964–1990

15

Master of my Fate

1964–1971

MANDELA'S LIFE SENTENCE was a more serious test of his resilience than his two previous years in jail. He was now cut off from the world in his prime, at the age of forty-six, with no end in sight. He had never been an ascetic like Gandhi or Lenin: in his letters he would constantly hark back to the delights of Soweto or the Transkei; to the food, the landscape, the women, the music. Now all the bright scenery and characters would contract into the single bare stage of his cell and the communal courtyard.

But there was a powerful consolation: he was not alone. With him were some of his closest friends, who could reinforce each other's morale and purpose, and develop a greater depth and self-awareness. At an age when most politicians tend to forget their earlier idealism in the pursuit of power, Mandela was compelled to think more deeply about his principles and ideas. In the microcosm of prison, stripped of all political trappings – platforms, megaphones, newspapers, crowds, well-tailored suits – and confined with his colleagues every day, he was able, as he put it, to stand back from himself, to see himself as others saw him.[1] He learnt to control his temper and strong will, to empathise and persuade, and to extend his influence and authority, not just over the other prisoners, but over the warders.

Between the black prisoners and their white guards, the balance of influence was constantly shifting inside the closed world. But gradually the prisoners, with much stronger motivation and cohesion than the warders, established their influence, with Mandela as their leader. There were many parallels with other twentieth-century political prisoners – with Gandhi in India, or the IRA in Northern Ireland's H-blocks – but the letters, prison records and recollections of the Robben Islanders over the next twenty years provide a unique record of the psycho-politics of a jail where the prisoners could ultimately dominate their guards.

The seven prisoners stayed for a few days in Pretoria Local, still buoyant after escaping the death sentence. At 1 a.m. on 12 June 1964 they were told to pack their belongings, because they were going immediately to Robben Island. The other six were put in handcuffs and leg-irons like slaves; but Mandela was not manacled.[2] They were herded into a police van and driven to the military airport. They were flown in an old, unheated military Dakota, landing just after dawn on a cold, windy island airstrip, surrounded by armed guards.

Robben Island had become a more inhuman place since Mandela had been there two years before. It had been prepared to receive many more long-term prisoners, and reorganised on strict apartheid principles, with the warders, all white, determined to impose their racial supremacy. There had been some brutal 'carry-ons' – as the warders called their assaults. They had recently beaten up the political prisoners, leaving one ANC activist, Andrew Masondo, with serious wounds.[3]

Mandela once again began with a confrontation. This time it was on the question of clothes, which he always saw as a part of his dignity which he would not give up. The seven were issued with the standard short khaki trousers – the uniform of the 'native boy' – except Kathrada, who as an Indian was entitled to long trousers. Mandela protested about the shorts, and a few days later found a pair of long trousers dumped in his cell. 'No pin-striped three-piece suit has ever pleased me as much,' he wrote. But when other prisoners were denied long trousers he protested again, and had his own taken away. It was not until three years later that they all wore long trousers.[4]

Mandela was treated more carefully than the others: he suspected that the prison authorities were concerned about his important friends and royal connections.[5] On the plane he had not been manacled, and when he arrived on the island he was offered a special diet because of his medical condition. He was allowed to continue his correspondence studies for his LLB at London University. He received law books via the British Embassy, arranged again by David Astor in London. 'I will do everything in my power,' he wrote to the Ambassador, 'to justify the confidence he has in me.'[6] Mandela was soon given a table and chair for his cell, though he was not allowed certain crucial books.[7] Granted these rare privileges, he felt all the more need to keep very close to his colleagues.

After a few days in the old jail building, the seven men were moved on 25 June – the day before the traditional protest day of the ANC. They were driven to a bleak new structure which had just been completed: a low rectangle built around a stone courtyard, with three sides containing rows of small cells; the fourth was a high wall which provided a catwalk for a warder with a gun. They were all given similar cells along one side, called the Isolation Section, or Section B. Mandela's cell was eight feet by seven feet, with a small barred window looking on to the courtyard, and was equipped with a straw mat and three threadbare blankets. It would be his home for the next eighteen years.

At first the prisoners and their lawyers expected they would serve ten years at the most.[8] On their way to Robben Island from Pretoria the friendly young investigating officer, Lieutenant Van Wyk, had assured them that world opinion would get them out in five years: 'the girls will be waiting for you'.[9] Some of the prisoners, Mandela noted, were seriously asking whether they would still be there at Christmas.[10] But they soon had to face the fact that they would be on Robben Island for a long time, and that their life would be 'unredeemably grim'.[11] He still had something to learn about brutality. 'You have no idea of the cruelty of man against man,' he said later, 'until you have been in a South African prison with white warders and black prisoners.'[12] They had no access to radio or newspapers, and at first could only write and receive one letter, of a maximum of five hundred words, every six months. They could only correspond with their immediate family; and Mandela's first letter – from Winnie – was blotted out by the censor. Censored portions of letters would be sent on to the Commissioner of Prisons to provide political background, while some letters to and from prisoners containing supposedly political information would be withheld, examined and then retained in the prison records – revealing both the doggedness and the pettiness of the surveillance.[13]

The political prisoners remained extraordinarily sure of the power of their cause and of their ideas, in total contrast to the common-law prisoners in other cells. 'What was important,' said Mandela after his release, 'was the fact that the ideas for which we were sent to Robben Island would never die. And we were therefore able to go through some of the harshest experiences which a human being can have behind bars – especially in a South African prison where the warders were drawn from a community which has always treated blacks like pieces of rag.'[14] 'We never lost confidence,' Sisulu recalled. 'Analysing Rivonia, we thought the policies for which we stood could be sustained, whether we were alive or dead. We had confidence in ideas.'[15] 'If you enter prison in a negative spirit every moment can be hell,' said Kathrada. 'Nobody had in mind that Mandela would be president, but we knew we would win.'[16] Despite the setbacks, Mandela was convinced, as he wrote in 1975, that 'In my lifetime I shall step out into the sunshine, walk with firm feet.'[17] 'Man can adapt to the worst of conditions if he feels he is not alone,' said Mac Maharaj, who arrived on Robben Island early in 1965, 'if he feels he has support in what he is doing.'[18]

After two weeks on the island the prisoners had a tantalisingly brief contact with the mainland when their lawyers Bram Fischer and Joel Joffe were allowed to visit them, to ask again whether they wished to appeal. They all said no, believing that a second trial would be an anti-climax; while Mandela was sure that an appeal would not succeed anyway.[19] He was delighted to see Fischer again, but was puzzled that when he asked Fischer about his wife Molly he turned away. After the lawyers had left, Mandela was told that Molly Fischer had just been killed in a car crash. He was allowed to write a letter of condolence, but the prison never posted it.[20] Soon afterwards Fischer – whose code-name was 'Shorty' – disappeared underground; when George Bizos, Mandela's other lawyer, visited the island, Mandela gave a questioning gesture with one hand, while holding the other hand low, meaning 'What's happened to Shorty?'[21]

The prisoners' routine was deliberately harsh, as part of the punishment. They were woken at 5.30 a.m. to clean their cells and wash and shave in cold water in an iron bucket. They were given breakfast in the courtyard, from a drum filled with maize porridge, which Mandela found almost inedible, accompanied by a drink of baked maize brewed in hot water. They were inspected by a warder, to whom they had to doff their hats. Then they worked till noon in the cold courtyard in midwinter, sitting in rows hammering stones into gravel while the warders watched them. It was a punishment which could (wrote Neville Alexander in his subsequent report) 'drive the most phlegmatic man into a state of fury . . . To have to sit in the sun without moving and (for months at the beginning) without being allowed to speak to one's neighbour was hell on earth.'[22]

At noon they had lunch of more maize, boiled in kernels. Then they worked again until four, when they washed for half an hour with cold sea-water in a bathroom, where they could exchange a few words. Then they had supper of more maize, sometimes with a soggy vegetable or gristly meat, in their cells. At eight the night warder patrolled the corridor to ensure that they were not reading or writing; though they could sometimes whisper to each other, and prisoners who were studying were soon allowed to read till later. A bare forty-watt bulb burned all night in each cell, and the prisoners were left with their bare beds and lonely thoughts until the morning.

In January 1965 they began much harder labour in the lime quarry, which was to be the centre of Mandela's daily life for the next few years. There they had to hack away the rock to reach the layers of lime, which they then dug out with a pick and shovel. As a workplace it was pitiless, with no escape or protection from the cold in winter or the dazzling glare and heat of midsummer. 'I was always thankful I never had to go into that hole, a veritable furnace,' said the warder James Gregory. 'In summer the walls deflected any cooling breeze sweeping in off the ocean. Not only were they being burned from above by the sun, but also within the quarry where the sun's glare rebounded off the white stone, reflecting into their eyes and burning them.'[23] For three years they were refused dark glasses, and many were left with damaged eyesight. Kathrada was refused dark glasses because, according to a letter from the Commissioner of Prisons, he belonged to the category of persons who wanted to be above his fellows by wearing dark glasses and carrying a folded umbrella and a briefcase.[24] After three years they were allowed sunglasses if they paid for them; Mandela's eyes never recovered, and even after an operation, he reads with difficulty.

Mandela preferred the exertion, the open air and the glimpses of nature in the quarry to enclosure in the courtyard. The prisoners were soon able to work at their own rhythm – for a short time with the help of African worksongs, which became a political contest. In 1965 they were joined in the quarry by three hardened criminals, who began to provoke them – clearly with the warders' approval – with a mocking worksong, '*Befunani e Rivonia?*' (What did you want at Rivonia?). The political prisoners responded with their own worksongs, which became bolder, including a Xhosa song which said: 'the white man's work is never finished: hold your knees' – that is, go slower. But one warder, Jordaan, understood Xhosa, and singing was soon banned.[25]

Mandela was in a very small, enclosed world. The thirty-odd political prisoners in the isolation section could briefly communicate with each other when they washed, or took their meals, or in the quarry. But they were cut off from the rest of the prison. All the changing pageants of their lives with their families, colleagues and communities contracted into the minimal scenery of a repetitive, long-running play. 'The only audience was ourselves and our oppressors,' said Mandela, always aware of his stage.[26] 'We were a universe of thirty people,' said one of them, Eddie Daniels.[27]

At the core of this universe were the seven men of Rivonia, who had known each other for ten or twenty years – including Mandela and his most trusted friends, Sisulu and Kathrada. Sisulu, six years his senior, was still Mandela's chief mentor: 'Nelson knew that it was really Sisulu who had made him and moulded him in so many ways,' thought Fikile Bam, one of the younger prisoners; 'I don't know of anyone to whom Walter was not acceptable as a leader.'[28] Mandela wrote in jail how much he admired Sisulu's clear vision and judgement, his accessibility and openness to new ideas, his simplicity and love of nature. He shared some of Sisulu's mannerisms, like the phrase 'what-you-call'. Sisulu had helped to teach Mandela how to see the best in everyone – which could exasperate more combative colleagues – but in any dangerous situation Sisulu was in the forefront.[29] 'He was a lamb at home,' said Bam, 'but when it came to the chase he was a lion. He was soft as a person, but never soft on principle.'[30]

Kathrada, much the youngest of the seven, and the only Indian among them, was equally steadfast, with an unselfishness and inner calm which may have owed something to his Islamic background. He had been a communist since his schooldays, but he could make fun of the dogmatists, and Mandela enjoyed his devastating repartee. He was always loyal to Mandela, whom he would call 'Mdala' (the old one), out of respect, but like Sisulu he felt free to criticise: Mandela saw them both as mirrors through which he could see himself truthfully.[31]

Govan Mbeki was the oldest and best educated. He was a big man with an innocent smile and a preacher's resonant voice. The son of a Christian peasant farmer, he had been educated by missionaries and named after the first principal of Lovedale, William Govan.[32] Like Mandela, he went to Healdtown and Fort Hare, after which he became a shopkeeper, teacher, journalist and political organiser. He found a new faith in Marxism, and devoured history, politics and economics, all with a strong Marxist flavour. His stubbornness could embarrass his colleagues, as it had when he had committed them to Operation Mayibuye; and his pedagogic style was at odds with Mandela's questioning approach. 'He had a more theoretical militancy,' said Sisulu, 'while we had to be realistic in assessing the situation.'[33]

Raymond Mhlaba was close to Mbeki, and was also from the Eastern Cape. The son of a policeman, he had bravely been one of the first to join the Defiance Campaign; Mandela enjoyed his down-to-earth approach as a 'son of the soil'.[34] He was more reluctant than Mbeki and others to join in political argument, and Mandela came to appreciate his conciliatory approach. He was still deeply influenced by his mission education, and Kathrada was once amused to hear Mhlaba, losing his temper with a warder, calling him 'You fu . . . fascist!' 'Those mission boys,' said Kathrada. 'They would rather be violent than swear.'[35]

The other two Rivonia prisoners, Andrew Mlangeni and Elias Motsoaledi, were working-class trades unionists who had sacrificed their livelihoods for the struggle. They had been less central to the Rivonia plots, and had expected to be acquitted. They both came from very poor backgrounds, and had educated themselves. Mandela went to some trouble to help in the education of Elias's children.

Other ANC members in the isolation section had been convicted in other trials. They included Dennis Brutus, a poet from Port Elizabeth, and two veterans of the Treason Trial: George Peake, a Coloured campaigner from Cape Town; and Billy Nair, a courageous Indian saboteur from Durban. Nair had already been on the island for four months, and the ill-treatment had made him very aggressive. When he joined the isolation section Mandela befriended him, and persuaded him to calm down. Nair was influenced by Mandela's stoical approach, but always found him maddeningly reticent about his personal life.[36]

Early in 1965 a batch of guerrilla fighters arrived in the isolation section. They had been sentenced following the so-called 'Little Rivonia Trials', and included Wilton Mkwayi, a trades unionist from Port Elizabeth who had commanded MK after the Rivonia arrests; Laloo Chiba, a former tailor who would prove to have invaluable skills in transcribing documents in tiny handwriting; and Mac Maharaj, a sophisticated Indian from Durban who became one of Mandela's trusted allies. A slender man with a neat goatee beard, educated at the London School of Economics as well as Natal University, Maharaj combined a sharp mind with great courage, and resisted severe torture. On Robben Island he would go through a short period of despair in 1970, when he was thirty-five, but he recovered his spirit to begin plotting new schemes for escape.[37]

The ANC members were mixed up with prisoners from other political parties, which gave Mandela a unique opportunity to get to know them better. It was an extraordinary decision by the government to concentrate all political prisoners on the island. 'Some people argued it would be better to spread prisoners over the 156 jails in the country,' General Willemse, one of the commanding officers on Robben Island, told me afterwards. 'But there would be a negative effect of spreading their influence. It was better to keep an eye on them.'[38] 'They thought we were so much poison we had to be kept in one bottle,' said one PAC prisoner, Dikgang Moseneke. 'And that worked wonders.'[39] Mandela thought it was the government's greatest mistake, for it allowed rival parties to find common ground, which they never had outside jail.[40] And Robben Island soon became a political laboratory, or workshop.

At first, prisoners from the ANC's chief rival body the PAC were in the majority. Their founder-President Robert Sobukwe was kept in a separate house on the island until 1969 – a cruel isolation which helped to disorient him later – but others were increasingly accessible. Many PAC members began by bitterly resenting the ANC prisoners, who included Indians and Coloureds. 'We saw things only in terms of the colour of the skin of an individual,' said Kwedi Mkalipi, who arrived in 1966. 'Then we came to Robben Island. It was a queer situation because now, for the first time, we were bundled together with the ANC, who we sincerely believed were all Marxists. So this led us to be chauvinistic in our approach.' Mkalipi would never forget his first approach from Walter Sisulu: 'I come from your area,' said Sisulu, 'and Mandela also comes from your area; and Mandela would like to talk with you. I know your attitude, but in here this is no place to voice our differences.'[41]

Mandela found most of the PAC prisoners very insecure, 'unashamedly anti-communist and anti-Indian'.[42] Kathrada thought they were 'colourless, bigoted, narrow and racialistic', with 'massive inferiority complexes'.[43] But Mandela was determined to establish dialogue, to provide the basis for unity later outside. He had talks with Zeph Mothopeng, a rugged ex-teacher with unbending principles who was one of the co-founders of the PAC; but made little impact before Mothopeng left the island in 1967. He had more success with Mothopeng's successor Clarence Makwetu (later President of the PAC), whom he found more balanced and sensible, but the dialogue collapsed after Makwetu left and was succeeded by John Pokela.[44] Most PAC prisoners would retain their differences with the ANC, but many came to respect their viewpoint and their leadership.

Mandela faced more abstract intellectual arguments from the Trotskyists of the Unity Movement, his old opponents. The most articulate was Neville Alexander, a Coloured academic from the University of Cape Town with a PhD from Tübingen in Germany, from whom Mandela learnt a lot.[45] Alexander had kept aloof from active protest until he rashly joined the small, eccentric group of conspirators the Yu Chi Chan Club (YCC), and had been sentenced for subversion and possessing literature about sabotage. He had been sent with five others to Robben Island in 1964. 'The poor YCC chaps (all of them),' wrote Kathrada to a friend in 1971, 'first woke to the reality of politics with the shock of their arrest and imprisonment. On the whole their approach still remains very naïve and idealistic.'[46] Alexander was a small man, young and hot-headed, as he described himself later, and the contrast with the slow-speaking, older Mandela was striking. Mandela sensed that Alexander was irritated by his height and sometimes 'wanted to throw a stone at him', but found he could disarm him with a smile.

Alexander began with a low opinion of the ANC as a racial body which had separated itself from the Indian and Coloured movements; but he welcomed the chance of arguing with Mandela himself. Over a year they argued man-to-man for more than thirty hours about 'the national question': was South Africa a nation? Alexander believed (like the rest of his movement) that there was no national consciousness, no national unity in South Africa: 'We were busy building a nation.'[47] Mandela insisted that the African people were a nation, while the others were minorities or national groups. When Alexander asked Mandela to define a Coloured person like himself, he replied that Coloureds were the progeny of a white and black union. Alexander retorted that this was a completely biological, racial argument, and that there was no point in continuing their discussion. 'Neville argued for non-racial political parties:

I said that was premature for ordinary people,' Mandela recalled. 'Look what happens at political meetings – they keep in their own groups. Let's go on pressing for a multi-racial society – but it will take time.'[48] The prison arguments would become much more topical in the eighties, when campaigners from all races made a common front against apartheid. In the nineties they would come closer together in the government of the new South Africa, as President Mandela took up the language of 'nation-building'.

On the island, Alexander soon revised his opinion of Mandela. 'In the first few months we were really terrible,' he admitted later. 'If it hadn't been for the statesmanship and maturity of Nelson and Walter and Govan and others I think we could have had a terrible situation in that prison . . . we would have been totally marginalised, marooned among all the others.' Alexander saw Mandela as a political animal, not a philosopher, but he was fascinated by his sensitivity and his skills in debate. Sometimes, he noticed, Mandela would concede a weakness in an argument, which he could then turn to his advantage – like a feint in boxing: 'The other person thinks you're weak, but actually your very acknowledgement of your weakness is a strength.' 'In terms of actual systematic rigorous attention to the logic of an argument,' Alexander thought that by the end, Mandela was 'way beyond any one of us'.

They argued with good humour until July 1967, when they learnt that Albert Luthuli, the President of the ANC, had died. Alexander thought that Luthuli had sold out by resisting armed struggle and accepting the Nobel Peace Prize: 'It was difficult to talk war and peace at the same time.'[49] When the ANC prisoners held a memorial service on Robben Island, Alexander attacked Luthuli caustically. Mandela resented the fact that he had not shown 'even perfunctory regrets at the man's passing', thus threatening the climate of co-operation between parties.[50] In retrospect, Alexander admitted that he had caused needless offence, but he was deeply hurt by Mandela's reproof in his 1995 autobiography, at a time when, as President, 'everybody he frowns on becomes a bit of a devil'.[51]

Most of Mandela's colleagues automatically regarded him as their leader, as he had led them from underground, and they would direct any visitor to his cell as their representative. 'He wasn't unquestioned,' said Govan Mbeki. 'We put him there. When we came to jail we said: "You are our spokesman."'[52] To some prisoners Mandela still seemed pulled between his two past roles of traditional chief and democratic leader. 'There was this arrogance about him which stemmed directly from the chieftaincy,' said Fikile Bam. 'It was Sisulu who saved him from the consequences.'[53] But Mandela's close colleagues saw his detachment as part of his search for unity and consensus: 'He tried to be a builder, to take a position which he thinks is more suitable for a leader of the ANC,' said Sisulu. 'He avoided expressing emotion: he would rather want a balanced picture.'

The ANC leaders were closer-knit than the others. 'We formed a very formidable team,' said Sisulu, 'because we knew each other so well, what the other was thinking.'[54] They soon recreated their own structure on the island, appointing a 'High Organ' of four prisoners as their ruling body, all of whom had served on the previous ANC National Executive: Mandela, Sisulu, Mbeki and Mhlaba. The High Organ decided on policy towards the prison authorities and discipline within the isolation section, and passed on their decisions to the other prisoners through the communications committee, led by Kathrada and including Michael Dingake and Joe Gqabi, who found ingenious ways to smuggle messages to political prisoners in the other buildings.

The morale of the ANC prisoners depended heavily on hearing good news from outside, which at first was rare, but in 1967 more guerrillas arrived on the island with exciting stories to tell of having actually fought in Southern Rhodesia as members of the 'Luthuli detachment', who were trying to get through to South Africa. One of the commanders of MK, Justice Mpanza, joined the isolation section, and Mandela as the first commander-in-chief was filled with pride to hear his accounts of the bravery and training of the troops, even though the incursion had failed.[55] In the communal cells the ANC prisoners were thrilled: 'We crowded round them, pumping them for every detail of the battles, of their training, and what kind of weapons they had used,' wrote Indres Naidoo. And they joined in 'The Soldiers' Song' (to the tune of 'Banana Boat'):

> Give him a bazooka and a hand grenade-o
> Take the country – the Castro Way.[56]

But the ANC prisoners had to be careful not to antagonise other groups. When members of other parties objected to the High Organ representing them, they formed a wider committee called 'Ulundi', which advised on common issues, and which had rotating chairmen, including Fikile Bam, who was a useful link between Mandela and the Unity Movement.[57] But the High Organ remained the main political power.[58] At first its members were all Xhosa-speakers, which could annoy others, who sometimes complained that the Xhosa language encouraged flattery by Mandela or Mbeki, even in English, which they called 'Xhosalisation'. Neville Alexander noticed that Mandela's stories, which sounded wooden in English, were much more vivid in Xhosa.[59] But Mandela spent time with non-Xhosa-speakers like Kathrada and Eddie Daniels, and the High Organ later added an extra rotating member – including in turn Kathrada, Laloo Chiba and M.D. Naidoo – who widened its scope.[60]

Mandela's friends were not all political. One of his closest was Eddie Daniels, a quiet and light-skinned Coloured from Cape Town who had once sailed on fishing trawlers. He had belonged to the Liberal Party but then joined a white group in its violent offshoot the ARM, which carried out acts of sabotage, for which he had been sentenced to fifteen years. He was the only Liberal on the island, lonely and distrusted by the more anti-white comrades, though he was not very politically-minded. On his second day he encountered a big man in short trousers, khaki shirt and sandals, whom he was thrilled to recognise as Mandela. When he said, 'Call me Nelson,' they were the first friendly words he had heard in prison. Mandela thereafter took trouble to brief Daniels personally about his meetings with visitors, so that he would not be isolated. Daniels was soon fortified by Mandela and Sisulu: 'When I felt demoralised I could hug them and their strength would flow into me . . . We couldn't see a future – it was blank. But Mandela always could.'

Once, when Daniels was too ill to get up, Mandela came to his cell and emptied his chamberpot. When a warder found that Daniels had been keeping a diary and summoned him to appear before the authorities the next morning, Daniels spent the night shivering with fear; but after breakfast he found Mandela sitting in his cell, to reassure him: 'Danny, I know you'll handle this.' Daniels, as he recalled, 'felt lifted, absolutely lifted'.[61] In return he was always trying to help Mandela and Sisulu. 'He was too good,' said Sisulu afterwards; 'it was embarrassing.'[62] Daniels became quite intimate with Mandela, whom he called Dalibunga. Mandela shared his letters from home with him, translating them from Xhosa, and talking about homely things. He also taught Daniels a song, 'Bonnie Mary of Argyle', which he had found in a book, and which Daniels still loves to sing:

'Tis thy voice my gentle Mary
And thine artless winning smile
That has made this world an Eden
Bonnie Mary of Argyle.

And he taught him the Victorian poem 'Invictus', by W.E. Henley:

It matters not how strait the gate,
How charged with punishments the scroll,
I am the master of my fate;
I am the captain of my soul.[63]

'When you read words of that nature you become encouraged,' Mandela said later. 'It puts life in you.'[64] He wrote in his memoir in prison: 'There is a profound truth in the idea that "man makes himself", a truth bound up with the whole history of mankind, that has shaped our own history.'[65]

Mandela had these close relationships with many of the thirty prisoners in the isolation block. A greater problem was how they should relate to the warders who dominated their daily lives, and who had the power to persecute them. They were unpromising material: usually young country Afrikaners, many from poor or broken homes, much less well-educated and confident than the prisoners, but therefore often all the more resentful and obsessed by the rules. Kathrada quoted Tolstoy: 'In prison the warders have regulations instead of hearts.' The guards had their own insecurities, rivalries and needs, and they lived in their own kind of prison on the bleak island.[66] That could provide some basis for communication.

Mandela had already realised from his earlier periods in jail that he could impress warders with a combination of assertiveness, respect and legal knowledge, and that he could retain his dignity in the most humiliating surroundings. When his lawyer George Bizos paid an early visit to the Island in October 1964, he was not allowed near the prison building. Instead, a truck arrived, from which eight guards jumped out, followed by Mandela, wearing short trousers and shoes without socks, who was then marched towards him, with guards surrounding him. But Mandela was walking very upright, with his hands behind his back, and setting his own pace. When he came near, Bizos went up to embrace him. Mandela said: 'George, let me introduce you to my guard of honour,' and named them. The incident summed up Mandela's relations with the warders from the start. He would respect them as human beings, like anyone else, but he would never be subservient. He would ensure that the prisoners set their own pace of work, and he would never call the guards '*baas*', as they demanded. All the prisoners tried to avoid saying '*baas*': some satisfied their pride by saying 'tard' after it, under their breath: 'Baastard'. Mandela simply refused to say the word.[67]

Mandela noticed a huge gap between the top and the bottom of the prison service. The Commissioner of Prisons in Pretoria, General Steyn, was a suave, well-mannered man who had travelled abroad; he wore elegant suits and shoes, and a fashionable short-brimmed hat, which he actually doffed to the prisoners. His etiquette, said the prisoner Michael Dingake, 'could be dazzling to inmates more acquainted with abuse from junior officers'.[68] But the General's visits to the island were rare, and Mandela soon realised he was turning a blind eye to the abuses. Mandela was more angry with senior officers than with the ordinary warders. His younger friend Fikile Bam thought it was due to his sense of superiority.[69] But Mandela had his own reasons: he reckoned that 'an ordinary warder, not a sergeant, could be more important to us than the Commissioner of Prisons or even the Minister of Justice . . . when you had a good relationship with the warders in your section it became difficult for the higher-ups to treat you roughly.'[70] When Mandela arrived on the island, Neville Alexander noticed, 'he had already come to believe that the warders were not uniformly evil'. In his earlier short stay in 1963 Mandela had encountered brutal warders like the sadistic Kleynhans brothers, but he had also come across others who were prepared to buck the system and show some humanity.

He now realised that there was a raging debate among the warders, between those who treated the prisoners humanely and those who were determined that they 'would never again resist white supremacy'. He was beginning to think that 'our occupation of the moral high ground could make it possible for us to turn some of the warders round.'[71] Alexander never bought that line completely, but Mandela was learning how to relate to the insecure young Afrikaner warders. 'I became relaxed in jail as I realised that the warders were not homogeneous,' he told me in 1996. 'Some warders wanted me to stay in jail for ever, but others wanted to keep in with me. It took some time to realise.' He saw a political opportunity in trying to argue with them and persuade them, and he was always hopeful of converting them. 'I soon realised that when an Afrikaner changes he changes completely and becomes a real friend.'[72] He began explaining the ANC's policies to visiting prison officials – which helped to develop his own skills in argument. Sisulu saw those talks as the precursor of the later discussions with government: 'The negotiation itself was a process which started from this source.'[73]

In December 1966 a new warder, James Gregory, arrived on the island. He had been brought up as a child among Zulus, and spoke Zulu and Xhosa fluently. He was later to achieve fame through his much-promoted book *Goodbye, Bafana*, which described conversations with his famous prisoner.[74] In fact Mandela had not known Gregory very well, but, as he put it, 'he knew us, because he had been responsible for reviewing our incoming and outgoing mail.'[75] In his book Gregory presented himself as a naïve country boy who was surprised to find the prisoners far better educated than himself, and soon recognised Mandela as a real leader, 'the perfect gentleman'.[76] But the warders who became genuine friends of the prisoners, like Christo Brand, were very suspicious of Gregory; and the prisoners were always aware that Gregory was spying on them, eavesdropping on visitors and intercepting mail, as part of the intelligence system of the Security Branch.[77]*

Mandela kept his cool with the warders. To respond in their own terms, he told others, was to come down to their level. Old colleagues, who had seen his temper in the past, watched with amazement how he could restrain himself in the face of humiliating provocations. Only rarely would he flare up with apparent fury. One day in 1968 prisoners were complaining to Captain Huysamen, one of the most intransigent officers, that warders were sabotaging their studies by withholding materials. Huysamen responded with an insult, and Mandela, who was standing at the back, exploded. Neville Alexander was standing near him: he had only ever seen Mandela in total control, and thought he had gone on a rampage: 'It was really amazing and astounding for everybody, because they'd never in public seen him losing his temper.' When Mandela had subsided, Alexander said, 'That was rather heavy,' but Mandela replied, 'No, no. It was deliberate.' It certainly had its effect: Huysamen went away with his

* Gregory's book, published in 1995, included intimate accounts of Mandela's family relationships which he had overheard. President Mandela, as he then was, decided not to apply for an injunction, but the Prison Department officially distanced themselves from the book.

tail between his legs. 'When Mandela goes off the deep end or loses his cool he can be quite a formidable person,' Alexander recalled, 'but not uncontrollable.'[78]

Mandela lost his temper genuinely seven years later, with Lieutenant Prins, the arrogant head of prison in 1975. Prins had refused him a visit from Winnie for the mendacious reason that he did not want to see her. When Mandela argued, Prins retorted that Winnie was only looking for publicity, and added some insults. Mandela was furious, moved towards him and nearly hit him. He restrained himself and instead let loose a stream of abuse, telling Prins he was contemptible, without honour, and strode out of the office fuming. Kathrada, who was watching with Daniels, was astonished to hear Mandela cursing.[79] When Mandela rejoined his colleagues in Section B he was still panting: someone whispered he needed tranquillisers.[80] Mandela was soon ashamed of having broken his self-control, which he saw as a victory for Prins. He paid a price: the next day he was charged with threatening the head of prison, but he retaliated – with very rational, legal tactics – with a counter-charge of misconduct against Prins and his superiors, and eventually the charge was dropped.[81]

Only a few foreign visitors ever penetrated into this self-contained world. But soon after the Rivonia prisoners arrived they were visited by an Englishman who they were told was an expert on prisons. They realised it was a special occasion when they were issued with jerseys for sewing, instead of the usual stones to break. As soon as the visitor left, recalled Andrew Mlangeni, 'stones and big rocks were brought into the yard on wheelbarrows'.[82] The Englishman turned out to be Bernard Newman, a travel writer and lecturer on espionage who was writing a book, *South African Journey*, and who had made friends with the police, who arranged for him to visit Robben Island. He talked to Mandela in his cell, which he found 'light and airy': but Mandela complained that it was 'cold and damp', that he was only allowed one bath a week, and that the food gave him stomach pains. Newman was convinced by the Governor Colonel Wessels that the 'settling-in troubles' would be rectified. He wrote a report in the London *Times*, and later told journalists that the conditions were better than in many prisons he had visited in Russia and Britain.[83]

Six weeks later, on 31 August, Mandela had a visit from a reporter supposedly from the London *Daily Telegraph*, before which he was again put on to sewing garments instead of breaking stones. 'On both occasions

I condemned conditions in this prison from beginning to end,' he wrote to the commanding officer. 'In spite of this fact press reports appeared which indicated that I was being satisfactorily treated.'[84] Later, in March 1965, he complained to the Commissioner of Prisons that he had told one of the journalists that Robben Island was being 'developed as a model prison', while in fact the food did not have adequate nutritional value: 'My physical condition has considerably deteriorated.' The commanding officer commented: 'He is posing as leader of his fellow prisoners and in so doing is also propagating these imaginary grievances.'[85]

The next month, in April 1965, the London *Sunday Times* published a half-page story about 'South Africa's Alcatraz', with a photograph of the prisoners sitting in a row with their hammers showing – Mandela alongside Billy Nair, Kathrada and Mbeki – together with another picture of Mandela in short trousers, sewing a jersey. Mandela had complained bitterly when his guards were out of earshot, according to the caption, pointing to his crumpled khaki shorts and saying: 'All part of the cruel method of destroying our dignity.' Some airmail copies of the newspaper slipped past the censors into South Africa, but they were soon seized by the police, who explained: 'The Mandela quote is dynamite and we have blacked it out on all remaining copies.'[86]

Another puzzling visitor in 1964 was an American lawyer called Henning, supposedly representing the American Bar Association. The prisoners assembled in the courtyard to meet him, with great expectations; they were shocked to find a rough, tousled figure, rather drunk, who kept spitting. Mandela had been chosen as the spokesman, but when he complained about the prisoners' conditions and the hard labour, Henning kept interrupting. Finally, Mandela burst out in exasperation: 'No, you don't listen!' Henning eventually explained that many American prisons were much worse, and that they probably deserved the death penalty anyway.[87]

Mandela had little reason to be grateful to lawyers' organisations, but he did know how to use the law. After two years working in the lime quarry he learnt that the Transvaal Law Society intended to strike him off their rolls because of his conviction – fourteen years after their earlier attempt following the Defiance Campaign. He demanded the right to defend himself, and to go to Pretoria, with access to law books. After months of correspondence, the prison authorities refused him permission. As Mandela saw it, the government dreaded the publicity he would receive by appearing in court, as it wanted him to be forgotten.[88] The Law Society eventually dropped its demand.

But the government was still harassing Mandela in jail. In July 1966 a sergeant hand-delivered a letter from the Department of Justice telling him that he had been included in a list of members and active supporters of the Communist Party, in terms of the Suppression of Communism Act of 1950. Mandela wrote back: 'I emphatically deny that I was a member of the Communist Party of South Africa since 1960 or at any other time,' and then put twelve questions, asking for details of any affidavits that made such allegations, and of any meetings he had supposedly attended. Four months later he was told that his name would not be included on the list.[89]*

But the Justice Department, after a long delay, came back with a different allegation: that Mandela had contravened the Suppression of Communism Act in the Defiance Campaign of 1952. Mandela replied in December 1969 that the campaign 'had nothing whatsoever to do with communism', and that the government were trying to victimise him. He was vindicated in a secret letter sent in July 1970 to the Commissioner of Police by D.P. Wilcocks, the official liquidator of the Communist Party, which was retained in the prison archives:

> I am of the opinion that on the available evidence Mandela cannot be described as an official, office-bearer, member or active supporter ['*actiewe ondersteuner*'] of the Communist Party of South Africa. Until such time as any further evidence in this regard comes to light the matter is regarded as closed.[91]

The island was a test-case for humanitarian organisations. A year after the Rivonia prisoners arrived their diet suddenly improved, and soon afterwards they were visited by the Red Cross. Mandela met the regional representative, Hans Sen, who was an odd choice: a Swiss Catholic who had emigrated to Rhodesia and was now disillusioned with his job. He told his friend the writer Doris Lessing: 'Knowing what went on everywhere was enough to make anyone a humanity-hater.'[92] Mandela gave Sen a list of the prisoners' requests – including better food, more visits

* In fact the files of the Justice Department show no real evidence of Mandela ever having been a member of the Party: only a statement by Fred Carneson, the former manager of the *Guardian*, that he once attended a meeting of the Central Committee at which Mandela was present, and a statement by Piet Beyleveld (an unreliable ex-communist who became a state witness) that Mandela had once attended the SACP's national conference.[90]

and letters, long trousers, socks and underwear. When Sen remarked that bread was bad for black people's teeth, Mandela began to suspect him of racist attitudes. There were some improvements including long trousers; but the diet soon went back to normal, and a later Red Cross report on Robben Island was so favourable that Pretoria publicised it at the UN.[93] It took the Swiss some years to realise the hardships and political significance of the prison.

The most effective visitor was from inside South Africa. Helen Suzman, the only member of the liberal Progressive Party in Parliament, insisted on visiting after hearing stories of wretched conditions. The prisoners welcomed her, and the rare waft of perfume in their cells. They told her that the thirty prisoners were facing over ninety prison charges. She was directed to Mandela's cell, where he spoke out against the poor food and clothing, the lack of newspapers and books, and about one brutal warder ('Suitcase' van Rensburg) with a swastika tattoo, while the prison commander and the Commissioner of Prisons listened. 'Mandela ignored their presence completely,' Suzman remembered. 'He had a commanding presence over both prisoners and warders, no doubt about it.'[94] Mandela was convinced that Suzman was basically on the prisoners' side. 'It was an odd and wonderful sight,' he wrote, 'to see this courageous woman peering into our cells and strolling around our courtyard.'[95]

Suzman reported back on the inhuman conditions. 'Things were bad then in the prison,' she recalls. 'They thought conditions had to be as tough as possible, as further punishment. Some of the warders really were Nazis.'[96] Soon afterwards, van Rensburg was transferred, and conditions began to improve. The prisoners saw Suzman's visit as a turning-point: had she not come, wrote Neville Alexander, 'there is no saying what might have happened'.[97]

Suzman would visit Mandela seven more times in prison, having lively arguments. They could never agree about violence. On her second visit, in 1969, Mandela maintained that the ANC prisoners should be released, just as the Afrikaner rebel Robey Leibbrandt had finally been set free despite his treachery during the Second World War. Suzman pointed out that Leibbrandt's rebellion had been defeated, while the ANC's struggle was continuing, and asked: 'Are you prepared to say that you'll abandon violence?' Mandela could not, so Suzman could not ask for his release.[98] But the prisoners would always be grateful to her for her practical help. 'I really had no idea,' she wrote to me thirty years later, 'what a long-lasting effect this would have on friendship with the chaps I met there . . . My jailbird chums remain staunchly loyal, despite my politically incorrect adherence to liberalism.'[99]

In September 1970 Mandela was visited by Denis Healey, the combative British Labour politician whom he had met eight years earlier in London. In 1967, as Minister of Defence, Healey had tried to resume selling some arms to South Africa (see p.270) – thus showing, he admitted later, 'gross insensitivity to the hatred of apartheid both in my party and in the Commonwealth'. Now Harold Wilson's Labour government had just been defeated, and Healey was opposing Edward Heath's Conservative administration's plans to start selling arms – as he explained, 'to expiate my own crime'. Healey was struck by Mandela's transformation since 1962: instead of the dark, bearded man he had met in London, Mandela was 'clean-shaven, close-cropped and pale'. But his morale was high, he was surprisingly well-informed about the outside world, and 'his moral authority, even over his warders, was immense'.[100]

After three and a half years conditions began to improve, and from 1967 the treatment of the prisoners was relatively civilised and relaxed.[101] They were allowed to wear long trousers and jerseys in winter, and could talk in the quarry and the courtyard. Sometimes they received eggs and fruit. But Mandela saw few of the changes which the Red Cross had promised: the diet was still minimal, there were no newspapers, and they were not allowed the recreation to which senior prisoners were entitled. The work was still exhausting, and prisoners were still being assaulted by the warders. In November 1970, after the Red Cross representative Philip Zuger had visited the island, he complained about the 'daily rounds of listless and aimless rock and lime-cutting'. He also noted that a prisoner's lack of outside news 'deep freezes him in the state in which he was put away for storage in prison'.[102]

Mandela had by now clearly become the spokesman for the political prisoners from all parties. The Commissioner, the elegant General Steyn, had warned him not to speak for the others, who, he said, could complain individually. 'And Nelson,' he reminded him, 'you are a *prisoner*!'[103] But Mandela refused to accept this prohibition, and in January 1970 he wrote a long letter of complaint to Steyn on behalf of all the prisoners. It reads like an official report from the head of a department. 'We have always accepted that firmness and discipline is a necessary instrument for the preservation of law and order in prison,' the letter began. 'But it is our firm belief that human beings are more likely to be influenced by exemplary conduct on the part of the officials than by brute force.' Mandela went on to complain about the assaults on prisoners, and the hard labour of his own group:

> For more than five years we have been forced to do heavy and uncreative work which sapped our energy and in some cases even adversely affected our health. Through this period you condemned us to a monotonous routine of either breaking stones, doing pick and shovel work, and denied us all opportunities for any kind of vocational training, or of any work that may encourage and develop a sense of self respect, industry and responsibility in the prisoner, and no efforts are being made to help us to lead respectable and meaningful lives when released.

He concluded with a serious warning:

> I sense rising tensions and growing impatience with the policy of a department which is clearly incompatible with our welfare, and I urge you to act with speed and to take appropriate measures to relieve the situation before matters go out of control.[104]

Pretoria responded by making things worse, appointing at the end of 1970 a new commanding officer: Colonel Piet Badenhorst, who arrived on the island with a reputation for brutality – and with some thuggish new warders. Mandela reckoned Badenhorst was the crudest of all his commanding officers, running Robben Island as if it were under martial law. It seemed part of a deliberate change of policy: Mandela had been told that the treatment of political prisoners was decided jointly by the prison authorities and the security branch, which was becoming more powerful since the formation in 1969 of the enlarged secret service BOSS.[105] 'They have launched a sort of reign of terror,' Ahmed Kathrada wrote to his friend Sylvia Neame; 'they only know one thing, and that is revenge and punishment.' The guards now picked on any excuse to persecute the prisoners, depriving them of meals and preventing their reading anything – including Shakespeare – which was not relevant to their studies.[106] Badenhorst soon stopped them from studying anything, because, he said, they were lazy. Unlike his predecessors, Badenhorst refused even to talk to Mandela, and when he saw him in the quarry he would shout at him in Afrikaans: 'Mandela, you must pull your finger out of your arse.'[107]

At the end of May 1971 the reign of terror reached a climax which tested all Mandela's restraint. It was the eve of the tenth anniversary of the Republic (and of the ANC's last abortive strike), and the warders had spread rumours that some sentences would be reduced as part of the celebrations. But the atmosphere in the isolation block had become tense since the arrival of a group of Namibian prisoners from the South-West African People's Organisation (SWAPO), led by its founder Toivo ja Toivo, who had begun a hunger strike which the other prisoners joined. On Friday 28 May a group of drunken warders burst into the cells, including the notoriously sadistic head warder Carstens, known as 'the Devil' (who showed, said Alexander, 'the narrow-minded viciousness of a henpecked husband').[108] They told everyone to strip naked, and kept them with their hands up for half an hour in the bitter cold while they searched every cell. Govan Mbeki collapsed and was taken to hospital in Cape Town. Fikile Bam wept with frustration. They could hear the warders beating up prisoners in the adjoining cells, hitting them and twisting their testicles. When Toivo fought back he was beaten to the floor, then forced to clean up his blood-spattered cell.[109]

'It was the worst day in my memory,' recalled Kathrada: 'It was terrifying, I'll never forget it.'[110] 'I felt angry and bitter,' said Sisulu; 'it was one of the most horrible invasions of our privacy.'[111] The prisoners never learnt the reason, but they suspected the warders had been provoked by some bad political news – which always made them (as one prisoner wrote) 'as dangerous as cornered scorpions'.[112] 'Brutality was always linked to some external event,' said Mac Maharaj: 'whether guerrillas, rugby or border troubles – anything which threatened the warders' view of their country.'[113]

Mandela remained calm, and Eddie Daniels was convinced that his authoritative presence saved him and others from many assaults.[114] Mandela was determined to stand up to Badenhorst's tyranny, and smuggled a message to friends outside to lobby for his dismissal. Soon afterwards he led a delegation of prisoners to see Badenhorst, threatening strikes if their conditions were not improved. They found him surprisingly conciliatory. A month later, three judges arrived on the island with the Commissioner of Prisons. When they asked to see Mandela privately he boldly insisted that Badenhorst should be present, and then described the recent brutal beating of a prisoner. Badenhorst burst out: 'If you talk about things you haven't seen, you will get yourself into trouble.' Mandela calmly told the judges: 'If he can threaten me here, in your presence, you can imagine what he does when you are not here.' The junior judge, Michael Corbett, protested sharply in Mandela's hearing about Badenhorst's behaviour, to obvious effect.[115] Thirty years later President Mandela reminded Corbett, by this time Chief Justice, of his intervention, and commented: 'Such courage and independence were rare.'[116] Three months after the judges' visit Badenhorst was transferred, together with his brutal gang of warders. Before he left, Badenhorst told Mandela: 'I just want to wish you people good luck.' Mandela was taken aback, but responded with his own good wishes. He felt fortified in his conviction that even apparently evil men could be changed: Badenhorst 'behaved like a brute because he was rewarded for brutish behaviour'.[117]

Mandela was not the only prisoner to see the warders as the slaves of the system. 'These people just somersaulted when they were given different orders,' said Neville Alexander: 'real brutes became doves and angels of peace.'[118] But Mandela went furthest in regarding warders with pity rather than hatred, and forgiving the worst excesses: even Kathrada could not go along with some of his tolerance. Mandela could see beyond the brutalities, to the insecurities and psychological deformities of the warders; and he was already seeing the prison as a microcosm of a future South Africa, where reconciliation would be essential to survival.

16

Steeled and Hardened

1971–1976

ROBBEN ISLAND soon acquired a reputation in the world outside as a 'hell hole' – the title of a book by the PAC prisoner Moses Dlamini, who spent two years there until 1969.[1] Yet by the seventies the conditions, though still grim, were not usually hellish. Robben Island, like the Bastille, or the Peter and Paul Fortress in St Petersburg,[2] became a powerful symbol abroad of the tyranny of the South African regime; but the legend became more terrible than the reality.

The balance of power was beginning to change. In December 1971 a new head of prison, Colonel Willie Willemse, replaced the hated Badenhorst. Willemse, with his clipped moustache and gentlemanly style, had a more conciliatory brief. The Commissioner of Prisons, still General Steyn, had told him to adopt a more enlightened approach because (as Willemse understood it) the government had to reckon with the political scene at home and abroad. 'I was told to change the atmosphere,' he said twenty-five years later. 'I made myself accessible: it was better to deal with complaints in prison, not let them go further up. I told them we must be professional, like the medical profession . . . I recognised they were political leaders. They weren't sissies.'[3] Willemse could suddenly switch from decency to harshness, but most of the prisoners respected him: as Neville Alexander said, 'We all realised that he was a quality person.'[4] The Red Cross visitors were soon convinced, as they told their headquarters in Geneva, that Willemse was 'trying to do his best to maintain a purely professional relationship with the inmates under his care. He has solved many problems.'[5]

Willemse knew he could not control the prisoners without their co-operation, and particularly Mandela's. Already, as Mandela described it, 'The inmates, not the authorities, seemed to be running the prison.'[6]

They had virtually stopped working, as there were now fewer warders to supervise them: 'We just go to the quarry and do nothing,' wrote Kathrada in 1971.[7] Willemse appealed to Mandela to help to impose some discipline in the quarry, and Mandela persuaded his fellow prisoners to resume work, but at their own pace. Willemse established his own relationship with Mandela: he too had been brought up in the Transkei, and could talk about the beautiful countryside and Xhosa dishes; Mandela would greet him in Afrikaans and talk about Afrikaner history. 'Mandela had a special stature,' Willemse recalled. 'He was experienced in the politics of change. I never felt he was waiting for revenge. I never experienced bitterness among any of them, but Mandela played a role in persuading them.'[8]

The Red Cross in Geneva was now playing a discreet role in improving the prisoners' conditions. In 1972 it appointed a new Delegate-General for Africa, Jacques Moreillon, who paid three visits to the island in three years. He carefully kept aloof from political lobbyists like Helen Suzman, but kept pressing for an end to the quarry-work and more freedom to study (both of which were achieved) and access to news (which would not be granted until September 1980). In 1974 he argued with the Minister of Justice Jimmy Kruger that political prisoners should be treated as normal inmates unless there were imperative security reasons: any hardening of conditions would 'contribute an additional punishment' to the judge's sentence.

Moreillon's critical but deadpan reports were summarised by the President of the Red Cross in Geneva, then sent to Pretoria. The government reacted very slowly: at one point, exasperated by its inaction, Moreillon was tempted to resort to the ultimate deterrent of stopping the Red Cross visits altogether, which would provoke international outrage. Mandela dissuaded him, with a piece of advice he would always remember: 'The good you bring is less important than the bad you prevent.' Moreillon was struck by Mandela's sense of superiority to his warders, and his special stature on the island: prisoners asked to shake Moreillon's hand, because he had shaken Mandela's. He was shocked to discover that a particularly cruel warder was censoring Winnie's letters, deliberately distorting their meaning, as a kind of mental torture, but Mandela merely said: 'I feel rather sorry for him: he's the last specimen of an extinguishing species, and doesn't know it.'[9]

By 1972 – just before a Red Cross visit – the prisoners were each issued with two new sets of underwear. By 1973 there was hot water for washing and for showers, though it would sometimes be cut off as punishment. By 1975 the prisoners were even allowed to improvise a tennis court in the yard. Mandela was now classed as an 'A' group prisoner, and was allowed three letters and two visits a month – but no 'contact visits', in which he could touch visitors, although he was officially entitled to them. On doctors' orders he was also allowed a special bed, some milk and a special salt-free diet for his high blood pressure.[10]

After more pressure from the Red Cross, the prisoners were allowed spells of alternative work, away from the lime quarry. They were taken down to the seashore to collect seaweed, which was shipped off to Japan as fertiliser. It was hard work, and the Atlantic could be icy in winter, but Mandela welcomed the view of the sea and the swooping seabirds. For lunch they picked mussels and clams, and caught abalone and sometimes even crayfish to provide their own seafood stew, which the warders shared. Away from the prison buildings, Robben Island has a wild natural beauty, like an unspoilt nature reserve – 'a tiny Garden of Eden', Denis Healey called it – and Mandela became fascinated by the wild birds.[11]

The political atmosphere on the island was beginning to change as younger warders arrived, some only seventeen, who were more easily influenced. The political prisoners tried hard to educate them. It was 'a tedious, burdensome duty imposed on all prisoners by the necessities of survival with dignity', said Alexander; but it had compensations: 'The patient, tactful, often hurtful, discussions occasioned by this need are one of the great human events on the island, for here many of the (black) prisoners and (white) warders for the first (and probably in most cases for the last) time are able to exchange ideas about the way of life of South Africa.'[12]

Kathrada saw the young warders as delinquents in need of rehabilitation. 'If they spend their impressionable years working with political prisoners,' he wrote in 1971, 'I am sure it will have a healthy impact on their outlook. Ironically it is in jail that we have closest fraternisation between the opponents and supporters of apartheid; we have eaten of their food, and they ours; they have blown the same musical instruments that have been "soiled" by black lips; they have discussed most intimate matters and sought advice; a blind man listening in to a tête-à-tête will find it hard to believe it is between prisoner and warder.'[13]

Mandela was becoming more clearly respected by most of the prison staff: when George Bizos visited the island now he lunched with Mandela on crayfish and other delicacies in the officers' club, served by prisoners in white gloves.[14] Mandela was a star attraction for newly-arrived warders. 'They were anxious to meet Mandela because they'd read about him,' said Billy Nair. 'As the years went by we'd have the warders having meals with him, playing tennis or table tennis when their superiors weren't watching. We'd have Madiba sitting with a warder in his cell, making the tea, giving biscuits, having long discussions, speaking Afrikaans – though not very well. He would win these chaps over.'[15]

Mandela was developing a special interest in the Afrikaner mindset. He urged the other prisoners to talk with the warders in Afrikaans, however much they disliked it, to understand more about their psychology and culture.[16] 'I realised the importance of learning Afrikaans history, of reading Afrikaans literature, of trying to understand these ordinary men . . . how they are indoctrinated, how they react,' said Maharaj. 'They all have a blank wall in their minds. They just could not see the black man as a human being.'[17] Maharaj was at first bitterly anti-Afrikaans, but came to realise that 'You must understand the mind of the opposing commander . . . you can't understand him unless you understand his literature and his language.'[18] Mandela himself studied Afrikaans systematically, reading many Afrikaans books, and spoke it quite well, though Kathrada thought his pronunciation was 'atrocious'.[19] He acquired an understanding of the Afrikaner which colleagues in exile would later envy. 'Mandela in his cell learnt much more about the Afrikaners than we who were fighting them,' said the MK leader Ronnie Kasrils. 'He knew he could negotiate with them.'[20]

Mandela's accommodation with the warders worried militant newcomers like Sonny Venkatrathnam, a Trotskyist from Durban who had been arrested for sabotage and was brutally tortured before arriving on the island. He was very sceptical about Mandela's negotiations with the prison authorities: 'Wow, Nelson is doing all that, how come we're in such shit?' He saw Mandela mainly from a distance, as he was in a separate section, but he learnt much from his behaviour. He regarded Mandela not as a revolutionary but as a Christian nationalist: 'I came out a different person: totally philosophical about things . . . What amazed me about Nelson and Sisulu and other people who had life sentences was the calmness, the equanimity with which they led their prison lives. They didn't throw in the towel. They didn't display bitterness. They showed me how to laugh at the tortures we went through.' At first Venkatrathnam had vowed to revenge himself on the policeman who had tortured him: 'I have no problems about that now. I said, "This guy's a lesser human being than I am: why bother about that stuff?" . . . I think I am a relatively calm person now.'[21]

The thirty prisoners cooped up in the isolation section faced their own strains. 'Living with the same faces day in and day out must be having adverse psychological effects on us,' Kathrada wrote after seven years in jail. 'We do get on one another's nerves and we have long exhausted all conversation relating to our experiences outside. All the jokes have been told, even gossip has become repetitive.'[22] But Mandela maintained his curiosity about other people. 'He was learning all the time,' Fikile Bam noticed, 'always going out and probing people. He schooled himself in our backgrounds.'[23] Mandela enjoyed hearing people's life stories: 'Few things are more exciting to me here,' he wrote in 1975, 'than to listen to a man's background, the factors that influenced his thoughts and actions, the unknown battles he has fought and won.' He was always amused when new versions kept coming up.[24]

Mandela had his own pressures and setbacks. His old friend Fatima Meer – later his biographer – came to visit him at a time when he was confined to his cell as a punishment. 'He looked terrible – emaciated, overworked in the prison yard. I knew Mandela as a strapping fellow; but now he was like a face in a pane of glass, or a squashed-up butterfly in a museum . . . He sat there looking sallow, emaciated. I said, "You've grown so thin." He said, "But you've grown fat."'[25]

The authorities tried to project a rosy picture of conditions on Robben Island to the world. In 1973 an Australian journalist, David 'Whiskers' McNicoll from the conservative news magazine the *Bulletin*, arrived on the island and wrote a glowing account of Mandela in his cell, 'scrupulously clean, like everything was on Robben Island'. Mandela looked to him to be in his mid-forties (he was then fifty-four), with smooth skin, alert, humorous eyes and hands which 'showed no particular signs of hard work'. Mandela complained to him about the lack of news from outside and the strict censorship – twenty articles had been cut out from a single issue of *Reader's Digest* – but sounded thoroughly optimistic: 'I can say I have never had a single moment of depression, because I know that my cause will triumph. I am satisfied with the way things are proceeding.'[26] McNicoll portrayed Mandela as preoccupied by his own status, resentful of being treated as inferior to Indians and Coloureds. (Neville Alexander, himself Coloured, accused McNicoll of having distorted 'the image of one of the least snobbish and most modest men in any South African jail'.)[27] All the prisoners were dismayed by the report. 'He certainly saw the prison through different eyes to our eyes,' said Mac Maharaj. After his visit the prisoners insisted that they must have forewarning of press visits, and must be allowed to choose their spokesmen.[28]

The prisoners still harboured dreams of escape – though only one man, Autshumao, known as 'Henry the Strandloper', had ever escaped from Robben Island, in the seventeenth century. They had to be doubly wary because at times they suspected that the government wanted to provoke a shoot-out: some prisoners noticed in 1967 that warders were pointing their rifles at them while they worked in the quarry, as if to incite them. And there was one wild escape scheme which was uncovered before it could be attempted. It was originated in 1969 by Gordon Bruce, a left-wing idealist who had become a friend of Mandela through the International Club in Johannesburg in 1950.[29] He devised a far-fetched plan to 'spring' Mandela from the island by bribing a warder to let him out. Bruce would then take him by speedboat to Cape Town disguised as a frogman, then drive him to an airstrip and have him flown off by a well-known aviatrix, Sheila Scott – after which Bruce proposed to involve Mandela in a crusade for world peace, based in South Africa.[30] Bruce advertised in the London *Times* for a 'competent organiser, prepared to execute unusual work'; but one of the applicants was Gordon Winter, an informer for the South African secret service BOSS, which planned to infiltrate the escape plot and have Mandela killed when he boarded the plane.[31] But the British secret service (according to both Winter and Bruce) was tipped off about the scheme by Sir Robert Birley, an ex-headmaster of Eton then teaching in South Africa, in whom Bruce had confided, and the whole plan was scrapped. After his release Mandela remained friendly with Bruce, and in 1992 arrived unannounced at his seventieth birthday party.[32]

In 1974 Mac Maharaj discovered a possible escape route after he had visited a dentist in Cape Town who turned out to be related to the wife of an underground ANC supporter, and who had insisted on the warders removing Maharaj's leg-irons and leaving the operating theatre. Soon afterwards Mandela arranged to be taken to the same dentist with Wilton Mkwayi and Maharaj, who armed himself with a knife he found in the truck. Their leg-irons were removed, the warders left, and Maharaj prepared to jump through the window to a side street. But then he noticed that the street was empty of people, and suddenly suspected that the police were waiting in hiding to shoot them as they emerged. Mandela agreed to abort it. Maharaj was certain afterwards that it had been a police ambush: 'I kicked myself that I could have got Madiba killed.'[33]

There were some diversions from the monotony of prison life, including religious services each Sunday conducted by chaplains from different denominations. After the third year they preached in the courtyard, which gave them the added attraction of fresh air: the more long-winded the priests, the more the prisoners liked them.[34] Mandela listened to them all: 'I started my own ecumenical movement in jail,' he joked afterwards. The Muslim priest was popular, Mandela recalled, because on special days 'he came not only with the Qur'an but with biryani, samosas and other lovely delicacies'.[35] (The warders clamped down when twenty-four prisoners suddenly declared themselves converts to Islam.) Mandela took the opportunity to learn more about the faith which had influenced many of his friends. He even got permission to visit a Muslim shrine on the island which commemorated one of the heroes of Islam in South Africa, Sheik Mantura, who had been banished to the island in 1744, and who had died there. Mandela was fascinated by the shrine, particularly by its murals, and insisted that the guard took his shoes off before entering.[36] Mandela also became quite friendly with the Dutch Reformed chaplain, the Reverend André Scheffler, a lean, craggy man who had begun by mocking the freedom fighters; but when he warned the prisoners against blaming everything on the white man, Mandela agreed with him. After Scheffler preached about Moses leading the Israelites out of Egypt, the authorities told him he was no longer acceptable; Mandela gave him a parting gift of guava for his wife.[37]

Mandela was disappointed by the Reverend Jones, the Methodist preacher, who kept insisting on reconciliation, without suggesting that whites should be reconciled to blacks.[38] But the Anglican, the Reverend Hughes, was (said Michael Dingake) 'everyone's darling'.[39] 'What a delightful man Rev Hughes is, and what sense of humour!' wrote Kathrada in an uncensored letter.[40] Hughes, a Welshman, who arrived on the island with his own organ, loved the prisoners' singing, which reminded him of home. He wove news from the outside world into his sermons, and delighted Mandela by quoting Churchill: 'We shall fight on the beaches . . .'[41] There was sometimes tension between warders and priests, and one thuggish guard objected to wine being served at communion. As Kwedi Mkalipi said: 'I had seen what I used to think the most sacred thing in Christianity now shattered.'[42]

Mandela's own faith was a matter of much speculation. Many of his basic principles – his capacity for seeing the best in people, his belief in the dignity of man, his forgiveness – were essentially religious. Some visitors, like Frieda Matthews, found him positively Christ-like.[43] And he was becoming more sympathetic to the Churches. He liked to talk about sympathetic priests like Trevor Huddleston, and defended missionaries against critics such as Nosipho Majeke, author of *The Role of the Missionaries in Conquest*. 'Is that really what we thought about missionaries?' he asked his young friend Bam, and his letters often harked back to his missionary teachers.[44] But he was not a formal believer like Oliver Tambo: he did not quote the Bible, or discuss theology. His interest in the Sunday services was more political than religious. 'He gave us hope when everything was rock bottom and we saw no future,' said Eddie Daniels. 'But character, not religion, was his strength.'[45]

Mandela's capacity for forgiveness already amazed visitors. Fatima Meer was exasperated when he asked after an earlier colleague in Durban, who had since been denounced as a quisling. 'Why do you want to know about him?' she asked impatiently. Mandela reminded her that the man had once provided a car to drive Luthuli to the airport. Fatima silently thought: 'Is he redeemed, for that?'[46]

Mandela's forgiveness was shared by many of his fellow-prisoners, who were determined to avoid bitterness and self-pity. 'Prison completely cured me of self-pity and of being self-centred,' said Bam.[47] They were reminded that their situation could have been much worse when prisoners joined them who had been tortured, or when they heard about many who had died in detention. Kathrada always remembered the Chinese proverb which Father Hughes quoted: 'I grumbled and groused because I had no shoes, until I met a man who had no feet.'[48] But it was Mandela who remained the model of tolerance.

If the Robben Islanders had a common culture and text, it was not the Bible or the Koran, but Shakespeare. 'Somehow Shakespeare always had something to say to us,' said Kathrada, who had once tried to argue that Shakespeare was a racist, but was soon shouted down.[49] 'We would recite long, long passages from Shakespeare,' Neville Alexander recalled.

'Usually the more militant passages: *Coriolanus*, *Julius Caesar*, of course, and *Henry V*.'[50] Shakespeare's political relevance to black South Africans was clear enough: *Julius Caesar* offered a kind of textbook for revolutionary theory. But his deeper understanding of human courage, suffering and sacrifice reassured the prisoners that they were part of a universal drama.

Sonny Venkatrathnam kept a copy of Shakespeare's works on his shelf, disguised behind Indian religious pictures. 'I'm not a religious person, but I wouldn't part with this, because it gave us such joys and countless readings,' he said later. He circulated it to all the inmates of the single cells, to autograph their favourite passages, providing a unique jailbirds' anthology. Kathrada chose Henry V's 'Once more unto the breach'. Wilton Mkwayi chose Malvolio's 'Some are born great', from *Twelfth Night*. Govan Mbeki chose the opening lines of the same play: 'If music be the food of love'. Billy Nair chose Caliban's lines from *The Tempest*: 'This island's mine, by Sycorax my mother'. Sisulu chose Shylock's:

> Still have I borne it with a patient shrug,
> For suff'rance is the badge of all our tribe . . .

Neville Alexander chose the sonnet beginning:

> Like as the waves make towards the pebbled shore,
> So do our minutes hasten to their end.

Andrew Masondo chose Mark Antony's

> O! pardon me, thou bleeding piece of earth,
> That I am meek and gentle with these butchers.

Mandela also chose a passage from *Julius Caesar*, with his signature for 16 December 1977:

> Cowards die many times before their deaths;
> The valiant never taste of death but once.
> Of all the wonders that I yet have heard,
> It seems to me most strange that men should fear;
> Seeing that death, a necessary end,
> Will come when it will come.[51]

Classical drama gained a new intensity in the prison; Sophocles' *Antigone* was seen as especially relevant to the struggle. The playwright Athol

Fugard wrote a short play, *The Island*, based on reports from the prison, which was performed in Cape Town in 1973, and later in London and on Broadway, in which two prisoners perform a minimal version of *Antigone*. On the actual island Mandela played the part of Creon in a full-length production of *Antigone*. He saw Creon as a leader who was originally wise and patriotic, but who showed himself merciless and inflexible in refusing to let Antigone bury her dead brother, while Antigone was a freedom fighter 'who defied the law on the ground that it was unjust'.[52]

The prisoners were gradually allowed more forms of recreation. After 1967 these included outdoor games such as rugby and cricket, though they were withdrawn for a time in 1971, and a court ruling defined them as privileges rather than rights.[53] They even played Monopoly, which helped to educate the socialists about capitalism. Mandela did not always excel at these games: he told Winnie in January 1975 that he had been trounced at chess, draughts and dominoes as well as tennis, explaining that he could not concentrate because he was thinking of her.[54] But he played a relentless game of chess or draughts: 'Nobody wants to play chess with Nelson because he takes three days to play a game,' reported Venkatrathnam. 'But that's part of the man's make-up. Sometimes he becomes very inscrutable, slow, but very smart, very adept.'[55] In one chess tournament Mandela played a game against a young ex-medical student called Salim, which went on for two or three days before Salim resigned from exhaustion. It was, said Kathrada, Mandela's war of attrition.[56] The Namibian leader Toivo ja Toivo complained that Mandela would use a lawyer's tactics: 'He would sit there the whole day and only move one piece. And I'm a man who likes to move about.'[57] 'I carefully considered the ramifications of every option,' said Mandela about his draughts technique. 'It is my preferred mode of operating, not only in draughts but in politics.'[58]

Mandela's happiest relaxation was the small garden which the prisoners were eventually allowed to establish in a corner of the courtyard, excavating the rocks above the soil. It gave him a sense of freedom and creativity, taking him back to his Transkei childhood and the garden at his mission school at Clarkebury, which he had tended for the headmaster, the Reverend Harris. 'Nowadays the garden is Nelson's baby and he is fanatical about it,' wrote Kathrada in November 1975. 'As expected he has read everything he could lay his hands on.' Mandela got seeds from the warders, and diligently practised horticulture, helped by a team of prisoners led by Laloo Chiba. Kathrada watched them 'trooping out each morning with rulers, ballpoints, labels, and other instruments, and carefully taking measurements and making copious notes'. By late 1975 they had raised two thousand chillies, nearly a thousand tomatoes, a few radishes, onions and sweet melons and two watermelons. Mandela's preoccupation with producing the best possible crops could be trying even for his fellow-gardeners. To provide compost he insisted on collecting the bones after any meal of meat, and asked colleagues to hammer them into powder. When he lacked volunteers he proposed a simpler form of compost: human waste. The prisoners dug a big hole in the courtyard, and every morning tipped their toilet buckets into it. But the stench, as Kathrada reported, 'did not endear this scheme to any of us', and soon it was abandoned.

The great excitement of 1975 was the arrival of a female chameleon, which moved from chilli to tomato to radish to lettuce, trying in vain (Kathrada observed) to alter her pigment accordingly. She gave birth to six babies, and promptly abandoned them – which (wrote Kathrada) 'excited all our parental feelings, and our concern for the orphan, the lowly, the helpless. Each morning, and throughout the day you'd find a cluster of chaps around one little baby, engaged in animated discussion.' But no one could solve the question: where was Papa chameleon?[59]

Mandela saw the garden as a substitute for cultivating human relationships with absent friends, including Winnie, but also as a metaphor for politics: a leader, too, he wrote, 'sows seeds, and then watches, cultivates and harvests the result'.[60] He wrote to Winnie about nursing a tomato plant which had been injured, and sadly pulling it out when it died: Winnie equated it with nursing a child in the midst of the struggle, only to see it mown down by the police.[61]

It was the opportunity to study that was most precious to the prisoners. Mandela had earlier urged the Commissioner to 'let the atmosphere of a university prevail', and by the late sixties that atmosphere was appearing: the quarry was becoming a kind of campus for what came to be called 'the university of Robben Island'.[62] The prisoners saw it as their own achievement, though the Red Cross liked to think it was 'the Red Cross University'.[63] Anyone with a degree or other qualification would teach his subject, and each morning they would plan their courses at the quarry. They could combine teaching even with hard labour: 'People could present actual lessons, even lectures, while they were swinging a pick or shovelling lime,' said Alexander. But as the work was relaxed, or stopped altogether, the teaching became more organised, and they could stand in groups, drawing diagrams in the sand, as Fikile Bam recalled: 'There was always movement as you got to the workplace, little groups assembling in different places, and you knew that there were classes in progress.'[64]

Mandela taught a course on political economy, tracing the development of societies from feudalism to capitalism to socialism – which he still saw as the most advanced stage. But he preferred arguing to teaching, and always welcomed questions from his pupils, which forced him to think harder about his views. He saw the Robben Island system as essentially Socratic, using dialogue to clarify the ideas of both teachers and pupils.[65] Michael Dingake, the Botswanan freedom fighter who took two degrees on the island, remembered Mandela as the most tireless participant in these discussions, with a fiercely candid approach which could offend his opponents: 'In argument against someone with insubstantial facts, Nelson can be vicious, by adopting a modified Socratic method. Very few people like to be cross-examined and exposed in their vagueness and ignorance. Quite a few times I have come out of an argument with Madiba "bloodied" and humiliated. None the less, I have found such an experience fruitful in the long term. For it has taught me to look at both sides of the question, to attempt to give an objective and honest answer to it.'[66]

Some prisoners were actually illiterate when they came to the island. At first, much of the education was informal and oral: 'simply talking to one another, sharing views about what we knew of politics, history, language', as Alexander recalled.[67] But for most illiterates, before long, learning to read and write became an engrossing interest. 'We took people from the lowest level, who came to the island illiterate, and they had to be taught,' said Govan Mbeki. 'And by the time they left Robben Island they were able to write letters home . . . And they spoke English.'[68] Dikgang Moseneke, a PAC activist who came to the island as a boy in 1963 (and who later became Chairman of South African Telkom), reckoned that everyone in his section could read and write within a few years.[69] Many progressed to more formal studies through correspondence schools, acquiring both the motivation and the opportunity for higher education which they might never have had outside. Several who arrived with a minimal education left with one or two degrees. Some of the young warders were also infected by the educational atmosphere. 'Many recruits volunteered for the island,' recalled Colonel Willemse, the prison head. 'It was a university for the warders too.'[70] Sergeant Aubrey du Toit, the warder who ran the Prisoners' Studies Department, recalled that Mandela was 'very strict about people studying – not only prisoners but warders'. When he told Mandela that he had only been studying practical Afrikaans, Mandela replied, 'Sergeant, you should be ashamed of yourself. I am Xhosa and I did Afrikaans and Nederlands.'[71] Later one of the prisoners advised du Toit to leave the prison service and to join the insurance company Sanlam – which he did.

The atmosphere of self-improvement and education helped the political prisoners to overcome the sexual strains and frustrations which caused ructions among common-law prisoners, who sometimes resorted to sodomy or violence. 'The sexual urge was sublimated into politics,' reckoned George Bizos, who was warned that the prisoners did not appreciate dirty jokes.[72] Many of the younger political prisoners undoubtedly felt frustrated by their enforced abstinence, but the discipline was strict. Mandela himself, as he explained later, had had plenty of experience of abstinence at his mission boarding-schools, but his friends were surprised by his ignorance about homosexuality. He had once, he said later, 'reacted with revulsion against the whole system of being gay'.[73] But when a prisoner boldly brought up the subject, he was glad to debate it. Dr Motlana, who saw many ex-prisoners after their release, believed that the body became accustomed to abstinence, though there were often problems with wives and girlfriends. Mandela would warn prisoners before they left that they would have difficulties adjusting to their wives.[74] The prevailing atmosphere remained puritanical and self-denying – reinforced by the complete lack of alcohol, which in some other jails could incapacitate intelligent prisoners.

The prisoners' isolation provided a unique opportunity for continuous and organised study, protected from all the interruptions and disconuities of urban life – the advertisements, magazines and sound-bites which normally provided constant distractions – what Coleridge called 'destroyers of the memory'.[75] The lack of written texts put a premium on memory, and many prisoners found they could recall quotations or verses they thought they had forgotten. 'The amazing thing is that people were remembering things,' said Fikile Bam. 'They came back in their sleep.'[76] Lesley van der Heyden, a former English teacher who gave classes on the island, found his mind bringing back forgotten poetry.[77] The need to memorise facts concentrated the mind. 'You had to listen to what they say outside: that listening had got to be sharp,' said Sisulu afterwards. 'I had to rely on my memory, now I rely on what I write.'[78] 'One thing a prisoner has is his memory,' recalled Raks Seakhoa, who came to the island as a barely-educated boy and emerged a serious writer. 'My memory was very intact – unlike now, when I forget both silly and serious things.'[79] Even Neville Alexander, who arrived as a highly-educated academic, found his memory improved on the island because he could not write anything down. Meanwhile his mind was being sharpened by argument: 'The challenge of debating and competing with people like Nelson was quite important for becoming rigorous and systematic.'[80]

Mandela already had an exceptional memory, as he had known since school. After his humiliations at university, he was able to study more systematically in his cell, pursuing his LLB degree until that privilege was withdrawn. He sometimes worried that his memory was failing, but his legal mind was honed by establishing an informal practice on the island, advising all kinds of prisoners, many of them illiterate, on matters such as how to appeal against their sentences, and even helping warders with their own legal problems.[81] More important, he was developing his intellectual powers and his interest in ideas. 'From year to year he was changing and revising his views,' said Fikile Bam. 'He didn't have ideological depth before he came in: he got that in prison.'[82]

The climate of discipline gave graduates of Robben Island an authority and confidence which never left them. It was, in the words of the historians Tom Karis and Gail Gerhart, 'a culture of comradeship, co-operation and learning, of fierce debate coupled with a political tolerance'.[83] It was this common culture, with Mandela as the role-model, which would be so important during the peaceful transfer of power twenty years later.

The quarry was not only a campus, but a debating club. After the first two years the warders became less strict in supervising the prisoners, and allowed them to talk as they worked. Mandela would join their small groups in discussing all kinds of topics. Should boys be circumcised? Were there tigers in Africa? Should homosexuality be tolerated in prison? But it was in the political arguments that he faced his real challenges. Within the isolation section there were always differences between the four ANC leaders who made up the original High Organ. Mandela and

Sisulu, both conciliators from the Transvaal, were often at odds with Govan Mbeki from the Eastern Cape, who as a convinced Marxist was impatient of consensus; but the High Organ had most trouble from Harry Gwala, a fiery communist from Natal known as 'the Lion of the Midlands', who was in the communal cells until he was released in 1973, but who returned four years later. Gwala combined a thorough knowledge of Marxist theory and history with a soapbox style which appealed to the younger prisoners; he organised lectures on 'the labour theory of value'.

By 1975 the left-wingers on the island, particularly Gwala's followers, were coming closer to challenging Mandela's leadership. They were reluctant to talk about it afterwards, but one anonymous prisoner with his own agenda smuggled a document off the island to Lusaka which painted a picture of 'gossip cells and mud-slinging camps', and of bitter complaints against the original four members of the High Organ for their lack of self-criticism and their 'casual blunders', resurrecting old arguments from the pre-jail period.[84] Fikile Bam reckoned that about 70 per cent of Section B supported Mandela; though if the political prisoners in the general cells had been counted in, he might have been in a minority.[85] Others thought Mandela's support was much higher. After 1975 the immediate crisis passed: the question of Mandela's leadership was put to all members of the Congresses, who reaffirmed it with an overwhelming vote of support. The motion, proposed by Sisulu and seconded by Kathrada, acknowledged him to be 'first among equals'. But the arguments were to surge up again when Harry Gwala returned to Robben Island in 1977.[86]

The most acrimonious question had worried Mandela since the fifties – the question which torments all revolutionaries confronting government bodies which try to co-opt their people. Should they boycott such institutions altogether, or infiltrate them and try to subvert them from within? Mandela was especially concerned about the Transkei, which the Verwoerd government was preparing as the showpiece of 'separate development', as the first of the Bantustans. Soon after he had first gone to prison in 1962 the ANC held a conference in Lobatse, Bechuanaland, where it had voted to boycott the forthcoming Transkei elections. Mandela opposed that decision: he thought the ANC could not enforce a boycott anyway, and that they should instead support the opposition party of Chief Victor Poto, which was challenging Pretoria's preferred candidate – Mandela's nephew Kaiser Matanzima. By exploiting the elections, Mandela argued, the ANC could gradually build up a mass organisation, and eventually make the Bantustan system unworkable.[87]

This argument was erupting again on Robben Island after 1969, when Mandela had what he tactfully called 'sharp differences' with Govan Mbeki and his supporters, which led to 'one of the longest and most delicate debates'.[88] For some time Mandela and Mbeki had strained relations. The more rigid communists, and the Trotskyists of the Unity Movement, argued that to participate in elections was to sell out to apartheid and to distract people from the armed struggle. They wanted to follow the example of the Bolsheviks who boycotted the elections to the Russian Duma before the revolution in 1917. Mandela conceded that participation could be dangerous, and could sow confusion among the people. But he insisted, as he had in the fifties, that the ANC must remain pragmatic; and they could use the electoral process to build up a mass following in the rural areas. He quoted the Sotho proverb 'A river is filled by little streams.'[89]

Mandela still refused to compromise on the basic issue of apartheid. He showed his strength when in December 1974 he had an unexpected visit from a Cabinet Minister: Jimmy Kruger, the Minister of Justice. Mandela described Kruger in a letter to Winnie, with an eye on the censor, as 'warm, cheerful and full of humour'; in fact he found him crude, ignorant and surprisingly unsophisticated. Kruger first tried to persuade Mandela and some of his colleagues to abandon the armed struggle. Mandela countered by explaining the history of the ANC and the Freedom Charter, which Kruger had never heard of. To Mandela's amazement, he did not even know about the Afrikaner rebels in the First World War.[90] 'Kruger tried to put us on the carpet,' Mac Maharaj commented, 'and Nelson put him on the carpet instead.' Kruger went on to ask Mandela, with unexpected deference, to recognise the legitimacy of the Transkei government, now under the autocratic rule of his nephew Matanzima, and suggested that he could soon be released if he went to live there. Mandela, with his colleagues' backing, had no doubts about his reply: he could not support the fraudulent policy of separate development. He gave the same answer when Kruger returned a month later. Mandela suspected that Kruger was simply playing white politics – a suspicion which was confirmed shortly afterwards when Kruger attacked Mandela in Parliament as a card-carrying communist.[91]

Mandela now had more time for reflection and analysis, which he could channel into writing his autobiography. It was the idea of Sisulu and Kathrada, and was endorsed by Maharaj, who suggested in 1975 that it should be published on his sixtieth birthday, in 1978, to encourage the liberation movement abroad.[92] Writing the book demanded all Mandela's powers of memory and concentration, but it was easier while the warders were more relaxed. He would sleep for part of the day and write energetically during the night, turning out a long book, complete with many complicated details, in four months. He wrote fluently, with only a few crossings-out. Some sections were headed as letters to his daughter, 'my darling Zeni'. 'I wish I could tell you more about the courageous band of colleagues,' he wrote in one chapter, 'but a curious warder is walking up and down the passage peering in from time to time to chat. I am working under heavy pressure and on strict deadline. Every completed sheet must leave the prison daily and I never see it again.'[93]

It was a remarkable and well-written document, first vividly recapturing his childhood in the Transkei, then describing his growing political commitment through protests, meetings and trials. He assessed the state of the struggle candidly, from the detachment of jail. 'Fourteen years ago, when I returned from abroad,' he admitted, 'we were confident that the movement inside the country would be far stronger than it is at present, and be able to exert a lot of pressure on the enemy.' But he was heartened by the massive international efforts for his release. He took a long historical perspective: he looked back at the past courage of the Afrikaners in fighting for their independence against the British, but saw them as 'a minority of oppressors heavily outnumbered here at home and isolated in the entire world'. Now it was the Africans who were fighting to regain their lost freedom. But he was careful to correct any impression that the struggle was motivated by revenge.

> The wheel of life is there, and national heroes from Autshumao to Luthuli, in fact the entire people of our country, have been working for it for more than three centuries. It is clogged with dry wax and rust, but we have managed to make it creak and move backwards and forwards: and we live in the hope and confidence that one day we will be able to turn it full circle so that the exalted will crumble and the despised be exalted. No – so that all men, the exalted and the wretched of the earth, can live as equals.[94]

Every day Mandela passed Maharaj ten pages of foolscap. He could not refer to the previous pages, as Maharaj recalled: 'He simply had to keep in his mind what he had already written and his train of thought.' Huddled under a blanket, Maharaj then copied out Mandela's work in tiny writing – less than half a millimetre high – and concealed the small pages among his study books. The original would be given to Kathrada and Sisulu for their candid comments and corrections. Maharaj then hid the revised miniature sheets inside the binding of a book of statistics, which he planned to smuggle out when he finished his sentence in 1976. Kathrada kept Mandela's original text as a standby, burying it, with the help of colleagues, in three plastic containers under the courtyard. Disaster struck when some other prisoners began digging the foundations of a new wall on that very spot. Mandela and his friends managed to destroy two of the containers, but the third was discovered and sent to the commanding officer.[95]

The Commissioner of Prisons wrote a confidential report to his Minister on 26 October 1977 – a very long delay – explaining that this 'undesirable literature' had been found, and verified by handwriting experts of the South African Police as having been written by Mandela, with additions by Maharaj and Kathrada. He summarised the ten chapters, emphasising the influences on Mandela, including the poet Mkwayi and Bram Fischer; his meetings with black leaders in Africa, and his critical remarks about Prime Minister Vorster. He believed that the trend of the writing 'certainly justifies a further case against Mandela' – which might not be useful, since he was already serving a life sentence for similar contraventions. He pointed out that as the prisoners had used paper supplied for studying, their study privileges might be permanently withdrawn. In fact Mandela, Sisulu and Kathrada were all stopped from studying for four years. (Mandela's manuscript, having been scrutinised, was kept among the prison records.)[96]

The loss of study privileges was a heavy price to pay for an adventure which was ultimately to be frustrated. The miniature pages were duly smuggled out by Maharaj in 1976. He sent them on to London, where they were retyped and forwarded to Oliver Tambo. The typescript was seen by very few people, but Joe Slovo and Yusuf Dadoo, the communists in exile, made it clear to Maharaj that they thought it did not give proper credit to the communists' role in the struggle.[97] It remained unpublished, and disappeared for twenty years. 'Naturally I'm surprised, disappointed and distressed,' Kathrada wrote from Pollsmoor when he learnt in 1989 that it had not yet appeared.[98] It was not until 1994 that it was to provide the basis for the first two-thirds of Mandela's published autobiography, *Long Walk to Freedom*.

By the mid-seventies most of the Robben Islanders had accepted a code of behaviour and co-operation. As Neville Alexander put it, confrontations were 'avoided and never provoked': 'Negotiations with the authorities, patient discussions and persuasion are the preferred methods. Civility and dignity are insisted upon, also voluntary discipline. On the other hand, no semblance of servility is tolerated. Rudeness is rebutted firmly but politely, as far as possible.'[99]

Mandela's complaints to the prison authorities could infuriate the staff. In July 1976 the commanding officer, Colonel J. du Preez, sent on a letter from Mandela to the Commissioner in Pretoria, with an exasperated comment proposing that Mandela's status be downgraded (which the Commissioner rejected):

> He systematically and in a psychological manner brought the reader under the impression of his own importance, self-esteem and the very high level at which he as a prisoner communicates and clearly creates the impression that the warders, the head of the prison and even the commanding officer are of no importance in solving his problems . . .
>
> I consider Mandela and the other prisoners in his section as extremely dangerous and as serious statutory offenders who do not hesitate to admit that they have no intention of rehabilitating themselves: their main aim is to create feelings of disloyalty, corruption, abuse of authority etc. against the department and its members . . . [100]

Three years later the Commissioner wrote to the Minister enclosing a letter which Mandela and Raymond Mhlaba had written complaining about racial discrimination on the island: 'In view of the sheer arrogance of the letter it is suggested that note be taken of the contents and that it be filed' – which it was.[101]

Mandela provided the model for the other prisoners, setting a style of confidence and dignity which rose above the daily tensions and humiliations, and appearing truly 'master of his fate'. Alexander claimed that prison could provide personal liberation – from convention, pettiness or self-consciousness – and Mandela did indeed feel liberated in many ways. The prisoners, he reckoned, were freed from the fear of the oppressor, which had so often paralysed the movement: 'Once you have rid yourself of the fear of the oppressor and his prisons, his police, his army, there is nothing that they can do. You are liberated . . . You don't want to be assaulted, you don't want to be hurt, and you feel the pain and humiliation. But nevertheless you feel that this is the price you have to pay in order to assert your views, your ideas.'[102]

After Mac Maharaj was released in December 1976, he described Mandela's state of mind. His cruellest punishment after coming from the heat of battle, thought Maharaj, was to be outside the area of deciding tactics: 'You now have to accept that you are in that sense on the sidelines, you have to trust to your comrades.' Mandela's ideas about basic strategy were becoming stronger and firmer: he saw the armed struggle as central to liberation, but felt sanctions would play 'a very important subsidiary role' by depriving the regime of support from international trade and investment. Maharaj had seen Mandela 'watching his enemy' – looking for any contradictions and divisions in Pretoria, while guarding against government attempts to divide the ANC through anti-communist scares.

Maharaj, like the others, was inspired by Mandela's morale, but his warm and welcoming style could be misleading: Mandela, he soon realised, took a long time to become an intimate friend, and even then he still kept his distance. He had developed almost total control over his anger, and behind his kind and gentle manner he had 'steeled and hardened' himself: 'As he has been living through prison, his anger and hatred of the system has been increasing, but the manifestations of that anger have become less visible to a person. They are more subdued, more tempered. They've become more cold and analytical in focusing on the evils of the system.'[103]

Mandela endorsed that assessment. He had successfully suppressed his emotions and maintained his rationality and self-discipline in the face of the most provocative encounters. 'When one is faced with such situations you want to think clearly,' he explained, 'and obviously you think more clearly if you are cool, you are steady, you are not rattled. Once you become rattled you can make serious mistakes.'[104]

But he was to face much more painful challenges within his family, from whom he could not keep his feelings.

17

Lady into Amazon

1962–1976

MANDELA WAS ABLE to relate to his fellow-prisoners, and even to his warders. But he found it harder to relate to his family. While he was underground or on trial, he had already become more distant from his children as his political life had absorbed him, like so many great leaders, and his divorce had left many resentments. But in jail he paid a still heavier domestic price. He was cut off from his second, younger family during their formative years; while they grew away from him, and began to see him as an impersonal myth.

Mandela had always been a demanding, ambitious father, an almost Victorian paterfamilias. He felt a heavy responsibility as head of the family, and set high educational goals for his children which they felt they could not attain. 'With his family he was conservative and authoritarian,' said one of them. 'He wanted a dynasty like the Kennedys.'[1] His seclusion in prison multiplied the distance and the obstacles. On their rare visits, the children appeared almost as strangers: he could not touch or feel them, and he could not keep pace with their adulthood as they went their independent ways. His emotional letters from jail to his wife and children, so different from his controlled political letters and statements, express all the anguish of a man who saw his family slipping away from him.

In his first five years on Robben Island Mandela faced two family tragedies. In 1968 his sister Mabel brought their aged mother from the Transkei to see him, together with his second son Makgatho and his daughter Maki. Mabel had been apprehensive about the visit, fearful of their mother's health being affected by the sea voyage and the attentions of the police, who took all her details as if they expected her to die.[2] Mandela had last seen his mother very briefly at the Rivonia Trial, as a bent, frail figure; in the prison his warder overheard him whispering to Mabel that he was worried by his mother's thin, haggard look, and he was unusually silent after she left.[3] A few weeks later a telegram told him she had died. Mandela was filled with self-recrimination about his past neglect of her. As her only son, he asked to be allowed to bury her in the Transkei – he recalled that Nehru had been let out of prison to take his wife to a tuberculosis clinic in Switzerland. But the government refused to grant him permission, fearing that he might escape. It was left for the tribal grandees, King Sabata and Paramount Chief Kaiser Matanzima, to arrange the funeral, while the Zulu leader Chief Mangosuthu Buthelezi sent a letter of condolence.[4]

Mandela was distressed that he received no visits from his eldest son Thembi, though he was living in Cape Town. Thembi had often seemed his favourite and brightest child. He had worshipped his father when he went underground in 1961, even wearing his jacket, proud to share his responsibility and secrets. But Thembi was upset by his parents' divorce, and was torn between his father's politics and his mother's religion. He was only sixteen when Mandela went to jail. He distressed his father by not writing to him, and by marrying very young, to the daughter of a Cape Town shopkeeper, with whom he had two daughters. In 1969, when the youngest girl was only six months old, Mandela was given a telegram with the news that Thembi had been killed in a car crash. He was devastated, and lay on his bed, taking no supper, until Sisulu came in, knelt by him and held his hand in silent sympathy. By the next morning he appeared to his colleagues to be his usual self. He sent Evelyn a message of sympathy – the only contact he was to have with her while he was in jail – but to his great sorrow he was again refused permission to attend the funeral.[5]

He felt all the more dependent on Winnie; but he was acutely aware that she was younger and less experienced than his contemporaries' wives, and that she was being persecuted by the police. They had been married for only four years when he went to jail, leaving her with two daughters. In passionate letters – at first limited to only two a year, later one a month – he seemed to idealise her, without considering her mistakes and shortcomings.

Winnie was all too conscious of her political responsibility and name: 'I was ready to deputise for Nelson,' as she put it. 'I had to think so carefully what I said – as his representative.'[6] She had some close women friends, including Helen Joseph, the veteran of the Treason Trials, and Fatima Meer in Durban, but she could be overbearing towards senior political women like Albertina Sisulu, and she often rashly looked to new men friends for support.[7] Most ANC activists were detained soon after Mandela's arrest, and Winnie longed for political allies. 'Anyone who showed any kindness was taken at face value,' as George Bizos put it.[8] But Winnie was in a social and political minefield, with spies and informers everywhere. She was especially friendly with Brian Somana, a journalist whose wife soon afterwards divorced him, naming Winnie as an adulteress, which she denied. Somana had earlier been close to ANC leaders, but after detention he had been turned by the police, giving away his ex-colleagues, and was suspected by some of revealing the hideout at Rivonia.[9]

It was in this confused state that Winnie made her first visit to Robben Island in August 1964, immaculately dressed, travelling with Albertina Sisulu. She had a brief half-hour encounter with Mandela in a bleak shed near the harbour, out of sight of the cells.[10] She was forbidden to speak Xhosa or to discuss anyone outside the immediate 'first degree' family. She and Mandela shouted through the window, while warders watched and listened on both sides, interrupting if they heard an unfamiliar name. Mandela, worried that Winnie had grown thinner and was under obvious stress, urged her to stop dieting. 'Oh, our men are shrinking here!' said Albertina Sisulu as they were being taken away, 'But their spirit is so strong.'[11] Mandela went back to his cell frustrated and bewildered by the lack of any physical contact with his wife. He could not stop worrying about Winnie, though he did not betray his emotions to his comrades.

Back in Johannesburg, Winnie was encircled by spies. The police had virtually crushed black political activity, but they saw her both as a likely underground channel and as a means of demoralising her husband. And the 'Dirty Tricks' department run by the secret service chief van den Bergh was determined (according to his agent Gordon Winter) 'to stifle the political life out of this troublesome woman'.[12] Winnie was banned from leaving Johannesburg, which prevented her from visiting her children's schools: she claims she never met a single one of their teachers. And the children, she said, 'kept being expelled once it was discovered who they were – but they were toddlers, they knew nothing. People were petrified.'[13] They were eventually sent to a convent school in Swaziland, out of the reach of the South African police. They thought the school, Our Lady of Sorrows, was well-named, and Zindzi complained that nobody was caring for them.[14]

It was two years before Winnie was allowed another visit to Robben Island, under still stricter supervision, tailed by the police from the airport to the boat. The warder James Gregory watched her talking to her husband through the glass, 'like seeing life through a 1950s black and white television screen'. She behaved with great decorum and dignity, Gregory said, but he was amazed to see 'the woman with a pride as fierce as any lioness, with tears rolling down her cheeks'.[15]

Mandela was worried by the hounding of the girls from school to school, and at this meeting they reluctantly agreed to send them to board at Waterford, a new multi-racial school in Swaziland – with the help of Helen Joseph and Winnie's new friend Elinor Birley, the wife of the ex-headmaster of Eton.[16] Mandela worried that Winnie could be too trusting, but he did not ask her about boyfriends: 'That was a question one had to wipe out of his mind,' he said. 'One must not be inquisitive. It is sufficient that this is a woman who is loyal to me, who supports and who comes to visit me, who writes to me.'[17]

Back in Johannesburg, Winnie was charged pettily with having failed to report to the police in Cape Town, and given a suspended sentence of a year's imprisonment – which cost her her precious job as a social worker. She was under constant pressure, and was beginning to turn to violence. One day a police sergeant invaded her bedroom in Orlando without knocking: she threw him on the floor (as she told it), and the dressing-stand fell on him, nearly breaking his neck. She was charged with resisting arrest. Mandela, she recalled, had once warned her: 'Zami, you are completely and utterly undisciplined! You need a great deal of taming!' Now there was no one to tame her. At her trial her lawyer George Bizos warned her to behave like a lady, not like an Amazon; and the magistrate acquitted her.[18]

Winnie remained banned from any political activity, but she could not keep away from it. She was helping the families of ANC women who had been jailed, and rashly arranged to print and distribute pamphlets for the ANC with the help of her friend Mohale Mahanyele, who worked for the US Information Agency. The police, now armed with the drastic powers of the Terrorism Act of 1967, were still determined to get Winnie. They laid an elaborate trap through their informers to provide her with a network of false friends. They included an Indian crook named Moosa Dinath, whom Mandela had originally recommended to her, not knowing about his criminal record, and his girlfriend Maud Katzenellenbogen, who were using Winnie to try to penetrate the Defence and Aid fund in London, which supported detainees. They also provided Winnie with an attorney, Mendel Levin, who turned out to be a government supporter with a shady past. On 12 May 1969 Winnie was arrested with twenty-one others whom she had rashly involved in her pamphlet-distributing operation. The police spy Gordon Winter, who had befriended her, had intercepted all their communications.[19]

The police came for Winnie at dawn, hauling her away from her children. 'They were grabbing my skirts,' she remembers, 'screaming, "Mummy, don't leave us! Mummy, where are you going?"'[20] She was held in solitary confinement in Pretoria, in a small cell with a bucket, a plastic bottle of water and a Bible. Later she was interrogated for five days and nights by the notorious torturer Swanepoel about her contacts with the ANC and communists, and with her women friends in jail.[21] The police had already extracted confessions from other prisoners, including Mohale Mahanyele, who had turned state witness. 'I could not believe his total betrayal of the cause we both worked for,' Winnie said later.[22]

The flamboyant lawyer Joel Carlson, whom Mandela had asked to represent her, was allowed to see her and her fellow-prisoners after they had spent two hundred days in solitary detention. They had not been allowed a bath or shower, and were kept in cells five feet by ten feet, sometimes with only ten minutes a day for exercise. 'They said the food was inedible and could only be eaten when they were driven to it by hunger.' The police pressed Winnie to make a radio statement calling on the black people to abandon illegal struggles and to co-operate with whites; in return Mandela would be released to the Transkei. She refused. 'Winnie wavered between sanity and insanity,' wrote Carlson afterwards, 'and never quite knew whether she would be able to live through her first period of detention.'[23]

At last, in December, she came up for trial with the other twenty-one in Pretoria, on broad charges under the Suppression of Communism Act, including reviving the ANC and receiving instructions from Mandela on Robben Island.[24] After two months the prosecution was withdrawn, but they were immediately re-arrested, and charged again in June 1970 under the Terrorism Act – by which time Winnie was in the prison hospital suffering from malnutrition, bleeding gums and fainting fits. In October she and the twenty-one were again brought to trial: but their counsel Sydney Kentridge was able to show that the indictment was almost identical with the first one, and the case collapsed.[25]

After thirteen months in solitary confinement, Winnie was still further out of control. On the surface she seemed extraordinarily carefree and vivacious. Joel Carlson, who gave a party for her release, remembers her 'filled with laughter, excitement and gaiety'.[26] She was gaunt, but with her eyes looking all the bigger. She insisted that she had gained strength from the ordeal. 'I got more liberated in prison,' she wrote later. 'My soul has been more purified by prison than anything else.'[27] But her liberation had a double edge. 'After that experience I never had respect for anyone in authority,' she explained. 'I then realised the brutality of apartheid and the fascisms of our harassment by the state . . . I knew at that point in time that I would not hesitate to use violence to attain my ideals.'[28] Some former admirers thought she had been unhinged. As Helen Suzman put it: 'They turned her from a warm-hearted person into a mad creature.'[29]

On Robben Island Mandela learnt something about Winnie's ordeal from newspaper cuttings the warders deliberately left in his cell. It was almost his worst moment when he heard that she too was in jail, under grimmer conditions than his. He had found his own brief solitary confinement 'the most forbidding aspect of prison life . . . there is no distraction from these haunting questions'. He felt helplessly guilty at not being there to defend Winnie. But he tried to keep cool and to remember that they were paying the price for being committed to the struggle.[30] And he and his colleagues had to admire Winnie for her courage in keeping the struggle alive, despite all the risks. 'However rash Winnie was,' said Bizos, 'they were proud of her.'[31]

Winnie was banned once again, for five years, but eventually received permission to visit Mandela – for only half an hour. She returned to Johannesburg in poor health, with bronchitis and high blood pressure, but was still being persecuted. Mandela learnt with anger that the police had kicked down her front door and hurled bricks at the window. White sympathisers who befriended her were harassed in turn, and some were put off by Winnie's paranoid moods and her escapades. Joel Carlson became exasperated by her unreliability, and warned her against political involvement; when she ignored him he gave up, and left for America. She would continue to be rash in her choice of friends. One of them, the journalist John Horak, helped look after the children, but his more serious career was as a police spy. (He later claimed that Winnie turned him into a double agent working for the ANC.)[32]

The police still harassed her and the children. 'Many times when the girls came home from school,' Winnie recalled, 'they found the house locked and had to look in the newspapers to see if I was detained.'[33] Since 1970 Mandela had kept up the pressure for her bans to be lifted, and in 1974 he asked for the police to be restrained, and for Winnie to be allowed a firearm to protect herself. The police headquarters could not recommend a gun: 'Mrs Mandela is known to be impulsive, quick-tempered and inclined to lose control.'[34]

Winnie had gained much moral support from her friend Peter Magubane, the *Drum* photographer, but he too was persecuted: he had been betrayed by Gordon Winter and was detained for 586 days, many in solitary confinement.[35] He remained loyal to Winnie, and in May 1973 he drove Zeni and Zindzi to meet her near the lawyer's office where she was working. The police saw them, and charged Winnie with illegal communication. She was sentenced to six months in Kroonstad jail, which was less harrowing than her solitary confinement, and she had proper food and weekend visits from the children.[36]

On Robben Island, Mandela was agonised when he heard about this new imprisonment. He could not concentrate on games, he told her, because he was thinking of her in jail. 'Although I always try to put up a brave face, I never get used to you being in the cooler,' he told her later. 'I will never forget the desperately distressing experiences we had from May '69 to September '70 and the six months you spent in Kroonstad.' He gave her some advice which reflected his own strict self-discipline in jail:

> You may find that the cell is an ideal place to learn to know yourself, to search realistically and regularly the processes of your own mind and feelings. In judging our progress as individuals we tend to concentrate on external factors such as one's social position, influence and popularity, wealth and standard of education . . . but internal factors may be even more crucial in assessing one's development as a human being: honesty, sincerity, simplicity, humility, purity, generosity, absence of vanity, readiness to serve your fellow men – qualities within the reach of

every soul – are the foundation of one's spiritual life . . . at least, if for nothing else, the cell gives you the opportunity to look daily into your entire conduct to overcome the bad and develop whatever is good in you. Regular meditation, say of about 15 minutes a day before you turn in, can be very fruitful in this regard. You may find it difficult at first to pinpoint the negative factors in your life, but the tenth attempt may reap rich rewards. Never forget that a saint is a sinner that keeps on trying.[37]

Mandela tried to organise the family from his jail while Winnie was in hers. Her sister Nobantu Mniki was looking after the house in Orlando, which he told her to cling to until Winnie returned. He warned Winnie that she would return to an atmosphere which might be 'more chilly and glum', but reassured her: 'Difficulties break some men but make others.' He arranged for Nobantu to 'prepare a dinner of ox tongue and tail and dumplings and champagne to wash it down' on the day she came out.[38] 'I wish I could be home the day you return,' he told Winnie, visualising the feast. 'I would then put you to bed with a song or two. Thereafter I would listen directly to you for days on end as you relate your experiences from Oct 14 to Apr 13. I would take you back to the very last day I saw you as a free man in July 62.' He seemed elated just by thinking about it: 'I feel like one who will live for another hundred years.'[39]

The two girls were confused: 'Our house was an extension of the police station,' said Winnie.[40] While Winnie was in jail Mandela warned Zeni: 'The wicked criminals that have repeatedly attacked Mum and ruined her health may now concentrate on you and Zindzi.'[41] They were cared for by friends, including Peter Magubane and Winnie's sister Nonyaniso, who were both in turn imprisoned. Fatima Meer in Durban helped out, to Mandela's relief: 'I would have been quite sure that . . . they would not be orphans as long as you were alive,' he told her.[42] But Fatima found the girls difficult. 'They were rarely happy with the arrangements,' she recalled, 'and often complained or became the targets of their benefactors' complaints.'[43]

The children were becoming more distant from their father, but remained loyal to their mother. When Zindzi was only thirteen she wrote to the UN's Special Committee on Apartheid in New York, asking them to protect her: 'The family and mummy's friends fear that an atmosphere is being built for something terrible to happen to Mum.' When Winnie was sentenced two years later, Zeni said, 'Now we are old enough to share her sorrow and grief with her.'[44] Mandela wrote affectionately to the two girls, but was stern about schooling, and was worried that they might be spoilt by the examples of richer children at Waterford. 'Judging from the girls' letters, travelling to Europe and America has become quite a craze at their school,' he wrote to a friend in 1974. 'I am tempted to remind them that they are my children, a fact that may place insurmountable difficulties in their path. But hard reality does not often coincide with the people's wishes, especially when these people are children.'[45]

After her release Winnie was eventually allowed to visit Mandela again, with both their daughters, in December 1975.[46] Zindzi was only fifteen – a year below the minimum age for visitors – but Winnie forged her birth certificate. Mandela had not seen her since she was three, and prepared himself with a new shirt and carefully combed hair: 'I did not want to look like an old man for my youngest daughter.' He was enchanted by Zindzi's beauty and resemblance to Winnie: 'I can imagine you sitting on my lap at home and having a Sunday roast with the family,' he told her. He reminisced about her babyhood, while through the glass she restrained her tears; but he noticed her reserve with a father who 'seemed to belong not to her but to the people'. He felt that 'somewhere deep inside she must have harboured resentment and anger for a father who was absent during her childhood and adolescence.'[47] And he soon learnt that Winnie could be jealous of his love for his daughters. When he wrote to her saying how beautifully they had grown up, he recalled to Fatima, Winnie was furious, as if this were treason, and retorted: 'I, not you, brought up these children whom you prefer to me.'[48]

He found it even harder to communicate with his two elder children, Maki and Makgatho, who moved between their mother Evelyn and their stepmother 'Mum Winnie'. Mandela had very limited news of them. With his memories of his own stepmothers, he seemed confident that they were all part of the same extended African family: he would remind them how Winnie had looked after them diligently while he was underground, and he reproved them for not being properly grateful.[49] But they had a different view: 'He didn't realise that Winnie wasn't doing what she promised him,' said Maki. 'We were at war with Winnie.'[50]

Mandela's son Makgatho visited him on Robben Island when he was sixteen in 1967, and once or twice a year over the next ten years. But he was soon disappointing his father with his school record: he was expelled for organising a strike, and kept failing his matriculation. Makgatho felt his father's pressure to succeed, all the more after his elder brother Thembi was killed in 1969, but at twenty-four he could not face going back to school. 'The real problem,' his father wrote from jail in November 1974, 'is that at his age and in my absence he finds it hard to resist the attractions of city life.'[51] He married Rayne Mosehle, who soon showed herself more studious than her husband, and more attentive in writing to Mandela. 'It is not easy to write to a person who hardly ever replies,' Mandela told Makgatho.[52] He told Rayne that his son was 'in most respects a sweet lad. But one of his weaknesses is his failure to write even when serious family problems are involved.'[53]

His daughter Maki visited Mandela in 1970, when she turned sixteen. She was a stronger character than Makgatho, more outspoken and more influenced by her mother Evelyn, who had brought her into her own faith as a Jehovah's Witness. After 1972 she often visited Evelyn in the Transkei, where Mandela's nephew Kaiser Matanzima had found Evelyn a grocery shop to run in Cofimvaba. Maki excelled at school, but she refused to go on to university, and married instead, to Camagu: she had two children by him before the marriage broke up a few years later. Mandela was sympathetic and helpful about the divorce, for which Maki was grateful. But he was disappointed that her greatest ambition was to be a nurse: 'Those without real ambition and drive,' he warned her, 'are left to work hard in inferior positions for the rest of their lives.'[54]

Winnie remained the chief outlet for his emotions, bringing out a romanticism he kept hidden from others. 'I have been fairly successful in putting on a mask behind which I have pined for the family, alone, never rushing for the post when it comes until somebody calls my name,' he wrote to her after a visit in 1976. 'I also never linger after visits although sometimes the urge to do so becomes quite terrible. I am struggling to suppress my emotions as I write this letter.' After she had visited him in August 1975, he told her: 'I said to myself: "There goes Msuthu like a bird in hand returning to the bush, to the wild jungle and the wide world."' 'I've plans, wishes and hopes. I dream and build castles,' he wrote the next month. 'But one has to be realistic. We're mere individuals in a society run by powerful institutions with its conventions, norms, morals, ideals and attitudes.'

Mandela felt deprived when Winnie did not write for over a month: 'You witch! You've numerous ways of keeping me hitched to you. But this is a new one.' He celebrated her birthday in September 1975 with 'a magnificent brew fit for a monarch' consisting of four teaspoons of powdered milk, three teaspoons of Milo and two teaspoons of brown sugar, all mixed in hot water. He dusted her photograph in his cell every morning. 'I even touch your nose with mine to recapture the electric current that used to flush through my blood whenever I did so.' And he pictured in his mind 'the shape of your forehead, shoulders, limbs, the loving remarks which come daily and the blind eye you've always turned against those numerous shortcomings that would have frustrated another woman'. 'My appetite is good and I sleep well,' he assured her next month. 'Above all, strength and supreme optimism runs through my blood because I know you love me and that I enjoy the good wishes of countless family members.' 'I light up immediately your letter comes,' he wrote to her in July, 'and I feel like flying where eagles cannot reach.'[55]

Other friends and relations helped to keep up his spirits. They made him realise (he told Winnie's sister Nobantu) 'that there are far more people wishing me well, and success in everything I do, than otherwise'.[56] 'Hope is the horse on which you travel to your destination to reach the winning post,' he wrote to Barbara Lamb, the daughter of his old friend Michael Harmel. 'My only fortune in life is to have friends who have taught me these things amongst whom was your darling pa.'[57]

But Winnie was his main source of strength, and of political information. She would bring him news in coded language, and he would reply with hints of his real views. 'The year 1975 started off badly and was disastrous from beginning to end,' he told her in 1976, 'and many fault-lines that had withstood the furious onslaught of the merciless forces of fate, caved in.'[58] Winnie was also the crucial messenger of political news for other prisoners: 'She was the best source,' said Kathrada. 'All other prisoners waited for her visits.'[59] After each visit they would wait anxiously for Mandela to reveal what he had learnt – which he would sometimes delay, with maddening self-control.

'Without Winnie, Nelson wouldn't have been what he is,' said Peter Magubane, who would remain the friend of both. 'When newspapers could not write about him, she could have his problems publicised. Without her, the ANC would have been forgotten. She was the only person who stood by the ANC and said, "I dare you to stop me." She was prepared to die for it.'[60]

Winnie, with all her faults, was becoming a major actor on the political scene in her own right, who could keep the name Mandela alive inside and outside South Africa. And in 1976, when the black opposition suddenly erupted in a new form, she would pop up in the thick of it.

18

The Shadowy Presence

1964–1976

THE PRISONERS CRAVED more news from outside. When Mandela was caught with a newspaper he had picked up from a bench he was sentenced to three days' solitary confinement with a diet of rice water. Newspapers were the most precious contraband, the raw material of the struggle, said Mandela afterwards. The prisoners would go to extreme lengths to get a newspaper: bribing warders, stealing them from visiting priests, or retrieving the newsprint wrapping from the warders' sandwiches. Maharaj even cajoled a warder, by getting his fingerprints on a cigarette packet, to smuggle in a newspaper every day, which he then summarised in his tiny writing to circulate among the other prisoners.[1] He managed to receive the *Economist* magazine in spite of the censors, on the grounds that he was studying economics; but it was often heavily censored, and was withdrawn for a time in 1967.[2] As Mandela wrote later: 'Our knowledge of current events was always sketchy.'[3]

What news they received was not encouraging. Since the Rivonia trial the police had almost obliterated any effective black opposition. 'There is scarcely an African political leader of note who is not in jail, in exile or under a restrictive order,' wrote Stanley Uys in the *Observer* just after Mandela had been sentenced. 'The security police have become extremely efficient, apparently with the aid of an extensive informer network, and no underground group seems able to get organised.'[4] Statements given after interrogation by ANC activists like Bartholomew Hlopane and Michael Dingake (later sent to Robben Island) show how deeply the police had penetrated the organisation. 'The present strength of the ANC is very weak indeed,' said Hlopane in an affidavit in October 1964. 'In my opinion there are no more than fifty members at present in Soweto.'[5]

Mandela soon learnt about the desolation from the captured saboteurs and guerrilla fighters who joined the island.

The hopelessness of resisting apartheid seemed personified by Mandela's friend Bram Fischer. Soon after visiting Mandela on the island in 1964 he had been arrested and charged with furthering communism. He was allowed bail, and disappeared underground: he owed it to the political prisoners, he later told the court, 'not to remain a spectator, but to act'.[6] After less than a year he was caught, and was sentenced in 1966 to life imprisonment. Had it really been worth giving up his family and career? George Bizos asked him. He replied sharply: 'Did you ask Nelson?' But Fischer paid a terrible price. In his all-white jail he was denied his human dignity, as Mandela said, 'by every means his jailers could imagine'. After Fischer contracted cancer in 1974 Mandela petitioned the Minister of Justice Jimmy Kruger to be allowed to see him, in vain. Fischer died the next year, and Mandela always deeply regretted that he had never conveyed his real feelings to him.[7]

The prisoners were always worried that they would disappear from the world's consciousness. 'Right from the outset, the prison department tried to bury us alive by cutting us completely off from the outside world,' Mandela wrote later.[8] 'At Rivonia we were told that no one will know the name Mandela in five years' time,' said Kathrada. 'There was collective amnesia: the world wasn't allowed to know anything about us, and vice-versa.'[9] 'We earnestly hope that they do not become forgotten men,' George Bizos wrote to me after the Rivonia trial.[10] But the prisoners were indeed soon almost forgotten by the media in Britain and America. In 1964 the London *Times* had fifty-eight references to Mandela, in 1965 two, in 1966 none, in 1967 four, in 1968 none, in 1969 two. The *New York Times* had twenty-four references in 1964, none in 1965 or 1966, one in 1967 – but to Winnie, not Nelson – and none in 1968. Without Winnie, Mandela would have been still more forgotten.

Within South Africa the name of Mandela was even more completely obliterated, through laws which forbade any mention of the ANC or its leaders. The activists seemed to have disappeared, and the poet Oswald Mtshali adapted the hippie song:

> Where have all the angry young men gone?
> Gone to the Island of Lament for Sharpeville . . .

It was all the more frustrating in contrast with the apparent liberation of the rest of Africa. '1964, a year that was the best of times for much of newly independent East and West Africa,' said the historians Karis and Gerhart, 'was the worst of times in the southern areas of the continent where the tides of empire had not yet receded.'[11]

'Verwoerd is dead!' whispered one of the ordinary criminals at the quarry in September 1966. The news gave the political prisoners a sudden ray of hope. Mandela was ambivalent when he learnt that Verwoerd had been killed by a deranged white messenger in Parliament, for assassination was not the ANC's policy. But he held some hopes for Verwoerd's successor Balthazar John Vorster: he had some fellow-feeling for Vorster, he wrote from jail, as a man who had been imprisoned for treason during the war: 'a man of strong beliefs prepared to fight for them'. He thought of him as 'deserving of the highest honours in so far as white conservative politics are concerned'.[12]

But Vorster's first acts gave little reason for optimism. He pushed through the new Terrorism Act of 1967, which gave the police still more draconian powers, and in 1969 established a ruthless new secret service, the Bureau of State Security (BOSS) under his old wartime colleague General Hendrik van den Bergh. His Minister of Defence, P.W. Botha, further extended the hold of the military. The news for the prisoners was nearly all bleak. 'The first few years on the island were difficult times both for the organisation outside and those of us in prison,' said Mandela afterwards.[13] 'The worst time was the sixties,' said Sisulu. 'But I didn't lose hope; I'm an optimist.'[14]

Mandela followed the news from the mainland with growing frustration, knowing that he was powerless to influence events. The prisoners had agreed from the start that they would not seek to interfere with the decisions of the ANC in exile, but Mandela did have fitful contacts with his former partner Oliver Tambo, by means of smuggled coded messages which have since come to light.[15] Through all the strains of separation he maintained his trust in Tambo, which would be a key to the ANC's unity and eventual success.

Mandela's first concern was with the progress of the armed struggle. Hopes rose in October 1967, when the prisoners learnt from the *Economist* that black South African soldiers were fighting along the Rhodesia–Zambia border. 'Although the terrorism has been contained easily enough,' it reported, 'the government seems unusually worried about it.'[16] ANC fighters in the 'Luthuli detachment' – the spearhead of MK – had, it turned out, crossed the Zambezi from Zambia to Rhodesia, personally supervised by Tambo, and joined by Zambian guerrillas. They had bravely fought the white Rhodesian army in the Wankie game reserve: Tambo announced optimistically on 19 August that they were 'fighting their way to strike at the Boers themselves in South Africa'. But the rebel force soon faced reinforcements from the South African army, and were eventually killed or captured after retreating to Botswana. Mandela did not learn the details until one of their commanders, Justice Mpanza, arrived on Robben Island.[17]

Tambo faced fierce criticism over the failed campaign when the ANC held a crucial conference at Morogoro, their headquarters in Tanzania, in 1969. The ANC reorganised the high command, and agreed to admit non-Africans for the first time – including Joe Slovo, who became commander of MK. The Robben Islanders were encouraged by this development. 'It had a tremendous impact on the whole question of Southern Africa and revolution,' said Sisulu.[18] But the new structure of the ANC would cause problems for Tambo by reviving suspicions that white communists were taking over the organisation.

Tambo remained a reluctant leader. He had been appointed Acting President of the ANC after Luthuli's death in 1967, but resisted becoming President. He insisted that the world assumed Mandela was really the President, but realised that Mandela could not be held responsible for conducting the armed struggle when he could not make crucial decisions, while if he were recognised officially as President he would be less likely to be released. The National Executive elected Tambo as President in his absence, which Tambo then challenged, but was overruled unanimously. He was worried that: 'I am the first and only President of the ANC to be elected by the NEC without a mandate from the available membership.'[19] He still called himself Acting President, and often referred to Mandela as 'Commander in Chief'.[20] It was not till 1977 that the decision was referred to the leaders on Robben Island, who confirmed Tambo as President; but he still avoided the title.[21] In his own mind Tambo had no doubt that Mandela was President-in-waiting, to whom he would defer.

Tambo's campaign against apartheid was made harder in the mid-sixties, when South Africa was enjoying a spectacular economic boom. The flight of foreign capital after Sharpeville in 1960 had been reversed, and by 1965 more investment was coming in than before the massacre. During the sixties South Africa's rate of growth averaged 6 per cent a year, outstripping nearly all Western nations, with an average return on capital of 15 per cent, much higher than in Europe. The biggest automobile manufacturers and other multinational corporations increased their presence, while West Germany became a major new investor.[22] The financial opportunities for overseas companies were extended by a huge increase in defence spending. The boom inevitably brought more blacks into the factories and cities, thus challenging the principle of apartheid. Vorster was all the more determined to press ahead with Verwoerd's plans for 'grand apartheid', which would give nominal independence to the new Bantustans while treating urban blacks as foreigners without rights.

Tambo's hopes of help from black South Africa were rapidly fading. The economic and military clout of Vorster's government enabled it to bully or seduce the much poorer new black nations to the north, which depended on it for trade, transport or migrant jobs. Tambo had expected increasing support from friendly neighbours as they emerged from being colonies to independence: more so when the three ex-British protectorates – Basutoland, Swaziland and Bechuanaland – achieved independence in 1966 and 1967. The United Nations swelled with new African members; the Organisation of African Unity (OAU), which emerged in 1963, made promises of boycotts and aid; and Zambia and Tanzania became the champions of black liberation. But by the end of the decade the harsh facts of economic dependence were asserting themselves. When fourteen heads of African states met in Zambia in May 1969 they proclaimed a 'Lusaka Manifesto', drafted without consulting the ANC, which stressed the need for compromise with South Africa and played down the armed struggle. At the ANC's Morogoro conference a week later Tambo warned about 'a sinister and vigorous counter-offensive' against the newly-independent states and liberation movements.[23]

Western governments could not resist the allure of the South African boom. South African businessmen, led by their biggest company, Anglo-American, liked to explain that South Africa was passing into a new stage of economic 'take-off', like Britain in the 1850s, in which prosperity would automatically compel reforms. This argument was taken up by the *Economist* in June 1968 in a long and influential study of South Africa by Norman Macrae. The whites, said Macrae, would become more liberal as they felt safer: 'richer and securer generally means lefter'. He described how the military seemed to have a complete grip on any black unrest: 'A few brave lunatics are sometimes infiltrated across the border with intentions of sabotage; they are then promptly picked up by the South African police which has informers in every one of those freedom-fighting camps.'[24]

Viewed from Robben Island, the outlook certainly seemed grim. 'It was the worst time,' said Maharaj, 'made worse by the numbers of fighters being caught, or failing to get in.'[25] By 1970 the South African prospects looked still grimmer, when the all-white general election showed no sign of the promised liberalisation. The United Party, led by de Villiers Graaff, were routed by Vorster's National Party and by the new right-wing Afrikaner party the Herstigte Nasionale Party (HNP). George Bizos, who visited the island periodically, was always struck by how morale fluctuated according to the black activity outside: now he found Mandela at his lowest ebb, worrying about the lack of opposition.[26] Resistance inside South Africa seemed almost to have disappeared. 'ANC' and 'PAC' were forbidden initials. Anyone seen with a Congress document could be detained indefinitely. No word by Mandela or Tambo could be published.

Western governments and observers had virtually written off the ANC. 'Occasional attempts to infiltrate South Africa have been unsuccessful,' said a secret American intelligence report in October 1969. 'Political organisation within the Republic is weak and infiltrated by government agents.'[27] 'By the end of the 1960s,' wrote the American historian Thomas Karis, 'the ANC seemed to be little more than a shadowy presence.'[28] When the *Washington Post* correspondent Jim Hoagland came to South Africa in 1970 he found that 'Luthuli, Mandela and Sisulu were perceived dimly, as if they belonged to another time, long past and long lost.'[29]

Mandela in jail admitted: 'During the harsh days of the early 1970s, when the ANC seemed to sink into the shadows, we had to force ourselves not to give in to despair.'[30] A draft ANC document in November 1970 conceded that their organisation inside the country was 'almost dead'.[31] When I visited black friends in Soweto in that year I found them far more reticent than six years before. 'You know I don't dare tell my own brother what I'm thinking,' said the son of the journalist Henry Nxumalo. Informers were everywhere, and young *tsotsis* (gangsters) were paid to give news of saboteurs or guerrillas. 'So you've come to pick up the old threads?' asked Mandela's old Indian friend Yusuf Cachalia. 'Well, they're broken.'[32]

Tambo now believed an eventual bloodbath was almost unavoidable. On 25 March 1970 he wrote to his friend Ronald Segal, who ten years earlier had helped him to escape from South Africa, that he could see how Vorster and white South Africans were driven to killings and torture by their fear of the unknown: 'I can understand the inevitability of a savage spilling of blood in South Africa which the developments of the last ten years have sealed irretrievably. The decade of the seventies will be soaked in blood – the blood of the innocent no less than of the guilty, unfortunately.' Tambo speculated on how different his own story might have been if Segal had not driven him across the border in March 1960: 'History builds on events that are in themselves totally insignificant . . . Perhaps the record would today stand as follows: Ronald Segal – serving a life sentence in Pretoria jail. Oliver Tambo – hanged in Pretoria, 1968, following a conviction under the Terrorism act. John Vorster – assassinated. Nelson Mandela – commander of a vast guerrilla army operating in different parts of South Africa.'[33]

The ANC, still placing hopes in military activity, was training more guerrillas in camps outside South Africa, and infiltrated propaganda through leaflets or broadcasts over 'Radio Freedom' from Zambia and Tanzania. But the small remaining groups of courageous internal activists were soon rounded up with the help of informers and torture.

The Robben Islanders received a huge boost to their morale in April 1974 from a completely unexpected event: a military coup in Portugal, which ousted the government of Marcello Caetano, soon followed by the promise of independence to the two Portuguese colonies in Southern Africa, Angola and Mozambique. It appeared to undermine Pretoria's strategy of using 'buffer states' to protect it from military infiltration. The ANC now saw the prospect of military bases in Mozambique, along the South African border, supported by the country's new revolutionary government, FRELIMO. The arrival of Marxist governments in Mozambique and Angola thrilled militant young black South Africans, who began chanting slogans like 'Viva FRELIMO!' or '*La lutta continua!*' On Robben Island, Mandela felt confident that 'the tide was turning our way'. He was delighted to hear that Tambo had attended a state banquet in Mozambique.[34]

But with all these hopes for the future, the MK was still ineffective inside South Africa. By 1976 it had not fired a single shot within the country's borders.[35] Mandela in his detachment was more realistic than most exiles about the immediate prospects, but he remained hopeful in the longer term. As he wrote in jail, in his remarkable unpublished paper on National Liberation in early 1976:

> Fourteen years after the first MK recruits were sent out, the armed struggle is still to begin inside South Africa. Even the independence of Mozambique and Angola is no guarantee that our problems in this regard have been solved. Newly independent states have numerous problems to contend with and they may find it quite difficult to do what they wish. The initiative is still in enemy hands and the most pressing task after the question of unity is to wrest that initiative from the enemy. I have the confidence that this historic moment will come, and that the results will more than compensate for the agonising moments of suspense and tension the movement has experienced for more than a decade . . .
>
> We cannot resist the optimism that the prospects of a new era have been greatly advanced by the liberation of Mozambique and Angola. It is only a question of time before the ideal conditions exist which the movement can fully exploit to come to grips with the last racialist regime in our continent. When that moment comes the enemy may be forced to fight on many fronts.[36]

But the South African Prime Minister John Vorster was sufficiently flexible to come to terms with the new black government in Mozambique, continuing to use the country's ports and to provide jobs for migrant workers in return for restraint of military activity. By now the economic boom had subsided, and South Africa's businessmen urgently needed markets in the rest of Africa. Vorster reached discreet agreements with countries further north, culminating in a secret visit to the Ivory Coast and Liberia. He also brought pressure on Ian Smith to negotiate with the black rebel movements in Rhodesia. At the UN in November 1974 Vorster's Foreign Minister Pik Botha boldly explained that his country was set on reform: 'We shall do everything in our power to move away from discrimination based on race or colour.' A few days later Vorster told black Africa: 'If you give South Africa a chance, you will be surprised where we will stand.'[37] Mandela had few illusions when he heard about Vorster's speech: he had seen how the government had ignored past opportunities to avert the threat of armed revolution, and was convinced there would be no fundamental changes.

Mandela remained preoccupied with maintaining unity, both within the ANC and with its partners. But there were growing tensions in the ANC in exile, once again between the communists and nationalists, and by 1975 Tambo was facing an imminent split. The immediate cause was the premature death in 1973 of Robert Resha, aged only fifty-three, the fiery nationalist from Sophiatown who had become the ANC representative in London, and who had often criticised the communists, particularly after he was ejected from the National Executive. Mandela had admired Resha, and wrote a long, moving letter to his widow Maggie, comparing him to his other dead heroes like Luthuli, Z.K. Matthews and J.B. Marks: 'Together we took solemn oaths, shared intimate secrets, suffered common setbacks and enjoyed the fruits of victory.'[38] But Resha's memorial service in London became a battleground when the young nationalist Ambrose Makiwane, from the prominent Transkei family Mandela had known as a child, delivered a diatribe against the 'small clique' who had hijacked the ANC: 'The Africans hate the domination of the Communist Party.'[39] Soon afterwards a group of eight rebel ANC members formed, including Ambrose Makiwane and his cousin Tennyson. Tambo faced a 'venomous' campaign against himself, as he wrote to Mandela, which resorted to 'unbridled anti-communism and racism', using the same language as the white oppressors.[40] Tambo still tried to keep the anti-communist rebels inside the fold, but in September 1975 the National Executive voted to expel 'the gang of eight', as they were called. The 'treacherous faction', wrote Alfred Nzo, the ANC Secretary-General, was 'deliberately and publicly launched to try to confuse and divide our people'.[41]

Mandela was distressed by the breakaway: with his own nationalist past, he had some sympathy with the rebels, and hoped that the ANC would adopt 'a softer, more lenient attitude'. But he realised that they had deeply offended the leadership, and he was too late to intervene.[42] The rebels set up their own body, provocatively called the ANC (African Nationalists). They claimed Mandela as their true leader, but Mandela himself left no doubt that Tambo was *his* leader. 'There is only one ANC,' he wrote in a smuggled message, 'and that is the ANC which has its head office in Lusaka, and whose President is O.T.'[43] Eventually most of the rebels would rejoin the ANC, and Ambrose Makiwane would welcome

Tambo back to South Africa when he returned in 1990. But his cousin Tennyson joined the Transkei government under Kaiser Matanzima, and was killed in July 1980 by an assassin suspected of being an ANC gunman.[44]

Tambo was under heavy fire, attacked for dull and uninspiring leadership, and worried about further splits – as he wrote to Mandela using a code which described factions as 'sports clubs' and the ANC as 'the Federation': 'A proliferation of clubs are being formed, but they do not engage in profitable sport unless recognised and admitted into the sporting Federation.' But he was confident that members of the Federation would 'arrange private informal bilateral games with new clubs'.[45] He still looked to the Robben Islanders for leadership. 'The air resounds with the voices of our youth singing in praise of our jailed leaders,' he wrote to Mandela in 1975. 'You are making a glorious contribution to the unity of our people.'[46]

The prospects for the ANC on the mainland still looked bleak. But while the prisoners followed the ups and downs of the armed struggle, they were much less aware of the groundswells of social change within South Africa, which were slowly weakening the iron structures of apartheid and widening the opposition to it. The most obvious centres of unrest were the factories, where the recession and inflation of the early seventies had stirred up black workers to demand higher wages. Strikes were illegal, but black workers went on strike in Durban early in 1973, and later in East London. It was a broad and unexpected movement, with no formal leaders who could be picked up or victimised. These semi-skilled workers could not easily be replaced, so they quickly won wage increases. Their success made them more interested in trades unions. They were politically cautious, and linked themselves to white-led unions which the ANC had condemned. But as the ANC had foreseen, there now emerged 'the most turbulent period of industrial and political unrest'.[47] Mandela in jail appreciated the strikes' significance, and the role that Harry Gwala and his colleagues had played in fomenting them.[48] 'There was hardly any evidence that the workers were now looking beyond the limited horizons of purely local interest and concentrating their attention on the defeat of apartheid in general,' he wrote in early 1976. 'But the speed at which the strikes escalated, the stubbornness and solidarity among the workers, their defiant attitude, showed that in their respective factories they were no longer prepared to tolerate any kind of discrimination.'

Mandela also took heart from the opposition to apartheid from white liberals, churchmen and students. He was hopeful that the new Progressive Party, which had six MPs elected in the 1974 elections, would help educate whites about the evils of discrimination. He was particularly interested in the students, both black and white, who were defending civil liberties and demanding the release of political prisoners. Christian leaders, he noted, were becoming more outspoken in criticising apartheid. He urged his colleagues in exile to reach out to all possible friends: 'The problems facing us appear insurmountable only so long as we try to solve them through a liberation movement which is divided,' he wrote in his paper on National Liberation in 1976, 'and which cannot rally the people to concentrate all their resources on the defeat of the common enemy.'

Mandela was determined to open up lines to more liberal Afrikaners, all the more so after his contacts with warders. He warned his colleagues not to reject any dealings with Afrikaners, or to be misled by 'the well-known hostility and contempt of the Englishmen for this group'. In the same paper he was already anticipating the opportunity which would arise fifteen years later:

> Afrikaner politicians have no monopoly of their people just as we have none over ours. We ought to speak directly to the Afrikaner and fully explain our position. Honest men are to be found on both sides of the colour line and the Afrikaner is no exception. We have a strong case and the Afrikaner leaders will command undivided support only as long as their people are ignorant of the issues at stake . . .
>
> A violent clash is now unavoidable and when we have fought it out and reduced this country to ashes it will still be necessary for us to sit down together and talk about the problems of reconstruction – the black man and the white man, the African and the Afrikaner.[49]

Throughout all the setbacks of the sixties and seventies, Mandela continued to look to the Western powers for support, and saw economic sanctions as the main future weapon against apartheid. But neither the British nor the American government was encouraging. When Tambo had first arrived in London he had spent much time seeking support from the Conservative government, first under Harold Macmillan, then Alec Douglas-Home, and had waited endlessly for interviews with the Foreign Office: 'He never stopped knocking,' said his wife Adelaide.[50] But the diplomats were wary. One of them, I.J.M. Sutherland, discovered that he was living opposite Tambo's house in Highgate in 1964, and asked the Foreign Office for background about him: they had only a minimal reference, but they were prepared to meet him if 'he has anything interesting to say about South Africa'.[51] Tambo found deep suspicions in London about the ANC's links with the communists, and much support for the anti-communist PAC. In Western Europe he was helped only by the Dutch and Scandinavian governments – to whom Mandela would always be grateful. Tambo felt compelled to seek assistance in Moscow, where he was promised military training and weapons free of charge.[52] It inevitably strengthened Pretoria's argument that the ANC was on the communist side of the Cold War.

When the Labour Party came to power in Britain in October 1964, the full news took some time to reach the prisoners on Robben Island: a letter in which Kathrada's brother briefly mentioned it was delayed for eighteen months.[53] Mandela and Tambo had hopes that the British would take sanctions more seriously, and the new Prime Minister, Harold Wilson, swiftly ordered that 'all shipment of arms to South Africa should cease forthwith'.[54] But documents recently released show how effectively Whitehall obstructed further sanctions. George Brown, the Economic Secretary, was already concerned about the financial consequences of the arms embargo, and the Colonial Secretary Anthony Greenwood was worried that Pretoria would retaliate by moving against the three British protectorates on its borders. 'If Dr Verwoerd decided to "take it out on the Territories",' Greenwood reported, 'he could inflict very heavy damage on them.'[55] Lord Caradon, the British member of the UN Expert Group on South Africa, was pressing for sanctions, but the Foreign Secretary Patrick Gordon Walker asked the Prime Minister to speak strongly to him, and Caradon then agreed that the government was opposed to economic sanctions; though he still told the Foreign Office: 'We should on no account remove from the South Africans the ultimate threat of sanctions.' As he put it: 'The sword of Damocles, though perhaps tied firmly to the ceiling, should nevertheless be there.'[56] The fake sword may have helped to placate the Labour left, but it hardly fooled Pretoria.

Washington, under President Lyndon Johnson, appeared to be pressing more seriously for sanctions, which worried the Foreign Office in London. When a State Department paper suggested that selective sanctions 'would be an effective and relatively painless way of bringing pressure to bear on South Africa', the British diplomats quickly responded that sanctions would have no effect, while they concealed their real financial concerns: 'Britain would suffer by far the most,' said a confidential draft, 'because of the scale of our export and import trade with South Africa.'[57]

Harold Wilson was anyway soon distracted by a much more immediate crisis in Southern Africa. In November 1965 Ian Smith's white government in the next-door colony of Rhodesia defied all British pressures for democratic elections, and declared unilateral independence. Wilson, ruling out the use of force, imposed sanctions, including an oil embargo which was apparently enforced by a naval blockade; but he turned a blind eye to the flow of oil into Rhodesia via South Africa arranged by British companies.[58] Tambo was not impressed. 'The British Labour government,' he said in 1969, 'has permitted and encouraged the white minority to seize and monopolise political power.'[59]

Wilson's government had little time to think about South Africa, let alone the prisoners on Robben Island. In 1967 Pretoria had still less reason to believe in the 'sword of Damocles' when the British Minister of Defence, Denis Healey, reopened the question of supplying some arms to South Africa. The move was eventually quashed by Wilson, but not before raising further doubts about the Cabinet's moral stand on apartheid.[60] Three years later, after his visit to Mandela on Robben Island, Healey conceded to the ANC: 'I now think I was wrong even to support the matter being considered.' But by that time he was out of office.

The Americans were even less involved. Preoccupied with Vietnam and uninterested in Rhodesia, they entered a period of 'benign neglect' of South Africa, as Senator Charles Percy called it.[61] In the wake of the civil rights campaign, black Americans provided indignation and rhetoric against apartheid, and some white politicians, including the Kennedy brothers, maintained a radical stance. Bobby Kennedy paid a much-publicised visit to South Africa in 1966, after which he said: 'If I lived in this country I would gather up everything I have and get out now.'[62] But the rhetoric was at odds with the actions – as Roger Morris of the US National Security Council put it: 'Through the 1960s the public face of the Kennedy and Johnson administrations was to deplore the racist regimes at regular intervals at the UN and elsewhere while doing discreet business with them on the side.'[63]

By the seventies the prospect of Western intervention looked still more remote; and the return of a Conservative government in Britain in 1970 was a new setback. The new Prime Minister, Ted Heath, had been shocked by the inhumanity of apartheid when he first visited South Africa in 1954, but he believed that the British naval base at Simonstown, near Cape Town, was crucial to Western defences against the communist powers; and he had already pledged to resume arms sales.[64] Pretoria turned out at first to want only a few helicopters, since South Africa now had its own growing arms industry, augmented by Mirage fighters from France. But it also needed sophisticated communications technologies from Britain and America, which many companies were glad to supply; the ANC saw the West as underpinning the apartheid economy and its military-industrial complex. The return of Harold Wilson's Labour government in 1974 gave the Robben Islanders some new hope; but Wilson was again bogged down in the Rhodesian deadlock, and had little time left for South Africa. 'Without the backing of the imperialist countries,' Tambo said on the sixtieth anniversary of the ANC in 1972, 'South Africa would long ago have gone bankrupt even while we were fighting, literally, with our bare hands.'[65]

The Americans had become more conciliatory towards apartheid governments after the arrival of Richard Nixon's Republican administration in 1969. His adviser Henry Kissinger was bored by South Africa, which he did not mention in the first two volumes of his memoirs, and instinctively in favour of the status quo. He commissioned a secret policy review (NSSM 39) – an 'infamous document', said Tambo after it became public in April 1972 – which tilted towards white regimes in Southern Africa, and judged that: 'For the foreseeable future South Africa will be able to maintain internal stability and effectively counter insurgent activity.' Kissinger chose one of the five options which proposed to relax American pressures and to ease the arms embargo, while increasing aid to black Africa. It argued that the Americans could encourage reforms by opening doors to Pretoria, but the first result was simply to reassure Vorster.[66] Soon after the policy-shift the American Ambassador went pheasant-shooting with government leaders – on Robben Island.[67] American diplomats nicknamed the Kissinger policy 'the Tar Baby Option', because Washington was stuck with its new friends in Pretoria; it continued under the presidency of Gerald Ford.[68]

The State Department now scarcely mentioned Mandela and his fellow-prisoners: when the liberal Senator Dick Clark held eight days of hearings about South Africa in 1976, occupying a book of 792 pages, the name of Mandela was never uttered. It was left to Andrew Young, the black Congressman from Atlanta, to make the point that: 'If there is a rational solution to the problems of South Africa, it is going to have to be worked out with those men who are now imprisoned or detained or now being destroyed.'[69]

The Robben Islanders still put more hopes in the East. The Soviet Union and Eastern Europe continued to welcome ANC leaders, to provide funds and weaponry for their armed struggle, and to educate ANC exiles in their universities. The East Germans were particularly supportive, and printed the ANC's magazine *Sechaba*, which was full of pro-Soviet propaganda and attacks on the imperialist powers. Tambo himself kept his distance from any communist influence, and was impressed that Moscow did not seek to influence ANC policy: he was personally convinced that Africans would not embrace communism when the time came.[70] But Sisulu and other Robben Islanders remained optimistic that their salvation would come from the socialist world. Mandela was more pragmatic, believing that the ANC should work with any friends it could find in time of need: he often recalled how Churchill had worked with Stalin during the Second World War. He remained preoccupied with unifying the opposition to apartheid; and his detachment in jail gave him a much clearer view of the challenge, as he explained in early 1976:

> My current circumstances give me advantages my compatriots outside jail rarely have. Here the past literally rushes to memory and there is plenty of time for reflection. One is able to stand back and look at the entire movement from a distance, and the bitter lessons of prison life force one to go all out to win the co-operation of all fellow-prisoners, to learn how to see problems from the point of view of others as well, and to work smoothly with other schools of thought in the movement. Thrown together by the fates we have no choice but to forget our differences in the face of crisis, talk to one another mainly about our background, hopes and aspirations, our organisations and the kaleidoscope of experiences in the field of struggle.[71]

19

Black Consciousness

1976–1978

It was Winnie, talking in her coded language on a visit to the island, who first told Mandela about the new generation of militant black rebels who were emerging inside South Africa, and warned him to take them seriously, as they were changing the character of the struggle.[1] She was in a position to know, for she was attracted both to their ideas and to their virile young leaders.

The 'Black Consciousness' movement had begun in 1969 when Steve Biko, a courageous young medical student at the University of Natal, had turned against the white leadership of the National Union of South African Students and formed the all-black South African Students' Organisation (SASO), which soon became the nursery for a new party, the Black People's Convention (BPC). Biko felt himself diminished by the paternalism of white liberals, and vowed that the black man must escape from his sense of inferiority and see himself as 'self-defined, not as defined by others'. Some of his rhetoric sounded like a replay of the revolt of the Youth League twenty-five years earlier, or of the PAC ten years before. But Biko had gained more intellectual depth and confidence than Robert Sobukwe, encouraged by the independence of black Africa, the civil rights victories in America and the growing literature of black power, particularly Frantz Fanon's *The Wretched of the Earth*. The confidence was expressed by pride in the word 'black', which would soon also be adopted by sympathetic Indians and Coloureds, and later by the media: the *Rand Daily Mail* used it as early as July 1972.[2]

The mood was heavily influenced from abroad, particularly America. 'In dribs and drabs we discovered the old voices of protest,' wrote one of Biko's followers, Patrick Lekota, who had become known as 'Terror' on the football field. 'We found Frantz Fanon, David Diop, Aimé Césaire of the negritude movement. Some us dug out W.E.B. du Bois, Julius Nyerere and Kwame Nkrumah. The younger voices of Stokely Carmichael, Eldridge Cleaver and George Jackson reached us.'[3]

Biko was determined to arouse his people from the 'great silence' of the sixties, and to give them self-respect in the midst of oppression. 'All in all the black man has become a shell,' he wrote in 1970, 'a shadow of man, completely defeated, drowning in his own misery, a slave and ox bearing the yoke of oppression with sheepish timidity.' He soon excited a militant new generation of black schoolchildren who saw their parents in this humiliating image, and were determined to escape from it. By 1973 Black Consciousness was sweeping through the black campuses, and the government banned eight of its leaders, including Biko and his lieutenant Barney Pityana. But the independence of Mozambique and Angola brought a new surge of hope: in 1974 the BPC organised rallies in support of the new black government in Mozambique. In response the government charged nine of its leaders, headed by Saths Cooper (later to be on Robben Island), with fomenting disorder under the Terrorism Act.[4]

The vestigial underground ANC within South Africa was wary of Biko's movement, with its echoes of the PAC, while many of Biko's followers despised the ANC's conservatism and inertia. But Winnie Mandela, banned from active politics, was inspired by the anger and assertiveness of the young rebels. 'There was a total vacuum,' as she recalled, 'and if Biko had not come into life then I shudder at the consequences for history. It was such a revitalising experience to communicate with that man . . . I was the only voice at that time that was brave enough to do so.' She shared the new pride in blackness: 'You felt your blood rise as you stood up and felt proud of being black, and that is what Steve did to me.'[5]

Barney Pityana took Biko to see Winnie, who responded warmly: 'Winnie had no ifs and buts, and opened her heart to us,' Pityana recalled. 'Steve always went to see her when he was in Johannesburg.'[6] After Winnie's bans expired in 1975 she gave speeches and interviews warning about a surge of anger among young blacks.[7] But the ANC had little to do with the build-up, and when the young activists Tokyo Sexwale and Naledi Tsiki approached Winnie for contacts with the ANC she said that her links had 'broken down'.[8] Mandela and his colleagues were sceptical when they first heard about Black Consciousness, partly because the Afrikaners originally welcomed the movement as a sign that blacks were 'developing on their own lines', in keeping with apartheid: he saw sympathetic articles by an Afrikaner professor and in the Afrikaans women's magazine *Huisgenoot*.[9]

But it was the government's insistence on teaching Afrikaans which was the breaking point for black schoolchildren. The violence of the revolt in June 1976 took nearly everyone by surprise. When pupils in Soweto went on strike against Afrikaans teaching, ten thousand young blacks marched in their support. The police fired on them, killing a thirteen-year-old boy, Hector Pietersen. Children ran riot, killing two whites. Soweto became a bloody battlefield, invaded by armoured cars and helicopters. In the next days strikes and riots spread to the Cape: by the end of the year the death-roll was between five hundred and a thousand. The government's report later blamed the ANC, the PAC and the communists, but the real inspiration came from Biko and the schoolboy leaders themselves, who knew little of the ANC.[10] 'We didn't deserve so much credit,' said Winnie, 'but we don't mind at all.'[11] She herself felt very personally involved, having been there when Hector was killed: 'I was part of that revolution . . . It was the contribution of those children who put us where we are today.'[12]

The Soweto revolt ran round the world, causing more outcry (Mandela reckoned later) than the Sharpeville massacres.[13] But on Robben Island the first indication of a crisis was a complete drought of news.[14] As stories gradually filtered through, Mandela wrote a statement which was smuggled out by Mac Maharaj when he left the island soon afterwards. It showed Mandela's first militant support for the revolt, stressing the need for both unity and action. 'The gun has played an important part in our history . . .' it began. And it concluded:

> We who are confined within the grey walls of the Pretoria regime's prisons reach out to our people. With you we count those who have perished by means of the gun and the hangman's rope . . . We face the future with confidence. For the guns that serve apartheid cannot render it unconquerable. Those who live by the gun shall perish by the gun. Unite! Mobilise! Fight On! Between the anvil of united mass action and the hammer of armed struggle we shall crush apartheid and white minority racist rule![15]

The first detailed news reached the prisoners in August 1976 from Eric Molobi, a young Black Consciousness rebel who arrived on the island after two years in prison, where he had been tortured almost to death. He was very critical of the ANC, and when he first told them about the revolt they would not believe it.[16] But soon a flood of young rebels arrived on the island, defiant and aggressive: some of them had escaped from South Africa to join ANC training camps, had returned as fighters for MK and been captured. 'We poured into the place, in truckfuls from everywhere, like a huge windfall,' said Terror Lekota.[17] Many of the young comrades saw the island as a place of honour. 'That was where our heroes were kept,' said Sifiso Buthelezi. 'We really equated Robben Island with freedom.'[18] But they had some disappointments with their leaders. As Lekota put it:

> We found the political prisoners steadfast in their fight, with defiant determination. But their morale had been dampened, and they couldn't see the horizons. They were allowed no news, and thought everything was dead: they didn't even know about the Durban strikes in 1973. We gave them hope and justified their determination, but also problems: a lot of us were bruised emotionally after being tortured; we were not refined politicians, only raw material. Lots of the comrades thought the Rivonia people were old conservatives, and that the PAC was more appealing with its call for Africa for Africans.[19]

Mandela was excited by the extent of the Soweto revolt, and by the reawakening of protest after the 'silent sixties'. He was gratified that Bantu education, far from making blacks subservient to white supremacy, had provoked a fierce reaction: it had 'come back to haunt its creators'.[20] He was impressed by the calibre of the young rebels, who revealed new aspects of black South Africa: 'You feel you have been enriched, your horizons have been widened, your roots in your own country have been deepened.' And he realised that the ANC was being challenged to catch up.[21] Many of the young men had been tortured by the police, and showed the marks. Mandela, who had never been tortured, was impressed by their fortitude.

But the extent of the generation gap came as a shock to him and the other earlier prisoners. 'Although some of us were young,' wrote Mosibudi Mangena, who had come to the island three years before Soweto, 'we suddenly found ourselves looking very old and moderate.'[22] Even Harry Gwala thought that 'at times young people's actions sometimes bordered on anarchy.'[23] Many of them had consciously rejected their own parents, whom they regarded as cowards. They were uncompromisingly defiant and confrontational: some of them, the 'lumpen element', were not really political extremists at all, but minor gangsters or *tsotsis*.[24] 'We would punch the warders,' said Mike Xego, a Black Consciousness activist who later joined the ANC. 'If the warders touched us, we would quickly punch back.'[25] 'We messed up the whole code, we refused to study,' said Eric Molobi. 'We were too angry – we took two years to change.'[26]

Mandela had foreseen the rise of a more radical generation. During the Rivonia trial he had warned that the government would face much fiercer rebellions, which would make it long for the old ANC leaders. But he was shaken to find that these rebels were almost as sceptical of the ANC as they were of the government. 'Before we went to the island we were told that Mandela was a sell-out, and that he believed in Xhosa domination,' said Tokyo Sexwale, himself an ANC fighter, who came to the island in 1978.[27]

'To be perceived as a moderate,' said Mandela, 'was a novel and not altogether pleasant feeling.'[28] He realised he must try to come to terms with the young rebels, and asked some of them, including Saths Cooper of the BPC and Strini Moodley of SASO, to give lectures to the older prisoners. He became more aware of the appeal of Black Consciousness; recalling his own experience in the Youth League, he thought the young men would soon come round to the broader policies of the ANC. He tried to visualise their influences: 'The toddlers I left behind have become serious-minded adults,' he wrote to Chief Buthelezi. 'They live in the milieu of rapid change and development of science and technology . . . Perhaps education and the influence of the mass media have helped to close the generation gap. We must, therefore, allow for what may appear superficially to be excesses of the youth. Wordsworth succinctly said, "the child is father to the man".'[29]

But Mandela faced the greatest test of his political skills in trying to relate to these courageous, but impatient and angry, young men with whom he had had no previous contact, but whom he needed to bring into the broader movement. He had some important links among their leaders, and responded warmly to a friendly message from Hlaku Rachidi, the President of the BPC, who was in prison in Modderfontein.[30] But he found many of the young rebels sectarian and immature in their preoccupation with blackness and their exclusion of whites.[31]

He was careful not to respond to the young lions with aggression, which would make them fight back: he did not campaign for the ANC or try to recruit from the new organisations. Instead he relied on a softer approach of gradual persuasion. He always remembered a fable which he had learnt as a child, about the wind and the sun challenging each other to make a man take off his clothes. First the wind blew a gale right through him, but he only clutched his clothes to himself more firmly. Then the sun shone on him until he eventually took all his clothes off.[32]

Mandela and his colleagues set about trying to convert the young comrades to more moderate policies. 'It was not the regime but the ANC that cracked us,' said Mike Xego. 'One by one, the ANC underground on Robben Island worked on us – on individuals – talking with us and smuggling notes to us.'[33] Most young comrades came to admire the sheer resilience of the veterans: 'It was amazing to us that in spite of so many years on the island they were still so courageous, mentally alert and determined to fight on,' said Dan Montsisi, who came to the island in 1979. 'We developed a deep comradeship with them through discussions and understanding of the problems we face in South Africa. We also felt great respect. They were like fathers to us.'[34]

'How I changed!' said Seth Mazibuko. 'All because I met Nelson Mandela and learnt from him and the others. I had been brought up to believe that Mandela was an animal. Our parents taught us: "Don't get involved in politics because you'll end up a terrorist and go to prison like that Mandela" . . . I heard this voice, deep and strong, saying, "Which ones are Seth, Murphy, and Dan?" I looked up and there was Mandela . . . It was then that I began to question some of my Black Consciousness beliefs, because here was our leader preaching unity and non-racialism.'[35]

The attitude to warders was a key issue. At first many of the young rebels were determined to defy them on principle: some would even provoke the guards to set the dogs on them. The Red Cross inspectors, visiting in March 1977, reported that the new inmates 'brought into the prison a new emphasis on prisoners' human dignity. They were frequently in conflict with the prison authorities, not because they wanted to make trouble at all costs, but because they were not prepared to accept the degrading and racist treatment they said they often received from their warders.'[36]

Some of the new prisoners regarded Mandela as a 'sell-out' because he had reached understandings with the warders, and helped to keep discipline. But they gradually began to listen to their elders. Eric Molobi was enraged by one warder who always swore at him and laughed when he swore back, until Sisulu asked him: 'Why do you think he laughs at you? It's because warders are the vermin of the Afrikaners, and like to see you come down to their level. Why don't you try not swearing back?' The next time, Molobi restrained himself and just looked at the warder, who soon lost interest in him. 'But I still wasn't emotionally convinced,' said Molobi, 'because Black Consciousness had taught me always to fight back.'

Gradually the comrades came to recognise many of the warders as human, and vulnerable, particularly to humour: when they discovered that they enjoyed dirty jokes, they arranged for their best joke-tellers to walk beside them and make them laugh. 'It broke through the wall,' as Molobi said. 'Most of them came round in the end, and helped us. It changed our views of the raw system.'[37]

'We were all convicted, prisoner and jailer . . . we were chained to one another,' said Tokyo Sexwale. He noticed that the warders were shocked to find a Catholic prisoner who wanted to see his priest, or a prisoner who spoke Afrikaans: 'They thought we only spoke Russian or Cuban . . . Eventually we were able to find common ground, and strong friendships were built.'[38]

Terror Lekota soon realised that most of the warders were uneducated, and that many were from orphanages, with miserable backgrounds. 'Eventually they wanted to understand why we were there. It was tremendously refreshing and inspiring to see these ordinary people appreciating our cause. The experience led to my belief that South Africa had a promising future.'

The influence of the veterans gradually took effect. 'After four to six months, the excitement died down,' said Terror Lekota. 'They had long debates and began to change their views.'[39] Lekota himself was a critical influence. Before coming to the island he knew little about the ANC: he had read Mandela's speech at Rivonia, but had only ever heard his name spoken in whispers. When he arrived he smuggled a note to Mandela asking him some political questions. Mandela, who had heard about his bravery, wrote back with three pages about the ANC's history, explaining its long attempts at peaceful persuasion before it turned to unconstitutional methods. 'I read it over and over,' remembered Lekota, 'till I knew it by heart, and I knew I'd join the ANC.' Mandela was impressed by this strong, articulate young leader. He advised him not to leave his own organisation, SASO, but Lekota was determined to join the ANC.[40] 'It was a painful self-appraisal,' said Dullah Omar, a Cape lawyer who talked to many Black Consciousness members on the island. 'It sounded simple, but it wasn't.'[41]

Lekota's switch provoked an assault which reverberated through the island. He tried to persuade his BC comrades in the cell of the merits of the ANC's non-racialism; but some of them planned a ferocious revenge. While they played music and watched out for warders, one of them set upon Lekota with a garden fork, hitting him on the head: 'I fell like a brick: I nearly died.' His head still shows the bruise. The prison authorities charged the culprits with assault, but Mandela and Sisulu wanted to avoid an open rift, and asked Lekota not to make a complaint. Lekota refused to testify, which undermined the charge and brought him closer both to Mandela and to the younger people. Many other young comrades soon followed Lekota into the ANC – including his attacker. Soon afterwards Lekota was transferred to Section B, where he was closer to Mandela and the 'old people'. He was sometimes impatient of their slowness, including their leisurely games of tennis, but was deeply influenced by their ideas.[42]

Sport was a crucial catalyst in the unifying process. It had first been allowed in 1967, and an elaborate system of teams and tournaments had developed, with constitutions, minutes and records, under the supervision of Steve Tshwete, the President of the Robben Island Amateur Athletic Association until he left in 1979. Sport helped to impose discipline, as is revealed in the detailed minutes of meetings. 'The unsportsmanlike and ungentlemanly conduct showed by some of our members was discussed,' said a report of February 1972. 'Mr A. Suze left the field in the midst of the play without informing his captain.'[43] The organisation of sports extended into choirs, musical groups, films and ballroom dancing. The Chairman of the Prisoners' Record Club, Michael Kahla, thanked the members in his annual report of 1974: 'You have given me a schooling in administration, patience and understanding that no formal school could have given.'[44] 'I learnt how to organise and make things happen,' said Raks Seakhoa, who came to the island as 'a rural village boy'. 'The way we lived on Robben Island, you became an all-rounder.'[45]

Mandela saw sport primarily as a way to overcome political rivalries. The teams were originally divided into ANC, PAC or other organisations, with a joint committee supervising. But they were later integrated, and sport and culture could avoid political deadlocks: 'It was not an uncommon sight to find a group of ANC sitting with PAC, talking earnestly and cracking jokes about everything except politics.'[46]

But many Black Consciousness prisoners continued to have clashes with the ANC, often coming together with the PAC. The tension came to a head when several ANC members were beaten up in the general cells. The prison authorities again brought charges, this time against the ANC men for provoking the fight. The accused hired a lawyer from the mainland and asked Mandela to give them a character testimonial, but he was embarrassed, dreading a new rift with Black Consciousness, and decided not to testify. This disappointed some ANC supporters, but impressed the BC with his determination to achieve unity.[47]

Mandela continued to worry about the divisiveness of Black Consciousness prisoners who were still attacking the ANC's multi-racialism and communist influences. Two years after the Soweto revolt he wrote a lucid and eloquent fifty-five-page essay, still unpublished, which analysed the roots and significance of the Black Consciousness movement. He was very conscious that he had been cut off from crucial events; but he was all the more aware of the theatrical aspect, and the importance of images and performances – as he made clear in a vivid paragraph at the beginning, which throws light on his own view of politics:

> It is often desirable for one not to describe events, but to put the reader in the atmosphere in which the whole drama was played out right inside the theatre, so that he can see with his own eyes the actual stage, all the actors and their costumes, follow their movements, listen to what they say and sing, and to study the facial expressions and the spontaneous reaction of the audience as the drama unfolds. Although this privilege is far beyond the reach of a prisoner the matter is sufficiently significant for us to run the risk of daring where the more cautious would hesitate.

In his essay Mandela tried to make a balanced judgement between the extreme views of Black Consciousness, whether as racialist reactionaries or as the only really revolutionary black movement in South Africa. But he provided a hard-hitting critique. He traced the development of black pride back to the eighteenth century, when Africans defended their freedom against whites. The Black Consciousness students, on the other hand, were heavily influenced by the international student revolt of the sixties and the American campaigns against the Vietnam war. Their ideas, he felt, had been imported from America and 'swallowed in a lump' without any understanding of the different conditions in South Africa, where whites had joined the liberation movement. By adopting the American concept of black power the Black Consciousness Movement 'assumed the character of a racialistic sect which blindly bundles a section of the progressive forces with the enemy'.

He was impatient with the arrogance of some BC prisoners: one of them had delivered 'an address to the nation' to a meeting of ten people. He was annoyed by their confused theories and their belief in existentialism: 'a philosophy of superstition, individualism and chaos'. He was worried that they might in future become collaborators, supported by Western imperialists to counter communism and liberalism in black politics.

He reasserted his belief in 'scientific socialism', and insisted that 'the socialist countries are the best friends of those who fought for national liberation.' But the ANC could defend its own policies and freedom of action, he said, and it had been dominated throughout its long history by non-communists: 'We can tame the most ultra-leftist radical just as we can rebuff the rightist elements who glibly warn us of communist danger and who at the same time collaborate with our enemies.' The ANC was 'the oak-tree of South African politics'.

But Mandela accepted the historical importance of Black Consciousness: 'The black student had found his feet, his slogans appealed to the black man's emotions, flattered his national pride and inspired him to assert his identity with confidence.' And he remained hopeful that it would become part of a united liberation movement. 'Realists amongst them,' he concluded, 'accepted that the enemy would not be defeated by fiery speeches, mass campaigns, bare fists, stones and petrol bombs; and that only through a disciplined freedom army, under a unified command using modern weapons and backed by a united population, will the laurels be ours.'[48]

20

Prison Charisma

1976–1982

BY THE LATE SEVENTIES, after the Soweto rebels had subsided, Robben Island was a calmer place. Conditions were less brutal than when the Rivonia prisoners had first arrived, and Mandela had acquired a quiet authority over the younger inmates.

The journalist-prisoner Thami Mkhwanazi, who came to the island in 1980, gave a vivid description of Mandela's style. He walked slowly, wearing the prison-issue fawn trousers and green shirt, looking straight ahead as if in deep thought. He now had a slight stoop and a lick of grey hair, but without any paunch. He was often deep in conversation, giving legal or personal advice to other prisoners, who might have made an appointment a long time ahead. He took their problems very seriously, sometimes preparing a lengthy paper in tiny handwriting. He could speak '*fly-taal*', the township slang with phrases like *okau boy*. Mandela, said Mkhwanazi, was 'a gentleman through and through'. He never seemed to be angry, and would persuade other prisoners to cool off before they reacted to crises. The prison officials called him 'Mandela', or sometimes 'Mr Mandela', but his fellow-prisoners called him by his clan name, 'Madiba'.

His tiny cell was always neat, with legal documents piled on his cupboard and boxes of books under his bed, a sculpture made by a prisoner, and a colour photograph from the *National Geographic* magazine of a tribal African woman: it would, he joked, make Winnie jealous. When other prisoners came to his cell he would offer them 'niceties' from the prison shop, while he himself would chew dry bread. He knew a lot about the other inmates and their family histories, and was also well informed about world events, closely following the struggles in Cuba, Nicaragua and elsewhere.[1]

Michael Dingake was amazed by Mandela's indefatigable concern with human rights: 'Every day, but every day, in addition to his organisation's programmes, he had numerous appointments with individuals, always on his own initiative, to discuss inter-organisational relations, prisoners' complaints, joint strategies against prison authorities and general topics.'[2]

Mandela still maintained his streak of stubborn rebelliousness and independence. Just when the Soweto upheavals had subsided and the prison atmosphere had become relatively peaceful, he proposed a provocative new confrontation. The ANC prisoners, he argued, should behave more like leaders of a movement: they should defy prison regulations, refusing to stand up in the presence of warders or to let them call them by their first names. His closest friends in Section B were taken aback: 'I said it was unacceptable, it could lead to a massacre,' Sisulu recalled, and Kathrada was equally opposed.[3] Only Toivo ja Toivo, the SWAPO leader, and Mandela's loyal friend Eddie Daniels were in agreement. The prisoners in the general cells were also against it: Laloo Chiba, whom Mandela always respected, even went on hunger strike in protest. Eventually, after weeks of feverish debate, Mandela dropped the idea, to general relief.[4]

The warders' treatment of the prisoners was anyway becoming less provocative. They were overstretched by the number of new inmates, and had become more relaxed. The diet was also improving, and political prisoners were allowed to work in the kitchens, which reduced the food smuggling. Africans were now allowed the same food as Indians and Coloureds, including a spoon and a half of sugar for breakfast. The Red Cross's confidential reports still included many complaints about food, censorship, lack of access to lawyers, abusive warders and inconsiderate treatment: prisoners without teeth were unable to eat mealies; and one prisoner who refused to shave because he had acne was put into a straitjacket and forcibly shaved.[5]

But the pressure from the Red Cross and elsewhere was gradually taking effect. Many prisoners were now allowed the opportunity for serious study; and Robben Island was looking more like an austere but intense university. Scores of prisoners were doing courses with the correspondence college the University of South Africa (UNISA), and some took several degrees: Eddie Daniels, Billy Nair and Michael Dingake each took two degrees, Kathrada four. Beyond the formal courses, the senior prisoners would provide their own seminars and lectures, as well as basic education for barely literate recruits. Raks Seakhoa owed his whole education to the island: 'We would write papers about anything, not just politics: literature, art, sport, religion, philosophy. They would respond to our papers.'[6] Murphy Morobe called the island 'a boiling cauldron of ideas'.[7]

They staged their own plays. They obtained a copy of Beckett's *Waiting for Godot* and performed it, wondering about its message for the liberation movement: 'Is the tramp trying to show us that we can go on hoping against hope?' asked Mkalipi.[8] They could see old movies in an improvised cinema in Section B, mostly safely non-political films like *The Ten Commandments, The King and I* and *Caesar and Cleopatra*: Mandela was enchanted by Vivien Leigh as Cleopatra, though some of the comrades complained that she did not look like an African queen. He also loved *Mary Queen of Scots*, with Vanessa Redgrave as Mary and Glenda Jackson as Queen Elizabeth. He saw a political message, he told his daughter Zindzi: 'It marks the end of feudalism and the beginning of the contemporary era of capitalism.'[9] Another film led to more serious political argument: *The Wild One* (long banned in Britain), in which Marlon Brando played the leader of a lawless motorbike gang. The ANC leaders were firmly on the side of law and order, and many of the young comrades also saw the bikers as villains, like the white South African biker gangs who enjoyed beating up blacks.[10] But one of the militants from Black Consciousness, Strini Moodley, insisted that the bikers really stood for the defiant spirit of the Soweto revolt. Mandela disapproved of the bikers, but defended Moodley's argument.[11]

They were allowed to buy and play their own musical instruments: the authorities did not realise, said Tokyo Sexwale, who played the classical guitar, 'that in allowing us these instruments they were giving us another avenue to conduct our struggle. We sang songs against apartheid.' Mkhwanazi recalled listening to Govan Mbeki strumming Afrikaans folk songs on a guitar, Zeph Mothopeng humming Mozart, and Mandela singing Handel's 'For unto us a child is born', waving his hands about like a conductor.[12]

Mandela was prevented from formally studying for four years until 1980, but before then he spent still more time discussing, writing letters, providing legal advice for his colleagues, tending his garden, and above all reading voraciously. Most of the books in the small prison library were trivial: when the Red Cross donated funds for thirty books in 1976, twenty-five of those purchased by the prison authorities were by Daphne du Maurier.[13] But Mandela found more serious novels which broadened his political knowledge, like those of Nadine Gordimer, Steinbeck's *The Grapes of Wrath* and the great Russian writers, who provided parallels with South Africa. He admired Dostoyevsky's novels, but they left him depressed, and he preferred Tolstoy: he read *War and Peace* in three days, and sent a copy to his daughter Zeni for her twenty-first birthday. He realised that Tolstoy was more interested in aristocrats than in the common people, but he enjoyed his jibes against them ('dripping jewels and venom'); and he would partly identify with General Kutuzov, who allowed Napoleon to capture Moscow but thus encompassed his defeat, and who understood the Russian soul.[14]

Mandela also read Afrikaans writers, in order to understand their language and culture: he enjoyed the poetry of Opperman and the novels of Langenhoven. But he read mainly in English. He read Dickens and the English poets, including Wordsworth, Tennyson and Shelley, reviving his own mission education: he could quote from *In Memoriam* or 'Daffodils'. Most of all, he enjoyed political biographies. 'While the comrades were reading *Das Kapital*,' said Eric Molobi, 'Madiba was reading Churchill's war memoirs, or biographies of Kennedy or Vorster.' He loved Churchill's style – 'just like music' – and his humour. He also read biographies of Lincoln, Washington, Disraeli and several Boer War leaders, including Smuts and Koos de la Rey; but the one who really fascinated him was Christiaan de Wet, who led the 1914 rebellion.[15] While the Afrikaner government was accusing Mandela of being a communist, he was studying not Marx but their own heroes.

He became more comfortable with English than Xhosa, which he regretted.[16] He had *The Oxford Book of English Verse* by his bedside, but nothing (he complained) by the Xhosa poets 'who gave expression to my own aspirations and dreams, who flatter my national pride, and who give me a sense of destiny and achievement'.[17] But he promised that 'Western culture has not entirely rubbed off my African background.'[18]

By 1977 the government felt confident enough about the relaxed atmosphere on the island to invite twenty-five South African journalists to visit, in the hope that this would dispel rumours about the harsh treatment of the political prisoners.[19] They were taken round by Major-General Jannie Roux, the Deputy Commissioner of Prisons, a psychiatrist with a degree in criminology. Roux was a persuasive tour guide, but the prisoners resented being stalked like big game in a political zoo. Eventually the journalists spotted Mandela, wearing dark glasses and a floppy hat, clearing weeds from a gravel path with a shovel, but he hid behind a bush as they passed. 'We have located him for you,' said General Roux, 'but he doesn't want to see you, and we won't drag him.' The cameras followed Mandela around the bush, where (the *Star* reported) 'with spade in hand he looks unsmilingly at the intruders and then bends to scoffle a weed'. The Reuters correspondent looked inside Mandela's cell, where he found 'a small pile of prison clothing lay neatly folded beside a picture of three young children. Books included the New English Bible, an economic history of Europe and *Great Stories of Mystery and Suspense*.'[20] The journalists were easily impressed. The *Natal Mercury* reporter found that Robben Island was 'run in a humane and enlightened manner that bears comparison with the best penal institutions in the world'.[21] But none had been allowed to talk to a prisoner; and none revealed that they had to submit their reports to the Commissioner.[22] Foreign correspondents, who had not been invited, were more sceptical; and Mac Maharaj, now in London, complained to the British Press Council about the misreporting, and asked for the press to publish a factual description, but without success.[23]

With all the improvements, the conditions remained grim, and the monastic lifestyle, cut off from wives, girlfriends and children, caused many psychological strains. 'You long for children more than anything else,' said Sisulu. 'It makes you happy just to hear the voice of a child.'[24] Neville Alexander only heard a child's voice once in ten years: 'We stood dead still and everyone was waiting for the moment when we would glimpse that child. And of course it wasn't allowed.'[25] 'There would be a sudden anxiety,' said Lekota, 'that one could die on Robben Island without ever being able to make contact with one's child.'[26] Many of the veterans, including Mandela, worried that their children would never forgive them for their absence. 'Their deepest fear,' wrote Lekota to his daughter, 'was that their own children might grow up to look with bitterness and contempt upon a struggle so dear to themselves.'[27]

In 1981 the younger prisoners went on a hunger strike, inspired by the IRA's Bobby Sands, demanding, among other things, to be allowed visits from younger children. Mandela warned them that it was their duty to survive, to preserve their intellects and to protect weaker prisoners.[28]

But he joined in the strike, which went on for six days. Eventually he negotiated an agreement which included allowing children as young as three to visit the island.[29]

The monastic conditions provided an apt setting for concentrated teaching and debate. Many other political leaders, from Jawaharlal Nehru in India to Robert Mugabe in Rhodesia to the IRA rebels in Northern Ireland, had developed their political theories in jail. But Robben Island, with hundreds of political prisoners serving long sentences, provided a more sustained opportunity to sharpen political ideas with dialectic and polemic, and to put the struggle in a wider context. It was like a protracted course in a remote left-wing university. The isolation and shared predicament of the prisoners, with no scope for consumerism, money-making or rabble-rousing, encouraged idealism and egalitarianism, and developed human sensitivities and communal attitudes. But the island had limitations as a school for practical government. It preserved much of the innocence and naïveté of the powerless, who had little experience of the complexities of administration, the drawbacks of state bureaucracies or the dangers of corruption. It encouraged theory rather than practice.

In this questioning university atmosphere, Mandela was soon challenged. Many of the young comrades were ardent Marxists when they arrived, inspired by the coming to power of communist governments in Mozambique and Angola, and by stories of Eastern Europe, Cuba and the Soviet Union. Some were startlingly innocent: 'Do they really catch colds in Russia?' Kathrada was once asked.[30] But they saw their belief in revolutionary Marxism justified in South Africa by the fascistic government, by the evident collusion between capitalists and apartheid, and by the long tradition of communist heroes of all races, from Moses Kotane to Yusuf Dadoo to Bram Fischer.

On the island they were stirred up by the veteran Stalinist Harry Gwala, who after finishing his sentence in 1973 had joined a secret network to recruit MK fighters and organise strikes; only to be caught in 1975, and sentenced to life imprisonment back on the island in 1977. He returned more fiery than ever, and captivated the young comrades with his rhetoric. 'We crammed daily into his tiny cell, analysing nearly all political conflicts in the world,' said Thami Mkhwanazi. 'Whenever Gwala roared, the young lions roared with him.'[31] 'He was a good writer, a good Marxist with a fantastic memory,' said Billy Nair. 'But he was a hard-liner, with a sectarian approach. He endeared himself to the youth. He didn't hesitate to take a swipe at anybody: he would go for Madiba.'[32] 'He was the best-read man I've ever met,' said Eric Molobi. 'He knew all the details about the Second and Third Communist International. And he didn't conceal that he was challenging Mandela.'[33]

Gwala saw himself as the protector of the true revolutionary flame from bourgeois reformists. 'There was no way of reconciling ideological differences,' he said later.[34] He was determined to achieve a genuine workers' democracy in South Africa, which would control the means of production: when the Freedom Charter said 'the people shall govern', it meant that the workers must rule. 'He had kept a hawkish eye on the non-communist Rivonia trial leadership,' said Mkhwanazi. 'He would bark at the slightest move that appeared to be threatening his dream.'[35] Mandela would later praise Gwala as a 'stalwart of the struggle', but Sisulu would be openly critical: 'He was a real Stalinist and took a narrow view. He was intellectually able to analyse, but alas he analysed wrong. The majority of the young people who took an ultra-left line would follow him.'[36] The Marxists saw the island as offering a unique opportunity for political education: 'A crying need was felt for a theory that would correctly interpret the world,' said Gwala. 'Such a theory was the labour theory as propounded by Marx and Engels and developed by Lenin.'

At first the young militants had no time for 'the dusty manuscripts of Marx and Engels', as Govan Mbeki complained, and were not well-informed about either the ANC or the Communist Party.[37] But Mbeki, Gwala and others were determined to educate them. Political classes would be provided surreptitiously, sometimes while prisoners were walking in the exercise yard. They managed to remove a copy of *Das Kapital* from the library, and a team then copied it out through the night.[38] The High Organ had already prepared a 'Syllabus A', which provided a history of the ANC, and a reading course which Mbeki reckoned would take three years to complete thoroughly.[39] 'Syllabus B' provided a history of human society, much influenced by Marx and Engels.

Gwala's return to the island in 1977 sparked off a fierce new round of debates between the pure Marxists and the 'nationalists' – as they called Mandela's group – of which details and documents have only recently come to light. Gwala was put among the young militants in Section E, which was called the '*Klipgooier*' (stone-thrower section), and it became a hotbed of Marxism. 'It was the most like the Soviet Republic in South Africa,' said one of them, Naledi Tsiki.[40] Gwala continually called for the 'seizure of power' – the battle-cry of the guerrilla fighters – which would require a decisive military victory, as in Cuba. Mandela, on the other hand, always saw the armed struggle as a means to force the government to the negotiating table.[41] It was an angry debate. 'Young people became more and more hot about the issue of seizure of power,' said Sisulu. 'Any doubts about it created problems for them, though they had high respect for the leadership. Because we were firm, and had examined the situation, we were able to keep to our line. The greatest danger was to attempt the impossible, to be defeated completely, and to ruin the country.'[42]

A more fundamental issue was the relationship between the Congresses and the Marxists, which resurrected all the arguments that had raged about the Freedom Charter twenty years earlier. Mandela always saw the ANC as a distinct national party, with its own proud history and policies, which 'welcomed all those with the same objectives'.[43] But Gwala and Govan Mbeki regarded the Communist Party as the dominant force, increasingly closely bound to the ANC: Gwala even wanted to replace the ANC anthem '*Nkosi Sikelel' iAfrika*' with 'The Internationale'. 'He saw the ANC as a passenger,' Eric Molobi thought, 'who'd get off before the revolution.'[44]

It was not a straight confrontation between communists and anti-communists, or between the SACP and the ANC. Many past loyal members of the SACP, like Maharaj and Kathrada, believed in the primacy of the ANC; while the ANC itself had many different strands, including Christians, Muslims, trade unionists, small businessmen and academics. Nor was it a racial division: since 1969 the ANC had admitted non-African communists like Joe Slovo (provoking some pure Africanists to retreat into the PAC or BPC); while the presence of courageous Indian and Coloured leaders on the island made racial arguments harder to sustain. The real issue was about the integrity of Marxism: the hard-line communists stood out against any dilution of Marxist principles and workers' control.

The argument raged among the thirty prisoners in Mandela's block, Section B. The rival camps exchanged documents, or 'polemics'. Document 1/B set out the position favoured by Mandela: that the Freedom Charter was always intended to establish a 'bourgeois democracy', which could be the prelude to a socialist state, as in Europe; but in the meantime the Congresses must fight on the broadest front possible, against racial barriers, rather than against capitalism.[45] Document 2/B went further, emphasising that Congress was a national front, not a party, and must work together with all enemies of fascism, including the PAC and new groups including the Zulu movement Inkatha and Black Consciousness. 'I do not think we can afford,' wrote its author, 'the lordly metaphysical categorisation of fixed enemies and fixed friends.'[46] But Document 3/B from the Marxist side, which showed the clear influence of Govan Mbeki, insisted that the Freedom Charter represented the workers and the oppressed, confronted by the white capitalist class.[47]

Mbeki was always strongly opposed to a broad front against apartheid: race oppression, he insisted, was born of class conflict, and so-called allies like Black Consciousness were really linked to 'far-flung imperialist forces'. He denied that blacks could benefit from capitalism: he strongly contradicted Mandela's notion, in his now famous 1956 article in *Liberation*, that after victory African free enterprise would 'flourish as never before' (see p.95). And he wanted to hear rival views from other sections, following Mao's professed principle: 'Let a hundred flowers bloom.'[48]

The leaders in Mandela's section put forward their views in a document with the code-name 'Inq-M' – 'Inq' (for '*inqindi*', meaning fist) was the Congress Movement, and 'M' (for Marxist) was the Communist Party. It explained that the immediate struggle was against racial oppression, not capitalism, and was based not on Marx but on the Freedom Charter, which promised a democratic system in which the communists could put forward their own policies.[49]

The High Organ in Mandela's section then extended the debate to the other cells. They were not supposed to communicate with each other, but the prisoners copied texts in tiny writing on thin pieces of paper, which they smuggled between cells, watching the warders like hawks: 'They had a greater number of eyes and ears than the jail authorities.'[50] Kathrada, who had been appointed a librarian, was able to move between cells with his books. One group of young militants asked him, 'What is a people's democracy?' The question helped to set off the fiercest debate.[51] Books were the ammunition in the battle of ideas. 'If we laid our hands on any book, however thick,' said Mbeki, 'it was copied out and distributed to our membership throughout the various sections.'[52]

The debate raged through the general cells, magnified by Harry Gwala, and taken up by his militant young comrades, who had more recent experience of the mainland than the veterans, who soon felt disadvantaged. 'We didn't have enough ammunition,' said Kathrada. 'We unearthed everything we could find.'[53] The militants complained that 'Inq-M' was thoroughly misleading and out of date: South Africa had changed greatly over the last decade while the veterans had been in jail. Supermarkets, hypermarkets and chain stores had helped to obliterate small entrepreneurs; big monopolies were buying off the middle class; industries were turning the peasantry into a rural proletariat; and even whites were becoming more removed from the ownership of industries and finance houses. As a result, the Marxists claimed, most South Africans had moved to the left politically, and now rejected capitalism. And elsewhere in Africa communism was gaining ground, controlling governments in Angola and Mozambique, and inspiring rebel forces in Zimbabwe and Namibia. Within South Africa, they argued, apartheid was a fascist movement which threatened all democratic values, so it must be countered by a people's democracy, not a bourgeois one. They quoted from *Sechaba*, the organ of the ANC in exile, which said in 1969 that 'On the wake of the victorious revolution a Democratic People's Republic shall be proclaimed.'[54]

Mandela was worried by the growing acrimony among the prisoners. He always encouraged debate, but the arguments were becoming increasingly tense. Within his own section he and Mbeki were barely on speaking terms, and sometimes Sisulu had to act as peacemaker.[55] The tension was spreading through the cells. 'You got a helluva debate,' said Raks Seakhoa, 'but sometimes it could be very ugly. It would go down the ranks.'[56] Mandela always saw his role in prison as promoting unity, both within the Congresses and between the parties. 'He always tried to be a builder,' said Sisulu. 'He avoided expressing his emotions: he would rather want a balanced picture.'[57] But he was now hard-pressed to maintain balance.

Eventually Kathrada was asked to write a summary of the arguments, to try to reach a consensus. He produced a masterly document of twenty-one closely-written pages. It began by welcoming the 'ferment in our own ranks', praising the alertness and knowledge of the comrades and humbly admitting that 'Inq-M' contained mistakes and confusions which arose from the isolation of the prisoners in Section B. It re-emphasised that Congress was leading the national struggle, while the Communist Party led the class struggle, and that the ANC's tactics would be decided by the concrete conditions inside South Africa. The Freedom Charter could under certain conditions provide a 'qualitative leap towards socialism', but in the meantime it allowed for the sharing of power among all classes and groups who had supported the struggle; it also allowed for Africans to own freehold land, factories and businesses, as stated in Mandela's article in *Liberation* – which, the document stressed, had expressed the views of the whole board of the journal.

Kathrada's document attempted to dampen the most revolutionary expectations of the comrades from the battlefields. South Africa, it warned them, was not yet ready to replace capitalism with a workers' state. The growing black middle class were investing in long leases, cars, television sets and refrigerators – which would make them more conservative and less political. The South African struggle was quite different from the revolutions in Eastern Europe, where the Communist Parties had overthrown Nazism with the help of the Red Army. And the Congresses had never said that they stood for the dictatorship of the proletariat. The document encouraged the comrades to study revolutions and Marxism, which could (echoing Mandela's words) 'operate like a bright searchlight in a dark tunnel'. But it stressed too that 'To fully harness the people's patriotism we should first be clear of our priorities.'

Kathrada's document was passed to the other sections, with a covering note in Mandela's handwriting:

> This document was unanimously approved by the High Organ and we are now sending it to you for attention. We are also circulating it again to the membership here and, should there be any additional comments, we will prepare an addendum and forward it to you in due course.
>
> Amandla![58]

The warders intercepted the document as it was on its way to Tokyo Sexwale's cell. Surprisingly there was no punishment, and nothing was said about it. But the general conciliation between the two sides was relaxing the tension, as prisoners in other cells noticed: 'Suddenly in about 1978 Nelson and Govan were walking and talking,' said Sonny Venkatrathnam. 'This was a strange sight to us.'[59] Govan Mbeki would insist that there had been no challenge to Mandela's authority: 'The decision was taken by the High Organ that Nelson would be our spokesman,' he wrote later, 'and that position continued until we parted in 1982.'[60]

In spite of the fierce arguments, Robben Island was acquiring a special spirit of tolerance and discipline. Many of the young rebels had acquired from the veterans the habits of self-control, team spirit and rational argument, which became the distinctive marks of the Robben Islanders who would later exert such influence on the New South Africa. In Western terms, it was as if the military discipline and camaraderie of the Guards or West Point had been combined with the intellectual stimulus of Oxford or Yale and the moral conviction of the French wartime resistance. There was also an African element of '*ubuntu*' in the concern for human relationships – 'a person is a person because of other people' – which was shared by the other races. Kathrada had often thought about Oscar Wilde's desolate lines:

> The vilest deeds, like poison weeds
> Bloom well in prison air;
> It is only what is good in man
> That wastes and withers there.[61]

'It hasn't applied in my experience,' said Kathrada. 'On the contrary, I learned a great deal about human relationships while in prison. Political prisoners generally have a positive approach that carries them through.'[62]

The spirit of self-discipline and tolerance would still flourish after Mandela left the island in 1982. 'We all had the same view of forgiveness,' said Eric Molobi, 'because the level of debate, with logic and ideas, was extremely high. I've never again seen the same intensity of discussion.'[63] Mandela's contemporaries had developed similar control and tolerance. But Mandela himself was the chief role-model, adding his own authority and insistence on reconciliation, based on strength: after all his sacrifices and uncompromising confrontations, it was hard to depict him as a sell-out.

The prison graduates would retain much of the same spirit after they left jail. Terror Lekota, when faced with his own setbacks as a premier in government, would return to the island to recapture the atmosphere of reflection and reconciliation.[64] 'I can spot a Robben Islander a mile away,' said Raks Seakhoa. 'When they find themselves in a conflict, they have this containment of anger, which is then channelled. I'm really thankful for it. It has had quite an impact on conflict situations, including my home life.'[65]

Mandela remained the prototype of this self-control, and his presence radiated authority. His physique was still formidable as he approached his sixties, with the help of rigorous early-morning exercises. His family doctor, Nthato Motlana, had visited him in 1976 under trying conditions, warned that he was forbidden to mention politics. When he began talking about boxing and Muhammad Ali, the warder quickly told him he could only talk about the family. 'It was the most miserable two hours ever,' Motlana said later. 'When it came to an end I think Mr Mandela was glad to go away.' But he found him in strikingly good health, with a diet which, though bleak, conformed to nutritional requirements. 'Oh, powerful, powerful!' he described Mandela afterwards. 'Except for a few grey hairs he was the same Nel I have known for many years. Absolute dignity, a grand Xhosa chief! Extremely fit, mentally and physically.'[66]

Priscilla Jana, a family lawyer, was impressed the next year by both Mandela's 'fantastic physique' and his legal mastery. 'He hadn't been acting as a lawyer for fifteen years, but I must tell you, he commented on the documents as a lawyer, which was amazing, without letting emotionalism have an effect on him whatsoever.' Instead of asking about his wife and children he enquired about 'my people', and asked Jana out of the warders' hearing, 'Tell them that there is still hope and it's not going to be long, and they must know he is still with them.'[67]

But there were occasional scares about Mandela's health. The Red Cross inspectors saw him on their annual visit in March 1977, together with a doctor, and reported that he 'looked poorly, was slow in speaking and in all his movements. BP 180/100, regular pulse rate 78/min. After sublingual administration of 2mg of Valium he felt and looked better and the pains had diminished.' The doctor saw him again on the following day. He looked well, felt much fresher and had no more pains but was still tired. The Red Cross had the impression that 'Mr Mandela did not like to complain about his health and should be kept under close observation'.[68]

Mandela was certainly dismissive of minor ailments. 'I don't believe very much in medicine,' he said later; nor, he added, did his doctor, Motlana.[69] But he could be too stoical. Once when he was pulling bamboo on the shore he slipped and fell, injuring his knee, which became swollen. The specialist told him not to allow the pain to get the better of him: 'Just use that leg.' After he had limped for a long time the pain disappeared, but the knee never fully healed, and it would give him much trouble twenty-five years later.[70]

In 1979 he discovered a virus 'had been eating up my eye', but after he saw a specialist it disappeared: 'The poor creature,' he told Winnie, 'had no idea of just how strong in me is the will to live.' In the same year, while playing tennis he felt a sudden pain in his heel, which was given urgent medical attention: the prison authorities, he wryly noted, were worried that he might die in prison. He was taken to Cape Town, handcuffed and surrounded by warders, on a rough crossing during which (he told Winnie) 'an army of demons seemed to be on the rampage'.[71] A young surgeon removed a bone fragment which dated back to his time at Fort Hare, and insisted that he stayed overnight in hospital, where he enjoyed the attention of the white nurses and the atmosphere of racial equality. He concluded that 'science had no room for racism'.[72]

On 18 July 1978 Mandela celebrated his sixtieth birthday, with speeches from comrades such as Sisulu and Kathrada. He received only eight messages from family and friends. One came from Govan Mbeki's son Thabo, to whom he could not safely respond, and another from Chief Mangosuthu Buthelezi, to whom he wrote a warm reply, recalling their friendly meeting in 1960 and saying he felt like a thirty-year-old.[73]

The birthday rang round the world. Winnie was not allowed to visit him, but she was more than ever his spokesman, presenting the image of dedicated wife and long-suffering activist. 'He's as upright and proud as the day he was arrested,' she told the *New York Times*. 'Oh, he's just divine.' She received piles of birthday messages from both governments and individuals abroad, prompted by E.S. Reddy of the UN's Special Committee on Apartheid, who had called for the occasion to be celebrated.[74] From Britain, anti-apartheid campaigners sent ten thousand birthday cards (which never arrived). The London *Times* called Mandela 'the colossus of African nationalism'.[75]

In 1980 Mandela was at last allowed to resume his LL.B. course at London University, which had been suspended four years earlier: he planned to tackle jurisprudence, international law, African law and mercantile law or family law, he told Winnie, and reckoned he would hold the record for long-term studies.[76] He received an unexpected tribute from the same university the next year when students proposed him as a candidate for Chancellor. He did not expect to get a hundred votes, he told Winnie, let alone the seven thousand he eventually received: he lost out to Princess Anne, who was supported by the more conventional students and academics, prompted by the Vice-Chancellor Lord Annan, but he enjoyed the long-distance royal rivalry, which he thought would inspire Winnie in her small house in Brandfort, 'turning that miserable shack into a castle, making its narrow rooms as spacious as those of Windsor'.[77]

Mandela was now receiving more news of the outside world. By February 1978 prisoners were allowed to hear tapes of selected South African radio news, though still heavily censored. 'The general policy pursued,' Mandela wrote to a friend, 'is still that of isolating us physically and spiritually from the outside world.'[78] But at last, in September 1980, he could receive his most precious contraband: newspapers. Prisoners were allowed to get the *Cape Times* and the Afrikaans *Die Burger*, and later the Johannesburg *Star*, the *Rand Daily Mail* and the Johannesburg *Sunday Times*. But they were full of holes cut out by the censors, and he found the reporting very incomplete.* 'I have some rough idea of what goes on in the country and the world,' Mandela told Dr Motlana. 'Occasionally the news coverage is quite good and some of the editorials and feature articles are fairly objective and outspoken. But most of the time the best editorials and reviews leave many pertinent questions unanswered. The greater and more decisive part of our political work is done from underground or behind the scenes, and the mass media are generally not aware of it.'[79]

Mandela was himself learning wider lessons from the University of Robben Island. Constantly up against other prisoners, he became more sensitive to other people's insecurities and resentments – like a business executive exposed to 'sensitivity training', but extended over years. He seemed much less arrogant: no longer the chiefly autocrat, but the flexible democrat who could listen and take note of the majority view. He was insistent on loyalty to the ANC: the only grounds for leaving it, he told Maharaj, would be the abandonment of the struggle against apartheid.[80] But he was always reaching out to other groups, trying to find common ground in the context of the nation.

Above all he was reaching out to the Afrikaners. The warders – the only whites on the island – represented racial domination in its most absolute form; but Mandela was able to see them as individuals to whom he could relate, who could teach him about Afrikanerdom. He urged his

* Some puritan groups imposed their own censorship: Harry Gwala forbade prisoners in his section to read the girly back page of the Johannesburg *Sunday Times*.[81]

colleagues to try to understand the Afrikaners, their language and culture. In his still-unpublished essay on Black Consciousness in 1978 he reminded them how the ANC's past ignorance and contempt for the Afrikaner had made them over-confident. He warned that the 'black Englishmen' with their liberal education could be too readily influenced by the English, 'who have their own reasons for despising the Afrikaner'. And with remarkable foresight, only two years after the Soweto uprising, he looked forward to a quite different future: 'Today South Africa has almost three million Afrikaners who will no longer be oppressors after liberation but a powerful minority of ordinary citizens, whose co-operation and goodwill will be required in the reconstruction of the country.'[82]

The Afrikaner government in Pretoria had been receiving confidential reports from the prison authorities giving character assessments of Mandela. In June 1980 Jannie Roux, the Deputy Commissioner of Prisons who had already had several conversations with Mandela, talked with him for two and a half hours, with particular interest since the agitation for his release. Roux reported that Mandela took strong exception to being called a 'self-confessed communist' by the Prime Minister P.W. Botha – though he was openly opposed to capitalism, private land-ownership and the power of big money, and was impressed by Soviet education. He appeared to see a place for white people in a future South Africa, but not as the holders of political power: he had in mind a five-year transition during which they would be accustomed to the transfer of power; but he understood Roux's warning that whites would not just capitulate. 'He appears to have relatively rigid thinking patterns [*betreklik regiede denkpatrone*],' Roux reported, 'and it's difficult to get him to accept an opposite viewpoint.' Roux sent a confidential report to the Minister, who noted: 'This kind of thing must be immediately brought to my attention.'[83]

In February 1981 the Justice Department received a summary in Afrikaans about Mandela's background. It said that he had so adjusted himself to prison regulations that he gave the impression of good behaviour ('*die beeld het van 'n gevangene wie se gedrag goed is*'), and no contraventions of prison regulations had been recorded against him up to 1976.

> He adopts a persistent [*knaende*] attitude by making repeated representations about conditions, but in a way that no steps can

be taken against him. But this should not be seen as good behaviour: he gives the orders and then withdraws to regard his actions from a distance. Mandela sticks to his chosen course and influences everyone with him not to deviate from this . . . It is clear that Mandela has in no way changed his position and that imprisonment so far has had no positive effect on him.[84]

The new Minister of Justice, Kobie Coetsee, asked for further background, and was given a more detailed analysis, which made eleven specific points:

A. Mandela is exceptionally motivated and maintains a strong idealistic approach.
B. He maintains outstanding personal relations, is particularly jovial and always behaves in a friendly and respectful way towards figures of authority.
C. He is manipulative, but nevertheless not tactless or provocative.
D. There are no visible signs of bitterness towards whites, although this may be a fine game of bluff [*blufspel*] on his part.
E. He acknowledges his own shortcomings, but nevertheless believes in himself.
F. He is a practical and pragmatic thinker who can arrive at a workable solution on a philosophical basis.
G. He has a capacity for integrated [*integrerende*] and creative thought.
H. He has an unbelievable memory, to reproduce things in the finest detail.
I. He has an unflinching belief in his cause and in the eventual triumph of African nationalism.
J. He regards himself as called to the task and this elevates him above the average white who, according to him, has apparently lost his idealism.
K. He believes self-discipline, and continually taking the initiative, to be the prerequisites for success.

'There exists no doubt,' the document continues, 'that Mandela commands all the qualities to be the Number One black leader in South Africa. His period in prison has caused his psycho-political posture to increase rather than decrease, and with this he now has acquired the characteristic prison-charisma of the contemporary liberation leader.'[85]

It was a remarkably accurate analysis of Mandela's personality and thinking, which would help to change the Minister's attitude towards his prisoner. But it gave no answer to the crucial question of what to do with such a formidable opponent. And it would be another nine years before Coetsee would release the 'number one black leader'.

21

A Family Apart

1977–1980

WINNIE WAS more than ever Mandela's lifeline to the outside world. 'Sometimes I feel like one who is on the sidelines,' he told her, 'who has missed life itself.' But she could help to connect him. On her visits he eagerly asked after old friends, avoiding any political references. And each year he carefully totted up her letters and visits, now more often allowed: in 1978, he told her, he had a harvest of fifteen visits and forty-three letters, fifteen of them from her.[1]

She could also convey his views, as she interpreted them, to the outside world, through journalists who came to see her. 'Winnie would visit Nelson and then discuss matters,' said Harry Gwala, 'and if you said, "Nelson saw it this way," it would tend to be the law, because his name was venerated. That's how Robben Island exercised influence.'[2] She was always outspoken: President Reagan, she told the *Christian Science Monitor* in 1981, was 'no friend of the black people'.

And she could give Mandela some indication of the political mood in the country after the Soweto uprising, as she was in the thick of it. Immediately after the first riots a Black Parents' Association was formed in Soweto to liaise with the children, and Winnie joined the executive – as the only woman member – with other prominent Sowetans, including her neighbour Dr Motlana. South Africa was in upheaval. The police killed hundreds of young blacks, and thousands escaped from the country. Winnie spoke out without inhibition: 'We shall fight to the bitter end for justice,' she told a protest meeting in Soweto.[3] Motlana, who would always remain loyal to her, was astonished by her fearlessness and her physical strength: 'She has got the kind of guts I don't have, many of us don't have. She would stand before police captains with machine guns and tell them to go and get stuffed . . . She is not scared of anything!'

But he was also struck by her ability to control herself: 'Sometimes she behaved like an Englishman, stiff upper lip, very dismissive.'[4]

The police still saw her as a mastermind of resistance: two months after the Soweto uprising, she was imprisoned in the Fort with other women, including Motlana's wife Sally. She found Winnie a great leader, defying the warders while reassuring the other prisoners: 'She was for ever ready to listen, to smile, to comfort.'[5] Winnie spent nearly five months in the Fort, to Mandela's distress, without being charged, in squalid conditions though without the earlier brutality, before she was released in December. She returned to Soweto as militant as ever among her young friends, and still closely watched by the police.

Five months after her release, in May 1977, she was banished. On Robben Island Ahmed Kathrada heard from a Hindu priest that she had been picked up by the police and driven 250 miles to Brandfort, a bleak Afrikaner town in the Orange Free State where most of the blacks spoke Sotho, which Winnie did not understand. She and her daughter Zindzi, now sixteen, were dumped with her furniture in a small, bare house in the black township with no heating, no running water. 'When I opened the front door there was a mound of dirt in the living room,' she wrote to Mandela. 'Most of the windows have been knocked out and the toilet is outside.'[6] In Brandfort Winnie was kept under surveillance, and was banned from meeting with more than one person. Mandela saw this banishment as a 'brazen and shameless act'.[7] 'I can't believe it,' he wrote to Zindzi. 'Mum has lost almost everything; she'll never get any job there except perhaps as domestic or farm hand or washerwoman; she'll spend all her days in poverty.'[8] He was convinced that the government had deported her to this bleak spot in order to force her to return to the Transkei, where she was born, to help give legitimacy to the 'independent homeland'.[9] But Winnie was contemptuous of the idea: 'The audacity of it! If anybody should leave, it's the settler government.'[10]

Winnie stuck it out in the Brandfort house – 'my cells' as she called it – for seven years. Her neighbours were warned against mixing with her, while a police sergeant watched her constantly. When a man tried to sell her a chicken while she was talking to a neighbour, she was charged with attending a gathering. 'In what other country would the price of chickens be entered as evidence?' she told the *New York Times*. 'They probably thought I was buying a Rhode Island Red,' she joked later.[11] She soon regained her fighting spirit, challenging the police, championing local grievances and enlivening the township with her bright clothes – some in the ANC colours of black, green and yellow. She refused to pay for her services and rent, on the grounds that the house was not her home but a jail.[12]

Winnie's banishment did not diminish her national popularity: from 1977 to 1979 opinion surveys showed her to be the most important political activist after the Zulu leader Chief Buthelezi.[13] And in Brandfort she gained some friends, not just among her black neighbours, but also among Afrikaners. She was befriended by an Afrikaner doctor, Chris Hattingh; but he was killed in a car accident – which some people suspected was engineered – and his sister, who had befriended Zindzi, was scared away by the police.[14]

Winnie also became friendly with Piet de Waal, the only lawyer in Brandfort, who was an old friend of the Nationalist MP Kobie Coetsee, who had a farm nearby. When Winnie needed a lawyer de Waal was at first reluctant to take the case, but her Johannesburg lawyer Ismail Ayob warned him that he was ethically obliged to represent her, since she could not move out of Brandfort. De Waal, very embarrassed, explained his 'unfortunate position' to Coetsee, and also to the Minister of Justice Jimmy Kruger, and tried to get her banished somewhere else. His attitude gradually changed. When Winnie first came to his office he complained about the huge crowd outside; but as she paid more visits he began to regard her as a friend, as did his wife Adele, who came from a well-known Afrikaner family. They were amazed by this warm and intelligent black woman, and championed her against the police.

Piet de Waal's advocacy of Winnie became more important in 1980, when Kobie Coetsee became Minister of Justice. De Waal began pressing him first to lift Winnie's bans, and then to reconsider Mandela's imprisonment. Coetsee began rethinking his attitude to Mandela. 'You could say,' he observed later, 'that's where the whole process started.'[15] But in the meantime the police did not let up in their persecution of Winnie and, through her, of her husband.

On Robben Island Mandela felt all the more guilty about not being with Winnie. He was always grateful to people who dared to visit her at Brandfort, like Fatima Meer and Amina Cachalia. For two years from 1976 he had anxious dreams about Winnie. He was haunted by one recurring nightmare, in which he was trying to get home from Johannesburg without transport, and had to walk to Soweto: he would race to his house, only to find the door open, with nobody inside, and would worry desperately about what had happened to Winnie and the children.[16] 'I had hoped to build you a refuge, no matter how small,' he wrote a month after her arrival at Brandfort, 'so that we would have a place for rest and sustenance before the arrival of the sad, dry days. I fell down and couldn't do these things. I am as one building castles in the air.' 'You have spent twenty-one years of your best years,' he told her on their wedding anniversary in June 1979, 'rolling about in the treacherous whirlpools of an unfriendly sea.' 'Every time I see you carrying visible signs of suffering,' he wrote after a visit, 'I am tortured by a sense of guilt and shame.'[17] Winnie, on her side, was struck by Mandela's insights and discipline. 'He would have been one of the greatest psychologists,' she wrote. 'He is a complete lawyer through and through. He is a perfectionist without imposing himself. He philosophises a great deal. This is his natural self.'[18]

But Mandela longed for physical contact, and poured out his emotions in letters which were quite unlike his measured political messages. 'At my age I would have expected all the urges of youth to have faded away,' he wrote to Winnie when he was sixty. 'But it does not appear to be so. The mere sight of you, even the thought of you, kindles a thousand fires in me.' 'I spent a lot of time on this day thinking of you,' he wrote in June 1980. 'Every time I do, I literally glow and long to embrace you and feel the electric shocks that your flesh rubs onto me, your navel and heartbeat.' He was sensitive about his age: 'I am not used to seeing parts of my body loose and sagging as if I am sixty-two,' he wrote to Winnie in December 1976. 'You know well that I am only forty-five and hardly anyone will have the courage to challenge that statement when I resume my exercises.'[19] But Winnie was more conscious now of the difference in their ages: 'Nelson is sixty-three now,' she told the journalist Allister Sparks in 1982, 'and I am like a young girl, still longing for the experience of married life.'[20]

Despite his apparent self-sufficiency in jail, Mandela seemed dependent on Winnie's support. 'Had it not been for your visits, wonderful letters and your love,' he wrote the month before, 'I would have fallen apart many years ago.' And two months later: 'Your love and devotion has created a debt which I will never attempt to pay back.' He felt luckier than some of his fellow inmates: 'Not all of us are as fortunate,' he wrote in February 1980. 'But I'd like you to know that you have spoilt me very much and a spoilt baby is always difficult to control.' 'There is far less steel in me than I had thought,' he told her in June 1980. 'Distance and two decades of separation have not strengthened the steel in me and [have] deepened my anxiety over the family.'

Mandela liked to remember Winnie's violent jealousy as well as her love: 'like a Penelope whose chastity has been questioned'.[21] He recalled to Zindzi how he had once been asked to give an attractive woman a lift to Sophiatown, and Winnie had retired to the bedroom shaking with anger; or the time when he was waiting in the office to see a beautiful secretary, and she had discovered him and dragged him out. 'Today we've a high-souled and tolerant shepherdess,' he reckoned, rather prematurely, 'who has made a man of me.'[22] He had always admired strong women, and when Winnie wrote to him about 1979 being Women's Year he reflected on the powerful women emerging around the world: Simone Veil, the President of the European Parliament, and Rosalyn Carter, the American First Lady, who 'seems to be wearing the trousers' – not to mention Margaret Thatcher. He looked back to earlier female rulers like Elizabeth I and Catherine the Great, but preferred the new women who had pulled themselves up by their bootstraps.[23]

Winnie appeared on the surface to have overcome the isolation and hardship of Brandfort, with as much self-control as Mandela. In May 1979 she vividly described her 'little Siberia' to her friend Mary Benson in London: 'The empty long days drag on, one like the other, no matter how hard I try to study. The solitude is deadly, the grey matchbox shacks, so desolate, simply stare at you as lifeless as the occupants, who form a human chain of frustration as they pass next to my window. From the moment the bar opens until it closes at eight p.m., they are paralytic drunk.' 'How grim that must sound,' she went on, 'yet there's something so purifying about exile . . . What could be greater than being part of such a cause no matter how infinitesimal our contribution is.'[24]

Winnie was making use of her experience as a social worker to build up such communal activities as a crèche, a sewing group and a clinic, assisted by donations which flowed in as journalists and diplomats began to visit her. She started studying for a degree in social work by correspondence, but faced many obstacles. 'I feel disappointed and even disgusted for I know that social work is second nature to you,' Mandela wrote to her. 'To get your degree would be such a compensation for the rough and raw deals that you have experienced during the last twenty-two years.'[25]

Visitors found Winnie indomitable. 'I was gladly surprised and impressed by her very pleasant disposition, her calmness and complete composure,' said her old friend Ellen Kuzwayo when she met her again in 1982. 'Her charm, her singing laughter, her unchanging face and her ever-present dignity are those of the Winnie Nomzamo of the 1950s when I first met her.'[26]

But Winnie's public image was misleading: she was not quite the upright and controlled heroine that she seemed to the world; and some friends thought the exile in Brandfort, and her ordeals in jail, had fundamentally changed her. Away from reporters, and unknown to Mandela, she was behaving more recklessly, flaunting her fame in white shops, suddenly erupting into violence, and drinking more heavily. The mayor of Brandfort, who ran a liquor store, said: 'She comes in here to buy things, champagne, Cinzano, things like that.' Her bills were said to amount to R3,000 a month.[27] Her righteous contempt for the police, together with her international acclaim, were combining to give Winnie a heady sense of being above any law; and in the armoury of the ANC she was becoming a much looser cannon – which would soon be firing off some dangerous explosives.

The children were suffering less visibly, but they were equally worrying: 'I never stop thinking that some of the children are unable to fulfil their life dreams,' Mandela told Winnie in 1979, 'simply because I am not there to help them solve their numerous problems.'[28] He was preoccupied with their education, Kathrada noticed, to the point of blackmail: 'When one seemed either reluctant or slow to carry out his admonitions, he virtually prohibited her from visiting until she satisfied him that she was studying seriously.'[29]

He was less worried about Zeni, his elder daughter by Winnie, after she became engaged to Prince Thumbumuzi, the son of the Swazi King Sobhuza, whom she had met at Waterford School. Mandela was concerned that Zeni was too young for marriage at eighteen, and that she had not finished high school: 'Priority number one is your studies,' he told Zindzi.[30] But he was proud to be linked to 'one of the most famous families in South Africa', as he told Winnie, and he saw Sobhuza as a popular monarch who supported the ANC.[31] With chiefly formality he asked his lawyer George Bizos to ask the Prince how he would support his daughter; Bizos reported that Thumbumuzi's prospects were good, and that he was genuinely in love.

Mandela saw it as a dynastic marriage, between a Swazi prince and a Tembu princess.[32] He was frustrated that he could not give his daughter away in the traditional marriage ceremony in 1977, but was thrilled by the birth of their daughter, whom he insisted should be called Zaziwe ('hope'): 'We will not feel happy until you assure us that you have accepted the name.'[33] He arranged for his old friend Helen Joseph, now seventy-three, to be godmother: in a photograph of the christening he 'immediately spotted a tall lady who stood upright like a field marshal'.[34] As the other godparent he chose, with characteristic forgiveness, the ninety-one-year-old Dr James Moroka – the former ANC President who had betrayed him and other leaders of the Defiance Campaign in 1952 by branding them as communists.

Zeni's new status as a foreign princess gave her the precious diplomatic privilege of being allowed to see her father in the same room, not from behind glass. When she arrived on the island with her husband and their baby daughter Mandela was able to embrace Zeni for the first time since his imprisonment, and held the baby with delight throughout the visit. He still worried, he wrote, about her 'lack of ambition and finesse', but was partly reassured after she left with her young family for America. And he was thrilled when more grandchildren arrived.[35]

Zindzi was more of a problem. Like Winnie she was spirited, bright and passionate. She was apprehensive when at the age of sixteen she first visited him in jail, but was reassured by his warmth: 'Oh, darling,' he said, 'I can see you now as a kid at home on my lap . . . We started dreaming and dreaming and then I felt so free.'[36] 'She has a lot of fire in her, and I hope she will exploit it fully,' he told a friend afterwards.[37] But he worried about her in Brandfort, away from her friends, alone with her harassed mother. 'How does poor Mum show her love to our last-born in a strange place where she has no income, where she faces numerous problems?' he wrote to her on her seventeenth birthday in 1977. 'In such circumstances, is it at all correct to talk of a birthday?' He could be solicitous: when Zindzi was embarrassed by the prospect of attending Zeni's wedding with bare breasts, following Swazi royal custom, he reassured her: 'Your breasts should be as hard as apples and as dangerous as cannons.' And he was pleased when she told him that she wanted to become a writer, which was 'a prestigious profession': Jim Bailey, the owner of *Drum*, had invited her to become a columnist for his new women's magazine *True Love*, and she had also begun writing poetry.[38]

The next year, 1978, she published a book of poetry, *Black as I Am*, which began with a poem about her father:

> A tree is chopped down
> And the fruit was scattered
> I cried . . . [39]

The book was awarded a $1,000 prize in America, and was well reviewed by Alan Paton and others. Mandela found the language simple and crisp, but advised Zindzi to polish the rough edges.[40] He did not welcome the news that she planned to write a family biography; he had been distressed by recent controversial autobiographies by Margaret Trudeau, the separated wife of the Canadian Prime Minister, and Sophia Loren, his favourite film star, and he dreaded sensationalism: 'A happy family life is an important pillar to any public man.'[41]

Mandela loved Zindzi's visits to Robben Island. 'You make a wonderful impression to me whenever I see you,' he told her in March 1979. 'You were really striking in your pantaloons,' he wrote six months later. But behind her exuberance Zindzi was suffering from confusion and sporadic depression: she had to see a psychiatrist, and her studies were set back. Mandela tried to reassure her that moodiness was common, and was quite understandable in her circumstances. He praised her inquisitive mind and lovely sense of humour, and sympathised with her anger at her disrupted life. He urged her: 'There are few misfortunes in this world that you cannot turn into a personal triumph if you have the iron will and the necessary skill.'[42] But Zindzi did not have her father's iron will: her writing had dried up, and she had backed off from going to Wits University. She had fallen in love with an odd-job man, Oupa Seakamela, by whom she had a daughter, Zoleka; she later had a son, Gadaffi, by a Rastafarian called Mbuyiselo, who would physically assault her.[43] She left Winnie in Brandfort to go back to the family house in Orlando. Mandela was anxiously protective: he understood Zindzi's longing to return to her childhood home, but did not want her to live alone: he hoped that an elderly aunt, or some friendly couple, might join her, but he knew that the police would harass anyone associated with the Mandelas.[44]

He also worried about his two eldest children by his first wife, Evelyn. 'It was always a matter of deep pain,' said Fatima Meer, who remained friends with most of the family, 'that those whom he loved . . . did not love each other as much as they should.' Makgatho, Mandela's eldest son, was still disappointing. After his wife Rayne ('Rennie') returned to her studies, Mandela hoped that he would realise that he was 'the only black sheep in the family', and asked Makgatho's sister Maki to keep urging him to think of his future. 'When he does actually enter a school I will do everything in my power to help him, but definitely not before that,' Mandela wrote in 1979.[45] But Makgatho continued to resist education, which his father valued above everything.

Maki was hardly more communicative. Mandela was surprised, he wrote to her after his sixtieth birthday in 1978, that she should 'attach no significance whatsoever to such important things as birthdays and Christmas cards'. In 1978, after her marriage collapsed, he urged her to divorce without delay: 'You are still young with a bright future, if from now on you plan carefully and are really determined to go forward.'[46] She eventually decided that 'Life without a profession is futile,' and was admitted to Fort Hare in late 1978, 'through Mum Winnie's manoeuvres'. She told him that this made her 'the happiest soul'.[47] He was very relieved, and advised her to read at least two newspapers a day.

Mandela was worried that Maki's husband Camagu was not supporting the children, and poignantly warned her about the traumas of divorce: the children would be 'tortured by the stigma of growing up without the security of a home where both parents live together'. He urged Maki to be strong: 'Divorce may destroy a woman but strong characters have not only survived but have gone further.'[48] In some ways Maki was the most independent-minded of Mandela's children, always ready to argue with him. 'Don't make me regret I am here,' he once wrote to her sadly. 'I do not want to come to the point where I regret what I am doing. What I need to do is worthwhile, not only for you and the rest of the family but for all black people.'[49]

In the loneliness of his cell Mandela was often racked by remorse as he looked back over his earlier years. 'One of the things that tortured me,' he said afterwards, 'was how I have treated people who have been very kind to me, specially when I was in difficulties, went out of their way to make me happy, under no obligation at all. Once I was a lawyer I forgot about them.'[50] He would never quite lose that remorse: 'I didn't show sufficient gratitude to those who were kind to me when hard times were knocking at my door,' he said later.[51]

He gained strength from thinking about his children and his increasing number of grandchildren: he would often talk about them with his fellow-prisoners, and would try to imagine their lives. 'I am at my best when the sun goes down to rest and the big gates slam,' he wrote to Winnie. 'This is the time for relaxation when I choose to gloss over my shortcomings and count my fortunes one by one instead.'[52] But he desperately missed the physical contact which could express simple love between himself and his children, and soften the sterner side of his parental ambitions. 'How can a child grow up,' he asked his friends, 'without ever touching its father?'[53] The steely political resolve that he had hardened in prison, which so inspired his comrades, did not easily mix with the softer side of parenting: and he would continue to blame himself for being an absent head of the family, who had sacrificed them for his political purpose. Already when he went underground in 1961 he knew that he was choosing a path which would separate him from any settled family life. But his isolation in prison distanced him from his children, and from Winnie, much more even than he realised at the time.

22

Prison Within a Prison

1978–1982

FROM HIS ISLAND PRISON, Mandela peered out at the mainland with very incomplete information, but with stubborn optimism. 'The little that filters through these grim walls convinces us that our forces are making progress,' he wrote to his friend Sheila Weinberg in 1978. 'Our people are fighting back courageously, so much so that I often wonder whether it is those inside or outside jail who suffer most.'[1] 'We have pestered almost every newcomer to the island about information relating to the political situation,' he told Rhadi, the wife of his old Durban communist friend J.N. Singh, the next year. 'And we have constantly sought information about the men and women who are the driving force behind our organisation.'[2]

In his sixties, Mandela was very aware that he had to come to terms with a quite new generation, particularly after his arguments with the Soweto rebels. He desperately needed to keep in touch with the politicians outside; particularly with the ANC President Oliver Tambo, who was now based in Lusaka and London, where his wife Adelaide and his children lived in Muswell Hill. Mandela was sometimes able to smuggle out political letters through visitors, departing prisoners or other intermediaries still not disclosed. He wrote to Adelaide (under the name 'Matlala') as a cover for Tambo (called by his middle name, Reginald). The censors soon rumbled this subterfuge, as he told Adelaide in 1980: 'The department of prisons wants to break all kinds of contact between Reggie and myself.' But messages still got through.

Mandela's first concern was that Tambo should not overwork himself, since he was not strong. 'I appeal to him once more to take a holiday, even for a fortnight,' he wrote to Adelaide in December 1980. He was also worried about Adelaide's own health, after a fall which had required several operations and which might confine her to a wheelchair: 'Only a woman of steel could have pulled through such a horrible experience.'[3] But Mandela's main preoccupations were that the ANC must hold together, and avoid the lethal rivalries which had undermined so many liberation movements; and Tambo must be the unquestioned leader. In 1978 some exiles were claiming that the Robben Island prisoners were critical of the handling of the struggle, and wanted to lead it themselves; but Mandela and Raymond Mhlaba wrote to Tambo denying this. Some prisoners, they conceded, had complained about the inactivity outside, but they appreciated the very difficult conditions, and accepted that the leaders in exile must move 'cautiously and patiently'. They were confident that 'the organisation has never been so strong in its history', and were encouraged by 'the high level of political consciousness on the part of our people who come into jail, including men in their early twenties'.[4]

Mandela knew that Pretoria was doing its best to divide the Africans, and to co-opt their leaders into the apartheid system. He was specially concerned about the new tribal homelands, or Bantustans, the showpieces of 'grand apartheid' which were being offered 'independence' under Pretoria's control, with rich rewards for collaborators. The prisoners watched the process with agonising frustration and anger. 'With "independence" for Bantustans,' wrote Walter Sisulu in 1976, 'the Nats will have gone a long way in dividing our people along ethnic lines and further sown seeds that may well become a time bomb that will explode in our midst, long after the Nats and white minority rule have been vanquished.'[5]

Mandela suffered a very personal anguish when in October 1976, four months after the Soweto uprising, his own home region the Transkei became a so-called independent republic (though it was not recognised as independent outside South Africa). His nephew Kaiser Matanzima was elected its first President, and was soon to establish himself, with his brother George, as a virtual dictator, supported by Pretoria. Matanzima saw himself as a friend of the Afrikaners, and thought his uncle Mandela deserved to be in jail for having broken the law.[6] He continued to press him to accept Pretoria's offer to release him to the Transkei. Mandela now had no illusions about his nephew, but he still maintained the family friendship. When in September 1977 Matanzima asked to visit him on the island, which Pretoria was glad to allow, Mandela was tempted to agree, optimistically believing that he might persuade him to turn to democracy if they talked face to face. He consulted his close colleagues, but Sisulu and Kathrada were against the visit, Mbeki and Mhlaba were also unhappy about it, and most of the other prisoners were opposed to having any dealings with a sell-out such as Matanzima.[7]

In 1980 Matanzima showed his full ruthlessness when he deposed the Thembu King Sabata – whom the young Mandela had been expected to serve as counsellor, and who had become increasingly supportive of the ANC.[8] After Sabata's dismissal a group of Thembu chiefs came to Robben Island to ask Mandela's advice, and he urged them to support Sabata against Matanzima. Sabata soon afterwards escaped and made his way to the Zambian capital Lusaka, where he formally joined the ANC and became known as 'Comrade King'.

Mandela still kept in touch with Matanzima, and even sought financial help for Matanzima's daughter, who had written him warm letters in jail.[9] But he was sure that the Bantustans would never win popular support. As he wrote in 1980:

> The so-called independent Bantustans are no more than glorified reservoirs of cheap labour crippled by overpopulation, soil erosion and poverty. They are pseudo-states that have been snubbed and humiliated by the international community and that have hardly any prospect for economic growth. It is for this reason mainly that several Bantustans are now reluctant to take independence.[10]

Mandela had equally ambivalent feelings about Mangosuthu Buthelezi, the Zulu chief who by the seventies had become the most prominent black leader inside South Africa. Buthelezi was the first Zulu chief – as Matanzima was the first Xhosa chief – to go to university, and Mandela had admired him ever since he had been expelled from Fort Hare for belonging to the ANC. Now a shrewd politician, combining intellectual agility with tribal understanding, in 1970 he had agreed to become Chief Executive of the new Zulu Territorial Authority, thus collaborating with Bantustan policies, and he was increasingly ambiguous towards the ANC. He kept in contact with Tambo, however, and in 1973 called for Mandela's release, so as to 'create a wholesome climate for meaningful dialogue'.[11]

Buthelezi was thriving on the government's patronage and publicity while the ANC was silenced. In 1975, with Tambo's encouragement, he relaunched an earlier Zulu cultural body, 'Inkatha', as a means of mobilising the Zulu masses, adopting the ANC flag and uniform.[12] But Buthelezi, as Tambo lamented, 'built Inkatha as a personal power base far removed from the kind of organisation we had visualised'. He controlled Kwa-Zulu as his own fiefdom, and presented himself abroad as the key black leader, meeting a number of heads of government, including the American President Jimmy Carter. In 1978 a team of West German researchers found that 44 per cent of urban Africans in three main South African cities admired Buthelezi more than any other political figure, compared to only 19 per cent for Mandela.[13] By 1980 Inkatha could claim 350,000 members in nearly a thousand branches. But young black militants began to see Buthelezi as a Quisling: at the funeral of Robert Sobukwe in 1978 he was forced to flee by furious youths shouting 'stooge' and 'sell-out'.[14]

Mandela remained personally friendly to Buthelezi, as he was to Matanzima. When Buthelezi sent him greetings on his sixtieth birthday he replied cordially, mentioning that he had seen pictures of him in government publications and films. Realising the letter was politically sensitive, he showed it to his close colleagues, only two of whom objected, and then had it smuggled out via Tambo, leaving him to decide whether to forward it to Buthelezi.[15]

Buthelezi continued to claim support from the Robben Islanders. 'From jail I hear a message from Nelson Mandela and Walter Sisulu,' he said in Soweto on 21 October 1979, 'telling me to go on doing what I am doing on behalf of millions of black people.' But only ten days later he was in headlong collision with the ANC. He went to London for a secret meeting with Tambo, which seemed cordial, although Buthelezi fundamentally opposed the armed struggle and sanctions. But on his return he leaked details of the meeting to the Johannesburg *Sunday Times*, which proclaimed 'Buthelezi Plans a Black Front', and made him appear to be the dominant black leader. He soon turned against the ANC, and in July 1980 Tambo announced that Buthelezi had 'emerged on the side of the enemy against the people'. Mandela still kept in touch with him, as an old chiefly friend; but Inkatha would remain at loggerheads with the ANC for the next sixteen years, the biggest single obstacle to a unified black opposition to apartheid.

Mandela could find more encouragement elsewhere, particularly from the Churches, which had been so cautious in opposing apartheid at the time when he had gone to jail. Now 'the winds of change were howling inside the churches', as the Catholic Father Smangaliso Mkhatshwa had foreseen in 1968, and black priests were breaking the pattern of white domination. The Catholics had produced a 'black priests' manifesto' attacking racism within their Church, and were becoming much more vocal against apartheid.[16]

The Anglicans had appointed the irrepressible black cleric Desmond Tutu as Dean of Johannesburg; he later became Secretary of the interdenominational South African Council of Churches (SACC). Tutu, a neighbour of the Mandelas in Soweto, was fearless in predicting black rule. 'We need Nelson Mandela,' he said in April 1980, 'because he is almost certainly going to be that first black prime minister.'[17] Mandela wrote gratefully to Tutu recalling other Anglican heroes – Michael Scott, Trevor Huddleston and Ambrose Reeves – and noting that the Churches were undermining the government's excuse that it was persecuting freedom fighters as part of a global communist conspiracy: 'The rising indignation of churchmen against all kinds of racial oppression has deprived the government of its only propaganda weapon.'[18]

Mandela was reaching out to all the main Churches, with a politician's eye for future friends. He congratulated Dr Gqubule on becoming President of the Methodist Church, noting that his new secretary Stanley Mogoba had been 'steeled through suffering' on Robben Island. He was glad that the Methodists had started 'the momentous task' of putting their house in order: he recalled his own Methodist upbringing, and welcomed the recent conference, which he saw as 'vindicating the great principles upon which the early apostles built the Christian Church'.[19]

Mandela especially welcomed the wind of change within the Dutch Reformed Church, the original seedbed of apartheid. He was inspired by the courage of Dr Beyers Naude, a fashionable preacher whose father had been a founder of the Broederbond, who rebelled against his own Church and became the first Director of the new Christian Institute, befriending many black leaders including Steve Biko. He was delighted by a report of the DRC's Synod which denounced all forms of racial oppression, and recognised that the Church could not isolate itself from other problems; and he wrote to Sam Buti, a black preacher affiliated to the Dutch Reformed Church whose father he had known well, to congratulate him on joining the South African Council of Churches.[20]

Mandela was also extending his diplomacy abroad, in letters full of understanding and flattery. When he was awarded an honorary doctorate in Lesotho he accepted it as 'a tangible expression of the unqualified and consistent support our struggle has always enjoyed among the people of Lesotho'. He praised the great Basuto King Moshoeshoe, who was 'one of the very first black statesmen to appreciate the dangers of divisions among our people in their struggle against imperialist aggression'. He recalled that the Basuto King Griffiths was a founder-member of the ANC in 1912, and how he had met the Basuto Queen in Johannesburg.[21]

After the death in office of Seretse Khama, the first President of Botswana, in 1980, Mandela wrote to his successor recalling his friendship with Sir Seretse and congratulating Botswana on its government. It was remarkable, he said, that in Africa 'men who had no previous experience whatsoever in government as it functions today should be able to run modern states with such success'. And he was grateful to Botswana for providing a haven for South African refugees from political persecution.[22]

Mandela was becoming reassured by more signs of recognition from around the world. In 1979 he was awarded the annual Nehru Prize for International Understanding, whose previous laureates included Mother Teresa, Martin Luther King and Marshal Tito. Tambo flew to Delhi to deliver Mandela's acceptance speech, in which he recalled how much Nehru had influenced him, and how Nehru in prison had refused to succumb to mundane hardships, or a closed mind: 'The most terrible walls are the walls that grow up in the mind.'[23] Mandela himself was not even allowed to see the album commemorating the award ceremony, but a warder sneaked it into his cell overnight.[24] 'You have to know this place well to appreciate the value of photos to prisoners,' he told Adelaide Tambo. 'They are among those things that minimise or even remove altogether the feeling of rejection and isolation.'[25]

In December 1980 the city of Glasgow provoked a fierce Scottish dispute by awarding him its freedom.* Mandela fulsomely thanked Dr Michael Kelly, the Lord Provost, praising the Scots and recalling how as a child he had learnt about Scots patriots like William Wallace, Robert the Bruce and the Earl of Argyll. He gave a vivid picture of his present predicament:

* When the Lord Provost of Glasgow wrote a letter, released to the press, to the South African President asking for Mandela to be allowed to come to Scotland to receive his award, the South African Consul in Glasgow reported to Pretoria with pride that 'the response (even in Labour newspapers) has been one of neutrality, disapproval, hostility or, now, of disinterest.'[29]

> I live in a prison within a prison, on a notorious island in a country where my people are virtually imprisoned by a minority of racial fanatics who are preoccupied with issues of colour and creed; the phantom gods who have made racial prejudice a religion. In my own country, and because of the colour of my skin, I have never enjoyed the freedom of the streets, let alone the freedom of the city.[26]

In his letters Mandela was sounding not at all like a prisoner serving a life sentence, and much more like the leader of a government in exile who was waiting to create a new unified nation. He had some reason to be more optimistic about international support. Western liberal opinion had been outraged by the torture and murder of the Black Consciousness leader Steve Biko in September 1977, which revealed all the brutality of the apartheid state. Two months later the United Nations had imposed a mandatory embargo on all arms sales to South Africa – the first in its history.[27] The new American Ambassador to the United Nations, the black Congressman Andrew Young, denounced the Pretoria government as 'illegitimate', while the American Vice-President Walter Mondale warned Pretoria not to have 'any illusions that the United States will, in the end, intervene to save South Africa'.[28] In London the new Labour Foreign Secretary David Owen was increasingly critical of apartheid, although he was frustrated by Whitehall, which he found 'adamantly opposed to the application of any sanctions'; and by the British Ambassador to Pretoria, David Scott, who later became Vice-President of the trading lobby UKSATA.[30]

In South Africa itself, the government appeared to be undermined from within by deepening scandals. The Minister of Information, Connie Mulder, had connived with his flamboyant director Eschel Rhoodie and the intelligence chief General van den Bergh, to create their own corrupt web of media and undercover diplomacy with a huge secret budget. By 1978 the 'Infogate' scandals were incriminating the Prime Minister himself, and Vorster was forced to resign, pushed upstairs to become briefly State President.[31]

It looked as if Mandela's hopes of a split in Afrikaner ranks were at last being realised, and that liberal Afrikaners might begin to break up the solid front of apartheid. 'With proper planning and better knowledge of Afrikaans,' he wrote in 1978, 'we can speak directly to a wider audience and win more Bram Fischers, Jack Simonses, Piet Vogels and Breyten Breytenbachs.'[32] He and Sisulu were particularly encouraged by Afrikaner writers like André Brink and Jan Rabie, who were attacking oppression. 'In the field of literature,' wrote Sisulu in 1976, 'Afrikaner writers appear to be rapidly showing themselves more forthright and outspoken on questions of oppression and racial discrimination than their English-speaking counterparts who have delved somewhat delicately into such questions over a much longer period.'[33]

But in place of Vorster the National Party chose the Minister of Defence, P.W. Botha, as Prime Minister, who soon proved a much tougher opponent. Botha was a fierce champion of his people, a big, bullying man with a loyal army behind him, who saw himself as both fighter and reformer. He soon launched reforms aimed at placating local businessmen and world opinion, and at establishing a more docile black middle class. He allowed blacks in urban areas to buy long leases, and agreed to legalise black trades unions. Despite these reforms, the CIA noted in its publication *Africa Review*: 'The government's failure to meet demands by black labour for equality in the workplace will damage prospects for economic growth and political stability.'[34]

Botha also massively strengthened the military machine under the new Minister of Defence General Magnus Malan, stepping up the campaign to combat the 'total onslaught' of communist powers. And he soon co-opted business leaders into the security system and growing arms industry.

Mandela had no confidence in Botha's reforms. 'There is not even a whisper about majority rule or any kind of direct representation for blacks in the country's Parliament,' he told Dr Kelly in Glasgow, and recalled the last twenty years of bannings, killings and torture: 'Every upheaval such as school boycotts and demonstrations is violently suppressed and turned to a bloodbath.'[35]

The ANC in exile was now facing a more formidable military force. But Tambo had gained strength from the Soweto uprising. He had been more sympathetic to the young rebels than Mandela, recalling his past in the Youth League: 'In a way we started from the point of Black Consciousness too,' he wrote in the ANC magazine *Sechaba* in late 1977.[36] And as thousands of young refugees escaped from South Africa, the ANC recruited large numbers into their training camps. Few of them were able to penetrate back into South Africa, where the military was increasingly effective, with the help of informers and torture. But since Soweto the ANC had been giving more emphasis to political mobilisation inside South Africa to complement the armed struggle. In October 1978 Tambo led an ANC delegation, including Joe Modise, Joe Slovo and Thabo Mbeki, to Vietnam after its reunification. On their return they produced a 'Green Book' of new priorities which were largely accepted by the National Executive. They foresaw a 'protracted people's war' rather than a 'nationwide insurrection', and identified the main task as being 'to concentrate on political mobilisation and organisation so as to build up political revolutionary bases throughout the country'.[37]

Mandela saw a new ray of hope for himself in March 1980 when the editor of the Johannesburg *Sunday Post*, Percy Qoboza, launched a petition for his release under the headline 'FREE MANDELA'. It had been inspired by the ANC in Lusaka, which had broken with the tradition of promoting only collective leadership, though some Robben Islanders were worried about creating a personality cult.[38] The campaign quickly gained momentum inside South Africa. At a meeting at Wits University twenty years after Sharpeville, Mandela's daughter Zindzi explained that the purpose of the petition was 'merely to say there is an alternative to the inevitable bloodbath'.[39] Support came from surprising quarters: many whites put 'Free Mandela' stickers on their cars, and even General van den Bergh, having been ousted from the secret service after the 'Infogate' scandal, now said that Mandela should be freed: 'I know the man's history well,' he told Kitt Katzin of the Johannesburg *Sunday Express*, 'and I challenge anyone to produce one shred of evidence to prove that Mandela was a member of the Communist Party.'[40] But the Minister for Police, Louis le Grange, insisted that Mandela 'remains just as staunch a communist . . . as he had been all his life'. P.W. Botha, after being heckled by Afrikaner students, reiterated that he would not release the 'arch-Marxist'.[41]

The campaign led to renewed allegations about Mandela's communism, against the evidence. 'There are nevertheless strong presumptions that Mandela in fact is a member of the Communist Party,' said a top secret ('*uiters geheim*') report from the State Security Council in May 1982. But they relied on the old charges that he had attended a meeting of the Central Committee in 1962, and on his transcription of 'How to be a Good Communist', exhibited at the Rivonia trial (see p.190).[42]

The Free Mandela campaign reverberated around the world. In New

York the UN Security Council joined the call to release him, as the only way to achieve 'meaningful discussion of the future of the country'.[43] In London Tambo appealed for 1980 to be 'a year of united mass struggle', and republished the statement which Mandela had written after the Soweto uprising, with its militant call: 'Those who live by the gun shall perish by the gun. Unite! Mobilise! Fight on!'[44]

The ANC was beginning to cause more effective sabotage, in keeping with its new policy of 'armed propaganda' while avoiding civilian targets and terrorism. In June 1980 ANC guerrillas put bombs in three major oil-from-coal installations: the explosions lit up the sky fifty miles away. South Africa, said the *Rand Daily Mail*, was now in a 'state of revolutionary war'.[45] Such attacks, Mandela wrote to Tambo, had 'considerably enhanced the ANC profile and made us walk tall. We are undoubtedly a force to be reckoned with.'

But Botha's government was determined to stamp out ANC bases beyond the country's frontiers. In January 1981 their forces invaded Mozambique, attacking three buildings in the capital Maputo and killing thirteen ANC people. Mandela saw this as being clearly linked to South Africa's forthcoming April elections. 'P.W. Botha is prepared to violate the territorial integrity of an independent country,' he wrote to Tambo, 'and to kill unarmed refugees in order to remain in power.' He believed Botha was trying to curry favour with the Reagan administration in its crusade against communism. But Mandela still seemed optimistic: 'Our next blow will be so devastating that more and more government supporters will realise that the Nats are leading the country to complete disaster.'[46]

By 1981 the attacks and reprisals were stepping up. Joe Gqabi, an ex-MK fighter and the ANC representative in Zimbabwe, was murdered in Harare; soon afterwards a bomb exploded in a Port Elizabeth shopping centre. Tambo announced that 'combat situations' might arise in which civilians could be killed. In four and a half years there had been 112 attacks and explosions. It was, wrote the historian Tom Lodge in 1981, 'the most sustained violent rebellion in South African history, and all the indications are that it will continue into a full-scale revolutionary war'.[47]

The rebellion was approaching a kind of insurrection within the townships. But it was also coming up against the global Cold War, as Western powers were watching black South Africa through red-tinted telescopes. P.W. Botha's anti-communist crusade was gaining more support from the neo-conservative governments in London and Washington, and from right-wing organisations and companies in America and Europe. They saw Mandela as an arch-enemy, and Buthelezi and Botha as champions of free enterprise.

When Margaret Thatcher came to power in Britain in 1979, she was sympathetic to the white South Africans – influenced by her husband Denis, who had good friends in Natal – and she became implacably hostile to the ANC, whom she saw as communist terrorists, threatening a stronghold of capitalism. Her friend the Afrikaner mystic Laurens van der Post advised her that while the ANC were Xhosa communists, the Zulus were a proud, separate nation, ably led by Buthelezi. 'She listened to him rapt,' said her Private Secretary Charles Powell, 'her lips parted.'[48]

In Washington, Ronald Reagan was 'not too steeped' in South African issues (as his Secretary of State General Alexander Haig delicately put it). Chester Crocker, in charge of Africa at the State Department, told a South African reporter: 'All Reagan knows about South Africa is that he's on the side of the whites.' Nevertheless, Crocker embarked on an ambitious policy of 'constructive engagement' aimed at getting the Cubans out of Angola and the South Africans out of Namibia, which involved dealing closely with P.W. Botha and his Foreign Minister Pik Botha, but left out the ANC entirely: Crocker would not meet Tambo until 1986.[49] And Crocker's patient negotiations were undermined by the hawkish CIA Director William Casey, working with Reagan's close aide Pat Buchanan. Casey was backing covert anti-communist plots throughout the continent. In South Africa he befriended Pretoria's intelligence chiefs and supported P.W. Botha – to whom he presented a signed copy of his book.[50]

The ANC's hopes of support from independent black states were being dashed by the failures of their governments, and by successive coups and counter-coups. Over two decades twenty-eight African countries had experienced *coups d'état* and fifty governments had been overthrown; some were taken over by dictators who ignored all human rights, like Idi Amin in Uganda.[51] By the early eighties only Nigeria, with huge oil revenues and a new civilian government, appeared economically hopeful. Western businessmen were writing off most of black Africa, while white South Africa depicted itself as the only viable part of the continent. The more mature Robben Islanders were learning lessons about the problems of democracy from the coups, wars and dictators to the north, and were determined not to take the same routes.

But the Cold War was now distorting policies all through Africa, as the Soviet Union supported Marxist regimes while the Americans financed anti-communist leaders like Mobutu in Zaire, thus providing coffers for corruption. The Marxists on Robben Island saw African setbacks in terms of American interference. They had looked to the communist government in Somalia, for instance, as a utopia; when in 1977 the Somalis threw out the Russians and brought in the Americans they simply could not believe it.[52] (Harry Gwala explained that the Somalis had not properly adopted Marxism-Leninism, and were held back by bourgeois democracy.)[53]

Mandela had hoped that the Cold War would evaporate as the two rival systems were forced to co-operate in space and elsewhere: he told Zindzi in 1978 that 'the Cold War is now melting away'.[54] But it became hotter round the edges of South Africa after Angola and Mozambique acquired Marxist governments. Mozambique under President Samora Machel briefly appeared to be a socialist dream, but then white technicians and managers left the country, and the incursions of rebel soldiers reduced large areas to chaos. Angola became a battlefield for the rival superpowers: the central government brought in Cuban troops, while the Americans and South Africans supported the rebel UNITA army of Jonas Savimbi. Angola was torn apart, and the battle for the country polarised both sides.

Most Robben Islanders regarded the CIA as the chief villains. Mandela saw the CIA as the agent of American imperialism, which (he wrote in 1975) 'props up right-wing elements in all countries, which tries to undermine and topple legitimate progressive governments through violence, intrigue and dollars'.[55] He still praised the American democratic system, as he had in his Rivonia speech, and educated the young comrades about the American constitution and the separation of powers. But the general mood on the island was very anti-American. 'America was the most hated country,' said Eric Molobi. 'No one looked for help from them.' 'We were unanimous in our negative attitude towards the United States,' said Kathrada.[56]

By March 1982 Mandela had been in prison for almost twenty years. From his isolation he had watched the Western world swinging from right to left, and back to the right, ending up with Reagan and Thatcher. Most governments had denounced apartheid, but none had held out much support for the prisoners or for the ANC in exile. In the meantime communist fighters in Vietnam and Cuba had shown the way to triumphant revolution, and the Russians, the East Germans and other Marxists were training ANC guerrillas and providing them with weapons. The ANC continued to look east rather than west for their salvation: the KGB reported that black Southern African leaders saw the Soviet Union as 'the only major power that could assist them'.[57]

The map of Africa had been transformed over two decades by the retreat of the old empires. 'The African Revolution which swept through Africa knocked at the doors of Southern Africa,' wrote Sisulu in 1976. 'The door remained bolted.'[58] Another door opened when Zimbabwe became independent in 1980, leaving only South Africa and its colony Namibia as the rump of the old 'white redoubt'. But successive white South African governments – under Verwoerd, Vorster and Botha – had fought back with growing ingenuity and ruthlessness, and had found friends among other pariah states and right-wing groups in the Western democracies. With all the protests around the world, the apartheid government was still very well fortified, and the Robben Islanders, who had lived on hope, could see no easy prospect of the walls tumbling.

23

Insurrection

1982–1985

IN APRIL 1982 the Commanding Officer of Robben Island, Brigadier Munro, came into Mandela's cell to tell him to pack his belongings because he was being moved from the island. Mandela, puzzled, stowed his accumulated things into a few cardboard boxes, and had no time to say proper goodbyes. He was taken with three others – Walter Sisulu, Raymond Mhlaba and Andrew Mlangeni – to board the ferry to Cape Town. From the boat they looked back in the dusk at the island which had been their home for eighteen years. In Cape Town they were rushed past armed guards to a huge truck with a cage on it, into which they were herded. After being kept standing for an hour's drive, they arrived in the lush suburb of Tokai, full of vineyards and gardens, where they were taken inside Pollsmoor prison, a huge complex built for 6,000 common-law prisoners.[1] From the outside, Pollsmoor looked sunny and cheerful. Inside, it was a self-enclosed underworld of dark corridors and clanging metal doors leading to rows of barred cells. They were taken to the top floor, to find a big room with four beds with sheets and towels, and their own separate washroom. From this isolated fortress Mandela would soon watch his country hurtling into much more serious violence, which he was helpless to control.

The prisoners' treatment at Pollsmoor was much more civilised than it had been on Robben Island. They were given meals of proper meat and vegetables; they were allowed more newspapers and periodicals, including *Time* and the *Guardian Weekly*; and there was a long rooftop terrace, where they could relax during the day. They enjoyed new gadgets which they had never seen before, including television, videos and FM radio.[2] Mandela even had a separate cell where he could read and write letters.[3] Compared to the island, it seemed to him like a five-star hotel. But he felt disoriented and much more isolated. He missed the camaraderie and arguments, and even the wildness, of the island, which was much closer to nature than this concrete compound.

When Winnie came to see him soon after his arrival she found him looking 'very, very well'. She was impressed by the handsome prison structure, which resembled a modern technical institution, and by the polite warder James Gregory, who had been with Mandela on the island. She also appreciated the more humane conditions for visits: she and Mandela could see and hear each other properly, through clear glass and loud amplifiers. But she felt he was worse off than before, cut off from his friends and subjected to 'harassment of the soul'.[4] He complained about the cold, damp cell and the lack of any view: he had not seen a blade of grass, he complained, since he arrived. Winnie thought Pollsmoor made the island look like a paradise.

The four prisoners assumed they were being deliberately detached from their comrades as ringleaders, and their suspicions were reinforced when they were joined a few months later by Kathrada, another member of the ANC's High Organ (which Mlangeni had not been). Govan Mbeki remained the most notable absentee: the leading Marxist. On Robben Island Major Harding thought the government had decided that 'these guys have got so much influence on the others. We must now get rid of them and isolate them from the others.' But he suspected they had acted far too late: they had believed their own myths about the troubles being caused by a small group of leaders.[5]

The three veterans – Mandela, Sisulu and Kathrada – were still together after four decades, having been through the Defiance Campaign, the Treason Trial and the Rivonia Trial. They knew each other backwards. 'After all the disagreements and tensions,' wrote Kathrada in June 1985, 'we were always able to successfully and satisfactorily resolve the problems.'[6] Kathrada, much the youngest of the three, sometimes found 'the old geezers', as he called them, rather too serious. 'The geezers don't read Andy Capp, or Hagar, Blondie . . . and they don't listen to the Bickersons, Morecambe and Wise, Lily Tomlin, all my favourite characters. Mercifully they do watch and enjoy *The Cosby Show* on TV.' But they were ageing gracefully: 'Prison life may not have altogether arrested the ageing process; but it certainly seems to have slowed it down.'[7]

Mandela made several complaints about the grim conditions, with six in one cell, and water seeping through the cement floor. Helen

Suzman, who had recently said on British television that Mandela was being well treated, passed on his complaint to Kobie Coetsee, warning that she might have to retract her comment; later she visited Pollsmoor, and agreed that the cells were bleak and the amenities worse than Robben Island.[8] Mandela kept up his complaints. A year later his lawyer Ismail Ayob wrote a seventeen-page memo to the Minister. Five years later he was still being refused more time out of his cell. 'The Department of Prisons,' Mandela protested grandly to the head of prison, 'had failed to apply its mind to the matter.'[9]

But he eventually came to terms with his new surroundings. 'I feel fine and ten years younger than I am,' he wrote to Fatima Meer in June 1983. 'The only difference is that I am not as active as I used to be on Robben Island.'[10] 'Morale is high,' he wrote in February 1984, 'and as I write this letter the body is literally boiling with optimism and hope.'[11] He was on friendly terms with Pollsmoor's commanding officer, Brigadier Munro, though he had a dispute once again on the question of clothes, when he was not allowed a woollen cap. He appealed to Munro 'not to make a caricature of myself by compelling me to see my family and legal representatives without a suitable head-cover'.[12] Munro allowed him to make a garden on the roof, and supplied him with sixteen oildrums, sliced in half and filled with good soil. Mandela spent two hours a day, in a straw hat and gloves, turning the roof into a small farm, eventually growing nine hundred plants, with all kinds of vegetables, including broccoli and carrots.[13] He was proud of his 'garden in the sky', he told Lionel Ngakane.[14] 'He has a sort of obsession with his garden,' wrote Kathrada. 'You can't imagine the amount of time and energy which he expends on his plants.'[15]

Mandela was now able to receive and send fifty-two letters a year. He wrote in his round hand, in a formal, almost Victorian style, full of compliments, reminiscences, condolences and felicitations to friends and children, whose names he always remembered. He looked back on his past life and tried to catch up with the new. From his cell he seemed to be reaching out to every possible constituency, including liberals. He asked about past members of the Institute of Race Relations, such as his Soweto friend and neighbour Barney Ngakane; Mrs Quintin Whyte, who taught him Latin at Healdtown; and Ellen Hellman, who had raised funds for the Treason Trial.[16] But he was especially interested in the Churches, which were becoming more political. He congratulated Desmond Tutu on his appointment as Bishop of Johannesburg. He wrote to the Methodist Peter Storey recalling a wayside pulpit he had seen forty years before outside the Central Methodist Hall displaying the words: 'The greatest glory of living lies not in never falling, but in rising every time you fall.' He remembered too how a priest on Robben Island had described a saint as 'a sinner who keeps on trying'.[17] He wrote to Stephen Naidoo, the Catholic Archbishop of Cape Town, remembering his meeting with Bishop Clayton.[18] He wrote to Sheikh Gabier, the militant chairman of the Moslem Judicial Council, recalling how he was first introduced to Islam by Congress leaders, and realised its full importance when he toured Africa in 1962. He had read the Qu'ran in English in prison, as well as books about Islam.[19] He wrote to Sister Bernard Ncube, a political Catholic nun who was frequently detained, saying how he was looking forward to the forthcoming film *King David*, and was glad that Sir Richard Attenborough was making a film about Gandhi.[20]

He longed for more letters. 'There are hardly any men to correspond with,' he complained to Kepu Mkentane, his friend in the Transkei. 'The few that can still be contacted seem to be totally unaware of the fact that letters were meant to be answered. By comparison, women have proved to be far better correspondents, more aware of the needs of prisoners.'[21] In his loneliness he could be touchy: Amina Cachalia wrote describing how her husband Yusuf, the former Congress leader, was doing well in business, and Mandela wrote back with a comment about the ringing till which Yusuf took as a reproof. Amina wrote back understandingly: 'Clearly you had your belly filled with news, and the honest man that you are made it necessary for you to spit it out to me.' And she translated an Urdu poem which Yusuf had quoted:

> Watch the rising sun
> witness the lustre of its crystal clarity
> hidden behind the veil.

But Mandela complained sadly about Amina's cold letter: 'There is a frozen lump inside me which nothing, save a letter from you, can melt away.' He assured her that he approved of Yusuf's business: 'Even in societies where the profit motive is not the dominant object of economic activity, business executives nevertheless strive for a good business day.' He concluded sadly that if only he had been with them, 'I would have simply hugged Yusuf and kissed you.' It was a poignant reminder of the need for physical contact in relationships. Five years later Mandela was still harking back to the reproof: he did not dare to ask about the shop, he wrote, 'lest I should get another tongue-lashing and a biting quotation from an Urdu bard . . . in the loneliness of a prison cell a rebuke from a loved couple can be as painful as a dart going through the heart.'[22] But he put on a bold face after two decades in prison, in letters which he knew the censor would read. 'If I had to I would be prepared to spend another twenty-one years without any regrets,' he told Kepu Mkentane. 'In spirit I live far beyond these walls and my thoughts are rarely ever in the cell.'[23] 'To be shut up behind bars for twenty-two years,' he told Barney Ngakane, 'is by any standard a shattering experience in which one misses virtually all the exciting joys of being alive . . . But as you know a human being has an amazing capacity for adaptation, getting used, in due course, to some of the most impossible situations.'[24] 'If I had been able to foresee all that has since happened, I would certainly have made the same decision,' he told another friend. 'But that decision would certainly have been far more daunting, and some of the tragedies which subsequently flowed would have melted whatever traces of steel were inside me.'[25]

Winnie's visits and letters were still Mandela's chief lifeline. 'You looked really sparklingly attractive in your outfit during your last visit,' he told her in March 1983. 'Your letters are more than a tonic. I feel different every time I hear from you.' He even enjoyed her stings, which 'have come to be part of our life, our mutual love and our happiness'. 'There are precious things worth dying for,' he told her two years later. 'Right on the top of the list is my beloved country and my darling Mum.'[26]

But he also needed friends. 'To appreciate just how very precious friendship can be,' he told his Indian friend Adelaide Joseph in London, 'you must be in prison and cut off from your beloved wife and children.' When he could not help his family in their problems, he added, 'life becomes torture in the proper sense of the term'.[27] 'In the final count it is a man's inner resources, the certainty that you have a million friends, which gives you the faith and conviction that you are on duty even behind these grim walls,' he wrote to an American friend, Arthur Glickman, on his farm in Maine. 'I wish I could be on that farm.'[28] He always felt fortified by his memories of his country upbringing. 'The country boy in me refuses to die, despite so many years of exposure to urban life,' he wrote to Effie Schultz in 1986. 'The open veld, a bush, blade of grass and animal-life make it a real joy to be alive.'[29]

He lamented the death of friends, particularly those like Yusuf Dadoo and Ruth First who had sacrificed themselves to the struggle. 'The world we once knew so well seems to be crumbling down very fast,' he wrote to Barney Ngakane's son Lionel in London. 'We were so busy outside prison that we hardly had time to think seriously about death. But you have to be locked up in a prison cell for life to appreciate the paralysing grief which seizes you when death strikes close to you.'[30]

He could now read more copiously, less restricted by political content. He had four volumes of J.D. Bernal's *Science in History*, Schapera's *Government and Politics*, Schurmann and Schell's *Republican China*, and Samir Amin's *Neo-Colonialism in West Africa*.[31] In May 1985 he told a friend that he had been reading Tom Lodge's *Black Politics in South Africa Since 1945*, Eddie Roux's *Time Longer than Rope*, and Karis and Carter's *From Protest to Challenge*, which had been smuggled into jail by Kathrada.[32] He was delighted to hear that Mary Benson was writing about ANC history: 'We are still fascinated by Greek literature of ancient times, and a work on AJL [Luthuli] or Tshekedi [Khama] may arouse fresh interest after the harvest has been saved . . . Twilight reading has become a phenomenon of our life, especially during the last thirty-seven years, so that the labours of all those who specialise on this theme have not been vain after all.'[33] He needed relaxation, he told Adelaide Joseph, 'in the form of novels and autobiographies'.[34] But he preferred political novels. He enjoyed Nadine Gordimer's 1979 novel *Burger's Daughter*, which was partly based on his friend Bram Fischer, and was reassured by Gordimer's growing political involvement: 'She has turned out to be a forthright and formidable communicator whose message reaches far beyond the visible horizons,' he told Helen Joseph. 'How such girls are so precious today!'[35]

But the more Mandela picked up about the outside world, the more frustrated he was to be cut off from any involvement as his country came closer to civil war: all the more so since the ANC was now at last flexing its muscles, invoking his own name and leadership.

The 'Free Mandela' campaign which had begun in March 1980 was proving efficient at publicising the ANC cause. It was, as Govan Mbeki said afterwards, 'the clear signal that the ANC was back at the very centre of the political stage'. Tambo had declared 1980 the 'Year of the Freedom

Charter' – twenty-five years after its first promulgation – and 'Charterists' were reappearing, pledged to a non-racial democracy. The next year, an 'Anti-Republic' campaign was launched for the twentieth anniversary of the founding of the Republic. Prisoners released from Robben Island were now playing key roles on the mainland. Before his assassination in Harare in 1981, Joe Gqabi had established a 'study group' in Soweto that included many former Black Consciousness activists from Robben Island, among them Popo Molefe, Eric Molobi and Murphy Morobe. In Durban young Indians and Africans were planning mass action, encouraged by Mac Maharaj, who was now in charge of 'political reconstruction' for the ANC in Lusaka. The rebellious spirit of the eighties came from disparate political groupings, including Black Consciousness, communists and churchmen. But Tambo in Lusaka was determined that the ANC must embrace the widest possible front, must 'bring under its revolutionary umbrella all actual and potential allies, inspire, activate, conduct, direct and lead them in a united offensive against the enemy'.[36]

The revolt had been further provoked by a wrong turning taken by P.W. Botha in 1982, soon after Mandela arrived at Pollsmoor. Botha proposed to change the South African constitution to allow Indians and Coloureds to elect their own MPs to separate parliaments which would have voting powers over education, housing and welfare. But the reforms excluded Africans, who would still have no vote. It was a move clearly intended to divide the non-white population, but it had the opposite effect, leading to new calls for a united front from all races and parties, particularly from the ANC. Tambo declared 1983 the 'Year of United Action', and called for 'one front for national liberation'.

It was the Coloured people based in Cape Town who provided the most surprising new protest. Traditionally they had always been conservative, looking towards the whites more than the blacks; and many of them were tempted by the new constitution. But the more far-sighted Coloured leaders were determined to resist dividing the ranks of apartheid's opponents, and to join the Africans. They included one surprising new recruit whose courage Mandela would never forget.

The Reverend Allan Boesak, a preacher in the Coloured branch of the Dutch Reformed Church, had recently become President of the World Alliance of Reformed Churches. A theologian of only thirty-seven, with a high-pitched voice, he would soon turn out to have expensive tastes and a dubious private morality; but he was a brilliant orator, often compared to Martin Luther King, and was eloquent in defending human rights. It was at a big meeting in Johannesburg in January 1983 that he first called for a 'united front'. The phrase was originally an aside, but it set off an immediate response from activists, who formed a steering committee from all races and many different groups including the Release Mandela Committee. As P.W. Botha's government pressed ahead with its plans for the tricameral parliament, they stepped up their protests. On 20 August 1983, a few days before the white Parliament debated the proposals, they held a mass rally in Mitchell's Plain, the Coloured suburb of Cape Town, to launch a new organisation, the United Democratic Front (UDF). The opening speaker was an ANC veteran, Frances Baard, who reminded them of Macmillan's 'Wind of Change' speech twenty years before, said she could now smell 'the freedom air' sweeping through Africa, and called for the release of 'our leaders'.[37] A message was read out from Mandela in Pollsmoor, who was named as one of the movement's patrons. But the most electrifying speech was by Boesak, who emphasised the 'God-given rights' of the people: 'We want all our rights, we want them here and we want them now.'[38] Sisulu heard about the event with delight from his son Zwelakhe, who visited him on the same day: 'It was a link between exile and the people in the country.'[39]

The ANC's contribution to the UDF would often be debated, but it had a clear influence on the movement's leadership.[40] The three joint Presidents were all ANC people: Albertina Sisulu, Walter's wife, from Johannesburg; Oscar Mphetha, a released Robben Islander from the Western Cape; and Archie Gumede from Natal. Popo Molefe and Terror Lekota, released from Robben Island in 1982, had converted from Black Consciousness to the ANC, and respectively became General Secretary and Publicity Secretary before being re-arrested.

The government put the new 'tricameral' constitution to a referendum of white voters in November 1983. It was opposed by a few business leaders, including Harry Oppenheimer of Anglo-American, and by some white liberal politicians including Van Zyl Slabbert of the Progressive Party, who foresaw that it would antagonise Africans. But it was supported by most businessmen, and by the influential English-language papers the *Sunday Times* and the *Financial Mail*. Both the British and American Ambassadors, Ewen Fergusson and Herman Nickel, lobbied for a 'step in the right direction'.[41] In the event 76 per cent of the votes said yes to the new constitution, a triumph for P.W. Botha. He was installed with his new title of State President, presiding over whites, Indians and Coloureds, while Africans felt still more shut out than before.

Soon afterwards Botha achieved a diplomatic victory over the ANC by signing a non-aggression treaty with President Samora Machel, at Nkomati in neighbouring Mozambique, that effectively excluded ANC bases. Photographs of the short figure of Machel beside the tall Botha seemed to symbolise the triumph of Pretoria's bullying power, a crippling blow to the armed struggle which (as the ANC put it) 'surprised the progressive world'. But the treaty helped to concentrate the ANC's efforts on the internal revolt. 'Its diplomatic defeat at Nkomati,' said the sociologists Heribert Adam and Kogila Moodley, 'turned into a psychological victory at home.'[42]

Mandela heard about these setbacks with all the frustration of his detachment. He saw Botha pretending to reform apartheid while actually extending it by separating Indians and Coloureds from the Africans. He saw the new assemblies as new 'toy telephones', like the Natives Representative Council forty years earlier.[43] But he was relieved by the small turnout of non-whites for the tricameral elections in August 1984: only 31 per cent of the eligible Coloureds voted, and only 20 per cent of the Indians. And the new Parliament soon turned out to be unifying rather than dividing the militants. The UDF leaders were subjected to arrests, detentions and assassinations, but they held together; and their loose and decentralised structure soon showed its advantage, for as the top layers were removed, small local groups and clubs were constantly throwing up replacements. The formation of the UDF, Walter Sisulu reckoned later, 'decisively turned the tide against the advances being made by the P.W. Botha regime'.[44]

From his jail isolation, Mandela was brought closer to developments, as he was allowed more frequent visitors. He suspected that Botha and his cabinet were using these visitors to 'test the waters', but he himself could use them to show his strength and reasonableness to different constituencies, and to catch up with the world.

He could connect up with journalists when in August 1984 he was visited by Benjamin Pogrund of the *Rand Daily Mail* (Mandela visualised him as 'a busy executive glued to some posh office in Main Street'), but he was not allowed to report the visit. Pogrund had not seen Mandela for twenty years: he was surprised to find his hair virtually all grey-white and his face very lined, with deep clefts running from his nose to his mouth, while his eyes looked rather dead. But his mind was very alert: he was interested in everything, from Robert Sobukwe's widow to the computerisation of newspapers. The *Mail* was closed down by its owners soon afterwards, but Mandela wrote that he was confident its tradition would be kept alive.[45]

He could connect up with Christians when in October 1984 he was visited by Professor H.W. van der Merwe, a Quaker from the University of Cape Town who had befriended Winnie and who was dedicated to political reconciliation. Van der Merwe was amazed by Mandela's sense of power, which manifested itself even through thick glass: 'in his eyes, his features, the way he leans slightly forward as if to bring home his message, his voice, the inclinations and tone, the choice of words, intense warmth – the smile, the greetings, the repeated gratitude'. After the Professor had praised President Kenneth Kaunda of Zambia as a sincere Christian, he asked Mandela outright: 'Are you a Christian?' 'Very definitely,' he replied; and the warder James Gregory confirmed that he hardly ever missed a service. Van der Merwe left the prison inspired, and convinced that 'This man will come out to participate in the government of this country in the near future. We must pray for it.'[46]

He could connect up with British conservatives when in January 1985 he had a visit from Lord Bethell, a portly peer (he reminded Mandela of Churchill) who the government clearly hoped would be sympathetic to their position. Bethell was surprised when 'a tall man with silvering hair, in impeccable olive-green shirt and well-creased navy blue trousers, came into the room, shook my hand and greeted me in precise, educated English'. He could almost have been a general in the prison service: 'Indeed, his manner was the most self-assured of them all. He was, however, black.' Mandela reassured him that the ANC was restraining the armed struggle, and deeply regretted a bomb which had killed innocent civilians in Pretoria two years before. He was interested in Margaret Thatcher's success, and in Neil Kinnock, the Labour leader. He showed Bethell his vegetable garden – 'like a landowner showing me his farm' – and praised one of the officers as 'really an excellent gardener'. After their two-hour meeting Bethell 'felt poorer at being so suddenly deprived of the man's exhilarating company'. He reported back favourably to Mrs Thatcher, but still she would not support calls for Mandela's unconditional release. Mandela wrote to Bethell in April, enquiring about Mrs Thatcher's links with both Gorbachev and Reagan; but the letter was never delivered – Bethell had been told that 'a response from Mr Mandela could possibly experience delay.'[47]

He could connect up with Americans when Professor Sam Dash of America's Georgetown University visited him soon afterwards. Dash too was surprised by his dignity: 'I felt that I was in the presence not of a guerrilla fighter or radical ideologue, but of a head of state.' Mandela, 'in a soft British accent', very openly criticised the government's promised reforms, including the repeal of the law against mixed marriages: 'You are speaking about pinpricks. Frankly, it is not my ambition to marry a white woman or to swim in a white pool.' He assured Dash that the ANC accepted that whites belonged to South Africa: 'We want them to live here with us and to share power with us.'[48] He was clearly longing to be involved, and worried (as he wrote to Dash afterwards) about the unprecedented loss of life: 'I am prepared to play my role in the effort to normalise the situation, and to negotiate over the mechanics of transferring power to all South Africans.'[49] But the South African police were closely watching Mandela's correspondents: even when Professor Dash wrote harmless thank-you letters to Helen Suzman and John Dugard for their hospitality, they were intercepted discreetly ('*op 'n delikate wys*') by the Special Branch, and forwarded to the Minister with a top-secret minute from the Commissioner, General Willemse.[50]

The protests and violence were now escalating, driven by a new mood of defiance. The exclusion of blacks from the tricameral elections had provoked resistance in the townships – particularly against Bantu education and the payment of rents. The protests were stimulated by the UDF, but spontaneous local outbursts of anger were spreading across the country. The old ANC idea of the stay-away was revived with some success, particularly in the Vaal Triangle south of Johannesburg. The government appeared to be rapidly losing any black support, and had to call in troops to control the townships. 'Things are cracking up,' Winnie Mandela said in the New Year. 'They are losing control.'[51] But she herself would soon prove to be one of the most uncontrollable elements.

The ANC leaders in Lusaka could not afford to lag behind the masses, as they had done in the past, and they were watching developments closely. In early January 1985 Tambo issued a dramatic New Year message: 'Render South Africa Ungovernable', and claimed that the ANC had already 'taken impressive strides' towards this goal.[52] The prisoners in Pollsmoor fully endorsed Tambo's message, but there were obvious dangers in such a policy for a party which, it now appeared, might itself have to govern before long. As Sisulu recalled: 'It did worry me, the strategy of ungovernability: the negative aspect – and people were also having necklaces* and things like that, which I thought was very negative and dangerous . . . I think Madiba shared that.'

At the time, though, the prisoners saw no real alternative to the policy of rendering South Africa ungovernable. 'The position internationally was very much in our favour,' Sisulu recalled. 'If we played our cards well there would be no reason why we should not succeed.'[53] The strategy was criticised by white liberals and businessmen: Harry Oppenheimer, the former Chairman of Anglo-American, would come to regard it as the ANC's most serious mistake.[54]

Meanwhile, the campaign to release Mandela gathered momentum. President Botha felt pressed to make some response, and seized an opportunity to project himself as a peacemaker. While touring Europe he had been encouraged by a group of right-wing German leaders including Franz-Josef Strauss – a good friend of the Afrikaners – to offer to release Mandela provided he renounced all violence. This was a brilliant solution, he told the Cabinet on his return, 'because if Mandela refused the whole world would understand why the South African government would not release him'. Kobie Coetsee and Louis le Grange, the Ministers of Justice and of Law and Order, warned him that Mandela could not give up his strongest bargaining chip.[55]

On 31 January 1985 Botha told Parliament that he was offering Mandela his freedom, provided he 'unconditionally rejected violence as a political instrument'. Mandela was called to the office at Pollsmoor to be given a copy of Hansard reporting it. He was determined to make a public response, and the same evening he carefully prepared a speech which rejected the offer while keeping open the option of negotiation and dispelling any suggestion of a division within the ANC. He gave it to Winnie when she next visited him, and on 10 February his daughter Zindzi read it out at the huge Jabulani stadium in Soweto, beginning with the words 'My father says . . .'. The speech firmly reasserted Mandela's loyalty to the ANC and to Tambo, 'my greatest friend', and insisted that it was Botha who must renounce violence, by dismantling

* 'Necklacing', the practice of placing a tyre filled with petrol around a victim's neck and setting it alight, came to be the most infamous characteristic of township violence.

apartheid and unbanning the ANC, before Mandela could accept freedom: 'I cannot and will not give any undertaking at a time when you, the people, are not free.'[56]

It was the first time in over two decades that Mandela's own words had been heard publicly, linking his policies directly to the ANC and the UDF. The huge crowd was ecstatic. Terror Lekota, now released from Robben Island, watched the scene with wonder: 'I recall several clusters of very old men, supported by walking sticks, shuffling with determination to the edge of the open-air stage,' he wrote to his daughter. After Zindzi had spoken, many of them walked away with tear-stained faces: 'They had heard what they wanted to hear.'[57] Tambo was delighted with the speech's reception, and wrote via Adelaide to Mandela in his code which called the ANC 'the Church' and Mandela 'Bishop Madibane'. He praised the Bishop's 'brilliant and stirring message which spread from congregation to congregation . . . it struck a powerful unifying note, and revealed a remarkable degree of identity of approach to the ever-changing terrain of the church-going world'.[58]

It looked like a total deadlock. But Botha, it turned out, was not quite as intransigent as he appeared in public. Soon after Zindzi's speech, he summoned the Minister of Justice Kobie Coetsee to his office and told him (according to Coetsee): 'You know, we have painted ourselves in a corner. Can you get us out?'[59]

In the meantime Mandela was still in jail, and the violence mounted. It reached a new climax in March 1985, on the twenty-fifth anniversary of the Sharpeville massacre, when the police in Uitenhage killed nineteen protesters. At the ANC conference at Kabwe in Zambia three months later Tambo warned that the violence would escalate, and that the ANC would have more difficulty in distinguishing between 'hard' and 'soft' targets. He did not call for a general uprising (he explained afterwards), because he knew he could not achieve it; but he warned that black policemen must prepare to turn their guns against their masters.[60]

An ungovernable South Africa was looking much more credible, but also more alarming to both sides. Police terrorism and torture were countered by young black activists extending their own counter-terrorism against black police and suspected informers, including the use of the notorious 'necklace'. Pretoria described the violence as 'black on black', but many of the worst atrocities later turned out to have been engineered by government agents. One young woman, for example, Maki Skosana, was stoned and burnt to death in July 1985, allegedly by ANC supporters. Years later her murder proved to be part of an elaborate government dirty-tricks operation which was responsible for hundreds of deaths.[61]

The government was also still using Kaiser Matanzima to attempt to persuade Mandela to be released to the Transkei. Mandela found his nephew's persistence 'highly disturbing, if not provocative', and warned him in December 1984 that if he continued it would cause an unpleasant confrontation: 'We will, under no circumstances, accept being released to the Transkei or any other Bantustan.'[62] Mandela was saddened by the break with the man he had once regarded as a hero. 'We are still very close to each other,' he told Fatima Meer two months later. 'But something snapped inside me when he went over to the Nats. Indeed, politics have split families, hero and worshipper.'[63] In 1985 Mandela refused a visit from Matanzima, who complained that he was grossly insulted. But Mandela warned him again not to use their relationship to involve the ANC in Bantustan politics: 'A public figure whether – as you would put it – he is "a dangerous revolutionary" or a mere Bantustan leader, who allows his image to be so severely dented by recrimination, touchiness and intemperate language can be no model for my own approach to people and problems.'[64] Four months later Matanzima wrote again in his huge handwriting from the Great Place, Qamata:

> I am happy to advise you that it will please me to meet you under conditions of strict confidency and secrecy. I shall be pleased also to hold the meeting away from the confines of your prison.
>
> Missing you. Yours Sincerely[65]

By July 1985 many townships were becoming seriously ungovernable, as Tambo had called for, and around Johannesburg they were close to anarchy. Many black police had fled from their homes in the townships and were living in tented camps on the outskirts. The government warned that the ANC was planning a classic two-staged revolution, culminating in the seizure of power. 'Law and order had virtually broken down,' recorded the well-briefed BBC correspondent Graham Leach, 'with even the simplest burglary unable to be investigated unless an officer entered the township accompanied by armoured personnel-carriers carrying police and troops.'[66]

On 20 July the government declared a state of emergency, allowing the police to detain and interrogate suspects without restraint; but the rebels did not appear to be cowed. Talking to black activists in Soweto a month later, I sensed a basic shift of mood: both schoolchildren and their parents now seemed confident of victory, while the collaborators were worried about being on the losing side. 'The emergency is preparing conditions for a much more violent conflict,' said Tambo, 'moving towards a real explosion.'[67]

Revolutionary ANC leaders, including Govan Mbeki on Robben Island, now expected the rebellion to cause a 'rolling revolution' which would bring the government to its knees. But the most serious blow to Pretoria came from a quarter where the ANC was least expecting it – from international bankers and investors. It was very rare for global capital to become associated with a moral crusade: 'The markets aren't sentimental,' the financier George Soros would often say. But in this case, he conceded, the markets moved against apartheid, though in a curious way.[68]

The battles in the townships had attracted massive television coverage in Britain and America, which was rapidly undermining Botha's assurances about the country's stability, while anti-apartheid protesters were pressing depositors and clients of the multinational banks to withdraw their custom, to force them to stop lending to and investing in South Africa. This had an immediate effect, as for two years Pretoria had been rashly relying on short-term foreign loans. One of the biggest lenders was the Chase Manhattan Bank of New York, with loans of $500 million. Twenty-five years earlier the Chase had been seen as a friend of apartheid, and it lent a large sum to the Verwoerd government soon after the Sharpeville massacre. But on 31 July 1985, eleven days after Botha proclaimed the emergency, the Chase quietly decided to stop rolling over its loans, and to recall its credits as they became due. It was not a political decision: the bank's bluff Chairman, Willard Butcher, had little interest in South Africa, and only wanted to placate complaints from New York investors and depositors. But it was disastrous for Pretoria. Other banks began to withdraw credit, the rand began falling, and the South African Reserve Bank had to renew loans from Swiss and German banks, at much higher interest rates.[69]

When Mandela heard the news in Pollsmoor he was surprised and delighted: 'I must be frank: I did not expect such massive support from bankers,' he said five years later. 'It was an indication of the impact which the ANC and other political organisations had made on the international community.'[70] 'We underestimated the importance of bankers,' said Sisulu. 'They gave a signal to South Africa to be careful.'[71] In Lusaka, Oliver Tambo declared that 'the refusal of the banks to roll over their loans is an important victory in our struggle.'[72]

President Botha could only reassure the bankers by making major concessions, which were expected to be announced at the next National Party Congress, in Durban on 15 August. His Foreign Minister Pik Botha drafted a speech which promised to begin to dismantle apartheid and to release Mandela, and which included the phrase 'today we have crossed the Rubicon'. Pik Botha personally reassured American diplomats, including Chester Crocker, that his President was 'on the verge of momentous announcements'.[73] Inside Pollsmoor prison, the five political prisoners waited expectantly for Botha's speech. Winnie had just visited Mandela, who had reiterated that he would accept no conditions to his release, and suggested that Botha should visit him: Botha was 'one man who has no problems whatsoever about seeing him in Pollsmoor.'[74]

In the event Botha's speech was a total anti-climax. He refused to take what he called the 'road to abdication and suicide', blamed the country's unrest on 'barbaric communist agitators' and wagged his finger as he threatened: 'Don't push us too far.' Mandela was a communist, he warned, who must promise not to plan, instigate or commit acts of violence before he was released. For the expectant world the speech was, as Pik Botha said later, 'a bucket of iced water in the face'.[75]*

For a few weeks it seemed that anything could happen. A poll conducted by MORI in mid-August showed that 70 per cent of South African blacks, and 30 per cent of whites, expected civil war; but a majority of blacks and half the whites still thought that their country could be ruled by a joint government of blacks and whites. Ninety per cent of blacks wanted Mandela released without conditions, though 57 per cent of whites did not want him released on any terms.[77] There was even speculation that Mandela might shortly be sharing power with Botha: on 22 August the conservative Johannesburg *Star* included a spoof issue purporting to be dated 1990, with the headline: 'MANDELA THREATENS TO PULL OUT OF PROVISIONAL GOVERNMENT'.[78]

* P.W. Botha's successor F.W. de Klerk was later rumoured to have told Botha to toughen the speech, although he strongly denied this to me. Botha insists that he wrote the speech himself, with some ideas contributed by Ministers, and that when he read it to them beforehand 'none of them complained'.[76]

By manipulating the media, the government did its best to depict Mandela as a violent terrorist. After Botha's speech Mandela was visited by two right-wing American journalists from the *Washington Times*, John Lofton and Cal Thomas, who had come out to South Africa with the fundamentalist preacher Jerry Falwell. Mandela tried to explain to them why he had had no alternative to taking up arms, and how a Christian had 'the right to use force against evil'. America, he said, had a deeply entrenched democracy, while black South Africans had no vote, and were ruled by 'a colonial power crawling on crutches out of the Middle Ages'. The resulting *Washington Times* article proclaimed 'Mandela Urges "Violent" Revolution', and began: 'Nelson Mandela, the South African terrorist and revolutionary, sees "no alternative" to violent revolution.'[79]

Western investors were now losing confidence in Botha, and they faced a new shock two weeks after his speech. The eloquent preacher Allan Boesak was due to lead a march on Pollsmoor demanding Mandela's release and promising to 'turn South Africa upside down'. But just before the march Boesak was arrested, and more riots broke out. In the Johannesburg stock exchange, which I visited on that 'Black Tuesday', foreign confidence collapsed, and the rand started plunging. By the close of business the rand was down to half its value against sterling compared to a year before. Most stockbrokers, including Afrikaners, saw Mandela's release as the only solution. It was an extraordinary alliance: international capital was now siding with Mandela, the old communist bogey.

The South African economy, which relied on foreign investment and loans, was now crippled. A small group of business leaders, led by Gavin Relly, the new Chairman of Anglo-American, took the bold step of flying to Zambia to meet Tambo and his ANC colleagues. Harry Oppenheimer, Relly's predecessor, felt 'twitchy' about the expedition, but the businessmen were surprised by the ANC leaders' sensitivity and intelligence: 'A more attractive and genial group it would be hard to imagine,' said Tony Bloom of the Premier Group. Tambo explained that he hated violence and suffering – 'I even take insects out of the bath' – but that the ANC had to counter the state's violence. Releasing Mandela was the only way to begin negotiations. But Relly took fright soon after the visit when another ANC bomb exploded. Tambo was puzzled by this reversal: 'It was because of the violence that Relly came to Zambia.'[80]

The financial crisis worsened. The Governor of the Reserve Bank, Gerhard de Kock, toured the world's bankers to try to raise loans, but

In 1962 Mandela toured Africa to gain support for the ANC's guerrilla army. At a conference in Ethiopia he was joined by his exiled colleague Oliver Tambo.

At the military headquarters in Algeria, where the bitter civil war was ending, Mandela and his colleague Robert Resha (*second from left*) met revolutionary leaders and received advice about guerrilla warfare.

Mandela spent ten days in London in June 1962; his friend Mary Benson took his picture outside Westminster Abbey. Many well-wishers warned him not to return to South Africa, where he would almost certainly be caught by the police.

ABOVE Mandela's mother came to Pretoria in 1964 for her son's trial, and watched him being sentenced to life imprisonment. Four years afterwards she visited him on Robben Island, and died a few weeks later.

OPPOSITE Eight men were sentenced to life imprisonment at the Rivonia trial in 1964. Six were Africans. *Top row*: Nelson Mandela, Walter Sisulu, Govan Mbeki, Raymond Mhlaba. *Bottom row*: Elias Motsoaledi, Andew Mlangeni, Ahmed Kathrada (the one Indian), Dennis Goldberg (who was imprisoned separately in a white jail in Pretoria).

Two photographs taken on Robben Island in 1965 provided virtually the only images of the Rivonia prisoners for almost three decades. For the first, the prisoners in the second row in the courtyard were put onto sewing clothes, instead of breaking stones. Mandela has been identified as fifth from the left in the second row, Ahmed Kathrada is seventh, Govan Mbeki eighth, Walter Sisulu eleventh. Soon afterwards they were put back to stone-breaking. The second photograph shows Mandela and Sisulu talking together in the prison courtyard.

Kaiser ('K.D.') Matanzima (*in blazer*), Mandela's nephew and earlier his hero, became leader of the 'independent' Transkei while Mandela was on Robben Island. He visited Winnie in Soweto. Mandela's son Makgatho is on the right.

Mandela (*left*) was working in the garden on Robben Island in 1977 with the Namibian leader Toivo ja Toivo (*centre*) and Justice Mpanza (*right*) when they were photographed against their will while visiting journalists were being escorted around the prison.

With Mandela out of sight in jail, the varied images from his past became more powerful: whether the handsome man-about-town with his glamorous young wife Winnie; the bearded 'Black Pimpernel' emerging from underground; or the Xhosa prince appearing in tribal regalia for his trial in 1962.

OPPOSITE The larger-than-life bust on London's South Bank, unveiled by Oliver Tambo in 1985, showed a thick-set, heroic Mandela, in keeping with his superhuman mythology.

Mandela emerged from prison on 11 February 1990, hand-in-hand with Winnie, bewildered by the crowd. He soon showed a much subtler and more sensitive face.

The first meeting between the ANC and the government in May 1990 was surprisingly amicable, with old enemies exchanging jokes. Among those in the front row are (*left to right*) Pik Botha, Joe Slovo (*in glasses*), Alfred Nzo and F.W. de Klerk.

he was treated as a pariah. P.W. Botha then brought in a negotiator, Fritz Leutwiler, the former head of the Swiss National Bank, who tried to make a deal with the lenders: but he refused to meet Mandela or Tambo, saying: 'I'm reluctant to shake hands with a communist without counting my fingers afterwards.' Eventually Botha convinced Leutwiler that he would produce new reforms, and Leutwiler negotiated for debts to be temporarily rolled over. But foreign bankers would never regain their confidence in South Africa's future under apartheid. Western conservatives continued to argue that sanctions would not bite; but the bankers' withdrawal would exert decisive pressure on Pretoria to reach a settlement.[81]

Anti-apartheid lobbies in America and Europe stepped up their demands for sanctions and for Mandela's release, using more sophisticated leverage. American campaigners were compelling pension funds to withdraw their investments in South Africa, while the Black Caucus in Congress was mobilising its political clout. But the American and British governments firmly resisted the popular pressure. President Reagan told Mrs Thatcher that he was content to leave it to her.[82] She had her own convictions. She was impressed by South Africa's thriving free-enterprise economy compared to the chaos in Marxist black states elsewhere in Africa; and she kept warning that a million whites were entitled to British passports, and would leave South Africa if the country collapsed, like the Portuguese from Angola or Mozambique.[83] Her right-wing advisers continued to stress the communist menace from the ANC and the tribal divisions among South African blacks.

Mrs Thatcher still rejected sanctions, and insisted that she could influence P.W. Botha in private, as a sympathetic friend. They had first met when she had visited South Africa as Minister of Education in the early seventies, when Botha, then Minister of Defence, had shown her round Cape Point. Now she met him again in June 1984 when he lunched at Chequers, her official country house, along with the Foreign Secretary Geoffrey Howe. She did not warm to him, she said: her Private Secretary Charles Powell thought he appalled her. But she still felt she had a special influence on him. She listened to him sympathetically before telling him to release Mandela and to stop forcibly removing blacks from their homes and bombarding neighbouring states. Botha, however, came away reassured: 'I know from the goodbyes of her and her husband that they respected me.' And he was struck that 'she did not deny that Mandela was a communist.'[84]

When Botha declared the state of emergency a year later Thatcher was more seriously worried, and in September 1985 she held a special seminar on South Africa; it was attended by academics, diplomats and politicians, but no one sympathetic to the ANC. The next month Tambo visited London to talk for the first time with businessmen and bankers as well as politicians – a major breakthrough. But Thatcher forbade anyone in her government to talk to him or any other leaders of the ANC, whom she still described as a group of communist terrorists: anyone who thought the ANC could ever form a government, she said, was 'living in cloud-cuckoo land'. It was not surprising that Mrs Thatcher should be suspicious of terrorists: she had nearly been killed by an IRA bomb in Brighton the year before. But the ANC never resorted to that kind of terrorism, and unlike the IRA they had no votes to bring about peaceful change.

In October Thatcher faced her toughest challenge over South Africa, at a Commonwealth Conference in Nassau which Mandela saw as a key event. She was determined to stand out against the 'gadarene rush' towards sanctions, and succeeded in limiting them to 'a tiny little bit', as she triumphantly put it. With those four little words, Geoffrey Howe complained afterwards, she 'humiliated three dozen other heads of government, devalued the policy which they had just agreed, and demeaned herself'.[85] But she did agree to the idea that a group of 'eminent persons' should visit South Africa in search of a settlement; and rather grudgingly President Botha agreed to let them in.

A team of seven was selected, including Lord Barber, the ex-Chancellor from Britain; Malcolm Fraser, the former Australian Prime Minister; and General Obasanjo, the ex-President of Nigeria. They were determined to visit Mandela in jail. The prisoner in Pollsmoor was now much more famous than ever before, both in South Africa and throughout the world. 'You all must be wondering what it is like to live with a "celebrity" like Uncle Nelson,' wrote Kathrada in September 1985. 'Not a single day goes by without something about him in the papers or radio.' He 'unfailingly makes a great impression upon people', Kathrada explained, yet he 'has the ordinary, normal interests, desires, hopes, likes, dislikes etc'.[86] With all the world's expectations resting on him, Mandela appeared in total control over his emotions – sometimes exasperating his fellow prisoners. 'No matter how affected or excited he may be about a particular incident or event he still manages to display a calm which is unbelievable,' Kathrada told Fatima Meer's daughter Shehneez in February 1986. 'We are convinced (and we have told him) that if he were to be called to the office and told that he would be released tomorrow, he would return to his cell and tell us after an hour or so . . . nothing in his talk or demeanour gives us the slightest hint that he is the man about whom there is such an upsurge of feeling throughout the world.'[87]

It was now difficult to imagine any settlement that did not involve Mandela, and his survival was crucial. At sixty-seven he appeared to be in unusually good health. But late in 1985 a medical examination at the Volks Hospital showed an enlarged prostate gland – a common ailment for men in their sixties – which the urologist Dr Willem Laubscher insisted required surgery. Cabinet Ministers were alarmed at the thought that they might be blamed if anything went wrong: the commanding officer of Pollsmoor, Brigadier Munro, warned that civil war would break out if Mandela died. Three more doctors converged on the hospital to give their opinions: Nthato Motlana, the Mandelas' family doctor, and two specialists from Switzerland and Johannesburg. They all agreed an operation was necessary – but who should perform it? To Motlana's surprise, Mandela insisted on the Cape Town Afrikaner Dr Laubscher.[88]

Winnie flew down to visit him the day before the operation. On the same plane, as it happened, was the Minister of Justice, Kobie Coetsee, who already knew much about Winnie through his friend in Brandfort Piet de Waal. He was in the first-class section, but he recognised Winnie and stopped to reassure her about the government's concern for Mandela's health. Later Winnie firmly walked into the first-class section and sat beside him, talking for most of the two-hour flight. Mandela had earlier asked to see Coetsee, but had received no reply. By the time the plane reached Cape Town, Coetsee had decided to visit him in hospital.

Coetsee arrived at Mandela's bedside unannounced. He was amazed to be greeted as if Mandela were a host welcoming an old friend. 'He came across as a man of Old World values,' Coetsee said later, 'an old Roman citizen with dignitas, gravitas, honestas, simplicitas.' Coetsee was struck too by Mandela's interest in Afrikaans and Afrikaners. Mandela found Coetsee far more polite than his predecessor Jimmy Kruger, and realised that he was subtly putting out feelers: Mandela suspected that he might want to make some kind of deal, but did not let on. He asked Coetsee for help in allowing Winnie to live in Johannesburg. Coetsee invited Winnie to his official mansion and offered to allow her to return provided she was not disruptive: Winnie made no such promise, but returned to Johannesburg anyway, more militant than ever.[89]

Mandela took a robust interest in his prostate operation. 'The surgeons tore up my abdomen mercilessly,' he wrote to a friend. 'They cut the pubis open, removed a vital organ, dug a deep hole just below the navel and inserted a thick pipe. There was a second one through the front, and a needle as long and dangerous as a javelin was embedded in the forearm.' But he 'came to love and respect all the nurses in that unit. If I was wealthy I would adopt all of them as my children.'[90] The nurses in the intensive care ward, he noticed, 'treated each person as if they were the only patient'. If he were to die, he reflected, he would prefer to be in the open veld, surrounded by the bush and wildflowers; but if he died in the city he would leave with a broad smile among such nurses.[91]

Mandela's illness, and the resulting flurry of official activity, produced a new wave of rumours that he would soon be released, and crowds gathered outside the jail. The Johannesburg *Sunday Times* urged President Botha to 'seize the opportunity of Nelson Mandela's illness – before the man dies and all hell breaks loose – and ship him out of the country on a one-way ticket to medical treatment abroad'.[92] The Ministry of Information ascribed the rumours to 'a continuing campaign of disinformation by propaganda experts behind the Iron Curtain'.[93] The prisoners themselves had seen enough hopes come and go. 'The only people who remain unconvinced and thankfully unperturbed by the excitement,' wrote Kathrada in February 1986, 'are ourselves.'[94] Mandela reminded Winnie of their hopes back in 1964. He still visualised his homecoming and recalled Winnie's delicious meals, warning her: 'If I don't get that dish when I return some day I will dissolve the marriage on the spot.' But by April 1986 he was writing to her: 'There is not a living soul in South Africa today, no matter how highly placed he may be, who knows when we will be released.'[95]

24

Ungovernability

1986–1988

Your logic frightens me
How coldly you disdain legerdemains!
'Open Sesame' and – two decades' rust on hinges
Peels at the touch of a conjuror's wand?

Wole Soyinka[1]

AFTER HIS OPERATION Mandela was not taken back to rejoin his colleagues on the top floor of Pollsmoor, but to a separate section on the ground floor. His new quarters were spacious, with three big cells, one for sleeping, one for exercise, one for studying; but they were damp, dark and bleak, with little view, and there were still fifteen locked metal doors between him and the entrance.[2] He now had no roof-terrace to exercise on, only a yard surrounded by prison cells, from which the ordinary prisoners would shout abuse at the old man in a straw hat – 'Hey kaffir, why are you ignoring us?' – until the commanding officer had blinds put on the windows.[3]

For the first time in his twenty-four years in jail Mandela was alone, while the crisis outside bore down on him. He insisted that he did not see himself as the chosen leader: 'He never called himself a man of destiny,' said George Bizos, who often visited him. 'He always speaks in the plural . . . I don't think I've ever heard him say "I did this."'[4] But the government had now put him into this Olympian isolation, and he was convinced that the time had come for him to play a leading role. When his old friend Amina Cachalia visited him, she sensed he was on a new peak: 'I have a feeling that the change came then. He had to take responsibility and try to make a breakthrough. He realised that he would get out, and that he could make a democracy. That's why he took the initiative.'[5]

Mandela was alarmed by the escalating violence in the country, which he feared could soon become uncontrollable by anyone. 'If we did not start a dialogue soon,' he reflected, 'both sides would soon be plunged into a dark night of oppression, violence and war.' He respected the government's armed strength: he did not, like many younger prisoners, believe that the ANC could seize power through a rolling revolution or a military victory. But he thought that the enemy were beginning to see themselves as being 'on the wrong side of history'. He believed, having once been a herd-boy, that 'there are times when a leader must move out ahead of the flock.'[6] But dare he move without consulting his colleagues? It was his most difficult decision. 'I knew that if I asked their permission they would say no,' as he put it to me. 'If I continued they could take action and expel me. But I was confident that the enemy itself wanted a retreat, through a silver bridge.'[7]

After a few days of lonely reflection Mandela was allowed to meet with the other four ANC prisoners, led by Sisulu. They had planned to protest on the day he was separated from them, rightly suspecting that the government was trying to divide him both from them and from the Robben Island revolutionaries like Harry Gwala. 'I knew that it's the strategy used the world over by rulers, to divide and rule,' said Sisulu, who correctly assumed that the intelligence service had bugged the prisoners' conversations on Robben Island. But he had confidence in Mandela – 'You must be a very powerful man to dictate your terms to Nelson,' as he said later – while he knew he could repudiate Mandela if he blundered. Mandela himself did not complain about being segregated. He told his old comrades with deliberate vagueness that the government would find it easier to approach him alone – not that he planned to approach the government. He only told them: 'Something good may come of this.'[8]

Mandela first had to reassure Tambo, so he enlisted George Bizos to make the journey to Lusaka. Bizos, having first informed Kobie Coetsee – who questioned him carefully about Mandela – made two visits to brief Tambo about Mandela's discussion with Coetsee, assuring him that Mandela would not commit himself without the ANC's approval. Tambo consulted his colleagues, who approved the principle of preliminary talks, and sent back the message to Mandela to carry on. Bizos then reported to both Mandela and Coetsee that Tambo had no differences with Mandela. That was not good news for the government. A few weeks later Mandela wrote to Coetsee to suggest 'talks about talks'. There was no reply.[9]

But in the meantime a new opening had appeared. In February 1986, just before Bizos's second visit to Tambo, three of the Commonwealth's seven 'eminent persons' had arrived in South Africa to try to find ways of beginning a political dialogue. They found widespread evidence of police intimidation and provocation. 'We came to a country in turmoil,' they reported later.[10] But the Nigerian member of the group, General Obasanjo – a big, bulging chief wearing robes and open sandals in which he wiggled his toes – quickly gained the trust of the Foreign Minister, Pik Botha, who saw him as a realist: Obasanjo depicted the conflict, Pik Botha later wrote, as 'between two nationalisms, both wishing the best for their country, but fighting each other for power'. The General was allowed to see Mandela in Pollsmoor, and was much impressed. He assured Pik Botha that Mandela was no communist, simply an African nationalist leader.[11]

President Botha was now appearing more conciliatory, and seemed to be looking for a way to release Mandela. He had already lifted the state of emergency by the time the eminent persons arrived, and soon afterwards the government abolished the hated pass laws, which Washington hailed as a 'major milestone'.[12] 'Mandela is of more use to the ANC inside prison than outside,' Botha admitted. 'Then why keep him in jail?' retorted Helen Suzman.[13] He told the sympathetic British Conservative Lord Wyatt, a friend of Mrs Thatcher, that he had good information that Mandela would be killed if he was released, and that he, Botha, would be blamed.[14]

On 12 March all seven eminent persons were allowed to visit Mandela. Kobie Coetsee, who accompanied them, was gratified to see their amazement at finding Mandela in such powerful form. 'For me it was a moment of glory. I felt that I had trumped them: they expected this emaciated person, and there he was completely in control.' Coetsee himself discreetly left the room, despite Mandela's entreaties, leaving an official to take notes.[15]

The eminent persons found Mandela 'isolated and lonely', but they were surprised by his immaculate appearance and commanding presence. He was wearing a three-piece grey pinstripe suit, which a tailor had hurriedly made for him, and matching grey shoes. 'You look like a prime minister now,' commented Brigadier Munro, the prison commander. 'He exuded authority,' said the eminent persons' report, 'and received the respect of all around him, including his jailers.'[16] Lord Barber, the most conservative member of the group, was struck by Mandela's self-confidence and humour, and was delighted when one of his first questions was about cricket: 'Is Don Bradman still alive?'(he was). Barber promised to send Mandela a copy of his book about escaping from Colditz during the Second World War.[17] But what most impressed the visitors was Mandela's lucid analysis of the crisis. 'There is nothing like a long spell in prison to focus your mind,' he explained, 'and to bring you to a more sober appreciation of the realities of your society.'[18]

The eminent persons were shocked by the growing violence in South Africa, as terrorism was met by counter-terrorism, and judged that 'events had increasingly passed out of the government's control'. The ANC seemed to be achieving its aim of making South Africa ungovernable, which provided its main weapon against the government; but it was a dangerous and two-edged weapon. Obasanjo had helped to draft a carefully-worded 'negotiating concept' which would link the government's release of the prisoners with the ANC's suspending violence. Mandela quickly accepted it as a starting point, without consulting his colleagues (which impressed Barber), while explaining that they must give their consent. Pik Botha was encouraged by the concept, which embodied (as he later conceded) all the elements which the government would accept four years later. But the hawks in the Cabinet balked at the ANC agreeing only to suspend violence, not to terminate it: they dreaded (according to Pik Botha) that the ANC would use violence as a bargaining counter: 'Keep talking . . . or else.'[19]

The danger of uncontrolled violence seemed to be personified by Winnie Mandela. She now showed two very different faces. On the one hand she was emerging as an international heroine, 'the Mother of a Nation' – the title of a book about her in 1985.[20] She insists now that she never called herself that: 'I couldn't stand on the platform and say, "Don't call me that because I am not so." I have never competed with mother Albertina [Sisulu] or mother Lilian [Ngoyi].' But she was confident of her unique role as Mandela's representative. 'I would proudly say, "I am the African National Congress," because I was the lone voice, and my people were killed for even mentioning the name . . . In order to save Nelson, in order for his name to stay on the lips of babies on their mothers' breasts, I had to expose myself deliberately to all the harshness.'[21] Winnie was now still more outspoken, overwhelming nearly everyone who saw her. She appeared to sail into dangerous storms like a ship in full sail, towering over both her acolytes and her adversaries. And she could show clear-sighted judgment about the developing crisis. When I telephoned her in Brandfort during her banning, she would comment sharply on visiting politicians, from Teddy Kennedy to Malcolm Fraser. Her criticism of the government was vivid: 'The Afrikaners make blunder after blunder,' she told me in September 1985. 'We thank them for unifying us. Botha said he had crossed the Rubicon; but it is we who crossed the Rubicon.' Six months later she reported: 'The government are now the prisoners, and the prisoners are the jailers.'[22]

But she was also acquiring a taste for violence, which the police could exploit and manipulate. She seemed wilder when she returned to Soweto in 1984 after her exile in Brandfort. She had taken to wearing a khaki military outfit, with soldier's boots and a beret. 'I think I will get her a toy gun and a holster,' joked Zindzi, 'for her to walk round and appear in court like that.'[23] But her show of combat was becoming all too real. On 13 April 1985, at Munsieville near Johannesburg, she made her most provocative statement, with fire in her eyes: 'We have no guns – we have only stones, boxes of matches and petrol. Together, hand in hand, with our boxes of matches and our necklaces we shall liberate this country.'[24]

Winnie was clearly inciting the crowd to violence. Even to report such words was a serious offence under the emergency laws, but after the overseas press and television recorded her speech, the government was glad to publicise this example of the ANC's brutality. South African papers were outraged: the Johannesburg *Star* called Winnie's words 'irresponsible in the extreme' – though the paper's commentator Rex Gibson explained that at other times she had said much that was 'better, warmer, more helpful'.[25] The ANC felt ambivalent in the face of the government's own violence, and Oliver Tambo was reluctant to criticise the speech publicly. 'We are not happy with the necklace,' he told a summit meeting of non-aligned nations in Harare, 'but we will not condemn people who have been driven to adopt such extremes.'[26] Privately Tambo was appalled, and in London he asked Winnie's neighbour and friend in Soweto Dr Motlana to shut her up.[27]

Winnie did back down slightly, claiming the speech had been quoted out of context, but she did not withdraw it. 'The statement was not necessarily an approval of the method,' she claims now. 'It was to say that we are now exposed to situations such as this because of the harshness of apartheid.' She was aware, however, that she was defying the party line. 'The ANC was beginning to speak a language of reconciliation, and extreme people like myself were beginning to be an embarrassment to those who were pulling the strings, the machinery, trying to put into place a peace process.'[28] And she was herself embarking – as it emerged later – on still more violent adventures with her bodyguards.

Mandela himself, as he told his lawyers George Bizos and Ismail Ayob, was shocked by any encouragement of necklacing, as were the other prisoners in Pollsmoor: 'We wanted ungovernability, but not necklacing,' said Kathrada.[29] On the battlefield, the line was harder to distinguish.

When the eminent persons returned to South Africa in May they were struck by the escalation in violence, particularly by vigilantes who, encouraged by the police, were attacking UDF supporters in Crossroads, the squatter camp outside Cape Town. The need for an agreement seemed all the more urgent: and Pik Botha seemed optimistic. He said later that the eminent persons 'came closer to success than most people realise'.[30] There were new rumours that Mandela would be let out. 'Talk of impending release has been on the lips of everybody,' Mandela wrote to a friend on 12 May. 'But the plain truth is that we are still here.'[31]

On 16 May Mandela was again visited by the eminent persons, in the comfortable prison guest house, where savouries were served. He asked them whether President Botha was taking their 'negotiating concept' seriously. They were not sure, and Mandela suspected that Botha simply wanted to delay negotiations. He assured them that he could control the violence if he was released; but he wanted to be sure that the government would withdraw troops from the townships and allow him to travel freely.

The eminent persons were encouraged, and flew up to Lusaka to tell Tambo about the concept. He too suspected Botha of employing delaying tactics, and doubted his good faith; but he thought the concept would command the support of his ANC colleagues. The visitors returned to Cape Town on 19 May to put their proposals to a committee of Cabinet Ministers. The hawks again insisted that the ANC must renounce violence altogether, not merely suspend it; but the eminent persons replied that they could not reasonably ask the ANC to 'forswear the only power available to them should the government walk away from the negotiating table'.[32] It was a classic deadlock.

Mandela, however, saw a real chance of peace. On that same morning he asked permission to see his colleagues to discuss the proposal, and later he talked to his attorney Ismail Ayob and to Winnie. He was puzzled that his people were hesitating. Ayob explained that they needed time to consult others, including the ANC executive and the UDF.[33]

But President Botha, Kobie Coetsee believed, was now torn: he realised that he must soon release Mandela; but he did not dare appear weak. He felt hurt that the British and Americans did not appreciate the extent of his concessions, and his aggressiveness was encouraged by the recent American air-strike on Libya: 'Crocker forgets that his own country made use of cross-border attacks,' he told me later. Botha now suddenly turned tough. When the Minister of Defence Magnus Malan proposed that the military should strike at ANC bases in neighbouring countries, Botha approved the suggestion without discussing it with either the Cabinet or the State Security Council.[34]

While the eminent persons were talking, South African forces were striking, with raids on Lusaka, Harare and Gaborone – all Commonwealth capitals which the eminent persons had recently visited. The raids confirmed their worst forebodings about not being able to trust the South African government; and Pik Botha later admitted that they were 'just one provocation too much'. In London Mrs Thatcher saw them as 'an unmitigated disaster'. In Washington Chester Crocker reckoned that President Botha had 'turned decisively toward the road of repression'. In Pollsmoor, Mandela was convinced that the raids had 'utterly poisoned the talks'.[35]

The eminent persons gave up. They had lunch with Winnie Mandela and flew back home that evening, knowing that their four-month mission had collapsed. Ten days later they heard from Pik Botha that the government had rejected 'the threat of violence as a bargaining counter', and was 'not interested in negotiating about the transfer of power'. They replied that they saw no merit in further discussions. The Commonwealth Secretariat prepared an outspoken report (which Lord Barber very reluctantly signed, to Mrs Thatcher's disgust) concluding with a sombre warning: 'If the government finds itself unable to talk with men like Mandela and Tambo, then the future of South Africa is bleak indeed.'[36]

President Botha was now determined on a total crackdown; and on 12 June he imposed a nationwide state of emergency, giving the police much more drastic powers. They surrounded the townships, blocked main roads, searched houses and detained 4,000 blacks in three weeks. P.W. Botha warned that he had still not used a tenth of the force available to him, but it was enough to create terror. Visiting Johannesburg at that time, I found that all the black leadership was either in hiding or in jail. The only gatherings permitted were in churches: the Bishop of Johannesburg, Desmond Tutu, preached a militant sermon in the cathedral, asking with his arms outstretched, 'Why are we allowing this country to be destroyed?'[37] All hope of talks seemed to have crashed.

It was just then that Mandela decided on a new approach. He was not put off by Botha's use of brute force. 'The most discouraging moments,' he insisted, 'are precisely the time to launch an initiative.' He was encouraged that the eminent persons had believed there was enough common ground for negotiations.[38] Niël Barnard, the head of the National Intelligence Service, would later maintain that he had already prepared the way for talks, and that from the early eighties the NIS had advised the government that 'there was no answer in trying to fight it out'.[39] But it was Mandela who took the first step – as he would often remind his opponents.[40] He asked to see the Commissioner of Prisons, General Willemse (the former commander of Robben Island), 'on a matter of major national importance'. Four days later Willemse flew down from Pretoria to meet him in his official house at Pollsmoor. Mandela told him he wanted to see P.W. Botha to discuss a meeting between the ANC and the government. To his surprise Willemse immediately rang Coetsee, who offered to see him straight away.

Mandela was driven quickly to Savernake, the Minister of Justice's official residence in Cape Town, where Coetsee was waiting for him. The Minister listened carefully and asked searching questions for three hours: could Mandela speak for the ANC? Under what conditions would the ANC suspend the armed struggle? Would they give constitutional guarantees for minorities? What was the next step? About that, Mandela had no doubts: he must see President Botha. Coetsee promised to pass on the request, and shook hands warmly. Mandela was driven back to his cell. He told no one about the meeting, but prepared for further talks, still confident that his colleagues would accept a *fait accompli.* But for months he heard nothing.

There were signs that the government was preparing him for more freedom. The deputy commander of the prison, Lieutenant-Colonel Gawie Marx, offered to drive him through Cape Town, where he had his first glimpse of ordinary life for twenty-four years, feeling like a tourist in a strange land: 'It was absolutely riveting to watch the simple activities of people out in the world: old men sitting in the sun, women doing their shopping, people walking their dogs.' But he noticed too that the whites were enjoying a much richer and more luxurious life after his quarter-century of imprisonment, while the black townships were poorer than ever. When Marx briefly left Mandela in the car while he went to buy a Coke he was tempted to escape into the woods, but soon realised the risk.[41]

Mandela's warder James Gregory also took him on several excursions outside Cape Town, followed by a police car with four guards armed with machine-guns. They looked at the gardens of Kirstenbosch from the car, visited the salt town of Langebaan, and even walked along the beach near the seaside town of Paternoster, while guards watched along the road. After Mandela had urinated behind the rocks, a group of German tourists walked past him. Gregory recalled him saying: 'They've just missed the scoop of the century.'[42] Mandela thought the excursions were designed to acclimatise him – and perhaps to make him long for freedom, and therefore look for a compromise. But he was prepared to wait.

He was now allowed more visits from friends and family – even 'contact visits', during which he could kiss Winnie and hug the children. But there was no relaxed setting where he could get to know them again. His children, all now parents themselves, had grown further away from him after twenty-five years. His son Makgatho (or Kgatho) had given up visiting him in 1983, having opted out of school and university. After his marriage to Rennie broke up he married again, then went to stay with his mother Evelyn in the Transkei – taken there by Kaiser Matanzima – where he helped her run the trading store. Mandela was more ambitious for Mandla, Makgatho's eldest son, who was doing well at school in Swaziland. He thought Mandla should move to Johannesburg, where he could pick up languages more easily and 'be free from religious indoctrination which can discourage clear thinking, which is so necessary to one's progress.'[43] (Was he thinking of Mandla's grandmother Evelyn?)

Mandela's eldest daughter Maki (Makaziwe) had married a school principal in the Transkei, Isaac Amuah, whom she brought to the prison in July 1985. Soon afterwards they both went to America to study as post-graduate students. 'I'm concerned, but I'm not a political person,' she told the *New York Times*.[44] She was more assertive than her brother Makgatho, and felt undervalued by her father. 'What's wrong, is old age setting in, or is your health failing you, that you are in no position to write to your beloved daughter?' she wrote to him in January 1987. She asked him not to interfere with her children, and defended her brother's autonomy: 'You have to give him the opportunity to exercise his privilege and right as a father,' she wrote in February 1988. 'I suspect that Kgatho feels neglected emotionally by both his parents.'[45] Their relationship was complicated by Winnie, who complained that her stepchildren were ungrateful. 'Why don't you have the courtesy to thank Mum Winnie for the funds?' Mandela asked Maki.[46] But Winnie was a more difficult stepmother than Mandela in jail could know.

He felt more confident about Zeni, his elder daughter by Winnie, married to her Swazi prince, who now had three children. Zeni began studies with her husband at Boston University in 1987, arranged by the neo-conservative President Silber. She was amazed by the Americans' ignorance of her country: 'Some think it is somewhere in the Caribbean,' she wrote to her father. 'Others think it is stuck somewhere near Nigeria. I really think it is unfair when we know so much about America.' She still half-longed not to have a famous father: 'If I had it my way I probably would have been a very ordinary person living an ordinary life somewhere in nowhere land. I always fantasised about being a model . . . I think you would have had a fit.'[47]

Mandela was concerned about Zindzi, who was headstrong and dashing like her mother, and who could not face university. 'I was more than disappointed when Mum told me that you have not moved to Campus,' he wrote to her in a mood of exasperation in May 1987. 'Of all the unspeakable errors you have made in your life,' he told her six months later, 'what you have done during the last nine months is the most disastrous.'

He had more sympathy for the next generation, including Zindzi's daughter Zazi. 'It is quite reasonable for Zazi to be puzzled by my refusal to leave prison,' he told Zindzi in March 1985: 'but she will soon be able to appreciate the reasons.'[48] His multiplying tribe helped to compensate him for his inactivity in other fields. Writing to Mary Benson in London about his benefactor David Astor, he boasted: 'I have twelve grandchildren and he and Bridget only have five.'[49] A year later he was telling Fatima Meer about his two great-grandchildren: 'At last, I have something which puts me head and shoulders above you.'[50]

Mandela's horizons were opening up further, through more visits, newspapers and films. He was delighted when Frieda Matthews, the eighty-year-old widow of his old mentor Z.K., visited him in November

1986 'with an entire library'; and she in turn felt uplifted by his lack of bitterness or regrets. 'I could not help thinking that Christ must have had the same attitude after his crucifixion,' she wrote to him afterwards.[51]

He often took solace in movies. He did not much like westerns, which were shown frequently in the prison, but he could now order his favourite films from outside. In 1986 his choices included *Shaka Zulu*, the Bolshoi Ballet and the Vienna Boys' Choir, the football World Cup in Mexico, *The Pirates of Penzance*, and the 1975 world heavyweight championship bout between Muhammad Ali and Joe Frazier in Manila. He was particularly keen to see Bernardo Bertolucci's Chinese epic *The Last Emperor*, and was eventually given a 16mm copy of the film by the Italian Ambassador for his birthday.[52]

But movies were no substitute for the reality outside, where the turmoil continued. For four years President Botha kept renewing the state of emergency, and his 'securocrats' established a more thorough police state, with soldiers permanently stationed in the townships, reinforced by new municipal black police and vigilante thugs. The UDF was effectively crippled after 25,000 people were detained in six months, while 50,000 more activists were said to be in hiding.[53] 'This time we have arrested all the right people,' the head of the security police General van der Merwe told the British Ambassador Robin Renwick.[54]

Despite the level of repression, there was still vigorous resistance. The UDF threw up new leaders and devised protests which were harder to suppress, including boycotts of shops and rent payments. The newly formed Congress of South African Trades Unions (COSATU) was feeling its muscles: and in August 1987 the mineworkers, under their leader Cyril Ramaphosa, launched a three-week strike. It was a show of strength, although it failed to achieve its demands. As Ramaphosa said afterwards: 'We felt the power surging in our veins.'[55] In the same month a militant youth organisation called SAYCO was formed, led by the young militant Peter Mokaba, a Robben Island graduate. Church leaders were becoming increasingly vocal, led by Desmond Tutu, who became the first black Archbishop of Cape Town in 1986. And the ANC guerrilla fighters were now having more success, with 231 attacks within South Africa in 1986, and 235 in 1987, according to police figures.

But the UDF had been seriously weakened by the detentions. In August 1987 their chief spokesman Murphy Morobe was arrested after a year on the run. In February 1988 the UDF and seventeen other organisations were banned. The government publicised the 'black on black' violence to show that the ANC had been responsible for anarchy. White businessmen who had been fearing a major upheaval decided with relief that the government was in control after all. Many observers, including the respected political scientist Tom Lodge, thought the revolt had been crushed.[56]

The ANC also now appeared to be seriously challenged by Chief Buthelezi's Zulu Inkatha party, and the rivalry between the two organisations led to escalating murders and atrocities on both sides. Buthelezi still portrayed Mandela as a friend and publicly called for his release, but he had condemned the 'Release Mandela' campaign as a gimmick, and privately warned the military that it would be 'irresponsible' to let him out.[57] In 1986 Buthelezi announced that he had been given permission to visit Mandela in Pollsmoor. Mandela tactfully but firmly replied through his lawyer Ismail Ayob that it would be best to meet after he had been released.[58]

Inside South Africa, Buthelezi was being built up as a serious rival to Mandela. He was given access to television and the press, and was free to travel abroad. He hired public-relations advisers, invited conservative journalists to his Zulu capital Ulundi, and welcomed rich foreign supporters. He sent a glossy magazine called *Clarion Call* around the world, publishing his marathon speeches. His publicity machine was much more effective than that of the ANC, whose embattled officials in Lusaka could exasperate the most sympathetic foreign journalists, who found it hard to get through to them: even the *New York Times* was once kept waiting in Lusaka for three days.[59] The ANC's magazine *Sechaba*, printed on shabby paper in East Germany, was addressed only to the left. The fitful communications of the ANC led many foreign journalists and politicians to underestimate its real popular support.

Buthelezi became the favourite of Western conservatives. In America and Germany he was welcomed as the desirable alternative to Tambo and Mandela, while in February 1985 he had been received by President Reagan. But it was Margaret Thatcher who, after meeting him with her mentor Laurens van der Post, became his most influential overseas ally, welcoming him as a champion of free enterprise and encouraging businessmen to put their hopes in him. She praised him as a 'stalwart opponent of violent uprising', while her Foreign Secretary Geoffrey Howe thought him 'extremely clear-sighted but firmly independent'.[60]

It was not until years later that the full truth was revealed: that the Pretoria government had been systematically arming Zulu forces against the ANC. Buthelezi (the Truth and Reconciliation Commission found in 1998) had conspired with President Botha and his Minister of Defence Magnus Malan to 'create an unlawful and offensive paramilitary force to be deployed against the ANC'. In early 1986, it emerged, Buthelezi had selected two hundred Inkatha soldiers for secret training near the Caprivi strip in the remotest part of Namibia, where they were taught by the South African army how to use rockets, mortars and hand-grenades and to terrorise communities: including how to attack houses with the aim of killing all the occupants.[61] While the government was publicly deploring the violence, its own security forces were fanning the flames, by arming and encouraging the Zulus to attack ANC supporters.

But behind the scenes, Western governments, and President Botha himself, were beginning to accept that there could be no solution without coming to terms with the ANC – and releasing Mandela.

25

The Lost Leader

1983–1988

As South Africa came ever closer to civil war, the clamour to release Mandela resounded across the world. Anti-apartheid boycotts were spreading, campaigns for disinvestment and sanctions were biting. And the cause of black South Africans was receiving more publicity, through television programmes, films and stage shows, including Richard Attenborough's film about Steve Biko, *Cry Freedom* (1987), and the Broadway hit *Sarafina* (1988), about a girl student who worshipped Mandela.

Mandela was the world's most famous prisoner, all the more romantic because hardly anyone had seen his face for a quarter of a century: no new picture of him had been published since 1965. The Mandela icon was free to develop as a symbol of heroic resistance to oppression, quite independent of physical reality. His generalised image seemed to transcend all the sectarian and national rivalries of Africa, and came to represent the universal black leader, the last great freedom-fighter. The icon is expressed in the larger-than-life bust unveiled by Oliver Tambo beside the Royal Festival Hall in London in 1985: its big-lipped, thick-set head is quite unlike Mandela's sensitive face. A whole generation of children had been told about Mandela as the lone champion of freedom, celebrated by Mandela streets, songs and concerts. They knew nothing about the actual man in Pollsmoor, grappling with complex realities. Could the real Mandela, if he ever emerged, possibly live up to the myth?

The anti-apartheid campaigns in the West, particularly boycotts of banks, had done much to extend sanctions. The British and American governments were still reluctant to have a showdown with Pretoria, and were strongly influenced by conservative lobbies which continued to denounce the ANC as terrorists or communists. But divisions were appearing.

In Washington the Secretary of State George Shultz and his African expert Chester Crocker were losing patience with Pretoria; but they were frustrated by Ronald Reagan's White House and by CIA chief William Casey, who was friendly with President Botha and who worked closely with South African intelligence. When Crocker prepared a strong anti-apartheid speech for Reagan in July 1986 it was rewritten by his right-wing aide Pat Buchanan so as to emphasise the sacrifices made by white South Africans and to blame the emergency on 'the calculated terror by elements of the ANC'. The State Department had effectively lost control over US diplomacy. Crocker called it 'the Great Foreign Policy Robbery of 1986', and Shultz had to be restrained from resigning.

But it was Congress, not the White House, which was soon making foreign policy. In August 1986 the Senate voted eighty-four to fourteen for a comprehensive sanctions bill imposing bans on new investment, loans, airport landing rights and exports of oil. It was a body-blow to Pretoria, closing off future international trade. When at last Shultz saw Tambo for the first time, in January 1987, he told him he did not want the ANC to become isolated like the PLO. He reassured him that Pretoria would eventually have to deal with the ANC, and warned him that the Soviets were 'sure losers'. Tambo asked Shultz for joint action from Washington and Moscow against Pretoria.[1] News of the meeting brought fresh encouragement to Mandela in prison.

The confusion in Washington put more emphasis on the role of Mrs Thatcher; she was in a stronger position than Reagan to influence Botha, but remained determined to resist sanctions. In spite of the 'unmitigated disaster' of the eminent persons' mission, in July 1986 she had insisted on sending her reluctant Foreign Secretary Geoffrey Howe, representing the European Community, to South Africa to try again to conciliate. But the ANC, including Mandela and Tutu, refused to see him; and President Botha was bad-tempered and offensive, haranguing Howe that he 'would not force South Africans to commit national suicide'. When in August 1986 Mrs Thatcher faced a special Commonwealth meeting in London, the deadlock was obvious: 'The Botha government had still not made the quantum leap for which we all looked,' wrote Howe afterwards. 'Mandela and his colleagues were still in jail, and the ANC and its parallels were still banned.'[2] Mrs Thatcher still resisted sanctions, encouraged over dinner beforehand with Laurens van der Post, and insisted that apartheid was 'if not dead, at least rapidly dying'.[3] But she had to accept a set of sanctions endorsed by the European Community which included a ban on new investment.

She continued to press Botha to release Mandela, but regarded his detention as an issue quite separate from recognising the ANC, which she still refused to do. It was not until February 1986 that a British diplomat, John Johnson, had been allowed to meet three ANC officials (including Thabo Mbeki) in Lusaka.[4] And it was not until September 1987 that Geoffrey Howe was permitted to talk to Tambo. The meeting took place at Chevening, the Foreign Secretary's official country residence. Tambo, in a well-tailored suit, was polite and moderate, but Howe was very cautious, pessimistic about any change, and worried about offending the Tory Party. They politely agreed to differ, as two lawyers, on the issue of violence.[5]

In July 1987 Mrs Thatcher appointed a much more proactive Ambassador to Pretoria: Robin Renwick, who would play an intricate role over the next four years. A subtle and charming man with an enigmatic smile, he was well informed about Africa, having helped to negotiate Zimbabwe's independence in 1979. Privately he saw the ANC as crucial to any settlement, and he kept discreetly in touch with it through intermediaries like Enos Mabuza.[6] But Thatcher prevented him from publicly approving the ANC, and he went along with her support for Buthelezi. Renwick's main task, Thatcher told him, was to press President Botha towards reform, but his first meeting was not encouraging. He was eventually received, as he put it, 'in a study lit only by his desk lamp, conjuring up images of what it must have been like calling on Hitler in his bunker'. Botha appeared unworried by sanctions, but fearful of losing control of the country: he had no intention of releasing Mandela, he said, unless he was critically ill. Renwick thought Botha would fight to the finish, and saw little chance of influencing him.[7]

Mrs Thatcher still set herself against the ANC. At the next Commonwealth Summit, in Vancouver in October 1987, the ANC representative Johnny Makatini provoked her with a question, and she snapped back that the ANC was 'a typical terrorist organisation'.[8] British diplomats were exasperated by her outburst. Geoffrey Howe complained that she had 'once again set back the prospect of dialogue', and Renwick had to remind Downing Street that he was developing private contacts with the

ANC – which he quietly continued to do – and British intelligence agents in Lusaka were befriending ANC leaders.[9] Thatcher's demonising of the ANC helped Botha's propaganda, while frustrating the moderates of the ANC, including Tambo, who wanted closer contacts with conservatives and business leaders in the West. 'If she goes on calling them communists it will be self-fulfilling,' the conservative Jamaican Prime Minister Edward Seaga commented after the Vancouver meeting.[10]

In fact the old Soviet menace in Africa, such as it was, was rapidly evaporating. 'Southern Africa is, practically speaking, well outside the Soviet Union's zone of primary interest, indeed of its secondary interest,' wrote Frank Wisner, the Deputy Assistant for African Affairs in Washington, in January 1984.[11] After Mikhail Gorbachev came to power in 1985 he soon realised that the Soviet Union could no longer afford expensive adventures in Africa, and at the Reykjavik Summit in October 1986 he told Reagan that he wished to retreat from regional conflicts. In 1986 British Ambassadors in Africa first met their Soviet counterparts, and were struck by the new mood of détente and disengagement – which soon showed itself in hopeful cooperation towards independence in Namibia. As for South Africa, Moscow was withdrawing its previous support for revolution. 'In the past it was always assumed that there would be a classical revolutionary overthrow of the white minority regime,' said Boris Asoyan, the deputy head of the Southern African Department in Moscow in 1988. 'Now we accept that there will have to be a political settlement.'[12]

The South African Communist Party itself was rethinking its revolutionary policies. At its sixty-fifth anniversary in London in 1986, the Chairman Joe Slovo shocked revolutionary British comrades by warning against 'the Pol Pot philosophy', which held that you could 'pole-vault into socialism and communism the day after the overthrow of white rule'. The next day he explained to me: 'I've never believed it's the job of a revolutionary to make a revolution; only to lead it . . . I've never relished the escalation of violence.'[13]

From jail, Mandela had followed the prospects of détente with high hopes. He had long thought the Cold War was ending, as he had told his daughter Zindzi in 1978. He had been delighted by Gorbachev's friendly meeting with Mrs Thatcher in December 1984 and by the prospect of his meeting with Reagan, as he told Lord Bethell and Sam Dash. In 1987 he enjoyed a television programme in which two professors who were visiting South Africa, Roger Fisher from Harvard and John Erickson from Edinburgh, discussed the changes inside Russia, though a South African academic, Dirk Kunert of Wits, 'sounded much like the ghost of Senator McCarthy'.[14]

Tambo had been encouraged in Moscow in 1986 by a talk with Gorbachev, whom he found very well-informed and open to argument: more like Kissinger than Brezhnev. Tambo did not feel at all pressurised to pursue Marxist policies: a year earlier a key Soviet official had commented for the first time on the ANC's economic policy, by advising him – to his great surprise – to put less emphasis on nationalisation. Tambo himself never believed that black South Africans would embrace communism. 'Our people will decide,' he said privately in New York in January 1987, 'and they're not very interested in a socialist state. The communists know they're only one group among many.'[15]

Pretoria's rhetoric about the 'total communist onslaught' was looking very hollow. But Reagan and Thatcher continued to play up the communist bogey, which both encouraged President Botha's ruthlessness and helped to scare off Western businessmen and politicians from any contact with the ANC. The ban was more tragic in view of the ANC's obvious need for management and professional skills, a need which became more urgent as they faced the likelihood of coming to power. Tambo's wish to provide training and work experience for young ANC people, to equip them for government and business, led to the setting up in late 1986 of the South African Advanced Education Project (SAAEP). It was funded by some far-sighted donors, including the Rockefeller Brothers Foundation, David Astor and Shell (which ironically the ANC were then boycotting). But the British and American governments offered no help.

In fact, the apparent non-contact between the ANC and the Afrikaners was not as complete as it seemed. While Botha and Thatcher kept up their attacks on the communist revolutionaries, a few enterprising non-governmental bodies were building secret bridges which promised to change the political scene. The Ford Foundation in New York, under its black President Franklin Thomas, was responsible for a dramatic breakthrough. In June 1986 it had arranged a discreet meeting between Afrikaners – including Pieter de Lange, the Chairman of the influential society the Broederbond – and ANC leaders including Thabo Mbeki, Mac Maharaj and a fiery freedom fighter, Seretse Choabe. When Choabe encountered de Lange he leapt to his feet and shouted, 'I'll shoot you, Broederbonder.' Maharaj tactfully asked the Afrikaners to understand the roots of Choabe's anger; the conference ended emotionally, with Choabe apologising and embracing de Lange. Thabo Mbeki subsequently had a long private dinner with de Lange which left the Afrikaner, as Mbeki put it, with a 'normalised perception of the ANC as human beings'.[16]

Another bridge was built by Frederik van Zyl Slabbert, the former leader of the liberal opposition, who had left Parliament in February 1986, when he called for a negotiated settlement. 'He has broken with a tradition of Afrikaner and white leadership which has sanctified racism,' said the ANC Secretary-General Alfred Nzo. In August 1987 Slabbert organised a meeting in Dakar, Senegal, where fifty Afrikaner intellectuals met with ANC leaders. They issued a joint communiqué calling for a negotiated settlement and the unbanning of the ANC. President Botha responded with apparent fury: 'The ANC is laughing up their sleeves at the naïveté of "useful idiots".' But in fact the National Intelligence Service had discreetly assisted the meeting. As its Director Niël Barnard later explained: 'We believed there could be no political solution without the ANC.' And Botha explained that he was happy for them to 'burn their fingers'.[17]

Some big companies were also feeling a need to reinsure themselves. Gold Fields, Cecil Rhodes' old mining company, still cultivated a reactionary style under its London chairman Rudolph Agnew: it celebrated its centenary in 1987 with a history by the right-wing historian Paul Johnson, who lambasted the ANC for its 'systematic violence'.[18] But behind the bluster Agnew had agreed in June 1986 to finance secret meetings, organised by his political adviser Michael Young, to bring the ANC together with Afrikaners. In November 1987 a team of Afrikaner intellectuals met with an ANC group at the Compleat Angler hotel at Henley, in Oxfordshire. Over the next two years further meetings established trust between the groups, which soon included Thabo Mbeki.[19] While Thatcher was denouncing the ANC as terrorists, hard-headed Afrikaners were learning to do business with them.

Even President Botha's attacks on Mandela were not what they seemed. In 1987 the Minister of Justice Kobie Coetsee at last responded to Mandela's request for talks, by inviting him to his official residence in Cape Town. The meeting was kept secret from the other four prisoners in Pollsmoor, but their friendliest warder, Christo Brand, could not resist talking to Kathrada, mentioning Mandela's secret excursions. 'I can't tell you who Mandela saw last night,' he teased them, but eventually revealed that it was the Minister of Justice.[20] Coetsee was not altogether trusted by President Botha. 'He was a funny little man,' Botha said later. 'I always felt after talking to him that it was a case of confusion worse confounded.'[21] But Botha needed Coetsee to get him out of his corner, and they kept in touch.

Thus began the loneliest stretch of Mandela's ordeal. It is common enough in world history for heads of government to maintain apparently intransigent attitudes to their enemies, while holding clandestine talks with them: as Nixon had done with the Vietnamese, or as John Major would soon do with the IRA. But Mandela was in an especially exposed position. He was facing the government alone, knowing that they were trying to split him off from his colleagues, with whom he could not come clean. From his cell he was now caught up in intricate talks, interlocking with other talks in Pretoria, Lusaka and Britain, of which he could not be properly informed. One false move could destroy his leadership.

Coetsee was now clearly looking for a way to release his famous prisoner: between 1987 and 1990 he would have twelve meetings with Mandela in jail.[22] Mandela pressed him to let out his colleagues as a first step, beginning with Govan Mbeki, who was now seventy-seven and in poor health on Robben Island. The government, worried that Mbeki might die in jail, eventually released him without conditions in November 1987, supposedly on 'humanitarian grounds', but also to test the public reaction. Mandela had advised Mbeki to act with restraint, but he was greeted by ecstatic crowds at big rallies, and openly presented himself as an ANC leader. Three weeks later he was put under twelve-hour house arrest, and confined to Port Elizabeth. The Commissioner of Police complained that he was encouraging young people to continue the struggle, and providing the ANC with a platform.[23] In Lusaka the ANC realised that 'something went wrong', and that the regime appeared to have taken fright – which could put them off releasing Mandela. But as Tambo said: 'If Mandela were released, he couldn't agree to say nothing.'[24]

The government clearly hoped that Mbeki's release would help to drive a wedge between the Marxist wing of the ANC and the moderates; and there was certainly more tension. Before Mbeki left Robben Island Mandela had told him only that he was talking with the government, without giving any details;[25] Mbeki's release was soon followed by a spate of rumours that Mandela was selling out, which reverberated over the next two years. Even Tambo in Lusaka seemed shaken. But Mandela kept talking to the government, confident that Tambo would understand; and Tambo held the party together.

Late in 1987 Coetsee had proposed that Mandela should begin more serious discussions with a team of four, chaired by himself and including the two top prison officials – who could pretend to be talking about jail conditions. But the key member would be the head of the National Intelligence Service Dr Niël Barnard, only thirty-six, who was close to the President. The NIS had already made a tentative contact with the ANC in Geneva in 1984, and had kept sporadically in touch, with Botha's approval. Barnard was convinced that a deal must be struck with the ANC 'before our backs were against the wall'.[26] Mandela knew that Barnard's joining the talks would be raising the stakes; but he did not want to alienate the President, who was his eventual target. So he agreed to meet the 'Team', as they were called, while insisting on first consulting with his four prison colleagues upstairs. He asked them separately, one by one, what they thought about talking to the government, without mentioning Barnard and his team. Raymond Mhlaba and Andrew Mlangeni were delighted: they had wanted talks long ago. Sisulu wanted to wait for the government to make the first move, and suspected a subtle plan to use Buthelezi and others against the ANC; he told Mandela he hoped he knew what he was doing. Kathrada was more worried: he thought the ANC might appear to be giving in. But Mandela never thought he was talking from a position of weakness, and went ahead.[27]

Mandela's desire for talks was partly echoed by new thinking from the ANC in Lusaka, and from the Communist Party. 'I believe that the transition in South Africa is going to come through negotiation,' said Joe Slovo in a thoughtful interview in March 1987. 'If there was any prospect of settling it peacefully tomorrow, we would be the first to say "Let's do it."'[28] But the ANC were worried that the Western powers as well as Pretoria had hidden agendas, and they saw indications that America, Britain and Germany were preparing their own plan which they would try to force the ANC to accept; they had also had visits from previously unknown intermediaries, including Allen Weinstein, a conservative professor from Boston University (which had CIA links), who proposed informal talks with Botha's Cabinet. In October 1987 the ANC produced its own document: 'Possible Response to Negotiations Initiative'. It restated their overriding aim: 'The defeat of the apartheid regime and the transfer of power to all the people.' But it stressed that they must 'prepare, on time, for the possible eventuality of negotiations, initiated by forces other than ourselves'.[29]

The ANC in exile were now making closer contacts with their UDF colleagues inside South Africa. In September 1987 a 'Children's Conference' in Harare, Zimbabwe, provided the first opportunity for Tambo and the Lusaka leaders, including Joe Slovo, to meet with activists who flew up from South Africa. The atmosphere was more Christian than communist: it was presided over by Father Huddleston from London, with the Church activist Frank Chikane from Johannesburg as the star. Huddleston had conceived the conference to draw attention to the suffering of black children; but it also provided unique contacts between the external and internal leadership. Tambo spoke optimistically, encouraged by his get-together with Afrikaners at Dakar, but he saw no signs of movement from P.W. Botha, who was still branding the ANC as Marxist murderers.[30]

Behind the scenes Tambo now for the first time showed himself worried by Mandela's actions. He knew that he enjoyed Mandela's complete trust: when his wife Adelaide compiled a book of Tambo's speeches Mandela smuggled out an introduction in his own handwriting, praising the 'brilliant exposition' of ANC policy which Tambo had given in an interview with Tony Heard of the *Cape Times*, and explaining how his commitment had 'inspired us beyond words'.[31] But Tambo was concerned to hear about Mandela's secret talks, and smuggled a message into jail asking him what he was up to. 'The tone was quite hostile,' Mandela recalled, 'so I decided to be very firm . . . I just added a sentence: "a meeting between the ANC and the government".' 'I felt,' Mandela told me later, 'that this had reached a point where we had to be very strong.'[32]

In May 1988 Mandela met the Team for the first time, in the comfortable surroundings of the officers' club within the Pollsmoor compound. They met almost once a week over the next months, sometimes for seven hours at a time. Mandela prepared carefully for each meeting, turning his cell into an improvised office. Niël Barnard was clearly the government mastermind, tougher and cleverer than the others, cold and smooth. But he developed an admiration for his opponent. He was moved to see Mandela relishing the sandwiches: 'I felt deep down a sense of sympathy for this man in prison overalls and boots. And he was *thin*.' Mandela was impressed by Barnard's 'controlled intelligence and self-discipline', but surprised by his misconceptions about the ANC, gleaned from biased police and intelligence files.[33] There were still negative reports about Mandela's state of mind. In May 1988 Colonel J.G. Lourens reported that his emotional condition remained stable, with no indications of mental illness ('*geestesiekte*') ; but 'his attitude towards the S.A. government is still unchanged and dismissive. He will not be prepared to disavow violence.'[34]

Mandela and Barnard went over the old arguments. Barnard reiterated that President Botha could not meet Mandela until he had agreed to renounce violence; Mandela explained once again that the state had begun the violence, and that the ANC would respond peacefully to peaceful methods. Barnard complained that the ANC wanted to nationalise everything; Mandela once again quoted his 1956 article in *Liberation*, which looked forward to African business flourishing as never before. Barnard insisted that the ANC was controlled by communists, and the government could not negotiate until the ANC broke with them. Mandela explained that the ANC's communists were far from any 'evil empire'; and that he would never be turned by any outside body. The Team must realise that, he suggested, since they had failed to change his mind: 'What makes you think the communists can succeed where you have failed?'[35]

Mandela knew that Barnard was pursuing other ANC contacts. 'We hear Thabo Mbeki is somebody who wants negotiations,' Barnard told him. 'Have you any objection if we talk with him?' Mandela asked why that was necessary: 'He is a young man, very able, very talented and very devoted; but if you are going to have a confidential discussion with him it will leak before he reports to his people and you can destroy him.' He preferred that Barnard should talk to Tambo himself. But Barnard went ahead with his contacts with Thabo.[36]

Thabo thus became a key player in the intricate game. Mandela felt well able to trust him, having first watched him when he had organised students for the anti-Republic strike in 1961. Thabo had first learnt politics from his father Govan, and had escaped into exile, taken a degree in economics at Sussex University, done military training in the Soviet Union, and then worked closely with Tambo in Lusaka and London, developing into a masterly diplomat. He became adept at reassuring Afrikaners that he understood their problems: he learnt, as he put it, 'to start off from where they were'. He would drink with them, puffing his curved pipe, listening, sharing their jokes, understanding their history, gradually disarming their fears about black extremists. But he never lost sight of the ANC's fixed objectives. When Thabo began talking to Barnard's friends, Mandela became aware that 'he was very acute and reported to the organisation. He was very correct.'[37]

Barnard, on his side, soon learnt more about Thabo's ideas from reports of the ANC's meetings with Afrikaners in England arranged by Gold Fields – about which Professor Willie Esterhuyse of Stellenbosch University kept him informed, with the knowledge of the ANC. At the second meeting in Kent, Thabo led the ANC team, while the Afrikaners were augmented by a constitutional expert and a businessman. Mbeki was surprised by the Afrikaners' ignorance: he tried endlessly to reassure them that they would not be selling out their own people, and that Mandela's release would unlock the door to peaceful talks.[38] 'Thabo ran rings round them,' Michael Young recalls. 'It was quite embarrassing. The Afrikaners just hadn't seen anyone like him: he moved in the international circles to which they aspired.' But the two sides came closer. The Afrikaners accepted that the ANC could not renounce violence unilaterally before they negotiated – the point which President Botha had refused to the eminent persons. And Thabo assured them that when released the ANC leaders – including his father Govan, who had just been let out – would restrain their followers from violence.[39]

Inside South Africa the public knew nothing of the secret talks or the activities of the real Mandela, as opposed to the mythological demon, or hero. But his name was now creeping back into the headlines, and the ban on his photographs had been broken. Ancient photographs from the sixties had re-emerged since 1986, when the *Weekly Mail* had challenged the law by reproducing one which had appeared in a government propaganda booklet.[40]

Mandela's international fame was enhanced by his seventieth birthday in July 1988. In London the BBC planned to televise a huge rock concert on 11 June called 'Freedom at 70' at Wembley Stadium, with star performers including Harry Belafonte, Whitney Houston, Roberta Flack and Stevie Wonder. Pretoria was so angry that they threatened to eject the BBC from South Africa altogether, and twenty-four British Tory MPs attacked the BBC for encouraging terrorists; the columnist and Tory peer Lord Wyatt wrote in the *News of the World* that Mandela and the ANC were trying to establish 'a communist-style black dictatorship'.[41] But the concert went ahead – with a smuggled message from Mandela – watched by 72,000 spectators and 200 million television viewers in sixty countries.[42]

'Has it struck you that apart from the birthday of the Lord Jesus,' Kathrada wrote from Pollsmoor to Paul Joseph, 'no birthday has ever been as widely celebrated as Nelson's 70th?'[43] The South African Broadcasting Corporation commented that the campaign to glamorise Nelson Mandela had 'descended to a new level of emotional silliness nurtured by ignorance'.[44]

Even conservative South African newspapers were calling for his release as the outbreaks of violence became more menacing. Just before his birthday, a powerful car-bomb had exploded outside the Ellis Park rugby stadium in Johannesburg, killing two whites and injuring thirty-five.[45] The Johannesburg *Star* warned that if he died in jail he would be canonised, while 'Once he is freed the Mandela myth would be cut down to size by political realities.' Even the pro-government Afrikaner daily *Beeld* said there would never be a better time to release him: he had acquired a status larger than life, which he would find hard to keep up if he were released.[46] The Minister of Information replied that the government could not see its way clear to release Mandela 'at this stage', and that no editor had the government's intimate knowledge of the circumstances.[47] Neither did the Minister, as it turned out.

Black South Africans now saw Mandela more clearly as their lost leader waiting in the wings. Just after his birthday he was visited by Yusuf and Amina Cachalia, who had not seen him for twenty-six years. 'He remembers everything and is alert as ever,' said Yusuf. 'His health is good and he is as charismatic as ever.' 'Nelson looks absolutely smashing,' said Amina publicly, 'though he now has lots of grey hair on his head.' Privately she was more worried, for he looked lean and pale, and she missed his chubby cheeks. But she was convinced that 'he had an inner strength which had taken over.' And he gave the Cachalias a message to his supporters: 'I am very grateful to you all and have very great hope for the future.'[48] A few days later he was visited by Dr Mamphela Ramphele, the partner of the murdered black leader Steve Biko and mother of one of Biko's two sons. She was amazed to see the warders defer to him, and was overwhelmed by his presence, 'oozing authority and grace . . . his great social skills were in evidence at every turn – he put me at ease without patronising me.'[49]

But Mandela was not well: he was coughing frequently, which he blamed on his damp cell. Three weeks after his birthday, on 4 August, the four other Pollsmoor prisoners were allowed to spend a few hours with him. He was cheerful, full of news about old friends, and very sharp. 'The lawyer in him is as keen, wise and dynamic as ever,' Kathrada wrote later. But Kathrada was concerned for the first time about Mandela's health: 'He coughed quite a bit, and his voice was just above a whisper.'[50] Ismail Ayob was even more worried when Mandela suddenly vomited. He summoned the warder, Gregory, who arrived (he recalled) to find Mandela struggling to stand up, sweating and pointing to the mess on the floor which he wanted to clean up.[51]

A few days later Mandela was visited by a doctor, who examined him briefly, after which he was driven, protected by a military convoy, to Tygerberg Hospital in Stellenbosch, where a whole floor had been cleared and surrounded by armed guards. He was examined by a genial young doctor who after a few tests assured him he was perfectly fit. But the next morning a gruff Professor de Kock appeared. He tapped Mandela's chest, noticed that one side was larger than the other, and diagnosed water on the lung. He pushed a needle through Mandela's ribs and drew out some brownish liquid. He then took him straight to the operating room under anaesthetic, and removed still more fluid to clear the lungs. He found early signs of tuberculosis, which he thought had been partly caused by the damp conditions. Mandela stayed at Tygerberg for six weeks for recuperation and treatment under de Kock's supervision. He was confident that he was 'in the hands of an expert', and by the time he left the hospital he saw de Kock as a close friend.[52]

A medical bulletin gave minimal information, explaining that Mandela had 'left-sided pleural effusion', or fluid in the left lung, with no more details. The doctors described his condition as satisfactory. But Winnie, who arrived at the hospital with Ismail Ayob the next day, soon gave a more worrying account, blaming the prison for neglecting him. The speculation and anxiety were intense, and the government seemed alarmed. The Minister of Information saw no reason why they should keep Mandela in jail. The Minister of Justice, Coetsee, was 'deeply perturbed', and was giving it his 'personal attention'. A Swiss professor of pneumology was rolled in, and said that the chances of a complete recovery were excellent. The government clearly realised, said the London *Sunday Times*, that 'the only thing worse than a free Mandela is a dead Mandela'.[53]

Tambo in Lusaka made plans for Mandela's imminent release; but the ANC suspected that President Botha had a hidden agenda, and their working committee discussed it at a key meeting in late November. They thought 'the regime intended to trigger a political realignment and start off a sterile negotiations exercise in order to play for time'. Pretoria would pressurise the ANC to act 'responsibly', backed by Mrs Thatcher, who planned to visit South Africa after Mandela was released, and who visualised the British as referees for a new constitutional formula.

Tambo was specially worried about the role of Buthelezi. Mandela, after putting off Buthelezi's visit in 1986, had sent messages that he wanted to talk to him. Tambo had opposed such a meeting, but realised that Mandela would want to see Buthelezi when he was released. 'NM thinks he can mobilise people into our ranks,' Tambo told the working committee, 'and he has been able to do so in the past.' He felt Mandela should be warned that Buthelezi was looking for acceptability before going his own way. 'Buthelezi is power-hungry and he would want to use NM for as long as it suits him . . . Margaret Thatcher is astute enough,' Tambo added, 'to realise that hostilities between ANC and Buthelezi would continue while NM is not there.'

The ANC were determined to maintain their military power. They had to ensure that 'the course of the struggle is not derailed by the release'. They considered organising a rally in Soweto, 'associated with explosions all over the place', and saw a need to plan for 'a sustained insurrectionary situation'. Mandela must defy any restrictions. 'The armed struggle would have to be stepped up even before NM goes out,' said Tambo, 'so that there is no question of his release being conditional on renouncing armed struggle.' Mandela, the working committee concluded, must set out a clear programme of action, in consultation with the leadership: 'Unanimity of views between him and the movement as a whole is of crucial importance.' There should be a tremendous nationwide welcome upon his release, with clear slogans like 'Welcome back people's leader!'[54]

But the prisoners in Pollsmoor were still sceptical about the likelihood of their release. 'Based on past experience there is no reason for optimism,' Kathrada told his friend J.N. Singh on 16 September.[55] And Mandela in hospital soon realised that the government had different plans. After six weeks at Tygerberg he was moved to the still more comfortable Constantiaberg Clinic, the only black patient in an expensive all-white establishment. He was very well cared for, and was admired by the white and Coloured nurses, who even managed to give a party in his room. Some of them kept in touch with him afterwards. 'Dear Mr M,' wrote Fiona Duncan, reminding him, 'no hamburgers, pizzas or chocolate mousse!'[56]

But at Constantiaberg, Mandela realised that he would not be set free. Kobie Coetsee visited him on his first day, after which Barnard and the Team resumed their meetings with him. Coetsee explained that he would now move Mandela to yet another prison, where he would be 'in a halfway house between prison and freedom'.[57] He was entering a strange limbo, on the edge of events and yet in the centre, knowing that he held the future peace of the country in his hands.

26

'Something Horribly Wrong'

1987–1989

IN THE MIDST of his political negotiations, Mandela was being faced with more insoluble problems by his wife Winnie, who was still further out of control. The 'she-elephant' now appeared to be taking ungovernability to its extremes, involving herself in outbreaks of violence and murder which gave a nightmare picture of an alternative South Africa. Her wild behaviour would precipitate a political crisis which would soon involve the ANC leaders both inside and outside the country.

Mandela had a glimpse of Winnie's financial irresponsibility just after his birthday in July 1988, when she made a deal with a plausible American entrepreneur, Robert Brown – who had links with Boston University – to exploit the Mandela name, giving him, as his press release stated: 'full power of attorney for the Mandela family worldwide'. Brown had visited Mandela in Pollsmoor with Winnie on 22 July, but Mandela had been warned from London to steer clear of him. He firmly rejected the agreement with Winnie and told Brown to deal only with Tambo, his 'closest friend and colleague'.[1]

Mandela faced a more fundamental problem with Winnie's violence, which was harder to face up to. In Soweto Winnie saw herself on the front line of the battlefield of the armed struggle, with her house as a stronghold. The township was coming close to civil war as young people took up weapons. As Azhar Cachalia, the Treasurer of the UDF, later described the problem: 'By mid-1985 thousands of unaffiliated youths lacking direction or cohesion, many of them badly affected by their experience of detention, saw themselves as soldiers in the liberation struggle.' They formed their own armed gangs, staking out territories and fiefdoms, and no-go areas. Many gangs claimed to be linked to the armed struggle and MK, but the UDF leaders, undermined by mass arrests and detentions, could not control them. As Cachalia said: 'Our linkages with youth groups in particular became tenuous.'[2] And the police clearly had their own agenda. They had penetrated some gangs with informers and agents provocateurs, playing them against each other, provoking suspicion, betrayal and reprisals, while not intervening against Winnie.[3]

The ANC leaders were anxiously watching Winnie, who since her return from Brandfort seemed even fiercer and more reckless. She had become still more militant since her 'necklace' speech in April 1986, pursuing her own campaigns against the government. She depicted herself as a guerrilla soldier, sometimes in uniform, harbouring MK refugees from the north and claiming to take orders from Chris Hani, who was leading MK beyond South Africa's borders.[4] She saw acts of violence as necessary for the battlefield. 'The woman clearly thought she was fighting a war,' said Helen Suzman, who still admired her total courage.[5]

The local leaders had given up trying to discipline Winnie, or to keep her within the structures of their organisation. Nine years later, the Truth Commission would partly blame them for 'not bringing her into the fold or disciplining her when things were beginning to go wrong'.[6] But she was hard to discipline, and she had powerful friends.

Her friends had warned her to protect herself, and from 1987 she surrounded herself with a gang of boys, called the 'Mandela United Football Club', who lived in the back of her house, which they called 'Lusaka', or 'Parliament'.[7] Visitors would see gangs running in and out of the front rooms in footballers' tracksuits. At first they appeared to be genuinely defending Winnie against violent rivals. 'When they started the Football Club everyone admired them. I did too, we all loved Winnie,' said her neighbour Mrs Dlamini. 'She used to be a mother, she used to be a loving person,' said Nicodemus Sono: 'You will go to Winnie with your grievances: she will help you if she can.'[8] But her neighbours soon suspected that the Football Club was terrorising other Sowetans more than the police: its members had menacing names like Ninja, Killer, Scorpion and Slash, and they often carried guns. Football seemed peripheral: their 'coach' Jerry Richardson had recently left jail, where (it was later revealed) the police had paid him R10,000 to become an informer, and several members were later sentenced for murder or kidnapping. Mandela in jail had been warned about the existence of Winnie's dangerous club, and had said that it should be disbanded.[9] But it was not. The

Football Club was one of many gangs of vigilantes that had grown up in South Africa, but it was one of the most lethal.

Already in early 1987 the back room of Winnie's house was associated with gruesome stories of torture and murders, which neighbours linked to Winnie and the Football Club. And it was clear, as the Truth Commission reported, that 'the chaos emanating from the Mandelas' backyard had useful political ramifications for the police, as it created a discord within the liberation movement that the authorities themselves had never been able to achieve.'[10] Winnie, after all her earlier persecution by the police, now seemed to have little trouble from them as she and her gang drove round Soweto in her minibus with apparent immunity. 'We were running away, struggling to keep our organisations alive,' said Cachalia, 'and Mrs Mandela was driving this Kombi around Soweto. Yes, it was strange.'[11]

By 1988 the Football Club were engaged in a turf war with a rival gang from the neighbouring Daliwonga High School. After fights, beatings and rape, a mob of Daliwonga supporters with petrol cans descended on the Mandela house in July 1988 and set it on fire. The police and fire brigade stood by and watched. Winnie arrived distraught to see her home destroyed, along with the family papers, letters and a slice of cake from her wedding. The young Church leader Frank Chikane, who was at the scene, worried about a further eruption of violence. He summoned a group of leaders including Cyril Ramaphosa, Sydney Mufamadi, Aubrey Mokoena, Sister Bernard Ncube and the Reverend Beyers Naude, who became known as the 'Mandela Crisis Committee'. They suspected that a sinister 'third force' was behind the house-burning, trying to distract the community from the liberation struggle by dividing them.[12] But their first aim was to get Winnie to disband the Football Club.

Mandela soon learnt in jail about the attack on his house, and was mortified by the loss of family treasures. 'The gutting of the house was a wicked act which I deeply detest and condemn,' he wrote to Winnie on 1 August.[13] 'Prison had robbed me of my freedom but not my memories,' he wrote afterwards. 'And now I felt some enemies of the struggle had tried to rob me of even those.' But he told his lawyer Ismail Ayob that he wanted no report to the police, no prosecution or witch-hunt: 'It is a matter that will be resolved by the people of Soweto.'[14]

While the old house was being rebuilt Winnie moved into a more luxurious rented house in Diepkloof, complete with jacuzzi, organised by her entrepreneurial American friend Robert Brown. Her gang moved with her, and they appeared still more uncontrollable, embarking on a 'reign of terror', as the community called it, over the next seven months. A young activist, Lolo Sono, the son of Nicodemus, had worked with Winnie helping MK fighters who had come down from the north. After one of them had been killed by a rival gang Lolo was suddenly accused of being a spy: on 16 November 1988 Winnie came to his home in her minibus, with Lolo inside, bruised and badly beaten, and told his father that he was being taken away. Nicodemus pleaded with her, but 'she wasn't the Winnie that I know. She was very aggressive. She was completely changed in her face.' She drove away. Lolo was never seen again.[15] Five days later the Sonos' neighbour Nomsa Tshabalala came home to find that her son Sibuniso, a friend of Lolo's, had also been taken away after some young men had called looking for him, with his name written on a matchbox. He too was never seen again.[16] The Truth Commission would later hold Winnie responsible for the disappearance of both Lolo and Sibuniso.[17]

Winnie was dominating her home territory, and she resented the influence of the Methodist Mission House in Orlando run by a dedicated priest, Paul Verryn, which provided a sanctuary for local African boys. In mid-December 1988 a fourteen-year-old boy known as 'Stompie' Seipei moved into the mission house: soon afterwards Verryn went on holiday, leaving the place in the charge of a powerful woman, Xoliswa Falati, who spread rumours that Verryn was a homosexual who was interfering with boys; and also that Stompie was a spy. She began interrogating him, and on 29 December he and three other boys were abducted by the Football Club and taken to the back rooms of Winnie's house in Diepkloof, where they were severely beaten by members of the club, led by Jerry Richardson, while Winnie watched. Stompie was singled out as an informer, thrown up and down and brutally assaulted. A few days later his decomposing body was found in a riverbed on the edge of Soweto, riddled with wounds; he had been stabbed three times in the neck. One boy, Katiza Cebekhulu, later claimed to have seen Winnie herself stabbing him twice in the moonlight.[18] But Jerry Richardson claimed to have slit Stompie's throat with shears 'as if slaughtering a sheep', on Winnie's instructions: 'Mami was the main decision-maker . . . I would be instructed to kill and I would do as I was told.'[19]

The Stompie Seipei murder was, said the Truth Commission later, 'one of the most serious crises ever experienced by the internal and external liberation movements'.[20] The Crisis Committee, together with the respected Methodist Bishop Peter Storey, were determined to discover the truth and to defend the other three kidnapped boys, who were still in Winnie's house. On 11 January 1989 they visited Winnie, who assured them that she was merely protecting the boys: but the visitors noticed they had fresh wounds. The Committee sent an agonised report to Tambo in Lusaka, explaining the evidence and Winnie's intransigence: 'She seems to think she is above the community! She shows utter contempt for both the Crisis Committee and the community.' They implored Tambo to act, to 'meet this new ghastly situation that is developing before our very eyes'.[21] On 14 January Frank Chikane wrote to Mandela: 'I have been asked to plead for your intervention . . . Even the lives of the Crisis Committee are at stake.' Mandela was seriously worried: he suspected that Winnie was guilty, but felt obliged as her husband to stand by her unless she was convicted.[22]

By the middle of January Soweto was buzzing with stories about the disappearance of Stompie, while the assaults and murders continued. One hundred and fifty community leaders met to protest against the outrages of the Mandela United Football Club.[23] On 27 January a well-known Indian doctor in Soweto, Abubaker Asvat, was found murdered in his surgery, discovered in a pool of blood by his assistant Albertina Sisulu, the wife of Walter. Two unemployed young Africans had come to the surgery as patients, and were seen running away after the murder; they were later convicted and sentenced. Winnie suggested that Dr Asvat was killed because only he could have proved that the boys in Verryn's house might have been raped.[24] In fact Asvat had earlier seen Stompie's wounds, and had refused to corroborate homosexual rape.

The Crisis Committee had to face an agonising showdown over the Stompie murder, confronting the famous wife of their venerated leader. 'We had to do something bold and imaginative,' said Azhar Cachalia. 'It was one of the most difficult decisions I have ever made.' 'People were at the end of their tether,' said Murphy Morobe, the Publicity Secretary of the Mass Democratic Movement (MDM), which had taken over from the UDF. 'One thing we couldn't afford was for our people to do something on their own.' Morobe called a press conference on 16 February. Winnie would never forgive the 'Indian cabal', as she called them, sneeringly referring to 'Murphy Patel'.[25] Their statement was devastating.

> We are outraged at Mrs Mandela's complicity in the recent abduction and assault of Stompie . . . Had Stompie and his three colleagues not been abducted by Mrs Mandela's 'football team' he would have been alive today . . . We are not prepared to remain silent where those who are violating human rights claim to be doing so in the name of the struggle against apartheid.[26]

How would this affect Winnie's relationship with Mandela, Morobe was asked, and replied: 'Comrade Nelson, in consultation with all the parties, will have to make a decision.'[27] The demands to control Winnie were joined by the weekly *New Nation*, edited by Walter Sisulu's son Zwelakhe: 'Any structure that claims to represent our leaders MUST submit itself to the discipline of the people.'[28]

In Lusaka, Tambo was appalled, and especially worried about the fate of Katiza Cebekhulu, who had now disappeared. He telephoned Frank Chikane in Johannesburg and told him to visit Winnie immediately, and not to leave until she had handed over Katiza. After five painful hours with Winnie, Chikane discovered the boy's whereabouts, and arranged urgent medical attention.[29] Tambo issued his own criticism of Winnie, more subdued than that of the MDM: 'It is with a feeling of terrible sadness that we consider it necessary to express our reservations about Winnie Mandela's judgement in relation to the Mandela Football Club.' She had failed to disband the Football Club, he explained, and had not co-operated with the movement: 'She was left open and vulnerable to committing mistakes which the enemy has exploited.' But he still hoped that Winnie would be reintegrated into the movement. She now appeared briefly under control. 'Comrade Tambo and Comrade Mandela have decided that the best thing the family should do is keep quiet,' she told the Johannesburg *Sunday Times* on 19 February. 'From now on we will be guided by Lusaka.' But she told Dutch television on the same day: 'I am convinced Stompie has not been killed.'[30]

Mandela advised her to be patient and to give no interviews, and wrote to her on 16 February telling her to put the case entirely in the hands of the Crisis Committee, adding: 'Under no circumstances should the tracksuits be used again.' But he partly blamed the conservative media for distortions: their 'real purpose is to destroy images, to sow divisions among the people, and to extend to the Rand the carnage that has plagued certain areas in Natal for several years now. WE MUST BE ABSOLUTELY VIGILANT.'[31]

Fatima Meer, who saw Mandela in jail, was struck by 'his distress, his capacity to assess the situation objectively and his unswerving love for his wife'.[32] When Amina Cachalia saw him in February with her husband Yusuf she found him wanting desperately to believe in Winnie's innocence, and to get her back on track.[33] 'It was a painful time,' said Dullah Omar, who also saw him in jail. 'He was absolutely loyal to Winnie, tirelessly concerned for her welfare, in spite of the movement's distancing itself.'[34]

On 23 February the Methodist priest Stanley Mogoba, who was closely in touch with his bishop Peter Storey, visited Mandela, whom he had known on Robben Island. Mandela accepted that Winnie was at fault. Mogoba explained that Storey had tried to meet her, and that it was she who had broken the press silence. Mandela thanked the Church for all it had done. 'It is an ugly situation,' he agreed. He suggested that Winnie might ask forgiveness at a press conference, and promise to begin again; but Mogoba thought it might be too late.[35] Mandela still hoped to help Winnie. She 'is a wonderful girl; like you,' he wrote to a friend on 28 February. 'I would accordingly urge patience and that you be as supportive as you have always been.'[36]

But in Lusaka, Tambo was now deeply worried about Winnie: 'I knew things were bad,' his wife Adelaide said, 'when he told me, "We must pray for her."'[37] After reports in the Johannesburg *Saturday Star* and *Sunday Times*, Tambo noted in his diary:

Image in tatters w top level
ANC image damaged
Major Gen Joubert investigation: this followed
'Very difficult to find witnesses'
Downward spiral
Nel poised to seek divorce
Thuggery . . .
= Stompie, unearthed
Crisis committee admitted it had dead boy to deal with.
Statement serious allegations against WM
Process interrupted by police announcement
Mandela should act to save himself and ANC

People think divorce imminent
WM denies rift
Tensions in marriage
Political raids[38]

In April the Afrikaner pastor Beyers Naude visited Mandela and then flew up to Lusaka to report to Tambo. Naude warned him that Winnie was 'prone to irrationality', that she was hostile to the Crisis Committee, and that her 'irresponsible behaviour had raised suspicions that she may be co-operating with the enemy'. Tambo asked him, 'Can people seriously think she is working with the system?' Naude replied that some thought so, and that they were angry that Winnie had started her own breakaway women's organisation. Tambo was exasperated, having wanted the new group dissolved: 'It is exactly what we tried to prevent – division.'[39]

By April the Winnie crisis had retreated from the headlines, overtaken by speculation about Mandela's release. The police continued to investigate the Stompie Seipei case, while Sowetans still watched Winnie with mixed feelings. Many of them retained great sympathy for a woman who had been so courageous. Her neighbour Archbishop Tutu, who had asked her to be godmother to a grandchild, was one of them. 'She was a tremendous stalwart of our struggle, an icon of liberation,' he said nine years later, yet 'something went wrong, horribly, badly wrong.'[40] But the Truth Commission would later find that Winnie 'became embroiled in a controversy that caused immeasurable damage to her reputation'; and had no doubt that she was 'politically and morally accountable for the gross violations of human rights committed by the MUFC'.[41]

Mandela himself could never forget how Winnie had kept the struggle alive through the worst days, and had borne the brunt of the government's attacks in his absence. He realised that she had made serious mistakes, and suspected she was guilty; but he would remain loyal, and expected his friends to be loyal, until she was convicted. The murder of Stompie Seipei, and the lawless brutality of the Mandela United Football Club, would haunt his peaceful negotiations over the next decade, as an alternative nightmare of violence.

27

Prisoner v. President

1989–1990

On 9 December 1988 Mandela was driven from the Constantiaberg Clinic to Paarl, the vineyard town thirty-five miles from Cape Town, to the Victor Verster prison, named after a former Director of Prisons. Like Pollsmoor and Robben Island it was a jail with tantalisingly beautiful surroundings. And this time he was taken not to a cell, but to a warder's house, a large, whitewashed bungalow with a spacious garden and a swimming pool. When his four colleagues from Pollsmoor visited two weeks later they were amazed by the comfort and modern gadgetry. Kathrada wrote to his nephew: 'The house itself is big and luxuriously furnished, and has wall-to-wall carpeting throughout. Even the guest rooms have their own bathrooms. The kitchen is high-tech – with stove, microwave, fridge, deep freeze, toaster, percolator . . . He also had a washing machine and a tumble-dryer.'

Mandela was now looked after by friendly warders, including a personal cook, Warrant Officer Jack Swart, who made his favourite breakfast – fishcakes, poached eggs and tea with freshly-baked full-grain bread – and provided elaborate lunches and dinners with wine for visiting guests. Mandela maintained his austere habits: he drank very little, preferred sweet white Nederburg wine, and only reluctantly agreed to order better dry white wine for his guests. He insisted on still making his own bed, and wanted to wash the dishes; he and Swart argued, said James Gregory, like an old married couple. Mandela was surrounded by comfort, but he was now still more cut off from his colleagues. As Kathrada wrote: 'The inescapable fact remains – he is still a prisoner in his lone luxury prison. In some ways we are better off.'[1]

In this privileged isolation, Mandela knew he was being prepared for freedom, but his situation was all the more difficult. He was determined to keep talking with the government, but they had their own agenda of dividing and ruling, and could easily misrepresent his position. He could only fitfully communicate with his allies inside South Africa and in Lusaka; while he had no direct contact with Western governments, which had their own objectives and misunderstandings. He was the spider in the middle of a broken web. But for fourteen extraordinary months he was at the centre of intricate diplomacy with his colleagues, two Presidents and foreign leaders – which would transform his country.

His long secret talks with the government team continued. He told them to stop seeing him as part of the problem, and to accept him as part of the solution. But they remained fearful of releasing him, and still stuck to three conditions which he could not possibly accept: the ANC must renounce the armed struggle, break with the Communist Party and abandon the principle of majority rule.

Mandela still insisted he must talk directly with President Botha, and prepared a careful memorandum for him, which he discussed with his four Pollsmoor colleagues and then gave to the government team. It was accepted in March 1989 as a 'non-paper' rather than an official document, a preliminary to eventual talks. It warned that South Africa was being split into two hostile camps, with blacks and whites slaughtering each other. It went on to explain Mandela's objections to the government's three conditions: 1) The ANC could not renounce violence while the government was not ready to share political power with blacks. 2) The ANC was not controlled by communists – 'at no time has the organisation ever adopted or even co-operated with communism itself' – and it could not break with them. 'Which man of honour will desert a life-long friend at the insistence of a common opponent and still retain a measure of credibility with his people?' 3) The government must accept the principle of majority rule. 'Majority rule and internal peace are like the two sides of a single coin.'

But Mandela ended on a positive note. He recognised that white South Africans were concerned about the ANC's basic demand for majority rule in a unitary state. And he proposed preliminary talks to create the right atmosphere for negotiations. It would be 'a time when all leaders will rise above the setting of preconditions and become themselves part of a great debate for a new South Africa'.[2]

The government team expressed itself disappointed by 'the revolutionary rhetoric in which the ANC has always conducted its propaganda', and claimed to have 'hard intelligence facts' that since 1964 the Communist Party 'had gradually strengthened its grip on the ANC'. They were more encouraged by the last part of the document, which showed 'a readiness to put national interests above sectional interests' and to normalise the situation, and they agreed that South Africans should 'solve their problems without foreign intervention'.[3] But there was no progress towards talks.

In Lusaka, Tambo was becoming more anxious. Mandela had smuggled out to him a copy of his memorandum to P.W. Botha; but Tambo did not show it to the National Executive, worried that they would misunderstand it. He was also concerned that the commitment to secrecy put Mandela at a disadvantage. 'Whereas NM was observing confidentiality,' he said, 'they were not.' Mandela tried to reassure him with a message to Lusaka through Beyers Naude, the trusted Afrikaner pastor. He told Tambo that the country was sliding into civil war, but that the government was 'in deep trouble and looking for a way out'. Mandela's own talks were only trying to bring the major parties to the table, and only the ANC could handle the negotiations, which would be 'a matter of life and death'. Mandela had already had ten meetings with the government team over the past year, he explained: now he had given them a list of people, some in jail, whom he wanted to consult.[4]

Soon afterwards Mandela was visited by his attorney Ismail Ayob – they both assumed they were being bugged. Ayob went up to Lusaka to report to Tambo and the 'President's Committee'. There were anxious discussions. ANC leaders who had seen Mandela's document thought it would get in the way of their campaigns, and Tambo was still worried that Mandela would appear to be giving in, as the minutes recorded: 'It is not for us to ask for negotiation . . . We would be displaying awareness of weakness and disposition to surrender . . . As of now there's no indication that they want to negotiate seriously.' There were concerns too about Mrs Thatcher's objectives. Tambo was suspicious that she was pressing for negotiation now, 'while the movement seems (to her) in disarray'. But Joe Slovo noted that even Thatcher was refusing to visit South Africa unless Mandela was released and the ANC unbanned.

The ANC were especially worried by Mandela's list of people he wanted to consult, including 'kingmakers', which he had given the government. Slovo thought these meetings could be used to divide the ANC, and that Mandela might be 'knocked off his pedestal'. Chris Hani too suspected that the government were trying to destroy Mandela, by leaking their talks with him. Tambo remained concerned about the secrecy, but still trusted Mandela: 'Let him continue; but his whole handling requires adjustment.'[5]

Was Mandela selling out? The ANC inside South Africa were apprehensive about his lone diplomacy. 'He had not consulted,' said Allan Boesak, 'and there was no greater sin in the UDF.' Some leaders, including Govan Mbeki, wanted to visit the people whom Mandela had asked to talk to and tell them not to see him. Mbeki had spent several hours in Mandela's bungalow, and was distressed: 'He seemed either not to have sufficient confidence in me to tell me the full story, or alternatively the other side might have come to some arrangement with him which he felt he couldn't break.' Mbeki insisted that 'no meaningful consultations are possible at Victor Verster.'[6] The rumours about Mandela's ill-health and tuberculosis encouraged suspicions that he was being psychologically weakened and manipulated. No one had seen a photograph of him since 1965. 'His eyes looked so dead,' said one aide in Lusaka. 'We thought he might really have changed.'[7]

But Tambo had now found a way of breaking through the communications barriers and achieving more direct contact. In 1988 he sent Mac Maharaj, the Indian veteran from Robben Island, back into South Africa together with Siphiwe Nyanda, an experienced MK guerrilla known as 'Ghebuza', to establish 'Operation Vula', a top-secret military mission which could connect up with internal activists and provide an 'insurance policy' if negotiations failed. Maharaj had been to Moscow and Amsterdam, where he had acquired false passports and new teeth and lost his beard. He had also been equipped with a laptop computer and a modem, brought out through a friendly KLM hostess, with which he could send coded messages through telephones. The system, devised by two ANC experts in Britain, Tim Jenkin and Ronnie Press, could secretly make a link between Tambo and Mandela.

By April 1989 Tambo was ready to communicate directly with Mandela in his prison-house. Mandela was reluctant to begin underhand activities in the midst of his delicate secret talks; but Maharaj sent a message explaining how he could send memos to Tambo concealed inside book-covers, which could reach Lusaka through a coded computer system. Eventually messages from Mandela began miraculously appearing on the screen in Lusaka. 'The two were now talking in confidence,' said

Tim Jenkin, 'for the first time since the early sixties.' The messages helped to reassure Tambo about Mandela's objectives; but he could not share his top-secret source with his colleagues without jeopardising the system; and he still had great difficulty in persuading his left wing that Mandela was not selling out.[8]

On 28 April there was another tense meeting of the 'President's Committee' in Lusaka, with more worries about Mandela's memorandum. Tambo, summing up, thought that Mandela was incorrect to give the government the names of people he wanted to see, and hoped that he would break the confidentiality of his talks; but 'we really have no reason to say he should discontinue,' and he concluded that 'we cannot really as a matter of policy say he can't ask anybody to see him.'[9]

Tambo encapsulated his own thoughts in his diary:

1. We are not against negotiations in principle but the conditions therefor have not matured.
2. Mandela is not negotiating but is facilitating a meeting of the SAR and ANC – to forestall a bloodbath, as he sees it. He makes that clear.
3. The problem for us is not what he tells the team when they visit him, but that we do not know what they say to one another. This is vital information without which we could not in any case meet the regime, especially because they would be fully briefed about the nature and content of the talks over these many months.
4. Therefore we agree he should continue to maintain the contact but that he must confide in us about the discussions with them.[10]

The worries and bewilderment in Lusaka were hardly surprising. In the words of Barbara Masekela, who was there at that time: 'There's always a paranoia in exile. You know it's about to happen, but you're not in control. You have to take a step forward which may be wrong. There's guessing and second-guessing. People have sacrificed their whole youth for the struggle, and they're reluctant to make the leap: some people can pose themselves into the new situation, but some can't.'[11]

Their suspicions were well-grounded. The government certainly hoped to detach Mandela and split the ANC, and to make a separate deal with Buthelezi. But they had misread Mandela's ability and toughness. 'They'd never dealt with black people of that calibre,' said George Bizos, who was seeing Mandela frequently at his bungalow (he noticed that even the flowerbed was bugged). 'They thought they could corrupt him, like Matanzima or Mangope. He did not deceive them. It was their misjudgement which led to his release. Once they had started to negotiate they couldn't go back, because of the ungovernability. At Victor Verster Mandela was already taking charge.'[12]

Sisulu, who in Pollsmoor had sporadic contact with Mandela, shared that view: 'They would have misjudged him. They regarded us as wild people including Madiba. When they saw a reasonable tone, they misjudged the person. It's easy to underestimate Madiba when he's nice – without knowing his stubbornness in approach . . . They look at the softness of the soft line: he is not aggressive, he is not wild. Then the possibilities are imagined to be there: to get Mandela. The National Party were prepared to discuss because the leadership would come from them, not from the ANC.'[13]

Whatever the government's expectations, they were soon thrown into confusion: for in January 1989 P.W. Botha had a stroke. It incapacitated him for a month, while the diehard Cabinet Minister Chris Heunis became Acting President, spreading further gloom among foreign diplomats. 'With his lugubrious moustache,' said Robin Renwick, 'he always reminded me of a dead walrus.'[14] After a month Botha stood down from the leadership of the National Party, unwisely assuming he could remain State President.

The party had to elect a new leader, and they chose not the moderate candidate, the liberal Minister of Finance Barend du Plessis, but the apparently conservative Minister of Education F.W. de Klerk. He looked unpromising to most foreign leaders, including Thatcher: 'She thought he was just another bloody Boer,' as her Private Secretary Charles Powell put it.[15] De Klerk had resisted many of P.W. Botha's reforms, and had been shocked when the Foreign Minister Pik Botha had said he was prepared to serve under a future black president. De Klerk was not imposing: 'a small man with bad skin and worse taste in clothes', the *Financial Times* correspondent Patti Waldmeir noted. 'He spoke English badly, smoked heavily, and seemed, somehow, shifty.' British diplomats were encouraged that he listened, was accessible and had no 'side'. And the ANC were hopeful when he promised the National Party caucus a 'great leap forward' and insisted that he had a mandate to talk to everyone.[16] But he gave little promise of a bold change of policy.

Mandela and Tambo both looked to the world outside, particularly to Britain, to avert a bloodbath through the pressure of sanctions. But Tambo was becoming exasperated by Mrs Thatcher's intransigence, all the more after she branded the ANC as terrorists at the Commonwealth Summit in Vancouver in October 1987. She wanted to visit Mandela in prison, but Tambo was strongly opposed to it, suspecting she would try to separate him from the ANC: 'We couldn't allow it,' he said in December 1988. 'She must get him *out* of jail.' Tambo was baffled by British attitudes, as he explained in London in January 1989: 'I don't know what is going to change diplomatic attitudes in London, they're so insensitive. I suppose a horrific massacre. It's very difficult to excuse Mrs Thatcher for saying that the ANC are terrorists, because we are the victims. She's totally blind: she can only see the violence of the ANC. It was Britain which landed us with this racism.'

There were further rumours that Britain planned to broker an eventual negotiation in London, where Southern African states would press the ANC towards agreement.[17] In late March Thatcher toured Africa for a week, ending in Namibia, which was moving towards independence, where she sharply warned Pik Botha against a counter-attack on SWAPO. She could not visit South Africa, she said, until Mandela was released. But her line was not encouraging to the ANC. She talked about one man one vote, but not necessarily under a unitary state.[18] She discussed with Buthelezi and other visitors the possibility of alternative federal constitutions, like the Swiss system of cantons. There were growing signs of 'divide and rule'.

The ANC were all the more puzzled by Thatcher's hostility when so many influential Afrikaners were in touch with them and wanted de Klerk to start talks; they included Pieter de Lange of the Broederbond, Johan Heyns, the head of the Dutch Reformed Church, Willie Esterhuyse of Stellenbosch University and Wimpie de Klerk, the future President's brother. 'So why is Mrs Thatcher moving in a different direction,' Thabo Mbeki asked, 'apparently accepting group rights and rejecting talks with the ANC?' Mbeki still hoped that Thatcher could play a peacemaking role: when he met again with leading Afrikaners (including Wimpie de Klerk) at a Gold Fields conference in April, he thought that Mrs Thatcher might be a mediator between the ANC and the South African government;

but she decided that 'any attempt to play a direct role from outside would be unwelcome'.[19]

The ANC achieved a new breakthrough in June 1989 when a conference of lawyers met in Oxfordshire, funded by the Ford Foundation and chaired by the lawyer-philosopher Ronald Dworkin, on the Concept of Law in South Africa. It was attended by senior South African judges and ANC lawyers, and a British Law Lord, Lord Oliver – with Tambo and Thabo Mbeki in the background. But it was shunned by Thatcher. Other British Ministers, including Geoffrey Howe, Chris Patten and Lynda Chalker, wanted to recognise the ANC: 'It's only Mrs Thatcher who stops them,' said one of her staff. 'She really *is* conservative.'[20]

Mandela was reluctant to criticise Mrs Thatcher openly. He had admired the strong woman who could do business with Gorbachev, and realised she could have a unique influence on Pretoria. He was impressed by accounts of her Ambassador Robin Renwick, and in March 1988 he sent a message through his Cape Town lawyer Hymie Bernadt welcoming Thatcher's stand against apartheid 'notwithstanding his difference of opinion on the sanctions issue'.[21] But after the message was misleadingly leaked Mandela wrote to Renwick on 10 April, firmly denying that he had written directly to Thatcher: 'I would have preferred to do so in the course of a face-to-face discussion with you in person.' He still concluded: 'I am happy to request you to pass my very best wishes to the Prime Minister.'[22]

The ANC were now putting more hope in the new American administration under George Bush. The new man in charge of Africa at the State Department, Herman Cohen, soon committed himself publicly to equal political rights for all South Africans, and described apartheid as 'an outrageous human rights catastrophe'. By May Bush was distancing himself from Pretoria by talking to a delegation of black South Africans led by Archbishop Tutu, and by inviting Albertina Sisulu to report on human rights.[23]

The CIA were becoming more sceptical of the right-wing depiction of the ANC as dangerous communists. In March 1988, when Bush was Vice-President, they had produced a secret analysis of the ANC (partly declassified in 1996) which showed a clear respect for Tambo's leadership. While seventeen out of twenty-seven members of the National Executive were probably communists, said the report, there were 'only a handful of committed black members inside South Africa', and Tambo had 'long been subtly curbing and channelling SACP influence'. The ANC's consensus system, said the CIA, worked remarkably well; the ANC was becoming less patronising to the UDF and the internal opposition; and was likely to 'continue to pursue its two-track policy of maintaining close ties to [Soviet] Bloc countries while expanding contacts in the West'. In sum, the ANC had met the challenges of the last few years 'by maintaining its organisational cohesion, retaining its dominant position in the anti-apartheid movement, and broadening its contacts with the West'.[24] But ten months later, in January 1989, the CIA noted that the 'stalemate' in South Africa would not be broken 'barring a dramatic shift . . . such as the unconditional – and highly unlikely – release of jailed ANC leader Nelson Mandela'.[25]

Both Washington and London seemed to be playing a double game by building up Chief Buthelezi. The ANC saw this as supporting de Klerk's policy of group rights – which would enable him to release Mandela while dividing the tribes, and thus maintain the government's control of them. Sisulu reckoned afterwards: 'Not only Thatcher, I think America and Germany too were working on a definite plan to promote Buthelezi in every possible way, and receiving reports of the reaction of Mandela.'[26] Mandela seemed more trusting of Buthelezi: after receiving his greetings on his seventieth birthday he thanked him warmly and hoped his cordial relations with Tambo could be restored, while stressing the crucial need for unity: any act or statement which worsened division, he warned, would be a fatal error.[27] But Tambo, having once been betrayed by Buthelezi, feared that the Zulu leader would exploit the friendship with Mandela.

What was de Klerk really up to? In May Tambo tried to assess him, in his careful handwriting in his notebook:

> - Typical Nationalist Party politician – conservative. – Differs from PW in that he relies on argument and reason instead of wagging a finger and silencing debate.
> - Is therefore capable of being persuaded by reality.

But he also reckoned that de Klerk was 'firm on group rights – not negotiable'; and that 'majority rule was totally unacceptable' to him. Colleagues had warned Tambo to 'be careful, be cautious, do not rush into negotiations . . . be careful what you give away now, you may wish you had not done so should in future the balance of forces turn in your favour'.[28]

De Klerk's links with the British government continued to worry the ANC. In June he toured Europe to reassure foreign leaders, including Mrs Thatcher, who said afterwards that 'there is a new climate in South Africa.' But the ANC now worried that she wanted a solution based on 'group protection', backed by Buthelezi, as they explained in a 'Report on Consultations' on 6 June. 'We don't see how she can be an honest broker,' said the ANC diplomat Aziz Pahad, 'when she is so closely allied to the regime.'[29]

Back in South Africa de Klerk was now taking control of government. He presided over his party's federal congress and unveiled a five-year plan of action to prepare for the elections in September 1989. It promised to end discrimination and to introduce a democratic constitution, but put more emphasis on 'group rights', which would effectively divide the non-white population. President Botha was being very visibly sidelined, and he reacted bitterly by refusing to attend a gala banquet in his honour.

The internal black rebellion was now showing signs of a strong revival after the devastating crackdowns. Tambo had heralded 1989 as a 'Year of Mass Action for People's Power', and his call was followed by a new surge of protest. In January prisoners on Robben Island went on a prolonged hunger strike which eventually persuaded the government to release nine hundred detainees, including key UDF leaders. In February the UDF regrouped, in alliance with the trades unions of COSATU, into a 'Mass Democratic Movement' (MDM) which quickly launched a Defiance Campaign to challenge segregated institutions, beginning with processions of black patients arriving at white hospitals – where doctors and nurses agreed to treat them. The Churches were becoming more militant, with Archbishop Tutu in the van. And the armed struggle was becoming more effective, with attacks on policemen and government buildings, culminating in a successful mortar attack on a radar station in May. It was, wrote Tom Lodge, 'a remarkable upswing in the movement's fortunes'; while the new government, facing growing international criticism and a continuing economic crisis, appeared to lack the resources and resolve for more ruthless military suppression.[30]

P.W. Botha was still State President, even though politically weakened; and it was in this uneasy interim that Mandela received the invitation he had been waiting for for two years. Botha had often (he told me) asked his intelligence chief Niël Barnard: 'When is Mandela coming to see me?' to be told that the time was not ripe. But in mid-1989 Barnard said that

Mandela wanted to talk to him, and that the time was ripe. Botha agreed to 'a general discussion'.[31] On 4 July the gentlemanly General Willemse told Mandela he would be seeing President Botha for a 'courtesy call' early the next morning. Mandela, conscious as always of his image, was determined to make the right impression; he asked for a new suit, reread all his notes, and rehearsed what he would say.[32] It was the ultimate test of his dignity, to outface the man notorious for his bullying and finger-wagging: the prisoner confronting the President. 'He'd always felt that the government had treated blacks as children,' said one of his colleagues. 'He was determined to meet the President on a basis of equality.'[33]

Mandela was driven first to breakfast with General Willemse, then to the garage below the President's offices in the Tuynhuys, next to Parliament. Entering secretly by lift, he found Kobie Coetsee, Niël Barnard and others waiting nervously for him in the anteroom. Major Marais, the prison commander, carefully retied his shoelaces. 'I was tense,' Mandela recalls, 'because I was expecting a fight.'[34]

But Botha was in his most courteous mode. He strode towards the famous prisoner he had never met, smiling, hand outstretched, with disarming friendliness. They sat down at the table with Coetsee and Barnard; while Botha to Mandela's amazement poured the tea himself. They talked relaxedly for half an hour about South African history and culture: about the Boer War, African Presidents and Matanzima in the Transkei. Mandela suggested that the Afrikaners were really 'the first freedom fighters', and compared his own struggle (as he had often before) with the Afrikaner rebellion against the government in the First World War. He explained how he had come to know the Afrikaners better in prison. Botha said that Mandela could contribute to a peaceful solution; but he must not forget the contribution Afrikaners could make. At the end, Mandela, more tensely, asked for the release of all political prisoners, which Botha politely refused. But they agreed about the need for peace, prepared a minimal statement, and parted genially. 'It was one of the pleasantest interviews I have had,' Mandela recalled. 'He treated me with respect, very correctly. That is the image I have of him.'[35] Niël Barnard thought the atmosphere was so convivial that it must be 'just a matter of time' before Mandela was released. But there was some tension when Mandela brought up the subject of immediately releasing Sisulu. Botha seemed sympathetic, but Barnard had to explain to Mandela on the way back to prison that it would take time to persuade the bureaucracy, which infuriated Mandela. The meeting was photographed by one of the aides, recording a genial, informal scene. It was also tape-recorded by Botha's staff, but Barnard afterwards had the tape destroyed (to the fury of Botha, who claimed Barnard 'stabbed me in the back').[36]

Mandela saw Botha crossing the Rubicon he had shirked three years before. And his relationship with the 'Crocodile' proved oddly enduring. The official statement blandly described the meeting as an 'informal courtesy visit' in which the two men 'availed themselves of the opportunity to confirm their support for peaceful developments in Southern Africa'. Mandela endorsed it, while explaining that it showed 'no deviation from the position I have taken over the past twenty-eight years': that only a dialogue with the ANC could bring peace to the country.[37] But the promise to support peaceful developments was not hollow: Mandela and Botha would trust each other more than either trusted de Klerk; and many of Botha's colleagues, including Barnard, would insist that Botha did much more to achieve reconciliation than de Klerk.[38]

Most journalists and politicians assumed that President Botha's talk with Mandela was intended to upstage de Klerk. If so, it was to no avail. Six weeks later Botha resigned in a furious televised speech, complaining that 'I am being ignored by ministers serving in my cabinet,' and was succeeded, much against his will, by de Klerk.

The new President still showed no desire for a fundamental change of direction: he was concerned (said his brother Wimpie) about the impracticability of apartheid, not its immorality.[39] But he was a clear-sighted pragmatist and he was very aware of the economic crisis. He soon realised how circumscribed were his choices: all roads led to Mandela.

In his prison bungalow Mandela was becoming more accessible to family and friends. In July he celebrated his seventy-first birthday, spending four hours with Winnie and fifteen other members of his family, including children and grandchildren. His four colleagues from Pollsmoor were also brought to see him – for the first time since December. Kathrada was allowed a brand-new suit for the occasion: 'It does a great deal to boost one's individuality,' he wrote. 'More important is the ability to *choose* something . . . It gives one a nice feeling even to be able to specify the colour of a tie, or a pattern of a jersey.' The arrival of suits had encouraged rumours of release, though Kathrada remained sceptical as always. 'There is absolutely nothing to indicate that anything will happen in the foreseeable future,' he insisted to Eddie Daniels.[40] There was a special expectation that Sisulu would be released. Since 15 March he had been in Mandela's old cells in Pollsmoor, separated from the other three. 'Beware the Ides of March,' Kathrada joked with him. But the government were still worried about releasing Sisulu before the forthcoming elections: the team asked Mandela several times to warn Sisulu not to make trouble.[41] But they did not let him out.

The government dithered. On 19 August Mandela again met with the team, led as before by Coetsee and Barnard, who produced their own document or 'non-paper' in reply to his memorandum to Botha. It recognised that the two sides had points of contact about a 'pre-negotiating stage', while rejecting many of Mandela's arguments: but it proposed further discussions after the elections in September.[42]

Up in Lusaka, Tambo was now under more stress, trying to hold the ANC and its allies together. He remained totally loyal to Mandela: he still insisted on calling himself Acting President, keeping the presidency vacant for his friend. 'He willed that Mandela should be a giant,' said Barbara Masekela. 'If he had wanted to be President he would have taken better care of himself.'[43] He was now visibly exhausted as he flew constantly between Zambia, Europe and America, battling for recognition and support. His doctors were repeatedly warning him to rest. He was the same age as Mandela, but the strains outside jail were greater, as Mandela had foreseen. And Tambo faced his hardest task in rallying the ANC behind the commitment to talks, which Mandela had begun.

To open the way to a negotiation, Tambo had to bring the ANC together with the front-line states with a definitive statement. On 21 August the Organisation for African Unity met in Zimbabwe and endorsed a document Tambo had carefully prepared and which Mandela had been shown in draft. The 'Harare Declaration' was strikingly conciliatory in both tone and content: while it still backed the armed struggle, it emphasised that hostilities could be suspended after the release of political prisoners, the unbanning of the ANC and the removal of troops from the townships. It clearly distanced itself from the revolutionary wing that believed in the 'seizure of power'. African leaders, it said, 'have repeatedly expressed our preference for a solution arrived at by peaceful means'. In fact the armed struggle was ineffective; the guerrillas of MK were infiltrating across the borders into South Africa only to be ambushed, captured and tortured as the South African army tightened its intelligence through informers and interrogation.[44] The ANC were looking to sanctions, rather than war, to press Pretoria to negotiate.

Mandela saw the Harare Declaration as a crucial breakthrough, putting the onus on Pretoria to provide the conditions for talks, while foreseeing a peaceful context for his own release.[45] And the world welcomed it. 'It establishes both climate and framework,' as the *Financial Times* commented, 'for negotiations in which he is expected to play a key role.'[46] It was a personal triumph for Tambo, but it nearly killed him. A few days before the meeting he collapsed with a serious stroke and was flown to the London Clinic, where 'Mr Reginald' began his long therapy and convalescence, gradually relearning to speak and to walk. Mandela was deprived of his most trusted link with the outside world.

De Klerk was now moving more quickly. In the general elections on 6 September the National Party achieved an uncertain victory, with only 48 per cent of the popular vote, while both the right-wing Conservative Party and the more liberal Democratic Party made gains. But de Klerk saw the result as a mandate for change. He was being pressed from all sides to release Mandela – by the central bank, by Western governments, and by Afrikaner intellectuals who included his own brother Wimpie, who had been meeting the ANC in Britain. Wimpie was on tenterhooks, watching de Klerk's conversion step by step: 'I couldn't believe my ears at some of the things he told me in confidence.'[47] De Klerk was soon showing himself much more realistic and rational than Botha. 'I've learnt the lesson of Rhodesia,' he told Robin Renwick: 'Don't leave it too late to negotiate with the real leaders.'[48] And in the meantime the Afrikaners were becoming more isolated than ever, as the world's scapegoats: in a blockbuster movie of 1989, *Lethal Weapon 2*, the villains had Afrikaner accents.

The talks between the ANC and government officials had been continuing under their own momentum, masterminded by Barnard, without de Klerk being fully informed. The contacts reached a new intimacy a week after the elections in a dramatic meeting in Switzerland. Barnard's deputy head of intelligence, Mike Louw, together with his spymaster Maritz Spaarwater, met secretly in a room at the Palace Hotel in Lucerne with Thabo Mbeki and his ANC colleague Jacob Zuma. 'Well here we are, bloody terrorists – and for all you know fucking communists as well,' Mbeki joked as they met. He and Louw talked through the night, clearly indicating that they were prepared to negotiate, and Louw passed a message personally to de Klerk at the Tuynhuys. De Klerk was at first shocked to hear about the breakthrough: who had given Louw permission to negotiate? But when Louw produced his authorisation – to investigate, not to negotiate – de Klerk listened eagerly and (Louw noted) 'took the ball and ran with it'.[49]

De Klerk knew he must release the ANC leaders, but Mandela was now calling most of the shots, as the secret correspondence shows. A week after the elections Mandela again met Coetsee, and told him that de Klerk should highlight the release of ten political prisoners – including Sisulu and Kathrada – whose political behaviour would be 'low key'; while he urged the prisoners not to stir up the crowds as Govan Mbeki and Harry Gwala had done.[50]

The ANC both outside and inside South Africa were concerned about the low-key approach, for they wanted to generate 'heightened activity'. On 9 October the leadership in Lusaka put out their own plan of action, which stressed that the released leaders should reaffirm their commitment and mobilise support for the Harare Declaration. When the working committee discussed it, Thabo Mbeki thought the released leaders must 'take their place at the head of the struggle'. Chris Hani insisted that the comrades 'can't afford to diffuse the spirit of the people', and Jacob Zuma warned that the government had deliberately counterposed Mandela and Harry Gwala. Joe Slovo maintained that Mandela would only be released as a result of 'heightened activity'.[51]

But while the ANC were talking, the government announced on 10 October that they would soon release eight prisoners, including Sisulu and Kathrada, without conditions. Kathrada refused to believe it until he saw it announced on television.[52] But they were released, into an atmosphere which was far from low key. Supporters marched through the cities, the banned flags of the ANC and the Communist Party were unfurled. Sisulu promised that the country's political future would be 'determined by the leadership of the movement', and called for an intensification of economic sanctions.[53] The ANC remained very wary of the government's motives for the releases. 'They represent a coldly-executed political manoeuvre,' said the *New Nation*, 'a desperate effort to take the initiative away from the people.' But if this was so, the manoeuvre showed no signs of succeeding; and none of the eight released prisoners showed any weakening of their resolve. 'If it is necessary for me to go back to prison, I'll go tomorrow,' said Andrew Mlangeni.[54]

They had some difficulty in adjusting to normal life after a quarter of a century in jail: Sisulu could never again sleep in the dark after getting accustomed to the lightbulb in his cell. Kathrada could never face driving on the motorways which now criss-crossed Johannesburg.[55] But they were also surprised by the lack of changes. Sisulu returned to the same small house he had always lived in with his wife Albertina, picking up where he had left off.* 'Much of Soweto has not changed since I first came to live here in the thirties,' said Sisulu. 'With few exceptions the matchbox houses are very much the same. A government who is not addressing the basic issue of decent housing is not seriously committed towards political change.'[56]

Their freedom opened up new contacts with the West: President Bush even wrote to Sisulu to congratulate him. Mandela had wanted Sisulu and his colleagues to fly to London to see Mrs Thatcher, but they resisted, still suspicious of her agenda, with some reason.[57] Thatcher had remained totally opposed to sanctions: at the Commonwealth Summit in Kuala Lumpur in October she issued her own separate statement which left her new Foreign Secretary John Major (according to his officials) 'gobsmacked' and 'flabbergasted'.[58] And just before Sisulu's release Thatcher had again pointedly welcomed Buthelezi, as her ally against sanctions.

Though still largely confined to Kwazulu-Natal, Buthelezi's Inkatha Party was becoming more threatening as the ANC came closer to recognition. On 19 November a rally of 70,000 Zulus in Durban celebrated their King's twenty-year reign. The King, the nephew of Buthelezi, called for talks with the ANC, but the lethal attacks on ANC supporters continued. Mrs Thatcher continued to depict Inkatha as a force independent of Pretoria, but American intelligence was already aware of its links with the government and the development of a 'third force'. Mrs Thatcher was openly supporting Buthelezi while he was known to be secretly conniving with Pretoria to destabilise the country. A CIA *Africa Review* in January 1990 reported:

> We believe South African security forces have trained and armed Inkatha paramilitary groups. Reporting from a variety of sources

* When I revisited him in Soweto after twenty-six years he warned me to lock my car: 'Remember how Patrick Duncan had his coat stolen there.'

> suggests that, at a minimum, government security forces aided Inkatha by selectively allowing the violence to continue.[59]

Mandela was now the only major opposition leader left in prison. It reinforced his unique authority and leadership. It was harder for anyone to accuse him of betraying his own people, as he had spent longer in jail than anyone. And he was still pressing for talks. Many hard-liners or bitter-enders within the ANC wanted to intensify the armed struggle to achieve the 'seizure of power', and saw the continuing violence as the beginning of the 'rolling revolution'. But Mandela warned all his visitors about the dangers of civil war: 'In any country, even if there is war, there is time for negotiations,' he told Albertina Sisulu.[60]

Mandela was watching President de Klerk like a hawk. He was impressed by his concessions. De Klerk had allowed a big protest march in Cape Town on 13 September, led by Tutu and Boesak, to take place without police interference. In the next months he dismantled many restrictions of 'petty apartheid', including segregated beaches, parks, lavatories and restaurants, and dissolved the semi-military network, the National Security Management System, which secretly controlled the townships. In his inaugural speech on 20 September de Klerk had promised to talk to any group committed to peace, and Mandela immediately asked for a meeting, writing to de Klerk restating that the time was ripe 'to negotiate an effective political settlement', while emphasising that he could not consult with the ANC, and refusing to break the ANC links with the Communist Party.[61] 'No self-respecting freedom fighter will take orders from the government . . . on who his allies in the freedom struggle should be.'[62] In the meantime Mandela continued to talk to the government team, now augmented by de Klerk's Minister for Constitutional Affairs Gerrit Viljoen, while he waited for the President to respond and extended his own contacts.

Mandela could now welcome friends to his prison-house in much more comfortable style. Fatima Meer, who was revising her biography of him, was amazed by the peaceful setting: she and Ismail were met at the main gate by Gregory in plain clothes, driven past rows of staff cottages, along an avenue of conifers and an orange grove, past cows and ducks to the bungalow, where they were embraced by Mandela. He appeared much fitter than when she had last seen him, looking sallow, on Robben Island seventeen years earlier. 'Tall, debonair and without a trace of fat on his lean frame. His hair is flecked with grey; his face remains unwrinkled; he smiles readily and often, his eyes crinkling at the corners; his laughter is deep-throated and spontaneous.' In his house 'every appointment bore the mark of decorative comfort'.

'What was this all about?' Fatima asked herself. 'It dawned on me that it was not only South Africa's disenfranchised who saw their hopes reflected in him but that the government too was hoping to resolve its problems through him.' Mandela was worried, he told her, that people would expect too much after his release; but 'if all these super-expectations can be overcome, I can work nicely'.[63]

He could re-meet friends from every stage of his life. One was his first employer in 1941, the lawyer Lazar Sidelsky. Mandela introduced him to his warder as 'the only white man who's my boss', and Sidelsky noted that Mandela was giving orders to a white warder. He recalled to Mandela how he had warned him fifty years earlier that if he went into politics he would find himself in jail: 'Look where you ended up!'[64]

Mandela's new friend Mamphela Ramphele brought her two sons (at his insistence), with whom he chatted about tennis and TV. She and Mandela agreed on most subjects, but she argued against the ANC's policy of reviving the old chiefs through the Congress of Traditional Leaders, which she thought was both anti-democratic and sexist. Mandela was upset, and defended the policy on her next visit, explaining how the ANC needed to bring the chiefs into the fold of liberation politics.[65]

He was visited by Eddie Daniels, his old friend from Robben Island, who was now a teacher and married to a Scots woman; Daniels's whole school gathered to give him messages to Mandela before his visit. 'I went there to cheer him up, to take his mind off his huge responsibilities,' said Daniels. He recited the poem 'Invictus' ('I am the master of my fate'); they hugged each other and sang 'Mary of Argyle'. Daniels found Mandela's face tighter with the anxiety of his lonely decisions, under tremendous strain and tension. But 'he was still the same Nelson.'[66]

Mandela had some apprehensions about not recognising the South Africa he had left three decades ago. 'I sometimes fear that by the time I return, the world itself will have disappeared,' he wrote to the owners of Kapitans restaurant, his old haunt in the fifties. He had heard that Kapitans was being closed down: 'There are many palates and tummies inside and outside the country which will justifiably be outraged by the disastrous news.' (The restaurant survived, and his letter is now framed on the wall.)[67]

De Klerk now knew that he must release Mandela and recognise the ANC, but he had to bring his cabinet with him. In early December he assembled them for two days in a game lodge near Botswana for a *bosberaad*, or bush conference. Some ministers argued fiercely against the plan, particularly Magnus Malan, the hawkish Minister of Defence who opposed legalising the Communist Party which he had so long been fighting. But the Red Menace was not what it was: the previous month the Berlin Wall had come down, which gave de Klerk a new impetus to act. 'It was as if God had taken a hand – a new turn in world history,' he told his brother Wimpie soon afterwards. 'We had to seize the opportunity. The risk that the ANC was being used as a Trojan horse by a superpower had drastically diminished.'[68]

Soon after the bush conference de Klerk agreed to Mandela's request for a meeting. Mandela again carefully prepared a memorandum, updating his earlier one to Botha, welcoming de Klerk's call for reconciliation and his commitment to peace. But he was concerned that the government was continuing apartheid by other means, by conspiring with black homelands and co-opting their leaders. The violent conflict, said Mandela, was draining the country's lifeblood, and peace could only be achieved through talks with the ANC, without preconditions. As the first stage, in keeping with the Harare Declaration, he called for de Klerk to end the emergency, to lift all bans and to remove troops from the townships.[69]

On 13 December he was driven again to the Tuynhuys to see the President – again with Coetsee and Barnard. The atmosphere was more relaxed than with Botha. De Klerk had studied the psychological profiles of Mandela's personality, so was not surprised (he told me) by his courtesy and magnanimity; what impressed him was his comprehension of Afrikaner history and sufferings, as a parallel to those of his own people.[70] Mandela knew something about de Klerk's political pedigree, and had heard from black friends that he had a reputation as a decent lawyer. He tried to see the problems from de Klerk's viewpoint, and was surprised to find de Klerk actually listening, and responding. Mandela criticised the National Party's commitment to 'group rights', which the world would rightly see as an extension of apartheid. De Klerk explained that he was trying to allay white fears of black domination – which Mandela himself had told P.W. Botha the ANC must do. Mandela insisted that 'group rights' would only increase black fears. In that case, said De Klerk, 'we will have to change it'.

Mandela then reiterated that he could not accept any conditions, and that the ANC must be unbanned. De Klerk made no promises, but Mandela left the meeting reassured. He believed (as he reported to Lusaka) that de Klerk was a genuine departure from his predecessors, with whom he could do business.[71] De Klerk on his side seemed unmoved by the encounter, according to his aides. But he told his brother Wimpie that Mandela was 'a man with tremendous style... He is a politician to be reckoned with.'[72]

Mandela was now being allowed to see all kinds of politicians in his prison-house – though no diplomats or journalists, for Pretoria was nervous that the UN or foreign governments might try to intervene. Robben Islanders still serving sentences, leaders of the Mass Democratic Movement, lawyers, clerics, trades unionists, academics and youth leaders all converged on the bungalow. It was now not so much a prison, said his lawyer George Bizos, as the office from which the leader of the ANC was conducting his business. 'He held court like Peter the Great of Russia,' said his old friend Dr Motlana.[73] Mandela spent much time with his Cape Town lawyer, Dullah Omar, a Muslim with big soulful eyes who worked out the details of his likely release.

Mandela caused some alarm within the ANC when in November he saw Richard Maponya, a rich black businessman and racehorse owner who had been accused of collaborating with the government. But Mandela recalled gratefully how Maponya had held a party for him and his friends in 1960.[74] Mandela told him (as Maponya reported it) that he was concerned about the problems of running big businesses, and suggested that nationalisation was not the best way to black empowerment: an independent South Africa must not, like some of its neighbours, become economically bankrupt.[75] That disturbed many ANC leaders, who saw the Freedom Charter being betrayed. But two months later Mandela made a statement reaffirming the ANC's commitment to nationalising mines, banks and monopoly industries. That remained the official policy, but Tambo and others in Lusaka had been considering ideas about a mixed economy; and like the British Labour Party's old Clause Four, nationalising was not to be taken too literally. (When businessmen asked Tambo about it, he would reply that the ANC's policies were similar to Robert Mugabe's in Zimbabwe; and Mugabe, while preaching state ownership, had nationalised nothing.) Businessmen anyway were not too worried: by late January 1990 the Johannesburg stock market was reaching record highs.[76]

Mandela was even allowed to telephone Lusaka and speak directly to banished friends who after nearly thirty years were now in closer contact with the country. Sisulu and his other released colleagues were given passports to fly to Lusaka, where they were received with ecstasy. Sisulu embraced his son Max after twenty-seven years, and Govan Mbeki was reunited with his son Thabo.[77] The three strands of the struggle which had been separated for nearly three decades – exiles, prisoners and internal activists – were beginning to intertwine.

But radical leaders, both outside and inside South Africa, still suspected that Mandela might be selling out, and betraying the revolution. When eighteen internal activists visited him in late 1989 some who had last seen him in prison clothes on Robben Island were shocked by his immaculate suit and conservatism, and his praise of de Klerk. 'This man is finished,' Eric Molobi said to himself. Guerrilla fighters within MK were more worried that before they had even begun the real battles, Mandela's negotiations would forestall their 'seizure of power'.[78] Within South Africa the ideological arguments were coming into the open, as the government relaxed its controls over protests and red flags; and the old debates in Robben Island re-emerged in public as the prospect of power became more realistic. Govan Mbeki was working with a Marxist 'collective' in the Eastern Cape which became more vocal, and remained uncompromising. 'The aim of the working class,' Mbeki reminded his followers in early December, 'is to take over the entire surplus value it has created.'[79]

But Mandela took care to leak a copy of his ten-page memo for de Klerk to Lusaka, and to make clear that he was committing himself to nothing. 'He is not negotiating,' said an ANC spokesman. 'He is facilitating the process for the government to sit down with the ANC.' And Mandela was using his splendid isolation to unify rather than divide. 'There is only one ANC,' Kathrada said on his behalf. 'It has been in existence since 1912 and it still exists today.'[80] Most of Mandela's visitors saw him as a conciliator and peacemaker, seeking to patch up old quarrels. He remained, above all, the loyal member of the ANC, determined to maintain party unity, as all his statements and talks had made clear.

Hopes for Mandela's release rose and fell over the New Year of 1990.

On 8 January Winnie, after visiting him for three hours, emerged to say: 'I don't think we are talking about months . . . this is the real thing.' But three weeks later there were still some problems, she explained, about the unbanning of the ANC. 'The price of his release is the change of history in this country.'[81]

The future of the country now rested on two lonely men. President de Klerk had kept to himself through the long Christmas summer holiday, preparing for the decision he could not avoid. The pressures from abroad were still building up and the economic crisis was becoming acute. 'Internationally we were teetering on the edge of the abyss,' de Klerk later told his brother Wimpie.[82] Mrs Thatcher, through her Ambassador Robin Renwick, promised de Klerk that when he released Mandela she would reciprocate by rescinding sanctions, including the ban on new investment.[83] By mid-January, de Klerk was writing by hand the speech he would make at the opening of Parliament on 2 February. He consulted only his close advisers, not his party caucus or his wife Marike, a conventional Afrikaner who was perplexed by his silence and his policies, and who compared Mandela to the Nazi prisoner Rudolf Hess.[84] When the British Minister for Overseas Development Lynda Chalker congratulated him on his courage, he replied that he had trouble persuading 'another woman': in fact, it turned out, the marriage was already in trouble.[85] On the day before his speech de Klerk had another row with his Minister of Defence Magnus Malan about legalising the Communist Party; but de Klerk insisted that maintaining the ban would only perpetuate political campaigns. At midnight on 1 February he sent Mrs Thatcher a message that she would not be disappointed by his speech.[86]* At last Parliament assembled for the speech. Despite all the predictions, it astonished almost everyone. In a few minutes de Klerk reversed nearly all his predecessors' policies over the past three decades. All political organisations, including the ANC and the South African Communist Party, would be legalised. All political prisoners not guilty of violent crimes would be released. All executions would be suspended. And the government had 'taken a firm decision to release Mandela unconditionally'.[88]

Mandela had won, while he was careful to give his people the credit. Winnie read out a message from him to a crowd in Johannesburg. 'You

* There were later claims that the draft of de Klerk's speech was negotiated with the British government, which Renwick emphatically denies.[87]

are the ones who have made the government give in to your pressure . . . It is not President de Klerk.' But he added: 'It is partly the international community which has forced these concessions.' The ANC's position was instantly transformed. It issued a statement from Stockholm (where Tambo was still recuperating) saying that de Klerk's speech went 'a long way toward creating a climate conducive to negotiations'.[89]

South Africa suddenly became a new country. The underground came overground, banned people proclaimed themselves, the ANC and red flags waved, and the papers published photographs of Mandela. Everyone speculated about his health and abilities, and when he would be released. There were rumours that he himself was delaying, but he told Bizos: 'Open the door, and see which way I walk.' Inside his prison-house he was making his last preparations for facing the crowds and the press: his photographer friend Peter Magubane gave him a booklet produced by *Time* magazine on how to handle the media.[90]

A week after his speech de Klerk summoned Mandela to his office and told him he would be flown up to Johannesburg to be released the next day. A tense argument followed. Mandela wanted another week for the ANC to prepare the reception (with good reason, as became clear), but the security forces feared it would create 'unrestrained tensions'. In fact Niël Barnard, the intelligence chief, was very worried that the ANC would organise mass demonstrations which would disorganise the whole country, like the followers of the Ayatollah Khomeini when he returned to Iran in 1979.[91] Mandela also insisted that he must walk out of the gates of the prison, alongside Winnie, and speak to the people of Cape Town. De Klerk was strongly against any postponement: he was fearful of demonstrations being stirred up by news items like the headline in the *Cape Times* that morning: 'Mandela Asks Release from Paarl'.[92] He consulted twice with colleagues, who said it was too late to delay; but he agreed to release Mandela at the prison gate. When Mandela returned to the prison his warder Gregory thought his mouth was harder, his eyes colder. He was determined to be released with dignity: as Kobie Coetsee noted, 'Dignity is a key word for Mandela.'[93]

The ANC had already appointed a Reception Committee to make the plans; and that night they came to his house to make final changes to his speech. Mandela wrote on the imitation-leather writing board which prisoners had made for him; but the speech was the collective work of the ANC, as was all too clear from its style. His Cape Town attorney Dullah Omar spent two hours with him, and found him 'subdued, quiet, deep in thought. He knew everything that was happening.'

The next morning Mandela got up at 4.30. After breakfast and a medical check-up he again met ANC colleagues, including Cyril Ramaphosa and Trevor Manuel, to finish the speech. He packed his books and papers, accumulated over the Pollsmoor years, into a dozen crates, and said his goodbyes to his warders. It was the most exciting moment of his life, he told Omar, who noted, 'he showed no emotion. He was very composed.'[94] Mandela was too preoccupied with detail, he explained, to realise how momentous was the occasion.

An ANC delegation, including Winnie and Walter Sisulu, had arranged to fly down from Johannesburg in two chartered planes: Winnie would meet her husband at the jail, and walk out with him at 3 p.m. But the second plane arrived late, and it was not till after four that he and Winnie emerged from the prison gate, to face a scene which took him completely by surprise.[95] At the age of seventy-one, after over ten thousand days in jail, he was rejoining a country which had grown up without him.

PART III

1990–1999

28

Myth and Man

> Wandering between two worlds, one dead,
> The other powerless to be born,
> With nowhere yet to rest my head.
>
> Matthew Arnold, 'The Grand Chartreuse'

MANDELA WALKED OUT of the prison gates on 11 February 1990, holding hands with Winnie. It provided the most powerful image of the time, even in an era of charismatic heroes overcoming tyrannies in Eastern Europe and Russia: of Gorbachev, Walesa, Havel and the fall of the Berlin Wall. For Mandela embodied a more elemental and universal myth, like a revolutionary opera or *The Odyssey*, depicting the triumph of the human spirit, the return of the lost leader. And his long isolation had allowed the myth to take off from the man, leaving everything to the imagination: a dotted outline within which anyone could fill in their own detailed picture of a hero. Only a few lawyers and visitors knew what he really looked like. Huge sums had been offered for his photograph to be smuggled out; and the old pictures had been endlessly recycled, turning into heraldic emblems. The first contemporary picture had been published only two days before, showing Mandela standing stiffly and smiling blandly alongside de Klerk. The world's journalists and television crews who converged outside the prison still did not know whom to expect.

When he finally appeared on the television screens, they showed scenes of confusion. The deliberately short notice, compounded by Winnie's late arrival, ensured a muddle. Crowds milled round the prison entrance, climbing up trees, clinging to wires and standing on tiptoe, waiting for his long-delayed exit. Television teams nervously tried to locate him. 'If we can just spot Mr Mandela . . .' said the normally unflappable David Dimbleby. At last his blurred shape appeared, unsmiling alongside a cheerful Winnie, wearing a light grey suit, looking tense and grim. 'Only when I saw the crowd did I realise,' he admitted later, 'that I had not thought carefully enough about the events of the day.'[1] One correspondent, John Battersby of the *Christian Science Monitor*, who was waiting inside the prison grounds, suddenly saw Mandela looming in front of him, and shook his hand. 'I lost all sense of ego,' he recalled. 'I saw history and legend merging with reality.'[2] Outside the gates, Mandela found his bearings and held up a clenched fist to the crowd. But two minutes later he had disappeared into a waiting Toyota. It was a tantalising glimpse for the millions who were watching across the world; but the symbolism remained as powerful as if he had walked out in orderly triumph. 'We clapped, cheered and cried,' wrote Roger Wilkins in Washington, 'at the sight of a king – our cousin, the king, walking in the sunshine.'[3]

The Toyota motorcade drove off to Cape Town. Along the road spectators, black and white, waved or clenched fists in the ANC salute. Once Mandela stopped the car to get out and chat with a white couple with two children by the roadside. But in the city the progress turned into chaos. Mandela was trapped inside his car by the seething crowds; the driver panicked, lost his way, and turned back to take refuge in the suburb of Rondebosch. The welcoming party at the City Hall tried to placate the waiting crowds who filled the square, but they were impatient. A shot rang out, and hooligans began looting shops and robbing spectators. Some whites saw it as a warning of black anarchy: 'an early example of the policy of appropriating other people's property,' wrote Ken Owen in the *Cape Times*, 'to which Mandela immediately gave his support.'[4]

Mandela eventually arrived at the City Hall in twilight to make his first public speech since his long statement from the dock in 1964. But this too was an anti-climax, read out in a deadpan style without rhetorical flourishes, as if he had not seen the text before. It was a more serious disappointment to white politicians and diplomats. Both de Klerk and Thatcher had expected Mandela to hold himself aloof from the ANC, and to distance himself from the armed struggle and the communists. But he insisted that he was totally identified with the ANC:

> I stand here before you not as a prophet but as a humble servant of you, the people. Your tireless and heroic sacrifices have made it possible for me to be here today. I therefore place the remaining years of my life in your hands.

He thanked many white liberals, including the women's 'Black Sash' movement; and – to the dismay of close colleagues – paid tribute to de Klerk as 'a man of integrity'. But he presented himself as 'a loyal and disciplined member of the African National Congress', and gave profound thanks to the ANC, the Communist Party and the soldiers of Umkhonto wa Sizwe. He had not been negotiating in jail, he assured his audience, only pressing to meet with the government. The ANC must keep up the armed struggle: 'We have no option but to continue.'

The total commitment to the ANC and the armed struggle alarmed the politicians and diplomats. De Klerk was shocked by Mandela's solidarity with the communists, and thought his speech had been written by hard-line ideologues: 'For once, Mandela completely failed to rise to the occasion.'[5] The British Ambassador Robin Renwick thought the speech had been written by the ANC. Mrs Thatcher was dismayed by the 'old ritual phrases', and cancelled a planned statement.[6] Her Afrikaner adviser Laurens van der Post, himself a former prisoner of war, said he was disappointed that Mandela had not learnt from the 'school of suffering'.[7]

The disappointment at the speech betrayed ignorance about Mandela's relationship with the ANC, and his true political importance: he would be powerless if he could not carry his movement with him, and his secret talks in jail made him all the more determined to show his solidarity with the ANC now. As a lone ranger, he would soon have been forced off the political stage, like Gorbachev. But as the acknowledged leader of the black majority he could use all his authority for a peaceful settlement. He could not yet abandon the armed struggle and sanctions, which provided his most effective leverage.

Mandela showed a more conciliatory and intimate aspect the next day at his first press conference. It was held in the garden of Bishopscourt, Archbishop Tutu's grand mansion in Cape Town, where he was staying: he had been worried about its associations with white grandeur, but was assured that it had now become 'a people's centre' for township blacks. He walked in, holding Winnie's hand, looking strained with his mouth turned down, and sat on a throne to face a barrage of reporters and television cameras. He had only been interviewed for television once before, in 1961. Now he was bewildered by the furry cylinders, which he did not recognise as microphones, and had no experience of rehearsed soundbites or photo-opportunities. But journalists were surprised to find him unfazed by the cameras, talking much more intimately than in his stiff speech from the City Hall. He spoke in complete sentences, said one correspondent, 'as though he spent twenty-seven years practising to address press conferences'.[8] He knew the names of reporters from their bylines, and thanked the press for having been a 'brick' to him in jail, keeping his name alive: 'It was the interest of the government that we should be forgotten. It was the press that never forgot us.' He insisted that the armed struggle was merely defensive. He reiterated that de Klerk was a man of integrity, though with an implied warning: 'He seems to be fully aware of the danger to a public figure of making undertakings which he fails to honour.' Most important, he emphasised his own lack of bitterness.

> It is not a nice feeling for a man to see his family struggling, without security, without the dignity of the head of the family around, but despite the hard times that were had in prison we have also had the opportunity to think about programmes ... and in prison there have been men who are very good in the sense that they understand our point of view, and they do everything to make you as happy as possible. That has wiped out any bitterness which a man could have.

It was, said the *Financial Times*, 'the first sign that black South Africa's reverence for Mandela – and faith in him as a leader – may not be misplaced'.[9]

He flew up to Johannesburg a few days later to address a crowd of 100,000 at the Soweto stadium, Soccer City. It was a tense test of the ANC's ability to control the crowd, employing a hundred of their own marshals since they would not tolerate the presence of the police. Walter Sisulu introduced Mandela to thunderous applause: 'This is a man who has sacrificed his life.' Mandela spoke more like a pedagogue than a demagogue: 'It is the policy of the ANC that the entire educational system is a site of struggle. All students must return to school and learn.' And he deplored the crime statistics: 'The level of crime in our country must be eliminated.' The crowd listened spellbound, without any outbreak of violence, and dispersed quietly.

Mandela left by helicopter to avoid the crowds, and descended from the sky near his old 'matchbox' house, 8115 Vilakazi Street in Soweto, awaited by the world's journalists and TV vans which clogged the rough street outside. In front of the house was an ANC poster: 'MANDELA IS

COMING!' Next door was a slogan: 'SOWETO IS NO ZOO FOR WHITE RACIST TOURISTS.' It was like a village homecoming. At home he appeared happily domesticated, with Winnie as the loyal housewife. Together they received an endless procession of visitors, who waited their turn in the little garden with an ANC flag flying over it, supervised by a reception committee including Zwelakhe Sisulu and Murphy Morobe. Winnie prepared meals in the kitchen, answered the door and hugged old friends before showing them through; her photographer-friend Peter Magubane snapped them. Mandela looked as formal as a head of state in a grey double-breasted suit, cosy in this small house, greeting friends with the ANC thumb-grip, sitting in the small dining room with his big boxer's hands on the table. He was obedient to his strict timetable ('Have you arranged with my colleagues?'); only his tailor Yusuf Surtee was able to jump the queue, arriving with a new pair of trousers on a hanger. Mandela's talk seemed relaxed and intimate, and his memory sharp: the three decades in jail appeared to have slipped away. 'I remember Tony as a bright young man,' he told my wife Sally. 'He didn't tell me about you. He's kept things from me.'

To old friends he seemed more at ease with himself than thirty years before, without defensiveness or arrogance. He looked softer and gentler, with a warm, humorous smile instead of the flashing grin. 'He's blossomed into a different personality, warm with everyone,' said Amina Cachalia.[10] 'He knew exactly who he was,' said Ismail Meer. 'He has gone through this period of fire and purified himself and emerged as a person who can hope to bring about change in this country.'[11] Many of his supporters had dreaded a let-down: the poster-hero commemorated round the world could turn out to be a frail, bewildered old man. But he did not seem trapped in the past. He soon became (as Nadine Gordimer put it) the 'personification of the future'.[12]

He was more sympathetic and human than the prison icon. 'We worried how Mandela could come out and match up to his saint-like image,' said Cheryl Carolus, the Cape activist who later became High Commissioner in London. 'Then he showed he had morality, integrity and value for human life.'[13] Like Ronald Reagan, he had a relaxed charm which made almost anyone feel better after meeting him; but his magnanimity and lack of bitterness conveyed a moral seriousness, particularly to white South Africans, as if he were a priest at confessional, forgiving sins and giving his blessing.

He was not alone in forgiving. 'Almost all the comrades I served with in prison have come out without any sense of bitterness,' he explained. 'If you were in our position you would never find the time to be bitter, because you are looking at problems.'[14] 'Bitterness would be in conflict with the whole policy to which I have dedicated my life,' said Sisulu later.[15] But Mandela went further than any of his prison colleagues, and would upset some of them when he reached out to his most ruthless former persecutors.

Mandela had his own sense of guilt at having neglected people who had helped him on his way up, and he now sought them out to thank them – from his first white employer Lazar Sidelsky to the friends who helped him in jail. 'It clears my conscience,' he explained, 'to be able to say: "Do you remember that this is what you did for me?" '[16] But after prison he seemed excited by all kinds of new faces, like Miranda in *The Tempest*: 'O brave new world, that has such people in it!' And he often seemed keener to meet enemies than friends. He looked for support from unlikely white politicians, diplomats and businessmen. When Robin Renwick, building British bridges to the ANC, gave Mandela lunch at the fashionable restaurant Linger Longer, he was apprehensive about the right-wing business lunchers, but Mandela made a point of touring the dining-room, shaking hands and co-opting them to his cause. 'It was a bravura performance,' said Renwick.[17]

Mandela seemed instinctively aware of the power of his icon: he could provide 'a symbolic expression of the confused desires of the people'.[18] But he guarded against the personality cult which had bedevilled so many young African states; he was careful to avoid the word 'I'. He realised, as Frantz Fanon had warned: 'The magic hands are finally only the hands of the people.'[19] He was always stressing that he was the servant of the ANC. 'They may say: well, you are a man of seventy-one, you require a pension; or, look, we don't like your face, please go. I will obey them.'[20] 'His life was never the struggle,' as Mac Maharaj said. 'The "I" never supplanted the organisation.'[21]

With his glittering image, Mandela set out on his travels. He would spend more time abroad than at home over the next half-year, but he had an urgent purpose: to rally support and funds for the ANC, translating his reputation into cash, and to maintain sanctions until negotiations were completed. He was also an old man in a hurry to see the world. He had only been outside South Africa once before, just before he was jailed.

When Bob Hughes, a British Labour MP, urged him to take more rest, he replied, 'I have twenty-seven years to catch up.'[22] Now he was in the midst of a high-speed world he had never seen before, of jumbo jets, computers, direct-dial telephones and global television, which made constant demands. And everywhere he had to live up to the media's legend, to connect the myth to the man.

He was also opening up South Africa to the world, which for years had treated it as a pariah state. Mandela could draw his own map of friends across the globe – beginning with Africa. Two weeks after his release he flew up to Lusaka in Zambia, to meet his ANC colleagues in exile, while Presidents of neighbouring countries and other leaders converged there to meet their hero. He embraced Yasser Arafat, who kissed him on both cheeks, and compared the Palestinian struggle to the ANC's. He was greeted ecstatically by huge crowds and old friends, and reiterated that he was merely the ANC's servant: 'If you tell me to sweep the streets, I will do so.' His first meetings with the ANC in exile were prickly, for many still suspected he had been selling them out in his talks with the government. But he soon reasserted his leadership and again committed himself to the armed struggle, despite arguments from Zambia's President Kenneth Kaunda.[23] Tambo, still formally ANC President, was slowly recovering from his stroke in Sweden, and Alfred Nzo, the veteran Secretary-General, was elected Acting President. Mandela himself became Deputy President; but to most ANC members he was the clear leader.

He visited Zimbabwe, where he spoke on 4 March at the National Sports Stadium, introduced by Robert Mugabe, who had become the country's President ten years before, in a similar atmosphere of reconciliation and expectation. But the two leaders already seemed very different. Mugabe introduced Mandela with a self-serving and hectoring speech denouncing his rivals, while Mandela, as one reporter described him, 'spoke with the quiet, dignified assurance of a great leader and appeared decidedly calm beside the sweating, twitching Mugabe'.[24]

He visited other states, including the brand-new Namibia, where he joined the independence celebrations on 21 March and met world leaders. Namibia's black government under Sam Nujoma was a further sign of the irreversible pressure for a democratic South Africa. The star visitor was Mandela, who showed all his diplomatic skills; when he was reported to have snubbed the British Foreign Secretary Douglas Hurd he quickly sent a message to assure him that it was not intended.[25]

He revisited Algeria, where he had been shortly before his arrest in 1962: he called on one Minister whom he had meant to see then, apologising for being twenty-eight years late. He ended with a visit to Sweden – the ANC's longstanding ally – staying at the beautiful small royal castle of Haga outside Stockholm, besieged by visitors from all over Europe. He had an emotional reunion with Tambo, who he believed had suffered and achieved more than he, and who was still speaking haltingly after his stroke. Mandela realised that at seventy-two he might never completely recover. Tambo implored him to take his place as President of the ANC, but Mandela refused: it would be misunderstood, he thought, for a leader to take over having just left prison.[26]

A few weeks later he went to London. Mrs Thatcher had sent an invitation, but his colleagues dissuaded him from seeing her, and instead he gave priority to loyal friends of the ANC. The Commonwealth Secretary Sonny Ramphal gave a reception in Mayfair, at which Mandela and Winnie worked the rooms like monarchs, shaking hands, while Jesse Jackson tried to steal the show. Mandela also addressed a packed ANC meeting, where he thanked and briefed party workers. 'While we were sitting comfortable in jail,' he told them, 'you were the people in the front line.' He warned that without a settlement, South Africa would witness a 'conflagration which has never been seen in Africa'. He dominated the meeting, but again said that he was only their servant: 'I've got bosses here today. Already I have a note passed to me: "You are long-winded."'[27]

His chief British date was a huge concert in Wembley Stadium on 16 April to thank the anti-apartheid campaigners for the earlier concert celebrating his seventieth birthday. The blend of pop music and radical politics was again televised live by the BBC: the Thatcher government warned them to avoid ANC propaganda or fund-raising, and the BBC2 controller Alan Yentob had to exercise 'sensible discretion', anxiously monitoring the pop stars' speeches.[28] Seventy-five thousand young people filled the stadium, singing and swaying in Mexican waves. International stars performed free, including the Manhattan Brothers, Mandela's friends in Soweto in the fifties – watched by an estimated billion viewers around the world. In a crowded reception room Mandela received old campaigners, tactfully prompted by Winnie, but he seemed more excited by pop singers than political leaders like Neil Kinnock. At the finale, Mandela strode up and down the platform with a clenched fist to thunderous cheers, and paid tribute to Tambo and Father Huddleston, the Chairman of the Anti-Apartheid Movement. 'You elected not to forget,' Mandela told the crowd. 'Even through the thickness of the prison walls . . . we heard your voices demanding our freedom.'

Back in South Africa he was soon down to earth, revisiting his home village of Qunu in the Transkei. He arrived in a dark suit and a black Mercedes to a scene of total contrast to London, a few round thatched huts in the bare countryside which seemed even poorer than before he went to jail, and was now defaced by plastic litter which clung to the fences. He was glad to see the children politicised, singing songs about Tambo, but was distressed that 'pride in the community seemed to have vanished'.[29] He visited his mother's grave, still remorseful that he had not properly cared for her, and was welcomed to a banquet, for which a nephew had slaughtered a precious ox, by local chiefs and Mandela relations, including his sister Mabel. He relaxed with a grandchild, pulling funny faces, and made a speech in Xhosa which he translated into English: 'My heart is very sore indeed on account of the poverty.' He shared the feast until a helicopter dropped down – to general amazement – to take him away.[30]

A few weeks later he was abroad again, to Europe and North America. He was on a serious mission to maintain sanctions and raise funds for the ANC, but he appeared more like a prophet, and South African Embassies watched him closely as he visibly eclipsed their own head of state, de Klerk. In France he was received royally by President Mitterrand, whose wife Danielle had backed the crucial Dakar meeting in 1987. In Rome he was received by the Pope. A Vatican official, Monsignor Menini, leaked confidential details of the audience to the South African Ambassador, assuring him that the meeting had no political significance, since the Pope saw all leading political visitors, even Arafat. The Pope, he said, had taken no notes, as he did with more serious visitors, and he had declined Mandela's request to endorse sanctions. The positive publicity, Menini claimed, 'fell short of [Mandela's] expectations'.[31]

Mandela stopped for two days in England to meet Tambo in a 'safe house' in Kent provided by the government, and had a long early-morning phone talk with Mrs Thatcher, urging her, without success, to maintain sanctions. But he was touched by her concern for his health and his overcrowded schedule, which she said was too heavy for a man half his age: 'If you go on like this,' she scolded him, 'you won't come out of America alive.' He realised she was 'a very powerful lady . . . one I would rather have as an ally than an enemy'.[32]

In America Mandela visited eight cities and was pulled between rival hosts, from African-Americans to churches and showbiz. In New York he was compared to Moses more than to Martin Luther King. He rode in a car with bulletproof glass in a forty-car motorcade up Broadway: computer printouts and twenty-five kilometres of tickertape – thought to be a record – showered down from the skyscrapers, with hundreds of thousands of spectators cramming the narrow streets. In the evening the Empire State Building was lit up with the ANC colours of green, black and gold. 'I have seen rallies, I have seen parades, I have seen huge crowds,' said New York's Governor Mario Cuomo, 'but this was something I have never seen before.' Mandela addressed the UN, thanking them for their Declaration on South Africa the year before. But in every speech he warned that the 'wall of sanctions' might crumble too soon. In Harlem he addressed a packed Africa Square, warning that the cancer of racism was still eating away. Mandela's visit, said the *New York Times*, 'touched and energised black Americans as much as anything since the height of the civil rights era'.[33] His quietly confident dignity was seen as a welcome contrast to the aggressive rhetoric of many African-American politicians, and he was hailed as providing the kind of leadership that was desperately needed; but he had the assurance of a black majority behind him, which black Americans could never have.

In Washington he was welcomed by President Bush, who had been the first head of state to congratulate him on his release. Bush criticised the ANC's use of violence against the apartheid regime, and Mandela replied that throughout history it was the oppressors who determined the method of political action: if they use brute force to suppress all the people's aspirations, and refuse all dialogue, they send the message to the oppressed that they must resort to force if they want liberation.[34] Bush and his Secretary of State James Baker were impressed by Mandela's willingness to compromise and negotiate seriously. Two days later Bush assured de Klerk by phone that Mandela was not trying to undercut him; but when de Klerk visited Washington three months later he would be anxious to show that he was more important than Mandela.[35]

In Washington Mandela also addressed a joint session of both houses of Congress, preceded by a three-minute standing ovation. He praised the black heroes like Marcus Garvey, Martin Luther King and W.E.B. du Bois alongside Washington, Lincoln and Jefferson: 'The day may not be far when we will borrow the words of Thomas Jefferson and speak of the will of the South African nation.' He annoyed the right by defending sanctions, but they did not walk out as they had threatened, and he received another standing ovation, while effectively postponing the lifting of sanctions. Conservatives continued to complain about his support for Cuba and Libya, but some accepted that he had to find friends where he could in time of need. As Charles Krauthammer wrote: 'We Americans, who once made an alliance of necessity with Stalin, should have no trouble understanding that.'[36]

Mandela was sometimes visibly exhausted by his crowded schedule, and was put out by the bodyguards who stopped him from talking to ordinary people. When he stayed with the Mayor of New York, David Dinkins, in Gracie Mansion, he tried to go for an early-morning jog alone, but the bodyguards insisted on accompanying him.[37] But he was revived by California and a last rally at Oakland Stadium, decorated with ANC banners: 'I feel like a young man of thirty-five. I feel like an old battery that has been recharged.' 'The struggle against apartheid,' he said, 'is the one issue uniting people with different political views in the US and throughout the world.'

Mandela had put South Africa briefly onto the centre of the American stage. He had, said the *New York Times*, been 'transformed into a popular hero hailed by millions who a few months ago were probably giving scant attention to apartheid in South Africa'.[38] *Time* magazine described him as a classic hero 'who has emerged from a symbolic grave reborn, made great, and filled with creative power. . . What Bolivar was to South America, what Lincoln was to America, Nelson Mandela is to Africa: the liberator.'[39] But he disowned the mythology: 'I am sorry if I am seen as a demi-god . . . I am a peg on which to hang all the aspirations of the African National Congress.'[40]

From America he travelled to Ireland, where he was soon in hot water: he could not believe that the problems of Ulster could not be resolved peacefully; he told a press conference in Dublin that 'There is nothing better than opposites sitting down to resolve their problems in a peaceful way.' He flew on to London, but his words caught up with him. 'There was a clear and pointless predictability about the mess Nelson Mandela got into in Dublin yesterday,' wrote the *Guardian*.[41] He would be wryly amused when Sinn Fein did sit down to talk with the British government seven years later.

In London he met British Members of Parliament at Westminster

Hall, where he was introduced by a brash Tory, Ivor Stanbrook, who immediately brought up the Ulster question but was sharply heckled by other MPs, including Dennis Skinner, with boos and cries of 'Nonsense!' and 'Rubbish!', which astonished Mandela: 'It's amazing what they say in the House of Commons.'[42] He reminded MPs that 'the ANC were outcasts only yesterday', and asked them to support sanctions and 'walk the last mile with us'. He went on to a small lunch given by the Foreign Secretary Douglas Hurd, including people who had helped Mandela, like the Archbishop of Canterbury and Father Huddleston. Mandela quietly dominated, explained the case for sanctions, drank water and ate an apple instead of the rich dessert.[43]

This time he did see Mrs Thatcher. Robin Renwick advised her that Mandela had been waiting for twenty-seven years to make his points, and she let him talk for fifty minutes without interrupting – a near record for her. He courteously thanked her for improving East–West relations, for achieving the independence of Zimbabwe and for pressing Pretoria to release him. He asked for her support in achieving a negotiated settlement, and explained the need for sanctions. She replied for half an hour, while Mandela remained motionless. She urged him to talk to Buthelezi, and to abandon the armed struggle and his plans for nationalisation, and promised to keep in close touch. The meeting had been scheduled to last an hour, but went on for three.[44]

Mandela realised that he had still made no headway on sanctions, but he was surprised to find Thatcher warm and charming, while truly an 'iron lady'. She found him 'supremely courteous, with a genuine nobility of bearing' and no bitterness. She warmed to him, but found him still 'stuck in a kind of socialist timewarp', and worried that he would prove another half-baked Marxist, like Mugabe in Zimbabwe.[45] Outside Downing Street a reporter asked Mandela how he could bring himself to talk to someone who had denounced him as a terrorist. He replied that he was working with South Africans who had done much worse things: 'I didn't even mention slaughters,' he said later.[46] He finished his trip in July in Mozambique, where for the first time he met Graca Machel, the widow of the former President Samora Machel (see pp.546–7).

In October he was off again for a tour of Asia, with his friend Ismail Meer among his party. India was the most important destination, as the traditional ally of black South Africans, and he was received there with the pomp usually reserved for a head of state, including a twenty-one-gun salute and a state banquet in Delhi. The President Ramaswamy Venkataraman promised to press for continued sanctions, and to support the ANC: later the Congress Party helped the ANC buy Shell House, their Johannesburg headquarters.[47] In Calcutta Mandela addressed a vast crowd, and thanked India for originating the South African struggle by sending them Gandhi. He drank holy water from the Ganges, slightly worried by seeing the carcasses of dead cows floating in it. He enjoyed Indian food, and publicly thanked Meer for having taught him to love curry.[48]

Other Asian countries were also generous, but more controversial politically. In Indonesia Mandela was so regally received by President Suharto that he asked him for $10 million for the ANC, which he received in front of the media. But Mandela kept quiet about the Indonesians' campaign against the East Timorese, who accused him of 'hypocrisy and opportunism'.[49] In Malaysia President Mahathir, having briefed him about economic development, gave him $5 million in cash. In Australia – where he failed to see his cricketing hero Donald Bradman – he steered clear of disputes about Aborigines and cancelled a visit to an Aboriginal community in Sydney, which led to more accusations of hypocrisy. But Aboriginals still proclaimed an alliance with the black people of South Africa.[50]

He was offended by his experience of Japan, where just before his arrival the Minister of Justice had been quoted as making a racist remark about America, where 'the neighbourhoods go to the dogs when blacks move in'. Mandela was shocked that the Minister had survived, which 'showed just how lukewarm Japan remained about fighting racism'. He was given a standing ovation in the Japanese Parliament, but was disappointed when the Prime Minister turned down a request for $25 million to the ANC. 'The contribution made by the Japanese government,' he said afterwards, 'is absolutely insignificant.'[51]

One country was notably missing from Mandela's journeys in the aftermath of the Cold War: the Soviet Union, which had loyally supported the ANC and had supplied arms and money for the last quarter-century. Gorbachev had invited him to Moscow in a message to Lusaka just after he was released; and Mandela had had a friendly meeting with the Foreign Minister Eduard Shevardnadze at the Namibian independence celebrations in March. But the plans kept being postponed. In fact Moscow, just when it might have reaped rewards from its long support for the ANC, was cosying up to de Klerk. Gorbachev's government, battered by economic crises, was desperate for immediate commercial opportunities. In 1990 they signed a direct marketing agreement with de Beers diamonds, and soon Gorbachev, breaking promises to the ANC, was establishing direct contacts with Pretoria, and stopped providing free training for ANC guerrillas. De Klerk paid a state visit to Moscow in June 1992, when the new Russian President Boris Yeltsin assured him that he would not receive Mandela as the ANC President, only as an international fighter for human rights. Behind these rapid changes (said the Soviet expert Vladimir Shubin) lay an upsurge of Russian xenophobia and racism which saw white South Africans as victims of black majority rule. It was not until 1993, when the ANC was coming closer to victory, that their relations with Moscow improved.[52]

Mandela still befriended enemies of the West like Muammar Qadaffi, Arafat and Saddam Hussein. He had visited Libya in May 1990, when he gave early warning that he would remain loyal to Qadaffi. In his tent he thanked him for providing the ANC with military training: 'We consider ourselves comrades in arms.' When Iraq invaded Kuwait in August 1990 Mandela accused the Europeans of hypocrisy: they had not objected to the US invasions of Grenada or Panama, 'but now the whole of the West is screaming and sending armies because of Iraq's invasion of Kuwait'. He did not condone Iraq's aggression, but suggested that Iraqis were treated differently because they were 'brown-skinned'. When the West eventually launched the Gulf War, President Bush courteously phoned Mandela, who 'agreed to differ'.[53]

Mandela showed a special fondness for Fidel Castro, who had inspired the ANC radicals with his daring revolution in 1959; on Robben Island he had been thrilled to hear that Cubans had intervened in Angola. He visited Cuba in July 1991 and gave an emotional speech thanking Cuba for helping the ANC, and recalling how Cuban troops had helped to defeat the South African invaders in Angola in 1988. That defeat, he said, 'enables me to be here today'. Castro replied by calling Mandela 'one of the most extraordinary symbols of this era', explaining that 'apartheid is capitalism and imperialism in its fascist form.' Castro spoke for three hours without a piece of paper, to Mandela's amazement, and no one left except to go to the toilet. Mandela found Castro 'a very happy chap': when they drove through Havana, 'he just sat down, folded his arms, and I was the person waving to the crowd'.[54]

Despite such embarrassing friends, Mandela was embraced by

Western governments with an enthusiasm which amazed him after their previous coolness towards the ANC. It was partly of course because of the geo-political transformation: the global communist bogey had evaporated, and the West no longer had to fear a hostile black South African government backed by Moscow. Cold Warriors who had built up Mandela as a communist ogre were disarmed – sometimes with pangs of guilt – to meet the genial old man with a conservative style and a close interest in Western democracies. And Western governments began competing belatedly to make friends with a possible black president.

But the ecstatic welcomes could not be explained by political science. Mandela's basic appeal was not as a man of power, but as a moral leader who had stood out for fundamental principles and who gave hope for the future to all oppressed people and all countries torn by racial divisions. His dignity and wish for reconciliation gave him an influence beyond ordinary politics, which was the more surprising because he was not religious. He had never offered himself as a spiritual leader, and he dismissed the label of saint: 'I'm just a sinner who keeps on trying.' 'I am not particularly religious or spiritual,' he told the professor of theology Charles Villa-Vicencio. 'I am just an ordinary person trying to make sense of the mysteries of life.'[55]

He seemed to enjoy and adjust his own icon, while not being fooled by it, as though he were watching a play with himself as the hero. He liked to tell stories about being cut down to size: about the American tourist in the Bahamas who recognised him but then asked: 'What are you famous for?' Or about the two white women in South Africa who asked for his signature and then said: 'By the way, what is your name?' His aides tired of the repeated anecdotes, but they were part of Mandela's determination to remain an ordinary man, and they delighted his audiences, particularly children. He loved telling stories about being put down by children. 'You know what the kids at school say about you?' a girl of thirteen asked him: 'That when you were young you were handsome. They say you are now old and ugly.' When a girl of five asked him why he spent so long in jail, and he explained, she replied, 'You must be a very stupid old man.' With children everywhere – despite or because of his own family problems – he could descend from his towering image to rediscover his own simpler self. But while he could sound like an innocent abroad, his instinctive ability to relate to all kinds of people made him a master-politician.

29

Revolution to Cooperation

As a political leader at home, Mandela had one overwhelming advantage: he had descended as if from the clouds, with all his principles intact, unsullied by intrigue or squalid manoeuvres, with no sense of his having climbed 'the greasy pole'. His unequalled period in jail had protected him from criticism and abuse, and earned him credentials which no one dared question. He had no serious rival in sight.

But in between his triumphant foreign tours he was soon facing more sceptical audiences at home. Like many world heroes – like both Churchill and Smuts after the Second World War – his global acclaim did not necessarily help his domestic career. Many white South Africans complained that he was too aloof, and could not control his own people's violence; while a few blacks thought he was forgetting the grassroots. And he faced a huge task in leading his disorganised party towards political power. He still had no vote, and no official status except as a rebel leader. His only effective levers against the Afrikaner government were sanctions, which depended on world support, and the threat of armed force, requiring guerrilla troops who were still ineffective. While he was acclaimed throughout the world as the great liberator, the new Moses or Messiah, he had no tangible power inside his own country, and no convincing liberation army.

De Klerk was still in command of a formidable military machine, police force and intelligence system: and he had no intention of giving way to a black majority unless he was compelled to. 'No government anywhere in the world,' Mandela said later, 'will surrender power without a tremendous amount of pressure.'[1] De Klerk was rapidly making his government acceptable to the West; and he was encouraged by Western leaders, including Mrs Thatcher in Britain and Helmut Kohl in Germany, to look for alternative federal or confederal systems which would prevent domination by any single party – that is, by the ANC. The Afrikaners had long looked to Europe for models of separate development: back in 1984 President Botha had said that Switzerland and Yugoslavia had 'found the key to cooperation and harmony'.[2] De Klerk still clung to a policy of 'group rights' which could play tribes against each other. Mandela had already argued with him before leaving jail that group rights really meant apartheid through the back door, and de Klerk's brother Willem, among others, soon persuaded him that 'group rights based on race or colour are unacceptable'. But de Klerk still supported 'the inalienable right of each cultural and language group to fulfil the imperatives of its identity': a right which could easily be stretched to encourage tribal divisions.[3]

Mandela quickly realised that de Klerk was in no hurry to begin negotiations, and suspected he was playing for time, hoping he would 'fall on his face'.[4] And he was soon suspicious of the role of the police: on 26 March 1990 they attacked a crowd of ANC demonstrators in Sebokeng, south of Johannesburg, killing twelve. He complained angrily to de Klerk that the President could not 'talk about negotiations on the one hand and murder our people on the other', and postponed the first talks. He thought de Klerk was looking for ways to retain a minority veto, to frustrate the majority.

South African military intelligence officers had their own secret plans for dividing the blacks. They had done so in Namibia, using 'dirty tricks' to weaken the majority black party, SWAPO, and build up a loose coalition of ethnic parties, the Democratic Turnhalle Alliance (DTA). Now they planned to weaken the ANC in the same way. They hoped to delay the transition long enough to allow the government to create an alliance with other black parties, including Inkatha, which could beat the ANC at the polls.[5] The South African security forces in Namibia were not demobilised, but moved back into South Africa. 'To all intents and purposes, then,' the Truth Commission later found, 'operatives and soldiers moved from one theatre of war to another.' And many members of military intelligence had a very crude notion of their role after the ANC was legalised. As one of them told the Truth Commission: 'We all thought: this is it, fuck the kaffirs, this is the time to sort them out.'[6]

Mandela urgently needed to rebuild and unify the ANC after its thirty-year ban, to bring together its scattered elements into a disciplined party, in order to begin negotiations with de Klerk. The leaders in exile were soon able to return, after talks with the secret service to ensure their safety. Most of them expected to come to power within five years. But they knew that the negotiations would be arduous, and set about selecting a team for the initial talks. Mandela was determined to include his old friend Joe Slovo, the Secretary of the Communist Party, now white-haired and mellowed: de Klerk at first absolutely refused, but he eventually agreed that each side must be free to choose anyone it wanted.[7]

On 2 May 1990 the ANC and government teams met to begin preliminary talks at Groote Schuur, de Klerk's official residence. It was a unique gathering: black leaders had, as Thabo Mbeki said, 'been striving for more than a century to sit and talk with the government'. Mandela and de Klerk stood in the garden in front of their delegations of eleven. They showed a striking racial contrast. All the government team were white male Afrikaners; while the ANC eleven included two whites, one Indian and one Coloured with the seven blacks: two of the team were women.

Both leaders made eloquent non-partisan statements. Mandela hoped they would 'engage in this sacred exercise without seeking advantage for their particular political organisation . . . All those of us who are hostages of the past must transform ourselves into new men and women who shall be fitting instruments for the creation of the glorious new South Africa which is possible and necessary to realise.' He talked briefly in Afrikaans, and gave his own account of Afrikaner history, which impressed the Foreign Minister Pik Botha, who was meeting Mandela for the first time.[8] De Klerk talked about 'the irreversible process of normalisation which has already started'. The two teams exchanged reminiscences and jokes: Afrikaner Ministers were visibly surprised by the fluency and knowledge of the black leaders, and both sides felt foolish (said Thabo Mbeki) that they had not had discussions years before, and surprised that 'nobody in the room had horns'. They were all in the same boat, said Pik Botha to an ANC delegate, surrounded by 'sharks to the left and right'. De Klerk was impressed to find Mandela a good listener who argued his case as a trained lawyer, though he would later complain that Mandela would 'admonish us with long monologues full of recriminations'; he would decide that Mandela had been 'scarred' by his experiences, and had no real vision of the future.[9]

After three days of talks the government team agreed to create a peaceful climate for negotiations by releasing political prisoners, removing repressive laws and lifting the state of emergency. These decisions were proclaimed in the 'Groote Schuur Minute'. De Klerk called it 'a great step forward', and Mandela said it was 'the realisation of a dream'. 'We went into these discussions in the spirit that there should be neither victors nor losers,' said Mandela. 'We are all victors, South Africa is a victor.' But he had to remind the government that apartheid was not dead, and that he still did not have the vote.

Mandela and the ANC leaders continued to feel the need to maintain an armed force in South Africa as a 'reinsurance' policy if negotiations collapsed. The military unit of 'Operation Vula' (see p.384) had remained intact, run by Mac Maharaj and Siphiwe Nyanda ('Ghebuza'); they had maintained communications with Mandela in jail, and after the ANC was legalised they were joined by the buccaneering Ronnie Kasrils. But some of the Vula activists had become complacent since the ANC had been legalised, and were feeling ignored by their leaders. The underground comrades in Durban had been careless with security, keeping confidential files on their computer disks. The police arrested two of them by chance, and extracted information about a secret meeting-place, where they ambushed others, and were soon raiding Vula houses in Johannesburg. Learning of the disaster, the Vula commanders quickly moved their arms caches and equipment to safer places. But on 25 July the police arrested Mac Maharaj and others, accusing them of plotting to overthrow the government. They released lurid details, reminiscent of the Rivonia trial, of an underground network designed 'to recruit, train, lead and arm a "people's" or "revolutionary" army to be used to seize power from the government by means of an armed insurrection'.[10]

De Klerk saw it as powerful ammunition against Mandela, exposing the revolutionaries and communists as still a sinister force; and he hoped to drive a wedge between the ANC and the SACP. He read out the police reports to Mandela, and insisted again that Slovo must be excluded from the ANC team, claiming that he had been at a secret meeting of the Communist Party in Tongaat in May. Mandela was aware of Operation Vula, which had provided his communication links with Tambo, and he had met Maharaj one-to-one in secret meetings, but at first he was taken aback by the extent of the operations which de Klerk revealed. Slovo was soon able to prove that he had not been at the Tongaat meeting: his passport showed he had been in Lusaka at the time, and the 'Joe' who was reported as being present was not him, but Siphiwe Nyanda. Mandela insisted that Slovo remain in his team, and argued that the ANC could not be disarmed while the government was deploying their own armed units against the ANC. The police continued to search for the other Vula suspects, including Kasrils, who was declared 'armed and dangerous'. But the arms caches remained undiscovered. Eventually, by March 1991, Maharaj and others were granted indemnity, and the case against them fell away.[11]

The affair had also given de Klerk crucial information about the ANC's negotiating strategy. Just before the arrest of Maharaj, on 19 July, Joe Slovo had proposed to the ANC National Executive that they should offer to suspend the armed struggle at the next meeting with the government. It was a historic compromise – all the more so coming from a leader of MK – designed to take de Klerk by surprise, and elicit major concessions. Mandela was at first dubious, but discussed it overnight, and after much soul-searching he agreed in the morning, and carried the National Executive with him unanimously. But the police found a handwritten document in Maharaj's briefcase outlining the strategy, which gave de Klerk time to prepare his response.[12]

Mandela and the ANC team met with the government in Pretoria on 6 August. Mandela promised an immediate ceasefire. De Klerk on his side promised to release political prisoners and to indemnify exiles for political offences. The two sides agreed on the 'Pretoria Minute', which proclaimed that the ANC was suspending all armed actions with immediate effect. But de Klerk, forewarned about the ANC strategy, inserted a reference to 'related activities', which would give him an advantage in later negotiations.[13] Still, the ANC offer had achieved what Slovo and Mandela had hoped for: a break in the logjam.

The ANC's offer of a ceasefire was not quite as generous as it appeared. Back in January 1990 Alfred Nzo, the Secretary-General, had admitted in public that 'we do not have the capacity within our country to intensify the armed struggle in any meaningful way'.[14] Mandela as MK's first commander-in-chief believed in the armed struggle's symbolic importance, although he thought 'it had a popularity out of proportion to what it had achieved on the ground'. 'We have never been under any misconception,' he said later, 'that we would be able to achieve a military victory against this regime.'[15] But he would not exclude underground activity. He drew a confusing distinction between 'action' and 'struggle': 'We have suspended armed action,' he explained in July 1991, 'but have not terminated the armed struggle, whether it is deployed inside the country or outside.' Slovo later explained that underground activities would be maintained until change was irreversible – a condition which de Klerk secretly accepted.[16]

The militant young comrades were outraged by the suspension of the armed struggle in return for minor concessions; and a hard core could not accept the whole idea of negotiation. Twenty-five prisoners still on Robben Island had refused the offer of amnesty, and insisted they would only leave after a victory on the battlefield. Mandela had had to return to the island in April 1990 to persuade them with difficulty to accept the government's offer.[17] On the mainland the ANC made a great effort to convince their more revolutionary members to switch from shooting to talking: they proclaimed the slogan 'Negotiations are Struggle' on T-shirts and car bumper-stickers, and published newspaper advertisements which stated that MK had not been dissolved.

The Pretoria Minute produced a wave of speculation about Mandela's apparent collaboration with de Klerk, and Mandela admitted on television: 'We have started some form of alliance already.' He was even rumoured to be joining the cabinet.[18] But the optimism was short-lived and premature. Mandela was becoming more distrustful of de Klerk, who clearly had his own strategy to weaken the black opposition, and could play up Mandela's serious problems within his own alliance; he would complain that 'the ANC had a very limited ability to ensure that its supporters and cadres honoured the undertakings it had given.'[19]

The ANC was still to some extent a revolutionary party. It was still allied with the SACP, which just before the Pretoria meeting had been triumphantly relaunched as a legal party, at the Soweto stadium on 29 July with a crowd of about 50,000. The white press saw the relaunch as all the more sinister in the light of the revelations about Operation Vula (which was depicted as a communist plot, though Vula was the creation of the ANC, not the SACP). Mandela addressed the crowd, welcoming the SACP as 'a dependable friend who respected the ANC's independence and policy', and insisted that the Party had never in his experience 'sought to impose its views on the ANC'. It was a spectacular resurrection: in the next fifteen months the SACP's membership would shoot up to 25,000 – at a time when most communist parties round the world were on the wane. The SACP's ideological commitment was now hazy: someone dubbed them the 'Sheepish about Communism Party'.[20] But they had a heroic record of confronting apartheid – they were more genuinely multi-racial than any other Communist Party in the world – while they provided a revolutionary cause for young militants in the townships. The SACP's rebirth as a popular party inevitably brought them into rivalry with the ANC, after their more discreet influence and exchanges in the past; and Mandela would soon become increasingly critical of them. 'They made a huge mistake,' said Ben Turok, a former Party insider, 'in trying to become a mass party.'[21]

The government, and much of the white press, continued to play up the communist menace; but it was much harder to believe in the world-wide 'total onslaught' since the collapse of the communist regimes in Russia and Eastern Europe. And Mandela warned Pretoria not to try to impede negotiations by 'whipping up anti-communist hysteria'. In fact it was simplistic to equate communism in South Africa with hard-line resistance, as Joe Slovo had shown. 'It has been communists,' claimed Mandela later, 'who have come out as the most moderate.'[22]

Mandela still faced great problems in unifying the ANC, and in bringing them round to negotiation and compromise. His personal leadership remained unassailable, and awesome: his friends had to encourage younger members to argue with him.[23] But he faced his most difficult task in trying to forge a unified party out of the many strands which had been separated by the thirty-year ban; and he took time to establish his own relationship with the National Executive, as an elder statesman who kept his distance while intervening on crucial issues.

All the complaints about the ANC's moderation came to the fore when it held a 'consultative conference' of 1,600 delegates in Johannesburg in December 1990. Tambo had returned to South Africa, still debilitated by his stroke, to formally open the conference as President. He made a bold speech, which had been approved by the National Executive, arguing that the ANC must modify its support for total sanctions: he warned that the Western countries were already retreating from sanctions, and that the ANC could not afford to be marginalised abroad. But the militants would not accept it, and the conference insisted on sanctions, even if they were not being enforced.

Mandela paid tribute to Tambo's leadership of the ANC through its darkest years. But it was left to him to hold the conference together. He tactfully praised all the different components: the guerrillas of MK, 'steeled by years of combat experience and sacrifice'; the long-term prisoners, educated in perseverance and patience; the exiles with their 'high level of political training'; and the leaders inside the country, with their experience of mass mobilisation, 'probably the most attuned to the popular mood'.[24] But the tensions were obvious: the younger internal activists resented the domination of the older exiles from Lusaka, while each section claimed credit for victory.

Mandela was already showing himself as a more conservative and moderate leader than the young comrades had expected, a very different man from the raw revolutionary who had been jailed as the leader of a guerrilla army. And he faced outspoken criticism from the delegates, particularly for having failed to consult them during his talks with the government. In his closing speech he promised that 'the leadership has grasped the principle that they are servants of the people.' But he was hurt that there was 'hardly a word of praise' for the National Executive, and he dismissed critics who thought he could negotiate without any secrecy, saying they 'do not understand the nature of negotiation'.[25]

Six months later, on 2 July, the ANC's policies came under fiercer fire at its full national conference in Durban – the first inside South Africa for over thirty years – with over two thousand delegates. Mandela's chief aim was to prepare the way for compromise and a peaceful settlement, to channel the energies of the militants into talks, not war. He depicted negotiations as 'a continuation of the struggle leading to our central objective: the transfer of power to the people'. He warned that the coming period of transition would be 'one of the most difficult, complex and challenging in the entire life of our organisation'.

But some younger members were impatient with his conservatism, or felt he was betraying the revolution. And he did not always welcome criticism. When he proposed a quota of 30 per cent of the executive for women, Terror Lekota, his old ally on Robben Island, argued boldly against 'tokenism'. Mandela responded quite angrily, and said he could have discussed the matter on Robben Island. 'Mandela taught us that argument is not a sign of disrespect or defiance,' Lekota said afterwards, 'though he wasn't easy to argue with.'[26]

Mandela had to deal with a disorganised political party which was under attack once again for incompetence. 'Does the ANC actually exist – as an organisation – beyond the rhetoric and the headlines?' asked the Johannesburg *Sunday Times*.[27] And Alfred Nzo, the retiring Secretary-General, gave his own devastating critique, which was accidentally leaked: 'We lack enterprise, creativity and initiative. We appear very happy to remain pigeonholed within the confines of populist rhetoric and cliché.'[28] Mandela insisted that they must be 'absolutely brutal' about their shortcomings, and was especially worried about the lack of effective communication between the ANC and the minority groups. But he promised 'to build our organisation into a strong and well-oiled task force'.[29]

The ANC was still dominated by the old guard, including Mandela, Tambo and Sisulu: the last elections for the National Executive had been in 1985. But three formidable younger contenders were competing for the future leadership, each from a separate theatre of the struggle: Chris Hani, the head of MK; Thabo Mbeki, who had been Tambo's key adviser in exile; and Cyril Ramaphosa, the head of the Mineworkers' Union. When delegates voted for the Secretary-General to succeed Nzo, they surprised many people by choosing Ramaphosa, who had outspokenly criticised Winnie and who was not then close to Mandela: before Mandela was released Ramaphosa had said that his status was 'no different from the status of any other member of the ANC'.[30] As a trades unionist he had shown both courage and skill as a negotiator. He could charm his opponents with his soft voice, friendly eyes and wide smile, while he never lost sight of his objective; and he created his own drama – he had been inspired to become a trades unionist by seeing Sylvester Stallone in the movie *F.I.S.T.* Mandela thought him 'very assertive but a born diplomat'; and he proved indispensable in the negotiations that followed.[31]

The ANC re-established itself, despite all the media predictions of splits. It was, Sisulu claimed, 'a unity of leadership unheard of anywhere, in any part of the world'.[32] The new executive of fifty contained a cross-section of the races, including seven Indians, seven Coloureds, and seven whites. White liberals complained that they were excluded and that the white members were all communists; but it was only the communists who had stood by the ANC through the whole struggle.

Tambo stood down as President, and Mandela was unanimously elected as his successor. 'I didn't see myself as leader until I was elected,' he said later. 'Now it was something that had to be done.'[33] Most people in fact already saw him as the real leader, and there were worries that he might become autocratic without Tambo's counterweight. But Mandela paid eloquent tribute to Tambo as the crucial unifier of the party: he had 'paved the way forward with gold, the gold of his humanity, his warmth, his democratic spirit, tolerance and above all intellectual brilliance, which in the end outwitted the racists in this country'. And Mandela remained deeply influenced by Tambo's legacy of reconciliation and consensus.

Mandela was presiding over a much bigger organisation than predecessors like Luthuli or Xuma had dreamt of: later in 1991 the ANC moved into Shell House, a tower block in central Johannesburg. Mandela insisted on having Sisulu and Tambo next door to him, and the three septuagenarians regularly slipped in and out of each other's offices, apparently as close as during the Defiance Campaign forty years earlier. Tambo still reflected more philosophically than Mandela about ANC policy, while Sisulu still assessed Mandela like a teacher with a pupil ('He's doing better than I expected').[34] But they were both backroom advisers, and Mandela was the star performer, the personification of policy. To run his own office he chose three strong women: 'It is no use for a leader to surround himself with yes-men.'[35] Frene Ginwala helped to set up his organisation before running the research department, while Barbara Masekela ran the Office of the President together with Jesse Duarte. They ran a punishing schedule: 'I sometimes think I had more freedom in jail than at the office,' Mandela joked. He found it difficult to operate within a bureaucracy, and treated his office more like a home, with his staff as daughters. He would often order lunch in the office, carefully counting out the coins, munching corn on the cob with childlike pleasure. He was a stickler for punctuality after his jail regime, determined to rebut jokes about 'African time': he insisted that 'lateness is a sign of disrespect for others.'[36] But he would sometimes evade his secretaries when he met old friends in the corridor and stayed talking, or gave visitors his secret home phone number. After his years of seclusion he enjoyed new faces, and he seemed to pay special attention to those who did not push themselves forward: at meetings he would seek out quiet people at the back.[37]

His staff were more worried by his continuing determination to see the best in everyone, as in jail. If they warned him that a visitor was incorrigible, he would feel all the more challenged to disprove it. Colleagues kept complaining that 'Madiba is too nice.' It could make him a bad judge of character, too easy-going with plausible exploiters and wheeler-dealers. But his generosity could often make other people more generous, and could turn hostility into loyalty. His sudden bursts of anger – whether real or assumed – were all the more alarming. He could flare up if his dignity was offended, or if he felt patronised. But he remained a consummate politician with a long-term perspective and unbreakable nerve. He seemed undeterred by bad news: he would make a joke of it, his secretaries noticed, and stand taller.[38]

His self-assurance seemed unassailable: even when low or exhausted, he would primp himself to greet a visitor. He remained instinctively aware of his image, with his aristocratic bearing and his well-tailored suits. 'His clothes were not peripheral,' Masekela said: 'they were central to his political life.' He still felt, as in the fifties, that 'clothes make the man'. Once in Oslo he wanted a furry hat and was brought a selection, none of which he approved. Later he disappeared from his hotel to return with his own choice – a Russian-type hat which he was still wearing in 1999. His vanity helped to keep him going. He could fish for compliments ('I'm an ugly old man'), but he knew that his handsome presence could outshine most politicians in the world.[39]

Would Mandela develop into another African autocrat, accumulating power around himself? South Africans and foreigners watched anxiously for the signs. Certainly Tambo had a genuine humility which Mandela lacked, and was much closer to a saint. Tambo was more loved within the National Executive, more equable, more inclined to listen to everyone, never resentful of being opposed. 'Tambo was a natural democrat,' as Albie Sachs put it; 'Mandela had to learn.'[40]

Mandela's style could offend some of his executive, and in August 1991, while he was travelling abroad, there was a reported plot to cut back his powers and put Ramaphosa in charge of the negotiations with the government. A neat organisational chart had been prepared, which put Ramaphosa as Secretary-General at the top, and Mandela below him; but it was a mistake, as Mandela explained it, based on a wrong analogy with communist parties abroad, where the Secretary was the most important leader. In fact there was never a serious plot or threat, and the story was blown up by deliberate disinformation. Mandela made light of it afterwards; but the executive found him more attentive.[41]

Mandela's regal style still owed something to his chiefly background and to his childhood in the Transkei, watching the Regent dispensing judgements to his subjects. The *Washington Post* correspondent David Ottaway thought Mandela had 'an authoritarianism typical of traditional tribal chiefs', and that he 'harboured a secret yearning to be treated as a chief'.[42] Certainly he often seemed to fill a psychological need in others for a monarch: the sociologists Adam and Moodley detected a 'clamour for royalty' when black car-workers devoted overtime without pay to build a luxury Mercedes for Mandela.[43] The regal style was often misleading: Mandela could sound autocratic, but he believed passionately in democracy. He remained the 'loyal and disciplined member' of the ANC, and when he talked about his 'bosses' he was not necessarily joking. His executive could put him down quite toughly, and his contradictory statements reflected their shifts more than his own. 'Sometimes I feel they are very wrong,' he explained in 1994, 'but I have to pay respect to the majority. I have to go to them one by one to try to persuade them.'[44] He could be very forceful in persuasion: he had been stubbornly right on one supreme issue – like Churchill or de Gaulle – when so many were wrong, and had reason to believe in his rightness.

But Mandela faced many painful transitions as the ANC moved away from revolutionary policies towards moderation and compromise. The most difficult arguments were about public ownership and nationalisation. The Robben Islanders had debated nationalisation in theory for years, but now the National Executive had to agree practical policies which could soon be implemented. Mandela himself still saw nationalising as the obvious means to reduce inequality and give economic power to blacks. Before he went to jail in 1962, he had seen how the British Labour Party embraced its constitution's Clause Four, and believed in capturing the 'commanding heights' through state ownership. And when in 1990 the British Ambassador Robin Renwick argued with him against nationalisation he replied: 'It was your idea. It was fashionable then.'[45] In prison through the seventies and eighties Mandela had not been exposed to the disillusion with state ownership which was being felt around the world; and he could see how South African corporations were working in league with apartheid governments.

By the time of his release in 1990 he was aware that South Africa desperately needed foreign investment to provide economic growth and more jobs, and he promised to campaign for investors as soon as sanctions could be lifted. 'Once the situation is settled,' he said in February 1990, 'investment in the country is the normal development – which we will want.'[46] But he was slow to see, as he admitted later, that the threat of nationalisation would scare away long-term investors. He reminded businessmen how Afrikaner governments had used nationalised industries, including railways, steel and South African Airways, to empower and enrich their own people. Why should blacks now be prevented from taking the same advantage?[47] But each time he called for nationalisation, the Johannesburg stock market turned down: a single speech drove the all-gold index down by 5 per cent.[48]

He became more flexible. He proposed that the ten big conglomerates which dominated the stock exchange need not be nationalised, but could be broken up by anti-trust laws. He harked back again to his own interpretation of the Freedom Charter, which would allow African business to 'flourish as never before'. He became friendly with business leaders including Harry Oppenheimer, the arch-capitalist. He asked Helen Suzman, his old Robben Island friend, to arrange a lunch with tycoons where (she noted) he 'charmed the bloody lot of them'.[49] They warned him that nationalisation was not the way to wealth creation, and several ANC colleagues including Thabo Mbeki pressed home the point. But his Marxist colleagues were still watchful; and the young comrades in the townships continued to equate capitalism with oppression.

Mandela's views could be confusing. He seemed more at ease with bankers than trades unionists, and to foreign visitors he did not sound like a socialist. 'He's one of the most conservative people I've ever met,' said the playwright Arthur Miller, who spent time with him in late 1990. 'Had he been born into a peaceful society he would have been a judge.'[50] But Mandela still believed in a classless society, while 'painfully aware' of the opposite trend.[51] He looked for ways to reduce inequality. In September 1991 he told businessmen that only nationalisation could redress the imbalances, though he would welcome an alternative. The confusing signals reflected arguments within the ANC which were more extreme than those that had raged through the socialist parties of Europe; for South Africa had long been an extreme case, both of inequality and of dependence on international capital.

It was not until February 1992, when Mandela went to the World Economic Forum in Davos, Switzerland, that he finally turned against nationalisation. He was lionised by the world's bankers and industrialists at lunches and dinners. He argued with them that other industrial countries, including Britain, Germany and Japan, had needed nationalised industries to restore their economies after world wars. 'We are going through a traumatic experience of war against the people,' he explained, 'and therefore we need nationalisation.' But he sounded, as one economist complained, like an early Fabian socialist; and he was outgunned by both de Klerk and Buthelezi, who made their own arguments for free enterprise at the conference.

He was finally turned by three sympathetic delegates from the left. The Dutch Minister of Industry was sisterly and understanding, but smashed his argument. 'Look, that's what we understood then,' she explained, 'but now the economies of the world are interdependent. The process of globalisation is taking root. No economy can develop separately from the economies of other countries.' Leaders from two Asian socialist countries – China and Vietnam – told him how they had accepted private enterprise, particularly after the Soviet Union collapsed. 'They changed my views altogether,' recalled Mandela. 'I came home to say: "Chaps, we have to choose. We either keep nationalisation and get no investment, or we modify our own attitude and get investment."'[52]

He still faced battles at home. When the ANC held an economic conference soon afterwards he proposed abandoning the option of nationalisation, but he was accused of betraying the Freedom Charter and he had to withdraw the proposal. The passionate old arguments were still raging through the executive and the townships. It was not until 1993, when the ANC was looking towards an election, that they accepted a more moderate policy of privatising some industries, and replacing nationalisation with the new Reconstruction and Development Programme. Mandela still stuck to his belief in a classless society; but he and his party had accepted that South Africa could not opt out of the global marketplace – which turned out to be more ruthless than they expected.

30

Third Force

WHILE MANDELA WAS trying to unify and moderate his own party, and prepare it for power, his prospects were being undermined by a terrifying escalation of political violence. The wave of killings through the late eighties surged rapidly after his release, and his inability to prevent them seriously damaged his credibility as a future leader. But the heart of the violence was impossible to penetrate, and the layers of evidence would only gradually be uncovered: it was not till eight years later that the truth became clearer.

At first most of the killings were concentrated in KwaZulu-Natal, the beautiful but impoverished heartland of the Zulu people, where the horrors seemed all the worse in the peaceful rural surroundings. Between July 1990 and June 1993, an average of 101 people a month died in 'politically related incidents' in KwaZulu-Natal, reaching a total of 3,653 deaths.[1] The violence was depicted by most whites as a straightforward tribal conflict between Zulu patriots and Xhosa interlopers seeking to dominate the nation through the ANC. The key to peace appeared to rest with Chief Buthelezi and his Zulu party Inkatha, which was extending its power. And Inkatha could hold the balance in the oncoming negotiations, for de Klerk's National Party clearly hoped to bring it, with other tribal groups, onto their side to outvote the ANC.

Mandela in jail had been careful to keep on good terms with Buthelezi, and before his release he had sent him another long letter, urging him to meet Tambo in London. 'In my entire political career,' he wrote, 'few things have distressed me [as much] as to see our people killing one another as is now happening.'[2] Tambo and Sisulu, like other ANC leaders, were very wary of Buthelezi after his past turnabouts, but Mandela had retained his chiefly relationship: he had defended Buthelezi for resisting the government's pressure to turn KwaZulu into a separate Bantustan, and believed he could persuade him to cooperate with the ANC. 'I don't think there was anybody who was more favourably disposed to Buthelezi than Madiba,' said Sisulu later.[3]

Mandela hoped for a personal rapprochement with Buthelezi, as chief to chief. He phoned him a week after he left jail, thanking him for refusing to negotiate with Pretoria until he came out and asking to visit him. A week later Mandela boldly went into the lion's den, to the Zulu stronghold of Durban to address a rally of 100,000 people, nearly all Zulus, at King's Park. He wanted Buthelezi to share his platform, but his colleagues opposed this, to Buthelezi's fury. Mandela suggested a future joint meeting, but the crowd gave 'an ominous rumble of disapproval'.[4] Mandela appealed to them: 'Take your guns, your knives and your pangas and throw them into the sea!' But his appeal, he lamented, 'fell on deaf ears'.[5] And soon afterwards, it turned out, the police secretly provided a grant of 120,000 Rand to Inkatha to fund their own counter-rally.[6]

Mandela had hoped also to deal direct with the King of the Zulus, Buthelezi's nephew Goodwill Zwelithini, with whom he had his own connections as a former lawyer to the Zulu royal house; but the ANC would not agree to his meeting him without colleagues, as the King insisted. And any meeting with Buthelezi was vetoed by the local ANC leaders led by Harry Gwala, the old Zulu Stalinist from Robben Island, now half-paralysed but still intransigent. 'The ANC wanted to choke me,' Mandela would often recall, 'when I mentioned Buthelezi.'[7]

De Klerk would always criticise Mandela for not meeting Buthelezi, which he blamed on Mandela's 'high-handed approach'.[8] Could the two leaders have stopped the massacres? 'History would have been quite different if Madiba had had his way,' said Buthelezi afterwards.[9] And Jacob Zuma, the ANC Zulu leader in Natal (who had also been on Robben Island), believed that the ANC was making a serious mistake: 'It was important for Buthelezi to feel welcomed, embraced and part of the process . . . You could have had absolutely the end of the problem.'[10] But the violence on the ground already had its own momentum, and many ANC leaders thought the conflicts could only be resolved further down. Thabo Mbeki was making discreet contacts with local Inkatha leaders, who met the ANC in September, for the first time since the break between the two groups in 1979. Mbeki insisted that Mandela and Buthelezi should not meet until they were part of the process; and it was Mbeki who would in the end produce agreement.[11]

The killings still escalated, coming closer to civil war, while the police appeared oddly reluctant to intervene. 'The attacks were launched blatantly in full daylight,' said a report by Amnesty International, 'and often in the presence of the police and in some cases with their active participation.' They spread further in July 1990, when Buthelezi launched the Inkatha Freedom Party (IFP), intended to bring the Zulu party onto the national stage. 'We will not allow the ANC and its SACP partner,' he proclaimed, 'to crush all opposition and emerge as the only viable party.' The IFP claimed to have recruited 300,000 members in its first few months, and would soon claim a membership of 1.8 million.[12] Shortly afterwards political killings erupted in the Transvaal, particularly in the urban areas embraced by Pretoria, Witwatersrand and Vereeniging: 4,756 people would be killed in 'politically-related violence' in the PWV region over the next three years, according to the Truth Commission's later report – more than in KwaZulu-Natal.[13] It was hard not to connect the violence with the IFP's national ambitions.

The single-sex hostels for Zulu workers in the towns provided hotbeds of violence, and a hideous massacre occurred in Sebokeng, south of Johannesburg, on 22 July, when hundreds of Zulus from hostels were bussed in for a mass demonstration. Anticipating trouble, the ANC tipped off the Minister of Law and Order, Adriaan Vlok, who took no action, and the resulting battle left thirty dead, mostly ANC. Mandela visited Sebokeng the next day, and saw the dead bodies in the morgue, hacked and disfigured. He blamed de Klerk rather than Buthelezi, and asked why he had done nothing; he received no proper reply.[14]

The killings were especially sinister because they seemed timed to upset the negotiations. Three days after Mandela had signed the Pretoria Minute with de Klerk in August a new wave of violence swept through the Transvaal townships, killing a thousand blacks in a month. While Mandela was talking with the government, his credibility was being undermined by massacres which he evidently could not control, and white South Africans were pointing to 'black-on-black' violence as a sign that the ANC were incapable of government. The plans of military intelligence officers to divide the black opposition appeared to be succeeding: many ANC leaders now seemed to regard Buthelezi as more of an enemy than de Klerk.

The police appeared still more ineffectual as armed gangs began to attack the packed trains which carried black commuters between Soweto and Johannesburg. In the most lethal battle, on 13 September, a band of gunmen rampaged through the carriages, killing twenty-six people and injuring a hundred. In all, 572 people would be killed in train violence over the next three years – for which the Truth Commission would later blame Inkatha, the police and the army.[15]

The ANC responded to the violence by creating their own paramilitary bands, called 'Self-Defence Units', or SDUs. They claimed to be based on local communities in response to 'grassroots demands for protection against the onslaught'. But the ANC authorised the supply of weapons, organised by Ronnie Kasrils, a member of the executive; and the SDUs, which were intended for self-defence, were not closely supervised: 'It was a very problematic situation,' Kasrils explained later, 'at times extremely confusing.' The Truth Commission would later partly blame the ANC for 'contributing to a spiral of violence in the country through the creation and arming of SDUs'.[16]

Mandela was now convinced by ANC intelligence that the attacks were not simply the work of Inkatha supporters, but were instigated by what he called a 'third force' inside the security services which was deliberately trying to prevent talks with the government.* He was becoming less sure about giving up the armed struggle: in September he told a press conference that the ANC might have to start fighting again. In October he warned de Klerk that people perceived that 'there are forces close to you, Mr President, with a double agenda'. De Klerk had in fact already been warned in January 1990, by the Minister of Defence Magnus Malan, about a murderous secret organisation within the defence forces, with the Orwellian name of the Civil Co-operation Bureau: de Klerk had commissioned an investigation by Judge Louis Harms, who reported in November 1990; but it was a whitewash, dismissing evidence of a death squad based on Vlakplaas outside Pretoria which later turned out to be perfectly true. Mandela found Harms's report unbelievable, and thought that de Klerk and others in government 'chose to look the other way or ignore what they knew was going on under their noses'. By the end of November he was accusing intelligence agencies of orchestrating 'the

* The expression 'third force' had been used by President Botha's State Security Council in November 1985, when they discussed setting up a separate paramilitary unit to enforce internal security. The police and defence could not agree about the control of the unit, and both later created separate organisations which effectively did the job. Ministers could thus claim that no 'third force' existed. But Mandela was talking about a less formally organised body.

slaughter of our people'. Western intelligence was also concerned: when de Klerk visited the White House in September 1990, President Bush soon said, 'I am concerned about evidence . . . on a "third force".'[17]

The rift widened between Mandela and de Klerk. Mandela kept telephoning de Klerk with new allegations, and often disbelieved the explanations he was given. De Klerk accused Mandela of hypocrisy, since the ANC had its own troublemakers, and resented his tirades: 'Mr Mandela, I did not telephone you to be insulted. Goodbye!'[18] Mandela felt all the angrier since he had earlier called de Klerk a 'man of integrity', against the advice of Sisulu and others, for which he was often criticised by the militants. 'When he felt betrayed,' said Sisulu, 'it was impossible to keep him on that line.' Sisulu was less surprised by de Klerk's behaviour, having always seen him as part of the National Party's intrigues; but Mandela had given de Klerk his personal endorsement, which he now withdrew. In fact he had never respected de Klerk, as he had P.W. Botha: now he thoroughly distrusted him.

De Klerk still hoped for Buthelezi's support as a counterweight against the ANC; but he was finding him a very awkward ally, a 'jumble of contradictions' who could be 'tenaciously obstinate and frustratingly sullen'.[19] De Klerk's Ministers, too, were often finding Buthelezi intransigent. 'We wanted an alliance with Inkatha, but he was impossible to deal with,' recalled the former Minister of Finance Barend du Plessis. 'One week he would agree to something, the next there'd be a fiasco.' 'Buthelezi was causing us a lot of trouble,' said the Foreign Minister Pik Botha. 'It was the Europeans and Americans who were building him up.'[20]

Certainly Buthelezi's ambitions were being openly encouraged by right-wing groups overseas. In America the Heritage Foundation and other anti-communist groups were still welcoming him as the scourge of ANC communists; while in Germany he was supported by the Konrad Adenauer Foundation and some rich businessmen. But it was Britain which provided his most enthusiastic backers on his frequent visits. Mrs Thatcher had seen him again early in 1990, against Foreign Office advice, and had praised him as 'a stalwart opponent of violent uprising in SA while the ANC had been endorsing the Marxist revolution'.[21] But British policy towards the Zulus was confused. Mrs Thatcher still argued for some kind of tribal confederal solution which would give more autonomy to Zulus and other tribes, while her more right-wing friends were encouraging a warlike defiance which seemed aimed at secession.

Zulu tribalism had a special appeal to a group of rich British right-wingers including Sir James Goldsmith and his friend John Aspinall, the casino and zoo owner who had bought a big estate outside Cape Town and called himself a 'White Zulu'. In July 1990 Buthelezi was the key speaker in London at a meeting of the Centre for Policy Studies, Mrs Thatcher's favourite think-tank, where he warned that the revolutionaries of the ANC were determined to 'shoot themselves into power' and told the British they had 'an unfinished job to do in South Africa'.[22] British speakers were even more inflammatory. The Tory journalist Bruce Anderson complained that the Zulus were not being violent enough, while Aspinall said that South Africa should be divided into over thirty tribal components – which went too far for Buthelezi.[23]

Four months later Aspinall gave a banquet for Buthelezi in London, ostensibly to discuss wildlife, attended by rich conservatives including Goldsmith, Jacob Rothschild and Marc Gordon of the International Freedom Front, which was championing Buthelezi's policies.[24] Aspinall continued to play the White Zulu: in May 1991, when the King of the Zulus addressed 40,000 people in Soweto, Aspinall made a speech warning the ANC that 'they have wakened the Zulu giant'.[25] Buthelezi had become a mascot of the far right in Britain and America, like Jonas Savimbi in Angola; but his patrons did not obviously seek to restrain him, and they had no visible plan to bring peace to the bloody battlefields.

Back in South Africa, Mandela had at last met Buthelezi personally on 29 January 1991, a year after leaving jail. Buthelezi maintained a chiefly respect for Mandela, deferring to him as an older person, in the African tradition.[26] They talked at the Royal Hotel in Durban for eight hours and agreed to promote peace, to stop 'killing talk' and to set up a joint monitoring committee; but Mandela thought afterwards that Inkatha 'never made any effort to implement the accord'.[27] In the first three months of 1991, four hundred people were killed, most of them after the Durban meeting. Inkatha's attacks on the ANC were increasingly provoking bloody reprisals, and both sides were retaliating with vendettas: the Truth Commission would later hold the ANC responsible for over a thousand deaths in KwaZulu-Natal and the Orange Free State, while Inkatha was blamed for nearly four thousand.[28]

Mandela and Buthelezi had much in common: both from proud chiefly backgrounds, both educated at Fort Hare, both with an articulate charm which could disarm white visitors. But Buthelezi remained much more the tribal leader, preoccupied with Zulu traditions and formal speech-making: he had never had to submit to the disciplines of party democracy, while his backers overseas had encouraged his tribalism. He was becoming increasingly erratic, with signs of paranoia, reacting furiously to critics, including journalists, who began to turn against him ('probably the most unpleasant politician on the African continent', judged David Ottaway of the *Washington Post*).[29] And Mandela was losing patience with Buthelezi's unpredictable moods: after a friendly man-to-man meeting, he would return to KwaZulu to deliver a ferocious attack in his tribal regalia. Mandela put it down to Buthelezi's insecurity: he had been deprived of parental love and care as a child, he explained, so that he became unsure if you were still his friend after he had left.[30] It was now the turn of colleagues like Sisulu to persuade Mandela to conciliate.

On 1 April 1991 Mandela met Buthelezi again. He warned him that the government had a hidden agenda to divide the blacks, but Buthelezi rejected the idea, as he explained in a confidential letter to Mandela two days later: 'I just do not believe that Mr de Klerk presides over cloak-and-dagger stuff in the employment of security forces in order to increase the white man's chance of continuing to dominate us . . . Do you really distrust Mr F.W. de Klerk and the SA government?'[31]

But Mandela *did* distrust de Klerk, with some reason. On 5 April, after Mandela warned his executive, the ANC wrote to de Klerk threatening to pull out of the talks unless the government purged the Ministers and police chiefs responsible for the violence. 'In no other country,' Mandela said at a press conference, 'would the government keep Ministers whose departments were responsible for the death of thousands of people.' When de Klerk refused, the ANC announced that they would break off the talks and embark on mass action, culminating in a general strike. De Klerk then organised a conference on violence which Mandela refused to attend, arguing that de Klerk already knew how to end the violence. 'He was still operating under the illusion, cherished by so many revolutionaries,' complained de Klerk afterwards, 'that possession of the levers of government enabled those in power to achieve whatever goals they wanted.'[32]

Mandela's image at home and abroad was now seriously dented, as he appeared incapable of controlling the 'black-on-black' violence. 'The image of the great deliverer has gone, perhaps for ever,' wrote the liberal journalist Shaun Johnson in September 1990. 'Everything the poor man says is interpreted in the worst possible light,' wrote *Business Day*, 'without the slightest consideration for the fine political line he must draw or for the inherent weakness of his position.' De Klerk, by contrast, was seen abroad as a statesman with growing authority. 'De Klerk's international standing,' the political scientist Stephen Ellis reckoned later, 'was higher than that of the head of any South African government for fifty years.'[33] He seemed thoroughly in control, and in April 1991 made a successful European tour, proclaiming that his government had re-entered the civilised world by dismantling apartheid and appealing to businessmen to start investing again. In London Mrs Thatcher, he said, 'did everything she could to support me'.[34] At dinner at Number Ten the Foreign Secretary Douglas Hurd was impressed by 'an amazingly wise and brave man' who had 'almost run out of aces'.[35] 'What the blacks need,' wrote Hugo Young in the *Guardian*, 'is a leader as competent as de Klerk.'[36]

But there were growing accounts in the more adventurous 'alternative press' in South Africa of secret conspiracies, particularly in the Afrikaans weekly *Vrye Weekblad*. And in June 1991 a disillusioned ex-military intelligence officer, Captain Nico Basson, claimed that his former bosses had planned to destabilise the black opposition with violence and dirty tricks as they had done in Namibia, masterminded by the chief of the defence forces, Kat Liebenberg.[37]

Basson's allegations could not be proved, but in July 1991 there was a spectacular breakthrough. The South Africa correspondent of the *Guardian*, David Beresford, obtained some top-secret documents from an ex-officer in the security police which showed clearly that the police had been financing Inkatha, through a secret bank account in Durban, with the knowledge of Buthelezi. The *Guardian* published the story jointly with the *Weekly Mail* in Johannesburg, which splashed it on 18 July: 'POLICE PAID INKATHA TO BLOCK ANC'. Rarely has any news story had such an immediate impact on a government. The Minister for Police, Adriaan Vlok, was forced to admit the payments, and ten days later de Klerk removed both Vlok and Magnus Malan, the Minister for Defence, from their jobs – though keeping them in his cabinet. In the following weeks the *Weekly Mail* produced still more damaging revelations about the defence forces' secret training of assassins for Inkatha.[38]

The disclosures vindicated all Mandela's suspicions about a third force. De Klerk's authority was weakened, and he would admit that 'our credibility had been seriously damaged'. Belatedly he 'began to suspect that some elements in the security forces might be dragging their feet'.[39] Two weeks later he appointed a new commission under Judge Richard Goldstone, which after a slow start uncovered much more serious conspiracies. The ANC wanted to press home their advantage by stepping up mass action. But Mandela still wanted to negotiate, while Churches and business leaders were clamouring for conciliation.

In September 1991 a national peace conference was held at the Carlton Hotel in Johannesburg, attended by twenty-four political bodies and including the three main leaders: de Klerk, Mandela and Buthelezi. Three days before, de Klerk had a fierce meeting with Mandela, accusing him of outrageous public attacks and complaining that Operation Vula was still infiltrating weapons. At the Carlton meeting the atmosphere was ominous, with hundreds of Inkatha supporters armed with 'traditional weapons' demonstrating outside without interference from the police, stamping their feet and smacking their shields. At the end of the conference all the parties agreed to a 'National Peace Accord'. It promised to 'actively contribute to a climate of democratic tolerance, refrain from intimidation and agree that no weapons . . . may be possessed, carried or displayed at any political meeting'. But the warlike crowds outside were not encouraging. At the televised press conference afterwards, Mandela furiously denounced de Klerk for not having them dispersed, while Buthelezi refused to join in a three-way handshake with the other two.[40] The killings went on, with three mass shoot-outs a few days later. Mandela continued to talk privately with de Klerk, but he was now much less trusting. At the Commonwealth Summit in Harare in October 1991 he said that de Klerk 'turned out to be a totally different man from what he was initially', and admitted: 'Perhaps there was a little bit of naïveté on our part.'[41]

Over the next year more evidence would emerge of secret conspiracies and hit-squads. In November 1992 Judge Goldstone uncovered more details of illegal acts by security forces, and the next month General Pierre Steyn would report to de Klerk that units of the army had secretly worked to attack and disrupt the ANC, and had probably been involved in the train massacres. De Klerk responded by retiring six top-ranking officers, but then appointed three Generals to investigate who had themselves been implicated by Steyn, an act which the Truth Commission would later call 'a serious error of judgement'.[42]

Much more evidence about a third force trickled out later, showing how the army had secretly trained assassins for Inkatha, how the police encouraged the massacres in Sebokeng and promoted tribal battles. But the full story never emerged. The Truth Commission, as it reported in 1998, 'did not make significant progress in uncovering the forces behind the violence in the 1990s'. It saw little evidence of a centrally directed, coherent or formally constituted third force. But it found that

> a network of security and ex-security operatives, acting frequently in conjunction with right-wing elements and/or sectors of the IFP, were involved in gross violations of human rights, including random and targeted killings.[43]

It was clear that groups of army officers and policemen had their own programmes for instigating violence, often using the same lethal tactics they had employed in destabilising neighbouring countries in the eighties, in order to divide the black opposition and weaken the ANC. After 1992, when the government clamped down on them more seriously, many of them would be effectively privatised, financing themselves through selling weapons or drugs, sometimes working with criminal gangs. And while the major parties began negotiating a peaceful settlement, the underground groups would establish their own network of corruption, which became a breeding ground for criminal activity, and would provide Mandela with his biggest problem in the following years.

31

Exit Winnie

IN HIS FIRST TWO YEARS of freedom, Mandela had taken many sharp knocks, as he appeared helpless to control the violence which had caused far more deaths than in any year of apartheid. Sometimes he seemed too weary to take the country into a new era. At the same time he was up against a domestic crisis which was even more stressful, and which was painfully being revealed.

Through all his public encounters and world travels, Mandela appeared to have the ideal consort. Winnie in her fifties was still strikingly beautiful, with the same powerful eyes and warm presence. To many people she had almost equal credentials in the struggle as her husband, in spite of the accusations over the murdered Stompie Seipei; while she could reach out further than Mandela, to younger and more radical spirits, and to the homeless and leaderless on the edges of society. The famous couple seemed mutually supportive: Winnie could tactfully guide Mandela to political friends, while he was attentive to her needs. He still felt guilty that she had borne the brunt of the family burdens and political persecution, and was grateful to anyone who had stood by her.

Only a few close friends saw the truth behind the façade, which he revealed in 1996 when he told the divorce judge that since he left jail 'not once has she ever entered my bedroom whilst I was awake'. He would have liked them to discuss their most intimate and personal problems, he would tell the judge, 'but she always refused. She is the type of person who fears confrontation.'[1] 'They never could talk things over,' their daughter Zindzi confirmed. 'From the day my father was free, we had to share him with the rest of the world.'[2]

Mandela's idealised Winnie (or 'Zami', as he called her) shone out from his prison letters; but that ideal soon faded in real life, while his own public image looked very different in the home. 'Zami married a man who soon left her,' as he said himself. 'That man became a myth;

and then the myth returned home and proved to be a man after all.'[3] 'While together in their separation,' as Fatima Meer put it, 'in their togetherness they began to discover how apart they had become.'[4]

Mandela was still visibly fascinated by Winnie: he was always looking at her, and when he was away he would frequently ring her up. Visitors to their house would see them together, romping with their grandchildren on the king-sized bed. Mandela, said Fatima, 'needed Winnie desperately to be with him, to love and be loved by her, to be at home when he arrived, in short to be a wife in the ordinary sense'.[5] But Winnie had no intention of settling down to a quiet domestic life, or giving up her liaisons with other men.

Winnie's unfaithfulness was very obvious to the press. 'How long can Winnie's demure image last?' asked the *Star* a week after Mandela's release. When a reporter from the London *Daily Mirror* interviewed Mandela in April 1990 in Soweto she noticed how affectionate he was towards Winnie, and how unresponsive and impatient Winnie was towards him; but the *Mirror* only published an idyllic version of their life together.[6] Winnie lived by a quite different clock from Mandela, who could not break his jail habit of rising very early and retiring early: on their very first night together in Soweto, one friend noticed, Winnie left the house at 10 p.m., returning in the early hours. And Winnie still kept open house to young people, who were constantly rushing in and out. Mandela was trying to pull her away from her connections with guerrilla fighters and MK, realising that many of her contacts were suspect. But he could not control her activities.[7]

It was not just with Winnie that Mandela had strained relationships. Behind his public accessibility, he had built high walls round his private personality while in jail; and he appeared an extreme case of the public leader who had left his private life behind: 'He combined extreme heartiness with impenetrable reserve' (as Arthur Schlesinger described Franklin Roosevelt).[8] He found it hard to relate casually to old friends and family, while his demanding schedule left little time for him to adjust and wind down. 'He had forgotten how to communicate,' said Amina Cachalia. 'At first he talked to me like a warder.'[9]

His children found him aloof, and his two younger daughters were much closer to their mother. 'Mummy, you know we were better off with Daddy in prison,' Winnie recalled Zindzi telling her a week after Mandela's release. 'We had access to him, we could talk to him as a father. Now that all has gone.' Six years later Winnie would still complain: 'My children still wait for the return of their father. He has never returned, even emotionally. He can no longer relate to the family as a family. He relates to the struggle which has been his lifetime.'[10]

Mandela's two eldest children, by his first wife Evelyn, had never come close to their stepmother. His son Makgatho, now in Natal, was still having difficulty with studying, in his forties, and saw his father only rarely. His eldest daughter Maki was bitter about not having had a father, she told the *Washington Post* in an interview just before Mandela was released: she suggested that he had deliberately chosen to be arrested in 1962.[11] It was not till she visited him on his seventy-first birthday in prison that she had felt his inhibitions fall away, and 'for the first time he opened to me as a father'. Maki was living in Boston in 1990, and was understandably hurt when Mandela visited the city and asked to see his grandchildren, but not her; though she blamed Winnie. After Maki returned to South Africa in October 1990 she saw her father occasionally, but she felt he did not know how to talk to her. 'It was easier with letters,' she said, though their letters were also strained.[12] Mandela recalled to Joe Slovo's daughter Gillian – who had likewise suffered from her father's commitment to the struggle – how he had tried to hug Maki, who had flinched away from him. 'You are a father to all our people,' she had told Mandela, 'but you have never had the time to be father to me.'[13]

After a few months in their old matchbox house Mandela and Winnie moved into the big house in 'Beverly Hills', a more spacious part of Soweto, which Winnie had had specially built for them, with seven bedrooms and a conference room with a boardroom table for twenty-five. 'See how right he looks in this house,' said Winnie, 'and his wife built it for him, all by herself.'[14] But Mandela had always been uneasy about the house's extravagance, and its upkeep soon proved a financial burden – particularly after October 1990, when an unnamed donor stopped payments.[15]

On New Year's Eve Winnie organised the 'Bash of the Year' at the big house, with five hundred guests who included Sisulu, Tutu and Slovo: but Mandela appeared uneasy, and gave an unfestive speech, warning that schoolchildren must go back to school after the holidays. Winnie liked to depict the big house as a family love-nest for the children and sixteen grandchildren. But stories emerged of her stumbling home in the small hours, and having to be carried to bed. The media were beginning to portray the famous couple as a national melodrama. They wondered, said Fatima Meer: 'How could a god-like hero live with a witch-like wife?' Mandela, said John Carlin of the London *Independent*, was 'blinded like Samson by love, seduced like Macbeth into betraying his better nature'.[16]

The ANC leaders faced a growing dilemma. They were well aware of Winnie's political appeal, particularly to the young. Mandela recognised that she had a populist flair that he lacked. Tambo saw her as a crucial link with the young and unemployed: he realised that some of Winnie's militant friends had dubious connections, but the ANC needed them inside their tent. And the support of Winnie and the firebrands was important to aspiring leaders, including Thabo Mbeki. Fatima Meer saw the Mandelas' marriage more threatened by the ANC power-struggle than by their personal relations.[17]

The political partnership still had its own electricity. 'Lunching with the Mandelas, you could feel a real pact between them,' said one of his aides. 'He seemed obsessed by her – and fascinated by his own obsession.'[18] But Winnie resented Mandela's total commitment to the movement. 'The ANC just took him over completely,' she complained later. 'He had been conditioned like Pavlov's dog to only respond to the call of the organisation.' From the start she was shocked that Mandela should call de Klerk 'a man of integrity', and claimed she argued with him about it on their first trip abroad: de Klerk was 'just as much a murderer as P.W. Botha'. When Mandela called for his supporters in Durban to disarm themselves, she was furious: 'I threw up my arms,' she recalled. 'You can't call upon the ANC to throw their spears into the sea whilst they're being killed by the enemy and our people are dying in hundreds.'[19] While Mandela wanted to end the armed struggle, Winnie liked to wear a kind of MK uniform, and talked about 'shooting our way to freedom'. She threatened to go back to the bush herself to fight the white man. But Mandela remained conciliatory to her: people outside the National Executive, he explained, did not find it so easy to understand the decisions.[20]

The 'she-elephant' ('Indlovukazi'), as Winnie was called, was becoming increasingly out of control. The ANC hoped to restrain her by bringing her inside the organisation, and in September 1990 they unwisely put her in charge of ANC welfare. It dismayed many large donors, including Bishop Trevor Huddleston, the Chairman of the Anti-Apartheid Movement in London, who thought Winnie was not reliable in handling large sums of money. Mandela defended her, saying that the opponents of the appointment could be counted 'on the fingers of one hand'.[21]

But Winnie had her own grudges against many ANC leaders, particularly those who had publicly condemned her after the murder of Stompie Seipei in 1988. She attacked Cyril Ramaphosa, and mocked Murphy Morobe as a friend of Indians: 'It's Morobe or me,' she told Mandela. She saw a cabal trying to tame Mandela and break up the marriage. 'They worked very hard to destroy that link with the family,' she explained later, 'because they wanted a Mandela who is what he is today. I was extreme, very extreme.'[22]

Winnie was due to come up for trial early in 1991 for the abduction of Stompie and five others in December 1988 (see Chapter 26). The preparations aroused intense speculation, with stories of witnesses disappearing or leaving the country. Some politicians and diplomats worried that Winnie's prosecution would undermine Mandela's morale, and de Klerk was rumoured to be trying to pressure the Attorney-General to drop it. But Mandela publicly welcomed a trial to settle the matter, and accused the government of deliberately putting it off while the press judged her instead.[23] When she was eventually charged – with kidnap and assault rather than murder – Winnie predictably retorted that it was part of the pattern of police harassment, which 'has never been a surprise to the Mandela family or to myself or to the oppressed people of South Africa. I know I have personally been their barometer through which they can measure the wrath of the people.'[24] Alfred Nzo, the ANC Secretary-General, condemned it as a political trial, which violated the spirit of the agreements with the government.

Mandela wanted Winnie to have the best possible defence. He asked George Bizos to take it on, and expected the costs to be paid by International Defence and Aid (IDAF), which was largely financed by the Swedes. But both the Swedes and the Chairman of IDAF, Trevor Huddleston, were doubtful that her case was eligible. In October Mandela rang the IDAF director Horst Kleinschmidt in London, clearly concerned that the funds had been refused. Kleinschmidt, as he reported to IDAF, 'felt uneasy and awkward beyond description', and explained that IDAF might soon be dissolved anyway. Eventually the Swedes were persuaded to pay much of the heavy cost of the trial, while part was paid by President Qadaffi of Libya. But the argument, said Denis Herbstein, the historian of IDAF, 'drove a wedge between the ANC and the IDAF board that soured relations once and for all';[25] and IDAF people were hurt that Mandela never mentioned them in his autobiography.

When Winnie finally came up for trial in February 1991, Mandela gave her maximum support, which he saw as a husband's duty, and urged his friends to turn up: on the opening day the audience included Joe Slovo, Alfred Nzo, Chris Hani and Fatima Meer. Only a few resisted: 'I was moved by his loyalty to her,' said Amina Cachalia, 'but she wasn't worth it.'[26] From London the Tambos sent messages of solidarity: 'We know you have told the truth,' wrote Oliver to Winnie. 'Whether the court decides in our favour or against us, you will continue to have our confidence and love.'[27]

The four-month trial had its own dramas, with disappearing witnesses and changing testimony. Winnie tried to distance herself from the Mandela United Football Club, and stuck to her alibi, that she was back in Brandfort on the night of Stompie's beating. The defence lawyers were puzzled by the apparent constraint of the prosecutors. 'Somebody tried to sabotage the case,' the assistant prosecutor van Vuuren testified seven years later. 'The security police obviously did not give us the evidence that should have been available to destroy her alibi.'[28] Just after the murder the police had enough evidence to arrest Winnie, as the prison records show. But were they withholding it to protect a possible First Lady, or keeping back ammunition for a future bombardment?

Winnie herself spent five days in the witness-box, remaining self-possessed and poker-faced, the judge observed, while showing herself to be 'a calm, composed, deliberate and unblushing liar'. The judge accepted her alibi, while finding her guilty of conniving in the assault, with a 'complete absence of compassion towards the victims'. He sentenced her to six years. She appeared unabashed as she left the court with her fist clenched. Mandela, listening to the verdict in court, appeared much more upset, but did not question the judgement: 'Once an appeal has been made, it is proper to leave the matter in the hands of the court.' Winnie continued to insist that the judge 'was not trying me as an individual. He was trying the ANC, criminalising the ANC and attempting to alienate me from the ANC.'[29]

Winnie appealed against the verdict, and in June 1993 the Appeal Court would deliver its judgement: it confirmed her conviction for kidnapping, but decided she was not an accessory to the assaults. And after 'careful and anxious' consideration the court reduced the sentence to only two years' imprisonment, suspended, and a fine of 15,000 Rand (about £3,000). The penalty was surprisingly lenient, but the judgement (including the acceptance of Winnie's alibi) would not be corroborated by the findings of the Truth Commission five years later. The Stompie murder still would not go away.[30]

Winnie was losing some of her political following. At the ANC's Durban conference after the trial she was elected to the National Executive; she tried to become President of the Women's League, against the advice of Mandela, who thought she would fail – which she did. In August the ANC reorganised its welfare department to cut back her powers. Winnie was becoming still more defiantly headstrong, consorting with her young lawyer lover, Dali Mpofu, with an openness which humiliated Mandela. When she planned to fly to America on a supposedly official trip he asked her not to go: she not only disobeyed him, but took Mpofu with her; when Mandela rang her in New York, Mpofu answered the phone.[31]

Mandela faced a new crisis when Winnie suddenly turned against Xoliswa Falati, her old ally against Paul Verryn in the Stompie affair, and threw her out of her house in Soweto. Falati appealed to Mandela, who thought Winnie had been unfair to her; he turned up at the house to find a reporter from the *Sowetan* newspaper, with a photographer recording Falati shut out of the house. Mandela tried to persuade the reporter to drop that story, and then asked the night-editor of the *Sowetan*, Moegsien Williams (later editor of the *Cape Argus*) to see him at the big house. Williams arrived to find Winnie hosting a big party to celebrate the engagement of her daughter Zindzi to Zwelibanzi Hlongwane, a Soweto businessman, with champagne corks popping, while Mandela sat sadly in his study, looking distraught. He implored Williams to spike the story, which he thought could damage Winnie's chances in the appeal. Williams was deeply upset but could not suppress it. The next Monday, 30 March 1992, the *Sowetan* blazoned the story of Winnie's wild behaviour, setting off a new wave of speculation about the Mandela marriage.[32]

Falati took her revenge on Winnie by retracting her supportive evidence in the trial: she now alleged that Winnie had not only connived in the torture of Stompie, but had ordered the murder of other enemies, including Abubaker Asvat, the Indian doctor in Soweto who could have contradicted her alibi. And Winnie's driver John Morgan also now contradicted his own evidence, to claim that Winnie had led the assault on Stompie.[33]

Mandela could not now ignore Winnie's misdeeds. On 13 April he summoned a press conference where, flanked by his two oldest friends Tambo and Sisulu (who had not tried to influence him) in front of the television cameras, he paid tribute to Winnie's fortitude and contribution to the struggle, but went on to announce that because of their differences and tensions 'we have mutually agreed that a separation would be the best for each of us'. He added: 'I part from my wife with no recriminations. I embrace her with all the love and affection I have nursed for her inside and outside prison from the moment I first met her.' He rose to leave with a look of total desolation: 'Ladies and gentlemen, I hope you appreciate the pain I have gone through.' It was the closest he ever came to publicly expressing his private tragedy.

For a time he seemed to have lost his confidence. The BBC correspondent Fergal Keane found him a changed man a week later, talking sadly about having to choose between his wife and the struggle.[34] He began a new life, and moved into a house which had been bought for him by a friendly African head of state, and which his aide Barbara Masekela carefully prepared for him, hoping it would 'hide his pain'.[35] It was a spacious but faded suburban house in the rich white suburb of Houghton, with a big garden and guards in a gatehouse, but it looked unlived-in. Mandela appeared isolated, while his close friends were 'tight-lipped and tense'.[36] Sometimes he seemed able to talk only to his guards, or to white neighbours he would sometimes drop in on. He was, said one friend, 'in a sea of loneliness'. He took solace from his grandchildren, with whom he could romp and relax, though their love was not always disinterested: 'Around Christmas they remember they have a grandfather,' he explained. 'They run around me and tell me how much they love me . . . and I know what question will follow: what are you going to give us?'[37]

Winnie still hoped for a reconciliation, and begged Fatima Meer – who remained friendly with both parties – to persuade Mandela to change his mind. But Winnie had now antagonised both her husband and the ANC, who insisted she resign from her official position. And there was another time-fuse fizzling away that would finally demolish her relationship with Mandela. Back in May ANC investigators had begun to look into misappropriated funds involving Winnie's lover Dali Mpofu when he was her deputy in the welfare department. They had come upon a passionate four-page letter that Winnie had written to him in March. In it she laid into Mpofu furiously for sleeping with another woman –

'running around fucking at the slightest emotional excuse . . . before I'm through with you you are going to learn a bit of honesty and sincerity and know what betrayal of one's trust means to a woman!' She had not been speaking with 'Tata' (Mandela) for five months now, she said in the letter, and 'the situation is deteriorating at home'. But more politically damaging was her reference to cheques she had cashed for Mpofu in the name of the welfare department, which Mandela had asked to be investigated.

It was a gift to her enemies. A copy of the letter was sent to the Johannesburg *Sunday Star* and *Sunday Times*, which confirmed the handwriting as hers. Winnie tried desperately to get the letter back, in exchange for another document. But it had been shown to Mandela himself, who realised it was 'incompatible with a marriage relationship'. It was published unedited by the *Sunday Times* on 6 September 1992, alongside a picture of Winnie with Mpofu. Four days later she resigned her positions in the ANC, 'in the interest of my dear husband and my beloved family', while blaming 'a vicious and malicious campaign against me'.[38]

Mandela appeared to find the letter the last straw, a betrayal and insult he could not ignore. Some close friends worried that he might be breaking down. He seemed physically depressed and inert, reluctant to get out of bed. It was a few days before he recovered his poise, with the help of a demanding schedule which left him little time alone. He kept up some appearance of normal family life. In October 1992, a month after the letter had been published, Winnie organised a wedding reception for Zindzi and her bridegroom Hlongwane, with 850 guests, in the ballroom of the Carlton Hotel in Johannesburg. Mandela appeared, without saying a word to Winnie. As he sat grimly at his table Helen Suzman sent him a note across the room telling him that he was looking like John Vorster, the former Prime Minister, and must smile – which he briefly did.[39] At the end of the party he made a moving speech. He described how one thread ran through the autobiographies of all freedom fighters: 'their private lives with their families are totally destabilised'.

> We watched our children grow up without our guidance, and when we did come out, my children, for example, said: 'We thought we had a father, and that one day he'd come back, but to our dismay our father comes back, and he leaves us alone almost daily, because he has now become the father of the nation.'

Again, one wonders whether it was worth it. But when those doubts come you nevertheless decided for the umpteenth time that in spite of all problems it was – still is – the correct decision that we should commit ourselves.[40]

32

Negotiating

History has many cunning passages, contrived corridors.

T.S. Eliot, 'Gerontion', 1920

NEARLY TWO YEARS after his release, Mandela saw the opening of the negotiations he had been working for. On 21 December 1991, in the middle of the midsummer Christmas holiday, the Convention for a Democratic South Africa (Codesa) was held in the World Trade Centre, a futurist building like a warehouse near Johannesburg airport. 'It was amazing,' said Helen Suzman; 'people who'd just been in jail negotiating with the people who put them there. But they'd decided on a new South Africa.'[1] Many ANC delegates were still surprised to be sitting on equal terms with their oppressors: 'I have spotted twelve policemen who were guarding me in jail,' said Murphy Morobe, who would later manage the convention. 'Now they see me chatting amicably with the Minister of Defence and Chief of Police.'[2]

Two hundred and twenty-eight delegates had assembled from nineteen political parties. It was the most important gathering, said Mandela, since the convention in 1909 which created the Union of South Africa; but the delegates then were all white, while now most were black. There were some dangerous absentees, including right-wing Afrikaner parties and Chief Buthelezi, who had unreasonably demanded three separate delegations for the Zulus. But the first key to peace was to reach some kind of understanding between the ANC and the government.

There was a worrying contrast between the peaceful, often boring atmosphere inside the convention centre and the massacres still raging round South Africa outside. But it was not a contradiction: for much of the violence was, in effect, a show of strength which was part of the bargaining process. 'South Africa is not the only country in the world,' as the political scientist Stephen Ellis wrote afterwards, 'where revolutionary struggles have been accompanied at various stages by intensive negotiation.'[3] Extremists wanted to show that there could be no settlement without them; while the ANC needed the weapon of mass action as their counter to the government's overwhelming military power. De Klerk had been warned by Felipe Gonzalez, the Spanish Prime Minister, to expect his opponents to resort to mass action and protest, and to say one thing round the conference table and quite another in public the next day, since this was the only way that resistance movements could level the playing field against the power of the state.[4]

But Mandela and de Klerk both accepted the basic logic behind any peace talks: that they could not win by force of arms without intolerable loss of life. Mandela was still convinced, as he had been in jail, that 'a military victory was a distant if not an impossible dream'. He warned ANC militants that they could not wait for the government to fall, and that negotiations would require fundamental concessions.[5] De Klerk told diplomats that he thought he could retain power if necessary for ten years, but the casualties would be too heavy.[6] They had both looked into the abyss. And Mandela faced the most demanding task of his career – to negotiate a peaceful revolution without a violent backlash from the white right or the black left.

The negotiations were rightly seen as a dramatic duel between Mandela and de Klerk, both master-politicians in lonely predicaments – and both, it turned out, enduring marital crises: while Mandela was separating from Winnie, de Klerk was falling in love with the wife of his Greek friend Tony Georgiadis.[7] Mandela and de Klerk came from totally opposite backgrounds, the ex-prisoner against the ex-jailer, and their mutual suspicions gave a special edge to the debates. But for much of the time they were arguing with their own parties more than with each other. De Klerk had to deflect his diehards and Generals from the confrontation which had been their chief purpose for forty years; while Mandela had to restrain comrades for whom armed revolution was their life's ambition.

It was one of the most spectacular negotiations in history, and Western governments watched it with fascination. While fighting continued in Northern Ireland, Yugoslavia and the Middle East, South Africa was seen as 'the negotiating capital of the world', and academics, journalists and diplomats converged to observe it. But in the end the South Africans, unlike the Namibians or Zimbabweans, did not need other countries to make their peace for them; and they would always be proud that they had more to teach the world than the world taught them.

The two leaders opened the convention with carefully prepared televised speeches. De Klerk emphasised the need for a democratic 'power-sharing' transitional government. Mandela gave a hopeful overview, with parts in Afrikaans and Zulu, looking forward to 1992 bringing the first democratic elections in homely terms:

> The process of moving towards democracy is unstoppable. History grants all of us a unique opportunity. To exchange this opportunity for a bowl of lentil soup of the past, and negative bravado, is to deny the future.

Most of the parties then endorsed a Declaration of Intent, 'to bring about an undivided South Africa, with one nation sharing a common citizenship, patriotism and loyalty'. The two main teams agreed to accept decisions by 'sufficient consensus' – a deliberately vague phrase. Mandela interpreted it as an agreement between the ANC, the government, and most other parties. But the ANC's chief negotiator, Cyril Ramaphosa, put it more bluntly: 'It means that if we and the National Party agree, everyone else can get stuffed.'[8]

Ramaphosa, the new Secretary-General, had been chosen to head the ANC's team; and he soon made an impact on the Afrikaners, who were unprepared for such intelligence in a black man. His eyes were coldly calculating, as de Klerk saw them, and 'seemed to be searching continuously for the softest spot in the defences of his opponents'.[9] He was backed up by a powerful team including Joe Slovo, Mac Maharaj and Valli Moosa, who were soon working intensely in their offices next to those of the government team, while Thabo Mbeki was also frequently in play. But Mandela himself, they explained, 'was always a phone call away'. They kept thinking, 'What would the old man say?', and in crises they went to his house to find out.[10]

The first day of Codesa ended ominously, with an explosion between the two leaders. De Klerk claimed he had passed a message to Mandela beforehand warning him that he would be sharply critical of the ANC for maintaining its private MK army; but Mandela insisted that de Klerk 'never even hinted' that he would make such an attack.[11] Certainly the ANC were taken aback by de Klerk's closing speech, which lammed into them for secretly keeping arms caches and for breaking the accord reached three months before. Mandela was outraged that de Klerk should exploit his opportunity as the last speaker to reprove him 'like a schoolmaster admonishing a naughty child'; all the more because he had reached a secret understanding with de Klerk in February 1991 – criticised by many colleagues – which allowed MK to remain intact until the transition.[12] After de Klerk finished, Mandela, tense with suppressed fury, strode to the podium, in full view of the TV cameras, to demolish him in the third person without even looking at him, in a masterpiece of invective:

> Even the head of an illegitimate, discredited minority regime, as his is, has certain moral standards to uphold . . . If a man can come to a conference of this nature and play the type of politics as is in his paper – very few people would like to deal with such a man . . .

Mandela insisted that the ANC would only turn in their weapons when they became part of the government collecting those weapons, and accused de Klerk once again of secretly financing violent organisations including Inkatha: if a man in de Klerk's position did not know about that, he said, 'then he is not fit to be the head of government'. But he was still prepared to work with him in spite of all his mistakes.

Mandela's ANC colleagues were amazed. 'He was quivering,' said Barbara Masekela. 'You could see all those years in jail, coming out.' 'Never had a head of state been publicly attacked like that,' said Frene Ginwala, who was on his staff. But whatever Mandela's personal anger, the outburst served a crucial political purpose, for it made forcefully clear that the ANC were there, as Kathrada said, 'not as a defeated party but as a proud participant'. And some journalists saw the aura of power already shifting to the ANC.[13]

De Klerk was quietly furious, hurriedly taking notes and whispering. 'I was hard put to control myself,' he told me later, 'but luckily I received the grace to keep a grip.'[14] He gave a short reply, explaining that unless the issue of arms was resolved, 'we will have a party with a pen in one hand while claiming the right to have arms with the other.'

The next morning both sides were carefully conciliatory: 'We are like the zebra,' said Pik Botha. 'It does not matter whether you put the bullet through the white stripe or the black stripe. If you hit the animal, it will die.' Mandela shook de Klerk's hand and promised to work with him, to the relief of other Afrikaners. But de Klerk reckoned afterwards that 'Mandela's vicious and unwarranted attack created a rift between us that never again fully healed.'[15] The convention adjourned with some pessimism, leaving five negotiating groups to work out detailed agreements before the next full meeting in May.

De Klerk soon received a humiliating defeat from white voters when in February 1992 his National Party was defeated in a by-election at Potchefstroom, one of its strongholds, by the Conservative Party, which opposed any talks with the ANC. He then made a bold decision: to declare a referendum for all white voters on the simple issue of negotiating a new constitution. Many ANC leaders saw it as a cynical diversion from the actual talks, as the government went into campaign mode. Mandela, though he could not approve any all-white election, gave tacit support to de Klerk. On 17 March de Klerk won a triumphant victory – 68.7 per cent of the vote, with an 86 per cent turnout, and declared: 'The nation rises above itself.' Liberal whites saw it as his finest moment. But Mandela knew it was not a vote in favour of black majority rule, and that it strengthened de Klerk's position.[16] De Klerk would never again be so strong; but he still seemed to be playing for time.

On 15 May 1992 the second full meeting of the convention, Codesa 2, was held at the World Trade Centre. De Klerk and his team seemed buoyant after the white referendum, and were insisting on a three-quarter majority vote for the passing of key points in the constitution. Mandela suspected that de Klerk was simply dragging out the talks, to frustrate majority rule: he complained that no progress had been made over the last five months. He was aware of criticism from the left that the ANC was conceding too much for too little. And the working group on the constitution was now reaching deadlock. De Klerk was still looking to Swiss or German models, with formulae for 'power-sharing', including rotating the presidency, and appointing a senate of regional representatives to safeguard minorities. They were designed to avoid control by a simple majority, or 'winner takes all'; Mandela saw them as perpetuating white rule by dividing the blacks. He suspected that de Klerk hoped to keep the National Party in power even after he had lost an election, which he had called a policy of 'loser takes all'.[17]

At the end of the first day of Codesa 2 Mandela and de Klerk met to avert an impasse. 'The whole of South Africa and the world is looking at you and me,' said Mandela. 'Let us leave the door open and say we have made progress.' De Klerk agreed that the negotiations must be kept going, and they both made hopeful statements; but de Klerk was convinced that the ANC was trying to break up the talks. The convention adjourned in deadlock. 'The essence of the problem is not one of percentages or arithmetic,' Mandela said in Sweden five days later. 'It is that the National Party is trying to hold on to power at all costs.'[18] But de Klerk insisted that the communists and militants in the ANC had now taken over, and would reject the concessions: 'They still favoured the revolutionary expulsion of the government and the seizure of power by the people.'[19] In fact the ANC executive were divided at their next meeting about continuing negotiations. Albie Sachs argued that since the government were not serious, the ANC should break off the talks until they agreed on key conditions. Mandela persuaded Sachs not to put it to the vote.[20]

But a few days later, on 17 June, a band of Inkatha supporters, heavily armed, invaded the Vaal township of Boipatong and killed forty-five people. White men with blackened faces joined the attack, and the police clearly colluded (as the Truth Commission later confirmed).[21] Mandela visited the desolated township in disgust, convinced that the government had connived in the massacre, and comparing apartheid to Nazism and genocide. He was met with placards saying 'MANDELA GIVE US GUNS'.[22] 'I can no longer explain to our people,' he said at the victims' funeral, 'why we continue to talk to a regime that is murdering our people.' He wrote to de Klerk, breaking off the negotiations, repeating the ANC's constitutional demands and insisting that the culprits of the massacre be brought to trial. De Klerk asked to meet him, but Mandela saw no point, accusing him of 'factual inaccuracies, distortions and blatant party political propaganda'.[23] De Klerk's lack of control was exhibited when he visited Boipatong in an armoured Mercedes, to be greeted by shouts of 'Kill the Boers!': he had to turn back. He was told that one of the Afrikaner Generals in the next car said: 'Now he can see what his fucking new South Africa looks like!'[24]

The negotiations seemed back to square one, while the whole country appeared to be on the edge of chaos, with continuing violence and an economic crisis. Each leader was now questioning the other's command over his own party. De Klerk complained that he had to deal with two different ANCs.[25] Mandela thought that the right-wing Afrikaners were enforcing their own policies – particularly after further evidence emerged about the third force. When he asked de Klerk why he had not prevented Zulu violence he replied: 'Mr Mandela, when you join me you will realise

I do not have the power which you think I have.' But Mandela thought de Klerk was paralysed: 'He has got the capacity to put an end to the violence.'[26]

Mandela was disturbed, he had told the people of Boipatong, that 'the international community is so quiet about the ongoing massacres', and he now looked abroad for support. He called on the UN Secretary-General, Dr Boutros Boutros-Ghali, to summon a special session of the Security Council. He flew to Senegal for a meeting of the Organisation of African Unity, which endorsed the request. Mandela discussed the situation with Boutros-Ghali, and proposed a UN peacekeeping force. In London the Anti-Apartheid Movement, led by Trevor Huddleston, lobbied the British government to press for UN intervention.

On 15 and 16 July the Security Council met in New York to hear representatives from the different South African parties, including Pik Botha from the government and Buthelezi from Inkatha. Mandela made an aggressive speech, warning members against the 'sweet-sounding words' from a government whose constitution 'the Security Council has declared null and void'. He insisted again that: 'This violence is both organised and orchestrated. It is specifically directed at the democratic movement . . . It constitutes a cold-blooded strategy of state terrorism.'[27]

The UN passed a resolution calling for the perpetrators of Boipatong to be brought to justice, and appointed a special representative – which Mandela had asked for. They sent out Cyrus Vance, the former US Secretary of State, who pressed all parties to resume their talks. It was a reminder to de Klerk of Mandela's global clout, and his own need for international acceptance; but the UN would never play a decisive role in the negotiations.

The deadlock gave more scope to the militants, or 'insurrectionists', within the ANC who were arguing for a return to the armed struggle. Ironically many communists now supported the 'Leipzig option', so called after the East German rebels who had launched mass demonstrations in the streets of Leipzig three years earlier which helped to unseat the communist dictatorship. But while de Klerk blamed the communists, there were many non-communists within the ANC who were equally militant. Mandela was faced with a critical balancing-act; as his friend Fatima Meer explained: 'He cautiously balanced negotiation and mass mobilisation, knowing full well that the responsibility for both fell on his shoulders.'[28] He achieved a compromise: a programme for 'rolling mass action' to press the government to give way. Mandela launched it himself on 16 June, the anniversary of the Soweto uprising, addressing the packed Soweto stadium in a baseball cap. The programme culminated on 3 August in a general strike – the biggest in the country's history – when over four million workers stayed away, a triumphant contrast to Mandela's abortive strike thirty years earlier whose failure had driven him to embrace the armed struggle. This time he led a march of between 50,000 and 100,000 people to the Union Buildings in Pretoria, where he told the huge crowd that the demonstration must not overspill into violence or 'allow any of us to become dizzy with success'.

The militants now wanted to extend the campaign into the homelands, which were technically outside South Africa, to rally ANC supporters. The National Executive authorised a march to Bisho, the capital of the corrupt republic of the Ciskei, while de Klerk sent Mandela messages pleading for restraint.[29] On 7 September an ANC procession of 70,000 crossed the border and entered a stadium outside Bisho. The local magistrate had ordered them to go no further, but the buccaneering Ronnie Kasrils led a group through a gap in the fence and headed towards the capital. It was not a prudent decision (the Truth Commission later judged), for it 'contributed to the volatile and unpredictable situation'.[30] Ciskei soldiers opened fire without warning and killed twenty-eight of the marchers, many of them shot while running away.

Mandela appeared angry, both with de Klerk and his own militants, but he defended Kasrils against critics: 'It was a decision of the organisation,' he said a week afterwards, 'which he was merely carrying out.'[31] He recognised the frustration: 'My people are beginning to say to me: what was the value? Let's abandon negotiations; they will never be able to take us to our goal.' But he thought that the Bisho confrontation had brought both sides close to disaster, and had damaged the ANC's image with friends at home and abroad. He blamed both the ANC and the government for having 'embarked on an electioneering campaign while we are negotiating'.[32] The Bisho massacre led to a painful reappraisal, and the *African Communist* re-examined the Leipzig idea: 'How realistic is this option?' asked the editor Jeremy Cronin. 'We must be careful not to fetishise mass insurrection or see it as the only possible revolutionary way.'[33]

The massacre strengthened Mandela's case for resuming negotiations, and de Klerk saw Bisho as a turning point, which strengthened the hand of the ANC moderates. There was now some hopeful movement behind the scenes. Cyril Ramaphosa had been working very closely with his Afrikaner opposite number Roelf Meyer, through their 'back channel', to reach agreements in forty meetings between June and September. Ramaphosa had his own firm principles about negotiation – as he would tell the Northern Irish in Belfast three years later. You must maintain the threat of the armed struggle, but not use it, while you must establish personal trust with your opponents.[34] Like Mandela, Ramaphosa could empathise with the Afrikaners' own past suffering under their British oppressors, while Meyer understood the blacks' grievances much better than de Klerk. The common memory of oppression helped to bring the two men closer together.

De Klerk's bargaining position was weakening after his delaying tactics. He had made the same kind of mistakes as Gorbachev in Russia – or Ian Smith in Rhodesia – even though back in 1990 he had specifically warned against Smith's short-sightedness.[35] His cabinet was already much diminished. The right-wingers Magnus Malan and Adriaan Vlok had both been forced to resign. The original chief negotiator Gerrit Viljoen had retreated. De Klerk's loyal Minister of Information Stoffel van der Merwe also departed. His Minister of Finance, Barend du Plessis, had resigned. P.W. Botha, the ex-President, who still had some allies, watched from retirement with contempt, telling de Klerk: 'You left South Africa in the lurch.'[36] Many of de Klerk's colleagues were disillusioned with him. 'He had complete confidence in his ability to control the situation, but no real strategy,' recalled Barend du Plessis. 'He misread the Mandela situation completely,' said Leon Wessels, the young Deputy Foreign Minister. 'He thought he could retain his authority, and share his power. When that failed, he had no fall-back position. He didn't understand black politics.'[37]

Mandela's purpose, by comparison, was straightforward and unwavering, while his team was united. 'I am a politician, and politics is about power,' he explained in July 1992. 'I would like to see an ANC government.'[38] He wanted one person, one vote in a unitary system. He remained aloof from the detailed negotiations, leaving them to the experts; but whenever they sought his advice, they found him a tower of strength. 'He sets his mind on doing something and he becomes unshakeable,' Ramaphosa said afterwards. 'We would never have been able to negotiate the end of apartheid without Mandela.'[39] Mac Maharaj, a key negotiator, had learnt by heart the crucial sentences of Mandela's original letter to P.W. Botha in 1989, in which he insisted on the principle of majority rule, while assuaging the fears of the white minority. 'His zig-zags were always leading to the same object,' Maharaj recalled. 'When I went to see him, he would ask, "Where does that take us towards majority rule? How long will it take?" He was my compass, through all the talks. The Nats had no compass: in the end they became preoccupied with their selfish interests.'[40]

Both sides were now strongly pressed to resume talks. By September 1992 South Africa was racked by continuing violence and a growing economic crisis. Behind the scenes, constitutional experts and committees were trying to resolve the tensions between central and federal systems, under the aegis of the Constitutional Business Movement, which consulted with the political parties and business leaders. Mandela was persuaded that the deadlock could ruin the economy, making it hard for any future government to succeed. But de Klerk was under greater pressure. 'De Klerk needed us more than we needed him,' Mandela reckoned later. 'He desperately needed that summit.'[41] De Klerk's previous strategy had depended on an alliance with Buthelezi, but the Zulu leader was proving impossible to deal with, while the revelations about the third force had discredited the relationship. Roelf Meyer began to have some success in persuading de Klerk that the Afrikaners could live with majority rule, provided they could share some of the power.[42] And de Klerk realised that he depended on the ANC for peace.

Mandela remained the key to any solution: 'The search to get back on track,' as one ANC delegate said, 'always led back to Madiba.' De Klerk claimed he invited Mandela to meet him, but Mandela said he took the initiative, by phoning de Klerk. It was Mandela's turn to be patronising. 'He sounded a bit down,' he explained two days later in an 'olive branch' interview with the *Star* which was seen by some as a turning-point. 'He is a very brave chap, you know, very bright and confident, and it was worrying.' De Klerk insisted that Mandela was climbing down, so 'I could afford to be magnanimous.'[43]

On 26 September Mandela and de Klerk held their summit at the World Trade Centre, which soon led to another dramatic duel. Mandela thought de Klerk could not afford to let the talks collapse again. He stuck to three preconditions for resuming talks, of which the most contentious was the release of all political prisoners. De Klerk balked at letting out some, including Robert McBride, the maverick saboteur who was still in a death cell for having bombed Magoo's Bar in Durban in June 1986, killing three white women. The ANC negotiators, including Ramaphosa and Maharaj, were prepared to concede the point, but Mandela felt a special loyalty to McBride, whom he had visited in prison in May 1990 to assure him that he was demanding the release of prisoners. Mandela had been tipped off that the government team were split on the question, and told de Klerk there would be no meeting unless McBride was let out. Maharaj warned that it might jeopardise the negotiations, but Mandela chuckled, as Maharaj recalls, and told his colleagues not to lose their nerve. He was dismissive of de Klerk: 'This chap, I have had enough of him. We hold the line here today.'[44] De Klerk wanted to turn Mandela down flat, and resented his 'blustering and bullying tactics'; but he realised that his colleagues were now in favour of a far-reaching compromise, and reluctantly agreed to Mandela's terms.[45] The ANC team were very impressed. 'Mandela has nerves of steel,' Ramaphosa recalled. 'He can be very brutal in a calm and collected sort of way.'[46]

The ANC's remaining two preconditions – the fencing-off of Zulu hostels and the banning of Zulu traditional weapons – were bound to antagonise Buthelezi. But de Klerk was being pressed to curb Zulu violence by others, including Cyrus Vance and Judge Goldstone, and he felt impelled to agree. The summit meeting ended with Mandela and de Klerk signing a Record of Understanding which accepted all three preconditions: but more importantly, it agreed on a constitutional assembly and a transitional government of national unity. De Klerk saw it as a victory over the ANC militants, while the ANC team saw it as a watershed on the way to democracy. 'It prepared the way for one man, one vote,' said Maharaj, 'and gave Mandela the ascendancy.'[47] Mandela himself was exultant: 'This is what our people want, this is what our economy needs, this is what our country yearns for.'[48]

But Buthelezi was furious, seeing himself excluded from the deal, and announced he would withdraw from the talks. He led a protest march through the centre of Johannesburg, and the next month joined a strange coalition with the right-wing Afrikaner parties and two homeland leaders, called the Concerned South Africans Group (COSAG), pledged to abolishing Codesa. The Record of Understanding, in fact, produced a fundamental realignment. It not only ended de Klerk's political alliance with Buthelezi; it also rapidly reduced the political violence outside Kwa-

Zulu-Natal, including train attacks, hit-squads and massacres. The Truth Commission would later find circumstantial evidence that 'the signing of the Record of Understanding led to a fall in the rate of random and anonymous attacks associated with "third force" violence.'[49] That clearly suggested that de Klerk was able to curb the violence when he wished to.

The ANC on their side made a historic concession, as de Klerk recognised: they agreed to 'sunset clauses' which would safeguard the jobs of white civil servants and allow for a coalition government between Afrikaner Nationalist and ANC Ministers. The idea was not new: Thabo Mbeki had quietly slipped it into the discussions some time before.[50] But it was surprisingly relaunched by the communist Joe Slovo in the *African Communist* for August. Slovo argued persuasively that 'we are not dealing with a defeated enemy', and that white soldiers and civil servants could still destabilise a democratic government – so the ANC should get them on their side by offering safeguards and sharing power. It was the more persuasive, as de Klerk said, coming from 'a communist with impeccable revolutionary credentials'.[51] It certainly seemed extraordinary for the left to suggest sitting in the same cabinet as the enemy. To many fellow-communists it seemed a betrayal: 'The only thing that is red about Slovo,' it was said, 'is his socks.' The Marxist Pallo Jordan accused Slovo of being 'charmingly ignorant of the history of the twentieth century', and Ronnie Kasrils feared with some reason that the policy would allow the Afrikaner Generals to entrench themselves.[52] Mandela was at first sceptical of the plan, but he came round to it. He was becoming more worried by 'the already incipient counter-revolutionary movement', and he saw a coalition as a means to hold the country together, and to avoid deadly challenges like Savimbi's in Angola.[53]

In November the ANC executive debated the 'sunset clauses' for two days: sixty-two of the eighty members spoke, with much feeling from the grassroots. But Mandela argued strongly that all democratic parties should have a stake in government, and that a coalition would defuse the threat of civil war.[54] On 18 November the ANC endorsed Slovo's proposals. There were still fierce critics. 'The National Party elite is getting into bed with the ANC,' said Winnie Mandela, 'in order to preserve its silken sheets.' And Harry Gwala would not accept the 'drastic departure from what we have always known the ANC to stand for'.[55] Certainly the limitations and compromises of the sunset clauses would prove much costlier than many of their proponents realised, as Afrikaner bureaucrats and military officers dug themselves in. But the huge compromise did turn the key to a democratic settlement.

By December 1992 the ANC was negotiating with the government in a more hopeful atmosphere, culminating in five days of bush conferences where black and white leaders worked and relaxed together. De Klerk was giving way to the idea of simple majority rule, which Mandela tried to soften by promising him a continuing role in government. 'You will notice there has been a sobering up of the politicians,' Mandela explained, in his most conciliatory style. 'All of us have made mistakes in the past.'[56] By February 1993 the two sides had agreed in principle that elections would be followed by a five-year government of national unity, whose members would include all parties polling over 5 per cent of the total vote cast. In March they convened a negotiating council with twenty-four other parties to work out the details.

On 23 March de Klerk made a dramatic announcement, which seemed to many ANC leaders to presage the abandonment of white domination. He told Parliament that over the previous nine years the government had secretly developed seven nuclear bombs, similar to the Hiroshima bomb, to provide a credible deterrent; but that they had now been effectively dismantled and destroyed. South Africa, de Klerk said, was thus the first country to renounce and abandon its own nuclear weaponry.[57] But to the ANC the overriding reason was clear: to prevent it passing into black hands.

Then, on 10 April, the whole process of negotiation was threatened. Chris Hani, the General Secretary of the Communist Party and former commander of MK, who was widely seen as the second most popular black leader, was shot dead in Boksburg, near Johannesburg. By an amazing chance an Afrikaner woman noted the assassin's licence-plate number. She immediately reported it to the police, and fifteen minutes later they stopped the car, driven by a Polish immigrant who still had a smoking gun with him. The murder seemed bound to precipitate race riots and abort any talks. De Klerk, on holiday in the Karoo desert, issued a statement of condolence, but he knew that only Mandela could calm his own people: as he wrote later, 'This was Mandela's moment not mine.'[58] In Johannesburg Tokyo Sexwale went to the SABC with a police Brigadier to demand that they televise a statement he was preparing.[59] Mandela flew back from the Transkei to make one of the most crucial speeches of his career. It was cut back by the SABC, but later, at Mandela's insistence, repeated in full. It began:

> A white man, full of prejudice and hate, came to our country and committed a deed so foul that our whole nation now teeters on the brink of disaster. A white woman, of Afrikaner origin, risked her life so that we may know, and bring to justice, this assassin.

Mandela's statesmanlike speech, set against de Klerk's silence, suggested that he was already the real leader, and the protector of peace.

There was an outburst of rioting and looting in the Cape and Natal, which left seventy dead; and in the prevailing panic hundreds of whites made plans to leave the country. Mandela appealed to them to stay. But the bloodbath did not happen. 'At the time of Chris's death prophets of doom predicted that our country would go up in flames,' Mandela said two years later at the unveiling of Hani's tombstone. 'They said that the leadership of our people could not control "young militants". The political maturity of our nation has disproved them.'[60]

It was a lonely time for Mandela. Two weeks after Hani's murder, his closest friend Oliver Tambo died of another stroke. Mandela said he had 'kept up a life-long conversation with him in my head', and now felt again 'the loneliest man in the world'. The ANC gave Tambo their own kind of state funeral, with a huge rally in Soweto. Mandela was moved by the presence of high-level foreign delegations; but the British Ambassador was noticeably absent: he was in London, accompanying Buthelezi on a visit to the Prime Minister, John Major.[61]

Mandela and de Klerk now seemed, said one foreign observer, like 'two exhausted heavyweight boxers at the end of a long title bout, both bloodied and badly bruised'.[62] But Mandela was more secure in his own party. 'He had been elevated to a new lofty status,' wrote David Ottaway of the *Washington Post*, 'above the day-to-day administrative concerns and internal squabbles of the NEC. He was now the distinguished elder statesman of the movement.'[63] The ANC were determined to press their advantage. 'After Chris Hani died,' said Ramaphosa, 'we went for the kill.'[64] When the parties met again at the World Trade Centre in late April, Mandela insisted on setting a date for an election – even before agreeing on an interim constitution. De Klerk stalled, but Mandela realised that his Afrikaner colleagues were now quarrelling openly among themselves. Mandela mobilised all his authority, at home and abroad. In early May he addressed British MPs in London, asking them to use their influence with the Afrikaners 'to persuade them to abandon their selfish and sectarian positions'. 'History demands,' he said, 'that you help us.'[65] By 3 June most of the parties had agreed to hold South Africa's first fully democratic elections on 27 April 1994. Mandela saw the signal for which he had been waiting. 'The countdown to the democratic transfer of power to the people has begun,' he told black Americans in the United States a month later.[66]

But there were still serious obstacles, for two disruptive parties had kept out of the negotiations. The Conservative Party, mostly Afrikaner, was threatening de Klerk, while Buthelezi's Inkatha Freedom Party was threatening Mandela. In KwaZulu-Natal the Zulu gangs were still killing, provoking bloody reprisals from ANC supporters; and Mandela accepted that the ANC must share some of the blame. When twenty people, including six schoolchildren, were massacred near Table Mountain in March 1993, Mandela admitted that all parties had made mistakes, and condemned the people responsible for mass slaughters: 'Whether they are members of the ANC, members of the IFP or members of the state security services,' he said, 'they are no longer human beings. They are animals.' 'I am not going to blame the IFP and the government only,' he said at Mamelodi in April. 'We must find the truth – our people are just as involved in violence.'[67] Mandela was prepared to stake his leadership on the question of talking to the IFP. 'Do you want me to be a leader or do you want me to stand down?' he asked. When they said no, he replied: 'You will have to listen to me, to talk to the IFP. If not you can ask me to resign: I will do so.'[68]

But Mandela now saw Buthelezi moving towards regional autonomy and possible secession, which he could not accept: 'Any threat to force conclusions down our throats, that we will reject without any reservation.'[69] De Klerk, too, was becoming increasingly worried by Buthelezi's plans to establish a separate state. Mandela again tried a personal appeal to Buthelezi; in June 1993 he met him for the first time in two years. Buthelezi remained intransigent, while he was still supported by conservative friends in the West: the month following his visit to John Major in London he was the guest of Prince Charles at his country house, Highgrove.[70] Right-wing journalists continued to build up Buthelezi: 'Preparing for Civil War', headlined *The Times* above an article by William Rees-

Mogg in October: 'A unitary state probably means a civil war. The Zulu people would fight for their independence, probably successfully.'[71]

But the election deadline spurred on the talks to settle the constitution, while the intricate technical discussions helped to disguise the drastic implications of a transfer of power. Negotiators on both sides would often find it harder to persuade their own colleagues than their opponents: as Frene Ginwala said, 'A camaraderie develops when your constituency is seen as your enemy, and the enemy is your ally.' By the end, observed van Zyl Slabbert, 'de Klerk's negotiators were really part of Mandela's team in facilitating the transition to majority rule.'[72]

As a settlement came closer, extremists on both sides became more violent. On 25 June three thousand Afrikaners converged on the World Trade Centre, carrying banners with the Swastika-like symbol of the AWB (Afrikaner Weerstands Beweging), and led by their potbellied leader Eugene Terre'Blanche. An armoured car smashed through the plate-glass entrance, followed by a rowdy crowd who surged into the building, shouting insults against kaffirs and urinating in the conference chamber. General Constand Viljoen, the leader of the new right-wing Freedom Front party, tried vainly to restrain them. After Terre'Blanche had delivered a fiery speech, the invaders retreated outside to light barbecues and drink beer.

A month later there was a deadlier outrage, when on 23 July five masked black men rushed into St James' Church in Cape Town and fired into the packed congregation, killing eleven and maiming many others. The massacre was blamed on a local branch of APLA, the military wing of the PAC which had boasted of earlier murders of whites; an eighteen-year-old APLA member was later sentenced to twenty-three years for his part in it. These and other murders provoked further panic among whites; but they also gave a new urgency to a settlement.

While their teams negotiated, Mandela and de Klerk were still barely on speaking terms. They were both in America in July 1993, where they were each received by President Clinton, but de Klerk found himself being escorted out of the White House by a roundabout route, to avoid meeting Mandela who was on his way in.[73] The next day in Philadelphia they were both presented with the Liberty Medal; and Mandela effectively snubbed de Klerk at a press conference: 'We don't regard him as the President of South Africa but as a leader put there by only 15 per cent of the population.'

But the negotiations progressed, and by early September de Klerk was giving more ground: he agreed to a 'transitional executive council' (TEC) to prepare for elections. It was the cue for Mandela to finally agree to the lifting of sanctions. He flew to the UN in New York to deliver a historic speech to the General Assembly, with deadpan delivery. He warned that South Africa was still not out of the woods, and that 'the very fabric of society is threatened by a process of disintegration'. But the transition to democracy was now enshrined in the law, and he asked the UN 'to take all necessary measures to end the economic sanctions you imposed'.[74]

The negotiators agreed on an interim constitution which many saw as a model document, incorporating a strict separation of powers, a bill of rights on the American pattern, and also a constitutional court. But it made compromises which would prove very expensive: there would be over four hundred Members of Parliament; and nine provinces would be created, each with its own premier and civil service; one would be the Eastern Cape, which embraced two of the most corrupt former homelands, the Ciskei and Transkei. Establishing nine provinces in place of the previous four was a concession to the federalists, but they would strain the future administration beyond the limit.

The most crucial clause was the last, about majority voting and safeguarding minorities. Mandela and de Klerk argued through the final night of 17–18 November. De Klerk still insisted that the winning party must have a two-thirds majority for crucial issues, but Mandela argued that he could not govern anyway without the support of de Klerk ('Whether I like him or not is irrelevant. I need him').[75] Some ANC negotiators were prepared to concede a 60 per cent majority, but Mandela stood firmer than any: he told de Klerk that he could not run a cabinet without a simple majority of 50 per cent. De Klerk by now was more willing than many of his colleagues to accept simple majority rule, and he gave way, putting his hopes on the 'consensus-seeking spirit' mentioned in the constitution. 'It was something I thought we should never win,' said Joe Slovo. 'Majority rule will apply,' said Mandela. 'We just hope we will never have to use it.'[76]

The next day de Klerk's cabinet colleagues were close to mutiny. 'You've given South Africa away,' the negotiator Tertius Delport had told him beforehand.[77] But eventually de Klerk persuaded them to accept, and at midnight both sides passed the new constitution. The ANC celebrated into the small hours – it was also Ramaphosa's birthday. But there remained ominous absentees from the feasting, including both Inkatha and the Conservative Party, who would not recognise the agreement.

The agreement certainly marked a fundamental retreat by de Klerk. 'The decision to surrender the right to national sovereignty,' he said in London three years later, 'is certainly one of the most painful that any leader can take . . . we had to accept the necessity of giving up the ideal on which we have been nurtured.'[78] But he could claim that it marked an almost equal retreat for the ANC militants who at the beginning had appeared to dominate their party. 'In a sense Mandela and his negotiators sold out the "National Democratic Revolution",' wrote Adam, Slabbert and Moodley, 'whereas de Klerk and his negotiators sold out Afrikaner minority domination. The one sacrificed ideological purity and correctness, the other political power.'[79]

Certainly the ANC had come a long way from the radical economic policies they proposed in 1990. Although Mandela had rejected nationalisation at the world forum in Davos in February 1992, the ANC had retained hopes of ambitious state planning. They set up a Macro Economic Research Group (MERG) under their economic adviser Vella Pillay, with strong support from the trades unions and the communists, which made bold plans for expansion. But Pillay soon became conscious of unseen pressures. ANC leaders including Trevor Manuel and Tito Mboweni visited the International Monetary Fund in Washington; tycoons from the 'Brenthurst Group' – first set up by Mandela and business friends – met with the ANC to discuss economic problems; while the British and American Ambassadors kept enquiring about MERG's plans. Many former ANC communists, including Joe Slovo, were disillusioned with Marxist economics after watching the collapse of the Soviet Union. And as ANC leaders faced the prospect of power, they were worried about state spending in the face of galloping inflation and a growing deficit under de Klerk's government. By the time Pillay launched the MERG document 'Making Democracy Work' in November 1993 Mandela had withdrawn his offer to write a foreword – just when the ANC negotiators at the World Trade Centre were agreeing on a secret 'Letter of Intent' which committed them to reducing the deficit, to high interest rates and to an open economy, in return for access to an IMF loan of $850 million, if required.[80] The settlement with international capitalism was almost as important as the settlement with de Klerk. 'Just as the ANC saw power within its grasp,' wrote the journalist John Matisonn, who analysed the changes, 'globalisation was taking away some of the sovereignty of all governments.'[81]

Mandela and de Klerk were both praised round the world for averting catastrophe and making peace at a time when killings were continuing in Northern Ireland and Bosnia. Where, it was asked, was their Mandela, or their de Klerk? So it was not surprising when, at the end of 1993, they were proclaimed joint winners of the Nobel Peace Prize. The prize put Mandela in the tradition of Luthuli and Tutu, both earlier laureates. But some militants were outraged. 'It was an insult to give it to him jointly with his jailer,' Winnie Mandela said afterwards. 'It was a bribe, part of a gigantic plot to make him an instrument of peace for the white man.'[82]

The Nobel ceremony in Oslo in December did not reveal much reconciliation between the two leaders. De Klerk told the Norwegian assembly that both black and white had 'repented' the past, but he made no apology himself, while his wife Marike objected to Mandela sitting next to the Norwegian Prime Minister. When the two prizewinners appeared on the hotel balcony a crowd of Norwegians gathered below, holding candles according to the tradition. But de Klerk was put out when he heard ANC slogans and shouts of 'Kill the Boer!'; and when the crowd sang '*Nkosi Sikelel' iAfrika*' he went on talking to his wife, and soon withdrew from the balcony.[83] Mandela described the occasion as 'a milestone for two former enemies building a new South Africa'. But they still sounded rather like enemies. When Mandela was asked on Norwegian television whether de Klerk was a political criminal, he replied: 'Almost everybody in government is a political criminal.' And in Stockholm soon afterwards, Mandela gave a combative impromptu speech in which he blamed de Klerk for being involved in the continuing violence. De Klerk bit his tongue, he recalled later, 'with the greatest self-control'.[84]

Back in Cape Town, de Klerk was still angered by the ANC's 'derogatory utterances': they showed, he said, that 'the ANC has no political message for the future'. Mandela explained why his relations with de Klerk were strained: de Klerk had allowed 'the slaughter of innocent people because they are black. It will remain a stain against him.' De Klerk would note the irony that they were both receiving the world's highest accolade as peacemakers while their relationship 'was characterised by so much vitriol and suspicion'.[85]

De Klerk was convinced that Mandela was overwhelmingly responsible for the vitriol. He was exasperated by the contrast between Mandela's global charisma as the man of peace and forgiveness, and his unforgiving attacks on himself and his party. Certainly Mandela often seemed harsh with de Klerk. His wife Marike (whom he later divorced) was 'dumbfounded' by the humiliations: 'Whenever Nelson Mandela telephoned him to say that evidence of a third force had been found, or that police had discovered some sinister activity or other, he had to decide: is this enough reason to put an end to negotiations?'[86] But Mandela had to be the 'man of steel' through the negotiations: the more he made compromises and retreated from the armed struggle, the more he had to show his militant followers that he was being tough with the enemy. More important, he still felt personally betrayed by de Klerk. The more facts that emerged about the third force and secret police plots, the less convincing he found de Klerk's protestations that he knew nothing about them. Meanwhile the deadly results became still more apparent.

Who deserved the most credit for the settlement? The debate still continues. De Klerk, having inherited the process begun by P.W. Botha, had seen the historic necessity and followed it to its conclusion, taking risks without losing his nerve, and narrowly keeping his fractious party together. Mandela had more able lieutenants, and a clearer goal to unify his movement. But it was doubtful whether anyone but Mandela, with his unique credentials and history of sacrifice, could have persuaded revolutionaries to abandon the armed struggle and the 'seizure of power' without a violent political backlash. 'Without Mandela South African history would have taken a completely different turn,' said Joe Slovo in 1994, despite his Marxist's scepticism of the role of any individual in history:

> And that is not just because of his charisma or his status, but basically because of his leadership and initiative from Robben Island. It is a fact that it was he who triggered the negotiations . . . Tambo was absolutely irreplaceable: he kept the organisation going, he kept the people together. But when it came to facing the post-1990 period, the role of Mandela is absolutely unique.[87]

33

Election

MANDELA WAS FIGHTING his first general election in 1994 at the age of seventy-five – two years older than Ronald Reagan during his second US presidential campaign in 1984; the same age as William Gladstone in his last campaigns as British Prime Minister in 1894 and 1895. They were at the end of their electioneering: Mandela was at the beginning. But the opportunity for equal political rights had been his chief demand for the past fifty years, for which he sacrificed much of his life; and his whole career had been leading up to this election.

The ANC set up a professional campaign through a hundred offices, organised by three veterans of UDF campaigns in the eighties, Popo Molefe, Terror Lekota and Khetso Gordhan. They hired Stanley Greenberg, a fast-talking American expert with a humorous moustache who had worked on Bill Clinton's 1992 campaign. He advised them to listen to the grassroots and to set up People's Forums all over the country.[1] But everyone knew that their crucial asset was Mandela himself, who personified his party and whose bright aura had recovered from all the blows of the past four years.

His previous varying images – Mandela the chief, the showman, the revolutionary, the guerrilla leader, the prisoner, the statesman – were now subsumed by Mandela at the hustings, who could play a different role to each audience. He sometimes addressed four People's Forums a day: they reminded him of the Chief's meetings he had watched as a boy. And he still enjoyed seeing new faces after his prison years, particularly young faces. 'I want to put you all in my pocket,' he would say again and again. 'I am seventy-five, but among you I feel like a young man of sixteen,' he would repeat. 'You are the people who inspire me every day of my life.'

Mandela had his own team travelling with him, including Barbara

Masekela; Joel Netshitenzhe, who wrote some of his best speeches; and Carl Niehaus, who looked after the media. The campaign was often exhausting and lonely. 'The private meetings could be horrible,' said one of the team, 'with little genuine about them; each person wanted a little bit of him.' But in public Mandela showed respect for all kinds of people: when spectators laughed at a group of Griqua chiefs who were singing tribal songs, he was furious. 'He had a sense of his own image,' said Carl Niehaus, 'but in public life the icon never seemed separate from the human being. Madiba *was* the campaign.'[2]

Mandela's public speaking was far from thrilling: Patti Waldmeir of the *Financial Times* judged him 'one of South Africa's most boring speakers. By the time he has finished, he has often lost half the crowd.' He could sometimes sound like a headmaster reproving young people: 'I make my own bed every day,' he told a crowd of six thousand in a Cape Town township. 'I can cook a decent meal, I can polish a floor. Why can't you do it?'[3] But once he mingled with the crowds and talked to individuals, particularly with children, he projected all the concentrated charm of a born politician. His card-index memory could identify names and faces he had last seen half a century ago; while like other lonely leaders he seemed to gain warmth from the crowds that he lacked at home. 'Was it real human feeling, or was it brilliant PR?' his aide Barbara Masekela wondered. 'You will never know, but does it matter?'[4] Mandela seemed much more at ease than when he first left prison: he often abandoned his suits to relax in the bright-coloured, loose-fitting shirts which President Suharto had first introduced him to in Indonesia, when he gave him six. When a child asked him why he wore them, he replied: 'You must remember I was in jail for twenty-seven years. I want to *feel* freedom.'[5]

His rapport with young people had led him into a stubborn one-man crusade to reduce the voting age from eighteen to sixteen, or even fourteen. 'They say that a person under eighteen can't think correctly and make a wise choice,' he said in May 1993. 'We reject that, and demand the voting age should be from fourteen.' 'I am going to fight and win this battle,' he said two months later. It gave useful ammunition to his critics: 'an ageing, erratic black liberation leader', the London *Sunday Times* called him, while a newspaper cartoon showed a baby in nappies putting a ballot paper into the box – which Mandela much enjoyed.[6] And the ANC executive refused to endorse the proposal. Only sixteen countries gave the vote to sixteen-year-olds, Albie Sachs pointed out – including Albania and North Korea, which were worse than none.[7] 'The organisation gave a resounding no,' recalled Maharaj, 'and the matter was never raised again.'[8]

But most of Mandela's electoral instincts were shrewd; and he was uniquely able to muster militant blacks while also reassuring white voters. He kept urging young whites to stay in South Africa, where they were needed; while he warned black audiences that they could not do without the whites. 'Those who do not know how useful whites are,' he told a crowd in the shack-town of Khayelitsha, 'know nothing about their own country.' He took special pains with his speeches in Afrikaans, which he rehearsed with his adviser Carl Niehaus, though he still spoke with a strong Xhosa accent. He was far from a demagogue, and was easily outbid by fiery young populists – and particularly by Winnie, who had bounced back into politics when she was elected President of the ANC Women's League in December 1993. She was a tireless campaigner, visiting remote, impoverished voters whom other politicians ignored, and telling them she would ensure that the ANC would deliver its promises. But most ANC speakers avoided crude demagogy, and Mandela still could not be seriously challenged as the people's hero.

Mandela was determined to show that the ANC was a responsible party, ready to rule. He warned his colleagues to be cautious in their policy-making: 'The Third World is littered with the relics of liberation movements which have successfully liberated their countries from the yoke of colonial oppression,' he said in May 1992, 'only to be defeated at the polls in the first post-colonial elections.' The ANC had worked out an ambitious Reconstruction and Development Programme (RDP) which promised 'a better life for all'. The programme, which aimed to build a million houses over the next five years, to extend electricity and water, and to provide free education for everyone, was discussed with industrial tycoons, including Harry Oppenheimer. Mandela explained that it had 'not a single reference to nationalisation ... not a single slogan that will connect us with any Marxist ideology'.[9]

Mandela knew he depended heavily on the media, and he had learnt much about handling journalists after his three decades away from them. He knew how to adjust to each medium, when to be discreet or indiscreet, when to put his hand in front of the tape-recorder. He recognised and related to individual journalists – particularly attractive women – with his instinct for flattery, or 'Xhosalisation'. They found it hard when writing about Mandela, said the BBC correspondent Fergal Keane, 'to exercise anything remotely resembling real detachment'. 'We are completely, hopelessly, charmed by Mandela,' admitted John Carlin of the London *Independent*.[10]

But the white South African editors and owners were not seduced: the English-language *Argus* group (except for the Johannesburg *Star*), together with the Johannesburg *Sunday Times* and *Business Day*, supported the small, white Democratic Party; most of the Afrikaans papers supported de Klerk's National Party; only the *Weekly Mail* and the *New Nation* endorsed the ANC. The conservative press thrived on doomsday stories about the inevitability of bloodshed between the ANC and both Zulus and right-wing Afrikaners – which were taken up by the conservative media overseas. In London the *Daily Mail* and the *Sunday Times* competed with scare-stories, encouraged by the Zulu lobby including John Aspinall and Laurens van der Post: 'BLOOD SET TO FLOW AS ZULUS TALK WAR', announced the *Sunday Times* in December. 'CHAOS LIES AHEAD, SAYS "WHITE ZULU"', it headlined in February above an interview with Aspinall ('It's all going to break up. Then it will be a loose confederacy like Switzerland and it will work very well'). And it quoted van der Post ('a confidant of Prime Ministers and royalty') saying: 'The world has become hypnotised by the mythological figure of Mandela even as South Africa slides into chaos.'[11] The ANC compiled its own report on the *Sunday Times* stories. Mandela would never forget the 'prophets of doom who thought there would never be changes in this country without bloodshed'.[12]

Mandela was especially valuable to the ANC as a fund-raiser, showing a mercenary persistence which surprised colleagues. He was not fastidious about his contacts with businessmen like Sol Kerzner, the gambling tycoon of Sun City, who expected favours in return. He seemed to enjoy extracting money from old supporters of apartheid, like a chief expecting tribute; and he had no compunction about rejecting inadequate gifts. After one big company with a pro-apartheid record had given the ANC 250,000 Rand they invited Mandela to lunch; he pulled out their cheque and told them it was an insult: he expected seven figures.

He had been fund-raising for the ANC overseas since his first travels, but now he stepped up the pace. In July 1993 he toured the United States for ten days, appealing for funds in each city. 'I want a seven-figure cheque and I want it now,' he was quoted as saying. In Britain he was supported by old ANC allies like Richard Attenborough, the director of *Cry Freedom*, and David Potter, the founder of Psion computers; but he also reached out to ultra-conservatives, to the chagrin of many anti-apartheid activists. In May 1993 he welcomed tycoons at a fund-raising reception at the Dorchester Hotel, including old opponents of the ANC like Lord King of British Airways and Lord Weinstock of General Electric, who now competed to shake his hand. Mandela's old friend Trevor Huddleston, who believed in 'holy anger', was dismayed to watch him forgiving men who had opposed sanctions and connived with apartheid. Mandela collected large sums from Europe, America and Asia, nobbling the Presidents he met on his travels. De Klerk, whose National Party had collected so much from South African businessmen in the past, was vexed by the ANC's 'enormous election budget'.[13]

The campaign formally opened on 12 February 1994. No one doubted that the ANC would win more votes than de Klerk's National Party: 'We are dealing with a mouse,' said Mandela. 'We in the ANC are like an elephant.' The more serious question was whether they would win the two-thirds majority which would enable them to revise the constitution. But would the election happen at all? Two major parties had not registered: Buthelezi's Inkatha and the Afrikaner Volksfront. Together they were capable of pulling South Africa apart. Accommodating these two dangerous forces was to prove Mandela's most testing and precarious task behind the scenes of the election campaign.

Mandela had always seen the right-wing Afrikaners as formidable enemies. Even if they could not mount an armed rebellion, they could deploy their many supporters in the military and the civil service to bring a black government to a halt. The most publicised resistance was from the AWB led by Eugene Terre'Blanche, who had crashed into the headlines when they invaded the World Trade Centre. With their horses, their fake swastikas and bloodcurdling rhetoric they played up to the TV cameras, evoking memories of the Boer War. But their stage-army of overweight thugs did not risk their own lives, and had little of the courage or resourcefulness of the lean, brave commandos who defied the British ninety years before.

A more serious danger came from the Volksfront, the broad alliance of right-wing groups formed in May 1993, which included the AWB but also the Conservative Party under its new leader Ferdi Hartzenberg, a hard-line Afrikaner farmer. The Volksfront was led by General Constand Viljoen, an elegant, white-haired soldier who had recently retired as head of the defence forces and who was much more popular than Hartzenberg. Viljoen could not believe in a multi-racial democracy; he thought it was an artificial invention, like instant coffee: 'a little bit of coffee, a little bit of milk, a little bit of brown sugar'.[14] He demanded a separate Afrikaner nation, or 'Volkstaat', and was prepared to defend his own people against the police: he twice stated in public that no Afrikaner should shoot another Afrikaner. Mandela saw him as a real threat to law and order, because 'the Afrikaners are like the Zulus: they are very loyal to their leaders.'[15]

Viljoen's Volksfront worried Mandela still more after October 1993, when they allied themselves with Buthelezi and the two homelands Bophuthatswana and Ciskei, which were also boycotting the elections, in the odd coalition COSAG. Mandela saw the grouping as a 'grave threat' to the negotiating process, and told businessmen that the Afrikaner right could do more damage than the armed struggle in the eighties, through their supporters in the civil service, the army and the police. If they carried out their threat of civil war, he warned, 'thousands of whites could die'.[16] Privately he reckoned that if Viljoen were part of a plot, it would be difficult for an ANC government to make use of the army.[17]

But Mandela also had respect for some Afrikaner conservatives, whom he saw as more honest and straightforward than de Klerk. He had first met General Viljoen in August 1993, through the mediation of his twin brother Braam, who was friendly to the ANC. Mandela told Viljoen: 'General, you may defeat us now, but if you take the road of violence, some day you and your people will be destroyed.'[18] He recognised Viljoen as a real leader of men: 'He was a very popular chap, because he was simple, down to earth, religious and honest.'[19] Thabo Mbeki and Jacob Zuma began a series of friendly talks with Viljoen, who soon said publicly that he was making more progress with the ANC, who were more sincere than de Klerk. Mandela was under fire from his executive for talking to the Afrikaner right, but he insisted on continuing to talk to prevent the crisis from deteriorating. De Klerk was hurt that Viljoen, whom he knew well, should prefer to deal with Mandela; he saw Viljoen's power-base as essentially racist, and recalled how his followers had regarded Mandela as a communist terrorist.[20] But Mandela had established a personal rapport with the General which became a key to peaceful elections.

The issue of a 'Volkstaat', the old Afrikaner dream, remained contentious. Mandela left the way open for a referendum; though it would not bind him as President. Viljoen thought it an honest answer which he could take to his people. But Hartzenberg of the Conservative Party was not satisfied by Mandela's uncertain commitment, and told him openly that he would prepare to stop the elections by force.[21] In fact the ANC still did not think a Volkstaat practicable under democratic conditions, because its supporters were scattered across the country, with a majority nowhere; and it was hard now to define an Afrikaner who would be entitled to live there: 'It's not a state but a state of mind,' said one future Minister.

Mandela was reaching out to other Afrikaner leaders to avoid a showdown. He had three meetings with Pik Botha, the veteran Foreign Minister whom he found the most positive man in the government towards the ANC.[22] Pik Botha was sceptical about Afrikaner rebels: he thought they might take control of a few towns, but their resistance would not last. But he was keen to be helpful: he had said eight years earlier that he would serve under a black President, to the fury of President Botha; and he now took to calling Mandela 'Mr President'.

Mandela's boldest move was to visit ex-President Botha himself, the 'Great Crocodile' who had kept him in prison for so long. On 12 February, when the election campaign opened, Mandela went to Wilderness, the peaceful seaside resort on the Cape coast where P.W. Botha had retired. Mandela had maintained a surprising respect for the old man, two years older than himself and equally tall; and he suspected he could have negotiated more effectively with him, as a strong man he could trust, than with de Klerk. He seemed to regard Botha as a white chief: once, when his plane had made an emergency landing near Wilderness, he asked Pik Botha for P.W.'s telephone number, explaining jokingly: 'It is an African custom for a chief to inform another chief when he is travelling in his area.'[23] And now he thought P.W. Botha could exert a restraining influence over the Afrikaner right and the military.

P.W. Botha received him in the gloomy study adjoining his house. He still saw South Africa in Cold War terms and Mandela as a communist; but he also regarded him as a gentleman and a chief, like his nephew Matanzima. Mandela recalled how they had both committed themselves to peace when they had met in the Tuynhuys, and explained his worries about violence: 'If the election date is postponed people will slaughter us.' He was prepared to compromise over self-determination, and asked Botha to help him to persuade Afrikaner leaders.

Botha replied that South Africa was in a dangerous condition, approaching chaos: Mandela must '*hamba kahle*' (go slowly): otherwise 'things will turn too ghastly to contemplate'. But the world should leave South Africans alone to solve their own problems. Mandela stressed that 'the real crux of the problem is between the Volksfront, the government and the ANC: I would like to involve these people.' Botha proposed that Mandela should bring all the Afrikaner leaders to meet him, including de Klerk (though not Terre'Blanche, whom Mandela wanted to involve). They parted on friendly terms, after Botha presented Mandela with a copy of his book of speeches, *Fighter and Reformer*. Mandela wrote in the visitors' book: 'Had a constructive and fruitful discussion with ex-President P.W. Botha. Nelson Mandela, 51 Plein St.'[24]

Mandela could not persuade de Klerk to cooperate in the proposed meeting – 'he was emotionally opposed to P.W. Botha intervening' – and it never happened. In fact Botha was not very helpful, by his own account: he did not press Viljoen, who was 'a very independent person'. But Mandela remained very grateful to Botha for 'trying to bring about peace in our country'.[25]

It was the Afrikaner Generals who remained the key to peaceful elections and the transition afterwards. Their future loyalty remained in some doubt: they had waged war on the ANC for thirty years, and many felt betrayed by de Klerk's peacemaking. General Meiring, the head of the defence force, had made a tough speech in 1992 denouncing Modise, Kasrils and Hani; and Kasrils – who would soon become Deputy Minister of Defence – feared that the ANC might find themselves ambushed 'like Piet Retief in Dingaan's kraal'. They were reassured by some senior military leaders: the head of the Air Force promised if necessary to use his planes to bomb rebel forces. But the ANC still saw a real possibility of a military coup in the African or Latin American tradition.[26]

Mandela used all his authority and flattery to reassure the military and security leaders. Some time before the election he had visited the Police Commissioner, General Johan van der Merwe, at his office to ask if he would serve under him. Van der Merwe said he had already served longer than his original contract. Mandela also visited General Meiring, who answered yes without hesitation, and promised to be ruthless with anybody who tried to interfere with the elections.[27] Some colleagues thought he was too trusting of Meiring and others. But he was determined to placate ex-enemies, whatever their past misdeeds.

By March civil war was looking closer, as right-wing Afrikaners and Buthelezi's party boycotted the elections, together with the two homelands, Ciskei and Bophuthatswana, or 'Bop'. The people of Bop now came into the front line. They had been given South African citizenship to allow them to vote, but their dictator, Lucas Mangope, still resisted elections, while his people were in full revolt against him. Mangope decided to call on the Afrikaner Volksfront to defend him. General Viljoen rashly agreed, and mobilised his small private army to move into Bop to support Mangope's own forces. But Viljoen's army was outbid by much wilder troops from the AWB – led by Terre'Blanche – who swaggered into Mmabatho, the capital, brandishing handguns, pistols and rifles, shooting blacks in the streets. The Bop army, outraged by this white invasion, promptly rebelled against Mangope and fired back at the raiders. Viljoen's army discreetly withdrew, but the AWB went on the rampage until they were forced to retreat in disarray. Television cameras caught the full horror when three Afrikaners in a blue Mercedes who had been shooting through the car window were stopped by gunfire and then confronted by Bop policemen, one of whom shot them dead in cold blood. It was a devastating image. 'The bubble of adventure, the heroic re-enactment of historic Boer myths,' wrote Allister Sparks, 'was punctured in a day of blood and humiliation.'[28]

There was more talk of bloodshed. 'South Africa braced itself for a race war yesterday,' wrote the London *Sunday Times*, under the headline 'BOERS BAY FOR REVENGE ON "KAFFIRS"'.[29] But the fiasco of the 'Battle of Bop' soon proved a political godsend for Mandela – and peace. Mangope was overthrown; the ANC could operate freely in Bop; while the Afrikaner military rebels were disgraced. General Viljoen was appalled by the fiasco, and decided at the last minute, on 16 March, to leave the rest of the Volksfront and to contest the elections through his own party, the Freedom Front. Mandela would always be grateful to the General. 'When he pulled out,' Mandela said later, 'I knew that the question of the right wing was just for the police.'[30] But it was a very close-run rescue. De Klerk would have faced a serious situation, he said afterwards, if Viljoen had successfully intervened to re-establish Mangope's illegal authority in Bop. Would de Klerk have sent the South African army to move against Viljoen, and would they have fired against their former commander? He left the questions unanswered. Ironically, it was the thugs of the AWB who saved the day, by discrediting the whole expedition and Mangope's regime, along with the system that created it. 'With his removal from power,' de Klerk wrote later, 'the last remnants of Dr Verwoerd's elaborate edifice of grand apartheid came crashing to the ground.'[31]

There was still a serious danger of resistance from the white right, and there remained the other major obstacle to a peaceful transition: Buthelezi, who remained adamant against the election and the new constitution, which he saw as belittling the Zulu kingdom: 'No foreign forces shall come into it to rule over us,' he told an Inkatha congress in January. He was supported by the weak Zulu King Goodwill, who now wanted to rule over an enlarged sovereign kingdom including the whole of Natal, as in 1830. Hopes of a settlement had dwindled in a new turmoil of killings, and the transitional government sent troops to Natal to try to limit the violence. The massacres seemed all the more sinister after Judge Goldstone on 18 March reported a 'horrible network of criminal activity' linking Inkatha with South African police. 'It appeared at last to corroborate the long-held suspicions,' de Klerk admitted later, 'concerning the existence of a sinister third force within the security forces.'[32]

Mandela had tried to conciliate: 'I will go down on my knees to beg those who want to drag our country into bloodshed,' he told a rally. He went to Durban to try to charm Buthelezi, and discussed the possibility of international mediators. But the deadlock remained, and the King stayed close to Buthelezi, who was still boycotting the elections on the closing date, 11 March, when Viljoen had decided to join the campaign.

Buthelezi then planned a provocative demonstration on 28 March in the centre of Johannesburg. The day before, Mandela warned de Klerk, who in turn warned the police chiefs, who took no visible precautions. When the marchers approached Shell House, the ANC headquarters, Mandela gave orders to the security guards: 'You must protect that house even if you are to kill people.'[33] Some of the demonstrators fired handguns and shotguns into the building; the police disappeared, and the ANC feared that the marchers would invade them. ANC guards, after firing a warning shot, aimed straight at the crowd, killing eight people including some who were hit in the back as they fled. One journalist inside the building saw it as 'a bloody counter-attack from those in a building under siege'.[34] De Klerk phoned Mandela, and agreed that the police should not search for weapons inside Shell House: the next day Mandela personally stopped them from entering the building. But de Klerk then complained that Mandela reneged on a promise to co-operate fully with a police investigation.[35] The blame continued to be fiercely debated. Mandela believed that de Klerk had deliberately allowed the march, as he had allowed the massacre at Sebokeng in July 1990. Four years later the judge in a High Court inquest found that the ANC had been wrong in claiming that Inkatha had conspired to attack them; but he also blamed the police and Inkatha.[36]

The 'Shell House massacre' was followed by further killings and scare stories. 'Emergency plans are being made to airlift up to 350,000 Britons out of South Africa,' the London *Daily Mail* reported on 3 April, 'should the country slide into chaos after this month's elections.' Buthelezi appeared implacable: 'We have now entered a final struggle to the finish,' he warned, 'between the ANC and the Zulu nation.'[37] On 8 April Mandela and de Klerk met Buthelezi and the Zulu King in the Kruger National Park game reserve, where Mandela (said de Klerk) 'spoke in a careful and measured manner'. He promised the King 'more powers than the Queen of England', while insisting that the elections could not be postponed. But Buthelezi and the King were intransigent, and the summit ended with no breakthrough. 'South Africa prepared for civil war yesterday,' said the London *Sunday Times*.[38]

The expected bloodbath looked all the more fearful in the light of the massacres in Rwanda at the time; the security forces were privately warning that South Africa could see a million dead.[39] But there was a last hope. At the summit Buthelezi had agreed on inviting international mediators, to which Mandela consented, though other ANC leaders were wary. A team of seven arrived, led by Henry Kissinger and the former British Foreign Secretary Lord Carrington, and including a huge Kenyan professor, Washington Okumu. They were holed up for three days in the Carlton Hotel in Johannesburg, trying to conciliate. Kissinger met Mandela with Cyril Ramaphosa, who insisted that the mediators should not allow postponement. The ANC and Inkatha were playing a dangerous poker game, it seemed to Colin Coleman, one of the mediating team: 'We were looking into the flames.'[40] Kissinger and Carrington left after no progress had been made: 'If we had stayed we would have become part of the problem,' said Kissinger afterwards. 'In a way, our failure achieved success.'[41]

Buthelezi was now still more isolated. Old allies, including General Obasanjo and Mrs Thatcher, sent messages advising him to join the elections.[42] The last homeland, the Ciskei, gave in. The King of the Zulus was being wooed away from his uncle Buthelezi by Mandela, while Zulu civil servants were worried about their future paycheques under a separatist government.

Before Buthelezi left Johannesburg, Professor Okumu met him at the airport to make a last plea, warning him that the elections would leave him out, and that the outcome could be bloody. Buthelezi now suggested he might join, on three conditions: if Inkatha was not discriminated against; if the Zulu kingdom was enshrined in the constitution; and if international mediation was resumed after the election. The next day he confirmed his offer. A draft memo of understanding was quickly produced and approved by Buthelezi, and Okumu then flew down to Cape Town with Coleman and two executives of Anglo-American to present it to Mandela at the Cape Sun Hotel. Mandela had just returned distraught from a rally where a fence had collapsed and two people were killed, but he quickly agreed to the outline and rang de Klerk, who concurred, with some reservations.[43] On 19 April Mandela and de Klerk met in Pretoria with Okumu and Buthelezi, and agreed on the general terms, while experts prepared a revised text to meet concerns raised by Buthelezi. It was only a week before the elections, and the ballot papers had already been printed; but the electoral commission was still, amazingly, able to print stickers to add to the sheets with the name of Inkatha; while de Klerk generously agreed that his National Party would lose its special place at the bottom of the ballot paper.[44] The ANC leaders were intensely relieved, but they still did not know what had changed Buthelezi's mind.[45]

The final week of the election campaign was seen still more as a contest between Mandela and de Klerk, both of whom were in the full glare of world publicity. De Klerk had seriously misjudged the ANC's skills in presentation: he could only muster a handful of convincing spokesman in English on television, while the ANC could offer a wide choice. And Mandela showed all his skills as a performer who could adjust his image according to his audiences and questioners. 'He was overestimated as a statesman,' said one of de Klerk's team, 'but underestimated as a politician.' He would sometimes change his clothes three or four times in a day – from a suit for a business breakfast, to an open shirt for a village crowd, to a woolly cardigan for a visit to old people.

He even appeared in camouflage battle-dress alongside Joe Modise, to appeal to guerrilla voters. 'But de Klerk would wear the same golfing jacket,' complained an aide.[46] And de Klerk had an inevitable handicap in attempting to appeal to blacks. The American political consultant Stanley Greenberg reckoned that Mandela's stock rose every time de Klerk lammed into him: 'When the party of the oppressor attacks,' Greenberg noted, 'you get a protective reaction from the people who were oppressed.'[47] De Klerk had to restrain himself from all-out attacks on the ANC as a party which was not fit to govern, for he would have to work alongside Mandela in a coalition after the election – though it was not a prospect he relished.[48] It was, in the end, a muted election, in which neither side said quite what it thought.

The ANC would clearly be the victors in most of the nine provinces, but they were seriously challenged in the Western Cape, the stronghold of Coloured voters. Their local leader Allan Boesak, the preacher who had helped to found the UDF, had lost much of his following after divorcing his wife to marry a white woman and leaving the Dutch Reformed Church; and many ANC activists found him too vain and fond of high living. Mandela remained stubbornly loyal to Boesak, and insisted he remain the ANC leader; but many of the Coloured voters were alarmed by the prospect of a black government, and preferred to vote for de Klerk and the local National Party leader Hernus Kriel. 'I lost track of the number of people who told me that they would "not vote for a kaffir",' said one well-informed American observer, William Finnegan, 'or "would never call a black man *baas*".'[49] The ANC's setbacks in the Western Cape were a serious blow to their vision of multi-racialism.

Ten days before the election, Mandela debated with de Klerk on television, American-style. Mandela was coached by another ex-adviser of Clinton, Frank Greer, whose first rule was: 'Be presidential.' Greer told him to talk faster, not to wag his finger – which would remind viewers of P.W. Botha – and to keep smiling.[50] Mandela rehearsed the day before, with de Klerk played by the journalist Allister Sparks, who was worried about Mandela overrunning his two-minute quota: 'He would go on for thirty minutes if left alone.'[51]

In the actual debate, Mandela began with a wooden, unsmiling three-minute monologue which the moderator cut short, and de Klerk soon felt he was winning on points. But Mandela took de Klerk by surprise at the end when he reached out to take his hand, apparently spontaneously, but actually carefully rehearsed to embarrass de Klerk. 'We knew his body language would not look good,' said one of Mandela's advisers.[52] 'Suddenly what had been a certain points victory had been converted into a draw,' de Klerk later admitted. 'It was a masterful stroke.'[53] Mandela could conclude in the conciliatory style at which he excelled. 'I think we are a shining example to the entire world,' he told de Klerk, 'of people drawn from different racial groups who have a common loyalty, a common love, to their common country.' 'He had all the moments,' Greer said afterwards. 'He was tough enough to energise his base, but then he was also able to reach out and appeal for reconciliation.'[54]

For most of the last week before polling day the mood seemed miraculously peaceful. When Mandela held his final Johannesburg rally, in the stadium outside Soweto, the whole atmosphere was festive. Sixty thousand ANC supporters converged in teams, waving flags and banners, to listen to singers yelling through deafening loudspeakers, and to watch tribal dancers, drum majorettes and acrobats. Then a helicopter whirred overhead and landed outside, while the drums rolled, and young women in fur busbys led a procession around the stadium: at the end of it was the unmistakable tall figure of Mandela in a red shirt, beaming and shaking hands, then sitting among young children, smiling and clapping with them. Thabo Mbeki warmed up the crowd, and introduced Mandela to thunderous applause. Mandela reached out to all kinds of supporters, of all religions and ages, freely interpreted into Xhosa by Tokyo Sexwale, adding his own emotion and humour in his sing-song voice. The merriment suddenly vanished when gunshots went up from somewhere in the stadium: Mandela fiercely rebuked the crowd – 'Nobody should come to a meeting armed' – and insisted the culprits be seized and removed. But it ended in harmony; and he already looked like a head of state as he was driven away in his car, while security guards stopped anyone from reaching through the window to shake his hand.

On 26 April, the day before the election, Mandela gave his last press conference in Johannesburg. He remained reticent about his emotions – 'certain things can't be expressed in words' – and insisted that 'no single individual can be elevated above others.' But he granted that 'It *is* a very exciting moment,' and wished he could awaken the dead heroes like Tambo and Hani to enjoy the fruits of their labours. Afterwards he talked proudly about the ANC's unification: 'There used to be twenty-six parties pulling in different directions,' he said on election day. 'Now we will have a government of unity.'[55]

In the last few days several bombs exploded in and near Johannesburg, including a car-bomb which went off outside the ANC regional office. Twenty people were killed altogether.[56] All the bombs turned out to have been placed by an AWB cell intending to scare voters away. But black voters were undeterred, determined to participate for the first time in their hard-earned democracy. Before dawn on Wednesday 27 April they started lining up at the polling stations, sometimes to wait for five hours before voting. 'After nearly 350 years,' someone said, '350 minutes is nothing.' The patient, expectant voters seemed to show much more faith in the democratic process than did apathetic electorates in America or Europe; and on that hot morning the violence had almost disappeared, as if drained away by the democratic process. But they showed few signs of unreal expectations: when one BBC correspondent was asked to provide soundbites from voters expecting cars and houses after the election, he could find no one to oblige. It was not money, but the vote, so long denied them, that they were queuing for.

Walter Sisulu, Mandela's old mentor, spent the day with voters in Soweto: he felt that his whole life had been geared towards this victory of peace over civil war. 'What makes our revolution one of the greatest', he said later, was that 'the people were determined only on one thing, to make their cross'.[57] Mandela took special pleasure in seeing Afrikaner farmers lining up next to their African labourers: 'You can see a New South Africa has arrived.' He himself went down to Durban to vote at Ohlange High School, near the grave of John Dube, the co-founder of the ANC in 1912 – chosen with characteristic care for the symbolism, to recall the dead heroes who had enabled him now to vote for the first time: 'It was as though we were a nation reborn.'[58]

The world watched tensely. No election had ever been so closely monitored: an estimated 200,000 officials and volunteers were observing the twenty-three million voters. The Special Envoy from the UN, the suave Algerian Lakhdar Brahimi, supervised an army of young UN volunteers with blue armbands or caps scattered round the townships. Many polling booths were nevertheless chaotic. Forms, ink and papers failed to arrive. Reports flowed in – particularly from KwaZulu, which had only a week to prepare – of blunders or rackets, votes duplicated or lost. Mandela was quick to see a conspiracy: 'It is clear to me that there has been massive sabotage,' he said on television on election day, which was 'totally unacceptable'. The organisers feared they would need a third day of polling, and de Klerk dreaded that South Africa would look like 'just another African country'.[59]

But the broad verdict was clear. 'Every party has committed itself to change,' said Brahimi, 'and the result will be roughly what they can accept.'[60] The political parties eventually cobbled together a rough and ready result which provided an acceptable compromise. 'It was an impressionist election,' as de Klerk said. De Klerk's National Party had a majority of 53 per cent in the Western Cape – where as many as 69 per cent of Coloureds voted for him. Buthelezi's Inkatha had a majority of 51 per cent in KwaZulu-Natal. In the other seven provinces the ANC had a majority, and across the country as a whole they had 62.6 per cent of the votes, giving them 252 seats out of four hundred in the new parliament. The PAC, which had once been such a formidable rival, had only 1.25 per cent. The ANC was just short of the two-thirds majority which would allow them to change the constitution; but Mandela sounded genuinely relieved that they 'could not do what they like'. Such an overwhelming victory, he said later, 'would have created tremendous problems; de Klerk would have applied to the court to declare the result null and void'. And he was already concerned with reactions after the elections: 'We have to be very careful not to create the fear,' he told the *Guardian*, 'that the majority is going to be used for the purpose of coercing the minorities.'[61]

De Klerk magnanimously conceded defeat in Pretoria, praising Mandela as a man of destiny who knew that beyond this hill lies another and another: 'The journey is never complete. As he contemplates the next hill, I hold out my hand to Mr Mandela in friendship and co-operation.' Three hours later in Johannesburg Mandela, exhausted with 'flu, came to the ANC victory celebration at the Carlton Hotel and returned the compliment. He congratulated de Klerk on the 'good fight', and described how they could still after harsh words 'shake hands and sit down to drink coffee'. It was time, he concluded, to drink a toast 'to the small miracle'. The world would continue to proclaim the 'South African miracle', but the phrase was misleading. As Albie Sachs said later, it had in fact been 'the most predicted and consciously and rationally worked-for happening one could ever have imagined, and certainly the most unmiraculous'.[62]

Mandela faced immediate and difficult choices. As President he would have two deputies; and under the terms of the constitution one would be de Klerk, as leader of the second largest party. But Mandela had to choose the senior one from within the ANC. The choice would be crucial, because Mandela intended to serve for only one five-year term, until he was eighty. His deputy would be well-placed to succeed, although the NEC would have to endorse him. Mandela had to decide between two able rivals from almost opposite backgrounds. Thabo Mbeki, at fifty-one, was the most obvious heir among the 'aristocracy of exile', the favoured protégé of Oliver Tambo. He had shown himself a masterful fixer and negotiator, with the training in economics and diplomacy which Mandela lacked, and with the intellectual flexibility to adapt from revolutionary to administrator. As Govan's son he had links with the Transkei and radical politics; but he was not close to his father – who had left his upbringing to others – and he had abandoned his Marxist beliefs. His political father-figure had been Tambo.

Cyril Ramaphosa was ten years younger, the son of a Soweto policeman; but he had been through testing ordeals – as a lawyer, as the miners' leader, as Secretary-General of the ANC and as the chief negotiator who had brought the ANC to power. He had both the charm and the ruthlessness to outwit experienced opponents. But he was outside the mainstream of the ANC: he had begun with the Black Consciousness movement, and came from the relatively small Venda tribe. He was detached from the networks of the Transkei, the exiles from Lusaka and the guerrillas of MK.

It was a very difficult choice. Mandela appeared often to favour Ramaphosa, and saw the advantage of having a non-Xhosa as his deputy, who could be neutral between the ANC tribes and groupings. But he consulted closely with the top ANC leaders, with the trades unions through COSATU, and with the Communist Party, 'without indicating his own feelings'. Their consensus was clearly for Thabo Mbeki.[63] Ramaphosa was put out, and refused a cabinet job; but he still appeared to be in the running to eventually take Mandela's place as leader. It was not until two years later that Mandela would make clear to his colleagues that Mbeki was his chosen successor.

On 10 May Mandela was inaugurated as President in a resplendent ceremony outside the Union Buildings in Pretoria, organised by the outgoing government. It was introduced by Barbara Masekela, and was watched by an estimated billion viewers around the world. It was a triumphantly international occasion, unlike de Klerk's inauguration five years earlier, which was attended by only four 'foreign' delegations – one from each of the South African homelands. This time there were four thousand guests, some of them incompatible, including Hillary Clinton and Fidel Castro, Yasser Arafat and President Chaim Herzog of Israel, Prince Philip and Julius Nyerere; but also old friends, including Bishop Huddleston and three of Mandela's prison warders. In his presidential speech Mandela stressed regeneration and reconciliation: 'Out of the experience of an extraordinary human disaster that lasted too long must be born a society of which all humanity will be proud.' He went on to promise: 'Never, never and never again shall it be that this beautiful land will again experience the oppression of one by another, and suffer the indignity of being the skunk of the world.'

The Generals and police chiefs saluted and pledged loyalty: a few years before, Mandela reflected, 'they would not have saluted but arrested me'.[64] Jet fighters which had been bought to defend the country against black insurgents roared overhead in tribute to the black President – though some ANC guests seemed to flinch, as though expecting to be gunned down. But the four thousand armed police were preoccupied with protecting Mandela against assassination (a hitman from the AWB had in fact been approached to kill him, but had backed out). The crowd sang the two national anthems, '*Die Stem*' and the ANC's '*Nkosi Sikelel' iAfrika*': 'Neither group knew the lyrics of the anthem they once despised,' Mandela reflected, adding hopefully: 'They would soon know the words by heart.'[65]* But there was still a powerful sense of the new nation rallying behind the new President.

It was essentially a tribute to one man. 'We all see ourselves reflected in his glory,' said Thabo Mbeki. 'A glory that arises in his humility, his sense of forgiveness.'[66] And it was a solitary glory. Mandela was accompanied by his daughter Zeni, under a huge black hat, but Winnie – under a still bigger green hat – was placed among the less important guests until she made a fuss. Mandela's first wife Evelyn (who had not voted) was not invited. His only son Makgatho was absent, preparing for his law exam in Durban. Mandela was painfully aware that his political commitment 'was at the expense of the people I knew best and loved most'.[67]

* Mandela would have to wait. Four years later, at a memorial service for Trevor Huddleston in Johannesburg Cathedral, he angrily criticised the congregation for not singing the words of '*Die Stem*', and insisted on the full version.

The outside world reported the inauguration with romantic euphoria, as the triumph of democracy, each country influenced by its own memories of past liberations. 'It was like being alive in the time of Lincoln,' said the *New York Times*. For Africa it had a much deeper significance. It was, as de Klerk wrote, 'the last manifestation of white rule – not only in South Africa – but on the whole continent'.[68] The process of colonisation which had begun in the Cape in 1652 had finally ended in Africa. There were a few sceptical warnings about African democracy, recalling how many black states had first gone to the polls over the previous forty years with similar enthusiasm. 'Dawn of freedom, my foot!' wrote the conservative Peregrine Worsthorne in the *Sunday Telegraph*. 'Black majority rule in South Africa should send a shudder round the world.'[69] But the doubts were drowned in the prevailing relief. The predictions of a civil war and a bloodbath had been disproved, and it was difficult not to give Mandela credit for avoiding disaster.

34

Governing

> The age of chivalry is gone. That of sophisters, economists, and calculators, has succeeded . . .
>
> Edmund Burke, 1790

WHEN MANDELA BECAME President of South Africa, four years after leaving prison, the world saw it as the end of the fairy-tale, requiring him to be happy ever after. In fact it was the beginning of a quite different story, with bureaucrats and exchange rates instead of heroes and villains, against a background which was new to Mandela: 'We have no experience of elections, of parliamentary practice, and of state administration,' he had already told British MPs.[1] The suddenness of power took most of the ANC by surprise: 'We were taken from the bush, or from underground outside the country, or from prisons, to come and take charge,' Mandela said four years later. 'We were suddenly thrown into this immense responsibility of running a highly developed country.'[2]

There was nothing new in Africa about prisoners suddenly coming to power: from Nkrumah in Ghana and Kenyatta in Kenya to Mugabe in Zimbabwe – all had faced unfamiliar problems. Mandela still saw himself in the African tradition, proud that his people had accomplished their own liberation, and determined to identify himself with them. 'I matured politically within the ranks of a movement and a leadership that were critical in shaping my outlook,' he explained later. 'I am the product of the mire that our society was. On occasion, like other leaders, I have stumbled; and cannot claim to sparkle alone on a glorified perch.' He was determined to show that Africans could govern effectively: 'Yes, Africans, with their supposed venality and incompetence, have achieved this feat!' And he resented insinuations 'that I do not belong to these African masses and do not share their aspirations'.[3]

But he also knew he was taking over a much more complicated

industrial nation than any other in Africa; and that it would be some time until black South Africans could govern without support from white managers, technicians and professionals. He had seen other African states devastated by a sudden exodus of whites – particularly Mozambique, whose first President Samora Machel had warned fellow-Africans to avoid the same fate. And South Africa was much more dependent on white expertise. From the beginning Mandela faced the balancing act of pacifying the white elite without alienating the black masses.

Mandela soon occupied the presidency as if he had been born to it. He moved into the grand mansions and offices – 'the places where the most diabolical policies were hatched' – at first feeling unsure of his reception by white bureaucrats. He liked to recall how he arrived in the President's office in Pretoria looking forward to the smell of coffee, which he had enjoyed when he visited de Klerk; now he could smell no coffee, and found no staff around. In the late afternoon he summoned a senior civil servant and asked him to assemble the staff the next morning. He shook hands with them, reminded them that a new government had taken over, and assured them that no one would be thrown on the streets.[4] Soon he established excellent relations with the white staff he had kept on. Afrikaner secretaries and servants became totally loyal to the genial old man who remembered their names and their families. 'Look at the lady who brought in the tea,' Mandela told one visitor. 'It is really unbelievable the way they have adjusted to their new position.'[5] When de Klerk later accused the ANC of having dismissed scores of Afrikaners from government jobs, Mandela retorted angrily that he had two white secretaries from the old regime who were 'typical *Boeremeisies*', and that he had retained an Afrikaner Major on his staff even though the security service had warned him that he had helped to bomb an ANC building. 'So what?' he had replied. 'I work in government with people who have done worse things than that.'[6]

In Cape Town, Mandela took over the President's office in the elegant old Tuynhuys, where P.W. Botha had poured him tea as a jailbird in 1989. He made only a few changes, putting up pictures of his mother's kraal and of himself as a boxer in the fifties. He moved into the secluded Groote Schuur estate – the legacy of Cecil Rhodes – where Afrikaner Ministers had long lived in private privilege; but he allowed de Klerk to remain in the official presidential residence, the historic Groote Schuur mansion, and himself occupied Westbrooke, an elegant but gloomy Cape

Dutch mansion – soon renamed in Afrikaans, 'Genadendal' (Valley of Mercy), the name of the first Christian mission in the Cape. He worked in the small and cheerful 'Elephant Room' opposite his bedroom at the end of a long corridor upstairs, which had been the powder-room for women guests; he could relax there with his feet up. He still often got up at 4.30, made his own bed, and walked round the grounds before breakfast.

In Pretoria Mandela caused more resentment when he decided to take over Libertas, the official mansion where the de Klerks had been living, while the ANC also used the Presidency, the other traditional residence, for entertaining and formal occasions. De Klerk was interested to watch the old man who had spent three decades in a tiny cell being 'conducted through the echoing halls of the sprawling mansion'. De Klerk himself had to move into a third official house, Overvaal, which he found delightful; but his wife Marike was offended by the chopping and changing, which she saw as 'a calculated effort by Mandela to humiliate us'. Her resentment, de Klerk reckoned, was 'a very real factor in the growing tension between Mandela and me'.

Mandela amazed the staff and servants by shaking hands and chatting with all of them, including the gardeners. 'He had an exceptional ability,' de Klerk noted, 'to make everyone with whom he came into contact feel special.'[7] He became friendly with his Afrikaner bodyguards, whose loyalty could be seen in their anxious faces as they watched his movements. 'I used to do it for the money, now it's for him,' said one of them. 'I'd take the bullet for him.' On the presidential plane or helicopter he chatted with the crew and pilot, concerned about their meals and accommodation. In Pretoria he gave a new intimacy to Libertas, which was renamed 'Mahlamba Ndlopfu', which means 'washing of the elephant', or dawn of a new era, in the Shangaan language. But he was still living in the house in Houghton, where he could remain a private person.

His physique and stamina amazed his physicians, including his old family doctor Nthato Motlana, who was always urging him to slow down. He still had trouble with his eyes, which were not cured by an operation in 1994, and photographers were forbidden to use flashlight when photographing him. He felt more pain from his knee, which had not recovered from his fall on Robben Island, but which could not safely be operated on: eventually he could not walk upstairs without help. Sometimes he suffered from exhaustion, and his doctors insisted on total rest. But he would recuperate quickly, and treated his long flights in the presidential plane as a rest – he appeared unaffected by jet-lag. At seventy-six his energy and vitality, doctors agreed, were like those of a man twenty years younger.[8]

In his offices Mandela conveyed both intimacy and authority, closeness and distance. He would greet visitors by springing up from his armchair or from behind his desk, looking them in the eye, remembering where they came from, recalling mutual friends. His style was always homely and earthy, like a countryman, still with his open smile. 'He wants to see you because he loves you,' his secretary would say. But he seemed equally glad to see new faces. He made dramatic entrances, often already welcoming a guest as he walked into the room, creating immediate rapport. Once, when a British television crew were filming him, he ruined the footage by walking straight up to the cameraman to shake his hand. When he arrived at 10 Downing Street the door was opened as always by the policeman inside: he immediately shook his hand, and remembered him when he returned, asking about his family.

Mandela never seemed to lose his courtesy or self-discipline. 'The man and the mask were one,' said Richard Stengel, the American journalist who collaborated on his autobiography; diplomats waited for the mask to slip, but it never did. His personal feelings seemed to have been subsumed by his political life, infusing warmth and energy; like a celibate priest he seemed to relate to people more closely, lacking the intimacy of a home. He always preferred to deal with politics and diplomacy through one-to-one contacts, bypassing bureaucracies; and he still loved the long-distance telephone as a new-found toy, using it to surprise friends on the other side of the world – sometimes waking them up early in the morning. His secretary Mary Mxadana, a tall, commanding woman who conducted choirs in Soweto, tried to prevent him from transacting all his business personally: 'I've just tried to stop him from walking downstairs,' she told a visitor, 'to call someone to the phone.'

But behind his courtesy, his secretaries knew, Mandela could be moody and dejected. 'He's not always as glad to see people as he says,' as one of them put it. 'His body language and facial expression indicate his different moods,' said Mary Mxadana. The word would sometimes go round the office: 'Madiba's in a bad mood today.' Once alone, he could suddenly show a sadder face. One sculptor who had portrayed many world leaders spent hours watching his expression. He found him uniquely charismatic, but also uniquely hard to represent: in company he lit up with every visitor, but by himself he would suddenly look exhausted, as his welcoming smile turned into a grim circumflex. Which mouth should the artist show?[9]

Mandela as President was more cut off than ever from old friendships: the greater his fame, the more lonely his isolation. 'The sad thing is that nobody realises that my father is very lonely,' said his daughter Zindzi.[10] He was much older than most of his colleagues. Tambo was dead, and Sisulu was outside the Cabinet. 'It was excruciating to see him sitting alone at his big table at home,' said one close colleague, who recalled how Mandela had once told him: 'I have no friends.' 'He guards against emotional friendships,' his observer went on. 'If you raise a question with emotional overtones he can look stony: you know you won't get anywhere. He has developed a total politicisation of being. It was a price I wouldn't like to pay, but it gave him a remarkable integrity in political life.'[11]

It was partly the legacy of prison. Most Robben Islanders had become accustomed to communing with themselves. 'We all found afterwards we needed space between ourselves and others,' said Eric Molobi, 'to reflect and regain ourselves, which made life difficult for our families.'[12] Mandela had been separated from his family for over a quarter of a century, and they now found him still less accessible as President. He was acutely conscious of his loss, but could do little about it.

Winnie had played no part in Mandela's social life since they separated: 'It was as if they did not exist for each other,' said their daughter Zindzi.[13] But she still caused political problems. After campaigning vigorously and successfully as an ANC candidate at the election she had become a prominent Member of Parliament. Mandela unwisely appointed her Deputy Minister of Arts, but she soon became involved in financial scandals: shady diamond deals, a dubious tourist project for black Americans, and an anti-poverty programme which allowed her huge expenses. Mandela made no move until she became openly disloyal: she accused the ANC of being preoccupied with appeasing whites, and challenged them to show they were in power.

When Mandela insisted she apologise Winnie reluctantly signed a formal apology, but then complained she had done so under duress, and that the ANC were restricting free speech. Then, in March 1995, while she was visiting West Africa against Mandela's instructions, her house in Soweto was raided by the fraud squad, backed by armed police, who seized documents. Returning the next day, Winnie exploded against the 'diabolical vendetta' by 'charlatans and cowards', and soon attacked the government again for ignoring the poor: 'Your struggle seems much worse than before,' she told an African crowd. Mandela finally dismissed her from government – though because of a legal oversight she had to be reinstated before she was properly sacked. Winnie still claimed she was in the right, and that other MPs were anyway more corrupt than she was. 'We must expect Comrade Winnie to fight back,' Mandela explained sadly. 'But we have the situation under control.'[14]

It was the end of the marriage. They had formally separated three years before, and in August 1995 Mandela began divorce proceedings, hoping for a friendly settlement to avoid family recriminations. But Winnie blamed her enemies, including Ramaphosa, for creating the rift, and insisted they could be reconciled through tribal customs: she even asked Mandela's nephew K.D. Matanzima, still paramount chief of West Tembuland, to mediate.

In March 1996 President Mandela appeared in the Rand Supreme Court, only a few feet from his wife, to plead for his divorce: a unique public display of his painful private life. He had delayed it, he explained, because he did not wish it to be linked to Stompie Seipei's murder. He rejected any mediation by Matanzima, who had once been Winnie's suitor, and whom he regarded as 'a sell-out in the proper sense of the word'. 'Can I put it simply, my Lord?' he told the judge. 'If the entire universe tried to persuade me to reconcile with the defendant, I would not. And least of all from Matanzima . . . I am determined to get rid of this marriage.' He sadly described his misery when Winnie would not share his bedroom while he was awake: 'I was the loneliest man . . .'

Through her lawyer, Winnie described her own past sufferings. Mandela accepted this, but insisted that there were others, like Albertina Sisulu, who had suffered more, and asked the lawyer not to compel him to reveal the 'even more serious reasons why I left home'. When the judge refused a request by Winnie's lawyer for a few days' adjournment to gather witnesses, Winnie dramatically sacked her lawyer. Mandela waited grimly until the judge returned to the courtroom to grant him a divorce, ending the marriage that had once seemed so crucial to his political morale. But Winnie still imagined herself as his wife: 'To hear him saying in a white man's court that I was pretending to love him was the greatest betrayal of the century.'[15]

Mandela remained quite alone on his 'glorified perch', and sought relaxation with quite unpolitical people at weekends. 'His weekends are none of our business,' said one of his Ministers. Like many other master-politicians – such as Jack Kennedy or Harold Wilson – he relished the undemanding company of showbusiness people or the rich. After his bleak isolation in prison he seemed dazzled by Hollywood figures like Whoopi Goldberg or Gregory Peck, not realising that he was more of a celebrity than any of them. However busy he was with government, he would shock his more austere colleagues by making time for visiting pop stars like Michael Jackson or the Spice Girls, being photographed with them and greeting them with flattery ('I'm only here to shine her shoes,' he said of Whitney Houston). 'I won't wash this hand for a long time,' he said after shaking hands with Peter Ustinov, whom he had seen in a movie while in jail.

Mandela worried the left more by enjoying the company of the very rich. Harry Oppenheimer, the arch-capitalist of Anglo-American, who had met Mandela once before he went to jail, was now glad to entertain him in his luxuriant Brenthurst estate, close to Mandela's house in Houghton (though Mandela was reminded to wear a tie). Mandela became especially close to Clive Menell, the Vice-Chairman of the rival Anglo-Vaal mining group, who had been a patron of black drama, including the musical *King Kong*, in the fifties. He spent his first Christmas as President at the Menells' secluded Cape mansion Glendirk, below Table Mountain. When in 1996 Menell was dying of cancer, Mandela sat silently with him, holding his hand: and at his memorial service he read a tribute to the generosity of a man 'born into privilege of a kind that few people can ever know'. But Mandela maintained his austere regime; when Menell came to his bedroom early one morning, he found that the President had already made his bed and was folding his pyjamas.[16]

Mandela was not always fastidious in his friendships. After he was separated from Winnie he stayed for a time in the showy mansion of Douw Steyn, a brash, self-made insurance tycoon; and his daughter Zindzi's honeymoon was partly financed by the casino king Sol Kerzner, who was soon to be charged with bribery. But Mandela kept his distance from the values of the rich. When he was staying in a luxurious enclave in the Bahamas surrounded by expatriates, he gave a talk to pupils at a nearby black school which appalled his white neighbours by its militancy. He sometimes seemed to regard successful businessmen as fellow-chiefs:

in Johannesburg he surprised a group of them by saying: 'You are the traditional tribal leaders in this area.'[17]

Part of him was still an African chief; and it was at his newly-built house in Qunu, in the Transkei, that he was most obviously at home. The house is always described as being modelled on the prison-house where he spent his last year in jail, which it was; but it gives no hint of a prison. It is a long, cheerful red-brick house – with no stairs to trouble Mandela's knee – with round arches and a wide, low roof, set back from the main road from Umtata and surrounded by a well-kept garden and trees to provide privacy. It looks across the beautiful Transkei landscape, with a few mud-walled, grass-thatched huts, which was so familiar from his childhood. The Transkei is even poorer, and much more densely populated, now than in the 1920s, with very few trees or birds, and the towns have suffered from the corruption of the Bantustan years. But the open views still have their timeless splendour. 'This is really home, where my roots are,' Mandela says. 'It becomes more important, the older you get, to return to places where you have wonderful recollections.'[18]

At Qunu he would sometimes walk for five hours in the morning, recapturing his childhood memories around the Great Place at Mqhekezweni, greeted by children on the way. He was pained to see their poverty, rags and skinny bodies, but encouraged by their cheerfulness. At his house he would enjoy providing open hospitality for neighbouring families. Once he presided over a two-day feast for six hundred guests, prepared by his friend Bantu Holomisa, with ten cauldrons, sixteen sheep and a whole ox slaughtered for the occasion, and brandy for the elders afterwards. Many colleagues worried that he was never left alone, but Sisulu noticed that he was most at ease when surrounded by people.

On his home ground Mandela loved being involved in tribal politics, settling local disputes about chickens or cows. He took a close interest in roadbuilding, pressing the case for women roadbuilders and ensuring that a road was diverted to the former home of the paramount chief, Sabata. He would even sometimes see his nephew Matanzima, now quietly retired in his 'Great Place' near Queenstown, in a spacious modern house in its own estate. Mandela still saw Matanzima as a sell-out, and Matanzima talked of Mandela patronisingly as a jailbird who had broken the law, though explaining that 'Nelson is free to come here at any time.'[19]

Mandela was on much easier terms with Bantu Holomisa, the youthful General who had deposed Matanzima; he came from another chiefly family nearby, and helped organise Mandela's house at Qunu. He seemed to regard Holomisa as a reminder of his own impulsive youth: 'When I was your age,' he told him, 'I was impatient with old men.'[20] But Mandela's tribal feelings did not appear to influence his patronage: the inhabitants of Umtata, the former capital of the Transkei a few miles from his house, complained that he did little to help them.[21] His overriding loyalty was not to grand neighbours, but to the ANC: and Holomisa learnt to his cost that he could not defy the ANC without forfeiting Mandela's trust.

In these different worlds Mandela remained a star performer who could play all the parts: the African chief, the Western President, the sportsman, the philosopher, the jiver with the 'Madiba shuffle'. He still loved changing clothes as he had in the fifties, now switching dramatically from a dark suit to a loose flowery shirt to a rugby jersey to a T-shirt and baseball cap. He could be transformed quickly from the stern head of state to the people's favourite. Sometimes he could change sides unpredictably: when trades unionists demonstrated angrily outside the President's office in Cape Town he suddenly appeared among them, to the alarm of his Cabinet colleagues. 'But I've learnt never to underestimate his political skills,' said one of them. 'It probably means he will soon hit them all the harder.'

Mandela seemed able to adapt to any constituency. He stiffly read out most of his speeches, written by a multi-racial team led by Joel Netshitenzhe, looking through his spectacles without attempting to make eye-contact with his audience. But often at the end he would take off his glasses and say: 'That's what my bosses said.' Journalists would look up, aides would frown, and he would come out with homely thoughts or reminiscences. He liked to repeat favourite stories – about being criticised by a child, or about people mistaking him for Nelson Mandela – to remind his audience that he was only a fallible old man, an ex-prisoner who found himself by accident in this odd position. He could still handle his own charisma, without being fooled by it.

In his first months as President, he enjoyed a brilliant honeymoon, particularly with white South Africans, to whom this tolerant old man came as a wondrous relief. He was in no hurry to rename the streets, suburbs and airports which commemorated Afrikaner heroes like Botha, Strijdom or Malan, the old hate-figures of the black majority, or to rename the Verwoerd Building, which housed government departments in Cape Town. He generated an atmosphere of normality and stability which dispelled all the past white nightmares about a black revolution. At the end of his first hundred days in office the *Financial Times* could find no whites who had a bad word for him.[22] It was a normality which carried its own dangers, as black militants saw the revolution betrayed; and younger ANC leaders including Thabo Mbeki knew they must soon make reforms which would offend the whites. They recalled how Robert Mugabe had a similar honeymoon after he took over Zimbabwe in 1980, only to antagonise the whites when he began making drastic changes fifteen years later.

But Mandela now seemed above politics. The campaigning party leader, the hard man of the negotiations, had been transformed into the father-figure who could sympathise with everyone's problems. At white cocktail parties he could work the room, making everyone feel special – particularly the women. 'Now I know the secret of your husband's success,' he would say to the wife of a prominent figure – who would sometimes be disappointed to overhear him saying the same thing to another woman a few minutes later. 'But I would still have been charmed,' said one editor's wife, 'even if he'd said I'd got spinach on my teeth.' Most whites were reluctant to criticise him; however much they complained about the black government, they would exclude Mandela and blame his underlings. Like Ronald Reagan, he appeared to be a Teflon man, against whom no charge would stick; or like a traditional monarch, whose faults could be blamed on his courtiers.

Mandela often seemed more like a king than a politician; all the more so when he received the British Queen on a state visit in March 1995, and established a friendship which took her entourage by surprise. As a student forty-eight years earlier he had watched her when her father the King was making his state visit. Now they had both seen apartheid come and go, while the Queen had been sympathetic to black South Africans through the Thatcher years.[23] Mandela fitted in naturally with the regal celebrations, and took the opportunity to conciliate the African chieftaincy by inviting thirteen South African kings to his state banquet. The Queen awarded him the Order of Merit, the most coveted British honour, and invited him to make a return state visit: 'You are, of course, well versed in making history,' she said, 'but I hope that, even for you, it will be an important milestone.' Sometimes Mandela appeared to be stealing the show, but the Queen always seemed unusually at ease; later she would often recall her enjoyment of Mandela's company. She especially appreciated the fact that he had delayed his impending divorce to prevent it from overshadowing the occasion.[24]

Mandela sometimes sounded like a philosopher-king, as if part of him had never left prison and was still looking at his country from his solitary cell. 'They can take us out of Robben Island,' said his colleague Kathrada, 'but they can't take Robben Island out of us.'[25] He liked to talk about first principles – about reconciliation, human dignity and love. His secretaries sometimes found him quite naïve about world affairs; he tended to see diplomacy in terms of contact with individuals, from Clinton to the Queen, as if he were still in the nineteenth century. But his simple view gave him insights. 'Like other great men,' said a Cabinet colleague, 'he is not afraid of simplicity: he is willing to be unpretentiously simple, to see beyond the immediate future.'

Mandela liked to say – to the Queen among others – 'I'm only a country boy,' and there was some truth in it. 'I've realised he is very *rural*,' said one of his closest aides. David Beresford of the *Guardian* compared him to the home-spun gardener played by Peter Sellers in the film *Being There*, whom politicians regard as infinitely wise and whom they invite to become a presidential candidate. Mandela's greatness, said Beresford, lay not in political or military skills, but in simple identification with his country: 'a creation of the collective imagination, an expression of national identity deeply desired in a bitterly divided country'. To both whites and blacks he seemed to have emerged as the man of destiny, to rescue his people from disaster: 'Cometh the hour, cometh the man.'[26]

35

The Glorified Perch

PRESIDENT MANDELA had theoretically strong powers under the South African constitution: as both head of state and head of government he was like a French President, but without a Prime Minister who chose his own Cabinet. His first Deputy President, Thabo Mbeki, only had the powers which Mandela chose to delegate, which could be quickly taken away. The President could be aloof one moment and immerse himself in detail the next. He enjoyed the personal scope: he had never worked easily with bureaucracies, and disliked paperwork. He relished his personal patronage, offering old friends grand jobs like ambassadorships and watching their surprise. He made the most of his easy access to the media, sounding off with strong views, and sometimes forgetting he was part of a collective Cabinet. Some commentators became alarmed, and he was accused of being a 'reckless gambler' and 'shooting from the hip'.[1]

Mandela still showed some authoritarian tendencies which were at odds with democratic controls, and some feared that he might emerge as yet another African autocrat, like Nkrumah or Mugabe, exploiting the traditions of a tribal chief. His old friends from the fifties looked for signs of autocracy. Walter Sisulu still watched him like a trainer watching his champ, but was soon reassured: 'I have no fears that you're going to have a dictator arising from him,' he said in 1993.[2] Mandela had great respect – perhaps too great – for African democracy.

He quickly realised, as de Klerk had warned him, that a President had less power than he appeared to. He could only rule effectively through his colleagues and civil servants, who had to be patiently persuaded; and he could not force his policies through Cabinet. 'It is comparatively easy . . . to win an election,' he had warned ANC members a year before he became President. 'But when you do so, you merely hold political office. You don't have political power.'[3] He still had to carry the ANC with him through the transition from rebellion to responsible government, against accusations that he was betraying the revolution.

At the end of 1994 he opened the forty-ninth conference of the ANC in Bloemfontein. He admitted the problems of the historic compromise of the 'sunset clauses' which entrenched Afrikaner bureaucrats from the previous regime: it was still debatable 'whether we are today reaping the whirlwind of a terrible misjudgement'. But the ANC were so disorganised after the elections, he explained, that they 'could have endangered the revolution', and the leadership had speeded up the process of transition by the decision to first capture the beach-heads, then to strengthen their forces. The ANC should not see themselves as 'weak, tied hand and foot by some terrible agreements'.[4]

In his closing address he once again complained about the ANC's incompetence, as he had done forty years earlier; it was now more serious, since the ANC was in power. It was ironic, he said, that they should talk as a government about fiscal discipline, waste and inefficiency when 'there is no financial discipline in the African National Congress, when there is waste, where there is inefficiency'. He implored delegates to spend more time thinking, as he had in jail; to welcome opposition; and to remember that 'power corrupts, absolute power corrupts absolutely'. But he congratulated them on being more united than ever, while delegates for the first time in their history 'discussed, not resistance, but reconstruction and development'.[5] They elected a new National Executive of sixty, who were clearly more militant than their predecessors; the top five were Bantu Holomisa, Pallo Jordan, Peter Mokaba, Mac Maharaj and Winnie Mandela. But Mandela's own position remained unchallenged.

In choosing his own government, Mandela had first hoped to form the widest possible coalition, to include the Democratic Party, the Freedom Front and the PAC: he approached the PAC President Clarence Makwetu four times without success.[6] Under the terms of the Government of National Unity he had to include de Klerk and his National Party. There was some bitter disagreement about Cabinet posts, and de Klerk complained that Mandela did not consult him about ANC Ministers.[7] De Klerk wanted his party to control either the police or defence; but Mandela insisted that the ANC must control both, since only the ANC could deal with the question of the third force.[8] The National Party had to be content with lesser posts: Roelf Meyer as Minister of Provincial Affairs and Constitutional Development; Kraai van Niekerk at Agriculture; Dawie de Villiers at Environment; and Pik Botha, the veteran Foreign Minister, in charge of Minerals and Energy.

The ANC Ministers included old friends of Mandela from almost every stage of his career. Joe Modise, the Minister of Defence, had been a colleague in Johannesburg in the forties; Alfred Nzo, the Foreign Minister, had been a leader of the bus boycott in 1958; Joe Slovo, the Housing Minister, had been alongside Mandela since the Treason Trials; Mac Maharaj, the Transport Minister, had been his loyal friend on Robben Island; Dullah Omar, the Minister of Justice, had often visited him in Pollsmoor as his legal adviser. Two came from chiefly backgrounds: Buthelezi, now Minister for Home Affairs, and Stella Sigcau, the daughter of the King of Eastern Pondoland in the Transkei, the Minister of Public Enterprises. But Mandela had only recently met many younger Ministers, who came from every strand of the struggle, including exiles like Tito Mboweni, the Minister of Labour, and Jeff Radebe at Public Works. There were complaints that the exiles had been preferred to internal leaders, but Cyril Ramaphosa, the most eligible, had refused a Cabinet post, and several new Ministers had been prominent internal activists in the eighties, among them Jay Naidoo, Sydney Mufamadi and Trevor Manuel. The most striking feature of the ANC government was the range of background and race, including whites, Indians and Coloureds, Muslims, Christians and communists, brought together by the forty-year struggle. As director of his own Office of the President and Cabinet Secretary Mandela chose Jakes Gerwel, an outstanding Coloured academic, a philosopher and expert on Afrikaans literature, who had supported Black Consciousness before becoming Vice-Chancellor of the University of the Western Cape.

From the start Mandela relied heavily on his first Deputy President, Thabo Mbeki, twenty-five years his junior, and the leading exile. Mbeki had a difficult assignment: he was as dependent on his boss as an American Vice-President, but with much heavier responsibilities. Mandela was given credit for triumphs, while Mbeki took the blame for mistakes. He developed an almost opposite style to Mandela, working from behind, schooled by his mentor Tambo, while Mandela led from the front. Mbeki would inscrutably puff his curved pipe, fixing and bargaining behind the scenes through a small group of confidants. Even their daily habits were out of sync: Mandela rose early and went to bed early, and was strictly punctual. Mbeki was more casual about appointments, and liked to talk expansively into the night. But their skills were complementary: Mbeki was the troubleshooter, picking up the pieces and filling in the gaps. He would always suffer from the world's recurring question: 'After Mandela?' But like all deputies of strong leaders – like Truman under Roosevelt or Pompidou under de Gaulle – he was impossible to assess while still under the shadow of the great tree.

The ANC Ministers took time to get used to sitting in the Cabinet alongside their ex-enemies: 'I still have to keep pinching myself to remember where I am,' said Kader Asmal, the Minister of Water, a year later.[9] But some former revolutionaries proved the most effective administrators. Joe Slovo, the former General Secretary of the Communist Party and MK chief of staff, reorganised his Ministry of Housing, bringing in his own Director-General and negotiating with banks for easier loans. Mandela suffered a great blow when Slovo died of cancer in January 1995, after only eight months in office. His funeral displayed the paradoxes of the peaceful revolution: the white leader was mourned by thousands of blacks; the Afrikaners' most sinister enemy had first proposed the coalition with them; the revolutionary idealist had become the most practical and flexible of politicians. Slovo was a man, said Mandela later at his graveside, who 'knew when to fight and when to negotiate'.[10]

When Mandela presided over his mixed Cabinet of blacks and Afrikaners, he found most discussions surprisingly non-partisan, and the Afrikaners genuinely committed to making the coalition work: 'You'd think they were members of the democratic movement.'[11] 'The atmosphere wasn't warm, but it wasn't cool,' said Pallo Jordan. 'Most policy was in conformity with what the ANC wanted.'[12] The National Party, said Kader Asmal, 'had a ferocious eye for detail, which could prove useful in Cabinet deliberations, although its overall showing on many issues of significance was not terribly helpful'.[13] On their side, the Afrikaners were surprised to hear ANC Ministers arguing openly with each other, with no sign that a caucus had agreed their line beforehand. De Klerk was gratified to find himself sometimes adjudicating in disputes between them.[14] 'There was a boyish boarding-school camaraderie which was very South African,' said one participant. 'Ninety-nine per cent of the discussion was unideological, often quite boring: you couldn't tell they came from different parties. The differences were often due to their age, rather than their ideology.'[15] The coming to power remained exhilarating for the ANC Ministers. Kader Asmal was reminded of Seamus Heaney's lines:

But then, once in a lifetime
The longed-for tidal wave
of justice can rise up,
And hope and history rhyme.[16]

The ANC Ministers were not driven by Marxist dogma as their right-wing opponents had so often prophesied; and many past members of the SACP, like Thabo Mbeki and Mac Maharaj, showed little interest in Marxism. Scare stories about a communist takeover now looked irrelevant as Ministers of all political hues sat down together to resolve day-to-day problems.

Mandela dominated the Cabinet, not just as President but as an older man, twice the age of many of the others, with a unique experience and reputation. They talked about him as 'the Old Man': to his face they would call him 'Madiba', rather than 'Mr President', but always with deference. He was the same age as Churchill had been when he returned as Prime Minister in 1951 at seventy-six, to resign at eighty; and like Churchill he embodied a patriotic spirit which overarched daily politics. He would preside sporadically over the Cabinet, held every two weeks, with a light hand, only occasionally making a strategic intervention. 'He took it like a chief,' said Mac Maharaj. 'He listened impassively, took everything in, and then intervened.'[17]

Mandela had asked George Bizos to investigate how other heads of government had handled mixed Cabinets. Bizos came up with the example of Clemenceau in France from 1917 to 1920 – who after listening to all viewpoints would give his own opinion and then ask: 'Any resignations?' Mandela sometimes adopted the 'Clemenceau solution', and no one resigned.[18] He was proud that no issue ever had to be taken to a vote. He detached himself from most detail, but involved himself closely in the Cabinet committees on security and intelligence. 'He followed it obsessively,' said one participant. 'He was still the old underground operator, the guerrilla fighter.' In smaller meetings he intervened sparingly but decisively. 'His decisiveness is what I most like,' said the same colleague. 'Often the briefings take only ten minutes, then he would decide.'[19]

He had some difficulties with two old antagonists, de Klerk and Buthelezi. As second Deputy President, de Klerk took turns with Mbeki to preside over the Cabinet when Mandela was absent, or had decided to stand down. The two Deputies met frequently to settle problems:

overhearing them amicably arranging agendas, it was hard to remember that they had ever been deadly opponents. De Klerk was impressed by Mbeki's economic insights and grasp of 'the essential realities of modern government'.[20] But he was much less at ease with Mandela: he realised that Mandela distrusted him, and asked mutual friends why this was so. The reason was clear: Mandela still felt betrayed by de Klerk's connivance with the third force. 'One thing Mandela cannot forgive,' said one secretary, '– a stab in the back.' Mandela still saw de Klerk as trying to divide the ANC: 'His tactic is to praise the President, and then attack and undermine the ANC.'[21] And Mandela always resented being patronised: 'He is most cross,' said one aide, 'when he feels his dignity is offended.'

All the tension burst in January 1995, during a Cabinet meeting chaired by Mbeki. Mandela had discovered that just before the election 3,500 policemen had been granted indemnity from prosecution for crimes carried out during the apartheid years, and launched into a tirade about de Klerk's underhand amnesty and his disloyalty to the coalition government. He praised other Afrikaner Ministers, including Roelf Meyer and Pik Botha, concentrating his abuse on de Klerk. 'It was a bristling attack,' said one observer, 'but with paragraphs and sentences perfectly constructed.' De Klerk started putting away his papers, and said he must reconsider his position. But his colleagues urged him to stay in government, and the next morning he found Mandela 'was his old charming self again'. In the afternoon they gave a joint press conference, at which they agreed to clarify the police indemnities.[22]

De Klerk was reluctant to break up the coalition. 'We won't upset the apple cart,' he told me five months later, 'though a few apples will fall.'[23] Mandela would still lash into de Klerk when he demanded indemnity for Afrikaners' past crimes. When in November 1995 de Klerk defended Magnus Malan, his former Minister of Defence, who was being charged with murder, Mandela said de Klerk was becoming a joke: 'I am the President of this country. I will decide who gets indemnity, not him.'[24] De Klerk in turn was fed up with Mandela: he thought he flew off the handle without checking his facts, and papered over problems with charm and promises. 'Ours had never been a marriage of love,' he wrote later. 'Now the honeymoon was over.'[25]

Mandela's other old problem, Buthelezi, had been appointed Minister for Home Affairs, but his loyalty was still uncertain, and he criticised Mandela for reneging on his pre-election promise to allow international mediators to settle the autonomy of KwaZulu-Natal: 'He dishonoured a solemn commitment,' he said afterwards. 'It's as if you say to your wife "till death us do part" and she disappoints you.'[26] Buthelezi became dangerously disruptive: he boycotted the first constitutional talks, and then called on Zulus to resist central government: 'Our march to freedom has begun.' Mandela overreacted, threatening to cut off funds to KwaZulu and to impose a state of emergency; de Klerk thought he wanted to crush Inkatha by force.[27] Mandela and Buthelezi staged another reconciliation, but their personal clashes continued. It was left to Thabo Mbeki and Jacob Zuma to eventually make peace with Inkatha in their low-profile style.

Mandela was much more concerned with the broader problems of transforming the nation from a white oligarchy into a multi-racial democracy. Parliament provided a visible pageant of the 'Rainbow Nation', with four hundred MPs of all colours thronging the chamber, and the revolutionaries turned into legislators. 'I love this dream,' exclaimed Archbishop Tutu. 'You sit in the balcony and look down and count all the terrorists. They are all sitting there passing laws. It is incredible.'[28] The 252 ANC members, many in colourful robes or bright dresses, far outnumbered the National Party members in their sober suits. The annual opening of Parliament in February 1995 was transformed. The troops still paraded outside the building, the President arrived with an armed guard, and the guns saluted; but now a black choir sang in the entrance, and the 'Soweto Strings' played in the street. Inside, the Generals were downgraded, while the judges came to the fore. Mandela walked through the chamber, shaking white hands as well as black, and delivered his speech formally from the written text, occasionally adding an impromptu aside. When he stopped to drink some water the members waited in total silence until he raised his glass and said, 'Cheers!'

Mandela wanted to use Parliament to consolidate a non-racial democracy, and was concerned that 'the Government of National Unity doesn't go down to the grassroots'.[29] He was supported in this by the new Speaker, Frene Ginwala, a formidable Parsee lawyer who had served the ANC for thirty years in Tanzania, Lusaka and London, and who now wanted to educate the ANC to use a Parliament which they had long seen as their enemy.[30] She saw the parliamentary democracy as a fragile plant, surrounded by authoritarian traditions, and tried to go back to first principles, learning from European and American models. Mandela had his own friendly battles with Ginwala: she resisted yielding to the executive, and was committed to the separation of powers. When he kissed her on both cheeks she told him: 'I'm not sure you are allowed to kiss the Speaker.'[31]

Parliament's most important task was to approve a new constitution – which was to be confirmed and fortified by a constitutional court chaired by Arthur Chaskalson, the lawyer who had helped defend Mandela in the Rivonia trial thirty years before. It was a poignant reversal of roles: when Mandela formally opened the court in February 1995, he reminded the lawyers that the last time he had been in court he was finding out whether he would be sentenced to death. And it was the death penalty which soon provided the first argument within the constitutional court. Mandela had wanted Parliament to decide on the question of capital punishment: he thought it was a moral issue, and personally believed that no civilised country should permit it. But the Cabinet decided to send the question to the court, which gave its own ruling, that the death penalty was unconstitutional. The court was soon to assert its independence of the President: when Mandela issued two proclamations affecting elections in the Western Cape, the Premier Hernus Kriel appealed to the court, which found that the President had overreached his powers: within an hour Mandela accepted the judgement – as he would often recall.[32]

The new constitution, to replace the interim agreement, was slowly hammered out by Ramaphosa and his team, reaching compromises to reassure all the parties, and working out safeguards for the Afrikaners' language and culture. After some brinkmanship it came before Parliament in October 1996, with copies distributed literally hot from the press. Politicians from all parties, from the PAC to the Freedom Front, complained about its shortcomings, but subsequently endorsed it. De Klerk said it showed that governments cannot simply do what they want. Ramaphosa, saying farewell to Parliament, congratulated the parties on rising above their principles.[33] But the ratification of the constitution would not put an end to arguments, particularly about the death penalty, which right-wingers, both black and white, were soon clamouring to bring back.

While Parliament projected the rainbow, the real battles to transform the country were waged inside the government departments. The ANC soon realised the full limitations of the 'sunset clauses'. They provided a caricature of the problem of any radical new government trying to push reforms through conservative officials: ANC Ministers had watched videos of the British satirical series *Yes, Minister,* in which wily civil servants obstructed the reforms of their political masters; but the substructure of officialdom in South Africa was much harder to budge than Whitehall. Some black Ministers suspected their Afrikaner officials of refighting old apartheid battles on new fronts, sniping or ambushing through filing cabinets and shredding machines. Mandela was aware of pockets of Afrikaner right-wing resistance – in the police, the army and intelligence – holding out against any reforms; but he believed most civil servants were cooperative.[34]

There were disturbing clashes between the more headstrong reforming Ministers and their Directors General, often about administrative practice rather than ideology: the head of the Housing Ministry, Billy Cobbett, resigned after complaining about irregular contracts arranged by his Minister Sankie Mthembi-Mahanyele, who had succeeded Joe Slovo. The political obstacles were sometimes exaggerated by Ministers who were not sure what they wanted to achieve or how. 'The civil servants have their own routine and rhythm,' said one senior black civil servant, 'but they are basically obedient, waiting to be told what to do.'[35] The shrewdest ANC Ministers, like Joe Slovo, could impose their policies quite swiftly: Kader Asmal effectively drove through plans to bring fresh water to rural areas. The basic ANC strategy was to root out and neutralise the senior civil servants who were actively obstructive, but it took time to remove them, and still longer to train qualified black administrators to take their place. The lack of experienced black middle-managers, particularly in the provincial governments, was the greatest obstacle to the transformation of government: and it was here that the full cost of apartheid policies, and particularly of Bantu education, showed itself.

The ANC faced compromises in every Ministry, as revolutionary dreams gave way to harsh budgets, but the central battleground was the Ministry of Finance. Huge outflows of capital during the previous eighteen months had left reserves dangerously low, and the government had to reassure international investors quickly. Mandela had no experience in economics, but he accepted the imperatives of the global marketplace; de Klerk was impressed that the ANC 'accepted a broad framework of responsible economic policies'.[36] Mandela reappointed de Klerk's Finance Minister Derek Keys, a quiet businessman who became one of the best-liked men in the Cabinet until he resigned a few months later, pleading family reasons. Mandela had to persuade an orthodox banker, Chris

Liebenberg, to take his place, while preparing Trevor Manuel, the ANC's Minister for Trade, as his successor. Manuel, with a militant past as a UDF activist, at first scared the bankers by talking disrespectfully about the global marketplace; but he soon appeared a pillar of financial rectitude.

At the Central Bank Mandela had reappointed the very conservative Chris Stals – a former member of the Broederbond – who was committed to curb inflation through high interest rates. Stals and Manuel became bogeys of the left, but the ANC Ministers learnt to live with the strict constraints they imposed: the interest payments on the debts incurred by previous apartheid regimes consumed a fifth of the entire national budget. For a time Mandela had hoped for some kind of Marshall Plan, like the aid Europe had received from America after the Second World War. 'What we expect,' he told *Time* magazine in June 1993, 'is that the Western world, led by the US, should ensure that massive measures of assistance are given to the people of South Africa.'[37] But the ANC soon realised that they must provide their own finance. 'The ANC has been in every country in Africa,' said Frank Chikane, the churchman who later ran the Deputy President's department. 'We saw what didn't work. When international help didn't come we realised that we must do it ourselves.'[38]

The retreat was agonising. The Reconstruction and Development Programme, in which Mandela had placed so much hope, soon proved overambitious. The target of a million new houses in five years could not be reached, and the promises of more jobs proved hollow, as new technologies required fewer employees, and put a premium on skills which most blacks still lacked. Nationalisation was no longer seen as an option for creating jobs. It was a bitter pill for ANC Ministers brought up to believe in the benefits of public ownership – not just by the communists, but by Afrikaner governments which had provided thousands of jobs for Afrikaners in overmanned nationalised industries, developing their own version of affirmative action. Now the world told the ANC to privatise industries, to shed jobs, to reject affirmative action and to rapidly reduce the deficit through which apartheid governments had financed their extravagance and oppression.

Mandela faced some disillusion. He had seen how foreign businessmen had piled into the apartheid boom in the sixties while he was in jail, when labour was cheap and the price of gold was shooting up. Now gold was slumping and labour was more expensive, and Africa was shunned by investors, who were racing into the miracle economies of South-East Asia. He tried to attract investors by reducing exchange controls, preparing to privatise and confronting the unions: but in the end they put their money elsewhere anyway. Mandela had felt the full power of the nation-state, which had jailed him for half his adult life: now he was told that states were losing their power to improve people's lives or rectify past wrongs.

It was the Ministry of Defence which was Mandela's special concern, as the sharp end of political power. As Minister he chose Joe Modise, the former MK commander, with Ronnie Kasrils – whom Africans called 'the white man with a black heart' – as his deputy. Mandela caused surprise by appointing de Klerk's head of the defence forces General Meiring – who had fiercely attacked the ANC in the past – to continue in his post for five years; but Meiring had appeared helpful to Mandela before the election, and now promised loyalty to him (he boasted to fellow defence officers that the President had talked to him on the phone for forty minutes).[39] And Modise and Kasrils gave more powers to the new civilian Secretary of Defence Pierre Steyn, the ex-Air Force General who had effectively uncovered third-force activities.

Defence remained the trickiest territory, a potential base for a coup or revolt. Many Afrikaner Generals still controlled powerful military networks which could withhold crucial facts about secret operations, arms sales or lists of informers, while the ANC's own former guerrillas were hard to integrate with the Afrikaner army, and reluctant to accept stricter discipline. Mandela had to intervene personally when in October 1994 three thousand MK soldiers refused to return from leave, warning them that they would be charged if they did not return within a week. The British government sent a small military team to advise on integrating the white and black forces, which later warned about Afrikaner obstructiveness: some ANC politicians wished that they had involved the British more closely, as the Namibian government had. Mandela kept a close eye on intelligence reports, which were themselves subject to rival loyalties. He still seemed confident – perhaps too confident – of General Meiring's loyalty.

Mandela's government was being closely watched by the world's businessmen and diplomats, above all for signs of corruption. They dreaded that South Africa would descend into the economic morass that had swamped so many potentially prosperous African countries like Nigeria and Kenya. Mandela had inherited a much more venal system

The relationship between Mandela and de Klerk was never as warm as it first looked. The tension was evident at the national peace conference in Johannesburg in September 1991, where smiling turned to glowering. And they each had their own problems with the Zulu Chief Buthelezi, who refused to shake either hand at the end of the conference.

After Mandela became President in May 1994 he very publicly forgave the people who had persecuted him. He visited the ninety-four-year-old widow of Hendrik Verwoerd (*left*), and saw the statue erected to Verwoerd (*above*). He visited Percy Yutar (*opposite above*), who as prosecutor had helped to send him to jail for twenty-seven years . . .

. . . and he visited ex-President P.W. Botha (*below*), who had kept him in jail and had denounced him as a communist terrorist. Botha still practised his hectoring style, but Mandela was amused, and preferred Botha's straightforward aggression to de Klerk's more devious approach.

Mandela achieved a new peak of popularity with white South Africans after the Springbok rugby team defeated New Zealand in the World Cup final in June 1995. He appeared on the field in a Springbok jersey to present the delighted captain Francois Pienaar with the trophy.

BELOW Mandela remained publicly loyal to his wife Winnie, in spite of his private doubts. He stood by her after she was convicted in 1991 of kidnapping the boy Stompie Seipei (in this photograph they are flanked by her lawyers Ismail Ayob and George Bizos). But the marriage was doomed.

Mandela established very personal one-to-one relationships with other heads of state, who were glad of the support of his moral authority. He saw President Clinton as a real friend of blacks and of Africa, and took him to see his old cell on Robben Island. In Britain he added a popular appeal to the antique ritual of a state visit, and forged a special relationship with the Queen.

ABOVE Thabo Mbeki succeeded Mandela as President of the ANC in December 1997, at the party's fiftieth conference in Mafikeng.

ABOVE LEFT Mandela loved receiving celebrities whom he had read about in jail, apparently unaware that he was as famous as they were.

LEFT He often seemed more at ease with his grandchildren than with his children. They came in and out of his house in Houghton, Johannesburg.

BELOW Mandela's eightieth birthday banquet near Johannesburg in July 1998 also became the celebration of his wedding to Graca Machel the day before. Two thousand guests watched them cut the cake. His grandson Mandla (right) gave a speech, while African and international singers and stars provided a showbiz festival.

President-elect Jacob Zuma greets Mandela during his inauguration ceremony as South Africa's fourth President since the end of apartheid in Pretoria on 9 May 2009. In his inaugural speech, President Zuma vowed to follow Mandela's legacy of reconciliation.

Mandela, wearing a chapka hat, waves as he arrives to attend the 2010 World Cup Final on 11 July 2010 at Soccer City stadium in Soweto.

than those further north, who had taken over from reasonably honest colonial administrators. The Afrikaner governments had been notorious for receiving bribes ever since Kruger's republic in the nineteenth century, and Mandela rightly said that the apartheid administrations were 'stiff in corruption'. The ANC needed to clean up both the networks of bribes and favours in Pretoria and the poisoned Bantustan governments built up by black dictators; while white entrepreneurs were now dangling bribes in front of politicians to acquire business footholds, particularly for casinos. In August 1997 South Africa was reckoned by one international survey of corruption to be thirty-third out of fifty-two countries surveyed, with Denmark at the top and Nigeria at the bottom.[40]

Mandela himself was visibly self-denying: he lived simply, and gave a third of his presidential salary to the Children's Fund which was his special charity. During the elections he had promised an end to the political gravy train: 'We are not going to live as fat cats.' But MPs were soon under fire for accepting big salary hikes. The critics included Archbishop Tutu, who made the fierce quip: 'The government stopped the gravy train long enough to get on it.' Mandela snapped back publicly against Tutu's 'act of irresponsibility', and told him he should have raised the matter in private. Tutu replied that he had, and that Mandela had impugned his integrity. The two men soon settled their quarrel. Mandela rang Tutu, complaining, 'Why shout at me in public?' but was soon laughing. A few months later Mandela announced a cut in the salaries of MPs and the President. Tutu continued to deeply admire Mandela's leadership. 'If this man wasn't there, the whole country would have gone up in flames.'[41]

Much more serious were charges of embezzlement and misappropriation. The ANC were especially damaged by charges against Allan Boesak, their former leader in the Western Cape who had been the heroic co-founder of the UDF. After Boesak's marital scandal Mandela stood by him during the elections, against the advice of several colleagues, and afterwards appointed him Ambassador to the UN in Geneva. Then a Danish aid agency complained that funds sent via Boesak had gone astray, and asked a Johannesburg law firm to investigate. They found that Boesak had 'enriched himself substantially' to buy a house and pay for his second wedding. A government report found the accusations unproven, and Mandela insisted that Boesak was innocent. The law nevertheless took its course, and Boesak, while in America, was charged with embezzlement.

When he returned, the Minister of Justice Dullah Omar – who was also Chairman of the ANC in the Western Cape – welcomed him at the airport with a supportive speech. The opposition complained that Mandela was putting party loyalty above public probity; but the trial went ahead, and in March 1999 Boesak was found guilty on four counts of fraud or theft, and sentenced to six years' imprisonment.[42]

By the end of Mandela's first year as President, the honeymoon had ended. White South Africans were complaining bitterly about the crime wave, the falling rand, corruption scandals, upheavals in hospitals and schools. Liberals were disillusioned that a black government was ignoring their advice; other whites never thought it would work anyway. White South Africa had been a uniquely privileged society under previous regimes, protected both from black competition and from the world marketplace, and found it hard to adjust to an open democracy. 'There is a bizarre pessimism in the leafy suburbs of what was previously exclusively white South Africa,' said Kader Asmal in February 1997, 'a pessimism which totally fails to take account of the remarkably favourable arrangements made for whites.'[43]

Most blacks took a much less pessimistic view, with longer perspectives. The rural poor saw the extension of primary health-care and the arrival of water-taps; and in the cities the burgeoning black middle class saw expanding opportunities in industry and commerce. But their prospects looked less hopeful when unemployment increased and new jobs failed to materialise; and overseas investors were discouraged. As the *Financial Times* wrote in May 1996: 'Rising crime and slow employment growth, failure to deliver on promises to cut the country's huge housing backlog and illegal immigration from impoverished neighbours have all contributed to declining business confidence.'[44] By November 1996 the ANC had to admit serious mistakes, in a 'half-term performance review': 'The ANC has gone into government for the first time and we have a steep learning curve in matters of governance . . . When we went into government we expected problems but not of the magnitude that we have.'

Mandela was facing his own learning curve. 'It was more difficult to defend the freedom we have won,' he said in January 1996, 'than struggling or fighting to gain it.'[45] By January 1997 he was admitting that the ANC had made some 'fundamental and serious' mistakes, including its response to funding from Sol Kerzner and the costly sequel to the musical *Sarafina*, intended to publicise AIDS, which was never produced. It was crucial, he added, to admit mistakes and learn from them. But he remained overwhelmingly loyal to old ANC colleagues – unless, like his ex-wife or Bantu Holomisa, they had publicly criticised the leadership. And he shrugged off the calls to reorganise his government. 'I thought I had found a reason to reshuffle my Cabinet,' he said when he opened Parliament in February 1997. 'I saw some members of the Cabinet dozing off as I was speaking . . . But then I looked at the Premiers right in front of me here, as well as members of the opposition, and I saw the same thing happening here! I thought I should be fair and not discriminatory, so there will be no reshuffling.'[46]

Mandela's stubborn loyalties exasperated some colleagues as well as opponents, as he appeared to tolerate inefficiency and abuses of power. He was personally often shocked and disappointed by the new mood of financial ambition and the careerism of the younger political generation.[47] But publicly he preserved an Olympian tolerance. His priority was building a new nation, and reconciling former enemies – which he saw as his overriding historical role.

36

Forgiving

MANDELA HAD BECOME FAMOUS above all as the man who forgave the enemies who had jailed him. It was not an obvious role for him to play. In his years before jail he had been quite aggressive, whether in his boxing or in his militant speeches. The younger Mandela enjoyed confronting enemies, whether Afrikaner bosses, Western imperialists or African sell-outs; it was his colleague Tambo who was then the obvious conciliator: 'When I want a confrontation,' Tambo told a colleague, 'I ask for Nelson.'[1] Mandela had learnt his conciliation the hard way, in his years in jail: through his brains, as he put it, not with his blood. He changed his attitude to Afrikaners, with the help of a few warders, and realised that the future peace of South Africa would depend on forgiveness. It was his control of his aggression which gave his policies their special power: like George Washington (wrote Anthony Lewis), he was 'a man of strong emotions who suppressed them in the interest of creating a nation'.[2]

Mandela was the founder of a new nation, like Washington, Garibaldi or Bolivar, but he had not established it through military conquest or brute force; and he was very conscious of the consequence: 'In nation-building you sometimes need a bulldozer,' as he put it, 'and sometimes a feather-duster.'[3] The previous South African nation – which was eight years older than Mandela – had itself been the result of a much-heralded reconciliation between ex-enemies, the Afrikaners and the British, who had come together after a bitter war. But the cost of that settlement had been the exclusion of Africans from government; and the idea of a multi-racial South Africa was still young and fragile.

Mandela still faced arguments about what multi-racialism really constituted. He accepted the image of the 'Rainbow Nation', embracing all the colours, which had been popularised by Tutu and others; but he had never believed in 'colour-blind non-racialism', as advocated by many left-wing theorists. He still recalled his long debates on Robben Island about the 'national question' with Neville Alexander, who had since become a professor at the University of Cape Town. Alexander had now moved away from the extreme 'assimilationist' model which assumed that racial differences would melt away; he now preferred the metaphor of a great river, absorbing tributaries from all over the country. But he still resisted emphasis on racial definitions.[4] Mandela saw unifying South Africa as a more gradual process than Alexander did, in the ANC tradition. As Albert Luthuli had put it: 'From the beginning our history has been one of ascending unities, the breaking of tribal, racial and credal barriers.'[5] Mandela remained sensitive to the cultures of different races and tribes, and warned the ANC not to forget the minorities. 'During the transition,' he said in March 1993, 'minorities everywhere will say: "If the change comes, what is going to happen to me, to my spouse, to my children, to the national group to which I belong, to the values in which I believe, to my possessions?"' He hoped for a Government of National Unity under which everyone could say: 'I am represented in that government.'[6]

He was particularly concerned with conciliating the most dangerous minority, the Afrikaners with whom he was sharing government. He could not forget that they included, as he put it, 'all sorts of people whose hands are dripping with blood'. But he had to make peace with them and make them feel part of the new nation: 'We have to be alive to the sensibilities of the other group that has now lost power.' And his jail years had paradoxically left him with a special tolerance of the Afrikaners, and a belief that they could reverse their loyalties: 'Once they change,' he would say, 'they move 180 degrees.' Many of his friends were puzzled and sceptical. 'He just seems convinced,' said one of them, 'that the Afrikaners are a good thing.'

But Mandela also had good political reasons to reach out to the Afrikaners – to deal separately with their different groupings. He had already defused some right-wing politicians, including the leader of the Conservative Party, Ferdi Hartzenberg. 'He will soon realise,' Mandela said on the eve of the election, 'that he either talks to us or disappears into the wilderness.'[7] After the election Hartzenberg did have friendly talks with Mandela, and he did almost disappear. The more extreme Eugene Terre'Blanche of the AWB was left out in the cold, thoroughly discredited, and denouncing Hartzenberg as a traitor.

Mandela went out of his way to conciliate his ex-enemies in a succession of symbolic visits with a high sense of drama. He went to see ex-President Botha again in Wilderness in November 1995. Botha appeared still to be fighting the Cold War: he told Mandela that after being a prisoner in jail, he was now a captive in his own cabinet, encircled by a cabal of Indians and communists: 'They will destroy you.' And he warned him that if Afrikaner Generals were prosecuted for acts carried out under the apartheid regime it could lead to disaster. 'Mandela said nothing and looked me straight in the eyes,' Botha recalled, 'like a Matanzima.'[8] Botha wagged his finger in front of the cameras which recorded their meeting, while Mandela watched with amused tolerance: he knew that the old crocodile was now almost toothless.

Mandela welcomed many old opponents from his jail years. When Niël Barnard retired as head of intelligence, Mandela gave a dinner party for him in Pretoria, with guests including General Willemse, the former commander of Robben Island. 'It doesn't happen in everyone's lifetime,' said Willemse afterwards, much moved. 'It's a wonderful experience to live through.'[9] And Mandela made peace with the Afrikaner Churches. One Sunday he joined the congregation at a Dutch Reformed church in Pretoria, where he was delighted by his reception: 'The men all wanted to touch me. The women all wanted to kiss me. The children all wanted to hang on my legs.' A few years earlier, he reflected, he would have needed guards to protect him from being assaulted: 'This time they were there to protect me from being killed out of love.'[10]

With the help of Amina Cachalia he met the widows and wives of both black and white leaders, not only veterans of the struggle like Albertina Sisulu and Albania Mothopeng, but also the wives of Afrikaner leaders, to 'make them feel comfortable in the new set-up'.[11] In August 1995 Amina flew with him to the bleak Afrikaner enclave of Orania in the Northern Cape – which reminded her of the Indian township of Lenasia, which apartheid planners had plonked outside Johannesburg – to visit the ninety-four-year-old widow of his old persecutor Dr Hendrik Verwoerd. She gave Mandela tea, and made a short speech pleading for a Volkstaat, reading haltingly without spectacles until Mandela prompted her in Afrikaans. She showed him an unimposing sculpture of Verwoerd: 'You've made him so small!' said Mandela. As they flew back, Amina argued with Mandela that Afrikaners would never face up to the New South Africa; but Mandela insisted: 'They will, they'll come right in the end.'[12]

Three months later he gave lunch in Pretoria to the eighty-four-year-old Percy Yutar, the prosecutor at the Rivonia trial who had infuriated the accused with his vindictive and hectoring tirades. Mandela flattered the frail little lawyer – 'You still look young and fresh' – while Yutar marvelled at his magnanimity: 'It shows the great humility of this saintly man.'[13] In seeking out his persecutors Mandela seemed like the legendary ex-convict who hunts down all the people who betrayed him; but instead of murdering them, he forgave them.

Many ex-Robben Islanders balked at his more extreme acts of forgiveness, such as appointing General Jannie Roux – the prison chief who had been so callous on Robben Island – as Ambassador to Austria. And they were baffled by his leniency towards his former jailer James Gregory when he published his book *Goodbye, Bafana*, promoted with the help of a letter from Mandela thanking him for 'the wonderful hours that we spent together'. Gregory had 'hallucinated' in many of his accounts, Mandela said privately, and Gregory himself admitted that he had used 'author's licence'; more seriously, he had abused his role by disclosing confidential personal details. Mandela was urged to sue him, but was satisfied when the prisons department distanced itself from the book.[14]

Mandela remained adamant about the necessity to conciliate Afrikaners, which he saw as an act of courage, not of weakness. 'We don't need to remind ourselves about past evil,' he told me when I argued the point. 'Courageous people do not fear forgiving, for the sake of peace.'[15] Reconciliation was certainly crucial to his political strategy. The more he reached out to individual Afrikaners, the more he could divide and disarm them. Forgiveness was an aspect of power, establishing a moral supremacy which reminded everyone that the balance had shifted. 'You never quite know,' said one of Mandela's colleagues, 'whether he's a saint or a Machiavelli.'

But his reconciliation was also part of the basic optimism about human nature which Mandela had carried with him since his youth, and which was strengthened rather than weakened in jail. His close aides were still often exasperated by his willingness to support dubious friends, to see the best in unattractive opponents, and to welcome apparent charlatans. Ahmed Kathrada, who worked in the next office, wondered how far Mandela saw through the deceptions of false friends who came to see him, 'of a superficial acquaintance of decades past suddenly elevated to "close friendship"; of opportunists ingratiating themselves in order to promote their dubious and even fraudulent agendas; of fair-weather friends who were nowhere to be seen when their friendship was most needed'. Mandela, Kathrada suspected, was simply too busy with other priorities to notice their machinations.[16]

All these dramatic gestures of forgiveness were greeted by whites with surprise and relief, while arousing the anger and suspicion of some black militants who saw their President in league with their enemies. Mandela always insisted that reconciliation must be accompanied by transformation – a key ANC word – to enable blacks to share economic power and jobs with the whites; and he was becoming impatient with the absence of reciprocal concessions from the white side. 'We can neither heal nor build,' he said at the opening of Parliament in February 1996, 'with the victims of past injustices forgiving and the beneficiaries merely content in gratitude' – followed by loud black applause and a few white claps. Businessmen, he warned, could not simply continue business as usual, living in islands of privilege: they must think in terms of the rest of the population.[17]

Mandela saw sport as a critical area for both reconciliation and transformation, and he reached out to white sportsmen who were thrilled by the new opportunities: they had been cut off from international competition by anti-apartheid boycotts, and now saw their world opening up again. Rugby more than any other game had been associated with apartheid, and with Afrikaner thuggery towards blacks: one Robben Islander recalled his police torturers kicking him round the cell, saying, 'Now we're playing rugby.'[18] The name of the South African team, the Springboks, had symbolised white arrogance, and many blacks wanted it changed; but Mandela insisted that it should remain, and went out of his way to identify with the Springbok team, who were all Afrikaners except for one Coloured. In June 1995 the Springboks celebrated their re-entry into international rugby with a triumphant match against New Zealand in the World Cup final in Johannesburg. Mandela watched the close-run game with absorption: 'It almost shattered my nerves,' he said afterwards.[19] When the Springboks won Mandela walked onto the field wearing the green Springbok jersey, to present the amazed captain Francois Pienaar with the trophy. The crowd round the stadium, mostly Afrikaner, went wild, chanting 'Nel-son! Nel-son!'; that evening boozy Afrikaners were embracing blacks in the streets and in hotels with spontaneous welcomes. 'Mandela won the hearts of millions of white rugby fans,' admitted de Klerk.[20]

It seemed to promise a new era of multi-racial sport, in which black players would soon come through to be selected for the Springboks. But the euphoria was premature. The Chairman of the South African Rugby Football Union, Louis Luyt – an Afrikaner businessman who had been a front for the government's dirty tricks in the seventies – was set against black pressure. Three years later, when the National Sports Council sought to hasten the process of integration, Luyt took legal action against them, and the judge subpoenaed Mandela himself to appear in the court. Mandela was advised by his lawyers not to go, but he insisted on attending, to show respect for the rule of law – only to hear the judge find in Luyt's favour.[21] When the Sports Council threatened to bring back the international boycott of South African teams, Luyt dug in his heels until his colleagues finally forced his resignation, in an atmosphere of racial acrimony which recalled the era of apartheid rugby. The slowness of other sports bodies to encourage the selection of black players in national teams continued to exasperate the ANC: Lulu Xingwana, the head of the parliamentary committee on sport, complained in December 1998 that the government was 'tired of apologising internationally for all-white teams that are supposed to represent South Africa'.[22]

A gulf still yawned between the symbolic gestures of reconciliation and gratitude at the top, and the realities below. Most white businessmen remained resistant to any real changes in the racial balance in their offices, recreations or daily lives, and saw black promotions in terms of lowering standards and risking corruption.

The most exposed and visible frontier of transformation was the media. Mandela saw them as the crucial windows through which South Africans saw each other; and nearly all the media before 1994 had been controlled by whites. Television had been tightly supervised by Afrikaner governments since they first allowed it into the country in 1976. The ANC had appointed Zwelakhe Sisulu, Walter's son, as Chairman of the SABC, with a mission to cut it down and transform it; the corporation sold off many radio stations, and brought black faces and opinions to the screens.

But most newspapers remained white-owned, and Mandela observed the press more closely than television. He had learnt in the fifties how desperately the ANC depended on newspapers to report its protests, and had tried to influence reporters and editors then. When he was released in 1990 he warmly thanked liberal journalists who had kept the ANC cause alive: 'It was the press which never forgot us.'[23] Through the negotiations with the Afrikaner government and the election campaign which followed he cultivated and charmed journalists, who helped to present a shining image which most other world leaders would envy. But once in office, like most politicians Mandela became touchy about criticism of his government, and soon laid into the press for its reluctance to transform itself, its white-centred viewpoints, and its relentless reporting of scandals and setbacks, particularly its reporting of crime. For a time the ANC considered starting up their own daily newspaper to ensure fair coverage, and Mandela had discussed collaborating with the British-based tycoon 'Tiny' Rowland. But he was warned that such a paper would be 'hammered' by competitors and advertisers.[24]

Mandela was eloquent in favour of a free press, at a time when it was being threatened throughout Africa. Before the elections he had told the International Press Institute in Cape Town that 'a critical, independent and investigative press is the lifeblood of democracy.' But he also pointed to the overwhelming influence of white editors and owners: 'With the exception of the *Sowetan*, the senior editorial staffs of all South Africa's daily newspapers are cast from the same racial mould. They are white, they are male, they are from a middle-class background, they tend to share a very similar life experience.' Or, as Thabo Mbeki told editors: 'You are all sons of the same mother.'[25]

Mandela still continued to champion press freedom after coming to power: 'I don't want a mouthpiece of the ANC or government,' he said in 1996. 'The press would be totally useless then. I want a mirror through which we can see ourselves.' But he was soon distressed by the lack of change: 'There is a perception among the population that the mass media is controlled by a minority section of the population,' he warned editors in November 1996. 'It is a totally unacceptable situation in terms of our vision . . . I seem to feel that the conservative press is trying to preserve, one way or another, the status quo.'[26]

The biggest newspaper group – the Argus group, led by the Johannesburg *Star* – had been bought after the elections by the Irish tycoon Tony O'Reilly, with Mandela's blessing, and renamed the Independent group. O'Reilly and other proprietors gradually began introducing some black editors as well as more black journalists. But Mandela was sceptical about such changes: 'As long as the newspapers are owned by a white, conservative minority, those promotions are simply tokens without power,' he said on television in December 1997.[27] He often sounded more impatient with black editors than white, including those of the *Sowetan* – whose Chairman was now his old friend Nthato Motlana, to whom he often complained about what he saw as the paper's bias against the ANC.[28] Nor was he satisfied when Motlana, together with Cyril Ramaphosa, took control of the TML group, which owned the popular *Sunday Times*. 'Even if Ramaphosa and Motlana have a controlling share,' he explained in 1997, 'there are many areas where power is not with them.'[29] He suspected, with some justification, that black reporters' copy was still being heavily edited by conservative white sub-editors: 'We all know what happens in the newsrooms.'[30] But he also had occasional grievances against individual black journalists. The outspoken young columnist Kaizer Nyatsumba complained in the *Star* in October 1996 about the 'Old Man's wrath': 'The truth is out, and it is frightening: our saintly emperor has no clothes on!' Mandela was hurt, and his communications chief Joel Netshitenzhe accused Nyatsumba of 'wallowing in invective'.[31] Mandela complained when the black editor of *City Press*, Khula Sibiya, inaccurately criticised him for interfering in the appointment of the Chief Justice. Later he met twenty black editors including Sibiya, and made peace; he told them that the ANC did not want 'a lapdog press', but that they could not expect him to fold his arms when they impugned his integrity.[32]

He was angry when editors – like Brian Pottinger of the *Sunday Times* or Peter Sullivan of the *Star* – acquiesced with him in private, and then attacked the ANC in print: 'They say they agree with you and later say the opposite,' he complained. 'I'm an old man, and I don't want to be taken for a ride by young people,' he told Sullivan. 'Do you remember the article in the *Star* where you said there was nothing worthwhile Mandela had done except to dismiss his wife?'[33] (Mandela later apologised to Sullivan, after failing to trace the comment.)

Journalists worried that Mandela was seeking to muzzle opposition, like African governments elsewhere; but he tried to reassure them: 'It is a mistake that some of our neighbouring countries have made to crush opposition parties. If you do that, the whole process of transformation will slip away.'[34] But he saw himself as being entitled to a simple right to reply: 'If you feel I am wrong, you will say so...' he told Jim Jones, editor of *Business Day*. 'But give us the right to say what we think too.'[35] He accused the media of double standards, defending their own freedom of speech while regarding any government counter-attack as an attempt to suppress them.[36] In fact he remained personally averse to censoring anything, including pornography. The sleazy South African edition of *Hustler* magazine had already embarrassed his staff in 1996 when it showed one of his secretaries posing in the nude; she reappeared in a later issue as 'Nelson's Girl, in the buff . . . the horny secretary who rocked the Presidency.'[37] Then, in February 1998, *Hustler* rudely featured Mandela as 'Asshole of the Month'. Lindiwe Sisulu, the Deputy Minister of Home Affairs, slammed the issue as 'vile, outrageous and obscene', and considered banning it. But Mandela laughed the matter off, and said he preferred that the magazine should use 'its own sense of morality and values'. He surprised his Secretary of Cabinet, Jakes Gerwel, by asking: 'Have you seen this month's *Hustler*?'[38]

Mandela continued to be wary about the more conservative press. In December 1997 he accused it of conspiring with counter-revolutionary forces to undermine the multi-racial democracy.[39] 'The bulk of the mass media in our country has set itself up as a force opposed to the ANC,' he said at the fiftieth ANC conference at Mafikeng, to cries of 'You tell them, comrade!' and 'Paparazzi!' 'The media uses the democratic order as an instrument to protect the legacy of racism.' But his main concern was to defend his mission of reconciliation, and he was equally fierce with black editors who complained that he was neglecting the underprivileged masses and was too preoccupied with placating whites. 'It is about nation-building and reconciliation that senior black journalists attack me,' he told editors in November 1996. 'We would have had bloodshed unless we had made these into fundamental policy. This country would have gone up in smoke.'[40]

Mandela's reconciliation could never be a simple question of forgiveness; and the tens of thousands of victims of torture and the families of dead comrades could not agree to sweep the horrors of the past under the carpet. Mandela believed that with the exception of Hitler's genocide against the Jews, 'there is no evil which has been so condemned by the entire world as apartheid'.[41] The ANC had to find a way to forgive without forgetting. The result was Mandela's launch in February 1996 of his government's most controversial innovation, the Truth and Reconciliation Commission (TRC).

The Truth Commission – as many of its critics forgot – originated as part of the hard bargain of the 'negotiated revolution'. President de Klerk and his security forces had constantly insisted on a general amnesty, with a self-interest which exasperated Mandela; the ANC could not allow the apartheid regime 'to grant amnesty to itself'.[42] After fierce arguments de Klerk eventually agreed with Mandela on a formula: a commission would grant individual amnesties on condition that the perpetrators revealed the truth, and could prove that their actions had been politically motivated. Many ANC activists thought the bargain far too generous: 'Now I know that my wife's killers will go free,' said Joe Slovo, whose wife Ruth First had been killed by a letter-bomb.[43] His daughter Gillian would be appalled when she heard policemen callously testifying as to how they had murdered her mother, in order to gain amnesty. But, as she recognised: 'The TRC was never supposed to be about justice; it's about the truth.'[44]

The ANC wanted to avoid a trial of 'war criminals' like that of the Nazis at the Nuremberg trials, which could create martyrs. ANC lawyers looked at other models in Eastern Europe, Chile and Argentina, and came up with their own solution, 'between amnesty and amnesia'. The Truth Commission, unlike the Latin American investigations, would have quasi-judicial powers to grant individual amnesties, with subpoena powers and hearings in public. But applicants for amnesty would have to come out with the full truth. The Truth Commission was thus able to reveal a much more detailed and credible picture of torturers, murderers and victims than any previous investigations anywhere in the world. It also acquired a more religious character when Mandela appointed Archbishop Tutu as Chairman, with a Methodist preacher, Alex Boraine, as his deputy. De Klerk saw Boraine as 'a zealot and an inquisitor', and having first supported a Truth Commission, he argued angrily with Mandela about its membership.[45] Tutu's chairmanship turned the subsequent hearings into a mixture of trial, confessional and morality play, with an African dimension. *Ubuntu* was actually written into the South African constitution: 'a need for understanding but not for vengeance, a need for reparation but not for retaliation, a need for *ubuntu* but not for victimisation'.[46]

The Commission was dedicated in February 1996 in the Anglican cathedral in Cape Town, before a mixed and colourful audience including Winnie Mandela. 'I invite you to join in the search for truth,' said the motto written by the Minister of Justice Dullah Omar, 'without which there can be no genuine reconciliation.' Priests from several faiths, including Jewish and Buddhist, recited their blessings. Mandela gave a subdued address, repeating that 'We can forgive but we can never forget,' and promising that the Commission would be free from all political interference. Tutu spoke with untypical brevity: 'For once,' he said, 'the Archbishop does not have too many words, thank goodness.' He would keep his distance from Mandela and the ANC: by November 1996 he was threatening to resign when the ANC resisted seeking amnesties on the grounds that theirs was 'a just struggle'.[47] But de Klerk and most Afrikaners would increasingly depict the TRC as an arm of the ANC government.

Over the next two years the much-publicised hearings of the Truth Commission revealed more horrific stories than most politicians, including Mandela, had imagined, as both perpetrators and victims described the cold-blooded details of torture and assassinations, which were played out on TV, radio and the press. The ANC had its own dark history of political crimes, and eventually provided a report admitting that twenty-two members had been executed in camps abroad for offences including mutiny, betrayal, rape and murder.[48] But most of the evidence was inevitably about the atrocities committed by the forces of apartheid.

Officials and politicians who declined to apply for amnesty could still be prosecuted through the normal legal processes; the former Minister of Defence General Magnus Malan was charged with others with conspiring to order massacres in KwaZulu, in a sensational trial. The ANC faced a setback when Malan was acquitted, but Mandela immediately accepted the judgement. And the Truth Commission soon afterwards achieved a breakthrough when senior officers of the apartheid security forces began implicating others, including Eugene de Kock, known as 'Prime Evil', who ran the notorious Vlakplaas camp, where death squads were organised; he fingered de Klerk as his ultimate boss. Soon, in a flood of confessions, police and army officers revealed systematised torture and murder. Victims' bodies were cut up or burnt to ashes; documents called for 'elimination', 'neutralisation' and 'removing from society'; the assassins of Steve Biko described in gruesome detail how they murdered him.[49]

The commissioners tried to trace the responsibility to the top, and to persuade politicians to admit their mistakes. Some ex-Ministers made partial apologies: Pik Botha admitted that all Cabinet Ministers at least suspected that the police were killing or torturing opponents, but failed to take steps against it: 'I deeply regret this omission. May God forgive me.'[50] Adriaan Vlok, the former Police Minister, at first would only admit:

'We at the top took certain decisions and used certain terminology without thinking about it.'[51] But he later made clear that de Klerk himself had given orders. De Klerk remained evasive. He said that 'the National Party is prepared to admit its many mistakes of the past and is genuinely repentant;' but he insisted that the government's 'unconventional' strategies 'never included the authorisation of assassination, murder, torture, rape, assault or the like'.[52] After further revelations de Klerk still denied that the government had given the security forces a licence to kill: Tutu replied with emotion that he could not understand his denial, in the light of the 'avalanche of information'.[53]

The ultimate responsibility for many atrocities in the 1980s lay with the State Security Council (SSC), which had been chaired by President P.W. Botha; and the Commission insisted he should testify. But Botha denounced the TRC as a circus, attacked its religious basis and refused to appear. Botha's friends warned Mandela not to make the mistake of turning him into a martyr, as he had turned Mandela into a martyr in prison.[54] Both Mandela and Tutu tried to avoid a showdown: Mandela even offered to accompany Botha to the hearings. Botha still refused, after being charged in court with defying the summons. But the Commission released documents which showed how the SSC under Botha's chairmanship had instructed that opponents should be 'neutralised', and had listed people who might require 'methods other than detention'.[55] The Commission's eventual report, after listing the 'gross violations' under his leadership, found that 'Botha contributed to and facilitated a climate in which the above gross violations of human rights could and did occur, and as such is accountable for such violations.'[56]

The Truth Commission completed its report in October 1998, with five volumes of careful analysis and findings, which included serious accusations against the ANC. The report aroused furious reactions from both sides. De Klerk, who was accused of covering up bombings, successfully appealed to the Cape High Court to suppress the Commission's judgements on him, which were blacked out in the printed volume.[57] More worryingly, the ANC, having seen only part of the report, demanded a special hearing: the commissioners were divided, and Tutu used his casting vote against the ANC.[58] The ANC then decided to go to court in their attempt to stop publication, against the advice of Mandela, who spent an hour arguing with the party's Secretary-General on the phone. But the ANC application, unlike de Klerk's, was dismissed.[59] Tutu was furious at the ANC's 'abuse of power', and warned that 'yesterday's oppressed can quite easily become today's oppressors . . . We've seen it happen all over the world and we shouldn't be surprised if it happens here.'[60] Tutu may have overreacted, but the ANC certainly made a serious blunder: when the five volumes of the report were duly published the news reports gave the ANC little credit for having originated the investigation, and instead concentrated on their attempt to suppress its findings. 'In casting a pall over the truth and reconciliation process,' said the *Washington Post*, 'the party may have raised more questions about its own credibility than that of the Truth Commission.'[61]

Thabo Mbeki as President of the ANC was ultimately responsible, and his office boldly claimed that no ANC member could ever concur with 'scurrilous attempts to criminalise the liberation struggle'.[62] But Mandela did not conceal his disapproval: he agreed that the ANC had committed gross violations, and thought that Mbeki had been too hasty. If they had read the whole report, he said, 'perhaps the response of the ANC would have been totally different'.[63] Mandela continued to be totally supportive of the Truth Commission: 'We must regard the healing of the South African nation as a process, not an event,' he said next month. The TRC, he said, 'helped us to move away from the past to concentrate on the present and the future'.[64] As head of state he saw himself as having loyalties which went beyond the ANC, of which he was now no longer President. 'I am President of the country,' he told me in January 1999. 'I have set up the TRC. They have done not a perfect but a remarkable job and I approved everything they did.'[65]

In the aftermath there was much discussion about granting a general amnesty in order to forestall divisive prosecutions – particularly against members of Buthelezi's Inkatha party, who were now coming closer to the ANC. But Mandela had opposed a general amnesty ever since de Klerk had first offered it to the security police in 1994, and he still insisted that amnesties should only be given on individual bases: 'There is no question as far as I am concerned of a general amnesty,' he said in November 1998, 'and I will resist that with every power that I have.'[66]

Mandela's attitude was a reminder of his ability to override short-term party pressures, and of his fixed belief that the unity of the nation depended both on forgiveness and on facing up to the truth on all sides. And in spite of Mbeki's blunder, Mandela's attitude was shared by large numbers of Africans, including many ANC members who complained about the attempt to suppress the report.

How far was the forgiveness special to Mandela, and how far was it a characteristic of the African people? Samora Machel's widow Graca, who was now closer to Mandela than anyone, had her own experience of atrocities and reconciliation in Mozambique. She saw the South African forgiveness as widespread, and part of a pattern through Africa: 'It is there in our culture. When we are faced with such a challenge we draw from that culture which is very deep inside ourselves.' But she also believed that attitudes could have been very different without Mandela's leadership:

> He symbolises a much broader forgiveness and understanding and reaching out. If he had come out of prison and sent a different message, I can tell you this country could be in flames. So his role is not to be underestimated too. He knew exactly the way he wanted to come out, but also the way he addressed the people from the beginning, sending the message of what he thought was the best way to save lives in this country, to bring reconciliation . . . Some people criticise that he went too far. There is no such thing as going too far if you are trying to save this country from this kind of tragedy.[67]

37

Withdrawing

THE COLLABORATION between Mandela and de Klerk in the same government was a historic achievement, and the Government of National Unity was working better than most members had expected. But the two leaders were never easy together. De Klerk not surprisingly found it hard to accept that he was no longer president, and felt that Mandela deliberately humiliated him. Mandela found de Klerk unnecessarily provocative in cabinet, as did de Klerk's National Party colleagues Pik Botha and Roelf Meyer. Mandela sometimes flared up; but he tried to settle questions amicably afterwards, he insists, and appreciated de Klerk's role.[1]

The tension was revealed very publicly in September 1995, after Mandela had made a speech in Johannesburg criticising the National Party. De Klerk was angry, and tried to avoid Mandela, but Mandela asked to see him, and they eventually found themselves arguing fiercely in the street, waving their fingers at each other in front of the cameras, before Mandela was driven away. Mandela was sorry that they had argued in the street, as he told de Klerk afterwards, but he did not apologise. De Klerk felt that Mandela was more bitter, more scarred by his prison years, than he had publicly revealed.[2]

De Klerk was having troubles with his own party caucus. He was accused of neglecting the party while being part of the government; the complaints reached a peak in May 1996, when the ANC and other parties agreed on a new constitution which did not provide for the National Party to share power at the executive level until 2004, as they had wanted.[3] Many members of the party's executive committee, particularly from the Western Cape, objected strongly: and on 9 May de Klerk announced that the National Party would withdraw from the Government of National Unity. Most of his six Afrikaner cabinet colleagues were shocked: Pik Botha, after being in cabinet for nineteen years, suddenly found himself without a ministerial house, office or job. Leon Wessels, a more recent Minister, thought de Klerk had not tried hard enough to make the GNU work: 'He negotiated for it, but didn't work for it.'[4] Roelf Meyer, who had become General Secretary of the party in February, felt betrayed.[5]

De Klerk promised vigorous opposition to the government. He wanted, he told me, to ensure 'a proper multi-party democracy, without which there may be a danger of South Africa lapsing into the African pattern of one-party states'.[6] But within a few months the National Party was in growing disarray: Roelf Meyer had resigned, to co-found his own party; and de Klerk himself soon retired from politics. Later it turned out that he was in the midst of a passionate affair with Elita Georgiades, the wife of a great friend: 'For once in my life,' as he put it, 'my heart took control.' Soon after leaving government he divorced his wife Marike, and married Elita.[7]

Some ANC Ministers regretted the break-up of the coalition. 'There was a camaraderie developing,' said one cabinet member. 'Breaking it up was one of de Klerk's greatest disservices to the country.' Mandela himself had hoped, he said at the time, that the partnership could have lasted longer. But he thought that de Klerk's influence in cabinet had been declining, and saw the change as a 'coming of age'.[8] He certainly did not miss de Klerk's presence; but he would pay tribute to de Klerk's place in history, and his 'wonderful work' in helping the transformation of the country: 'We are grateful to him and others,' he said in 1999, 'for having worked together with us to avoid a bloody civil war.'[9]

Mandela seemed confident that the ANC could govern without the National Party. He kept the ANC Ministers in their existing jobs, and filled the gaps with more ANC men. Thabo Mbeki was now the sole Deputy President, and was more decisively running the country as Mandela became increasingly aloof from day-to-day government. Mbeki had been worried that the ANC would lose its dynamism in coalition, and saw the break with the Afrikaners as inevitable and useful. He did not feel the need of Afrikaner Ministers to ensure the support of civil servants: he thought they would be loyal to whoever paid them.[10] And the ANC were now much less worried about an Afrikaner revolt: 'The time is passed when the right wing could be a danger,' Walter Sisulu said. 'We have played our cards so well on this issue. Today we could work with the right wing better than with the Nationalists.'[11]

De Klerk had hoped that Buthelezi and his Inkatha party would follow him out of the government. 'When are you going to leave?' he asked Buthelezi in his office soon afterwards. But Buthelezi replied bluntly that he would not leave unless his party instructed him to, and he stayed on as Minister of the Interior.[12] His relationship with Mandela noticeably improved, and blossomed when Mandela had to be briefly out of the country at the same time as Mbeki, and appointed Buthelezi as Acting President. 'I hope the President will be able to come back,' joked a National Party politician. But Buthelezi seemed mollified by his temporary role, which was repeated several times afterwards, and Mandela would sometimes call him 'Mr Acting President'.

At seventy-eight, Mandela was visibly more detached. 'He really abdicated after the GNU broke up,' said one adviser. He enjoyed playing down his role, referring to himself as a mere decoration, or a ceremonial head of state. 'If I wanted to see real progress in our country,' he said in Singapore in March 1997, 'I should have stepped down three years ago. We have such capable young men and women.'[13] Certainly he often behaved more like a constitutional monarch than an executive president, as he referred more and more problems and visitors – even the President of the World Bank – to his deputy, and left Mbeki to preside over cabinet meetings. But he still held on to many of the levers of power, including hiring and firing, and he could dominate his colleagues when he wished to. 'It reminded me of the house cats on the farm where I spent my childhood,' said one close observer. 'One older cat spent most of the day just sitting among them, not looking at them. But when he moved, they all *cringed*.'

Mandela in his detachment was all the more determined to unify his people, and to take the long view. In July 1996, soon after de Klerk had left the government, Mandela gave a seventy-eighth birthday party in the grounds of the State House in Pretoria, for 'veterans of the struggle'. He gave an impromptu speech without spectacles, and with no media present to report it. During the negotiations, he explained, he had always said that there must be no winners and no losers: the South African people as a whole must win: 'You mustn't compromise your principles, but you mustn't humiliate the opposition. No one is more dangerous than one who is humiliated.' He had no regrets about the departure of de Klerk, but he wanted to bring in his old black rivals, Inkatha and the PAC (he had invited the widow of the late PAC leader Zeph Mothopeng to this lunch).[14]

Mandela was still acutely aware of how narrowly the country had avoided civil war two years earlier, and of his own scope as peacemaker. He was wary of a personality cult, and suspected that critics of the ANC were praising him in order to damn others: 'It is particularly unacceptable that this strain of hero-worshipping should be coupled with a systematic campaign to denigrate other ANC leaders such as Deputy President Thabo Mbeki,' he had said five months earlier. It was 'a campaign that is beyond any civilised norms of discourse, let alone objectivity'.[15]

Mandela was being pressed by colleagues and the media to reduce his workload, and to give up the presidency of the ANC, and by the time of the birthday party he had decided to stand down in time for the next ANC conference in December 1997, while remaining President of South Africa until the end of his five-year term in 1999. Would this not weaken his influence, I asked him, as head of state? He answered firmly: 'You don't lead by your position, but by the strength of your ideas.'[16]

When he made his decision public in August 1997, it inevitably opened up a political vacuum. It was clear that Thabo Mbeki would succeed him as the ANC President, but that would leave open the deputy presidency, a crucial step on the road to the top. Mandela could not prevent an embarrassing public leadership struggle.

Mbeki's own position now looked much more secure; since the middle of 1996 Mandela had been more clearly treating him as his political heir. Mbeki's chief rivals, including those who had appeared protégés of Mandela, were now out of the running. Cyril Ramaphosa, after pushing through the new constitution, left Parliament to become Deputy Chairman of the biggest African business group, New Africa Investments Ltd (NAIL). He denied a serious clash with Mbeki: 'We see eye to eye on many things. If we differ, it's just in emphasis.'[17] But he told friends that he would be back in politics in ten years.[18] Tokyo Sexwale, the Premier of Gauteng, the Johannesburg region, had previously promoted himself as a contender: in his house he hung a cartoon showing Mbeki and Ramaphosa boxing while a newcomer, labelled 'Tokyo', was slipping into the ring. He could still dazzle crowds with his huge white smile and exuberant rhetoric, but he overreached himself with attacks on Mbeki, who quietly undermined him; and by May 1997 he too had decided to quit politics for business.

Mandela still demanded total loyalty to the ANC, as he had since the fifties, and some colleagues thought he carried this to excess. For a time he had seemed to favour Bantu Holomisa, his chiefly friend in the Transkei with whom he spent Christmases, and whom he appointed Deputy Minister of the Environment. Holomisa, with his boyish, direct style, was very popular with the masses – and close to Winnie. But in July 1996 Holomisa told the Truth Commission that his fellow-Minister and rival Stella Sigcau had accepted a bribe from the casino-owner Sol Kerzner. Mandela asked Holomisa to apologise, and when he refused promptly fired him from the government. Holomisa retorted that the ANC was in Kerzner's pocket, and that Kerzner had paid two million rand into its election fund. The ANC reacted by calling him a 'blatant liar'; but then Mandela admitted that Kerzner had indeed secretly paid him the money for the fund – he was in fact one of several equally generous donors.[19] Mandela had to admit that the ANC had seriously mishandled the affair, but still he could not forgive Holomisa's treachery. Holomisa dared not confront Mandela face-to-face, and eventually formed a new party, the United Democratic Movement, jointly with Roelf Meyer, the ex-National Party Minister. It failed to have much national impact, but caused considerable trouble for the ANC.

There was no single obvious candidate for Deputy President. Joel Netshitenzhe, Mandela's Director of Communications, was talked of, but was never a contender. The executive backed Jacob Zuma, the Party Chairman, a former Robben Islander who had helped to make peace in KwaZulu. The Premier of Mpumalanga, Mathews Phosa, a lawyer and poet, was put forward by his province before he was persuaded to withdraw in favour of Zuma.

But a nightmare candidate was emerging: Mandela's ex-wife, now called Winnie Madikizela-Mandela, had bounced back to the political front-line. Through all her disgraces she had remained a heroine to many ordinary underprivileged people, who loved her forthright views and superhuman courage, even her extravagance: like Evita Perón in Argentina or Imelda Marcos in the Philippines she offered an escape from the drabness and squalor of the townships. She was again championing the revolution and criticising the complacency of the leadership, without compromise. 'We didn't know that the transition would be this bitter,' she said in 1997. 'Democracy is much more expensive than we thought.'[20] By April 1997 she had been elected President of the Women's League, which later nominated her as Deputy President of the ANC. At meetings of the National Executive she was very silent, but in mid-November she gave a long, provocative interview to her friend Newton Kanhema in the Johannesburg *Star*, lashing into the ANC leadership. She complained that the 'criminals are in control', criticised the Truth Commission – with 'Desmond Tutu hugging Pik Botha' – and urged a return to the death penalty, to which the leadership were firmly opposed.[21]

The ANC were outraged. 'I can't recall a challenge to the movement by one so senior,' said Steve Tshwete, the Minister of Sport – except, he added, from people on the way out. Tshwete wrote a devastating reply to Winnie's interview in the *Star* three days later, attacking the muddled thinking and armchair criticism of populists who 'may sound radical but are in fact right-wing'. He called Winnie 'an individual who does not respect rules and regulations', and complained that she had tried 'to denigrate the person of the President, after the terrible pain she has caused him'. And he restated the difficult realities of government: 'We achieved a victory that has got many limitations and constraints.'[22]

Winnie's past excesses were again being unearthed, this time by the Truth Commission, which was looking into the misdeeds of the ANC as well as those of past governments. New accusations were made that Winnie might have been responsible for the murder of Abubaker Asvat, the Soweto doctor who examined Stompie Seipei in 1988 before he died. In September 1997 new horror stories appeared in a sensational television programme, shown on the BBC and SABC and initiated by a passionate British crusader, Lady (Emma) Nicholson, and produced by a maverick journalist, Fred Bridgland. It was accompanied by a book, *Katiza's Journey*, based heavily on interviews with Katiza Cebekhulu, a young man who had worked for the police and then joined the Mandela United Football Club, and who gave an eye-witness account of Winnie attacking Stompie with a knife or scissors just before he died: 'I saw her lift her hand and stab Stompie twice.'[23] The programme also claimed – without evidence, and without Nicholson's approval – that Mandela himself had personally arranged for Katiza later to be deported to Lusaka, where he languished in jail.[24] The programme and book caused a furore within the ANC; but the fact that they had originated from right-wing foreign sources appeared to boost Winnie's popular image rather than damage it. Winnie dismissed Katiza as a 'lunatic', and Nicholson as a 'mad cow'.[25]

All eyes were now on the Truth Commission, which in late November began hearing witnesses' testimony about the murder of Stompie Seipei and others, in front of TV cameras and the world's press. The murderous events in Soweto ten years before were replayed, with bloody and contradictory accounts of abductions, tortures and murders, further implicating Winnie and also her daughter Zindzi as apparent accomplices. The Commission's Chairman, Archbishop Tutu, occasionally interrupted; Winnie listened apparently unmoved. Mandela was pained by the evidence, but did not try to intervene.

On the ninth day Winnie herself gave evidence, brazen and defiant. When her TRC questioner Hanif Vally told her not to play around with the facts, she replied: 'I will not tolerate you speaking to me like that,' whereupon Tutu threatened to clear the hall. Winnie insisted that 'most of the witnesses who testified here were lying'. Her own evidence was thoroughly evasive, and Tutu complained that one witness had been intimidated in the ladies' lavatory by members of the ANC Women's League. Winnie expressed regret, but not remorse, for the killings.

Tutu finally averted the questioning with a passionate interjection, explaining how he had lived in the same street as the Mandelas, and that Winnie was godmother to one of his grandchildren. She was 'a stalwart of our struggle, an icon of liberation . . . Everything was done to seek to break that spirit.' He appealed to her to apologise: 'You are a great person and you don't know how your greatness would be enhanced if you were to say: "Sorry. Things went wrong. Forgive me."' Winnie thanked Tutu as a father, and said she was deeply sorry to Stompie's mother and Dr Asvat's family – 'It is true that things went horribly wrong' – but made no further apology.[26] Tutu's sympathy raised some doubts about his neutrality, while Winnie's defiant attitude did not visibly disqualify her as a potential Deputy President.

It was a dramatic curtain-raiser to the fiftieth conference of the ANC, which would elect the new officials, and which took place at the end of 1997 in Mafikeng, near the border with Botswana. Mandela presided over his party for the last time. He emphasised again beforehand that his withdrawal from office would not mark a sudden break in leadership: 'Thabo Mbeki is already *de facto* President of the country. I am pushing everything to him,' he said on television. 'My stepping down will be very smooth.' But it was still a watershed.

The conference was on a much grander scale than the meeting forty-six years before, when African delegates had gathered in a bare hall in Bloemfontein to approve the passive resistance campaign which first launched the struggle. Now the great university hall was draped with yellow flowers, huge slogans reading 'All Power to the People', and a blown-up colour photograph of Mandela with his fingers clasped as in prayer. The 3,500 delegates surged into the hall, wearing yellow ANC T-shirts and green baseball caps, singing ANC songs. On the platform sat the National Executive, made up of all races, sizes and generations, including African veterans – Govan Mbeki, Raymond Mhlaba, Andrew Mlangeni – who had been in prison with Mandela; and the youthful-looking Winnie in a purple dress, who swayed to the music.

A huge praise-singer in tribal costume pranced into the hall, chanting extravagant compliments with long vowels which slowly expired like a siren. In the silence that followed the lean figure of Mandela appeared in his yellow shirt, walking slowly onto the platform. A row of inter-denominational priests blessed the conference, including veterans of the struggle like Carl Niehaus from the Dutch Reformed Church and the Catholic Father Mkhatshwa, who said that 'Christians and Marxist-Leninists expound the same values'. Then the Chairman, Jacob Zuma, warmed up the hall to introduce the President.

Mandela's speech took nearly everyone by surprise. He spoke, standing up, for four and a half hours in the stifling hall, with only a short break for lunch: 'I'm the only one perspiring,' he said as he mopped his face, but he seemed inexhaustible. He criticised nearly everyone, except his old rival Buthelezi. He warned his own party – to loud applause – of the dangers of corruption and greed: he pointed to other African countries with 'predatory elites that have thrived on the basis of the looting of national wealth', and called for a moral renewal to achieve an African renaissance. He warned against the 'careerism' of politicians who sought to use their positions to make money. He told the ANC to spend more time in attracting white voters, and not to surrender them to the white parties. He criticised white businessmen for the slow pace of transformation and black empowerment, which had only just begun. He blamed the media for perpetuating old hierarchies and neglecting black viewpoints. He criticised non-governmental organisations who were working 'to corrode the influence of the movement'. He warned that a 'counter-revolutionary network', run largely by Afrikaners, was deliberately trying to erode confidence, subvert the economy and use crime to make South Africa ungovernable. He claimed that the National Party aimed at 'the total destruction of our organisation', while the leaders of the new United

Democratic Party, Meyer and Holomisa, owed 'their political origins to a common apartheid home'.

It was a wide-ranging, bewildering speech which bore the marks of many contributors, most notably Thabo Mbeki. It was far from a radical tirade: it quoted the American arch-capitalists George Soros and David Rockefeller to describe the dangers of the global marketplace. But it was quickly presented by the white media as an attack on white enemies, and a clean break with Mandela's earlier conciliation. The speech destroyed much of the sympathy Mandela had built up since he took office, said the conservative *Citizen.*[27] 'Mandela is naïve,' warned *Business Day*, 'if he thinks whites will voluntarily take a drop in living standards to help the poor.'[28] It marked Mandela's low-water mark, said the Democratic Party.[29] British papers took up the attack, calling the speech a 'depressingly paranoid tirade' (*Daily Telegraph*), 'meaningless dogma' and 'antiquated gibberish' (*Independent*). Even the *Observer*, Mandela's long-standing ally, called it a 'profoundly depressing assault'.[30] The speech was certainly out of keeping with Mandela's earlier statesmanlike surveys; but it was not a policy statement. It was an analysis of the problems of three years of government, and a rallying call for the election in sixteen months' time.

In the evening the ANC put on a cultural tribute to Mandela, now relaxing in the audience. Frenzied drummers introduced a troupe of nubile girl-dancers swinging their leather skirts; a team of Zulu war-dancers, with fly-whisks and furry costumes, kicked their legs up to their chests. The Deputy Speaker recited a poem: 'Let Life Flow in Our Land'. The musician Abdulla Ibrahim, in a loose black suit, played old songs on the piano, and the trombonist Jonas Gwangwa, a veteran of the fifties, blasted wild jazz. Most of the cabinet came to the front to jive, to the amazement of Japanese diplomats.

Thabo Mbeki paid tribute to Mandela and his veteran colleagues, including his father Govan, who were now retiring 'to tend to the cultivation and domestication of the flowers of the veld'. He quoted W.B. Yeats on Ireland in 1916, adding that the African leaders 'refused that the sacrifice should make a stone of their hearts'.[31] Mbeki presented Mandela with a sculpture, and a woman singer sang in his praise: he came up from the audience to the stage to say only: 'All that I want to say is in her song.' He looked tearful, and the delegates seemed subdued as they saw the old men giving way to a much younger generation.

The next day Mbeki was confirmed unopposed as the new President of the ANC – at fifty-five, he was the representative of the new generation. He gave a short speech warning that 'the revolution has not been completed'. But the real excitement was over the deputy presidency. Winnie was nominated from the hall, but seconded by only about twenty delegates; overall she received only 127 votes from the 3,500 delegates. She asked Mbeki to be allowed to consult the 'structures', but he refused. Winnie responded defiantly: 'Comrade Thabo, I think I understand what's happening here. To those comrades who nominated my name, I apologise. I have to decline.' Delegates cheered and whistled, sang and danced. Winnie left the platform, with hugs and kisses from members of the executive, accompanied by her militant young friend Peter Mokaba. 'She will remain,' he said. 'She is an old iron soldier. She stood down to retain unity within the organisation that she loves.'[32] The delegates went on to elect the favoured candidate, Jacob Zuma. Later they elected Terror Lekota, another of Mandela's prison protégés, as Chairman of the party.

The real surprise was the voting for the new National Executive. Many commentators had predicted that the ANC under Mbeki would become more 'Africanist', less tolerant of white and Indian allies; and the overwhelming majority of the delegates were Africans. The existing executive was markedly multi-racial, and vulnerable to Africanist attacks: there were many prominent Indians, Coloureds and whites, including the Minister of Justice Dullah Omar, the Minister of Water Kader Asmal, the Minister of Finance Trevor Manuel and the Deputy Defence Minister Ronnie Kasrils. They had all made unpopular decisions, supporting the government's conservative economic policy including strict fiscal discipline and privatisation, which had antagonised the unions and the Marxists. Yet when delegates voted at the end of the conference they showed confidence in the rainbow government. The top vote went to Cyril Ramaphosa, Mbeki's chief rival, who was now an ambitious businessman. Next place went to Kader Asmal, while Manuel, Omar and Kasrils all increased their vote. Among the top ten, only three were Africans – and they were far from populists. Winnie dropped from fifth place at the previous election to fifteenth. More important, the delegates approved with few changes the government's orthodox economic policy, which was even endorsed by the communists and trades unionists. The revolutionary anti-capitalist movement appeared to be transmuting into a governing party which accepted the disciplines of the global marketplace.

On the last day of the conference, when many of the media had left,

Mandela gave his own moving farewell to the party which (he insisted) had made him:

> More often than not an epoch creates and nurtures the individuals who are associated with its twists and turns: and so a name becomes the symbol of an era. As we hand over the baton it is appropriate that I should thank the ANC for shaping me as such a symbol of what it stands for . . .
>
> We take leave so that the competent generation of lawyers, computer experts, economists, financiers, doctors, industrialists, engineers and above all ordinary workers and peasants can take the ANC into the new millennium. I look forward to that period when I will be able to wake up with the sun, to walk the hills and valleys of my country village Qunu in peace and tranquillity . . .

He paid a tribute to his successor Mbeki, which made some listeners uneasy: 'I am of course worried,' he began jokingly, 'by the fact that there should be two bulls in one kraal, even though I have the advantage that one is short.' He congratulated Mbeki on being elected without opposition, but went on to warn:

> There is a heavy responsibility for a leader elected unopposed. He may use that powerful position to settle scores with his detractors, to marginalise or get rid of them [applause] and surround themselves with yes-men and women [applause]. His first duty is to allay the concerns of his colleagues to enable them to discuss freely without fear within internal structures.

A leader, he explained, 'must keep forces together: but you can't do that unless you allow dissent . . . People should be able to criticise the leader without fear or favour.' He hastened to emphasise that 'our President understands these issues. He has taken criticism in a comradely spirit. He is not the man who is going to sideline anybody' (applause). And he asked his audience to make allowances for an old man: if he complained about younger people in the future, 'Just remember that I was once your colleague' (laughter). But he warned them that as an ordinary ANC member 'I will have the privilege to be as critical as I can be'.[33] With that, Mandela left for his Christmas holiday in Qunu with some favourite books: *War and Peace*, *The Brothers Karamazov* and Nadine Gordimer's novel *Burger's Daughter*, based on his friend Bram Fischer.

Mbeki was certainly a quite different kind of leader from Mandela. He was an introvert from a bookish background, without deep rural roots: 'He has never played in his youth,' said Mandela.[34] He loved quoting Shakespeare and Yeats, wrote poetry himself, and often talked enigmatically: some Africans complained that he had spent too long in England. He remained reluctant to lead from the front – at least while Mandela was there – and bore some marks of the underground leader who could only trust a small cell: he played his cards close to his chest. After his cosmopolitan past and overseas friendships he felt the more need to show himself as a true African. He kept his distance from white businessmen and journalists, and took many advisers from Black Consciousness, who sometimes interpreted his 'African Renaissance' as an exclusively African crusade. Indian and white colleagues worried that he would play the race card, and that the multi-racial vision of South Africa would fade, as it had in other African states.

But Mbeki belonged in many ways more closely to the ANC tradition than did Mandela. He remained deeply influenced by his mentor Tambo: he talked, walked and worked like him, patiently listening and seeking consensus with an unassertive style. He was always sensitive to the cross-currents within his party, and was skilful at defusing dangerous egos and tensions, as he had defused Buthelezi. He knew he could never play the same heroic role Mandela had done over the last nine years. Mandela, like Churchill, had been called upon by his party to meet a supreme challenge; he was loyal to his party, but remained above it. Mbeki was essentially the creation of the ANC; and he knew that the age of heroes had passed. He also knew that he would face angry, disappointed voters. 'What happens to a dream deferred?' he asked, quoting the black American poet Langston Hughes. 'It explodes.'[35]

38

Graca

AS HEAD OF STATE, Mandela had seemed more personally isolated than he was before. He had loyal and strong women friends like Fatima Meer, Amina Cachalia and Barbara Masekela; but it was difficult for them to break through the barricades of government. Fatima saw no one in his Houghton house who had been part of his former life, and found him hard to detach from politics or the television news.[1] He was becoming accustomed to the hectic pace of government, he explained, but 'it destroys your family life'.[2] His grandchildren were often in the house, but his contacts with his children were fitful. His son Makgatho was again studying law, in Durban, but rarely saw his father. His eldest daughter Maki still found him uneasy, worried that she might unleash complaints about the past. Zindzi and Zeni, his two daughters by Winnie, were torn between their parents after the divorce, though they came closer to their father. For a time Mandela was cared for in Houghton by his charming granddaughter Rochelle Mtirara, but she began to have difficulty in studying there, and moved out. 'People are always calling for her so that they can get to me,' Mandela explained. 'She has no life of her own.'[3]

Mandela could still flirt with an attractive woman. A week after divorcing Winnie he was welcoming the Irish President Mary Robinson at Cape Town airport when he spotted a pretty Irish journalist, Nicola Byrne, whom he had seen before, and asked her if she was married. When she said no, he smiled: 'Well, if you were to ask me to marry you I would consider the request very favourably.' Byrne said later: 'He is my hero. I would marry him tomorrow.'[4] But the 'proposal' looked less flattering when Mandela later appeared to mistake another reporter, Alexandra Zavis of the Associated Press, for Byrne.[5]

It was in July 1990, when he visited Mozambique six months after his release, that Mandela first met Graca Machel, the widow of the former

President Samora Machel. Machel had died in a mysterious air crash in 1986, after which the Mandelas had sent Graca a joint message of condolence. Graca had written back to Nelson: 'From within your vast prison, you brought a ray of light in my hour of darkness.'[6] To Winnie she wrote that 'those who have locked up your husband are the same as those who killed mine. They think that by cutting down the tallest trees they can destroy the forest.'[7] Graca already saw Mandela as her hero, and when he came to Mozambique she visited him with her family in a government guest-house. He was impressed, but she was still mourning her dead husband, and it was not love at first sight. It was two years before they met again, soon after Mandela had separated from Winnie, when Graca came to Cape Town to receive an honorary doctorate. He did not recognise her in the line-up, and when he was reminded he went back to talk to her, and was struck by her sensitivity and compassion. Soon afterwards they met again, and Mandela felt physically attracted to her. Thereafter he saw her whenever he could. Oliver Tambo had been custodian to Machel's six children, and after he died Mandela took over the responsibility – which gave him more opportunities to see Graca.

She was then forty-six, twenty-seven years younger than Mandela, with a wide smile, a piercing laugh and big eyes behind spectacles. She was a strong character, but not dominating like Winnie. She came from a humble rural family, the youngest of six children: her father was a peasant who was taught by Methodists to read and write as an adult. He died just before she was born, but he had asked his elder children to help her through school, and she eventually won a Methodist scholarship to Lisbon University, where she became politically active against the Portuguese colonial power. After taking her degree she trained as a freedom fighter for the liberation movement FRELIMO in Tanzania, and came close to its leader Samora Machel, whose wife had died. When Mozambique gained its independence from Portugal in 1975 FRELIMO became the government, and Graca was appointed Minister of Education at the age of twenty-nine: soon afterwards she married President Machel, looking after his six children. She was now at the heart of a young country which was being devastated by the rebel army Renamo and the mass exodus of whites, and destabilised by the South African government, which she suspected of being involved in her husband's death. She mourned him in black for four years, feeling empty and lonely, determined to continue his work. She became involved with children's welfare, and later wrote a report for the UN on the effects of war on children. This remained a central interest, and linked her to Mandela's Children's Fund.

By mid-1995, while Mandela was divorcing Winnie, he began dropping public hints about his new love. Graca was spotted with him at a banquet in Paris, and again at President Mugabe's wedding in Zimbabwe, where she and Mandela were seen kissing. Archbishop Tutu, who had given up on a reconciliation with Winnie, said: 'Madiba needs to have someone to give him his slippers and someone on whose shoulders he could cry.'

Mandela was visibly enchanted by Graca. He enjoyed her warmth, her grace, her love of children. He telephoned her every day. He formally proposed to her, but she was concerned about her obligations to her family and her country: 'I belong to Mozambique,' she insisted. 'I will always be the wife of Samora Machel.' Mandela had to concede: 'She has made a clear statement that she will not marry the President of South Africa. I cannot overrule her.' Eventually they agreed on an unconventional bargain: that she should spend two weeks every month with him in Johannesburg.

Their friendship was now public knowledge, and the love story was unfolding theatrically. In September 1996 Mandela was snapped on a Sunday afternoon walking near his Houghton home with his arm round Graca, laughing happily. 'It's just wonderful,' Graca told a radio programme, 'that finally we have found each other and can share a life together.'[8] Winnie was mocking about Mandela's 'concubine', or 'the Portuguese woman'. She said it was a huge joke, claimed that she was still Mandela's wife by African custom,[9] and warned that another marriage would undermine the children – although, as Mandela pointed out, they were now all fully adult. Mandela's first wife Evelyn, whom he had divorced nearly forty years before, also claimed that he was still her husband in God's eyes; though she herself would remarry a year later, aged seventy-seven. Some clerics complained about the President's half-time half-marriage, and urged him to tie the knot. 'People like Archbishop Tutu are making my life very difficult,' Mandela admitted, 'because they feel that I'm not setting a proper example for the young people.' But Graca seemed content: 'I think we are OK like this . . . We are two grown-up people who love each other.'[10]

By 1997 Graca had clearly become the President's consort. She officially accompanied him on his tour of South-East Asia: when a young journalist in the Philippines asked Mandela whether they would marry, he replied with a favourite reproof: 'My cultural background does not permit me to answer questions of this nature from someone younger than my grandchildren.'[11] Mandela also tried to fit in with Graca's own travel plans, 'playing second fiddle'. When she was offered an honorary degree from Essex University he hastily accepted an invitation from the Islamic Centre at Oxford to visit Britain – to their great surprise, and to the chagrin of Oxford University, who had tried to invite him earlier – so that he could accompany her.

Graca brought her own experience and sensibility to the foreign tours, noticing Mandela's friends, watching his health and his moods, remembering people from her own past travels. But she kept a firm base in Mozambique, where she lived in a spacious house with marble floors in the diplomatic quarter of Maputo, overlooking the Indian Ocean. She was still very popular there, sometimes even described as the next leader, and regarded warily by President Joaquim Chissano. Other Mozambicans were ambivalent about her friendship with Mandela. 'He is probably the only person they would accept in Samora's place,' she reckoned, 'but others are genuinely concerned that something is being stolen from them.'[12]

At home, Mandela's friends saw a more relaxed and carefree man. 'That's the real South African miracle,' one colleague said. Mandela was visibly proud of having attracted such a notable woman, and had long, loving conversations with her on the telephone, which he did not mind friends overhearing. He began talking openly like a young lover about his own transformation. 'I'm in love with a remarkable lady,' he said in a television interview in February 1998. 'I don't regret the reverses and setbacks because late in my life I am blooming like a flower, because of the love and support she has given me . . . She is the boss. When I am alone I am very weak.'[13]

On public occasions they seemed love-struck without embarrassment. When Graca was awarded an international prize in Johannesburg in February 1998 she began her acceptance speech with 'Madiba!' – to long applause. Afterwards he came up to whisper to her, clasping her hand, before leaving. 'We were all terrorists,' said the chairman of the ceremony, Andrew Young. 'Now we're all lovers.'[14]

Graca had some difficulty in adjusting to Mandela's lifestyle, particularly his early rising and bedtime: 'When you love somebody you really have to give up certain things. I'm not an early riser, but I'm getting used to it.' She did her best to stop him ringing people up from home at all hours of the day and night: 'I'm trying. I'm trying,' she said in March 1998. 'When I'm here I make sure he doesn't do it. Weekends have been much better since last year. Now he's really trying to slow down.' She looked forward to his retirement, stretching out their holidays: she spent Christmas 1997 with him in Qunu, and he spent the New Year with her in Maputo. 'I want to help him to do things he loves as a human being,' she said, 'and not what he is expected to do.'[15]

She could ease his relationships with his own family through her experience as a stepmother: 'I'm that kind of woman who never knew what it is to start a family. I got married and I was a mother of six immediately.' Her own two children were now both studying in Cape Town: her daughter Jozina had a flat in the President's mansion Genadendal, where she kept Mandela company and sometimes accompanied him on visits.

Graca was aware of the problems of other hero-parents, like the Nyereres in Tanzania or the Kaundas in Zambia, whom she knew well. She knew how Mandela's children had longed to have a father to touch and talk to, and how they resented sharing him with the nation: 'I think they have adjusted: they know what they can expect, and he is also trying now to make himself available.' She relished his grandchildren: 'This is a normal family with children running round and making noises,' she explained in their Houghton house as they shouted outside. 'Now you can take over,' she told the six boys as she let them into the drawing-room. 'We're taking over!' they yelled while she grinned. 'We're taking over the world!'[16]

Graca felt that she had broken through the defences and deep reserve which Mandela had built up in jail, to allow him to express his real emotions: 'He can love very deeply, but he tries to control it very well in his public appearance. In private he can allow himself to be a human being. He likes people to know he is happy. When he is unhappy he lets you know . . . He's a very simple person, very gentle . . . He is so down to earth. Even politically if you watch him sometimes you can feel there's a bit of naiveté.'

She saw him at last able to relax and stand back from the strains of office, no longer feeling defensive about what he could not achieve: 'You come to a point when you know who you are, and you know what is the space in which you can move. You reach out to others. You are quite secure. You have to have your emotional life in balance.'[17]

By the middle of 1998 the couple seemed established. They moved into a grander, modernised house in Houghton, a street away from Mandela's former home, with a curving staircase below a big portrait of Mandela, and large rooms separated by sliding glass doors. It was refurbished to their specifications – wherever possible by African artisans – and fitted with a lift so Mandela could avoid the stairs, which were becoming painful for his injured knee.

Mandela's friends were still pressing him to marry, but Graca continued to resist. Mandela was planning his eightieth birthday celebrations on 18 July, and a few days beforehand rumours began circulating that a magistrate and priests were preparing to marry him and Graca. This was vigorously denied, but in fact Mandela had settled it with Graca two months before, and with his usual sense of timing arranged it for his birthday.

They were married in the new house, Mandela in a gold-patterned open shirt, Graca wearing a long white dress with wide puffed sleeves, Elizabethan-style. They were blessed beforehand by the Chief Rabbi, and also by the Muslim Sheikh Nazim Mohammed and the Hindu Mrs Nanahchene. They were married by a Methodist Bishop, Mvume Dandala – since they had both been brought up as Methodists – assisted by Desmond Tutu, now retired as the Anglican Archbishop. Mandela's family and sixteen friends were present, including Ahmed Kathrada and the Sisulus, and a single photographer, Siphiwe Sibeko from the black magazine *Enterprise*. 'She has made a decent man of him,' Tutu said afterwards. 'Now you won't shout at me,' said Mandela.[18] Among the guests was Mandela's former warder Christo Brand, who was now running the Robben Island souvenir shop in Cape Town, and who had been flown up to Johannesburg for the first time in his life. He presented Mandela with some of his favourite 'Pantene' hair-oil – which Brand had bought for him while he was in Pollsmoor prison. Now a bottle had been obtained, with great difficulty, from Germany, and was presented to the President with a huge cardboard replica of the bottle.[19]

The next day, the Gallagher Convention Centre, between Johannesburg and Pretoria, was transformed into a banqueting hall for the eightieth birthday feast, now also a wedding party. Two thousand guests had been invited, the multi-racial elite of the New South Africa, with only a few notable absentees, like F.W. de Klerk and Winnie Madikizela-Mandela. The President had invited foreign dignitaries including ex-President

Kaunda of Zambia, Prince Bandar of Saudi Arabia and General Obasanjo, recently released from detention in Nigeria; but the atmosphere was set by showbiz, with the top South African stars eclipsed by African-American visitors including Michael Jackson, Danny Glover and Stevie Wonder. After the first course and a blast of music, Mandela's grandson Mandla gave a short speech of praise for his grandfather, followed by Thabo Mbeki, who, as so often, used Shakespeare to express his emotions. He imagined Mandela retiring as King Lear had hoped to,

> to tell old tales, and laugh
> At gilded butterflies, and hear poor rogues
> Talk of court news; and we'll talk with them too –
> Who loses and who wins; who's in, who's out . . .

Some of the guests were puzzled by the comparison with a mad old king, but Mbeki put the emphasis on Lear's sacrifices, upon which 'the gods themselves throw incense'.

Mandela himself had prepared a formal birthday speech, asking South Africans to 'rededicate themselves to the land of their dreams'. But he confined himself to a few words of thanks, beginning 'My wife and I' – to a burst of laughter. He then took to the dance floor with Graca for a brief 'Madiba shuffle', soon to be joined by other guests while the music roared. The next morning the newly married couple flew off to visit Argentina and Brazil, returning to Johannesburg five days later for a birthday concert before retreating to Qunu for a private honeymoon.

It had been an African celebration, with its casual mix of pageantry, music and fun. Some white conservatives complained that the festivities were inappropriate at a time of economic crisis. Others were very critical that Mandela had ordered the release of nine thousand prisoners, which they said would encourage crime. A few complained about the personality cult, reminiscent of other parts of Africa. But the gathering was a celebration disconnected from power, or fear: it was more like a nation redefining its image of itself.

Graca, having provided a happy ending, could connect the icon with the ordinary person. She had seen Mandela in both roles, like her first husband Machel; and she knew his faults: 'Sometimes he is not very patient in discussions of very important things . . . Once he has made up his mind he tends to be very stubborn. He doesn't accept that he's wrong.'

But she also understood the importance of his basic values and sense of human dignity, and how much they influenced ordinary people:

> The world needs symbols, probably nowadays more than before. He is a symbol and he is good at projecting what he represents, his values. But at the same time you have to look at him as a human being who has strengths and weaknesses. I want him as a human being. He is a symbol, that's correct, but he's not a saint. Whatever happens to him, it is a mark of the liberation of the African people, particularly the South African people. He makes the point that he should be treated with dignity because he's absolutely aware of what he represents.[20]

39

Mandela's World

DESPITE HIS PROBLEMS at home, Mandela travelled the world with his reputation undimmed: like earlier global heroes such as Churchill or Eisenhower, his influence abroad seemed unaffected by domestic setbacks. His moral authority as a peacemaker seemed unique as other countries were racked by racial conflicts; and he could make everyone feel better, left or right, black or white. His disarming smile beamed from showbiz magazines or posters for Hilton hotels as well as the *New York Times*, while his fairy tale seemed scarcely tarnished by his years in power. As he arrived in the presidential jet and inspected guards of honour he still managed to appear as the plain man with whom anyone could identify, like a Gary Cooper or a James Stewart, embodying simple values in a cynical world of technicians and manipulators: the Nigerian poet Wole Soyinka called it 'the unselfconscious emanation of uncluttered humanity'.[1]

Mandela revelled in personal diplomacy, relating directly to other Presidents and Prime Ministers, ringing them up as if bureaucracies and embassies did not exist: a conversation in his office was always liable to be interrupted by an international phone-call: 'My President! How are you?' Mandela would startle Ambassadors by asking, 'How's Fidel?' or 'How's Bill?', and he wrote to the Queen of England as 'Dear Elizabeth'. He himself seemed like a monarch from an earlier age, naturally at ease with foreign royalty. At a banquet in Oxford he sat alongside Prince Charles and Prince Bandar of Saudi Arabia – in whose house he was staying overnight – to whom he paid elaborate compliments; but he appeared more regal than either of them. His whole style was becoming more like a monarch's with a common touch than a politician's. South Africa had the advantage of a head of state who could express national values and policies with conviction and grandeur; but there were pitfalls in the diplomatic undergrowth.

Mandela had no difficulty in personifying his country, which he was opening up to the world after its long exclusion as a pariah state. He could justifiably boast: 'After 1994 you only have to say "I am a South African," whether you are black or white, and the doors of the world are wide open to you.'[2] Some foreigners knew his name better than his country's: one South African businessman who visited Thailand was amazed to find that people there knew about Mandela, but had not heard of South Africa: to them it was 'Mandela-land'.

And Mandela put his own stamp on South Africa's diplomacy. He chose many old friends and ex-colleagues to be Ambassadors: Mendi Msimang, the clerk in his law firm in the fifties, went to London; Ruth Mompati, his secretary in the firm, went to Switzerland; Barbara Masekela, who ran his ANC office, went to Paris; Carl Niehaus, who had been his press officer during the elections, went to The Hague. Mandela told them to extend his own conciliatory policies abroad, to reach out to make friends for their country, and also to persuade enemies to talk to each other. He would repeat his principle that disputes should be settled 'with brains, not blood'. He saw the art of peacemaking and persuasion in the wider world much as he had seen it with warders and prisoners in jail; and he saw no real difference between reconciliation at home and abroad. 'People understand the importance of discussing issues and resolving them,' he told me in 1997, 'so I haven't found it more difficult to reconcile people outside.'[3]

But he soon came up against the constraints of multilateral diplomacy and treaties, while his own white diplomats could put up obstacles. The Department of Foreign Affairs was an unreconstructed ministry, still full of Afrikaners conducting business in Afrikaans, under a conservative Director-General, Rusty Evans. The embassies were full of Afrikaner old-timers more accustomed to siege diplomacy than to reaching out for friends or conducting sophisticated negotiations, while the new ANC Ambassadors often found themselves reporting to Afrikaners in Pretoria who disapproved of their policies. There were only a few experienced African diplomats; and some of those came from former Bantustan governments which had given them the wrong kind of experience. It was not until 1998 that Mandela could appoint an African Director-General, Jackie Selebi, in whom he could have full confidence, to the Department of Foreign Affairs.

Mandela sometimes created his own confusions. When he rang up other Presidents he did not always tell his colleagues what he or they had said. The Foreign Minister Alfred Nzo, Mandela's co-activist in the fifties, could be quite shrewd, but he had a slow and somnolent style – he was nicknamed 'Nzzzz'. The real executor of foreign policy was often Thabo Mbeki, who as Deputy President was constantly persuading and negotiating behind the scenes. The different operations were often uncoordinated: 'Really we have three separate foreign policies,' complained one Ambassador. 'When I want something done, I ring up Madiba.'

It was Mandela who set the direction and priorities of South African diplomacy. He had strong ideals: 'South Africa's future foreign relations,' he told the American journal *Foreign Affairs* shortly before coming to power, 'will be based on our belief that human rights should be the core of international relations, and we are ready to play a role in fostering peace and prosperity in the world.'[4] He was determined to be loyal to friendly powers, as to people: 'My foreign policy is determined by the past,' he said in 1998. 'The relations I have had with the country, the contributions they have made to our struggle.'[5] Sometimes loyalty conflicted with human rights – for instance in Indonesia, Saudi Arabia or Libya. But Mandela saw himself with a moral mission to spread peace and tolerance round the world, convinced that South Africa had lessons for other countries. And he resisted the more cynical calculations of *Realpolitik*.

He could not ignore his African neighbours – if only because the poverty and instability beyond South Africa's borders were pressing millions of immigrants into the country. Mandela insisted that Africans must take charge of their own destiny: 'The time has come for Africa to take full responsibility for her woes,' he told the Zimbabwe Parliament in May 1997, 'and use the immense collective wisdom it possesses to make a reality of the idea of the African renaissance.'[6] The 'renaissance' had already been popularised by Thabo Mbeki, who insisted that Africa must face up to its past disasters. Mbeki looked back to the 'lost decade' of the eighties, when African politicians experimented with one-party states, military governments and expensive economic policies, none of which had worked; as he said in February 1997: 'Now I believe there is a new generation on the continent saying we are ready to turn things around.'[7] Mandela took up the theme: with his keen sense of dignity and faith in democracy, he provided an appropriate symbol for a continent seeking to escape from its colonial past and the legacy of the Cold War, and to develop stable systems of government. South Africa, by far the richest country south of the Sahara, was well placed to give leadership to a renaissance. Western businessmen, though, remained sceptical, conditioned to 'Afro-pessimism': they feared that South Africa would be dragged into the African morass of corruption and chaos.

Mandela's hardest case was Nigeria, the most populous African country. It had been taken over by the corrupt dictator General Sani Abacha, who had imprisoned his democratic predecessors and critics, including the much publicised poet-agitator Ken Saro-Wiwa. Mandela was bringing pressure behind the scenes, following (he explained later) the methods accepted by international law, to stop the violation of human rights.[8] The issue of Nigeria dominated the Commonwealth Summit in New Zealand in November 1995 – Mandela's first such meeting as President, where he renewed his admiration for the Queen. Some members called for sanctions against Nigeria, but Mandela still favoured 'quiet diplomacy', believing that Abacha would yield to pressure: but during the Summit Ken Saro-Wiwa was executed. Mandela was outraged, feeling personally betrayed, and was soon under attack for having been too soft: 'Were quiet diplomacy pursued in South Africa,' a lawyer for Saro-Wiwa wrote to him, 'I doubt you would be alive today.'[9] In New Zealand Mandela mustered all his moral authority to call for immediate sanctions against Nigeria, but was disappointed by the caution of the British Prime Minister John Major.[10] Back in South Africa, he said publicly that he was 'hurt and angry' with the action of 'an insensitive, frightened dictator': 'If Africa refrains from taking firm action against Nigeria, then talk about the renaissance in Africa is hollow, is shallow.' Abacha, he warned, was 'sitting on a volcano, and I am going to explode it under him'.[11] It was the first time, said the journalist Cameron Duodu who interviewed him, 'that an African head of state had publicly gone against trade union rules and insulted a fellow card-holder'.[12]

Mandela's frankness was refreshing, but his plans to impose sanctions through the UN Security Council were unrealistic. He wanted to involve China, as a member of the Council; but Pretoria did not then recognise Beijing. Other members, including Britain, were too interested in Nigerian oil to support sanctions, and South Africa soon found itself isolated. Nigeria was later suspended from the Commonwealth, but its tyranny was only ended by the death of Abacha in 1998 – which was followed by promising moves towards democracy. In the meantime Mandela had experienced the limits of moral authority as a diplomatic weapon.

Mandela's closest African dealings were with the eleven neighbouring states grouped as the Southern African Development Community (SADC), which were heavily dependent on trade and investment from South Africa. When Mandela became Chairman of SADC in 1996 he brought a welcome candour to its proceedings: he criticised the prevailing complacency, and even suggested sanctions against countries like Zambia and Swaziland which were resisting pressure towards democracy. 'Can we continue to give comfort to member states,' he asked the SADC Summit in September 1997, 'whose actions are so diametrically against the values and principles we hold so dear?'[13] But he faced growing resentment, particularly from Robert Mugabe of Zimbabwe, who had previously dominated SADC, and his hopes of a peaceful renaissance were soon dashed by the chaos in Zaire, which had rashly been admitted as a member.

Zaire's dictator President Mobutu had been supported by the Americans through the Cold War, but in 1997 he was threatened by the rebel army of Laurent Kabila, backed by Uganda and Rwanda. Mandela tried to bring Mobutu and Kabila together, providing a South African warship anchored off the mouth of the Congo River as a neutral meeting-place, on which he waited patiently. But both sides were intransigent, and Kabila failed to turn up at a second rendezvous. Mandela did help persuade Mobutu to leave Zaire, which averted further bloodshed; but Kabila failed to consolidate his victory or to control his borders. Uganda and Rwanda turned against him, sending in their own armies, while Zimbabwe and Angola came to his support. The tragedy of Zaire – now called the Democratic Republic of the Congo – threatened to involve all its neighbours in a single African war. Mandela again tried to calm things down, urging the Presidents not to send in troops; but each nation had its own conflicting interests in the disintegrating country. The Congo seemed once again to be the 'heart of darkness' which could infect its neighbours with its lawlessness; while across its border Angola, which had been riven by the rivalries of Cold Warriors, had gone back to civil war.

Mandela was also drawn into the problems of Lesotho, the mountain kingdom surrounded by South Africa. In 1998 its Prime Minister Pakalitha Mosisili asked for Pretoria's help to forestall a threatened rebellion. Buthelezi, who was Acting President at the time, consulted both Mandela and Mbeki (who were travelling abroad), who approved the intervention;

but the South African Army, dangerously lacking in intelligence, sent an inadequate force of six hundred men. They took several days to impose order, and in the process destroyed much of the capital, Maseru, while looters emptied the shops. There was an outcry of indignation, and in parliamentary hearings Ministers and the military candidly admitted to basic misjudgements. Mandela insisted that the intervention had achieved its object: 'We have handled it very well,' he said in January 1999. 'The military aspects may not have been properly arranged, but we have got peace in that country.'[14] But the bungled operation made South Africa look like a clumsy bully, and damaged Mandela's image as the peacemaker.

The optimism about an African renaissance was fading as civil wars raged again through the continent, and South Africa was seen abroad as part of a deteriorating continent. 'When pictures flash across the television screens of hunger, of poverty, of devastation, of the dependence on charity,' warned Mbeki in July 1998, 'they do not say it is occurring in the Republic of Kalahuta. They say it occurs in Africa.'[15]

Mandela still retained his unique prestige, not only in Africa but in most developing nations; and South Africa was a potential bridge to the richer countries. It had an opportunity to play its new role when the Non-Aligned Movement, including over a hundred developing nations, held its twelfth summit in Durban in September 1998, chaired by South Africa. Mandela welcomed an exotic gathering, including Fidel Castro and Yasser Arafat, and gave a challenging opening speech. He questioned the 'orthodox uniformity' of the global marketplace, with its language of budget deficits, capital movements and flexible labour markets, and warned that people might 'end up deifying the means to an end', and forget that the real purpose of development was to improve 'the material and spiritual life of every citizen'. He assured them of his independence; he also criticised 'the narrow, chauvinistic interests of the current administration in Israel' for blocking the prospect of a permanent peace in the Middle East; and urged India and Pakistan to resolve their bitter dispute over Kashmir through peaceful negotiations, offering his help.[16] The Israeli government quickly complained about Mandela's 'unpleasant and unhelpful remarks', while the Indian Prime Minister Vajpayee warned third parties to stay out of the Kashmir dispute. But Mandela received praise from Pakistan and the Palestinians, and later played host to a state visit by Arafat – now debilitated and shaking from Parkinson's disease.

'South Africa must be able to say that someone or some government is doing something wrong,' said Jackie Selebi, the new Director-General at the Foreign Ministry, 'without having the stock markets plunge.'[17]

Mandela had been redrawing South Africa's economic map of the world by forging new alliances. At first his most promising new financial friends were in the fast-growing economies of Asia, who had made generous donations to the ANC (see Chapter 28). But there were many complications. Taiwan, which had given the ANC $10 million in 1993, proved an embarrassing ally when Mandela's government sought to recognise mainland China. Mandela insisted that he would not stab his old friend Taiwan in the back, drawing the complaint from Tony Leon of the Democratic Party that 'Our whole foreign policy is based on the electoral debts of the ANC.' But Pretoria soon switched course, and was able to recognise China without completely alienating Taiwan.[18]

Mandela had more than party-political reasons to develop links with Asia, at a time when international investors and bankers were heaping praise on the wonder-economies of the 'tigers' of the East. He looked to reinvent the 'Indian Ocean Rim' which had played its part in earlier South African history when communities of Indians, Malays and Chinese settled on its shores. 'Long years ago, trade and relations existed between Asia and Southern Africa,' Mandela pointed out in Singapore in 1997, 'relations that we are only now starting fully to appreciate.'[19] And he had useful links with Muslim countries: there were three Indian Muslims in his cabinet, as well as two Hindus. 'Democratic South Africa, unlike its predecessor,' he told the Oxford Centre for Islamic Studies in 1998, 'accords Islam equal constitutional status with all other religions.'[20] Mandela had been lionised in Indonesia, where he had praised President Suharto as 'an able, patient and suave leader'. He refused publicly to condemn Suharto's abuses of human rights. But he privately raised with him the issue of East Timor, which Indonesia had annexed in 1975 against heavy world protest; and in 1997 he persuaded Suharto to allow him to see Jose Xanana Gusmao, the jailed leader of the East Timor Liberation Movement whose ordeals had some parallels with Mandela's own. He pleaded with Suharto to release him, with his familiar argument: 'unban, release, negotiate'[21] – which would be vindicated after Suharto's fall.

Malaysia developed a closer commercial relationship with South Africa. Mandela had been impressed by Prime Minister Mahathir Mohamed when he visited South Africa in 1990, and again at the

Commonwealth Conference in 1991; he was also attracted to the Malaysian concept of 'Bumiputera', or 'sons of the soil', which sought to give Malays a bigger share in the ownership of industry and to establish a prosperous Malay middle class to compete with the Chinese minority – a situation with obvious parallels for black South Africans. When Mandela visited Malaysia in 1996 he praised the country as a model for training, restructuring and empowerment. And Mahathir encouraged Malay businesses to reach across the Indian Ocean, in keeping with 'South–South' diplomacy. After the 1994 elections Malay companies moved into timber, property and other industries in South Africa, culminating in the purchase of a third of the energy company Engen and a major share in the telecommunications giant Telkom. Malaysia, it was said, was taking the place of Cuba in the ANC's intellectual geography.[22]

But the South-East Asian tigers were crippled by the economic crises of late 1997, which sent currencies tumbling, banks failing and companies collapsing into bankruptcy; and President Suharto was toppled. Western economists who had lavished praise on the Asian miracle countries now claimed they had always been flawed by corruption and 'crony capitalism'. For a time South Africa, with its sounder banking system, seemed much less vulnerable; but the collapses in Indonesia, Malaysia and Thailand soon scared Western investors away from all emerging markets, and they withdrew funds from South Africa, precipitating a new fall of the rand; while the openings to the East now looked much less promising. South Africa could not escape from its basic dependence on the West, whether for investment or diplomacy.

Mandela had an ambivalent relationship with the United States. Since his first triumphant tour in 1990 he had been encouraged by the reservoir of American goodwill, and he loved the visits of film stars, pop singers and friendly politicians. Presidents Bush and Clinton were both proud of their personal links with him. The past sins of the CIA had been forgiven, and the State Department wanted to use Pretoria as a surrogate power in Africa. But Mandela was resistant to American arrogance, and reacted fiercely to patronising attitudes or insults to African dignity. He was one of the few leaders who could publicly criticise Washington and get away with it; as one Ambassador said: 'He wants to exorcise the idea that America is unchallengeable.' And he knew that much of the developing world was behind him.[23]

Mandela spoke out against Clinton in November 1996, when he

vetoed the reappointment of the UN Secretary-General Boutros Boutros-Ghali, who was supported by most other UN members: if America defied the consensus, he warned, 'we could be plunged into chaos because, after that precedent, no country will observe majority decisions in the world body'.[24] Mandela was partly reassured by the appointment of an African Secretary-General, Kofi Annan from Ghana, but he continued to object to Washington's high-handed treatment of the UN.

Mandela also resented Washington's attempts to restrict Pretoria's selling of arms – where he was on shakier moral ground. The apartheid governments had built up an extravagant weapons industry which they subsidised by selling weapons abroad wherever they could; and after the ANC came to power the state arms company Armscor continued to make deals with dubious customers. The State Department was outraged in early 1997 when they learnt that Pretoria was planning to sell tanks worth $650 million to Syria, Israel's bitter enemy. The Americans warned that such an act would be 'extremely serious', and Senators threatened to cut off aid to South Africa. Mandela reacted angrily: 'We will conclude agreements with any country whether they are popular in the West or not . . . the enemies of countries in the West are not ours.'[25]

But Mandela's chief defiance of Washington was his championing of the two American *bêtes noires*, Qadaffi and Castro. He reasserted his friendship for them in February 1996 while he was visiting Robben Island with Gro Brundtland, the Prime Minister of Norway. It was a dramatic moment: speaking impromptu in the lime quarry, Mandela paid tribute to Norway for having supported the ANC when they were almost without friends. Warming to his theme with visible enjoyment, he announced that he would invite both Castro and Qadaffi to South Africa; he complained that President Bush had advised him not to support them, but said 'we will never renounce our friends'.[26]

Castro made a theatrical state visit to South Africa in 1998, after attending the Non-Aligned Summit in Durban, where he warned about 'an unavoidable and deep economic crisis' which was threatening the whole world. He addressed a joint sitting of Parliament, delivering an emotional speech, 'like a love letter that you write to a sweetheart you have been longing for'. The Democratic Party boycotted Castro as an 'enemy of democracy', but black South Africans applauded him with shouts of 'Cuba! Cuba!' Later he spoke for two hours in Soweto without taking even a sip of water.[27]

Qadaffi never visited South Africa, but Mandela continued to champion him as an old ally who had helped the ANC in the dark days of the sixties (though he had also helped the rival PAC). Qadaffi was still more demonised by the West after the bombing of the American airliner over Lockerbie in Scotland in December 1988, which was blamed on Libyan agents. But Mandela had visited Libya several times from 1990, partly to raise funds for the ANC. When the West demanded that the Libyan suspects be extradited and put on trial, Mandela argued with President Bush and insisted they should be tried in a neutral country.[28] The Americans' anger boiled over in October 1997 when Mandela was preparing for a state visit to Libya. The State Department said they would be 'disappointed' if the visit went ahead. Mandela reacted furiously at a banquet in Johannesburg:

> How can they have the arrogance to dictate to us who our friends should be? . . . Can you imagine what they would say if I said Boris Yeltsin should not visit Albania? They would say that I am the most arrogant black man . . . Notwithstanding the changes in the world, the contempt for blacks is still deep-seated.

He ended with an echo of his favourite poem on Robben Island: 'I am the master of my fate'. And he defiantly went ahead with his visit to Libya. Qadaffi embraced him, kissed him, held up his hand in solidarity and showed him the presidential palace which had been destroyed by American bombers. Mandela criticised 'countries that play policeman of the world', and argued that 'those who object to my visiting Libya have no morals . . . A politician must not lose his morals and must be ready for suffering, and this is the reason which made me remain twenty-seven years in prison.'[29]

From Libya, Mandela flew on to Edinburgh for a Commonwealth Summit hosted by Tony Blair, and put the subject of Libya into the forefront, arguing again that the bombing suspects should be tried in a neutral country: it was wrong, he said, for any country to be 'the complainant, the prosecutor and the judge at the same time'. He gained support from British families of the victims of Lockerbie, who resisted the American hard line. On his way back he stopped again in Libya, where he invested Qadaffi with the Order of Good Hope, and advised him to 'understand the importance of moderate language'.[30]

Mandela's defence of Qadaffi upset many Westerners: the saint of

Robben Island, as the *Guardian* put it, appeared to be in league with the mad dog of Tripoli.[31] His attack on American morality exasperated American conservatives: it was disgusting, said the *New Republic*, 'an example of moral absolutism at its worst'.[32] White South Africans were also outraged by his defiance of American policy. But Mandela saw the criticism as basically racist. 'Not a single African, Coloured or Indian has questioned my going to Libya,' he said; 'but they regard the interests of the whites as being the interests of the country: that you cannot challenge the United States because the interests of the country are going to be harmed. Not one black man has said so: only the white parties.'[33]

Mandela kept in touch with Qadaffi through Jakes Gerwel, his self-effacing Cabinet Secretary, who had experience of negotiating the non-negotiable, while Mandela would ring up Blair and Clinton directly, to the dismay of their diplomats. Mandela was able to reassure Qadaffi – who trusted him much more than he did the UN – and in March 1999 flew to Tripoli to clinch the deal: that Qadaffi would hand over the two suspects, in return for the UN dropping its sanctions. It was (as the conservative media conceded) a vindication of Mandela's personal diplomacy and friendly relations with Libya.[34]

Mandela's championing of Libya did not damage his growing friendship with President Clinton, which was based on mutual admiration. Clinton always remembered watching Mandela's release on television in Arkansas with his wife Hillary and daughter Chelsea (who became fascinated by Mandela's story).[35] Mandela found Clinton 'brilliant' when they first met, and soon saw him as the friend of minorities. 'Clinton has done something which has never been done in the United States,' he told me. 'He has brought in blacks, he has brought in women, disabled, and he has got solid support from blacks.'[36] Mandela would often ring Clinton, and could not remember him refusing any request.*

In March 1998 Clinton paid a state visit to South Africa as the climax of an African tour, which emphasised the special importance of Pretoria's role. 'South Africa's relationship with the rest of the continent,' said the American Ambassador James Joseph, 'is very much like our relationship

* Once he asked Clinton to help the South African journalist Philip van Niekerk, who was in serious danger during the civil war in Liberia. Van Niekerk soon received a message to go to the American Embassy, from which he was flown out with the American staff by helicopter.

with the rest of the world. We're both dominant powers.'[37] Addressing Parliament, Clinton paid tribute to the courage and imagination of the New South Africa, and insisted that Americans should stop asking what they could do *for* Africa and instead ask what to do *with* Africa – a point which particularly appealed to Mandela.[38] But Mandela soon broke with the usual exchange of compliments: at a press conference in the Tuynhuys garden he criticised American pressures and reasserted his independence over Libya, Iran and Cuba. Clinton appeared unfazed, and Mandela delighted him by telling his own South African critics to 'go jump in the pond'. Later he infuriated Clinton's aides by insisting on very private diplomacy: he first talked alone with the President, and then invited his Saudi friend Prince Bandar, who was waiting, to join them.[39]

Mandela could give Clinton the kind of moral support he desperately needed – as he displayed in Washington six months later, when Clinton was feeling the full heat of his persecutors, who were threatening him with impeachment. At a White House reception for religious leaders Clinton paid an emotional tribute to his guest: 'Every time Nelson Mandela walks into a room we all feel a little bigger, we all want to stand up, we all want to cheer, because we'd like to be him on our best day.'

Mandela replied, referring obliquely to the clamour to impeach the President. He insisted: 'It is not our business to interfere in this matter,' but went on to praise Clinton as 'a friend of South Africa and Africa', and to promise his loyalty, as he had done to Qadaffi: 'We have often said that our morality does not allow us to desert our friends. And we have got to say tonight: we are thinking of you in this difficult and uncertain time in your life.'[40]

Mandela, now eighty, did not lose his delight in foreign travel. In his last months as President he covered much of the world with his wife Graca, to say goodbyes to his friends. Some white South Africans complained or joked about his absences ('This week President Mandela is paying a visit to South Africa'); but he had made it clear that he was not now running the country. His international aura had hardly been blurred by his years in office. Insecure heads of government gained confidence and kudos from being seen with him, and he could reassure leaders from the right as much as the left. In Britain the Queen visibly appreciated his visits at a time when her own family was under fire, while Tony Blair could improve his left-wing image by making a quick visit to Mandela in January 1999.

How far were these enthusiastic welcomes translated into practical assistance? Could Mandela cash in on his charisma? South African Ambassadors tried hard to use their President's visits to attract investors or to improve terms of trade. But the image of the saintly Mandela was not necessarily helpful in the marketplace, for it implied that he was above worldly matters, like Mother Teresa or the Dalai Lama. 'St Nelson needs our cash,' warned *The Times* of London above an article about Mandela's 1996 state visit by the conservative columnist Simon Jenkins, who wrote him off as a serious head of government: 'A state can be represented by a saint but not ruled by one.'[41]

On the Continent there was an even wider gap between moral praise and economic support. When Mandela first became President in 1994 the European Union was full of goodwill for a prosperous and stable South Africa, and promised to open up a free-trade area which would be a model of enlightened development policy. But the negotiators in Brussels soon came up against German potato-farmers, Italian wine-producers and Dutch flower-growers; and after four years and forty rounds of talks they had still not made good their original promise to Mandela. The British, being less threatened economically, were the most supportive of South Africa, and in 1998 Tony Blair invited Mandela to the European Summit in Cardiff, hoping his presence might shame the Europeans into opening up their markets. The European heads of government, led by Helmut Kohl and Jacques Chirac, welcomed him with thunderous applause. The British EC Commissioner Neil Kinnock whispered to Mandela to press for the commitment to be honoured, but Mandela replied wryly: 'There is no ink in their pens.' The Europeans promised an agreement by the autumn, but then postponed it once again. At last, on 26 March 1999, the European heads of government approved an agreement which Pretoria welcomed as a 'massive statement of confidence' – a few hours before Mandela's final speech to Parliament.[42]

Western governments were glad to use Mandela's presence to burnish their images or to improve their race relations; but tight-fisted negotiators felt little obligation to make concessions in return to a fragile young democracy. The calculations of the global marketplace had no room for humanitarian issues. There remained a gulf between worshipping the Mandela icon and helping the people he represented.

But Mandela remained optimistic that the world was becoming less racist. He had always felt that the British were much fairer than colonials of British stock in Africa: 'The best way to receive protection against British settlers in any colony,' he recalled saying as a freedom fighter, 'is to go to London.' He was now reassured that America under Clinton was also moving away from racism: 'The case of the United States shows very well what the trend is,' he said in January 1991. 'The decision-makers in every country are moving away from that.'[43]

Clinton was glad to return the compliment, with an eloquent tribute to Mandela's influence when he welcomed him in Washington in 1998:

> In every gnarly, knotted, distorted situation in the world where people are kept from becoming the best they can be, there is an apartheid of the heart. And if we really honour this stunning sacrifice of twenty-seven years, if we really rejoice in the infinite justice of this man happily married in the autumn of his life, if we really are seeking some driven wisdom from the power of his example, it will be to do whatever we can, however we can, wherever we are, to take the apartheid out of our own and others' hearts.[44]

40

Mandela's Country

HOW BASICALLY AND PEACEFULLY had South Africa been transformed by Mandela's five years of government? In February 1999 Mandela gave his last annual speech to Parliament on the state of the nation. He looked back ten years to the time when 'one humble prisoner' had written from jail to the President to propose negotiations, and to address two central issues: the demand of the blacks for majority rule in a unitary state, and the concerns of the whites over this demand. He recalled his warning about South Africa being 'split into two hostile camps', and reflected with some pride on the extraordinary changes since that humble prisoner had himself become President: 'Things such as equality, the right to vote in free and fair elections, and freedom of speech many of us now take for granted.'

But Mandela still saw worrying divisions between black and white: 'We slaughter one another in the stereotypes and mistrust that lingers in our heads, and the words of hate we spew from our lips.' And he stressed once again that reconciliation was impossible without 'the dismantling of what remains of apartheid practices and attitudes'.[1]

Certainly most white South Africans took a much more negative view than blacks about the transformation of the country. Their euphoria after the elections in 1994 had been followed by growing complaints about the economy, corruption and crime, and the whites' diminishing prospects; and most Western journalists and visitors, who had few social contacts with the black middle class, took their perceptions from whites. Many whites had expected that their lifestyles would be unaffected by the political upheaval of 1994. But they could no longer belong to a quite separate society with its own privileges and rules, an appendage of the rich world of the West; they were now part of a developing country in a state of continuous change, like Brazil or Mexico, exposed to all the problems and hazards of a growing, impoverished population streaming into the cities. Mandela's government had faced a succession of crises which seemed like caricatures of the problems of the developing world, in the fields of race, immigration, finance, health and education.

The whites' preoccupation with their own problems made Mandela impatient of most of their politicians and their 'pessimism of armchair whining'. 'Opposition parties in this country are still concerned with promoting the interests of a white minority,' he told me in January 1999. 'You can quote a lot of examples to say: you are not loyal to the country, you are loyal to the interest of a white minority.'[2] He attacked the 'Mickey Mouse' white parties, to which Tony Leon of the Democratic Party replied that Mandela was 'running a Goofy government'. (Some weeks later, Mandela was visiting a hospital where Leon was recovering from an operation, and called out from behind the curtains: 'Mickey Mouse, this is Goofy!')

Certainly the future looked rosier to the burgeoning black middle class, which included much of the ANC leadership. Austere freedom fighters driving battered 'struggle' cars in the townships were transformed into well-dressed executives driving BMWs and living in the white suburbs, while black managers had adapted the lifestyle of big business.

It was a rapid transition from the years of self-sacrifice and hardship, and it shocked some observers. 'Many ANC leaders raced to catch up with the finer tastes of the former masters,' wrote the sociologists Adam, Slabbert and Moodley in their controversial book *Comrades in Business* in 1997. 'Anything less than a white bourgeois lifestyle would have appeared unequal.'[3] Phumzile Mlambo-Ngcuka, the Deputy Minister of Trade, told black businessmen not to be shy about wanting to become 'filthy rich'. Thabo Mbeki soon slapped her down, but the phrase continued to re-echo among the less privileged.[4] And the politicians were themselves becoming more separated from their voters. MPs' salaries were reckoned to be thirty times the average income, while cabinet members and top civil servants (said the political scientist Tom Lodge) were 'excessively well paid for a relatively poor country'.[5]

The black middle class appeared to embrace capitalism with an enthusiasm which would have been unimaginable twenty years earlier. It was true that hopes of rapid 'black empowerment' in business had been disappointed, whether by white resistance or by the acute shortage of trained black managers and accountants, or by the crippling effects of Bantu education. Liberal white businessmen insisted that the transformation, like that of the Afrikaners, would take time: 'Afrikaner empowerment and affirmative action started in the 1920s,' said Marius Schoon, the Afrikaner ANC supporter in the Development Bank. 'It took until the mid-1960s for Afrikaners to have a meaningful grip on the South African economy. It is crazy to expect rapid results.'[6] But a few black entrepreneurs had achieved real commercial power, like the veteran capitalist Dr Nthato Motlana, who became Chairman of the conglomerate, NAIL ('When I want to get hold of my old doctor now,' joked Mandela, 'I have to get through to the stock exchange').[7] He was joined for a time as Deputy Chairman by Cyril Ramaphosa, before he resigned in February 1999 to pursue his own business interests.

Mandela had his own worries about the excesses of commercial enthusiasm; having been in jail while consumerism had swept through the world, he was often distressed by the conspicuous consumption of the young generation, including some grandchildren. But he had been convinced that business enterprise and foreign investment were essential for jobs and prosperity. He saw finance and industry, like other institutions, in terms of individuals with whom he could relate personally. He was constantly ringing up business leaders to ask for their support, particularly for the Children's Fund, his favourite charity, which raised spectacular sums during his presidency, but also for other schemes to provide schools, clinics and scholarships for children. And he appreciated their response, as he told me in January 1999:

> Since 1990 when I came out of prison I have gone to big business, not as a member of the ANC or as President of the country, but as an old man. I said: 'I want you to deliver services to our people using your own resources.' . . . You ask them to do certain things and you judge them from their response whether they are taking part in transformation . . . Almost everything I have asked for from business they have responded to very positively.[8]

Left-wing critics thought that Mandela was being too cosy with businessmen as he welcomed their gifts to his favourite projects, while being too uncritical of their politics; but he was convinced that the ANC had to remain on friendly terms with big business if it were to create a thriving economy.

The greatest worry of the whites about the sudden commercial activity in black South Africa was the prospect of widespread corruption, such as had devastated so many African states. In fact it was initiated by white businessmen as much as black recipients, as ruthless entrepreneurs sought to gain contracts and short-cut the bureaucracy by offering bribes to Ministers or officials. But a succession of scandals soon revealed the weaknesses of several ANC leaders. Mandela was shocked by their venality. 'We came to government with the zeal of a group of people who were going to eliminate corruption in government,' he said in January 1999. 'It was such a sad disappointment to note that our own people who are there to wipe out corruption themselves became corrupt.' But he insisted that he and Mbeki were doing everything possible to root out the problem, including the appointment of a formidable judge, Willem Heath, to investigate all allegations of corruption in government: 'We cannot act on accusations which have never been investigated.' The ANC, he insisted, was quite different from the previous government – whose own corruption was rapidly coming to light – who 'tried to brush everything under the carpet'.[9]

It was true that the Afrikaner governments had been much more venal than had ever publicly emerged; and the ANC's policy of transparency, together with the newfound freedom of the press, gave an unfair impression of a rapid deterioration in standards. But the ANC was too lenient towards corrupt Ministers, and too slow to condemn and root out bribery and abuses of power, particularly in the provincial governments, which Mandela admitted were the 'Achilles heel of democratic governance'. Mandela became increasingly outspoken. As he put it in February 1999:

> Among the new cadres in various levels of government you find individuals who are as corrupt as – if not more than – those they found in government. When a leader in a provincial legislature siphons off resources meant to fund service by legislators to the people; when employees of a government institution, set up to help empower those who were excluded by apartheid, defraud it for their own enrichment, then we must admit that we are a sick society.[10]

The ANC's embrace of big business distressed many left-wing and Christian veterans of the struggle, who had looked forward to an ideal country without class barriers or personal greed. Idealists and revolutionaries abroad, who had imagined South Africa as a special Utopia, were still more disillusioned: the crusading Australian journalist John Pilger expressed all their anger in a television documentary shown in Britain and South Africa in April 1998. 'A small ANC-connected elite,' he wrote afterwards, 'has seized the opportunity of the "market" while the majority sink deeper into unemployment and poverty.'[11]

The left's attacks on the global marketplace gained ammunition from the crises in the 'tigers' of South-East Asia in 1997. When their economies and currencies collapsed South Africa at first seemed remarkably unaffected; but the reserves were dangerously low, and by May 1998 speculators saw a chance to gamble against the currency: in two months the rand lost a quarter of its value against the US dollar, forcing new cutbacks on the government and serious problems for companies which had over-borrowed abroad. The collapse could not be blamed primarily on the ANC's policies: 'The mugging of the rand is a classic act of bullying,' commented the *Financial Times*. 'The victim's main sin is its weakness.'[12] But the uncertainty about the currency was increased when Thabo Mbeki announced in July 1998 that the Governor of the Reserve Bank, Chris Stals, would be succeeded in a year's time by Tito Mboweni, the Labour Minister, who was a former trades unionist and an old friend of Mbeki. White businessmen worried that the Reserve Bank would be politicised and would become vulnerable to corruption – though the bank was already being investigated for having shored up Afrikaner-owned banks which had been close to the Broederbond, and Mboweni was known for his fierce independence. In fact the announcement was followed by some rallying of international support.[13]

The South African economy paid a heavy price for the growing distrust of all emerging markets, but it escaped the worst disasters that had overcome the Asian countries. 'South Africa did not experience what others did,' Mandela could claim in February 1999, 'because we have credible and sustainable fiscal and monetary policies.'[14]

Black South Africans nevertheless had some reason to be disillusioned with global capitalism after five years had failed to produce much investment or new jobs, while unemployment increased further. The setbacks might have been expected to give a new boost to the ANC's communist allies. As it happened, in June 1998, while the rand was falling, the Communist Party was holding its tenth conference, which Mandela was invited to address. Before he spoke, the militants were in a provocative mood, attacking the government's economic policy GEAR, and delegates were singing 'We don't want GEAR'. 'That song makes our guest angry,' warned the Party's Deputy Secretary Thenjiwe Mtintso. Mandela did indeed make an angry speech, wagging his finger at the audience. 'I will ensure,' he said, 'that the government continues to implement what we believe is good for the country.' He warned the communists that if they left the ANC's structures, they must be aware of the implications. The delegates were stunned: Mtintso complained that Mandela's speech was 'unmandated', and hoped Mandela was not 'going to disrupt this congress as you disrupted meetings of the Communist Party in the 1940s'. But Mandela's attack was fully supported the next day by Thabo Mbeki, who warned delegates not to dismiss it as the 'rantings of an old man'. The communists did not press home their attack: they were reluctant to split with the ANC, particularly since several Party members were in the government.[15] After all the scares about the Communist Party since its rebirth in 1990, they realised they were dependent on the ANC for their share of power.

There remained a clear danger that underprivileged blacks, who had seen none of the promised benefits of liberation, investment or job-creation, would eventually challenge the moderate ANC leadership with a militant programme laced with anti-white propaganda. But the old bogey of revolutionary communism, which had hovered over Mandela throughout the Cold War, appeared to be losing its fascination.

It was criminals rather than politicians who now appeared to pose the greatest threat to the peace of Mandela's South Africa. Gruesome headlines daily proclaimed murders, rapes, bank robberies and car-jacks, and Johannesburg was being described as the crime capital of the world, providing a growing deterrent to foreign investment. Crime waves had devastated other countries emerging from authoritarian rule, like Russia or Brazil, where criminals took advantage of new freedoms, and demobilised soldiers with guns and no jobs were quickly lured into crime. But South Africa was uniquely vulnerable. When Mandela was released in 1990 he had soon realised the danger: 'We are today witnessing a crime wave of terrifying proportions,' he warned in February 1991, 'which, if it continues and escalates, could quickly reduce South Africa to a pile of ashes.'[16] After 1994 international syndicates and drug networks systematically moved across the country's porous borders, exploiting a benign government and using the sophisticated financial system to launder their funds.[17] There was nothing new about crime in black Johannesburg. The townships which Mandela knew in the 1940s and 1950s were full of armed gangs, rapists and robbers. Soweto in the fifties had one of the highest crime rates in the world: one in thirty of the black population of the Johannesburg region could expect to be murdered.* But the police were too busy arresting blacks for offences against the pass laws to secure many convictions for serious crime, and the white media scarcely noted black murders or robberies.

It was not until the crime wave began seriously to affect the white population that it became more widely publicised. As criminals ventured into the suburbs, several prominent white citizens and foreign businessmen were assaulted or murdered: car hijacks and house burglaries soon alarmed everyone, and visiting tourists and businessmen all had stories about robberies and stolen cars. In some rural areas there was a spate of gruesome murders of white farmers: four hundred were killed in four years.[18]

Mandela as President was soon made aware of white fears about crime by his neighbours in Houghton, but the ANC were slow to grapple with the problem. 'We were always thinking about human rights,' the Minister of Justice Dullah Omar explained. 'We thought of law and order as being part of the apartheid system.'[19] Mandela was reluctant to interfere with his Minister of Security Sydney Mufamadi, but in 1997 he appointed a prominent industrialist, Meyer Kahn, to reorganise police resources. Kahn warned that the process would be slow, 'like making love to an elephant'.[20] By September 1998 he reckoned that 'the situation has stopped getting worse', and was confident that acceptable crime levels would be reached within three or four years.[21] In fact the total number of murders had been going down fairly steadily since the election of Mandela's government in 1994, but the number of serious robberies had later increased.† The basic problem was the police as much as the criminals: they were corrupt and incompetent, trained to track down political enemies through informers and torture rather than to patiently pursue

* I wrote this in an article on crime for the magazine *Drum* in October 1951, and discussed the problem in my book *Drum* in 1956. The *Survey of Race Relations in South Africa* in 1957–58 showed that the number of convictions of Africans in 1956 amounted to a fifth of the total African population, but that only 4.7 per cent of those convictions were for serious crimes.

† The annual number of murders reported to the police increased from 15,109 to nearly 26,832 in the four years of de Klerk's government (1990–94), but was down to 24,588 by 1997, and fell again in 1998. Serious robberies, after falling, went up from 151 per 100,000 people in 1996 and 1997 to 188 in 1998.

criminals. They were poorly deployed, with few visible on the streets, and they were underpaid and demoralised. In four years from 1994, 874 policemen were murdered, while three hundred committed suicide. When Sir Paul Condon, the Commissioner of the Metropolitan Police in London, visited South Africa in October 1998, he reckoned that: 'The scale of murder and violence committed against the police was unprecedented in the world.'[22] A quarter of the police left the service in four years.[23]

The crime wave was a challenge not only to the police, but to Mandela's liberal policy based on human rights; and it soon produced a clamour for a return to the death sentence, from both whites and blacks (including his ex-wife). Mandela, who had his own sharp memories of the death penalty, was totally against it, seeing it as 'a reflection of the animal instinct still in human beings'. What deterred a criminal, he insisted, was not the death penalty, but his knowing 'that if I commit an offence I will end up in jail'. And he thought that the white minority had the idea in the back of their minds 'that the death sentence is going to be used against blacks, not really against whites'.[24] He rejected any pressure to bring it back: 'This government,' he reasserted in February 1999, 'is not about to join the chorus baying for the death sentence or to reverse our human rights gains.'[25]

As the crime wave continued, it was seen as the main cause of the growing white emigration from South Africa: one survey in 1998 found that 96 per cent of emigrants gave crime as a reason for their departure, while in a later poll 74 per cent of skilled whites said they were ready to leave South Africa because of it.[26] The numbers emigrating were impossible to verify because many left the country as tourists, but did not return. According to the official figures of the Bureau of Statistics, only about ten thousand people left South Africa in 1997; but the real number was certainly larger, and it included doctors, accountants and computer experts whose skills were seriously needed.[27]

Mandela, who had always urged whites to stay, reacted angrily to the complaints of potential emigrants. In September 1998 he made a speech in Mauritius suggesting that those who left were cowards: 'The real South Africans are being sorted out.' He claimed that 'fear over crime is mainly a white preoccupation, fomented by a white-owned press.'[28] Some prominent Africans agreed that white emigrants showed a lack of patriotism: 'If their first option when faced with a difficult situation is to leave the country,' said Murphy Morobe, 'what does it say to us about the sacrifice we have made?'[29] But many whites were indignant: Tony Leon of the Democratic Party accused Mandela of being racially divisive, and asked him to retract his words. The widow of the liberal novelist Alan Paton, who had suffered horrific burglaries, explained why she was returning to England in an article in the London *Sunday Times* headed 'Fly the Beloved Country': 'President Mandela has referred to us who leave as "cowards" and says the country can do without us. So be it . . . We are leaving because crime is rampaging through the land.' But Paton's son David publicly contradicted his 'abrasive' stepmother's 'drab misleading picture', and blamed the apartheid government.[30] Mandela remained impatient with the preoccupation with crime in local right-wing newspapers. 'The idea is to frighten investors not to come,' he said in January 1999. 'It's absolutely deliberate.'[31]

Certainly the white protests about crime brought out all the differences between the races: they seldom made any reference to the blacks who were the overwhelming majority of victims; and some of the complaints sounded like a replay of the scare stories of the apartheid years about black hordes overwhelming the strongholds of white civilisation. For Mandela, as for most of the African majority, the problem of the crime wave was interlocked with the basic problem of transforming the country, and building up a police and a defence force with a common commitment and patriotism which would give equal value to black and white lives.

The basic security of the country still depended on the armed forces. Mandela remained worried about the loyalty of some Afrikaners in the army. Serious thefts of weapons and equipment from military arsenals showed signs of being inside jobs; and a wave of well-organised bank robberies and heists increased suspicions that the military were involved, with some ex-guerrillas from MK. 'We're not out of the wood,' Mandela told me early in 1998, 'because some of the Generals who led the army are behind the criminal syndicates.'[32] Two months later Thabo Mbeki warned that there were 'enemies of change still among us . . . Some structures set up by the former government to destroy the movement remain intact.'[33] Mandela could not give the media evidence for such claims, but a strange story was unfolding behind the scenes.

On 5 February 1998 Mandela was handed an intelligence report by General Meiring, the defence chief, bypassing the Minister of Defence Joe Modise. It suggested that senior black officers were unfit to command, including Sipho Nyanda, the former MK fighter who was expected to succeed Meiring the next year; and it described how a group of black leaders including Bantu Holomisa and Winnie Mandela had been plotting with Robert McBride, the ex-saboteur who had been condemned to death under the apartheid government but who had since been employed in the Foreign Ministry. The report claimed that the conspirators were planning to promote chaos in order to seize power after the next elections in 1999. Mandela was very sceptical about the report, particularly as it fingered black soldiers from the liberation movement, and suspected it was a diversion by old-guard officers who were defending the status quo.[34] But he bided his time.

Six weeks later Robert McBride was arrested in Mozambique and charged with gun-running: the charge sheet alleged that he had been involved in supplying bombs, pistols and rifles to conspirators, including Winnie Mandela, eighteen months before.[35] The government at first refused to comment, declaring that they would not feed the 'ill-intentioned frenzy and offensive'. In fact Mandela at first thought McBride's arrest gave credence to Meiring's report, but then he began to suspect that McBride had been framed.[36]

Then, on 27 March, Mandela revealed that he had received the report seven weeks earlier, and that it alleged 'organised activities with the aim to overthrow the government'. He asked three judges, headed by the Chief Justice Ismail Mahomed, to investigate how the report was prepared and verified. The judges, after questioning Meiring and others, decided that the report was 'without substance', that it was based on a single unreliable source, a spy who had been arrested with McBride, and that it had never been checked for its veracity.[37] General Meiring asked to be retired early, which Mandela agreed was 'appropriate and honourable', and soon afterwards Mandela appointed General Nyanda as his successor.

Some ANC colleagues who had never trusted Meiring thought that Mandela should have moved against him much earlier. But Mandela had handled the crisis shrewdly and characteristically. By leaving the decision to the law he had avoided a direct political clash with the Afrikaner old guard, and by discrediting them he had eased the succession of black commanders. It was a remarkable transition: eight years earlier Nyanda had been in charge of the secret military force, Operation Vula; now he was in command of all South Africa's defence forces.

There were still serious military threats from other quarters. Political killings had fallen sharply – from 3,794 in the peak year of 1993 to 470 in 1997.[38] But there were ominous alliances between criminals, politicians and religious groups. And Mandela still suspected that a residual third force was at work in some areas, destabilising the country by arming local warlords, and in league with criminal groups which could finance it. During 1998 the country town of Richmond in KwaZulu-Natal, which had a long history of faction fights, became a battleground between rival warlords; the trouble flared up again in January 1999 when the notorious warlord Sifiso Nkabinde was gunned down in broad daylight, quickly followed by the murder of eleven people in reprisal. Nkabinde was the Secretary of Bantu Holomisa's party, the UDM, and his assassination was blamed on the ANC, to which he had earlier belonged; but Mandela suspected that the 'third force' was engineering the killing to destabilise the region. And more murders of UDM and ANC leaders in the Western Cape in March 1999 aroused similar suspicions.[39] Certainly the encouragement of 'black-on-black' violence under the previous government had created lethal alliances between criminals and politicians which would be hard to obliterate.

South Africa was still far from peaceful by comparison with most European or North American countries. But compared to the predictions of bloodshed five years earlier, as Mandela would often recall, the transition from minority to majority rule had been relatively painless.

After all his fierce arguments, Mandela could still rise above party politics, as the father of his country's democracy. On 29 March 1999 he made his farewell speech to Parliament, before it adjourned to prepare for the elections on 2 June. He depicted himself as one of the generation 'for whom the achievement of democracy was the defining challenge', and recalled how South Africans 'finally chose a profoundly legal path to their revolution'. And he ended with the words: 'The long walk continues.'[40] Thabo Mbeki praised him as 'our nearest and brightest star to guide us on our way'.

But Mandela's opponents also competed to pay tributes. Marthinus van Schalkwyk, de Klerk's successor as leader of the National Party, called him 'everybody's President', and promised that his party would be co-builders of the new nation. Constand Viljoen of the Freedom Front said that 'Mandela has always acted as a lord to me.' Tony Leon of the Democratic Party, Mandela's most acerbic critic, saw him as a leader, like Gandhi or the Dalai Lama, 'born with a special kind of grace who seem to transcend the politics of their age'.

41

Image and Reality

How lasting and deep is Mandela's achievement, behind his dazzling image? A contemporary biographer cannot hope to provide a definitive historical judgement: he can only try to make the most of available sources and portray his subject against the background of his own time. It is easy to overestimate the importance of a living hero with a universal charisma, on a stage whose bright lights can fade soon afterwards. Africa has seen many short-lived saviours who have later been toppled from their pedestals, while Mandela's stature is harder to assess at a time when the world feels a desperate need for great men to admire.

Mandela, like most great leaders, has always been a master of images who knows how to project himself, whether as the Defiance Campaigner, the 'Black Pimpernel' or the guerrilla leader. His great occasions – like his long speech at the Rivonia trial or his inauguration as President – have been grandly operatic. Behind the scenes he has always owed much to modest colleagues: the liberation of his people, as he points out himself, was achieved while he was in jail. How far, then, did the imagery connect with the reality of Mandela's leadership?

Certainly he had to establish his own mythology as part of his challenge to a racist regime: for he was confronting powerful myths – of black inferiority, white invincibility, and incompatibility between races. He had to give confidence to a people who had been conditioned into submission, and to personify African dignity and self-respect. And he did that with panache: when he faced an all-white court, buttressed by the whole panoply of the law, he deliberately dressed up in tribal regalia, 'carrying on my back the history, culture and heritage of my people'.[1]

In that kind of showmanship Mandela seemed at first to be following the style of other post-war African nationalist leaders like Kwame Nkrumah or Jomo Kenyatta, who had been imprisoned before taking power in a blaze of glory, and presenting themselves as redeemers or fathers of their people. The fifties were years of heady optimism and illusions, before Africa had to face the difficult realities of government and economics; and many foreign observers as well as black South Africans had expected the apartheid government to crumble rapidly in the face of moral condemnation and the prevailing retreat of European empires.

Mandela, like his colleagues, took some time to realise that he faced a much more testing struggle than his predecessors, and more ruthless opponents than the British colonists to the north. His Afrikaner oppressors were not temporary expatriates, but entrenched landowners who had built up a powerful military and economic structure, supported by Western Cold Warriors, and who were determined to root out black opposition. With hindsight, Mandela was not a very realistic military commander: he seriously underestimated his enemy's strength, as his political writings make clear, and made careless mistakes which led to his own arrest. But the amateurishness was part of the false optimism of the time.

Some recent critics have judged Mandela's early career more harshly. The British television commentator Brian Walden accused him in 1998 of being first duped by the communists with whom he allied himself, then embarking on a military campaign 'with unbelievable amateurism and fecklessness', and leading the 'most useless and incompetent guerrilla army in history'. Walden argued that Mandela lacked the true ruthlessness of a great leader like Churchill, and that apartheid was brought down in the end not by the ANC, but by Afrikaner tycoons who realised it was bad for business.[2]

This critique does not stand up to the historical evidence. Mandela, like most shrewd politicians, was always more pragmatic than he sounded. He needed the communists at a time when they were the only available allies, and when white liberals and Western governments were scared away from supporting the ANC. The confidential despatches of British diplomats show how easily they were intimidated and duped by apartheid governments into joining their anti-communist crusade; while in the end Mandela used the communists, as he foresaw, more than they used him.

Mandela could not avoid committing himself to an armed struggle without losing his black support, when every other avenue of protest was closed; but he never thought it could by itself liberate South Africa. He knew that a truly ruthless military campaign of urban terrorism would have destroyed his country, as it nearly destroyed Algeria; and when from jail he saw South Africa facing chaos, he sought to negotiate – while looking to international pressure and sanctions to bring down apartheid, which they did. The belief that white politicians and businessmen would have put an end to apartheid without the threat of violence is not sustained by the facts. It was only because of the violence, as Oliver Tambo realised, that businessmen became seriously worried. The very limited 'armed propaganda', backed by sanctions, was effective without a major armed confrontation, and Mandela resisted the clamour from the militants for the seizure of power. His lack of military ruthlessness was the key to achieving the transition to democracy without a bloodbath.

Certainly Mandela had an over-optimistic view of the struggle before he went to jail in 1962; but his prison ordeal transformed him into a much more reflective and influential kind of leader, as this book has tried to show. He was cut off from mass audiences, public images and television cameras, stripped down to man-to-man leadership and to the essentials of human relationships, away from the trappings of power. He learnt about human sensitivities and how to handle the fears and insecurities of others, including his Afrikaner warders. He was sensitised by his own sense of guilt, both about his family and about friends he had used during his political career; but he was acquiring a deeper confidence, feeling himself 'master of my fate', like a classical hero. Unlike most politicians, in mid-career he had time to become much more thoughtful and questioning, reading biographies and histories. And he deepened his interest in the law, which, though it had put him in jail, he realised provided the only basis for a lasting settlement: the law, not war, was the basis of his hopes for his country's future.

Mandela's unpublished essays and writings from jail, as he watched the South African stage as a spectator, showed far more intellectual depth and originality than his early anti-colonialist clichés; and he was persistent in getting to the truth, however uncomfortable. He still understood the importance of his own image as he wrote his autobiography in jail, hoping that it would inspire others – though it was to be suppressed by colleagues abroad. He saw his own icon being built up across the world, quite separately from himself. But he was not fooled by it, and he was very aware of the dangers of the personality cult which had misled other African countries. He talked less about 'I' and more about 'we', and was determined 'to be looked at as an ordinary human being'.[3]

The fortitude and resilience of the Robben Island prisoners was a communal achievement, and Mandela might not have maintained his strength without his colleagues. His closest friends like Walter Sisulu and Ahmed Kathrada reinforced his courage, and his commitment to reconciliation and forgiveness. But in the end his personal leadership was decisive. When he took his most critical decision – to propose talks with the government – he took it alone. Joe Slovo was probably right in judging that 'without Mandela South African history would have taken a completely different turn.'[4] His conciliation emerged from his personal development: he had learnt how to control his aggression, to 'think with his brains, not his blood', and to channel his energy into the goal of a negotiated victory. He became a much more formidable politician by subordinating his emotions and feelings to his central purpose: even an intimate colleague like Kathrada found him impenetrable. He had been 'steeled and hardened', as Mac Maharaj observed, and his underlying toughness was essential to the success of the negotiations which followed.

But the Mandela who emerged from jail surprised most people who had known him before (including myself), not so much by his political shrewdness as by his humanity and simplicity. He had lost his defensiveness and arrogance as he became more confident of his powers, and he appeared at ease with himself, with a warmth and humour that gave him immediate rapport with all kinds of people, particularly children – which was all the more attractive in contrast to the superhuman images of him in the world outside. He sometimes projected an almost childlike innocence as he insisted on speaking his mind. He showed no signs of the familiar deformities of power: of the egomania, pomposity or paranoia which had afflicted so many leaders in the developing world. His mistakes came from the opposite direction: from being too trusting, and seeing the best in everyone, however unworthy. But he could also bring out the best in unexpected people, and his ability to convert past enemies proved essential to his policy of reconciliation.

'I'm no angel,' Mandela liked to remind me. Behind his acts of forgiveness and magnanimity he remained a politician to his fingertips. He still had a brilliant sense of showmanship and timing; and he could appear as the ultimate post-modernist leader, the master of imagery and performance, as he popped up in a Springbok jersey on the rugby field, or outwitted de Klerk by taking his hand at the end of a televised debate. He knew instinctively how to work a room or flatter a journalist: he was the master of the photo-opportunity, the soundbite, the intimate handshake and the rapturous smile. He could mix politics with showbiz almost too enthusiastically, as he favoured the Spice Girls or Michael Jackson over a visiting head of state.

But he had a moral authority and concern for the truth with which few could compete, as a rock of continuity in a discontinuous world. Through his three decades in jail he had remained true to his principles and beliefs in the face of all pressures and temptations, at a time when politicians in most countries were becoming more opportunist and changeable, and heroes and great causes were fading into history. He had been right about one big issue when so many had been wrong. His persistence had a difficult downside: he could be very stubborn in thinking he was right about everything, and sometimes remained loyal to doubtful allies who brought him much criticism. But his loyalty to his own principles and friends gave him the edge over other world leaders who had forgotten what they stood for.

Mandela was not so much post-modern, as pre-modern. He belonged to the much older tribal tradition in which he had been brought up, of a chief representing his people and accessible to them. He still recalled the boy Mandela sitting at the feet of his guardian the Regent, watching him hearing his tribesmen's outspoken criticisms and settling their disputes with careful courtesy, making them all feel part of the same society. His rural roots remained a crucial ingredient in his make-up: it was noticeable that he wrote best about his home territory. He still genuinely saw himself as the 'country boy' who had a sense of his own belonging and *ubuntu*, and his own rural values: it was no accident that his life would end as it had begun in his tribal village of Qunu. But Mandela was no ordinary country boy: he remained the son of a chief. His princely style could strike chords with white as well as black South Africans; and in Britain it could even help to reassure the Queen. He could evoke an earlier era when monarchs were identified with their people and there was no distinction between the imagery and the reality of kingship. Mandela's monarchic instincts could have drawbacks in running a complicated industrial state beset with economic problems and urgently in need of modern management. He could be devastatingly candid about his government's shortcomings, but he seemed in no hurry to rectify them. In his detachment from bureaucracies and diplomatic complexities, from economists or managers, Mandela sometimes seemed to belong more to the nineteenth than the twenty-first century. But his sense of leadership straddled the centuries, and he personified a country looking to the future.

In fact, for most of his presidency, as he often said, Mandela saw himself as a ceremonial head of state rather than a chief executive. He was more like a constitutional monarch, submitting himself with a strong sense of duty to the disciplines of party democracy through the cabinet or the ANC National Executive. He was not always obedient, and could often interfere, like Queen Victoria rather than Queen Elizabeth II; and he was often torn between being the democrat and the autocrat. But he was totally committed to democracy, and was determined – unlike most African leaders – to appoint a democratically elected successor: he allowed his deputy Thabo Mbeki, as he explained, to be chosen by the party leaders and their allies without revealing his own preference; and Mbeki was effectively running the country for most of Mandela's presidency. On some critical issues, particularly on crime and corruption, Mandela was strongly criticised for not intervening more decisively. But there was a built-in contradiction between the roles expected of him: to use his personal authority to the full, but also to establish a democratic tradition in which no single leader could prevail.

As head of state he saw a clear priority: to consolidate the new nation, to hold it together and transform it into a multi-racial democracy in which all citizens could live at peace. He knew that without that peace the machinery of government and the economy was useless; and the horrific civil wars which were breaking out again in nearby countries like Angola and the Congo provided fearful warnings. He was uniquely suited to the task of nation-building after his extraordinary journey through his country. He could relate personally to the very different communities through which he had moved over his eight decades: to rural tribesmen, to mineworkers and streetwise city-slickers, to African nationalists and freedom fighters, to Indian and white comrades, to Afrikaner warders, to international businessmen or to heads of state.

Mandela had learnt the hard way about the difficulties of reconciliation, and he had seen how narrowly the country had avoided a bloodbath. He did not believe, like many idealists on the left, that people of different races would readily abandon their communal loyalties to become members of a colour-blind non-racial society. But he had progressed from his early exclusive African nationalism to work closely with white and Indian colleagues and to trust them completely; and in jail he had seen how Afrikaners could be changed, as he put it, by 180 degrees, and how the same people who could not bear to touch black flesh could be reassured by a handshake. With all this personal experience he was uniquely able to establish a 'rainbow cabinet' which was one of the few genuinely multi-racial governments in the world; while he gave no indication of his own racial preferences. He seemed above race.

Mandela's life story had become central to his nation's story. He had been brought up with stories of the humiliations of his own tribe, before the nation of South Africa – the union between Afrikaners and English-speakers – had been established only eight years before he was born, creating a democracy from which Africans were excluded. He had lived through the rise and fall of apartheid, and seen how it controlled people's attitudes and lives. As President he had seen the persistence of apartheid attitudes, and how many strongholds of racialism remained – in the military, in business or in the media. But his experience had persuaded him that reconciliation could be achieved. He was effectively refounding a nation, stamping it with the concept of racial tolerance and cooperation as firmly as his predecessors had stamped it with intolerance and segregation.

Mandela remained a master of symbolic images, but they had become part of his own personality and history, acquiring more universal appeal as he retired from politics to become an ordinary old man. He had survived the most testing challenge to his reputation when he emerged from jail to face up to his overwhelming global icon; and he did so by presenting himself as a fallible human being. His biography in the end converged with his mythology; and it was his essential integrity more than his superhuman myth which gave his story its appeal across the world.

AFTERWORD

by John Battersby

Living Legend, Living Statue

RETIREMENT WAS NEVER going to be easy for Nelson Mandela. For a short time after he stepped down from the presidency in August 1999, Mandela appeared to contemplate retreating into family life with his graceful wife, Graca Machel, and his extended family. Time would be spent between his house in Johannesburg, his country retreat in Qunu – near his birthplace and what he saw as his natural resting-place – and his wife's house in Mozambique.

He dealt with the prospect of retirement by making light of it, describing himself as an 'ordinary pensioner', or joking about what would become of him now that he was no longer President. He even speculated aloud on several occasions that he might end up begging with a placard at the traffic lights, a common sight in Johannesburg's plush residential suburbs. When invited to speak before influential audiences he would often express surprise that the audience thought there was still use for 'an old man' like himself.

At last he had time on his hands. It was the commodity that Mandela missed the most after his release in 1990 into the maelstrom of political life, with the constant demands on his time and physical, mental and spiritual resources. The benefits of the routine of prison life and the lessons he learned from studying the minds of his oppressors had remained with him and influenced his understanding of leadership. 'Thinking is one of the most important weapons in dealing with problems ... and we didn't have that outside [jail],' Mandela said in an interview published nine months after relinquishing the presidency.[1] But there was a paradox in his newly regained time to think: the ability to act on the outcomes of his reflections diminished as he became, for the first time, a private individual without any political position. He was, however, the most extraordinary 'ordinary' member of the African National Congress, the organisation which he had led and to which he had observed lifelong loyalty.

In 1998 Mandela embarked on writing the sequel to his autobiography *Long Walk to Freedom*, which was to be known at his own request as *The Presidential Years*, and would cover the period from his inauguration as President in 1994 into the first years of retirement. Mandela was determined to write the second instalment himself (the first volume having been co-written with Richard Stengel) and use his own methods of research.[2] 'He was very protective of the writing,' said Verne Harris, director of the Mandela Centre of Memory. 'He did have a research assistant for a while, but grew impatient with the arrangement. Ultimately he simply ran out of steam.'[3] I got a call from Mandela's assistant, Zelda, during the research stages as Mandela wanted me to help him check some facts. (We had met previously on several occasions, in my capacity as a journalist and editor of *The Sunday Independent*.) But Mandela's post-presidential commitment to conflict resolution, the growing demands of his charitable work and a constant stream of visitors created sufficient distractions to disrupt work on the project and the sequel never got as far as publication.*

It was not long before Mandela had forgotten all ideas of a leisurely retirement and reverted to a demanding programme. He continued meeting and inspiring world leaders and celebrities, for whom he had lost none of the exceptional qualities of humanity and generosity of spirit that had made him a global icon. Some travelled to South Africa to meet him and others he met and engaged on his travels abroad. 'I have retired,' he told a BBC documentary, broadcast to coincide with his eighty-fifth birthday in 2003; 'but if there is anything that would kill me it is to wake up in the morning and to not know what I was going to do.'[4] Each day he had a long list of vetted requests to attend to. When in Johannesburg, he would report to the Nelson Mandela Foundation offices at around 11 a.m. daily, under the efficient and loving guidance of his Afrikaner Personal Assistant Zelda La Grange. 'The only thing that keeps me going is knowing that I have a programme,' Mandela said.[5] Graca tried to make him relax, but she soon gave up. 'I tried very hard until I realised I was

* The text of the rough drafts, originally mostly written in Mandela's own hand, were published as excerpts throughout *Conversations with Myself* (Macmillan, London, 2010).

making a mistake,' she said. 'He needs to be very busy. He is quite clear that if he slows down he will feel depressed. He'll feel he is not needed anymore.'[6]

Retirement gave Mandela the chance to build on his relationship with Graca, whom he had married in 1998. Though Mandela rarely discusses his third wife in public, the smile on his face and his obvious and deep respect for her says it all. 'She is a wonderful lady and I felt life together with her would be bliss,' he said in 2003.[7] Over recent years Graca has spoken movingly and candidly about their relationship, stressing how important it has been in sustaining one another after their respective life tragedies. 'Madiba was a lonely person when I met him,' she says. 'I was an aggrieved woman because of the sense of loss I had in life. So that loneliness and the need of a shoulder to cry on … I think it played a role to bring us together. So it was in one sense a meeting of minds and in another sense a meeting of hearts.'[8]

The couple shared another passion: they believed that education is the key to empowerment. Both are living examples of the primacy of education: Graca attended Methodist mission schools, as Mandela had, and was given the chance to excel through scholarships. 'Madiba is obsessed with education and the role it can play in changing people's lives,' says Graca. The same might be said of her. She would often tell the story in public of how education had transformed her life; how it had enabled her to transcend a life of rural poverty and become Minister of Education in Mozambique and a prominent ambassador for UNESCO. In 2007 she attended an event in Downing Street to mark the launch of a series of scholarships for young women in Southern Africa bearing her name.

Mandela's first charitable intervention after his release from jail had been to create the Nelson Mandela Children's Fund, which advances the cause of underprivileged children and creates educational opportunities. His first act after stepping down from the presidency was to set up the Nelson Mandela Foundation, which ran his peronal office and prioritised HIV/AIDS work, rural development and the building of schools. In 2003 the Mandela-Rhodes Foundation was created at Rhodes House, Oxford, to promote leadership in Africa by offering postgraduate scholarships to promising students. These took the place of the original Mandela scholarships which, over ten years until the scheme ceased in 2008, put more than a hundred students through their studies abroad. Other Mandela initiatives have been the Nelson Mandela Centre of Memory (now the core function of the Nelson Mandela Foundation), the '46664' global campaign on HIV/AIDS and the Nelson Mandela Annual Lecture, which began in 2002. Speakers have included three Nobel laureates, Archbishop Desmond Tutu, Kenyan Wangari Maathai and Professor Muhammad Yunus of Bangladesh, former US President Bill Clinton, the Chilean author and human rights activist Ariel Dorfman and former UN Secretary-General Kofi Annan.

Although Mandela's power to influence political decision-making at home and abroad was inevitably on the wane, his moral authority and legacy became more potent after his retirement. There was clear evidence of this in his firm intervention on the ANC's policies on HIV/AIDS which proved a turning point in attitudes towards President Thabo Mbeki's ambiguous leadership on the issue. It also placed the provision of anti-retroviral drugs, as well as prevention and care of HIV/AIDS sufferers, at the top of the government's agenda. Without provoking a crisis of leadership, Mandela made very clear that whatever his successor's personal views were about the relationship between AIDS and the HIV virus and the efficacy of anti-retroviral treatment, there should be no such ambiguity reflected in government's policy and actions. He repeatedly stressed that ANC policy had to prioritise the widest possible access to medical treatment and drugs for the country's millions of HIV-positive people. 'This is a war. It has killed more people than has been the case in all previous wars and in all previous national disasters,' he said. 'We must not continue to be debating, to be arguing, when people are dying.'[9]

Mandela's own legacy on the issue of dealing with the AIDS pandemic was something that he felt compelled to confront publicly. His critics argued that he had neglected the spread of AIDS during his five-year presidency and only become vocal on the issue once Mbeki took over. 'Mandela more than anyone – through his enormous stature and almost god-like status among young people in Africa – could have reached into the minds and behaviour of young people in the [black] townships,' said Edwin Cameron, a respected High Court judge and AIDS activist. 'He didn't do it. AIDS was the silent issue. And the epidemic burgeoned.'[10]

Although Mandela has always been quite forthright about discussing matters relating to sex, the ANC urged him not to break the taboo that operates in black society about discussing sex for fear of losing votes in the election. The pandemic had reached a serious stage but was certainly not a priority issue in the media during Mandela's presidency. Mandela responded openly to suggestions that he had not campaigned hard enough or acted early enough on the AIDS threat, saying: 'That may be true because as President you have got many duties. I had to concern myself with nation-building.'[11]

Mandela sought to undermine the taboo that exists around the disease when on 6 January 2005, his son Makgatho died of HIV/AIDS aged fifty-four. Hours later Mandela held a press conference at which he announced that the cause of Makgatho's death had been HIV/AIDS, saying: 'Let us give publicity to HIV/AIDS and not hide it, because the only way of making it appear to be a normal illness just like TB, like cancer, is always to come out and say somebody has died of HIV.' This represented a major break with convention in South Africa, where the related illness, such as tuberculosis or pneumonia, rather than HIV/AIDS itself, is given as the cause of death and recorded on the death certificate.

At the time of writing, more than a million people in South Africa have received anti-retroviral treatment and there are growing indications that the rate of infection is levelling out and could start falling. President Jacob Zuma, who had always been on-side politically with the AIDS issue, has continued to strengthen the implementation of HIV/AIDS policy since he took over as President in May 2009. Zuma has won widespread and deserved praise for the landmark decision in 2010 to provide universal access to anti-retroviral drugs for infants.

On the international front, Mandela in retirement proved no less forceful. In 2003 he intervened in the global debate around the British-backed US-led invasion of Iraq. He strongly criticised Prime Minister Tony Blair and President George W. Bush for undermining the United Nations by taking a unilateral decision to invade Iraq when UN consensus could not be achieved, and he described Bush's actions as 'a tragedy'. 'What I am condemning is that one power, with a President who has no foresight, who cannot think properly, is now wanting to plunge the world into a holocaust,' Mandela said.[12] He also attacked the United States for its poor human rights record and for dropping atomic bombs on Hiroshima and Nagasaki during the Second World War: 'If there is a country that has committed unspeakable atrocities in the world, it is the United States of America,' he said. 'They don't care.'[13]

Mandela's sharp comments created an international stir. He told *Newsweek* magazine's Tom Masland: 'The most catastrophic action of the United States was to sabotage the decision that was painstakingly stitched together by the United Nations regarding the withdrawal of the Soviet Union from Afghanistan. If you look at those matters, you will come to the conclusion that the attitude of the United States of America is a threat to world peace.'[14] It is difficult to think of another world leader who could have delivered this kind of tongue-lashing to a global superpower and still continue to have an open relationship with the country based on mutual respect. As Anthony Sampson wrote in 2004: 'Through all his interventions during his retirement, Mandela remained a consummate politician with a clear understanding of the realities of his power. His statements were usually more calculated than they appeared. He knew that he could now speak out more freely than any other government minister and he often expressed thoughts with which other leaders privately agreed but could not say so publicly.'[15] Mandela went on to angrily describe Tony Blair as the 'foreign minister of the United States' for Britain's unquestioning support of the US over the invasion of Iraq. Blair was clearly stung by the accusation and waited until Mandela's next visit to Britain to try to patch up their relationship: he tried to speak to Mandela on the phone, but Mandela was not keen to speak to the British PM.[16]

'I said that they can't solve differences by war. They need to talk to people and find out what they are quarrelling about,' Mandela told the BBC.[17] Once Britain and America finally went to war with Iraq, Mandela deliberately avoided further criticism of the Western leaders, though he remained deeply concerned that the two countries were acting as 'the world's policeman'.[18] 'Mandela still thought that South Africans had a special opportunity and responsibility to contribute to world peace through their own experience of reconciliation and negotiation,' Anthony Sampson wrote.[19] By the time of the launch of the Mandela-Rhodes Foundation in London's historic Westminster Hall in July 2003, Mandela, never one to bear grudges, appeared to have reconciled with Blair. Frail and needing assistance to walk, he was accompanied down the hall's long aisle by his friend Bill Clinton, steadying him on the one side, and Tony Blair on the other.

Mandela had aspirations to apply more broadly his philosophy of reconciliation and compromise which had seen South Africa through its most difficult period and avoided a widely predicted racial conflagration. Throughout his leadership – and that of President Mbeki after him – he mediated in conflicts, including in Ireland, Sri Lanka, Myanmar, Iraq, the Great Lakes region and the Middle East. 'He had become the unofficial spokesman,' Sampson said, 'not just for South Africans, but for the huge populations in the developing world who felt themselves unrepresented in a world dominated by Washington. He knew that he still had a moral authority in Western countries, including many parts of the United States, as a man who had stood out against oppression and racism to become the champion of reconciliation and multi-racial society.'[20]

Mandela's most high-profile intervention was on Libya, where he and his colleague, Jakes Gerwel, were instrumental in persuading Colonel Muammar Qadaffi to allow suspects in the bombing of the American airliner which crashed over Lockerbie in 1988 to stand trial in Holland. Mandela used his good offices to get the US administration to promise to lift sanctions against Libya if the deal went ahead. One of the suspects, Abdel Al-Megrahi, was sentenced to life in prison and served eight years in a Scottish jail before his controversial release on compassionate grounds in August 2009. In the interim, the Libyan leader had thrown large sums of money at lobbyists to secure Megrahi's release. US sanctions against Libya were lifted in stages from 2003 and the country was removed from the US terrorist list in 2006. The British government praised Mandela for negotiating the settlement but when he visited Megrahi in Glasgow's Barlinnie prison, he publicly criticised the conditions in which the Libyan was being held, describing them as 'psychological persecution'.[21]

In 2004 British Prime Minister Tony Blair led an international rapprochement with Qadaffi after he had offered to give up his nuclear weapons programme and cease support for Islamic terrorists. Blair visited Tripoli and embraced Qadaffi: gas exploration and arms deals followed soon afterwards. There was a deep irony for all concerned when the UN imposed a no-fly zone on Libya in March 2011 with the support of the Arab League and African nations following Qadaffi's vicious war of retaliation against an internal uprising against his rule. Britain and France went into battle against weapons they had been supplying to Qadaffi; Italy and the United States were also embarrassed by the economic support they had been providing to the Libyan leader since he had supposedly turned over a new leaf in 2004. It emerged too that South Africa had been providing Qadaffi with arms for several years in the run-up to the insurrection.

Mandela often faced criticism and raised eyebrows from Western leaders because of his warm embrace of certain leaders, including the late Palestinian leader Yasser Arafat, the Cuban leader Fidel Castro and Colonel

Qadaffi. A far more troubled relationship existed between Mandela and Robert Mugabe. The Zimbabwean leader's image had been seriously tainted over the years by his determination to stay in power seemingly regardless of the means or consequences. In contrast, Mandela had vowed to serve only one five-year term, and honoured his pledge. Tensions had existed between the two leaders from the time they first met at a regional meeting of the World Economic Forum in Cape Town in 1990. Mandela had learned the hard way that he could not vent his frustration with Mugabe in public after having once, in 2001, sounded off about a dictatorial leader without naming him. Mandela was later reined in by Mbeki and the leaders of Southern African Development Community (SADC) and never made a public attack on Mugabe after that.[22]

Mandela told me in an interview in 2002: 'We must understand the person we are dealing with. I have worked very closely with President Mugabe. If you attack him publicly he will never respond. The best way to persuade him to take any action is to respect him … to discuss it with him confidentially.'[23] He believed that Mugabe would have preferred it if he, Mandela, had stayed in jail and described Mugabe as a classic case of the 'big man in Africa syndrome': he didn't want to give up power because of an emotional inadequacy. Mandela failed in a bid to persuade Mugabe to leave office in 2007 'with residual respect and a modicum of dignity'. He then tried to use the Elders group, of which Mandela is patron, to persuade the Zimbabwean leader to step down. The Elders nominated Kofi Annan to make overtures, but Mugabe snubbed the former UN Secretary-General, and subsequent attempts by the Elders proved futile.

At a gala event in London to celebrate his ninetieth birthday in 2008, Mandela finally broke his public silence on Mugabe and referred to 'the tragic failure of leadership in Zimbabwe'.

* * *

Mandela's most valuable legacy by the time of Thabo Mbeki's inauguration as President of South Africa in June 1999, as Anthony Sampson acknowledged, was that most South Africans of all colours, unlike five years earlier, assumed that their country was a working democracy.

Mbeki's presidential inauguration in 1999 had a strong African feel both in the composition of those attending and in the celebratory events that followed. That continued to be the case with Mbeki's second inauguration in 2004. By the time a frail and ageing Mandela was hoisted onto the amphitheatre stage at the Union Buildings for Jacob Zuma's inauguration in 2009, it was a distinctly African occasion in every sense. The heavens opened several hours before the ceremony began and the crowd took shelter under umbrellas. Then the clouds cleared and the sun came through, as is the case in African mythology when the leader is about to make an appearance. The symbolism of Mandela, Zuma and Thabo Mbeki all on the same stage struck a powerful blow for democracy and continuity. It came in the aftermath of the acrimonious nature of Mbeki's 'recall' by the party following the turbulent ANC conference in the northern town of Polokwane in December 2008. Zuma knew that he needed to demonstrate continuity in terms both of the values that Mandela represented as well as his inclusive style of government.

As Zuma knelt before Mandela, his legs covered with a blanket in the chilly winter weather, and made a vow to follow in his footsteps, Mbeki sat on the other side of the stage with his elegant wife Zanele resplendent in a designer African dress. The clouds that unleashed the heavy showers before Zuma was sworn in were not the only signs of a gathering storm that day. In one of the alcoves of the Union Buildings' upper colonnade overlooking the amphitheatre, the fiery ANC youth leader Julius Malema had taken up position with a group of Youth League followers; he and his colleagues chanted and danced in African knees-up style at every opportunity throughout the ceremony. Malema would come to symbolise the impatience with Zuma's moderate approach and continually clash with the ANC leadership over the pace and direction of ANC policy. Malema wanted more state intervention, more pro-black economic empowerment and nationalisation of the mines. When he had emerged from prison, Mandela had supported these traditional policies of the ANC but had been persuaded by big business and international capital to take a more gradualist and liberal approach to ensure that South Africa became integrated in the increasingly globalised economy.

Thabo Mbeki had an almost impossible task stepping into Mandela's shoes and he often seemed exasperated when having to compete with the euphoria that the elder statesman's arrival at any event would inevitably cause. At the ANC's five-yearly conference in the Afrikaner town of Stellenbosch near Cape Town in 2003, Mbeki was about halfway through his long conference speech when a note was passed to the chair that Mandela, who had been expected earlier, had arrived by plane from the

Eastern Cape and his motorised ground convoy was circling the sports field seeking direction about the next move. The chair realised that there was no option but to invite Mandela into the conference hall in the middle of Mbeki's speech. Proceedings came to a standstill and the hall erupted into wild chanting and singing. Mbeki, with a characteristic roll of the eyes, mumbled something and sat down with a resigned expression. Eventually the crowd was subdued and Mbeki was able to continue his report of the five-year period.

There was a history of subdued tension between the two leaders. On one occasion Mbeki arrived forty-five minutes late for a gala evening held in Mandela's honour, shortly after his retirement in 1999. Addressing the audience, Mandela talked of a former ANC President from the 1930s (Alfred Xuma) who used to say that he was 'the Black Prime Minister' and needed to come late to meetings so that everyone could see him. Mbeki knew what was coming and looked up to the ceiling in his characteristic way of saying: *here we go again*. Mandela, aware that his public remarks were being recorded on the BBC television cameras, then gestured in the direction of Mbeki and said: 'I think that this President here has taken after that President of the ANC.'

While the transition from Mandela to Mbeki in 1999 was relatively smooth, that from Mbeki to Zuma was anything but seamless. The resentment that had built up against Mbeki by those who accused him of waging a conspiracy against Zuma and refusing to step down, divided the ANC into sharply opposing camps. There was disquiet in the society at large that the values that Mandela represented and fought for were becoming blurred in his own party as it descended into bitter infighting and acrimony. Although Mandela was more at ease with Zuma, there were fears among Mandela's advisers that as the elder statesman became more frail and his short-term memory deteriorated he would be more vulnerable to being a political football in the battle for supremacy between Mbeki and Zuma in the run-up to the 2009 election. Mandela refrained from commenting directly on the fraud charges that Zuma was facing, which were later dropped in April 2009, or the rape charges of which he was acquitted: he was clearly upset by the turn of events but did not want to add to the ANC's mounting problems.

In August 2008, at the height of the political power struggle between Mbeki and Zuma, the ANC organised a belated ninetieth birthday celebration for Mandela in a bid to heal the rift and restore a semblance of unity in the party. Zuma paid tribute to Mandela as a selfless leader and the glue that held the ANC together as well as being an icon to the nation at large. Friends of the ANC were invited to the event to show that it was not solely for the party faithful. Mandela described the ANC as a great organisation and made his point by saying that the ANC needed disciplined leaders as much as in any time in its history. In October, barely a month after Mbeki had resigned, Mandela was transported by plane from his home in Johannesburg by his grandson and head of the Mandela clan, Chief Mandla Mandela, to a political rally in the Eastern Cape where he shared a platform with Zuma. The Nelson Mandela Foundation only heard about the venture hours before it happened. Security regulations were flouted and the weather conditions were not favourable for flying. The plane had to make three attempts at landing. Jakes Gerwel, chair of the Mandela Foundation, was furious as were other Foundation staff and family members. They felt that Mandela's health had been jeopardised to boost Zuma's stature and the performance of the ANC in the upcoming election in April the following year. 'We were not aware that he was going until almost the last minute. We were taken as much by surprise as many other people,' Gerwel told the Johannesburg *Sunday Times*.[24]

Most of Mandela's ANC colleagues from the prison years and the anti-apartheid struggle had died; he was one of the last survivors. Oliver Tambo, the former president of the ANC in exile, and Joe Slovo, the Communist Party leader in exile and close adviser to Mandela during the negotiating process, both died in the 1990s. But it was the passing of his closest friend, mentor and political coach, Walter Sisulu, at the age of ninety-one in May 2003, that brought home Mandela's mortality more than any other loss he suffered in the years after stepping down as President. Mandela declared that with Sisulu's death part of himself had died. 'His absence has carved a void. A part of me is gone,' Mandela said in a lengthy obituary to his friend and mentor. 'He held his own; he interacted with ease and without a trace of inferiority,' Mandela said. 'He was courageous and his quiet self-confidence and clarity of vision marked him out as a leader among us.'[25]

Although Sisulu had been ill for a long time and his death was not unexpected, Mandela found himself going into a period of reflection about his own life. 'In a sense I feel cheated by Walter. If there be another life beyond this physical world I would have loved to be there first so that I would welcome him,' he said. Mandela told me that Sisulu was 'almost like a saint' when it came to taking care of the needs of others.[26] 'I learned a great deal from him. He led from behind and put others in front. But he reversed the position in times of danger. Then he chose to be in the front line,' Mandela said.

Sisulu once said of Mandela that if he had a flaw, it was a tendency to trust people too much. 'He develops too much confidence in a person sometimes,' Sisulu observed; 'when he trusts a person, he goes all out.' But on reflection, he said, it was not perhaps a failing, because Mandela had never let down his colleagues or the movement as a result of the confidence that he placed in people.[27]

* * *

Mandela had achieved his core goals of liberating the country and leading a transition to democracy between the ages of seventy-one and eighty-one, when most people would be enjoying retirement and reflecting on their life's work. He had done so in the face of major threats to his health, including suspected prostate cancer in 1985 and severe tuberculosis in 1988, which raised fears that he may die in jail. In 2001 he was diagnosed with prostate cancer but responded well to radiation therapy and made a full recovery. Following his eighty-fifth birthday in 2003, Mandela continued to make appearances at the series of concerts for his '46664' charity and receive dignitaries at the Foundation offices in Johannesburg. But by 2004 he was becoming visibly more frail: he was white-haired and walked with the help of a stick. His sharp recall was not what it had been when he stepped down as President. In June he announced that he was 'retiring from retirement'. He did not intend to hide away totally from the public, he said, but quipped: 'Don't call me. I'll call you.'

The Foundation discouraged invitations for his appearance at public events and requests for interviews were seldom entertained. He still saw his close friends, such as his lawyer and confidant George Bizos, Archbishop Desmond Tutu, and his fellow prisoners from Robben Island, Ahmed Kathrada and Mac Maharaj, amongst others. And Mandela would meet periodically with the former head of his office in the presidency and chair of the Mandela Foundation, Jakes Gerwel, and billionaire Tokyo Sexwale, a former Robben Islander and trustee of the Foundation.

As Mandela's life followed a set routine he had less opportunity for the spontaneous incidents in which he revels, though he still managed to steal the odd mischievous interaction with the public. One such occasion was after boarding a flight to France from London following the unveiling of his statue in Parliament Square in the summer of 2007. En route to a celebrity fundraising gala for his Children's Fund in Monaco and a pep talk for the Springbok team for the 2007 Rugby World Cup final against England, he was hoisted in a wheelchair onto a scheduled flight before the rest of the passengers had boarded. Mandela was positioned at the entrance to the short-haul plane at the front of business class, meaning that each of the boarding passengers had to pass him on the way to their seat. The astonished passengers, some literally at a loss for words to be confronted by a living icon, greeted him as they passed. Mandela took obvious delight in being the centre of attention and made a point of shaking the hand of each one individually in his inimitable way.

Mandela has managed to retain his humanity, sense of humour and natural affinity with people despite his frailty. When pushed to explain in an interview in August 2005 by Professor Tim Couzens, historian at the University of the Witwatersrand, how he had acquired such a mischievous sense of humour, given the seriousness of his upbringing as a member of the Thembu royal family and almost three decades in jail, he explained: 'People want to forget about the painful experiences which they've had and when they meet somebody who helps them to forget about their past, at least for the moment when you are talking to them, people like that,' Mandela said. 'So we have learned from the countryside to make people happy by making jokes and making them forget about their painful experiences. It's very important.'[28]

One of Mandela's most enduring qualities is to make those in his presence feel completely relaxed and at ease. He has developed some close friendships with a variety of celebrities and members of royalty, such as Queen Elizabeth II and with the late Diana, Princess of Wales, whose charity work with landmine victims he deeply respected. Following his last visit to Britain in 2008, Mandela stayed at Buckingham Palace as a guest of the Queen. Mandela made no secret of the fact that he was on first-name terms with the Queen but insisted that they only addressed each other by their first names when alone together. However, several house guests at Mandela's home were astonished on separate occasions to hear him declare 'Hello, Elizabeth', when the telephone was brought to the dinner table. The next question was invariably 'How are the boys?', referring to princes William and Harry, the second and third heirs to the British throne.

Despite professing to take his retirement 'seriously', in 2004 Mandela threw himself into campaigning for South Africa to host the 2010 FIFA World Cup, showing the sort of enthusiasm he had displayed towards the mainly white national rugby team in 1995. Mandela firmly believed that shared moments of triumph in sport were key to achieving reconciliation between black and white and forging in South Africa a common identity. South Africa had narrowly lost out to Germany in its bid for the 2006 World Cup; in May 2004 South Africa was taking no chances and put Mandela at the centre of its campaign. 'There could be few better gifts for us in the year of our celebration [on the tenth anniversary of the end of apartheid] than to be awarded the 2010 World Cup,' Mandela declared. In 1976 FIFA had suspended South Africa from the game in response to the apartheid state's bloody crackdown on the Soweto student uprising. FIFA President Joseph Blatter had no doubt that it was Mandela's stature and presence that had clinched the deal for 2010. 'You are the true architect of this FIFA World Cup,' Blatter told Mandela. 'Your presence and your commitment made it happen.'

In July 2007 Mandela embraced an idea proposed by the entrepreneur Richard Branson and the musician Peter Gabriel to form an independent group of former world leaders to promote world peace efforts. The Elders was launched on Mandela's eighty-ninth birthday as 'twelve wise men and women' with a remit to address global problems by offering their expertise and guidance, and included Desmond Tutu, former US President Jimmy Carter, former Irish President Mary Robinson and former UN Secretary-General Kofi Annan.* 'This group derives its strength not from military, political or economic power,' Mandela declared, 'but from the independence and integrity of those who are here.' All twelve members attended the Council of Elders' launch with founders Mandela and Graca Machel in Johannesburg in July 2007. Burmese Freedom fighter Aung San Su Kyi, released from detention in November 2010, was later named an honorary patron alongside Mandela. Over the years, the Elders have discussed and sent delegations to Zimbabwe,

* The other members of the Elders are: the former Brazilian President Fernando Cardoso; India's revolutionary development worker Ela Bhatt; Gro Brundtland, former Prime Minister of Norway; Nobel Peace laureate and former President of Finland Martti Ahtisaari; international peace envoy and former foreign minister of Algeria Lakhdar Brahimi; Graca Machel and the Nobel laureate economist and founder of the Green Bank in Bangladesh, Muhammad Yunus (who later withdrew).

Cyprus, the Sudan, Ivory Coast, Palestine and Myanmar, with varying, mainly modest, degrees of success.

While the former leader became physically weaker and more vulnerable, his legacy was increasingly evident as a fresh wave of events, artworks, books and films about Mandela's life, message and philosophy was launched ahead of the twentieth anniversary of his release from prison. In 2009 the Hollywood film *Invictus* (named after one of Mandela's favourite poems and by the English poet W. E. Henley) depicted Mandela's extraordinary orchestration of the South African victory in the 1995 Rugby World Cup, and saw Morgan Freeman play Mandela and Matt Damon in the role of Francois Pienaar, the Springbok rugby captain whose life was transformed by Mandela's support. In November 2009 the United Nations General Assembly declared 18 July, Mandela's birthday, 'Nelson Mandela International Day' 'in recognition of the former South African President's contribution to the culture of peace and freedom'.

When in January 2009 President Barack Obama was inaugurated as the first black President of the United States many saw it as the symbolic closing of a circle that had begun with slavery: the institutionalised form of racism could be said to have ended with the civil rights struggle in America and finally with the overthrow of apartheid in South Africa. In his foreword to Mandela's collection of writings and interviews, *Conversations with Myself*, President Obama said that long before they met, he had been inspired by the sense of possibility that Mandela's life demonstrated and awed by the sacrifices necessary to achieve his dream of justice and equality. 'Even when faced with the temptation to seek revenge, he saw the need for reconciliation and the triumph of principle over power,' Obama wrote.

It was fitting that the US law which still humiliated ANC leaders visiting America long after apartheid ended and democratic government installed was finally removed before Obama took his oath of office in January 2009. The law, introduced during the Reagan years, designated the ANC as a terrorist organisation and classified ANC leaders who had a conviction against them for terrorism, sabotage or treason as unwelcome visitors who would be stopped by immigration officials and interrogated unless they had applied for waiver in their country of origin. That definition under the law included Mandela and his senior colleagues. The law remained in force until April 2008 when the Berman Bill finally removed Mandela and his ANC colleagues from the watch lists. It was the moment at which the ANC finally became *kosher* in Washington – fourteen years after Mandela had been sworn in as the first black President of South Africa.

Mandela has already, during his lifetime, been immortalised in a number of sculptures and artworks around the world, including a larger-than-life statue outside the Drakenstein Prison (formerly Victor Verster) in Paarl near Cape Town, and a towering statue in Johannesburg's shopping centre at Sandton City. There is also a giant bust of Mandela at the Royal Festival Hall on London's Southbank and a nine-foot bronze in Parliament Square, facing the Houses of Parliament. The inner square is home to statues of British prime ministers spanning more than a century, with two exceptions: one of those is the former South African Prime Minister, General Jan Smuts, a close confidant of Winston Churchill and a co-founder of the League of Nations. The other is that of Nelson Mandela, in his own lifetime. While the somewhat light-hearted pose of the statue had come in for some criticism, the historic honour of its position is beyond debate. Abraham Lincoln looks on from across the street.

Mandela attended the unveiling of the statue in August 2007. As the eighty-nine-year-old former President rose to address the crowd, flanked by Graca Machel and Zelda La Grange, there was an audible sigh of relief as it quickly became clear that this was a return of the 'old Madiba'. Mandela found his prior form and authoritative voice as he was propelled by the history of the occasion to deliver a *tour de force*. Reading from a prepared speech he reminded the invited guests and celebrities that while he was underground in 1962 following a period in jail, he and Oliver Tambo had visited Westminster Abbey and Parliament Square. 'We half joked that we hoped that one day a statue of a black person would be erected here alongside that of General Smuts. Oliver would have been proud today if he had been here,' Mandela said to applause and cheering from the crowd.

As the twentieth anniversary of Mandela's freedom dawned, he made another rare public appearance and received a hero's welcome at the state opening of the South African Parliament, which he had helped transform twenty years earlier when he emerged from a prison warder's house near Cape Town a free and reconciled man. The theme for the 2010 parliamentary session was 'Celebrate the Legacy of Mandela – Contribute to Nation Building'. But the reality that prevailed was a far cry from the atmosphere of hope and expectation which had accompanied the opening of the first democratic Parliament in 1994. A deeply divided ruling party, regular service delivery protests in black neighbourhoods around the country, power outages and consistently high unemployment levels had detracted from the ANC's notable achievements in providing clean water, electricity and houses to millions of South Africans since the end of apartheid.

The year of the twentieth anniversary witnessed unprecedented focus and interest in Mandela's historic achievements and allowed South Africans to pay their respects for what many believed might be the last time in public. 'Let us pursue the ideal for which Madiba fought his entire life – the ideal of a democratic and free society in which all persons live together in harmony and with equal opportunities,' President Zuma said in his state of the nation speech. He then quoted Mandela's famous statement from the dock in the 1964 trial, in which he was sentenced to life imprisonment and in which he dedicated himself to fight against both white domination and black domination for a society based on equal opportunity. 'It is an ideal which I hope to live for,' Mandela said. 'But if needs be it is an ideal for which I am prepared to die.'

In the transition from the Mandela period to the Mbeki Government, the focus on Mandela's core values of reconciliation and inclusivity as guiding principles in the process of democratic transformation receded from the mainstream of public discourse and were replaced increasingly with a more thinly veiled racial dialogue which prioritised the need to replace white civil servants with black ones. The essence of Mandela's statement from the dock at the Rivonia trial faded as the clamour for wealth and status increased.

There were echoes of this Rivonia speech months later in a surprise intervention by Trevor Manuel, who served as Finance Minister under both Mandela and Mbeki and won widespread international praise for South Africa's macro-economic management and integration into the global economy. Mandela had singled Manuel out early in his presidency as one of the younger generation leaders of the ANC from the contested mixed-race 'coloured' community who should be nurtured as a future leader and he was one of five cabinet ministers of the Mbeki era who made it into the Zuma government. In March 2011 Manuel launched a blistering attack on a senior black official, Jimmy Manyi, appointed by Zuma to run government communications and act as the Cabinet's chief spokesman. Manyi, who had been pushed out as the chief official in the labour ministry, was an outspoken advocate of pro-black policies and questioned the broader definition of 'black' to include mixed-race 'coloured' and Indian South Africans. Manuel seized on a remark made by Manyi in an interview several months earlier in which he said that there was an 'oversupply of coloureds' in the Western Cape Province. The Western Cape Province is the only one of nine provinces in South Africa which is ruled by the opposition Democratic Party and the vote of the populous coloured community, more affluent than the black African community, is fiercely contested. Manuel, in a move which was not canvassed with the ANC leadership, accused Manyi of being a racist in the mould of the white architect of apartheid, Hendrik Verwoerd. He questioned where Manyi was during the liberation struggle and he cited Mandela's famous statement from the dock at the Rivonia treason trial and said that Mandela had been referring to people like Manyi when he said that he had fought against black domination.

Manuel at first appeared isolated within the ranks of his own party and the leadership distanced itself from his statement. But when an overzealous official launched a counterattack on Manuel, he was suspended from his post. There was much sympathy in the wider society for Manuel's sentiments. Manuel's marker could form the basis for a future political realignment which would see a new coalition of forces gathering around Mandela's values and a society ordered more on loyalty to these values than a return to race as a criterion for advancement, which dominated the country's political dynamics during the four decades of apartheid and some feel could be returning in the spirit if not in the letter of the law. The outcome of the May 2011 municipal elections, in which Mandela cast a special vote from his Johannesburg home, hinted at a possible step in this direction. Although the ruling ANC won more than 60 per cent of the vote, the election produced a modest reduction in its share of national vote at the expense of smaller parties and a significant increase in support for the Democratic Alliance of Helen Zille, premier of the Western Cape and the only political leader heading a non-ANC government.

Mandela always appeared to be aware that the momentous change that he had precipitated in the country in 1994 was a turning point in history and that dealing with the legacy of the past was going to be a long-term project. But what about his own legacy? At a political level, it is intensely practical. It is about clear principles, faith in what you believe in, a clear sense of what is right and wrong and the need for reconciliation and forgiveness as a viable means of achieving one's goals. It is unmistakeably founded in a deep-seated conviction about the importance of inclusivity, accountability and freedom of speech as the fundamentals of democracy.

In 2010 it was only an avalanche of international and domestic condemnation that finally persuaded the ANC to shelve plans for a government-controlled media tribunal to curb the media and regulate its criticism of government. In the same year, an innocuous-sounding Information Bill had to be repeatedly amended and resubmitted to Parliament to prevent it becoming a draconian secrecy measure which would enable government to shield itself from overzealous media scrutiny. There is little doubt that had Mandela still been leader of the ANC he would have resisted these measures. 'The media is the cornerstone and ground plan for democracy,' Mandela told me in 2002. 'Sometimes journalists say things about us that we don't like. But what hurts me is not the fabrications, but when I know that what they are saying about me and my country are correct.' His firm belief in freedom of expression is based on an equally strong conviction that leaders must be accountable to their organisations and to the people who elect them. 'I want people who are going to criticise me so that when we go out we have looked at the matter from all angles and we have the maximum support of our people, including those who had reservations,' he told me. 'If we take exception to the extent of stifling the freedom of the press to express itself, then we are killing democracy.'

Mandela has received mainly positive coverage in the media commensurate with the impact of his leadership and key role in South Africa's transition from apartheid to democracy. However there have been times when he has been at the receiving end of investigative articles examining statements he has made or initiatives being pursued in his name. In 2006 the American magazine *The New Republic* published a lengthy report in which Mandela was criticised for his comments on the diamond industry, which it was argued could benefit the cause of 'blood diamonds' emanating from conflict areas in Africa. Mandela had written to Edward Zwick, the director of the film *Blood Diamond*, and said that it would be an unfortunate outcome if the film led the world to believe that the solution might be to cease buying diamonds from Africa. The magazine argued that Mandela's comments, which coincided with industry campaigns to counter the negative impact of the film, were influenced by his friendship with the late Harry Oppenheimer, former chairman of De Beers, and by narrow national South African interests.

In 2010 a former CEO of the Nelson Mandela Children's Fund, Jeremy Ractliffe, stepped down from the Fund after being the subject of a criminal investigation: he had admitted that he was in possession of three uncut diamonds given to him thirteen years earlier by the celebrity model Naomi Campbell. Ractliffe was later acquited by a South African court of being in illegal possession of uncut diamonds. Campbell in turn claimed she had been given the diamonds as a gift by the deposed Liberian President Charles Taylor after a celebrity dinner hosted by Mandela at the presidential residence in Pretoria in 1997, at which Taylor and Campbell had both been guests. Campbell was subpoenaed to give evidence at Charles Taylor's high-profile war crimes trial in Holland, which sought to prove that he had profited from the sale of blood diamonds from Sierra Leone.

Other aspects of his legacy have been mired in controversy in recent years as Mandela, the various foundations and charities in his name, his lawyers and members of his family, have contested certain initiatives. The first cracks appeared in 2005 when Mandela sued Ismail Ayob, the attorney who had represented him throughout his prison years, for marketing and selling artworks – simple watercolours of Robben Island prison and an imprint of Mandela's hand bearing his signature. It was alleged that some of the paintings had been signed by a sophisticated autograph machine imported by Ayob's business partner and that not all the proceeds of the sales of the paintings had ended up with the charities earmarked to benefit from their sale. An exchange of legal letters followed in which Ayob and his partner denied acting unlawfully and in breach of Mandela's copyright and intellectual property rights. Ayob responded that he had never sold any prints nor was a partner of anyone selling prints and declared that he was a victim of a smear campaign. The matter was eventually settled in an out-of-court agreement.

The Nelson Mandela Foundation's Centre of Memory, meanwhile, often found itself at pains to strike a balance between acting as a gatekeeper and sole arbiter of the Mandela brand on the one hand, and custodian and protector of the Mandela legacy on the other. The Foundation has had to intervene repeatedly to prevent the exploitation of the Mandela brand for financial gain or to enhance the reputation and credibility of certain leaders and public figures. The most recent of these was the public spat in 2009 between the Foundation and President Denis Sassou-Nguesso of the Republic of Congo, in relation to flattering comments about the President included as a 'foreword' in a book about Sassou-Nguesso and attributed to Mandela. The Foundation initially denied that Mandela had penned the tribute, although the South African Government later confirmed that Mandela had described Sassou-Nguesso as a 'great African leader' in a speech given in 1996. It was words from that speech that had been used in the foreword. The Foundation continues to state that there is no archival record of this speech.

One of the most difficult parts of Mandela's legacy, often outside his control, has been the divided nature of Mandela's extended family. Tensions came to the fore with the tug-of-war over whether Mandela should attend the ANC election rally in 2009 after the Mandela Foundation indicated that he would not be taking an active role in the election run-up. On other occasions Mandela's former wife, Winnie, and his strong-willed grandson, Chief Mandla Mandela, have vied with each other to speak in Mandela's name. There was a row between Mandla and other members of the family over whether Mandela should attend the opening of the 2010 World Cup in Johannesburg. In the end, Mandela did not go: the tragic death of his great-granddaughter, Zenani, was given as his reason for his non-attendance. Mandela did, however, make a surprise appearance in a motor-drawn chariot at the closing ceremony. Graca assisted in lifting his arm to wave at the crowds as she had done back in 2008 when he attended a gala concert in London's Hyde Park to mark his ninetieth birthday.

In February 2011, at the age of ninety-two, Mandela's contracting of a respiratory infection made headlines worldwide when he was admitted to intensive care. Mandela rallied and returned home after several days in hospital, but during this time there were internal family disputes as to whether Mandela should be treated at a state military hospital in Pretoria or a private hospital in Johannesburg. The Zuma government was caught inevitably in the crossfire but was also widely criticised for the poor communication around the Mandela illness. The Mandela Foundation was stung by criticism in the media that it had misled the public by insisting that Mandela had merely been admitted to hospital for 'routine checks'. The deputy President, Kgalema Motlanthe, eventually stepped in to reassure the public that Mandela was in fact making a good recovery.

Although Mandela did not appear in public to mark the twenty-first anniversary of his release or attend the state opening of South Africa's Parliament in February 2011, his daughter Zindzi revealed that there was one particular item in his diary he was looking forward to. Mandela has always been an avid boxing fan and would be watching the Filipino boxer Manny Pacquiao's world title defence against the American Shane Mosley. 'My father is still very much aware of who the fighters are,' Zindzi said at a press conference; he 'sits up to watch a fight and he still loves the sport with a passion.'[29]

* * *

In a wide-ranging interview in February 2000, Mandela spoke frankly to me about how his experience in prison had shaped him and enabled him to change himself. He insisted that when it came to his legacy he was not able to control how future generations would see him. 'I would like to be remembered as part of a team, and I would like my contribution to be assessed as somebody who carried out decisions taken by that collective,' he said, adding that even if he wanted to be remembered in a specific way that was not a realistic option. 'As prisoners, we used our individual and collective positions to make friends with some of our jailers. But this must be understood against the bigger picture of what was happening outside – an organised and disciplined struggle by our organisation and the international community,' he said.

The key to understanding Mandela and his major role in initiating and overseeing the process that led to the liberation of South Africa, and the most enduring example of leadership and affirmation of human dignity in the face of racial oppression, lies in the transformation he underwent during almost three decades in jail. 'It is possible that if I had not gone to jail and been able to read and listen to the stories of many people … I might not have learned these things,' Mandela said of the insights that he gained during his imprisonment. Reading the biographies of great leaders who had been able to overcome their shortcomings and rise to do great things had inspired him. It also helped him to understand that behind every seemingly 'ordinary' person lay the potential of greatness. 'I have been surprised a great deal sometimes when I see somebody who looks less than ordinary, but when you talk to the person and they open their mouths, they are something completely different,' he explained.

Mandela said he had learned that when you had the moral high ground, it was better to sit down and talk to people and persuade them of the correctness of your cause. 'If you have an objective in life, then you want to concentrate on that and not engage in infighting with your enemies,' he said. 'You want to create an atmosphere where you can move everybody towards the goal you have set for yourself – as well as the collective for which you work. And, therefore, for all people who have found themselves in the position of being in jail and trying to transform society, forgiveness is natural because you have no time to be retaliative ... You want to mobilise everybody to support your cause and the aims you have set for your life.'[30]

In December 1999 Mandela addressed a gathering of religious leaders from the world's major faiths in Cape Town and spoke publicly about his views on religion for the first time. Though he had attended a mission school and was brought up as a Methodist, he had never broached the subject of religion or discussed his own religious views. 'I appreciate the importance of religion. You have to have been in a South African jail under apartheid where you can see the cruelty of human beings to each other in its naked form. But it was again religious institutions, Hindus, Moslems, leaders of the Jewish faith, Christians, it was them who gave us the hope that one day we would come out. We would return. And in prisons, the religious institutions raised funds for our children who were arrested in thousands and thrown into jail.'[31]

Real leaders, he said, were those who thought about the poor twenty-four hours a day and who knew in their hearts that poverty was the single biggest threat to society. 'We have sufficient cause to be cynical about humanity. We have seen enough injustice, strife, division, suffering, and pain, and our capacity to be massively inhuman. But this gathering counters despairing cynicism and reaffirms the nobility of the human spirit,' Mandela continued. 'Religion is one of the most important forces in the world. Whether you are a Christian, a Muslim, a Buddhist, a Jew, or a Hindu, religion is a great force, and it can help one have command of one's own morality, one's own behaviour, and one's own attitude.'

Mandela has also spoken increasingly about the importance of looking at oneself. In conversations with Verne Harris of the Foundation's Centre of Memory he has talked about his inner life and thoughts. Mandela, Harris says, felt an enormous 'burden of responsibility' when the ANC decided to use him as a symbol of the liberation struggle while he was still in prison. From that point everything that Mandela did in his private life impacted on his public representation. Mandela was acutely aware that he had contributed to creating the iconic image of himself and felt uncomfortable about having done so. One of Mandela's strongest attributes was that he understood the power of the image. 'He was also aware that you pay a price: the human being that you are starts to lose connections with that public representation.'[32]

Mandela has gone to some lengths during his retirement to acknowledge weaknesses and shortcomings in his own life, in his personal relationships with women, and with his immediate and extended family. 'One of the most difficult things is not to change society – but to change yourself,' Mandela said on the eve of retirement from the presidency. He gave similar advice to his wife Winnie in a letter in 1981, after she had been jailed by the apartheid regime. Ultimately Mandela's greatest achievement was that he changed himself fundamentally in the prison years and in doing so he changed South Africa, and the world, forever.

20 June 2011

SOURCE NOTES

CHAPTER 1 Country Boy: 1918–1934

1 R.S. Conco, letter to Mandela, 27 Jul. 1987
2 Mandela to Richard Stengel, 1994
3 Mabel Mandela, interview for Joe Menell and Angus Gibson, *Mandela* (film), 1994
4 Mandela to Richard Stengel
5 Mabel Mandela, interview for Menell and Gibson, *Mandela* (film); Fatima Meer, *Higher than Hope*, p.4
6 Mandela, interview with author, 8 Aug. 1997
7 Mandela, Jail Memoir (unpublished)
8 Mabel Mandela, interview for Menell and Gibson, *Mandela* (film)
9 Jail Memoir
10 Meer, op. cit., p.7
11 Mabel Mandela, interview for Menell and Gibson, Mandela (film); Heidi Holland, *The Struggle: A History of the African National Congress*, pp.13–14
12 Mabel Mandela, interview for Menell and Gibson, *Mandela* (film)
13 Jail Memoir
14 Clive Menell, Memoir (unpublished)
15 Archbishop Desmond Tutu (ed. John Allen), *The Rainbow People of God*, p.122
16 Mandela, interview with author, 8 Aug. 1997
17 Mandela, *Long Walk to Freedom*, p.27
18 Mandela, *The Struggle is my Life*, p.141
19 Frank Welsh, *A History of South Africa*, pp.74–5, 503
20 Noel Mostert, *Frontiers*, pp.203, 716
21 J.B. Peires, *The House of Phalo*, p.166
22 Mostert, op. cit., pp.1222, 1254, 1237
23 Mandela, interview for Menell and Gibson, *Mandela* (film)
24 J.A. Froude, *Lord Beaconsfield*
25 Z.K. Matthews, *Freedom for my People*, p.58
26 Mandela, interview for Menell and Gibson, *Mandela* (film)

CHAPTER 2 Mission Boy: 1934–1940

1 *Long Walk*, pp.31–2
2 Mandela, interview for Menell and Gibson, *Mandela* (film)
3 *Long Walk*, pp.34–5
4 Jail Memoir
5 Rev. Arthur J. Leonard, *A Brief History of Clarkebury*
6 Nosipho Majeke, *The Role of Missionaries in Conquest*, pp.34–5
7 Leonard Thompson, *A History of South Africa*, p.172
8 *Independent*, 29 Apr. 1993
9 Mandela, speech to the Oxford Centre for Islamic Studies, 11 Jul. 1997
10 Fikile Bam, interview with author, 30 Jul. 1997
11 Jail Memoir
12 Rector H.M. Nyali, Clarkebury, interview with author, 11 Mar. 1997
13 Jail Memoir
14 Mandela, interview for Menell and Gibson, *Mandela* (film)
15 Mavis Knipe, interview with author, 2 Feb. 1998
16 Mandela, letter to M. Knipe, undated
17 Mandela, speech at Clarkebury, 19 Nov. 1993
18 Jail Memoir
19 *Long Walk*, p.42
20 *Healdtown, 1855–1955: Centenary Brochure*
21 Phyllis Ntantala, *A Life's Mosaic*, p.66; Jack Dugard, 'Fragments of my Fleece' (unpublished)
22 Enid Webster, interview with author, 19 Feb. 1998; Leslie Hewson, 'Healdtown' (unpublished thesis)

23 Rev. A.A. Wellington, letter to Rev. George Ayre (London), 5 Feb. 1936 (Methodist Archive, School of Oriental and African Studies, University of London)
24 Dugard, op. cit.
25 Mandela, letter to Dr Michael Kelly, 1980
26 Mandela, letter to Kepu Mkentane, 25 Feb. 1987
27 Mandela to Richard Stengel
28 Jail Memoir
29 Ntantala, op. cit., p.67
30 Dugard, op. cit.
31 Ntantala, op. cit., p.66
32 Jail Memoir
33 Dugard, op. cit.
34 Mandela, interview for Menell and Gibson, *Mandela* (film)
35 Dugard, op. cit.
36 Mqhayi (trans. Robert Kavanagh), 'The Prince of Britain' (1925), in *The Making of a Servant and Other Poems*, pp.14–16
37 Meer, op. cit., p.9
38 Margery Perham, *African Apprenticeship*, p.44
39 Alexander Kerr, *Fort Hare, 1915–1948*, p.217
40 Z.K. Matthews, op. cit., p.62
41 *A Short Pictorial History of the University College of Fort Hare, 1916–1959*
42 Z.K. Matthews, op. cit., p.82
43 Kerr, op. cit., p.31; Z.K. Matthews, op. cit., pp.119–21
44 Mandela, interview for Menell and Gibson, *Mandela* (film)
45 Noni Jabavu, *The Ochre People*, pp.21–8
46 Z.K. Matthews, op. cit., pp.230, 54, citing Mandela, letter to Frieda Matthews, 1 Oct. 1970
47 Alfred Tennyson, 'In Memoriam A.H.H.', *The Poems of Tennyson* (ed. Christopher Ricks), pp.861–2
48 Ralph Bunche (ed. Robert R. Edgar), *An African-American in South Africa: The Travel Notes of Ralph J. Bunche*, p.126
49 Kaiser Matanzima, interview with author, 12 Mar. 1997
50 Meer, op. cit., p.9
51 Matanzima, interview with author, 12 Mar. 1997
52 Mandela, letter to Fatima Meer, 25 Feb. 1985
53 Joe Matthews, interview with author, 5 Aug. 1997
54 Mandela, letter to F. Matthews, 1985; Frieda Matthews, *Remembrances*, p.100
55 Mandela, letter to Winnie Mandela, 2 Sept. 1979
56 Jabavu, op. cit., p.90
57 *Long Walk*, p.55; Godfrey Pitje, interview for Menell and Gibson, *Mandela* (film)
58 Jail Memoir
59 South African Native College, 'Report of the Governing Council for the Year Ending 31 December 1940'
60 Govan Mbeki, *Student Politics at Fort Hare, 1916–1959*
61 *Long Walk*, p.58
62 Mary Soames, conversation with author, 25 Jul. 1997
63 Jail Memoir
64 Mandela, interview for Menell and Gibson, *Mandela* (film)
65 *Long Walk*, p.61
66 Meer, op. cit., p.9
67 James Kantor, *A Healthy Grave*, p.145; *Long Walk*, p.64
68 Jail Memoir

CHAPTER 3 Big City: 1941–1945

1 Alan Paton, *Cry, the Beloved Country*; Peter Davis, *In Darkest Hollywood: Exploring the Jungle of Cinema's South Africa*, pp.21–31, 38–47
2 W.K. Hancock, *Smuts: The Fields of Force, 1919–1950*, pp.479, 475–6, 488, citing Smuts, speech to the Institute of Race Relations, Cape Town, Feb. 1942
3 *Long Walk*, pp.74–5
4 Anthony Sampson, *Drum*, pp.32–3
5 Mary Benson, *South Africa: The Struggle for a Birthright*, pp.97–8
6 Mandela to Richard Stengel
7 Walter Sisulu, interview with author, 29 Nov. 1995

SOURCE NOTES

8 Meer, op. cit., p.29
9 Walter Sisulu, interview with George Houser and Herbert Shore, Sept.–Oct. 1995
10 Sampson, *The Treason Cage*, pp.156–9
11 Sisulu, interview with Houser and Shore, op. cit.
12 Sisulu, interview with author, 29 Nov. 1995
13 Kantor, op. cit., p.145
14 Lazar Sidelsky, interview with author, 23 Oct. 1996, citing Mandela, inscription in a book (14 Jan. 1995)
15 Martin Meredith, *Mandela: A Biography*, p.36
16 Tom Lodge, *Black Politics in South Africa Since 1945*, p.19
17 Jail Memoir
18 T. Dunbar Moodie, 'The Moral Economy of the Black Miners' Strike of 1946', *Journal of Southern African Studies*, Vol.13, No.1, Oct. 1986, p.15
19 Michael Dingake, *My Fight Against Apartheid*, p.56
20 Jail Memoir
21 Mandela to Richard Stengel
22 Mandela, letter to Zindzi Mandela, 1 Mar. 1981
23 Jail Memoir
24 *Long Walk*, pp.103, 89, 104
25 Frank Diamond, *Portrait of Mandela* (film for IDAF), 1980
26 Joe Slovo, interview for Menell and Gibson, *Mandela* (film)
27 Ismail Meer, interview for Menell and Gibson, *Mandela* (film)
28 [Johannesburg] *Sunday Times*, 10 Nov. 1996
29 Bruce Murray, *Wits: The Open Years*, pp.54, 56
30 George Bizos, interview with author, 22 Oct. 1996
31 [Johannesburg] *Sunday Times*, 10 Nov. 1996
32 *Long Walk*, p.105
33 [Johannesburg] *Sunday Times*, 10 Nov. 1996
34 Mandela, interview with author, 29 Nov. 1995
35 Sisulu, letter to author, 7 Oct. 1957
36 Albertina Sisulu, interview for Menell and Gibson, *Mandela* (film)
37 Es'kia Mphahlele, conversation with author, 16 Mar. 1997
38 Meer, op. cit., p.40
39 Mandela to Richard Stengel
40 Evelyn Mandela, interview with author, 24 Feb. 1997
41 Leabie Piliso, interview for Menell and Gibson, *Mandela* (film)
42 Phyllis P. Jordan (Ntantala), letter to F. Meer, 1989
43 Adelaide Tambo, interview with author, 13 Feb. 1997
44 Meer, op. cit., p.41
45 Sisulu, interview with author, 29 Nov. 1995
46 *Long Walk*, p.100
47 *Treason Cage*, p.46
48 Treason Trial transcript, p.15,766
49 *Treason Cage*, p.68
50 Dr Xuma, extracts from 'Autobiography', *Africa*, Dec. 1954
51 *Treason Cage*, p.71
52 *Long Walk*, p.111
53 Sampson, *Black and Gold: Tycoons, Revolutionaries and Apartheid*, p.75
54 *Treason Cage*, p.75
55 Mandela to Richard Stengel
56 A.P. Mda, interview with Gail Gerhart, 1 Jan. 1970
57 Martin Gilbert, *Finest Hour: Winston S. Churchill, 1939–1941*, p.1163
58 *Treason Cage*, p.160
59 Thomas Karis and Gwendolen M. Carter, *From Protest to Challenge, Vol.2: Hope and Challenge, 1935–1952*, by Thomas Karis, p.212
60 Meer, op. cit., pp.32–3
61 Karis and Carter, Vol.2, op. cit., p.401
62 *Treason Cage*, p.76
63 Karis and Carter, Vol.2, op. cit., pp.301–9
64 Treason Trial transcript, pp.15,762, 15,764
65 Lodge, op. cit., p.28
66 *The Struggle is my Life*, p.169; Rivonia speech, 20 April 1994
67 James Calata, comments on *The Treason Cage* in letter to author, 21 Jul. 1957

68 Brian Bunting, *Moses Kotane*, pp.138–9
69 Mda, interview with Gerhart, op. cit.
70 Govan Mbeki, interview with author, 15 Feb. 1996
71 Eric Hobsbawm, conversation with author, 28 April 1997

CHAPTER 4 Afrikaners *v.* Africans: 1946–1949

1 Moodie, op. cit.; Lodge, op. cit., pp.19–20
2 Benson, *South Africa*, pp.99–100
3 *Treason Cage*, p.78
4 *Long Walk*, p.118
5 Hancock, op. cit., p.485
6 Karis and Carter, Vol.2, op. cit., pp.236, 243, 253–5
7 For a comprehensive study of Indians in Natal, see Bill Freund, *Insiders and Outsiders: The Indian Working Class of Durban, 1910–1990*
8 Mandela, letter to F. Meer, 29 Jun. 1983
9 Ismail Meer, conversation with author, 6 Oct. 1997
10 Mandela, interview with author, 8 Aug. 1997
11 Jail Memoir
12 Kader Asmal, conversation with author, 19 Mar. 1997
13 *The Struggle is my Life*, p.169; Rivonia speech, 20 Apr. 1964
14 Lodge, op. cit., p.20
15 Enuga Reddy and Fatima Meer (eds), *Passive Resistance 1946: A Selection of Documents*, p.27
16 Mandela, letter to Mrs Bhalla (Indian Council for Cultural Relations), 3 Aug. 1980. In a postscript to the letter, Mandela notes that during December 1980 he had discovered that the Department of Prisons had failed to dispatch the letter because of its contents. He adds: 'For this reason I decided to use my own channels of reaching you.'
17 Meer, op. cit., p.43
18 Mandela to Richard Stengel
19 Mda, interview with Gerhart, op. cit.
20 Meer, op. cit., p.43
21 D.H. Darling, letter to Oliver Tambo, 27 May 1948
22 Karis and Carter, Vol.2, op. cit., p.323
23 T.R.H. White, 'Z.K. Matthews and the Formation of the ANC Youth League', *Kleio*, No.XXVII, 1995
24 Brian Lapping, *Apartheid: A History* (television documentary, 1986, directed by John Blake)
25 Karis and Carter, Vol.2, op. cit., p.329
26 *Long Walk*, p.124
27 Bunting, op. cit., pp.153–6
28 Sisulu, interview with author, 29 Nov. 1995
29 Bunting, op. cit., pp.138–9
30 Mandela, speech to ANC Conference, Mafikeng, 20 Dec. 1997
31 *Long Walk*, p.126
32 Jail Memoir
33 Karis and Carter, Vol.2, op. cit., p.362
34 Mandela to Richard Stengel
35 Jail Memoir
36 Karis and Carter, Vol.2, op. cit., p.368
37 Jail Memoir
38 Ben Pimlott, *The Queen*, p.111
39 Meredith, op. cit., p.67
40 Charles Douglas-Home, *Evelyn Baring: The Last Proconsul*, p.153; Mandela, interview with author, 24 Feb. 1997
41 [Cape Town] *Guardian*, 20 Feb. 1947
42 Mandela, interview with author, 24 Feb. 1997
43 Karis and Carter, Vol.2, op. cit., p.274
44 Esme Matshikiza, conversation with author, 10 Oct. 1996
45 Dan O'Meara, *Forty Lost Years: The Apartheid State and the Politics of the National Party, 1948–1994*, pp.40–57; Sampson, *Macmillan: A Study in Ambiguity*, p.186
46 Mandela, *Nelson Mandela Speaks: Forging a Democratic, Nonracial South Africa*, p. 76
47 Douglas-Home, op. cit., p.160
48 *Economist*, 5 Jun. 1948
49 *Long Walk*, p.128

50 *The Struggle is my Life*, pp.87–8; Treason Trial testimony, 1960
51 Karis and Carter, Vol.2, op. cit., pp.370–6
52 Mandela to Richard Stengel
53 Mandela, letter to Marie Naicker, 1978
54 Ahmed Kathrada, interview with author, 27 Nov. 1995
55 Mda, interview with Gerhart, op. cit.
56 Mandela to Richard Stengel
57 *Long Walk*, pp.131–2
58 Karis and Carter, Vol.2, op. cit., p.337
59 Meer, op. cit., p.48
60 [Bloemfontein] *Friend*, 17 Dec. 1949
61 Meer, op. cit., p.48
62 *Bantu World*, 1 April 1950
63 Benson, *South Africa: The Struggle for a Birthright*, p.129
64 Sisulu, interview with author, 29 Nov. 1995
65 Treason Trial transcript, p.15,775
66 F. Matthews, op. cit., p.46

CHAPTER 5 Nationalists *v.* Communists: 1950–1951

1 Les Switzer (ed.), *South Africa's Alternative Press: Voices of Protest and Resistance, 1880–1960*, p.254; see also Tim Couzens, *The New African: A Study of the Life and Work of H.I.E. Dhlomo*
2 Can Themba (ed. Essop Patel), *The World of Can Themba*; Nat Nakasa (ed. Essop Patel), *The World of Nat Nakasa*; Ezekiel Mphahlele, *Down Second Avenue*; Bloke Modisane, *Blame me on History*; Casey 'Kid' Motsisi (ed. Mothobi Mutloatse), *Casey and Company*; Peter Abrahams, *Return to Goli*; Todd Matshikiza, *Chocolates for my Wife*; Don Mattera, *Memory is the Weapon*
3 See *Drum*, op. cit.; Couzens, op. cit.
4 C.W. de Kiewiet, *The Anatomy of South African Misery*, p.37
5 Lewis Nkosi, *Home and Exile*, p.25
6 *Drum*, op. cit., p.233
7 Joe Matthews, interview for Menell and Gibson, *Mandela* (film)
8 Kathrada, interview with author, 7 Feb. 1997
9 Nthato Motlana, interview for Menell and Gibson, *Mandela* (film)
10 J. Matthews, interview for Menell and Gibson, *Mandela* (film)
11 The print shop is the subject of a short story by Nadine Gordimer, 'Which New Era Would That Be?', in *Six Feet of the Country*, 1958
12 [Johannesburg] *Sunday Times*, 29 Nov. 1992
13 *Long Walk*, p.207
14 Benson, *Nelson Mandela*, p.25
15 Karis and Carter, Vol.2, op. cit., pp.452–8
16 Benson, *South Africa*, p.130
17 Joe Slovo, *The Unfinished Autobiography*, p.52
18 Kathrada, interview with author, 7 Feb. 1997
19 Rusty Bernstein, 'Memory Against Forgetting' (unpublished manuscript)
20 Mandela, speech to South African Parliament, 7 Feb. 1997
21 *Long Walk*, p.134; Karis and Carter, Vol.2, op. cit., p.454
22 Benson, Nelson Mandela, pp.25–6
23 Jail Memoir
24 *Long Walk*, pp.134–5; Jail Memoir
25 Karis and Carter, Vol.2, op. cit., p.409
26 *Long Walk*, p.135
27 Modisane, op. cit., pp.141–4
28 Jack and Ray Simons, *Class and Colour in South Africa*, 1850–1960, p.606
29 Slovo, op. cit., p.51
30 Rusty Bernstein, interview with author, 29 Sept. 1996
31 Simons, op. cit., p.609
32 Brian Bunting, interview with author, 15 Oct. 1996
33 R. Bernstein, interview with author, 18 Aug. 1996
34 Mda, interview with Gerhart, op. cit.
35 J. Matthews, interview for Menell and Gibson, *Mandela* (film)
36 Mandela, interview with author, 11 Feb. 1997
37 Jail Memoir

CHAPTER 6 Defiance: 1952

1 *Drum*, op. cit., pp.104–5
2 Karis and Carter, Vol.2, op. cit., p.471
3 *Long Walk*, p.142
4 Bunting, op. cit., p.182
5 *Drum*, op. cit., p.106
6 Slovo, op. cit., p.87
7 A. Lerumo, *Fifty Fighting Years: The Communist Party of South Africa, 1921–1971*, p. 96
8 Mda, interview with Gerhart, op. cit.
9 Fatima Meer, interview with author, 27 Jul. 1996
10 *Long Walk*, p.147; Jail Memoir
11 Treason Trial transcript, p.16,047
12 Slovo, op. cit., p.88
13 Karis and Carter, Vol.2, op. cit., p.482
14 Benson, *South Africa*, p.141
15 Karis and Carter, Vol.2, op. cit., p.482
16 J. Matthews, interview with author, 18–19 Aug. 1996
17 Karis and Carter, Vol.2, op. cit., p.418
18 Jail Memoir
19 Treason Trial transcript, p.15,871
20 *Long Walk*, pp.153–4
21 Lodge, op. cit., p.55; Karis and Carter, Vol.2, op. cit., p.420
22 Mandela, 'We Defy', *Drum*, Aug. 1952, pp.35–7
23 *Long Walk*, pp.155, 159
24 Jail Memoir
25 Treason Trial transcript, pp.15,993, 16,088–9
26 Naboth Mokgatle, *The Autobiography of an Unknown South African*, p.307
27 Amina Cachalia, interviews with author, 29 Aug., 2 Sept. 1996
28 *Drum*, op. cit., p.108
29 Mandela to Richard Stengel
30 *Long Walk*, p.158; Jail Memoir; Helen Joseph, *Side by Side*, p.220
31 *Drum*, op. cit., p.108
32 G. Mbeki, *Student Politics at Fort Hare*, op. cit.
33 Mandela, letter to Lionel Ngakane, 1 Apr. 1985
34 *The Struggle is my Life*, p.35
35 J. Matthews, interview for Menell and Gibson, *Mandela* (film)
36 Karis and Carter, Vol.2, op. cit., pp.485–6
37 Treason Trial transcript, p.16,054
38 *The Struggle is my Life*, p.36
39 *Drum*, op. cit., p.110
40 C.J. Driver, *Patrick Duncan: South African and Pan-African*
41 *Long Walk*, p.160
42 Treason Trial transcript, p.15,789
43 *Long Walk*, p.161
44 Albert Luthuli, comments on *The Treason Cage* in letter to author, 1957
45 Karis and Carter, Vol.2, op. cit., p.486
46 *Drum*, op. cit., p.113
47 Extract Union Rep. Despatch, 13 May 1952 (PRO: DO 35/3259)
48 J.H. le Rougetel, British High Commissioner, letter to Sir Percival Liesching, 2 Jun. 1952 (PRO: DO 35/3137); le Rougetel, 'South African Racial Riots', 18 Nov. 1952; unsigned letter to N. Pritchard, Commonwealth Relations Officer, 24 Sept. 1952 (PRO: DO 35/3259)
49 Prime Minister's personal minute to Secretary of State for Commonwealth Relations, 16 Oct. 1952 (PRO: DO 35/3259)
50 T.W.L. MacDermot, Canadian High Commissioner in Cape Town, report to Secretary of State for External Affairs, Canada, 10 Feb. 1953 (PRO: DO 35/10575)

CHAPTER 7 Lawyer and Revolutionary: 1952–1954

1 Phyllis P. Jordan (Ntantala), letter to Fatima Meer, 1989
2 John Collins, *Faith under Fire*, pp.205–6
3 Mandela to Richard Stengel
4 Evelyn Mandela, interview with author, 24 Feb. 1997
5 Mphahlele, conversation with author, 16 Mar. 1997
6 Piliso, interview for Menell and Gibson, *Mandela* (film)

7 George Bizos, Notes for a Memoir (unpublished)
8 A. Tambo, interviews with author, 20 Oct. 1996, 13 Feb. 1997
9 Joe Mogotsi, interview with author, 7 Jan. 1997
10 Oliver Tambo, introduction to *Long Walk*, pp.ix–x
11 Mendi Msimang, interview with author, 30 Jun. 1997
12 Pitje, interview for Menell and Gibson, *Mandela* (film)
13 Ruth Mompati, interview with author, 26 Oct. 1996
14 Bizos, op. cit.
15 Pitje, interview for Menell and Gibson, *Mandela* (film)
16 Meer, op. cit., p.61
17 Bizos, op. cit.
18 *Long Walk*, p.190
19 Bizos, op. cit.
20 *Mail & Guardian*, 5 Dec. 1996
21 Bizos, op. cit.
22 *Nelson Mandela Speaks*, p.83
23 Jail Memoir
24 *Long Walk*, pp.186–7
25 *The Struggle is my Life*, p.148; Trial statement, 1962
26 Jail Memoir
27 *Long Walk*, pp.166–8; Jail Memoir
28 Treason Trial transcript, pp.15,800–1
29 *The Struggle is my Life*, p.40
30 Jail Memoir
31 Lodge, op. cit., p.75
32 Benson, *Nelson Mandela*, p.76
33 Treason Trial transcript, p.16,175
34 *Long Walk*, p.183
35 Treason Trial transcript, p.16,174
36 *Drum*, op. cit., p.135
37 Trevor Huddleston, *Naught for Your Comfort*, p.133
38 Trevor Huddleston, conversation with author, 27 Sept. 1996
39 Jail Memoir
40 Mattera, op. cit., p.140
41 Jail Memoir
42 Sampson, diary, 12 Feb. 1955
43 *Long Walk*, pp.193–4
44 Walter Sisulu, interview with author, 25 Jan. 1996
45 Mandela to Richard Stengel; *Long Walk*, p.184
46 Treason Trial transcript, p.15,791; *The Struggle is my Life*, pp.34–5
47 *The Struggle is my Life*, p.42
48 Mandela, interview with author, 8 Aug. 1997
49 Treason Trial transcript, pp.16,105–10, 8,503–5, 15,807–8, 16,022; Mandela, 'Africa and World Peace', *Liberation*, Dec. 1953

CHAPTER 8 The Meaning of Freedom: 1953–1956

1 *Treason Cage*, p.127
2 Meer, op. cit., pp.54–6
3 Z.K. Matthews, op. cit., p.169
4 F. Matthews, op. cit., p.55
5 Thomas Karis and Gwendolen M. Carter, *From Protest to Challenge, Vol.3: Challenge and Violence, 1953–1964*, p.105
6 Z.K. Matthews, op. cit., p.175
7 Jail Memoir
8 *Long Walk*, p.199
9 Karis and Carter, Vol.3, op. cit., p.115
10 *Long Walk*, p.200; Karis and Carter, Vol.3, op. cit., pp.19–20
11 Slovo, op. cit., p.89
12 Jail Memoir; Meer, op. cit., p.72
13 Mandela to Richard Stengel
14 Diana Collins, *Partners in Protest: My Life with Canon Collins*, pp.205–6
15 Alan Paton, *Journey Continued: An Autobiography*, p.68
16 Treason Trial transcript, pp.15,829, 16,041, 15,828; *The Struggle is my Life*, p.44
17 Mandela, 'Searchlight on the Liberal Party', *Liberation*, Jun. 1953, pp.7–8
18 Randolph Vigne, *Liberals against Apartheid: A History of the Liberal Party of South Africa, 1953–68*, pp.24, 48 and 51, citing David Everatt, '"Frankly Frightened": The Liberal Party and the Congress of the People', undated
19 Slovo, op. cit., p.89
20 Sydney Kentridge, interview with author, 2 Oct. 1996
21 Mandela to Richard Stengel
22 Jail Memoir
23 Karis and Carter, Vol.3, op. cit., p.128

24 Sampson, diary, 22 Jul. 1954
25 Karis and Carter, Vol.3, op. cit., pp.22, 135
26 R. Bernstein, op. cit.
27 Jail Memoir
28 Lerumo, op. cit., p.100
29 *The Struggle is my Life*, p.50
30 *Treason Cage*, p.106
31 Meer, op. cit., p.74
32 *Long Walk*, p.203; *Treason Cage*, p.107
33 R. Bernstein, op. cit.
34 *Africa X-Ray Report*, Sept. 1956, p.9
35 Lodge, op. cit., p.74
36 Karis and Carter, Vol.3, op. cit., pp.71, 242, 210
37 Meer, op. cit., p.76; *Africa X-Ray Report*, Nov. 1956
38 Albert Luthuli, letter to Mary-Louise Hooper, Jul. 1956
39 *Treason Cage*, p.113
40 *The Struggle is my Life*, p.54
41 Kathrada, Summary of Different Viewpoints (unpublished), 1977
42 *The Struggle is my Life*, p.55
43 Karis and Carter, Vol.3, p.247
44 The original version of Mandela's essay, 'In Our Lifetime' (*Liberation*, Jun. 1956, pp.4–8), was republished as 'Freedom in our Lifetime' in *No Easy Walk to Freedom* (1965, pp.55–60, ed. Ruth First). The missing lines were also excluded from *The Struggle is my Life* (1978). See also *Arise! Vukani: Magazine of Action Youth*, Vol.1, No. 5, Sept.–Oct. 1985, pp.5–7, which analyses the missing lines as being '. . . a denial that the Charter implies the overthrow of capitalism. In fact, it is positively interpreted as a programme of reforming capitalism.' The anthology also removed a number of significant sentences from Mandela, 'Searchlight on the Liberal Party' (*Liberation*, Jun. 1953, pp.7–8) before its republication as 'The Shifting Sands of Illusion' (*No Easy Walk*, pp.33–5). Ruth First told readers in an editorial note: 'The articles are reproduced here almost exactly as they were written, with light editing only here and there to omit repetition or local references' (*No Easy Walk*, p.xiv). The editorial note was not reproduced in *The Struggle is my Life.*
45 Mandela, 'Verwoerd's Grim Plot', *Liberation*, May 1959, pp.7–17
46 *The Struggle is my Life*, p.67
47 Jail Memoir
48 *Long Walk*, p.212
49 Jail Memoir
50 Mandela, 'Bluffing the Bunga into Apartheid', *Fighting Talk*, Jul. 1955, pp.6–7
51 Matanzima, interview with author, 12 May 1997
52 Jail Memoir
53 Allister Sparks, *The Mind of South Africa*, p.196, citing House of Assembly Debates, 1953, col.3576
54 Jail Memoir
55 *Long Walk*, p.196
56 *The Struggle is my Life*, p.86
57 Welsh, op. cit., p.447
58 Jail Memoir
59 *The Struggle is my Life*, p.65
60 Dugard, op. cit.
61 *Long Walk*, p.224
62 Jail Memoir
63 Mandela, letter to Minister of Justice, 13 Apr. 1956; J.J. Marais, Acting Secretary for Justice, letter to Mandela, 13 Jul. 1956 (Justice Archive)

CHAPTER 9 Treason and Winnie: 1956–1957

1 Karis and Carter, Vol.3, op. cit., p.259
2 *Drum*, Dec. 1956–Jan. 1957; Lionel Morrison, interview with author, 1 Nov. 1996
3 *Long Walk*, p.232
4 Jail Memoir; *Long Walk*, p.234
5 *Treason Cage*, p.202
6 *Drum*, Jan. 1957
7 Jail Memoir
8 *Long Walk*, p.237
9 Slovo, op. cit., pp.93–4
10 Kathrada, interview with author, 7 Feb. 1997
11 Jail Memoir

12 *New Age*, 9 May 1957
13 Morrison, interview with author, 1 Nov. 1996
14 Albert Luthuli, *Let my People Go: An Autobiography*, p.157
15 *Treason Cage*, pp.207–14; *The Struggle is my Life*, p.68
16 Mary Benson, *Guardian*, 16 Aug. 1962
17 Kentridge, interview with author, 2 Oct. 1996
18 F. Matthews, op. cit., pp.151, 137, 134, citing Z.K. Matthews, letters to F. Matthews, 5 and 10 May 1957
19 Luthuli, op. cit., p.170
20 Paul Joseph, interview with author, 6 Dec. 1996
21 Sampson, diary, Aug. 1957
22 Mandela, letter to Mrs Perlman, 5 Sept. 1983
23 Luthuli, op. cit., p.172
24 Private information
25 *Long Walk*, p.237
26 Jail Memoir
27 *New Age*, 17 Jul. 1957
28 See for example E.J. Emery, letter to R.G. Britten, 19 Jan. 1959: 'Judging from press reports (which is all we have so far to go by) . . .' (PRO: DO /35/10575)
29 Eleanor Emery, interview with James Sanders, 12 Dec. 1996
30 *Sunday Telegraph*, 25 Feb. 1990; Mandela, comments on text
31 *Long Walk*, p.242; Meer, op. cit., p.82
32 Joseph, op. cit., p.209
33 Meer, op. cit., p.94
34 Winnie Mandela, interview with author, 22 Oct. 1996
35 Meer, op. cit., p.104
36 Winnie Mandela, interview for Menell and Gibson, *Mandela* (film)
37 Emma Gilbey, *The Lady: The Life and Times of Winnie Mandela*, p.26
38 Ellen Kuzwayo, *Call me Woman*, p.159
39 *Sunday Independent*, 8 Sept. 1996
40 A. Tambo, interview with author, 13 Feb. 1997
41 J. Matthews, interview for Menell and Gibson, *Mandela* (film)
42 *Long Walk*, p.250
43 Adelaide Joseph, interview with author, 6 Dec. 1996; Amina Cachalia, interview with author, 29 Aug. 1996; R. Bernstein, interview with author, 18 Aug. 1996
44 Winnie Mandela, *Part of my Soul*, p.66
45 W. Mandela, interview with author, 22 Oct. 1996
46 *Long Walk*, p.252
47 Mandela, letter to W. Mandela, 2 Jun. 1986
48 Sisulu, interview with author, 25 Jan. 1996
49 W. Mandela, op. cit., p.65
50 Meer, op. cit., p.132
51 Kuzwayo, op. cit., p.160
52 A. Joseph, interview with author, 6 Dec. 1996
53 Lodge, op. cit., p.145
54 Bizos, op. cit.
55 *Long Walk*, pp.259–60, 591; Joel Carson, *No Neutral Ground*, pp.106–7
56 *Long Walk*, p.591

CHAPTER 10 Dazzling Contender: 1957–1959

1 *Long Walk*, p.248
2 Gail M. Gerhart, *Black Power in South Africa*, p.174, citing *Golden City Post*, 2 Mar. 1956
3 Mandela to Richard Stengel
4 Benjamin Pogrund, *How can Man Die Better: Sobukwe and Apartheid*, p.118; Gerhart, op. cit., p.166
5 Slovo, op. cit., p.113
6 Pitje, interview for Menell and Gibson, *Mandela* (film)
7 Peter Raboroko, interview with Gail Gerhart, 9 Sept. 1968
8 Mandela to Richard Stengel
9 Karis and Carter, Vol.3, op. cit., pp.284, 308
10 Gerhart, op. cit., pp.284, 178
11 Mandela, interview with author, 24 Feb. 1997
12 Nthato Motlana, interview with author, 3 Feb. 1997; Pogrund, *How can Man Die Better*, op. cit., p.85
13 Motlana, interview for Menell and Gibson, *Mandela* (film)

14 Mandela, interview with author, 24 Feb. 1997
15 Mda, interview with Gerhart, op. cit.
16 Mandela, letter to Momazoma Finca, Aug. 1974
17 Karis and Carter, Vol.3, op. cit., p.314
18 Pogrund, *How can Man Die Better*, op. cit., pp.37, 62
19 Karis and Carter, Vol.3, op. cit., p.508
20 Lewis Nkosi, 'Robert Sobukwe: An Assessment', *Africa Report*, Apr. 1962
21 *Long Walk*, p.268
22 E.J. Emery in Cape Town, report to R.G. Britten in London, 25 May 1959 (PRO: DO 119/1200)
23 Commissioner of the South African Police, report to Mr Gee, British High Commission, 17 Aug. 1959 (PRO: DO 35/10575)
24 Sampson, diary, Oct. 1958
25 *Long Walk*, p.101
26 Meer, op. cit., p.142
27 Mandela, interview with author, 24 Feb. 1997
28 Mandela to Richard Stengel
29 Mandela, 'The First Bram Fischer Memorial Lecture', 9 Jun. 1995
30 E. Matshikiza, conversation with author, 10 Oct. 1996
31 E.J. Emery in Cape Town, report to R.G. Britten in London, 4 Jun. 1959 (PRO: DO 35/10575)
32 *New York Times*, 28 May 1959; Karis and Carter, Vol.3, op. cit., p.293
33 Sisulu, interview with author, 29 Nov. 1995
34 'Banned Leader', 'Problems of Organisation in the ANC', *Liberation*, Nov. 1955, p.8
35 Mandela, interview with author, 11 Feb. 1997; Martin Leighton, interview with James Sanders, Jun. 1998
36 Karis and Carter, Vol.3, op. cit., pp.263, 453, 484
37 Mandela, interview with author, 11 Feb. 1997
38 Karis and Carter, Vol.3, op. cit., pp.445, 472
39 Sampson, diary, Jul. 1957
40 *Long Walk*, p.299
41 Karis and Carter, Vol.3, op. cit., pp.292, 473; Sampson, diary, 30 Mar. 1960
42 *The Struggle is my Life*, p.86
43 Karis and Carter, Vol.3, op. cit., pp.475, 546
44 Oliver Tambo, oration at Duma Nokwe's funeral, 22 Jan. 1978
45 Karis and Carter, Vol.3, op. cit., pp.475, 546
46 Gerhart, op. cit., p.229
47 Slovo, op. cit., p.114

CHAPTER 11 The Revolution that Wasn't: 1960

1 *The Struggle is my Life*, pp.76–7
2 Karis and Carter, Vol.3, op. cit., p.464
3 Sampson, diary, Feb. 1960
4 *Observer*, 20 Dec. 1959
5 Harold Macmillan, conversation with author, 31 Dec. 1959; Richard Cockett, *David Astor and the Observer*, p.201, citing PRO: CO 1027/143
6 Alistair Horne, *Macmillan, 1957–1986: Volume II of the Official Biography*, pp.189, 194. For the development of the speech see PRO: CO 1027/143
7 Harold Evans, *Downing Street Diary: The Macmillan Years 1957–1963*, p.102
8 Horne, op. cit., pp.195–6; see also Sampson, *Observer*, 7 Feb. 1960
9 Sampson, *Macmillan*, p.189
10 Driver, op. cit., p.172
11 Sir David Hunt, *On the Spot*, p.119
12 Sampson, diary, Feb. 1960; Sampson, *Macmillan*, p.189
13 Mandela, speech to British Parliament, 11 Jul. 1996
14 Sampson, *Macmillan*, p.190
15 Jail Memoir
16 Karis and Carter, Vol.3, op. cit., pp.564, 332
17 *Long Walk*, pp.279–80
18 Lodge, op. cit., p.207
19 Welsh, op. cit., p.454
20 Karis and Carter, Vol.3, op. cit., p.336
21 Mandela, interview with author, 24 Feb. 1997
22 Sampson, *Observer*, 24 Apr. 1960

23 *Long Walk*, p.281
24 Slovo, op. cit., pp.115–16
25 R. Bernstein, op. cit.
26 Jail Memoir
27 Sampson, diary, 30 Mar. 1960
28 Sampson, *Observer*, 3 Apr. 1960
29 Pogrund, *How can Man Die Better*, op. cit., p.144
30 Joseph Lelyveld, *Move Your Shadow: South Africa, Black and White*, pp.315–47; Karis and Carter, Vol.3, op. cit., pp.329–44
31 Kathrada, comments on text
32 R. Bernstein, op. cit.
33 Joseph, op. cit., p.83
34 Karis and Carter, Vol.3, op. cit., p.343
35 Sampson, *Observer*, 24 Apr. 1960
36 Mandela to Richard Stengel
37 Karis and Carter, Vol.3, op. cit., p.344
38 *Long Walk*, pp.294, 296
39 Kentridge, interview with author, 2 Oct. 1996
40 Mandela to Richard Stengel
41 Treason Trial transcript, pp.15,987, 15,983–5, 16,002, 16,012–13, 15,919, 16,138, 15,977, 16,118, 15,959
42 Joseph, op. cit., p.95; Treason Trial transcript, p.15,864
43 Treason Trial transcript, pp.16,143, 16,149, 16,112–13, 15,772
44 Kentridge, interview with author, 2 Oct. 1996
45 Ben Turok, interview with author, 26 Jul. 1998
46 R. Bernstein, interview with author, 29 Sept. 1996
47 D.P. Wilcocks, Liquidator, Department of Justice, letter to Mandela, 1 Jul. 1966; Mandela, letter to Liquidator, 15 Aug. 1966; Wilcocks, letter to Mandela, 15 Dec. 1966 (Justice Archive)
48 I. Meer, interview for Menell and Gibson, *Mandela* (film)
49 *Long Walk*, p.139
50 Jail Memoir
51 Mandela to Richard Stengel
52 Jail Memoir
53 Karis and Carter, Vol.3, op. cit., pp.341, 572–6
54 R. Bernstein, op. cit.
55 Ronald Segal, *Into Exile*, pp.278–81
56 *Long Walk*, p.289
57 Kathrada, comments on text
58 Jail Memoir
59 Karis and Carter, Vol.3, op. cit., p.359

CHAPTER 12 Violence: 1961

1 Mandela to Richard Stengel
2 W. Mandela, interview with author, 22 Oct. 1996
3 Lodge, op. cit., p.233
4 Bunting, op. cit., p.266
5 P.M. Foster, report to A.I.M. Davie, Commonwealth Relations Office, 23 May 1961 (PRO: DO 180/6); Karis and Carter, Vol.3, op. cit., p.355
6 Mandela, interview with author, 24 Feb. 1997
7 Harry Oppenheimer, conversation with author, 8 Aug. 1997
8 *Contact*, 4 May 1961; *New York Times*, 27 Mar. 1961; *Rand Daily Mail*, 27 Mar. 1961
9 Lodge, op. cit., p.232
10 Dingake, op. cit., p.65
11 *New York Times*, 27 Mar. 1961
12 *New Age*, 30 Mar. 1961; *Observer*, 26 Mar. 1961
13 Andrew Wilson, conversation with author, 25 May 1997
14 *Contact*, 6 Apr. 1961
15 Benjamin Pogrund, interview with author, 22 Oct. 1996
16 Denis Goldberg, interview with author, 13 Dec. 1996
17 *The Struggle is my Life*, p.21
18 Karis and Carter, Vol.3, op. cit., p.348
19 *Long Walk*, pp.309–10
20 Ibid., p.304
21 Sisulu, interview with author, 29 Nov. 1995
22 Benson, *Nelson Mandela*, p.78
23 Jail Memoir; John Sutherland, interview with author, 15 Mar. 1997; Tony Heard, interview with author, 6 Feb. 1997
24 P.M. Foster, report to R.G. Britten,

Commonwealth Relations Office, 20 Apr. 1961 (PRO: DO 180/8)
25 Driver, op. cit., p.195
26 Randolph Vigne, interview with author, 29 Oct. 1997; Vigne, op. cit., pp.143–4; Jail Memoir
27 P.M. Foster, report to A.I.M. Davie, Commonwealth Relations Office, 23 May 1961 (PRO: DO 180/6)
28 P.M. Foster, report to W.S. Bates, Commonwealth Relations Office, 30 Jan. 1961 (PRO: DO 180/6)
29 P.M. Foster, report to A.I.M. Davie, Commonwealth Relations Office, 23 May 1961 (PRO: DO 180/6)
30 Horne, op. cit., pp.392–3
31 Oliver Tambo, conversation with author, 26 Dec. 1987
32 P.M. Foster, memo to W.H. Young, Pretoria, 21 Dec. 1962, citing Ambassador's Policy Despatch No.17, Jun. 1961 (PRO: FO 371/161906)
33 Private information
34 House of Assembly Debates, 23 May 1961, col.6497
35 Karis and Carter, Vol.3, op. cit., p.636; Sir de Villiers Graaff, *Div Looks Back*
36 *New York Times*, 12 May 1961
37 Jail Memoir
38 Baruch Hirson, *Revolutions in my Life*, p.302
39 Meer, op. cit., p.165
40 Dingake, op. cit., p.66
41 *Star*, 12 May 1961
42 *Guardian*, 27, 29 May 1961
43 *Long Walk*, p.318
44 *Star*, 27 May 1961
45 *The Struggle is my Life*, pp.104–6
46 Benjamin Pogrund, 'Killing the Messenger' (unpublished); Pogrund, interview with author, 22 Oct. 1996
47 R. Bernstein, op. cit.
48 Lodge, op. cit., p.232
49 *Rand Daily Mail*, 3 Jun. 1961
50 Brian Widlake, interview with James Sanders, Jan. 1997
51 R. Bernstein, op. cit.
52 Benson, *A Far Cry: The Making of a South African*, p.129
53 *Long Walk*, p.320
54 Stanley Uys, conversation with author, 30 Apr. 1998
55 Robert Oakeshott, conversation with author, 6 Jan. 1997; Benson, *Nelson Mandela*, p.87
56 *Observer*, 4 Jun. 1961
57 A.I.M. Davie, note, 7 Jun. 1961 (PRO: DO 180/6)
58 Jail Memoir
59 Francis Meli, *South Africa Belongs to us: A History of the ANC*, p.144
60 Tom Lodge, Bill Nasson, Steven Mufson, Khehla Shubane and Nokwanda Sithole, *All, Here and Now: Black Politics in South Africa in the 1980s*, p.307
61 *Long Walk*, p.322
62 R. Bernstein, interview with author, 18 Aug. 1996
63 Slovo, interview for Menell and Gibson, *Mandela* (film)
64 R. Bernstein, interview with author, 18 Aug. 1996
65 *Long Walk*, pp.320–3
66 Jail Memoir
67 Sisulu, interview with author, 25 Jan. 1996
68 Apollon Davidson, interview with author, 15 Oct. 1996
69 Slovo, op. cit., pp.151–2
70 Jail Memoir; *Rand Daily Mail*, 29 May 1961
71 Slovo, op. cit., pp.147, 150
72 Karis and Carter, Vol.3, op. cit., p.701
73 *The Struggle is my Life*, pp.148–9, Trial statement, 1962
74 Wolfie Kodesh, interview with author, 13 Oct. 1996
75 Jail Memoir
76 Slovo, op. cit., p.147
77 Jail Memoir
78 Kodesh, interview with author, 13 Oct. 1996
79 *Long Walk*, p.329
80 Kodesh, interview with author, 13 Oct. 1996
81 Meer, op. cit., p.255, citing Rivonia trial testimony
82 Mandela, speech at Memorial Service for Joe Slovo, 23 Nov. 1995
83 Slovo, op. cit., pp.150, 153

84 Kodesh, interview with author, 13 Oct. 1996
85 Meer, op. cit., pp.228, 164, citing Rivonia trial testimony
86 Mandela, letter to Effie Schultz, 10 Mar. 1986
87 Meer, op. cit., p.248, citing Rivonia trial testimony; R. Bernstein, op. cit.
88 Holland, op. cit., p.135
89 Kathrada, *Star*, 17 Jul. 1998
90 R. Bernstein, op. cit.
91 P.and A. Joseph, interview with author, 6 Dec. 1996
92 Goldberg, interview with author, 13 Dec. 1996
93 Meer, op. cit., pp.165, 251
94 Benson, *Far Cry*, p.131
95 Vigne, op. cit., p.202; Slovo, op. cit., p.152
96 R. Bernstein, op. cit.
97 Karis and Carter, Vol.3, op. cit., p.656
98 Slovo, interview for Menell and Gibson, *Mandela* (film)
99 Karis and Carter, Vol.3, op. cit., pp.716–17
100 R. Bernstein, op. cit.
101 Jail Memoir
102 *Long Walk*, p.338
103 J.J. Hurley, Ambassador, Canadian Embassy, Pretoria, 'Conversation with Chief Albert J. Luthuli', 23 Nov. 1961 (PRO: FO 371/155546)
104 *Long Walk*, p.337
105 E.B. Boothby, Visit of Chief Luthuli memo, 11 Dec. 1961 (PRO: FO 371/155546)
106 R. Bernstein, interview with author, 18 Aug. 1996
107 R. Bernstein, op. cit.

CHAPTER 13 Last Fling: 1962

1 'The White Redoubt' (declassified US State Department document), 6 Jul. 1962
2 Mandela, Africa Diary (unpublished), 9–11 Jan. 1962
3 Mandela, letter to Mary Benson, 6 May 1987
4 Jail Memoir
5 High Commissioner, Cape Town, telegram to Secretary of State for the Colonies, 22 Jan. 1962 (PRO: DO 119/1478)
6 Jail Memoir
7 'Overt and Covert Activity by the South African Police within the High Commission Territories'; J.A. Steward, Cape Town, letter to V. Gillett, Maseru, 26 Apr. 1961 (PRO: DO 119/1222)
8 John Longrigg, interview with James Sanders, Apr. 1997
9 V.J.G. Matthews: Source of Funds – HC Telex, 10 Aug. 1962 (PRO: DO 119/1229)
10 Jail Memoir
11 Frene Ginwala, interview with author, 11 Oct. 1996
12 Jail Memoir
13 *Long Walk*, p.347
14 Jail Memoir
15 *The Struggle is my Life*, pp.116–24
16 *Star*, 3 Feb. 1962; see also Mandela's statement in *Star*, 10 Feb. 1962: 'The underground ANC is becoming stronger every day.'
17 *Observer*, 4 Feb. 1962; *Guardian*, 7 Feb. 1962
18 R. Bernstein, op. cit.
19 Meer, op. cit., pp.177–80; Jail Memoir
20 Mandela to Richard Stengel
21 Jail Memoir
22 R. Bernstein, op. cit.
23 Rivonia trial evidence, R13
24 Mandela, interview with author, 24 Feb. 1997
25 Rivonia trial evidence, R13
26 Meer, op. cit., p.246, citing Rivonia trial testimony
27 *Long Walk*, p.355
28 Jail Memoir
29 Africa Diary, 25 Mar. 1962
30 Jail Memoir
31 Neville Alexander, interview with author, 14 Oct. 1996
32 Africa Diary, 7, 30 Apr., 3–4, 17 May 1962
33 Mandela, interview with author, 11 Feb. 1997
34 A. Tambo, interview with author, 13 Feb. 1997

35 Sisulu, interview with author, 21 Feb. 1997
36 A. Tambo, interview with author, 20 Oct. 1996
37 Benson, *Far Cry*, p.144
38 Denis Healey, *The Time of my Life*, p.358; Mandela, interview with author, 24 Feb. 1997; Healey, conversation with author, 15 Jul. 1997
39 Jail Memoir; David Astor, conversation with author, 1 May 1996
40 Africa Diary, 15 Jun. 1962
41 Astor, conversation with author, 1 May 1996
42 Colin Legum, interview with author, 6 Jan. 1997
43 Benson, *Far Cry*, p.144
44 E. Matshikiza, conversation with author, 10 Oct. 1996
45 Vella Pillay, interview with author, 3 Dec. 1996
46 Jail Memoir
47 Africa Diary, 29 Jun. 1962
48 Meer, op. cit., p.199
49 Sampson, diary, Jul. 1962
50 *Long Walk*, pp.363–4
51 Kathrada, interview with author, 16 Oct. 1996; *Long Walk*, p.365
52 Rivonia trial evidence, R14
53 Kathrada, interview with author, 16 Oct. 1996
54 F. Meer, interview with author, 27 Jul. 1996
55 *Long Walk*, pp.370–1
56 Ronnie Kasrils, *'Armed and Dangerous': My Undercover Struggle Against Apartheid*, p.50
57 Billy Nair, interview with author, 20 Feb. 1997
58 Bruno Mtolo, *The Road to the Left*, p.40
59 *Long Walk*, pp.371–3; Nair, interview with author, 20 Feb. 1997
60 Mandela, speech at a luncheon before receiving the freedom of Howick, 12 Dec. 1996
61 *Rand Daily Mail*, 8 Aug. 1962; [Johannesburg] *Sunday Times*, 12 Aug. 1962
62 Slovo, op. cit., p.159
63 *New York Times*, 13 Oct. 1986; see also *Star*, 14 Jul. 1986; *Atlanta Journal and Constitution*, 10 Jun. 1990
64 Kathrada, interview with author, 16 Oct. 1996
65 *Long Walk*, p.379
66 Kodesh, interview with author, 13 Oct. 1996
67 *Long Walk*, pp.375–6
68 *Guardian*, 11 Jun. 1964
69 Joseph, op. cit., p.127
70 David Astor, letter to Sir John Maud, 10 Aug. 1962; Maud, letter to Astor, 20 Aug. 1962; Maud, letter to V.R. Verster (Commissioner of Prisons), 10 Sept. 1962; Mandela, letter to Maud, 14 Sept. 1962. The other books were J.M. Keynes, *Essays in Biography* and Theodore H. White, *The Making of the President* (PRO: DO 119/1478)
71 Lord Dunrossil, report to P.M. Foster, 7 Dec. 1962 (PRO: FO 371/161887)
72 W. Mandela, letter to A. Tambo, 5 Sept. 1962
73 R. Bernstein, interview with author, 18 Aug. 1996
74 Leaflet issued by the Free Mandela Committee, 1962
75 'Release Nelson Mandela', *African Communist*, Oct.–Dec. 1962
76 Slovo, op. cit., pp.159–65
77 *Long Walk*, pp.385–6
78 Lord Dunrossil, letter to Peter Foster, 23 Oct. 1962 (PRO: FO 371/161901)
79 *Long Walk*, pp.387–95; Jail Memoir. The first draft of Mandela's speech is held by the Cullen Library, University of the Witwatersrand
80 Douglas-Home, op. cit., pp.247–8
81 Jail Memoir; UN General Assembly resolution: The Policies of Apartheid of the Government of the Republic of South Africa (A/RES/1761 [XVII]), 6 Nov. 1962, *The United Nations and Apartheid, 1948–1994*, p.251
82 Sir John Maud, Note for the Record, 23 Oct. 1962 (PRO: FO 371/161886); Record of a Meeting Convened by Sir Roger Stevens on 6 June: Future Policy Towards South Africa, 1962 (PRO: FO 371/161884)

83 J.P.R. Maud, Farewell Interview with Dr Verwoerd, 29 Apr. 1963 (PRO: FO 371/167504)
84 Record of a Meeting Convened by Sir Roger Stevens on 6 June: Future Policy Towards South Africa, 1962 (PRO: FO 371/161884)
85 T.W. Aston, Notes on Meeting with Paul Eckel, 23 Jan. 1959 (PRO: DO 119/1209)
86 R.W.H. du Boulay, letter to P.M. Foster, 14 Jun. 1963 (PRO: FO 371/167503)
87 Joseph Satterthwaite, 'Country Internal Defense Plan' (declassified US State Department document), 18 Dec. 1962
88 Marcus Edwards, Note of Conversation, 5 Dec. 1962 (PRO: FO 371/161887)
89 Note of a Conversation with Joe Matthews, 5 Oct. 1962 (PRO: FO 371/161886)
90 P.M. Foster, letter to Hilary Young, 21 Dec. 1962 (PRO: FO 371/161906)
91 Donald Gordon (for Hilary Young), letter to P.M. Foster, 29 Dec. 1962 (PRO: FO 371/161906)
92 Mandela, interview with author, 24 Feb. 1997

CHAPTER 14 Crime and Punishment: 1963–1964

1 Jawaharlal Nehru, *Mahatma Gandhi*, p.42
2 *Long Walk*, pp.396–7
3 Pogrund, *How can Man Die Better*, op. cit., p.176
4 *Long Walk*, pp.398
5 Jurgen Schadeberg, *Voices from Robben Island*, pp.7–13; *Long Walk*, p.404
6 Neville Alexander, *Robben Island Dossier, 1964–1974*, p.20
7 Mandela, interview for Menell and Gibson, *Mandela* (film)
8 *Long Walk*, p.408
9 Ibid., p.413
10 Joseph, op. cit., p.154
11 Hilda Bernstein, *The World that was Ours: The Story of the Rivonia Trials*, p.54
12 Holland, op. cit., p.145
13 Mtolo, op. cit., p.73–7
14 Rivonia trial evidence, R71
15 W. Mandela, letter to A. Tambo, 16 Apr. 1963
16 R. Bernstein, op. cit.; Kathrada, comments on text
17 Slovo, interview for Menell and Gibson, *Mandela* (film)
18 H. Bernstein, op. cit., p.55
19 Mandela, comments on text
20 Stephen Clingman, *Bram Fischer: Afrikaner Revolutionary*, pp.302, 313
21 Joel Joffe, *The Rivonia Story*, pp.v, 19
22 Bizos, interview with author, 3 Aug. 1998
23 Jail Memoir
24 *Long Walk*, p.416
25 H. Bernstein, op. cit., p.108
26 Joffe, op. cit., p.37
27 *Guardian*, 24 Nov. 1995
28 Joffe, op. cit., p.190
29 Sir John Maud, valedictory report to Lord Home, 14 May 1963 (PRO: CAB 129/114)
30 Lord Home, letter to Sir Hugh Stephenson, 12 Jun. 1963 (PRO: CAB 129/114)
31 Private information
32 UN General Assembly resolution: Release of Political Prisoners, (A/RES/1881 [XVIII]), 11 Oct. 1963, *The United Nations and Apartheid*, op. cit., p.267
33 Clingman, op. cit., p.319
34 John Wilson, 'Trial of Nelson Mandela in South Africa', 5 May 1963 (PRO: FO 371/177036); Sir Hugh Stephenson, letter to Sir Geoffrey Harrison, 20 Dec. 1963 (PRO: FO 371/177122)
35 Leslie Minford, report to Lord Dunrossil, 13 Dec. 1963 (PRO: FO 371/167542)
36 *Long Walk*, p.422
37 Joffe, op. cit., pp.61–2
38 R. Bernstein, interview with author, 29 Sept. 1996
39 Rivonia trial evidence, T29, T14–16, T25; Mandela, comments on text

40 Bizos, interview with author, 21 Jul. 1996
41 Rivonia trial evidence, R12, R15, R18–19, R89–90, R20–23
42 Joel Joffe, interview with author, 23 Jan. 1997
43 R. Bernstein, op. cit.
44 Jail Memoir
45 Joffe, op. cit., p.72
46 Jail Memoir
47 Joffe, op. cit., pp.76–7, 88–9, 91, 125
48 Bizos, interview with author, 17 Jul. 1998
49 Joffe, interview with author, 23 Jan. 1997; Joffe, op. cit., pp.127, 122, 124
50 Mac Maharaj, interview with author, 19 Feb. 1997
51 The Jail Memoir contained a description of this incident
52 George Bizos, interview for Menell and Gibson, *Mandela* (film)
53 *The Struggle is my Life*, pp.155–75
54 Joffe, op. cit., p.133
55 John Wilson, minute to John Ure (Information Research Department), 22 May 1964; Ure, minute to Wilson, 25 May 1964 (PRO: FO 371/177122)
56 Joffe, op. cit., p.190
57 David Astor, letter to R.A. Butler, 2 Apr. 1964 (PRO: FO 371/177036)
58 R.A. Butler, letter to David Astor, 8 Apr. 1964 (PRO: FO 371/177035)
59 Leon Brittan, letter to Peter Thomas, 24 Apr. 1964 (PRO: FO 371/177035)
60 Record of a Meeting between the Minister of State and a Delegation from the Anti-Apartheid Movement held at the Foreign Office on 19 May 1964 (PRO: FO371/177036)
61 John Wright, draft letter, 14 May 1964 (PRO: FO371/177122)
62 P.W.J. Buxton, note, 13 May 1964 (PRO: FO 371/177065)
63 Hilary Young, Cape Town, report to Guy Millard, London, 20 May 1964 (PRO: FO 371/177122)
64 Clingman, op. cit., p.320
65 Bizos, interview with author, 17 Jul. 1998
66 Joffe, op. cit., pp.151, 144
67 *Star*, 22 Apr. 1964
68 Joffe, op. cit., pp.203–4
69 *Long Walk*, pp.450, 445
70 Mandela, Brief Notes in the Event of a Death Sentence (Institute of Commonwealth Studies, University of London)
71 *Long Walk*, p.444; Kathrada, comments on text
72 Meli, op. cit., p.158, citing Bram Fischer, letter, 24 Jun. 1964
73 Paton, *Journey*, op. cit., p.250
74 Jail Memoir
75 Clingman, op. cit., p.322
76 *Long Walk*, pp.448–9
77 *Daily Telegraph*, 12 Jun. 1964; *Guardian*, 13 Jun. 1964; *The Times*, 12 Jun. 1964
78 [Johannesburg] *Sunday Times*, 14 Jun. 1964
79 *Star*, 13 Jun. 1964
80 Sir Hugh Stephenson, telegram to Foreign Office, 12 Jun. 1964 (PRO: FO 371/177123)
81 R.A. Butler, note, 3 Jul. 1964 (PRO: FO 371/177124)
82 Donald McD. Gordon, letter to John Wilson, 1 Jul. 1964 (PRO: FO 371/177124)
83 Sir Hugh Stephenson, report to R.A. Butler, 8 Sept. 1964 (PRO: FO 371/177124)

CHAPTER 15 Master of my Fate: 1964–1971

1 Mandela, interview with author, 25 Jul. 1996
2 Jail Memoir; *Long Walk*, p.453
3 Alexander, op. cit., p.21
4 *Long Walk*, pp.460, 464
5 Jail Memoir
6 Mandela, letter to the British Ambassador, 4 May 1964 (Prison Records)
7 Mac Maharaj, in *The Struggle is my Life*, pp.182–3, 192; Jail Memoir
8 Clingman, op. cit., p.328
9 Kathrada, comments on text
10 Mandela, letter to Connie Njongwe, 12 May 1986
11 *Long Walk*, p.460
12 Mandela, speech to the Oxford

Centre for Islamic Studies, 11 Jul. 1997
13 Long Walk, p.475; for examples see Prison Records
14 Claudia Schadeberg, *Voices from Robben Island* (film, 1994, directed by Adam Low)
15 Sisulu, interview with author, 25 Jul. 1996
16 Kathrada, interview with author, 11 Feb. 1996
17 Jail Memoir
18 Maharaj, in *The Struggle is my Life*, p.191
19 *Long Walk*, p.461; Kathrada, comments on text
20 Clingman, op. cit., p.328
21 Bizos, interview with author, 3 Aug. 1997
22 Alexander, op. cit., p.32
23 James Gregory, *Goodbye, Bafana*, p.108
24 Kathrada, comments on text
25 Maharaj, comments on text; Gregory, op. cit., p.108
26 *Long Walk*, p.464
27 Eddie Daniels, interview with author, 9 Feb. 1996
28 Lodge and Nasson, op. cit., p.299; Bam, interview with author, 30 Jul. 1997
29 Jail Memoir
30 Bam, interview with author, 30 Jul. 1997
31 Jail Memoir
32 Govan Mbeki, *Learning from Robben Island: The Prison Writings*, p.ix
33 Sisulu, interview with author, 25 Jan. 1996
34 Jail Memoir
35 Kathrada, interview with author, 31 Jan. 1996
36 Nair, interview with author, 20 Feb. 1997
37 Maharaj, interview with author, 19 Feb. 1997
38 General Willemse, interview with author, 21 Oct. 1996
39 Fran Lisa Buntman, 'The Politics of Conviction: Political Prisoner Resistance on Robben Island, 1962–1991' (unpublished PhD thesis)
40 *Long Walk*, p.463
41 Lodge and Nasson, op. cit., pp.298–9
42 *Long Walk*, p.523
43 Kathrada, letter to Sylvia Neame, Jan. 1971
44 *Long Walk*, pp.523–4
45 Mandela, interview with author, 25 Nov. 1996
46 Kathrada, letter to Sylvia Neame, Jan. 1971
47 Alexander, interview with author, 14 Oct. 1996; Jail Memoir
48 Mandela, interview with author, 25 Jul. 1996
49 Alexander, interview with author, 14 Oct. 1996
50 *Long Walk*, p.523; Jail Memoir
51 Alexander, interview with author, 14 Oct. 1996
52 Govan Mbeki, interview with author, 15 Feb. 1996
53 Bam, interview with author, 30 Jul. 1997
54 Sisulu, interview with author, 25 Jan. 1996
55 *Long Walk*, p.522
56 Indres Naidoo and Albie Sachs, *Prisoner 885/63: Island in Chains – Ten Years on Robben Island as Told by Indres Naidoo to Albie Sachs*, pp.214–15; See also *Long Walk*, p. 551
57 Jail Memoir
58 *Long Walk*, pp.525–7
59 J. Schadeberg, op. cit., p.51
60 Thomas G. Karis and Gail M. Gerhart, *From Protest to Challenge*, Vol.5: *Nadir and Resurgence, 1964–1979*, p.32; Kathrada, interview with author, 7 Feb. 1997
61 Eddie Daniels, interview for Menell and Gibson, *Mandela* (film); Eddie Daniels, *There and Back: Robben Island*, 1964–1979, p.199
62 Sisulu, interview with author, 21 Feb. 1997
63 W.E. Henley, 'Invictus', 1875
64 Mandela to Richard Stengel
65 Jail Memoir
66 J. Schadeberg, op. cit., p.41
67 Bizos, interview with author, 21 Jul. 1996
68 Dingake, op. cit., p.218

69 Bam, interview with author, 30 Jul. 1997
70 J. Schadeberg, op. cit., pp.17–19
71 C. Schadeberg, *Voices from Robben Island* (film); Alexander, interview with author, 14 Oct. 1996
72 Mandela, interview with author, 12 Jul. 1996; Anant Singh, *Prisoners of Hope: Robben Island Reunion* (video, 1995, directed by Danny Schechter)
73 Sisulu, interview with Houser and Shore, op. cit.
74 Gregory, op. cit.
75 *Long Walk*, p.614
76 Gregory, op. cit., pp.84, 95; James Gregory, interview with author, 26 Jul. 1998
77 Christo Brand, interview with author, 16 Oct. 1996; Maharaj, comments on text
78 Alexander, interview with author, 14 Oct. 1996
79 Kathrada, interview with author, 7 Feb. 1997
80 Dingake, op. cit., p.222
81 *Long Walk*, pp.563–4
82 J. Schadeberg, op. cit., p.23
83 *The Times*, 14 Aug. 1964; Bernard Newman, *South African Journey*, pp.160–7
84 Mandela, letter to Commanding Officer, 12 Sept. 1964 (Prison Records). No articles originating from the visit to Robben Island appear to have been published in the *Daily* or *Sunday Telegraph*.
85 Mandela, letter to Commissioner of Prisons, 14 Mar. 1965; Commanding Officer, letter to Commissioner of Prisons, 19 Mar. 1965 (Prison Records)
86 *Sunday Times*, 25 Apr. 1965; *Rand Daily Mail*, 29 Apr. 1965
87 Dingake, op. cit., p.218; see also *Long Walk*, pp.471–2; Alexander, op. cit., p.90: 'Judge Henning, editor of *International Lawyer*, who gave evidence for South Africa in The Hague at the South-West Africa hearings, was downright rude, prejudiced, and probably embarrassing even to his hosts.'
88 Mandela to Richard Stengel
89 D.P. Wilcocks, Liquidator, Department of Justice, letter to Mandela, 1 Jul. 1966; Mandela, letter to the Liquidator, 15 Aug. 1966; Wilcocks, letter to Mandela, 15 Dec. 1966 (Justice Archive)
90 Fred Carneson and Piet Beyleveld's statements are contained in the Nelson Mandela files (Justice Archive)
91 D.P. Wilcocks, letter to Commissioner of Police, 2 Jul. 1970 (Prison Records)
92 Doris Lessing, *Under my Skin*, p.368
93 Kathrada, interview with author, 20 Jul. 1998
94 Helen Suzman, interview with author, 15 May 1996
95 Mandela to Richard Stengel; *Long Walk*, pp.518–20
96 Suzman, interview with author, 15 May 1996
97 Alexander, op. cit., pp.88, 34
98 *The Struggle is my Life*, p.200; see also Mandela, letter to Minister of Prisons, 22 Apr. 1969
99 Helen Suzman, letter to author, 20 Nov. 1997
100 Healey, op. cit., pp.336, 355, 358
101 Alexander, op. cit., p.14
102 Philip Zuger and Dr Roland Mart, ICRC Report on Visit to Robben Island, 24–29 Nov. 1970
103 Dingake, op. cit., p.216
104 Mandela, letter to General Steyn, Jan. 1970
105 Alexander, op. cit., p.30
106 Kathrada, letter to Sylvia Neame, Jan. 1971
107 *Long Walk*, p.544
108 Alexander, op. cit., pp.23, 96
109 Mandela to Richard Stengel; Lodge and Nasson, op. cit., p.309; Dingake, op. cit., p.219
110 Kathrada, interview with author, 16 Oct. 1996
111 J. Schadeberg, op. cit., p.27
112 D.M. Zwelonke, *Robben Island*, p.63
113 Maharaj, interview with author, 18 Feb. 1997

114 Daniels, interview with author, 9 Feb. 1996
115 *Long Walk*, p.548
116 Mandela, speech on the retirement of Chief Justice Corbett, 11 Dec. 1996
117 *Long Walk*, p.549
118 Alexander, interview with author, 14 Oct. 1996

CHAPTER 16 Steeled and Hardened: 1971–1976

1 Moses Dlamini, *Hell Hole, Robben Island: Reminiscences of a Political Prisoner*
2 Orlando Figes, *A People's Tragedy: The Russian Revolution 1891–1924*, pp.123, 204
3 Buntman, op. cit., p.289; Willemse, interview with author, 21 Oct. 1996
4 Alexander, interview with author, 14 Oct. 1996
5 Jacques Moreillon, Dominique Dufour, Nicholas de Rougemont and Dr Andreas Vischer, ICRC Report on Interview with Commissioner of Prisons, 5 Jun. 1974
6 *Long Walk*, p.536
7 Kathrada, letter to Sylvia Neame, Jan. 1971
8 Willemse, interview with author, 21 Oct. 1996
9 Moreillon et al., ICRC Report on Interview with Commissioner of Prisons, 5 Jun. 1974; Jacques Moreillon, interview with author, 30 Nov. 1997
10 Maharaj, in *The Struggle is my Life*, pp.182–4
11 Healey, op. cit., p.358
12 Alexander, op. cit., p.26
13 Kathrada, letter to Sylvia Neame, Jan. 1971
14 Bizos, interview with author, 21 Jul. 1996
15 Nair, interview with author, 20 Feb. 1997
16 Bam, interview with author, 30 Jul. 1997
17 Hilda Bernstein, 'Two South Africans from the Island', *The Times*, 18 Jan. 1978
18 Patti Waldmeir, *Anatomy of a Miracle: The End of Apartheid and the Birth of the New South Africa*, p.16
19 Kathrada, letter to Navi, 3 Oct. 1989
20 Ronnie Kasrils, interview with author, 12 Feb. 1997
21 Sonny Venkatrathnam, interview for Menell and Gibson, *Mandela* (film)
22 Kathrada, letter to Sylvia Neame, Jan. 1971
23 Bam, interview with author, 30 Jul. 1997
24 Jail Memoir
25 F. Meer, interview with author, 27 Jul. 1996
26 David McNicoll, *Observer*, 22 April 1973
27 Alexander, op. cit., p.90
28 Maharaj, in *The Struggle is my Life*, pp.191–2; Naidoo and Sachs, op. cit., pp.245–6
29 Meer, op. cit., p.62; Gordon Bruce, interview with James Sanders, Jul. 1998
30 Gordon Winter, *Inside BOSS: South Africa's Secret Police*, pp.274–6; Gordon Bruce ('Charles Metterlink'), letter to Gordon Winter ('Florrie'), 16 April 1970
31 *The Times*, 18 Mar. 1969; Winter, op. cit., pp.264, 275
32 Gordon Winter, 'Inside BOSS and After', *Lobster*, No.18, 1989; Bruce, interview with James Sanders, Jul. 1998
33 Maharaj, interview with author, 18 Feb. 1997; *Long Walk*, p.565
34 Dingake, op. cit., pp.191–2
35 Mandela, speech to the Oxford Centre for Islamic Studies, 11 Jul. 1997
36 Eddie Daniels, *Weekly Mail*, 21 Mar. 1986; Mandela to Richard Stengel
37 [Johannesburg] *Sunday Times*, 30 Oct. 1994
38 *Long Walk*, p.53
39 Dingake, op. cit., p.192
40 Kathrada, letter to Sylvia Neame, Jan. 1971
41 Dingake, op. cit., p.192; *Long Walk*, pp.536–7

42 Lodge and Nasson, op. cit., p.297
43 Frieda Matthews, letter to Mandela, 24 Nov. 1986
44 Bam, interview with author, 30 Jul. 1997; Majeke, op. cit.
45 Daniels, interview with author, 9 Feb. 1996
46 F. Meer, interview with author, 27 Jul. 1996
47 Lodge and Nasson, op. cit., p.295
48 Kathrada, interview for Menell and Gibson, *Mandela* (film)
49 Kathrada, interview with author, 7 Feb. 1997
50 Alexander, interview with author, 14 Oct. 1996
51 Venkatrathnam, interview for Menell and Gibson, *Mandela* (film); the original copy of Shakespeare, with annotations by the Robben Island prisoners, is held by Venkatrathnam in Durban
52 *Long Walk*, pp.540–1; Mary Benson, Athol Fugard and Barney Simon, *Bare Stage, a Few Props, Great Theatre*, pp.101, 154; Benson, *Far Cry*, pp.194–5
53 Alexander, op. cit., p.85
54 Mandela, letter to W. Mandela, 1 Jan. 1975
55 Venkatrathnam, interview for Menell and Gibson, *Mandela* (film)
56 Kathrada, *Star*, 17 Jul. 1998
57 A. Singh, *Prisoners of Hope* (video)
58 *Long Walk*, p.539
59 Ahmed Kathrada, letter to Tom, 22 Nov. 1975; Kathrada, *Star*, 17 Jul. 1998
60 *Long Walk*, p.583
61 W. Mandela, op. cit., p.86
62 Alexander, op. cit., p.50
63 Moreillon, interview with author, 30 Nov. 1997
64 Lodge and Nasson, op. cit., p.301
65 *Long Walk*, pp.556–7
66 Dingake, p.215
67 Lodge and Nasson, op. cit., p.300
68 G. Mbeki, *Learning from Robben Island*, op. cit., p.xx
69 Karis and Gerhart, Vol.5, op. cit., p.33
70 Willemse, interview with author, 21 Oct. 1996
71 J. Schadeberg, op. cit., p.47
72 Bizos, interview with author, 3 Aug. 1997
73 Jennifer Crwys-Williams (ed.), *In the Words of Nelson Mandela*, p.36
74 Motlana, interview with author, 26 Jun. 1997
75 Coleridge, *Biographia Literaria*
76 Bam, interview with author, 30 Jul. 1997
77 Lodge and Nasson, op. cit., p.300
78 Sisulu, interviews with author, 25 Jan. 1996, 25 Jul. 1996
79 Raks Seakhoa, interview with author, 29 Nov. 1995
80 Alexander, interview with author, 14 Oct. 1996
81 Jail Memoir
82 Bam, interview with author, 30 Jul. 1997
83 Karis and Gerhart, Vol.5, op. cit., p.34
84 Maharaj, comments on text; Thami Mkawanazi, *Weekly Mail*, 23 Aug. 1987; *Long Walk*, pp.509–11; Karis and Gerhart, Vol.5, op. cit., pp.406–11
85 Bam, interview with author, 30 Jul. 1997
86 Kathrada, comments on text
87 Jail Memoir
88 *Long Walk*, p.605; Govan Mbeki, letter to T. Karis, 4 Sept. 1995
89 Jail Memoir
90 Mandela, letter to W. Mandela, undated; Mandela to Richard Stengel
91 Maharaj, in *The Struggle is my Life*, p.199; *Long Walk*, pp.573–4
92 *Sunday Independent*, 25 Jun. 1995; *Long Walk*, p.567
93 Jail Memoir, draft version (Prison Records)
94 Jail Memoir
95 *Sunday Independent*, 25 Jun. 1995; *Long Walk*, pp.568–72
96 Commissioner of Prisons, letter to Minister of Prisons, 26 Oct. 1977, initialled by the Minister 30 Oct. 1977 (Prison Records)
97 Mac Maharaj, comments on text
98 Kathrada, letter to Bob and Navi, 15 May 1989

99 Alexander, op. cit., p.91
100 J. du Preez, letter to Commissioner of Prisons, 27 Jul. 1976 (Prison Records)
101 Commissioner of Prisons, letter to Minister of Prisons, 9 Oct. 1979 (Prison Records)
102 Mandela to Richard Stengel
103 Maharaj, in *The Struggle is my Life*, pp.195, 199, 201
104 Mandela to Richard Stengel

CHAPTER 17 Lady into Amazon: 1962–1976

1 Maki Mandela, interview with author, 21 Mar. 1997
2 Mabel Mandela, interview for Menell and Gibson, *Mandela* (film)
3 Gregory, op. cit., pp.138–9
4 *Long Walk*, p.529; Jail Memoir
5 *Long Walk*, p.531; Mandela to Richard Stengel
6 W. Mandela, op. cit., p.87
7 Gilbey, op. cit., pp.68–9
8 Bizos, interview with author, 3 Aug. 1997
9 Carlson, op. cit., p.298; Gilbey, op. cit., pp.69–70
10 Gregory, op. cit., pp.129–30
11 *Long Walk*, pp.477–8; Benson, *Nelson Mandela*, p.147
12 Winter, op. cit., p.237
13 W. Mandela, op. cit., p.89
14 *Sunday Star*, 27 May 1980; Gilbey, op. cit., p.99
15 Gregory, op. cit., pp.130–1
16 W. Mandela, op. cit., p.89
17 Mandela to Richard Stengel
18 W. Mandela, op. cit., p.88
19 Gilbey, op. cit., pp.72–3; Carlson, op. cit., pp.263–7; Winter, op. cit., pp.229–32
20 W. Mandela, interview with author, 22 Oct. 1996
21 Benson, *Nelson Mandela*, pp.152–3; Carlson, op. cit., pp.293–4
22 W. Mandela, interview with author, 22 Oct. 1996
23 Carlson, op. cit., pp.291, 295
24 Benson, *Nelson Mandela*, p.154
25 Gilbey, op. cit., p.90
26 Carlson, op. cit., p.355
27 W. Mandela, op. cit., p.105
28 W. Mandela, interview with author, 22 Oct. 1996
29 Suzman, interview with author, 15 May 1996
30 Mandela to Richard Stengel; *Long Walk*, p.494
31 Bizos, interview with author, 3 Aug. 1997
32 Gilbey, op. cit., pp.92–3, 97–8; John Horak, interview with author, 10 Jul. 1996
33 W. Mandela, interview with author, 22 Oct. 1996
34 Mandela, letter to W. Mandela, 18 Aug. 1974; South African Police, Pretoria, report, Oct. 1974 (Prison Records)
35 Winter, op. cit., p.230
36 Gilbey, op. cit., pp.100–1
37 Mandela, letters to W. Mandela, 1 Jan. 1975, 11 Mar. 1981, 1 Feb. 1975
38 Mandela, letter to Zindzi Mandela, 1 Dec. 1974
39 Mandela, letter to W. Mandela, 1 Dec. 1974
40 W. Mandela, op. cit., p.90
41 Mandela, letter to Zeni Mandela, 1 Dec. 1974
42 Mandela, letter to F. Meer, 1 Nov. 1974
43 Meer, op. cit., p.377
44 Ibid.
45 Mandela, letter to a friend, 1974
46 Meer, op. cit., p.383
47 Gregory, op. cit., p.165; *Long Walk*, pp.560–1; Benson, *Nelson Mandela*, p.161
48 Mandela, letter to Fatima Meer, 30 Jun. 1987
49 Mandela, letter to Maki Mandela, 31 Dec. 1978
50 Maki Mandela, interview with author, 21 Mar. 1997
51 Mandela, letter to a friend, 1 Nov. 1974
52 Mandela, letter to Makgatho Mandela, 1 Sept. 1974
53 Mandela, letter to Rayne Mandela, 1 Dec. 1974

54 Mandela, letters to Maki Mandela, 8 Jun. 1978, 6 Nov. 1978
55 Mandela, letters to W. Mandela, 26 Oct. 1976, 1 Oct. 1975, 1 Sept. 1975, 15 Apr. 1976, 24 May 1976, 19 Jul. 1976
56 Mandela, letter to Mrs Mniki, 1 Dec. 1974
57 Mandela, letter to Barbara Lamb, 1 Oct. 1974
58 Mandela, letter to W. Mandela, 12 Nov. 1976
59 Kathrada, interview with author, 31 Jan. 1996
60 Peter Magubane, interview with author, 22 Oct. 1996

CHAPTER 18 The Shadowy Presence: 1964–1976

1 *Long Walk*, pp.492–4, 509
2 Maharaj, comments on text
3 *Long Walk*, p.575
4 *Observer*, 14 Jun. 1964
5 'Bartholomew Moru Hlopane, Bantu male, 46 years, residing at 3037 Moroka location, Johannesburg, statement, 1 Oct. 1964'; 'Michael Kitso Dingake, Tswana male, Bobonong village, Bechuanaland, sworn statement, 25 Jan. 1965'
6 Clingman, op. cit., pp.413
7 Mandela, 'The First Bram Fischer Memorial Lecture', 9 Jun. 1995
8 Mandela, letter to Sheila Weinberg, 1978
9 Kathrada, interview with author, 11 Feb. 1996
10 George Bizos, letter to author, 16 Jun. 1964
11 Karis and Gerhart, Vol.5, op. cit., pp.358, 6, citing Oswald Mtshali, 'This Kid is no Goat', 1969
12 Jail Memoir
13 *Long Walk*, p.521
14 Sisulu, interview with author, 9 Feb. 1990
15 *Long Walk*, p.525
16 *Economist*, 28 Oct. 1967
17 Karis and Gerhart, Vol.5, op. cit., pp.375, 30; *Long Walk*, p.522
18 Sisulu, interview with Houser and Shore, op. cit.
19 O. Tambo, letter to Mandela, 1975
20 Albie Sachs, interview with author, 21 Jul. 1996
21 Karis and Gerhart, Vol.5, op. cit., p.299
22 *Black and Gold*, p.87
23 Oliver Tambo, *Preparing for Power: Oliver Tambo Speaks*, compiled by Adelaide Tambo, p.79; Karis and Gerhart, Vol.5, op. cit., pp.34–5
24 'The Green Bay Tree', *Economist*, 29 Jun. 1968
25 Maharaj, interview with author, 19 Feb. 1997
26 Bizos, interview with author, 28 Nov. 1995
27 *The Kissinger Study on Southern Africa*, p.111
28 Thomas G. Karis, 'Revolution in the Making: Black Politics in South Africa', *Foreign Affairs*, Winter 1983–84, p.383
29 Jim Hoagland, *South Africa: Civilizations in Conflict*, p.78
30 *Long Walk*, p.603
31 Karis and Gerhart, Vol.5, op. cit., p.51
32 *Black and Gold*, p.105
33 O. Tambo, letter to R. Segal, 25 Mar. 1970
34 *Long Walk*, p.596; Bizos, interview with author, 28 Nov. 1995
35 Karis and Gerhart, Vol.5, op. cit., p.7
36 Mandela, 'National Liberation' (unpublished essay), 1977
37 R.W. Johnson, *How Long will South Africa Survive?*, pp.114–15, 121–2
38 Maggie Resha, *My Life in the Struggle*, p.239
39 Karis and Gerhart, Vol.5, op. cit., pp.400–1
40 Luli Callinicos, Notes for a Biography of Oliver Tambo (unpublished)
41 Karis and Gerhart, Vol.5, op. cit., p.43; Stephen Ellis and Tsepo Sechaba, *Comrades against Apartheid: The ANC and the South African Communist Party in Exile*, p.64; Alfred Nzo, letter to Jonas D. Matlou, 4 Oct. 1975
42 Mandela to Richard Stengel

43 Callinicos, op. cit.; Mandela, interview with author, 28 April 1994
44 Karis and Gerhart, Vol.5, op. cit., p.44
45 Callinicos, op. cit.
46 O. Tambo, letter to Mandela, 1975
47 *Sechaba*, Mar. 1973
48 Mandela, 'Black Consciousness Movement' (unpublished essay), 1978
49 Mandela, 'National Liberation', op. cit.
50 A. Tambo, interview with author, 13 Feb. 1997
51 I.J.M. Sutherland, memo and response, Oct.–Nov. 1964 (PRO: FO 371/177122)
52 A. Tambo, interview with author, 13 Feb. 1997; *Black and Gold*, p.83
53 Kathrada, interview with author, 11 Feb. 1996
54 Oliver Wright, memo to P.W. Carey (Board of Trade), 17 Oct. 1964 (PRO: PREM 13/092)
55 George Brown, letter to Prime Minister, 19 Oct. 1964 (PRO: PREM 13/092); Anthony Greenwood, letter to Prime Minister, 19 Nov. 1964 (PRO: PREM 13/093)
56 Patrick Gordon Walker, letter to Prime Minister, 'Visit of Lord Caradon', 18 Nov. 1964 (PRO: PREM 13/093); John Wilson, report to R.W. Jackling (New York), 19 Nov. 1964 (PRO: FO 371/177071)
57 British Embassy, Washington, confidential draft, 'Sanctions Against South Africa', Dec. 1964 (PRO: FO 371/177071)
58 Martin Bailey, *Oilgate: The Sanctions Scandal*, pp.128–44
59 Tambo, op. cit., p.85
60 *Sechaba*, Jan. 1971
61 United States Senate Hearings Before the Subcommittee on African Affairs of the Committee on Foreign Relations, 94th Congress, Second Session on South Africa, *South Africa: US Policy and the Role of US Corporations*, p.142
62 Arthur Schlesinger Jr, *Robert Kennedy and his Times*, p.748
63 Roger Morris, 'Race War Diplomacy: South Africa Unmentionable', *New Republic*, 26 Jun. 1976
64 Edward Heath, *The Course of my Life: My Autobiography*, pp.619–21, 477–8
65 *Sechaba*, Apr. 1972
66 Tambo, op. cit., p.105; *Kissinger Study*, op. cit., pp.81, 66–70
67 *Black and Gold*, p.119
68 Anthony Lake, *The 'Tar Baby' Option*, p.129
69 *South Africa: US Policy and the Role of US Corporations*, op. cit., p.142
70 O. Tambo, conversation with author, 21 Jan. 1987
71 Mandela, 'National Liberation', op. cit.

CHAPTER 19 Black Consciousness: 1976–1978

1 *Long Walk*, p.576
2 Gerhart, op. cit., pp.272, 278
3 Patrick (Terror) Lekota, *Prison Letters to a Daughter*, p.140
4 Gerhart, op. cit., pp.286, 298
5 W. Mandela, interview with author, 22 Oct. 1996
6 *Black and Gold*, p.108
7 Benson, *Nelson Mandela*, p.164
8 Howard Barrell, 'Conscripts to Their Age: ANC Operational Strategy, 1976–1986' (unpublished D.Phil. thesis), p.114
9 Mandela, 'Black Consciousness Movement', op. cit.
10 On the Soweto uprising, see John Kane-Berman, *South Africa: The Method in the Madness*; Alan Brooks and Jeremy Brickhill, *Whirlwind Before the Storm: The Origins and Development of the Uprising in Soweto and the Rest of South Africa from June to December 1976*
11 *Black and Gold*, pp.111–12
12 W. Mandela, interview with author, 22 Oct. 1996
13 Mandela, 'Black Consciousness Movement', op. cit.
14 C. Schadeberg, *Voices from Robben Island* (film)
15 Mandela, 'Unite! Mobilise! Fight on!

Between the Anvil of United Mass Action and the Hammer of the Armed Struggle we Shall Crush Apartheid', in Sheridan Johns and R. Hunt Davis Jr (eds), *Mandela, Tambo and the African National Congress: The Struggle Against Apartheid, 1948–1990 – A Documentary Survey*, pp.211–13

16 Eric Molobi, interview with author, 27 Jun. 1997
17 Terror Lekota, interview with author, 8 Feb. 1997
18 C. Schadeberg, *Voices from Robben Island* (film)
19 Lekota, interview with author, 8 Feb. 1997
20 *Long Walk*, p.576
21 C. Schadeberg, *Voices from Robben Island* (film); Mandela to Richard Stengel
22 Karis and Gerhart, Vol.5, op. cit., p.298
23 Buntman, op. cit., p.158
24 Karis and Gerhart, Vol.5, op. cit., p.298
25 Buntman, op. cit., p.171
26 Molobi, interview with author, 27 Jun. 1997
27 Tokyo Sexwale, interview with author, 22 Oct. 1996
28 *Long Walk*, p.577
29 Mandela, letter to Chief Buthelezi, 1978
30 Mandela, letter to Hlaku Rachidi, 1978
31 *Long Walk*, p.578
32 Mandela to Richard Stengel
33 Karis and Gerhart, Vol.5, op. cit., p.298
34 *Weekly Mail*, 13 Jun. 1986
35 *Newsweek*, 23 Jun. 1986
36 Frank Schmidt et al., ICRC Report on Visit to Robben Island, 29 Mar.–2 Apr. 1977
37 Molobi, interview with author, 27 Jun. 1997
38 J. Schadeberg, op. cit., pp.34, 45
39 Lekota, interview with author, 8 Feb. 1997
40 Mandela to Richard Stengel; Lekota, interview with author, 8 Feb. 1997
41 Dullah Omar, interview with author, 12 Feb. 1987
42 Lekota, interview with author, 8 Feb. 1997
43 Buntman, op. cit., p.113
44 Karis and Gerhart, Vol.5, op. cit., p.296
45 Seakhoa, interview with author, 29 Nov. 1995
46 Karis and Gerhart, Vol.5, op. cit., p.295, citing Indres Naidoo
47 *Long Walk*, p.580
48 Mandela, 'Black Consciousness Movement', op. cit.

CHAPTER 20 Prison Charisma: 1976–1982

1 Mkawanazi, *Weekly Mail*, 23 Aug. 1987
2 Dingake, op. cit., p.214
3 Sisulu, interview with author, 21 Feb. 1997
4 Kathrada, interview with author, 24 Feb. 1997; Kathrada, *Star*, 17 Jul. 1998
5 Frank Schmidt et al., ICRC Report on Visit to Robben Island, 25–29 Sept. 1978
6 Seakhoa, interview with author, 29 Nov. 1995
7 Murphy Morobe, interview with author, 7 Feb. 1997
8 C. Schadeberg, *Voices from Robben Island* (film)
9 Mandela, letter to Zindzi Mandela, 10 Jul. 1978
10 Molobi, interview with author, 27 Jun. 1997
11 *Long Walk*, p.597
12 J. Schadeberg, op. cit., p.35; Mkawanazi, *Weekly Mail*, 23 Aug. 1987; Irwin Manoim (ed.), *'You Have Been Warned': The First Ten Years of the Mail & Guardian*, p.90
13 Maharaj, in *The Struggle is my Life*, pp.186–7
14 *Long Walk*, p.585; Mandela to Richard Stengel; Mandela, interview with author, 11 Feb. 1997
15 Molobi, interview with author, 27 Jun. 1997; Mandela, interview with author, 11 Feb. 1998

16 Mandela to Richard Stengel
17 Mandela, letter to Amanda Kwadi, Orlando, 12 May 1986
18 Jail Memoir
19 SAIRR, *A Survey of Race Relations in South Africa*, 1977, p.119
20 *Star*, 26 April 1977; *New York Times*, 27 April 1977
21 *South African Panorama*, Jul. 1977
22 Amnesty International, *Political Imprisonment in South Africa*, p.83; *The Times*, 26 April 1977
23 *The Times*, 26 April 1977; Maharaj, comments on text
24 J. Schadeberg, op. cit., p.27
25 Lodge and Nasson, op. cit., p.308
26 Lekota, interview with author, 8 Feb. 1997
27 Lekota, op. cit., p.ii
28 Molobi, interview with author, 27 Jun. 1997
29 J. Schadeberg, op. cit., p.45
30 Kathrada, interview with author, 26 Jan. 1996
31 *Sunday Independent*, 25 Jun. 1995
32 Nair, interview with author, 20 Feb. 1997
33 Molobi, interview with author, 27 Jun. 1997
34 Karis and Gerhart, Vol.5, op. cit., p.297
35 *Sunday Independent*, 25 Jun. 1995
36 Mandela, 'Message on the Death of Themba Harry Gwala', 20 Jun. 1995; Sisulu, interview with author, 25 Nov. 1996
37 G. Mbeki, *Learning from Robben Island*, op. cit., pp.vii, xxi
38 Morobe, interview with author, 7 Feb. 1997
39 G. Mbeki, *Learning from Robben Island*, op. cit., p.xxiii
40 Buntman, op. cit., p.187
41 Kathrada, interview with author, 27 Nov. 1995
42 Sisulu, interview with author, 25 Jan. 1996
43 *Long Walk*, p.510
44 Molobi, interview with author, 27 Jun. 1997
45 Kathrada, op. cit.; G. Mbeki, *Learning from Robben Island*, op. cit., pp.178–80
46 Kathrada, op. cit.
47 G. Mbeki, *Learning from Robben Island*, op. cit., pp.178–87
48 Ibid., pp.187, 196
49 Kathrada, op. cit.
50 G. Mbeki, *Learning from Robben Island*, op. cit., p.xxiii
51 Kathrada, interview with author, 31 Jan. 1996
52 G. Mbeki, *Learning from Robben Island*, op. cit., p.xxii
53 Kathrada, interview with author, 7 Feb. 1997
54 Kathrada, op. cit.; *Sechaba*, Jul. 1969
55 *Long Walk*, p.580; Molobi, interview with author, 27 Jun. 1997
56 Seakhoa, interview with author, 29 Nov. 1995
57 Sisulu, interview with author, 25 Jan. 1996
58 Kathrada, op. cit.; Mandela, covering note to Kathrada, Summary
59 Venkatrathnam, interview for Menell and Gibson, *Mandela* (film)
60 Karis and Gerhart, Vol.5, op. cit., p.57
61 Oscar Wilde, 'The Ballad of Reading Gaol' (1898)
62 *Weekly Mail*, 20 Oct. 1989; Kathrada, letter to Eddie Daniels, 22 Jul. 1989
63 Molobi, interview with author, 27 Jun. 1997
64 Lekota, interview with author, 8 Feb. 1997
65 Seakhoa, interview with author, 29 Nov. 1995
66 Motlana, interview for Menell and Gibson, *Mandela* (film); Motlana, interview with author, 26 Jun. 1997; W. Mandela, op. cit., p.130
67 W. Mandela, op. cit., p.131
68 Frank Schmidt et al., ICRC Report on Visit to Robben Island, 29 Mar.–2 Apr. 1977
69 Mandela to Richard Stengel
70 Motlana, interview with author, 19 Oct. 1996
71 Mandela, letters to W. Mandela, 27 May 1979, 2 Sept. 1979
72 *Long Walk*, p.601

73 Mandela, letter to Sheila Weinberg, 1978; Mandela, letter to 'Our Dear Reggie' (Tambo), 1978
74 *New York Times*, 19 Jul. 1978; United Nations Centre Against Apartheid Notes and Documents, 'Observance of Mr Nelson R. Mandela's Sixtieth Birthday', Aug. 1978
75 *The Times*, 19 Jul. 1978
76 Mandela, letter to W. Mandela, 1 Jun. 1980; *Long Walk*, p.585
77 Mandela, letter to W. Mandela, 1 Mar. 1981
78 *Long Walk*, p.595; Mandela, letter to Sheila Weinberg, 1978
79 Mandela, letter to Nthato Motlana, 1980
80 Maharaj, interview with author, 16 Mar. 1999
81 *Sunday Independent*, 25 Jun. 1995
82 Mandela, 'Black Consciousness Movement', op. cit.
83 Jannie Roux, letter to Minister of Prisons, 12 Jun. 1980 (Prison Records)
84 'Security Prisoner Nelson Mandela: Background', 12 Feb. 1981 (Justice Archive)
85 H.J. Coetsee, 'Nelson Mandela', 23 Mar. 1981 (Justice Archive)

CHAPTER 21 A Family Apart: 1977–1980

1 Mandela, letters to W. Mandela, undated and 21 Jan. 1979
2 Buntman, op. cit., p.247
3 Benson, *Nelson Mandela*, pp.187, 165
4 W. Mandela, op. cit., p.116; Motlana, interview for Menell and Gibson, *Mandela* (film)
5 W. Mandela, op. cit., pp.116–17
6 Kathrada, comments on text; Gregory, op. cit., p.170–1
7 *Long Walk*, p.586
8 Mandela, letter to Zindzi Mandela, 4 Sept. 1977
9 Mandela to Richard Stengel
10 W. Mandela, op. cit., p.127
11 Benson, *Nelson Mandela*, p.170
12 Ibid., pp.68–9
13 Meer, op. cit., p.306
14 Mandela to Richard Stengel
15 Allister Sparks, *Tomorrow is Another Country: The Inside Story of South Africa's Negotiated Revolution*, pp.17–20
16 Mandela, interview for Menell and Gibson, *Mandela* (film); *Long Walk*, p.590
17 Mandela, letters to W. Mandela, 26 Jun. 1977, 10 Jun. 1979, 1 Oct. 1979
18 W. Mandela, op. cit., p.137
19 Mandela, letters to W. Mandela, 21 Jan. 1979, 29 Jun. 1980, 1 Dec. 1976
20 *Observer*, Jan. 1982
21 Mandela, letters to W. Mandela, 6 May 1979, 21 Jul. 1979, 3 Feb. 1980, 28 Jun. 1980, 15 Apr. 1980
22 Mandela, letter to Zindzi Mandela, 4 Sept. 1977
23 Mandela, letter to W. Mandela, 2 Sept. 1979
24 Benson, *Nelson Mandela*, pp.185–6
25 Mandela, letter to W. Mandela, 1 Jun. 1980
26 Kuzwayo, op. cit., p.247
27 *Observer*, Jan. 1982; Gilbey, op. cit., p.134
28 Mandela, letter to W. Mandela, 9 Sept. 1979
29 Kathrada, *Star*, 17 Jul. 1998
30 Mandela, letter to Zindzi Mandela, 4 Sept. 1977
31 Mandela, letter to W. Mandela, 29 Jul. 1979
32 *Long Walk*, p.588
33 Mandela, letter to Zeni Mandela, 30 Oct. 1977; *Long Walk*, p.589
34 Mandela, letter to Helen Joseph, 15 Oct. 1978
35 Mandela, letter to W. Mandela, 26 Sept. 1979
36 W. Mandela, op. cit., p.136
37 Mandela, letter to a friend, 1 Jan. 1976
38 Mandela, letters to Zindzi Mandela, 30 Oct. 1977, 5 Mar. 1978, 4 Sept. 1977
39 Zindzi Mandela, *Black as I am*, p.14
40 Mandela, letter to Zindzi Mandela, 27 Jan. 1980
41 Mandela, letter to W. Mandela, 6 May 1979

42 Mandela, letters to Zindzi Mandela, Dec. 1979, 3 Feb. 1979, 25 Mar. 1979
43 *Independent on Sunday*, 3 Jan. 1993
44 Mandela, letters to W. Mandela, 10 Feb. 1980, 1 Jun. 1980
45 Meer, op. cit., p.371
46 Mandela, letters to Maki Mandela, 31 Dec. 1978, Feb. 1979, 8 Jun. 1978
47 Mandela, letter to W. Mandela, 19 Nov. 1978
48 Mandela, letters to Maki Mandela, 31 Dec. 1978, 26 Nov. 1978, 8 Jun. 1978
49 *The Times*, 3 Nov. 1998
50 Mandela, interview for Menell and Gibson, *Mandela* (film)
51 Ibid.
52 Mandela, letter to W. Mandela, undated
53 Mkawanazi, *Weekly Mail*, 23 Aug. 1987

CHAPTER 22 Prison Within a Prison: 1978–1982

1 Mandela, letter to Sheila Weinberg, 1978
2 Mandela, letter to Rhadi Singh, 1979
3 Mandela, letter to A. Tambo, 7 Dec. 1980
4 Mandela, letter to O. Tambo, 1978
5 Sisulu, 'National Liberation' (unpublished essay), 1977
6 Mandela and Raymond Mhlaba, letter to 'Reggie' (O. Tambo), 1978
7 *Long Walk*, p.484; Venkatrathnam, interview for Menell and Gibson, *Mandela* (film)
8 Karis and Gerhart, Vol.5, op. cit., p.256
9 Mandela, letter to A. Tambo, 1 Dec. 1980
10 Mandela, letter to Dr Michael Kelly, 1980
11 Karis and Gerhart, Vol.5, op. cit., p.675
12 Lodge, op. cit., p.351
13 Karis and Gerhart, Vol.5, op. cit., pp.256, 264–5
14 Lodge, op. cit., p.352
15 Mandela, letter to Chief Buthelezi, 1978; Mandela and Raymond Mhlaba, letter to 'Reggie' (O. Tambo), 1978
16 Karis and Gerhart, Vol.5, op. cit., pp.257, 273–4, 79–80
17 [Johannesburg] *Sunday Post*, 30 Apr. 1980
18 Mandela, letter to Bishop Tutu, 1980
19 Mandela, letter to Dr Gkubule, 1980
20 Mandela, letter to Sam Buti, 1980
21 Mandela, letter to Morenaka, 1980
22 Mandela, letter to Dr Masire, Jul. 1980
23 Mandela, letter to Mrs Bhalla, 3 Aug. 1980
24 Tambo, op. cit., p.197; Dingake, op. cit., p.170
25 Mandela, letter to A. Tambo, 1980
26 Mandela, letter to Dr Michael Kelly, 1980
27 *UN and Apartheid*, op. cit., pp.39, 347; Security Council Resolution: The Question of South Africa (S/RES/417 [1977]), 31 Oct. 1977
28 *Black and Gold*, p.125
29 SA Consul General, Glasgow, report, 'Nelson Mandela: Freedom of the City of Glasgow', to Director-General Foreign Affairs and Information, Pretoria, 8 Feb. 1981 (Justice Archive)
30 David Owen, *Face the Future*, p.144; David Scott, *Ambassador in Black and White: Thirty Years of Changing Africa*, p.195
31 O'Meara, op. cit., pp.229–49
32 Mandela, 'National Liberation', op. cit.
33 Sisulu, 'National Liberation', op. cit.
34 'The Black Labour Problem: South Africa's Achilles Heel' (declassified CIA document), *Africa Review*, 2 Sept. 1980
35 Mandela, letter to Dr Michael Kelly, 1980
36 *Sechaba*, Fourth Quarter, 1977
37 Karis and Gerhart, Vol.5, op. cit., pp.302, 304–5, 724
38 [Johannesburg] *Sunday Post*, 9 Mar. 1980; *Long Walk*, p.602–3
39 Benson, *Nelson Mandela*, p.182
40 [Johannesburg] *Sunday Express*, 20 Apr. 1980
41 Benson, *Nelson Mandela*, p.184.
42 Report on Mandela, stamped by

Secretary of the State Security Council, 18 May 1982; see also file on the 'Free Mandela' campaign (Prison Records)
43 Benson, *Nelson Mandela*, p.183
44 *Guardian*, 11 Jun. 1980; *Morning Star*, 11 Jun. 1980
45 Karis and Gerhart, Vol.5, op. cit., p.305
46 Mandela, letters to O. Tambo, 1980, 1981
47 Lodge, op. cit., pp.339–40
48 Sir Charles Powell, conversation with author, 3 Oct. 1996
49 Chester Crocker, *High Noon in Southern Africa: Making Peace in a Rough Neighborhood*, pp.328, 66; Jacob Heilbrunn, 'Apologists Without Remorse: American Conservatives on South Africa', *American Prospect*, Jan.–Feb. 1998
50 P.W. Botha, interview with author, 2 Mar. 1998
51 David Lamb, *The Africans*, p.109
52 Kathrada, interview with author, 31 Jan. 1996
53 Molobi, interview with author, 27 Jun. 1997
54 Mandela, letter to Zindzi Mandela, 10 Jul. 1978
55 Jail Memoir
56 Molobi, interview with author, 27 Jun. 1997; Kathrada, comments on text
57 Davidson, interview with author, 15 Oct. 1996
58 Sisulu, 'National Liberation', op. cit.

CHAPTER 23 Insurrection: 1982–1985

1 W. Mandela, op. cit., p.142
2 Kathrada, letter to Genghis (Eddie Daniels' dog), 22 Jul. 1989
3 *Long Walk*, p.613
4 W. Mandela, op. cit., pp.141–2
5 Buntman, op. cit., p.319
6 Kathrada, letter to Essop Jassat, 2 Jun. 1985
7 Kathrada, letter to Sonia Bunting, undated
8 Helen Suzman, letter to Kobie Coetsee, 4 Jul. 1982 (Prison Records)
9 Ismail Ayob, letter to Minister of Prisons, 16 Aug. 1983; Mandela, letter to Head of Prison, 2 Feb. 1988 (Prison Records)
10 Mandela, letter to Fatima Meer, Jun. 1983
11 Mandela, letter to Lwezi Vintela, 6 Feb. 1984
12 Mandela, letter to Brigadier Munro, 25 Feb. 1983
13 *Long Walk*, pp.614–15
14 Mandela, letter to Lionel Ngakane, 11 Jun. 1984
15 Kathrada, letter to Zohra, Sept. 1985
16 Mandela, letter to Mrs Perlman, 5 Sept. 1983
17 Mandela, letter to Peter Storey, 11 Jun. 1984
18 Mandela, letter to Stephen Naidoo, 4 Mar. 1985
19 Mandela, letter to Sheikh Gabier, 4 Mar. 1985; Ahmed Kathrada, comments on text
20 Mandela, letter to Sister Bernard Ncube, undated
21 Mandela, letter to Kepu Mkentane, 25 Feb. 1987
22 Amina Cachalia, letter to Mandela, undated; Mandela, letters to Amina Cachalia, 29 May 1983, 1 Mar. 1988
23 Mandela, letter to Kepu Mkentane, 24 Apr. 1984
24 Mandela, letter to Barney Ngakane, 11 Jun. 1984
25 Mandela, letter to Joy, 17 Feb. 1986
26 Mandela, letters to W. Mandela, 31 Mar. 1983, 13 May 1985
27 Mandela, letter to Adelaide Joseph, 25 Feb. 1985
28 Mandela, letter to Arthur Glickman, 31 Jan. 1985
29 Mandela, letter to Effie Schultz, 1 Apr. 1985
30 Mandela, letter to Lionel Ngakane, 11 Jun. 1984
31 Mandela, letter to a friend, 17 May 1983
32 Mandela, letter to Connie Njongwe, 14 May 1984
33 Mandela, letter to Mary Benson, 13 May 1985

34 Mandela, letter to Adie Joseph, 25 Feb. 1985
35 Mandela, letter to Helen Joseph, 1 Apr. 1987
36 G. Mbeki, *Sunset at Midday*, p.50; Buntman, op. cit., p.247
37 Jeremy Seekings, 'What was the United Democratic Front?' (unpublished seminar paper), 1994; see also Jeremy Seekings, 'The Fragile Front: The United Democratic Front and the Referendum Issue, 1983–84' (unpublished seminar paper), 1993
38 Lodge and Nasson, op. cit., p.51
39 Sisulu, interview with Houser and Shore, op. cit.
40 Mbeki, *Sunset at Midday*, p.54
41 *Black and Gold*, pp.151–2
42 *Sechaba*, May 1984; Heribert Adam and Kogila Moodley, *South Africa Without Apartheid: Dismantling Racial Domination*, p.250
43 *Long Walk*, p.618
44 Seekings, 'What was the United Democratic Front?', op. cit.
45 Mandela, letters to Benjamin Pogrund, 30 Jan. 1984, 22 Oct. 1985; Pogrund, interview with author, 22 Oct. 1996
46 H.W. van der Merwe, Report on Visit to Nelson Mandela, 11 Oct. 1984 (University of Cape Town Archive)
47 Nicholas Bethell, *Mail on Sunday*, 27 Jan. 1985; Nicholas Bethell, *Spies and Other Secrets*, pp.211–15, 218, 220
48 Samuel Dash, *New York Times*, 17 Jul. 1985
49 Mandela, letter to Samuel Dash, 12 May 1986
50 General Willemse, minute to Minister of Prisons, Apr.–May 1985 (Prison Records)
51 *Black and Gold*, p.160
52 Message of the NEC of the ANC, 8 Jan. 1985
53 Sisulu, interview with author, 25 Jan. 1996
54 Harry Oppenheimer, conversation with author, 8 Aug. 1997
55 Sparks, op. cit., pp.49–50
56 Mandela, 'I Am Not Prepared to Sell the Birthright of the People to be Free', 10 Feb. 1985, in Johns and Hunt Davis, op. cit., pp.214–5
57 Lekota, op. cit., p.194
58 Oliver Tambo, letter to Mandela, undated
59 Allister Sparks, *The Death of Apartheid* (film, 1994, directed by Mick Gold)
60 *Black and Gold*, p.161
61 *Mail & Guardian*, 2 Feb. 1996
62 Mandela, letter to Kaiser Matanzima, 29 Dec. 1984
63 Mandela, letter to Fatima Meer, 25 Feb. 1985
64 Mandela, letter to Kaiser Matanzima, 19 May 1986
65 Kaiser Matanzima, letter to Mandela, 19 Sept. 1986
66 Leach, *South Africa: No Easy Path to Peace*, p.174
67 *Black and Gold*, p.178
68 George Soros, conversation with author, 30 Jun. 1998
69 *Black and Gold*, p.32
70 Mandela, interview with author, 21 Feb. 1990
71 Sisulu, interview with author, 9 Feb. 1990
72 *The Sampson Letter*, 4 Feb. 1986
73 Crocker, op. cit., p.275
74 *New York Times*, 16 Aug. 1995
75 Roelof F. (Pik) Botha, 'His South Africa Connection', in Hans d'Orville (ed.), *Leadership for Africa: In Honour of Olusegun Obasanjo on the Occasion of his 60th Birthday*, p.57; *Black and Gold*, p.32
76 F.W. de Klerk, letter to author, 9 Dec. 1996; P.W. Botha, interview with author, 2 Mar. 1998
77 *Public Opinion*, Aug. 1985
78 *Star*, 22 Aug. 1985
79 *Washington Times*, 22 Aug. 1985
80 *Black and Gold*, pp.33, 193–5, 198–200
81 Ibid., p.40
82 Powell, conversation with author, 3 Oct. 1996
83 See also Geoffrey Howe, *Conflict of Loyalty*, p.479
84 Margaret Thatcher, *The Downing Street Years*, p.515; Powell,

conversation with author, 7 Jan. 1997; P.W. Botha, interview with author, 2 Mar. 1998
85 Sparks, op. cit., p.33; Howe, op. cit., p.483
86 Kathrada, letter to Zohra, 28 Sept. 1985
87 Kathrada, letter to Shehneez Meer, 23 Feb. 1986
88 Gregory, op. cit., pp.250, 156; Motlana, interview with author, 27 Jun. 1996
89 Sparks, op. cit., pp.21, 24–25, 32
90 Mandela, letter to Ayesha, 19 Mar. 1996
91 Mandela, letter to Connie Njongwe, 12 May 1986
92 Adam and Moodley, op. cit., p.282
93 *Weekly Mail*, 6 Dec. 1985, 7–14 Feb. 1986
94 Kathrada, letter to Shehneez Meer, 23 Feb. 1986
95 Mandela, letters to W. Mandela, 2 Feb. 1986, 4 Apr. 1986

CHAPTER 24 Ungovernability: 1986–88

1 'Your Logic Frightens Me', Wole Soyinka, *Mandela's Earth and Other Poems*, p.3
2 *Long Walk*, p.633
3 Gregory, op. cit., p.265
4 Bizos, interview for Menell and Gibson, *Mandela* (film)
5 Amina Cachalia, interview with author, 23 Jul. 1996
6 *Long Walk*, pp.626–7
7 Mandela, interview with author, 24 Feb. 1997
8 Sisulu, interview with Houser and Shore, op. cit.
9 Bizos, interview with author, 22 Jan. 1999; Sparks, op. cit., pp.29–31
10 The Commonwealth Eminent Persons Group on Southern Africa, *Mission to South Africa: The Commonwealth Report*, pp.56–62
11 Pik Botha, in d'Orville, op. cit., p.64
12 Crocker, op. cit., p.315
13 *The Sampson Letter*, 4 Feb. 1986
14 Woodrow Wyatt (ed. Sarah Curtis), *The Journals of Woodrow Wyatt, Vol.1*, p.95
15 Waldmeir, op. cit., pp.95–6
16 *Mission to South Africa*, op. cit., pp.67–8
17 Howe, op. cit., pp.484–5; Anthony Barber, *Taking the Tide*, pp.164–73
18 Waldmeir, op. cit., p.96
19 *Mission to South Africa*, op. cit., p.63; Barber, op. cit.; Pik Botha, in d'Orville, op. cit., p.67
20 Nancy Harrison, *Winnie Mandela: The Mother of a Nation*
21 Winnie Mandela, interview with author, 22 Oct. 1996
22 *The Sampson Letter*, 10 Sept. 1985, 4 Mar. 1986
23 W. Mandela, op. cit., p.92
24 Gilbey, op. cit., p.145
25 *Star*, 16, 19 Apr. 1986
26 See also Gilbey, op. cit., p.146
27 Private information
28 Winnie Mandela, interview with author, 22 Oct. 1996
29 Ismail Ayob, conversation with author, 19 Jul. 1998; Kathrada, interview with author, 24 Feb. 1997
30 *Mission to South Africa*, op. cit., p.61; Pik Botha, in d'Orville, op. cit., p.61
31 Mandela, letter to Connie Njongwe, 12 May 1986
32 *Mission to South Africa*, op. cit., pp.112, 114–16, 119
33 'Memorandum on Consultation with N.R. Mandela at Pollsmoor Prison, 19 May 1986' (Mayibuye Centre)
34 Sparks, op. cit., pp.32, 35; Crocker, op. cit., p.315; P.W. Botha, interview with author, 2 Mar. 1998
35 Pik Botha, in d'Orville, op. cit., p.67; Thatcher, op. cit., p.519; Howe, op. cit., p.485; Crocker, op. cit., p.316; *Long Walk*, p.630
36 *Mission to South Africa*, op. cit., p.135; private information
37 *The Sampson Letter*, 1 Jul. 1986
38 *Long Walk*, p.631; Sparks, op. cit., p.35
39 Niël Barnard, interview with author, 5 Feb. 1998
40 *Nelson Mandela Speaks*, p.154
41 *Long Walk*, pp.631–5
42 Gregory, op. cit., p.380

43 Mandela, letter to Rayne Mandela, undated
44 *New York Times*, 22 Jan. 1986
45 Maki Mandela, letters to Mandela, 23 Jan. 1987, 18 Feb. 1988
46 Mandela, letter to Maki Mandela, 18 Feb. 1987
47 Zeni Mandela, letter to Mandela, 25 May 1987; Mandela, letter to President Silber (Boston University), 30 Jun. 1987 (Prison Records)
48 Mandela, letters to Zindzi Mandela, 18 May 1987, 23 Nov. 1987, Mar. 1985
49 Mandela, letter to Mary Benson, 6 May 1987
50 Mandela, letter to Fatima Meer, 1 Mar. 1988
51 Mandela, letter to Kepu Mkentane, 25 Feb. 1987; Frieda Matthews, letter to Mandela, 24 Nov. 1986
52 Mandela, letter to a friend, undated; Kathrada, comments on text
53 Lodge and Nasson, op. cit., p.88
54 Robin Renwick, *Unconventional Diplomacy in Southern Africa*, p.113
55 Robert Harvey, 'The Great White Trek: A History of the Afrikaner Tribe from van Riebeeck to the Fall of Apartheid' (unpublished)
56 Lodge and Nasson, op. cit., pp.103, 109, 114
57 *Sunday Independent*, 21 Apr. 1996
58 *Financial Mail*, 20 Jun. 1986
59 Lelyveld, op. cit., p.356
60 Thatcher, op. cit., p.532; Howe, op. cit., p.490
61 Truth and Reconciliation Commission, *Truth and Reconciliation Commission of South Africa Report*, Vol.2, p.464

CHAPTER 25 The Lost Leader: 1983–1988

1 Crocker, op. cit., pp.321–4; George Shultz, *Turmoil and Triumph: My Years as Secretary of State*, p.1123; private information
2 Howe, op. cit., pp.489–91, 497
3 Thatcher, op. cit., pp.521–2
4 *Financial Times*, 5 Feb. 1986
5 Lord Renwick, interview with author, 2 Oct. 1996; O. Tambo, conversation with author, 29 May 1987
6 Enos Mabuza, interview with author, 24 Jul. 1996
7 Renwick, op. cit., pp.113–14; private information
8 See *Guardian*, 19 Oct. 1987
9 Howe, op. cit., p.489; Renwick, interview with author, 2 Oct. 1996
10 Edward Seaga, interview with author, 6 Nov. 1987
11 Adam and Moodley, op. cit., p.120
12 Waldmeir, op. cit., p.71; Sir Patrick Fairweather, interview with author, 3 Oct. 1997; *Observer*, 25 Sept. 1988
13 *Black and Gold*, p.246
14 Mandela, letter to Effie Schultz, 1 Apr. 1987
15 O. Tambo, conversation with author, 21 Jan. 1987
16 Waldmeir, op. cit., pp.63–4, 69
17 *Black and Gold*, pp.228–9; Chris Alden, *Apartheid's Last Stand: The Rise and Fall of the South African Security State*, p.267, citing Niël Barnard, *Die Beeld*, 19 Feb. 1992; Dr Daan Prinsloo, *Stem uit die Wilderness: 'n Biografie oor oud-pres. P.W. Botha*, p.280; P.W. Botha, interview with author, 2 Mar. 1998
18 Paul Johnson, *Gold Fields: A Centenary Portrait*, p.94
19 Michael Young, interview with author, 12 Apr. 1995
20 Kathrada, interview with author, 24 Jul. 1996
21 P.W. Botha, interview with author, 2 Mar. 1998
22 Reply from Kobie Coetsee to Advocate S.C. Jacobs in Parliament, 19 Apr. 1990 (Prison Records)
23 Mbeki, *Sunset at Midday*, p.86
24 O. Tambo, conversation with author, 26 Dec. 1987
25 Sparks, op. cit., p.60
26 Alden, op. cit., p.267, citing *Die Beeld*, 19 Feb. 1992
27 Sisulu, interview with author, 25 Jan. 1996; *Long Walk*, p.638
28 *Observer*, 1 Mar. 1987
29 Mbeki, *Sunset at Midday*, pp.103–4
30 Sampson, diary, 23–27 Sept. 1987

31 Mandela, foreword to Tambo, op. cit., p.xi
32 Mandela, interview with author, 24 Feb. 1997
33 *Long Walk*, p.640; Waldmeir, op. cit., p.101
34 Colonel J.G. Lourens, report on Mandela, 14 May 1988 (Prison Records)
35 *Long Walk*, pp.640–2
36 Mandela, interview with author, 24 Feb. 1997
37 Waldmeir, op. cit., p.67; Mandela, interview with author, 24 Feb. 1997
38 Thabo Mbeki, interview with author, 19 Oct. 1996
39 Young, interview with author, 12 Apr. 1995
40 Manoim, op. cit., p.86
41 *Guardian*, 30 Apr. 1994
42 *ANC News Briefing*, 12 Jun. 1988
43 Kathrada, letter to Paul Joseph, 26 Aug. 1988
44 SABC, *Comment: The Mandela Campaign*, 14 Jun. 1988
45 [Johannesburg] *Sunday Times*, 10 Jul. 1988
46 *Star*, 14 Jun. 1988; *Sowetan*, 19 Jul. 1988, citing *Die Beeld*, 18 Jul. 1988
47 *ANC News Briefing*, 24 Jul. 1988
48 Amina Cachalia, interview with author, 31 Jul. 1997; *Sunday Star*, 24 Jul. 1988
49 Mamphela Ramphele, *A Life*, pp.200–1
50 Kathrada, letter to J.N. Singh, 16 Sept. 1988
51 Gregory, op. cit., p.287
52 *Long Walk*, pp.645–6; Mandela, comments on text
53 *Sunday Times*, 14, 21 Aug. 1988
54 Emergency Meeting of the National Working Committee, 28 Oct. 1988, 'Nelson Mandela's Possible Release: Decisions of the National Working Committee', 28 Oct. 1988 (Mayibuye Centre, Cape Town)
55 Kathrada, letter to J.N. Singh, 16 Sept. 1988
56 Fiona Duncan, letter to Mandela, Nov. 1989 (Prison Records)
57 *Long Walk*, p.650

CHAPTER 26 'Something Horribly Wrong': 1987–1989

1 Ismail Ayob, press release on behalf of Nelson Mandela, 29 Jul. 1988
2 Azhar Cachalia, statement to the TRC, Nov. 1997
3 TRC Report, Vol.2, pp.578–9
4 W. Madikizela-Mandela, testimony to TRC, Dec. 1997
5 *Sunday Independent*, 30 Nov. 1997
6 TRC Report, Vol.2, p.582
7 Amina Cachalia, interview with author, 29 Aug. 1996
8 TRC Submissions: Questions and Answers, 25 Jul. 1996
9 W. Madikizela-Mandela, testimony to TRC, Dec. 1997
10 TRC Report, Vol.2, pp.579, 582
11 *Sunday Independent*, 30 Nov. 1997
12 Submission of the Mandela Crisis Committee to the TRC
13 Mandela, letter to W. Mandela, 1 Aug. 1988 (Prison Records)
14 *Long Walk*, p.645; *Independent*, 30 Jul. 1988
15 TRC Submissions: Questions and Answers, 25 Jul. 1996
16 TRC evidence
17 TRC Report, Vol.2, pp.565–7
18 Fred Bridgland, *Katiza's Journey: Beneath the Surface of South Africa's Shame*, p.69; TRC Report, Vol.2, p.567–8
19 *Business Day*, 25 Nov. 1997; *Daily Telegraph*, 4 Dec. 1997
20 TRC Report, Vol.2, p.567
21 Mandela Crisis Committee, report to Oliver Tambo, Jan. 1989; *Mail & Guardian*, 12 Sept. 1997
22 Frank Chikane, letter to Mandela, 14 Jan. 1989 (Prison Records); Mandela, comments on text
23 Manoim, op. cit., pp.122–3
24 Bridgland, op. cit., p.100
25 Azhar Cachalia, statement to the TRC; *Sunday Independent*, 30 Nov. 1997; W. Madikizela-Mandela, testimony to TRC, Dec. 1997
26 MDM press statement on Winnie Mandela and the MUFC, 16 Feb. 1989

27 Bridgland, op. cit., p.119
28 *New Nation*, 16 Feb. 1989
29 Submission of the Mandela Crisis Committee to the TRC; Frank Chikane, report to SACTU/ANC, 18 Feb. 1989
30 [Johannesburg] *Sunday Times*, 19 Feb. 1989; Bridgland, op. cit., p.120
31 Mandela, letter to W. Mandela, 16 Feb. 1989 (Prison Records)
32 Meer, op. cit., p.322
33 Amina Cachalia, interview with author, 29 Aug. 1996
34 Dullah Omar, interview with author, 12 Feb. 1997
35 Record of Stanley Mogoba's visit to Nelson Mandela, 23 Feb. 1989 (from a verbal report given to Peter Storey after visit)
36 Mandela, letter to a friend, 28 Feb. 1989
37 Sampson, diary, 6 Mar. 1989
38 Oliver Tambo, notes (Tambo Archive, Fort Hare)
39 Report of President's Committee meeting with Beyers Naude, 25 Apr. 1989 (Mayibuye Centre)
40 W. Madikizela-Mandela, testimony to TRC, Dec. 1997
41 TRC Report, Vol.2, pp.581–2

CHAPTER 27 Prisoner *v.* President: 1989–1990

1 Ahmed Kathrada, letter to Zohra, 25 Jan. 1989; Gregory, op. cit., pp.310–12
2 *Long Walk*, pp.653–4; government team document, 1 Sept. 1989 (Mayibuye Centre)
3 Government team document, 1 Sept. 1989 (Mayibuye Centre)
4 Maharaj, interview with author, 12 Feb. 1998; Report of President's Committee meeting with Beyers Naude, 25 Apr. 1989 (Mayibuye Centre)
5 Report of President's Committee meeting with Ismail Ayob, undated (Mayibuye Centre)
6 Sparks, op. cit., pp.60–1
7 Barbara Masekela, interview with author, 26 Oct. 1997
8 Tim Jenkin, 'Talking to Vula: The Story of the Secret Underground Communications Network of Operation Vula', *Mayibuye*, May–Oct. 1995; Sparks, op. cit., pp.62–7
9 Report of President's Committee meeting, 28 Apr. 1989 (Mayibuye Centre)
10 O. Tambo, notes, undated (Tambo Archive, Fort Hare)
11 Barbara Masekela, interview with author, 26 Oct. 1997
12 Bizos, interview with author, 21 Feb. 1998
13 Sisulu, interview with author, 27 Nov. 1995
14 [Johannesburg] *Sunday Times*, 16 Nov. 1997
15 Powell, conversations with author, 12 Feb. 1989, 3 Oct. 1996
16 Waldmeir, op. cit., pp.109–10; Fairweather, interview with author, 3 Oct. 1997
17 Sampson, diary, 26 Dec. 1988, 24, 26 Jan. 1989
18 Renwick, op. cit., p.133; *Daily Telegraph*, 25 Mar. 1989
19 Thabo Mbeki, interview with author, 25 Apr. 1988; Harvey, op. cit.
20 *Guardian*, 24 Jun. 1989; Sampson, diary, 8 Jun. 1989
21 Hyman Bernadt, interview with author, 13 Oct. 1996
22 Mandela, letter to Robin Renwick, 10 Apr. 1989; *Weekly Mail*, 14 Apr. 1989
23 *South*, May 1989
24 'South Africa's African National Congress: Weathering Challenges' (declassified CIA research paper), Mar. 1988
25 'South Africa Entering the 1990s' (declassified CIA document), *Africa Review*, Special Issue, 20 Jan. 1989
26 Sisulu, interview with author, 25 Jan. 1996
27 *Weekly Mail*, 21 Apr. 1989
28 O. Tambo, notes, May 1989 (Tambo Archive, Fort Hare)
29 *Weekly Mail*, 21 Jul. 1989; *Independent*, 23 Jun. 1989
30 Lodge and Nasson, op. cit., pp.110–15
31 P.W. Botha, interview with author, 2

Mar. 1998; Prinsloo, op. cit., p.285
32 *Long Walk*, p.657
33 Frene Ginwala, interview with author, 11 Oct. 1996
34 Mandela, comments on text; Mandela, interview with author, 24 Feb. 1997
35 Sparks, *The Death of Apartheid* (film); Prinsloo, op. cit., pp.286–7; *Long Walk*, p.659; Mandela, interview with author, 24 Feb. 1997
36 Alden, op. cit., p.271, citing *Die Beeld*, 19 Feb. 1992; Barnard, interview with author, 5 Feb. 1998; *Cape Times*, 18, 25 Nov. 1991; P.W. Botha, op. cit., pp.430–4; for the photograph of the meeting, see Albrecht Hagemann, *Nelson Mandela*, p.116
37 *Long Walk*, p.659; *Observer*, 9 Jul. 1989; *Star*, 13 Jul. 1989
38 Barnard, interview with author, 5 Feb. 1998
39 Robin Renwick, op. cit., p.137; Willem de Klerk, *F.W. de Klerk: The Man in his Time*, p.61
40 Kathrada, letter to Eddie Daniels, 22 Jul. 1989
41 Kathrada, interview with author, 7 Feb. 1997; Sisulu, interview with Houser and Shore, op. cit.
42 Government team document, 1 Sept. 1989 (Mayibuye Centre)
43 Barbara Masekela, interview with author, 26 Oct. 1996
44 Maharaj, comments on text; *Financial Times*, 22 Aug. 1989
45 *Long Walk*, p.663
46 *Financial Times*, 24 Aug. 1989
47 W. de Klerk, op. cit., p.22
48 Robin Renwick, interview with author, 2 Oct. 1996
49 Sparks, op. cit., pp.110–14
50 Sisulu, interview with Houser and Shore, op. cit.
51 Plan of Action After the Release of the Political Prisoners: Lusaka, Zambia, 9 Oct. 1989 (Mayibuye Centre)
52 Kathrada, interview with author, 26 Jan. 1996
53 *Daily Telegraph*, 18 Oct. 1989
54 *New Nation*, 13, 20 Oct. 1989
55 Sisulu, interview with author, 25 Jan. 1996; Kathrada, interview with author, 27 Nov. 1995
56 *South*, 19 Oct. 1989
57 *Weekly Mail*, 20 Oct. 1989
58 Anthony Seldon, *Major: A Political Life*, p.97
59 'South Africa: Political Violence in Kwazulu-Natal' (declassified CIA document), *Africa Review*, 19 Jan. 1990
60 *Independent*, 13 Oct. 1989
61 *Long Walk*, pp.662, 660
62 *Guardian*, 16 Oct. 1995
63 Meer, op. cit., p.xviii; Meer, 'Past-Postscript' to *Higher than Hope* (unpublished in English)
64 Sidelsky, interview with author, 23 Oct. 1996
65 Ramphele, op. cit., p.203
66 Daniels, interview for Menell and Gibson, *Mandela* (film)
67 Mandela, letter to Kapitans restaurant, 25 Sept. 1989
68 Sparks, op. cit., pp.105–6; Waldmeir, op. cit., pp.136–7
69 *Long Walk*, p.663
70 F.W. de Klerk, letter to author, Dec. 1996
71 Waldmeir, op. cit., p.147; *Long Walk*, pp.664–5
72 Waldmeir, op. cit., p.147; W. de Klerk, op. cit., p.80
73 *Business Day*, 5 Feb. 1990; Sparks, *The Death of Apartheid* (film); Motlana, interview for Menell and Gibson, *Mandela* (film)
74 Mandela, letter to Richard Maponya, 28 Jun. 1989
75 *Independent*, 24 Nov. 1989
76 *Black and Gold*, p.197; *Financial Times*, 27 Jan. 1990
77 *Citizen*, 16 Jan. 1990
78 Molobi, interview with author, 27 Jun. 1997
79 *New Nation*, 8 Dec. 1989
80 *South*, 11 Dec. 1989
81 *Guardian*, 9 Jan. 1990; *Independent on Sunday*, 28 Jan. 1990
82 W. de Klerk, op. cit., p.5
83 Renwick, op. cit., p.142

84 Marike de Klerk, *Marike: A Journey Through Summer and Winter*, p.153; Waldmeir, op. cit., p.148
85 Lynda Chalker, interview with author, 31 Oct. 1997
86 Renwick, op. cit., p.142
87 R.W. Johnson and Lawrence Schlemmer (eds), *Launching Democracy in South Africa*, p.6, citing 'private communication'; Renwick, letter to author, 1998
88 John Dugard (ed.), *The Last Years of Apartheid: Civil Liberties in South Africa*, p. 152
89 *Independent on Sunday*, 4 Feb. 1990; *Independent*, 3 Feb. 1990
90 Bizos, interview with author, 5 Feb. 1990; Magubane, interview with author, 22 Oct. 1996
91 *Long Walk*, pp.666–8; Barnard, interview with author, 5 Feb. 1998
92 W.H. Willemse, letter to Mandela, 10 Feb. 1990 (Prison Records)
93 *Long Walk*, pp.667–8; Gregory, op. cit., p.357; Kobie Coetsee, *Cape Times*, 1 Feb. 1991
94 Dullah Omar, interviews with author, 13 Feb. 1990, 12 Feb. 1997
95 *Long Walk*, pp.671–3

CHAPTER 28 Myth and Man

1 Ottaway, *Chained Together*, p.47
2 Battersby, conversation with author, 16 Nov. 1998
3 *International Herald Tribune*, 23 Feb. 1990
4 *Cape Times*, 19 Feb. 1990
5 F.W. de Klerk, *The Last Trek: A New Beginning – The Autobiography*, p.169
6 Thatcher, op. cit., p.532
7 van der Post, speech at Cape Town Press Club, 29 Nov. 1990
8 *Financial Times*, 13 Feb. 1990
9 Ibid.
10 Amina Cachalia, interview with author, 29 Aug. 1996
11 Meer, interview for Menell and Gibson, *Mandela* (film)
12 Gordimer, letter to author, 19 Dec. 1993
13 Cheryl Carolus, speech in London, 9 Mar. 1998
14 Mandela, interview for Menell and Gibson, *Mandela* (film)
15 Sisulu, interview with Houser and Shore, op. cit.
16 Mandela, interview for Menell and Gibson, *Mandela* (film)
17 Renwick, op. cit., p.149
18 Nehru, op. cit., p.42
19 Nixon, *Homelands, Harlem and Hollywood*, p.182
20 Mandela, interview with author, 21 Feb. 1990
21 Mac Maharaj, *Mayibuye*, Dec. 1997
22 Lord Hughes, conversation with author, 12 Jun. 1996
23 *Long Walk*, p.685
24 Graham Boynton, *Last Days in Cloud Cuckoo Land*, p.168
25 Private information
26 Mandela, interview with author, 28 Apr. 1994
27 Video of Mandela's 1990 visit to London (Mayibuye Centre)
28 *Independent*, 12 Apr. 1990
29 *Long Walk*, p.696
30 *Guardian*, 27 Apr. 1990
31 Confidential report from South African Ambassador in Rome, 28 Jun. 1990 (Justice Archives)
32 Mandela, comments on text; *Guardian* 16 Apr. 1990, 30 Jun. 1990
33 *New York Times*, 1 Jul. 1990
34 Mandela, comments on text
35 US State Department memo to US Embassy in Pretoria, 2 Jul. 1992
36 Krauthammer, *International Herald Tribune*, Jul. 1990
37 David Dinkins, conversation with author, 16 Feb. 1998
38 *New York Times*, 7 Jul. 1990
39 *Time*, 7 Jul. 1990
40 See also Nixon, op. cit., p.189
41 *Guardian*, 3 Jul. 1990
42 Mandela to Richard Stengel
43 Sampson, diary, 3 Jul. 1993
44 Sir Charles Powell and Lord Renwick, interviews with author, 1996; Mandela, comments on text
45 Thatcher, op. cit., p.533; Renwick, interview with author, 1996

46 Mandela, interview with author, 11 Feb. 1997
47 Kathrada, comments on text
48 I. Meer, interview with author, 6 Oct. 1997
49 See Dale McKinley, *The ANC and the Liberation Struggle*, p.112
50 *Independent*, 25 Oct. 1990; *Citizen*, 27 Oct. 1990
51 *International Herald Tribune*, 31 Oct. 1990
52 Vladimir Shubin, in *African Affairs*, 1996
53 Mandela to Richard Stengel
54 Ibid.
55 Ottaway, op. cit., p.50; Mandela, interview with author, 25 Jul. 1996

CHAPTER 29 Revolution to Cooperation

1 *Nelson Mandela Speaks*, p.228
2 P.W. Botha, *Fighter and Reformer*, p.50
3 de Klerk, letter to author, Dec. 1996
4 *Long Walk*, p.692
5 Sparks, op. cit., pp.153–4
6 TRC Report, Vol.2, p.69
7 Sparks, op. cit., p.119
8 P.W. Botha, interview with author, 21 Mar. 1998
9 de Klerk, BBC radio, London, 15 Sept. 1998
10 Jenkin, op. cit., p.21
11 Maharaj, interview with author, 21 Nov. 1998
12 Maharaj, comments on text
13 Maharaj, interview with author, 21 Nov 1998
14 Waldmeir, op. cit., p.137
15 *Nelson Mandela Speaks*, p.226
16 See also Mkhondo, *Reporting South Africa*, p.42
17 *Long Walk*, p.696
18 [Johannesburg] *Sunday Star*, 12 Aug. 1990
19 de Klerk, op. cit., p.188
20 Nixon, op. cit., pp.219–21
21 Turok, interview with author, 26 Jul. 1998
22 Mandela interview, *Prisoners of Hope* (video), Anant Singh.
23 Kathrada, interview with author, 21 Nov. 1998
24 *Nelson Mandela Speaks*, pp.53ff
25 Ibid., pp.68ff
26 Lekota, interview with author, 8 Feb. 1997
27 [Johannesburg] *Sunday Times*, 26 Aug. 1990
28 Waldmeir, op. cit., p.197
29 Mandela, closing address to ANC Conference, 7 Jul. 1991
30 *Leadership* magazine, Cape Town, Nov. 1989
31 Waldmeir, op. cit., p.210
32 Sisulu, interview with Houser and Shore, op. cit.
33 Mandela, interview with author, 28 Apr. 1994
34 Sisulu, interview with author, 29 Nov. 1995
35 *Sunday Independent*, 24 Nov. 1996
36 *Observer*, 17 Oct. 1993
37 Masekela, interview with author, 26 Oct. 1997
38 Author's interviews with Mandela's staff, 1997
39 Ibid.
40 Sachs, interview with author, 21 Jul. 1996
41 Ottaway, op. cit., p.158; Mandela, comments on text
42 Ottaway, op. cit., pp.32, 40
43 Adam and Moodley, op. cit., p.96
44 Mandela to Richard Stengel
45 Renwick, op. cit., p.146
46 Mandela, interview with author, 21 Feb. 1990
47 Mandela, speech to businessmen, 23 May 1990
48 *Citizen*, 15 Feb. 1990
49 Helen Suzman, interview with author, 16 May 1996
50 *Cape Times*, 8 Dec. 1990
51 Mandela, interview with author, 8 Aug. 1997
52 Ibid.

CHAPTER 30 Third Force

1 TRC Report, Vol.2, p.585
2 Mkhondo, op. cit., p.67

3 Sisulu, interview with Houser and Shore, op. cit.
4 Meer, 'Past Postscript', op. cit.
5 *Long Walk*, p.690
6 *Weekly Mail*, 19 Jul. 1991
7 Mandela to Richard Stengel
8 de Klerk, op. cit., p.199
9 Buthelezi, interview with author, 10 Feb. 1998
10 Waldmeir, op. cit., p.175
11 Mbeki, briefing in London, 20 Sept. 1990
12 Mkhondo, op. cit., p.68
13 TRC Report, Vol.2, p.585
14 *Long Walk*, p.704
15 TRC Report, Vol.2, p.708
16 Ibid., pp.681–4
17 Memo of Conversation, White House, 24 Sept. 1990 (declassified 22 Aug. 1995)
18 de Klerk, op. cit., p.200
19 Ibid., p.196
20 Pik Botha, interview with author, 21 Dec. 1997
21 Thatcher, op. cit., p.532
22 *The Times*, 18 Jul. 1990; personal recollections
23 Buthelezi, interview with author, 10 Feb. 1998
24 *Independent on Sunday*, 11 Nov. 1990
25 *Guardian*, 27 May 1991
26 Mandela, comments on text
27 *Long Walk*, p.708
28 TRC Report, Vol.3, p.326
29 Ottaway, op. cit., p.114
30 Mandela, interview with Bill Keller, *New York Times*, 12 Sept. 1994
31 Buthelezi, letter to Mandela, Apr. 1991 (ANC Archive, Johannesburg)
32 de Klerk, op. cit., p.206
33 *Business Day*, 18 Sept. 1990; Stephen Ellis, 'The Historical Significance of South Africa's Third Force', *Journal of Southern African Studies*, Jun. 1998, p.288
34 de Klerk, op. cit., p.184
35 Mark Stuart, *Douglas Hurd: The Public Servant*, p.281
36 *Guardian*, 25 Apr 1991
37 Sparks, op. cit., p.153
38 Manoim, op. cit., pp.143–53
39 de Klerk, op. cit., p.211
40 Mkhondo, op. cit., pp.93–4; see also photograph
41 Ottaway, op. cit., p.169
42 TRC Report, Vol.2, p.707
43 Ibid., p.709

CHAPTER 31 Exit Winnie

1 *Daily Telegraph*, 19 Mar. 1996
2 *Independent*, 8 Mar. 1995
3 *Long Walk*, p.719
4 Meer, 'Past Postscript', op. cit.
5 Ibid.
6 Noreen Taylor, interview with author, 27 Jun. 1998
7 Maharaj, interview with author, 21 Nov. 1998
8 Arthur Schlesinger, conversation with author, 10 Nov. 1997
9 Amina Cachalia, interview with author, 29 Aug. 1996
10 Winnie Mandela, interview with author, 22 Oct. 1996
11 *Cape Times*, 25 Jan. 1990
12 Maki Mandela, interview with author, 21 Mar. 1997
13 Gillian Slovo, *Every Secret Thing*, p.210
14 Meer, 'Past Postscript', op. cit.
15 IDAF memo, 14 Oct 1994 (IDAF Archive)
16 *Independent*, 17 Feb. 1991
17 Meer, 'Past Postscript', op. cit.
18 Mandela aide, interview with author
19 Winnie Mandela, interview with author, 22 Oct. 1996
20 *Sowetan*, 26 Sept. 1990
21 Ottaway, op. cit., p.153
22 Winnie Mandela, interview with author, 22 Oct. 1996
23 *Guardian*, 22 May 1990
24 *Star*, 20 Sept. 1990
25 Denis Herbstein, 'IDAF: The History' (unpublished)
26 Amina Cachalia, interview with author, 29 Aug. 1996
27 Tambo Archive, Cullen Library, Witwatersrand University, C3121
28 TRC hearings, 23 Jan. 1998
29 Winnie Mandela, interview with author, 22 Oct. 1996
30 See Chapter 37, pp.539–40

31 Gilbey, op. cit., p.272
32 *Sowetan*, 30 Mar. 1992; Moegsien Williams, interview with author, 17 Feb. 1997; Mandela, comments on text
33 See Gilbey, op. cit., pp.278–80
34 Fergal Keane, *The Bondage of Fear: A Journey Through the Last White Empire*, p.217
35 Masekela, interview with author, 26 Oct. 1997
36 Meer, 'Past Postscript', op. cit.
37 *Sowetan*, 16 Jul. 1993
38 [Johannesburg] *Sunday Times*, 6 Sept. 1992
39 Suzman, interview with author, 15 May 1996
40 [Johannesburg] *Sunday Times*, 1 Nov. 1992

CHAPTER 32 Negotiating

1 Suzman, interview with author, 16 May 1996
2 Mkhondo, op. cit., p.3
3 Ellis, op. cit., p.286
4 de Klerk, op. cit., p.185
5 *Long Walk*, p.626; video of Mandela's 1990 visit to London (Mayibuye Centre)
6 Renwick, interview with author, 2 Oct. 1996
7 de Klerk, op. cit., pp.365–7
8 *Long Walk*, p.588; Waldmeir, op. cit., p.241
9 de Klerk, op. cit., p.238
10 Mac Maharaj, interview with author, Jul. 1998; Maharaj, comments on text
11 *Nelson Mandela Speaks*, p.154; de Klerk, op. cit., p.220
12 Frene Ginwala, interview with author, 11 Oct. 1996; Albie Sachs, interview with author 21 Jul. 1996
13 See Waldmeir, op. cit., p.191
14 de Klerk, letter to author, Dec. 1996
15 Pik Botha, see Mkhondo, op. cit., p.12; de Klerk, op. cit., p.224
16 *Long Walk*, p.717
17 Ibid., p.692
18 *Nelson Mandela Speaks*, pp.164–5
19 de Klerk, op. cit., p.239
20 Albie Sachs, interview with author, 27 Feb. 1998
21 TRC Report, Vol.3, p.698
22 Meer (ed.), *The CODESA File*, p.109
23 *Nelson Mandela Speaks*, p.181
24 de Klerk, op. cit., p.242
25 Renwick, interview with author, 2 Oct. 1996
26 *Nelson Mandela Speaks*, p.210
27 Ibid., p.191
28 Meer (ed.), *The CODESA File*, pp.108–9
29 de Klerk, op. cit., p.245
30 TRC Report, Vol.3, p.144
31 Kasrils, interview with author, 31 Jul. 1997; Mandela, comments on text
32 *Star*, 15 Sept. 1992; *Nelson Mandela Speaks*, p.205
33 Ottaway, op. cit., p.224
34 Cyril Ramaphosa, conversation with author, 28 Jun. 1996
35 Ottaway, op. cit., p.250
36 Tim Du Plessis, interview with author, 26 Feb. 1998
37 Leon Wessels, interview with author, 27 Feb. 1998
38 Mandela, interview with Prof. Villa-Vicencio. See *Cape Times*, 1 Aug. 1992
39 BBC History Video
40 Maharaj, *Mayibuye*, Dec. 1997; Maharaj, interview with author, 21 Nov. 1998
41 Mandela, quoted in Waldmeir, op. cit., p.41
42 Waldmeir, op. cit., p.215; Sparks, op. cit., p.80
43 de Klerk, op. cit., p.248
44 Waldmeir, op. cit., pp.217–18; Maharaj, interview with author, 21 Nov 98; Maharaj, comments on text
45 de Klerk, op. cit., p.252
46 Waldmeir, op. cit., p.218
47 Maharaj, interview with author, 21 Nov. 1998
48 Sparks, op. cit., p.184
49 TRC report, Vol.2, p.708
50 Jeremy Cronin, conversation with author, 20 Nov. 1998
51 de Klerk, op. cit., p.257
52 Mkhondo, op. cit., p.163; Kasrils, interview with author, 12 Feb. 1997

53 *Nelson Mandela Speaks*, p.230
54 Albie Sachs, interview with author, 27 Feb. 1998
55 *Independent*, 18 Feb. 1993
56 *Long Walk*, p.727
57 de Klerk, op. cit., p.274
58 Ibid., p.276
59 *Star*, 14 Apr. 1993
60 Mandela, speech, 14 Apr. 1995
61 *Long Walk*, p.731
62 Mandela, speech to British Parliament, 5 May 1993; *Nelson Mandela Speaks*, p.256; Anthony Sampson, *Observer*, 9 May 1993
63 Ottaway, op. cit., p.249
64 *Observer*, 24 Apr. 1994
65 *The Times*, 6 May 1993
66 *Nelson Mandela Speaks*, p.261
67 Ibid., p.220; Kane-Berman, op.cit., pp.79–83
68 Mandela, comments on text
69 *Nelson Mandela Speaks*, p.231
70 *Independent*, 24 Jun. 1993
71 *The Times*, 21 Oct. 1993
72 Waldmeir, op. cit., p.227; Slabbert (reviewing Waldmeir), *Sunday Independent*, 25 May 1997
73 de Klerk, op. cit., p.280
74 Mandela, speech to UN, 24 Sept. 1993
75 Waldmeir, op. cit., p.231
76 Ibid., p.232
77 Ibid.
78 [Johannesburg] *Sunday Times*, 16 Feb. 1997
79 Adam et al., *Comrades in Business*, p.61
80 Vella Pillay, conversation with author, 7 Jan. 1999
81 *Mail & Guardian*, 6 Nov. 1998
82 Winnie Mandela, interview with author, 22 Oct. 1996
83 Nadine Gordimer, letter to author, 19 Dec. 1993; de Klerk, op. cit., p.299
84 de Klerk, letter to author, Dec. 1996
85 de Klerk, op. cit., p.300
86 Marike de Klerk, op. cit., p.200
87 Slovo, interview for Menell and Gibson, *Mandela* (film)

CHAPTER 33 Election

1 *Long Walk*, p.735
2 Carl Niehaus, interview with author, 30 Apr. 1998
3 *Citizen*, 21 Mar. 1994
4 Masekela, interview with author, 26 Oct. 1996
5 Buntman, op. cit., p.127 (quoting SA Press Association, 27 Sept. 1996)
6 Mandela, comments on text
7 Albie Sachs, interview with author, 21 Jul. 1996
8 Maharaj, in *Mayibuye*, Dec. 1997
9 Mandela, interview with Ken Owen, [Johannesburg] *Sunday Times*, 1 May 1994
10 *Independent*, 29 Apr. 1994
11 *Sunday Times*, 19 Dec. 1993
12 Mandela, speech at Johannesburg City Hall, 20 Feb. 1998
13 de Klerk, op. cit., p.330
14 Waldmeir, op. cit., p.238
15 Mandela, interview with author, 11 Feb. 1998
16 *Star*, 10 Oct., 24 & 26 Nov. 1993
17 Mandela, interview with author, 11 Feb. 1998
18 Mandela, interview with Anthony Lewis, *New York Times*, 23 Mar. 1997
19 Mandela, interview with author, 11 Feb. 1998
20 de Klerk, op. cit., p.311
21 Mandela, interview with author, 11 Feb. 1998
22 Mandela, comments on text
23 Pik Botha, interview with author, 21 Dec. 1997; Mandela, comments on text
24 P.W. Botha, interview with author, 2 Mar. 1998
25 *Observer*, 18 Dec. 1994; P.W. Botha, interview with author, 2 Mar. 1998
26 Kasrils, interviews with author, 12 Feb 1997, 31 Jul. 1997
27 Mandela, comments on text; *Star*, 25 Apr. 1994
28 Sparks, op. cit., p.214
29 *Sunday Times*, 13 Mar. 1994
30 Mandela, interview with author, 11 Feb. 1998
31 de Klerk, op. cit., p.315

32 Ibid., p.318
33 Mandela, speech to Senate, *Star*, 2 Apr. 1995
34 *Mail & Guardian*, 9 Jun. 1995
35 de Klerk, op. cit., p.322
36 *Guardian*, 9 Dec. 1997
37 Meredith, op. cit., p.514
38 *Sunday Times*, 10 Apr. 1994
39 Colin Coleman, interview with author, 30 Jun. 1998
40 Ibid.
41 Kissinger, interview with Ivan Fallon, *Star & S.A. Times*, 13 Nov. 1996
42 Private information
43 Colin Coleman, interview with author, 30 Jun. 1998
44 de Klerk, op. cit., p.326
45 Thabo Mbeki, conversation with author, 23 Apr. 1994
46 Author's conversation with member of de Klerk's election team, 15 Jun. 1990
47 *International Herald Tribune*, 16 Apr. 1994
48 de Klerk, op. cit., p.301
49 *New York Review of Books*, 20 Oct. 1994
50 *Star*, 25 Apr. 1994
51 Anant Singh, *Countdown to Freedom* (video, 1994)
52 Niehaus, interview with author, 30 Apr. 1998
53 de Klerk, op. cit., p.332
54 *International Herald Tribune*, 16 Apr. 1994
55 Mandela, interview with author, 28 Apr. 1994
56 TRC Report, Vol.2, p.662
57 Sisulu, interview with Houser and Shore, op. cit.
58 *Long Walk*, p.743
59 [Johannesburg] *Sunday Times*, 1 May 1994; author's conversation with member of de Klerk's election team, 15 Jun. 1990
60 Lakhdar Brahimi, conversation with author, 28 Apr. 1994
61 *Guardian*, 29 Apr. 1994
62 André Brink (ed.), *27 April: One Year Later*
63 Mandela, comments on text
64 *Long Walk*, p.747
65 Ibid.
66 *Time*, 13 Apr. 1998
67 *Long Walk*, p.750
68 de Klerk, op. cit., p.340
69 *Sunday Telegraph*, 1 May 1994

CHAPTER 34 Governing

1 *Nelson Mandela Speaks*, p.252
2 *Star & S.A. Times*, 1 Apr. 1998
3 [Johannesburg] *Sunday Times*, 25 Feb. 1996
4 Mandela, comments on text
5 Mandela, interview with John Carlin, *Independent*, 8 Jun. 1994
6 Hansard, South Africa, 12 Feb. 1997
7 de Klerk, op. cit., pp. 338–9, 346
8 BBC News, 31 Oct. 1997
9 John Doubleday, telephone conversation with author, 10 Jan. 1996
10 *Independent*, 8 Mar. 1995
11 Author's interview with a cabinet member
12 Molobi, interview with author, 26 Jun. 1998
13 *Independent*, 8 Mar. 1995
14 Ibid., 7 May 1995
15 Winnie Mandela, interview with author, 22 Oct 1996
16 C. Menell, op. cit.
17 Ibid.
18 See *Drum*, Johannesburg, Feb. 1996
19 Matanzima, interview with author, 24 Feb. 1997
20 Holomisa, interview with author, 19 Jan. 1997
21 Author's conversations in Umtata, 4 Feb. 1996
22 *Financial Times*, 18 Aug. 1994
23 At the annual Commonwealth party in London in March 1987 the Queen warmly greeted Archbishop Tutu, who was then at odds with Mrs Thatcher's government.
24 Private information
25 Kathrada, *Star*, 17 Jul. 1998
26 *Mail & Guardian*, 7 Nov. 1997

CHAPTER 35 The Glorified Perch

1 David Beresford, *Observer*, 5 May 1996

2 Sisulu, interview with author, Nov. 1995
3 Mandela, speech in Pietermaritzburg, 13 Mar. 1993; *Nelson Mandela Speaks*, p.229
4 Mandela, opening speech to 49th ANC Conference, Bloemfontein, 17 Dec. 1994
5 Mandela, closing speech, ibid., 22 Dec 1994
6 Mandela, speech at birthday party, Pretoria, 20 Jul. 1996
7 de Klerk, op. cit., p.342
8 Mandela, interview in *Time*, 16 May 1994
9 Asmal, interview with author, 26 Jan. 1996
10 Mandela, speech at memorial tribute to Joe Slovo, 4 May 1996
11 Mandela, interview with Keller, *New York Times*, 12 Sept. 1994
12 Pallo Jordan, interview with author, 12 Feb. 1998
13 Asmal, interview in [Johannesburg] *Sunday Times*, 19 Jul. 1998
14 de Klerk, op. cit., p.344
15 Author's interview with cabinet member
16 Asmal, conversation with author, 19 Mar. 1997
17 Maharaj, interview with author, 12 Feb. 1998
18 Bizos, interview with author, 19 Dec. 1997
19 Author's interview with cabinet member
20 de Klerk, op. cit., p.244
21 *New York Times*, 12 Sept. 1994
22 Author's interview with cabinet member; de Klerk, op. cit., p.350
23 de Klerk, conversation with author, 19 Jun. 1995
24 [Johannesburg] *Sunday Times*, 26 Nov. 1995
25 de Klerk, op. cit., p.352
26 Buthelezi, interview with author, 10 Feb. 1998
27 de Klerk, op. cit., p.353
28 Tutu, speech to Commonwealth Press Union, Cape Town, 15 Oct. 1996
29 *New York Times*, 12 Sept. 1994
30 Frene Ginwala, interview with author, 11 Oct. 1996
31 *New York Times*, 12 Sept. 1994
32 Mandela, lecture to Institute of Southeast Asian Studies, Singapore 12 May 1987
33 de Klerk and Ramaphosa, speeches to Parliament, 10 Oct. 1996
34 Mandela interview with author, 11 Feb. 1998
35 Author's interview with cabinet member
36 de Klerk, op. cit., p.345
37 Mandela, interview in *Time*, 14 Jun. 1993
38 Frank Chikane, speech to Commonwealth editors, Cape Town, 10 Oct. 1996
39 *Independent*, Jun. 1994
40 [Johannesburg] *Star*, 1 Aug. 1997, quoting Transparency International
41 Tutu, conversation with author, 17 Feb. 1998
42 *Independent*, 18 Mar. 1999
43 *Cape Argus*, 7 Feb. 1997
44 *Financial Times*, 9 May 1996
45 Raymond Louw, *Southern African Report*, Johannesburg, 12 Jan. 1996
46 Mandela, speech to Parliament, 7 Feb. 1997
47 See Mandela, speech to ANC Conference, 16 Dec. 1997

CHAPTER 36 Forgiving

1 Denis Goldberg, conversation with author, 2 Jan. 1999
2 Anthony Lewis, *New York Times* magazine, 2 Mar. 1997
3 Mandela, interview with author, 24 Feb. 1997
4 Alexander, interview with author, 14 Oct. 1996
5 Rich Mkhondo, *Reporting South Africa*, p.65
6 *Nelson Mandela Speaks*, p.229
7 *Independent*, 18 Aug. 1994
8 P.W. Botha, interview with author, 2 Mar. 1998
9 Willemse, interview with author, 21 Oct. 1996
10 C. Menell, op. cit.

11 Amina Cachalia, in *Madiba*, op. cit., p.76
12 Ibid., p.80
13 *Guardian*, 24 Nov. 1995
14 Gregory, interview with author. 26 Jul. 1998; Kathrada, interview, 16 Oct. 1996
15 Mandela, interview with author, 28 Apr. 1994
16 *Star*, 17 Jul. 1998
17 Mandela, speech to Parliament, 9 Feb. 1996
18 Naidoo and Sachs, op. cit., p.21
19 Mandela, interview with Anthony Lewis, *New York Times*, 2 Mar. 1997
20 de Klerk, op. cit., p.346
21 *Mail & Guardian*, 14 Aug. 1998
22 *Independent International*, 22 Dec. 1998
23 Mandela, press conference, Cape Town, 12 Feb. 1990
24 Author's talks with ANC officials, 18 Nov. 1991
25 [Johannesburg] *Star*, 15 Feb. 1994; T. Mbeki, conversation with editors, 17 Feb. 1998
26 Mandela to National Editors, 1 Nov. 1996; *Rhodes Journalism Review*, Grahamstown, Dec. 1996
27 *Star*, 20 Dec. 1997
28 Motlana, conversation with author, 2 Feb. 1996
29 *Business Day*, 19 Dec. 1997
30 Mandela, speech to ANC Conference, 16 Dec. 1997
31 *Star & S.A. Times*, 6 Nov. 1996
32 *Independent*, 1 Oct. 1996
33 *Rhodes Journalism Review*, Nov. 1997
34 Report by Peter Sullivan, 11 Jun. 1997
35 *Rhodes Journalism Review*, Nov. 1997
36 Mandela, speech to ANC Conference, 16 Dec. 1997
37 *Hustler* magazine [South Africa], Vol.4, No.1
38 *Cape Argus*, 6 Feb. 1998; Jakes Gerwel, conversation with author, 13 Feb. 1998
39 Mandela, speech to ANC Conference, 16 Dec. 1997
40 *Rhodes Journalism Review*, Dec. 1996
41 *Sunday Independent*, 6 Dec. 1998
42 Kader Asmal et al., *Reconciliation Through Truth*, p.18
43 Esther Waugh, conversation with author, 28 Jul. 1998
44 Gillian Slovo, in *Guardian*, 11 Oct. 1998
45 de Klerk, op. cit., pp.369–72
46 TRC Report, Vol.1, p.126
47 *Independent*, 5 Nov. 1996
48 *Guardian*, 13 May 1997
49 Ibid., 31 Mar. 1998
50 Ibid., 15 Oct. 1997
51 Ibid., 16 Oct. 1997
52 *The Times*, 22 Aug. 1996
53 *Star & S.A. Times*, 21 May 1997
54 Private information
55 *Mail & Guardian*, 17 Apr. 1998
56 TRC Report, Vol.5, p.225
57 Ibid., pp.225–6
58 *Sunday Independent*, 8 Nov. 1998
59 *Mail & Guardian*, 30 Oct. 1998
60 *Financial Times*, 31 Oct. 1998
61 *International Herald Tribune*, 2 Nov. 1998
62 *The Times*, 2 Nov. 1998
63 *Financial Times*, 4 Dec. 1998
64 Mandela, interview with John Carlin, *Sunday Independent*, 6 Dec. 1998
65 Mandela, interview with author, 21 Jan. 1999
66 *Sunday Independent*, 6 Dec. 1998
67 Graca Machel, interview with author, 22 Feb. 1998

CHAPTER 37 Withdrawing

1 Mandela, comments on text
2 de Klerk, op. cit., p.355; Mandela, comments on text
3 de Klerk, letter to author, Dec. 1997
4 Leon Wessels, interview with author, 27 Feb. 1998
5 Roelf Meyer, conversation with author, 17 Feb. 1998
6 de Klerk, letter to author, Dec. 1996
7 de Klerk, op. cit., p.365
8 *Independent*, 10 May 1996; Mandela, speech in Pretoria, 20 Jul. 1996
9 Mandela, interview with author, 21 Jan. 1999
10 Thabo Mbeki, conversation with author, 18 Oct. 1996

11 Sisulu, interview with Houser and Shore, op. cit.
12 Buthelezi, interview with author, 10 Feb. 1998
13 Mandela, lecture to Institute of Southeast Asian Studies, Singapore, 12 May 1997
14 Mandela, speech at birthday party, Pretoria, 20 Jul. 1996
15 [Johannesburg] *Sunday Times*, 25 Feb. 1996
16 Mandela, interview with author, 25 Jul. 1996
17 *Mail & Guardian*, 11 Oct. 1996
18 Ramaphosa, conversation with author, 21 May 1996
19 Mandela, comments on text
20 Winnie Mandela, interview with author, 22 Oct. 1996
21 *Star*, 17 Nov. 1997
22 Ibid., 20 Nov. 1997
23 Bridgland, op. cit., p.69
24 Lady (Emma) Nicholson, conversation with author, 30 Sept. 1997
25 *Star*, 17 Nov. 1997
26 Winnie Mandela, testimony to TRC, 12 Apr. 1997, pp.2197, 2390, 2217, 2249, 2408–12
27 *Citizen*, 18 Dec. 1997
28 *Business Day*, 18 Dec. 1997
29 *Citizen*, 18 Dec. 1997
30 *Daily Telegraph*, 18 Dec. 1997; *Independent*, 18 Dec. 1997; *Observer*, 21 Dec. 1997
31 Thabo Mbeki, speech to ANC Conference, 16 Dec. 1997
32 *Sowetan*, 18 Dec. 1997
33 Mandela, speech to ANC Conference, Mafikeng, 20 Dec. 1997
34 Mandela, breakfast talk at Rockefeller Center, New York, Sept. 1998
35 Thabo Mbeki, *Africa: The Time has Come*, p.76

CHAPTER 38 Graca

1 Fatima Meer, interview with author, 27 Jul. 1996
2 *Star*, 20 Aug. 1995
3 Ibid.
4 *Star & S.A. Times*, 3 Apr. 1996
5 Kathrada, in *Star*, 17 Jul. 1998
6 *Guardian*, 8 Jul. 1997
7 *Observer*, 17 Sept. 1995
8 Graca Machel, interview with author, 22 Feb. 1998
9 Winnie Mandela, interview with author, 22 Oct. 1996
10 *Independent*, 14 Jan. 1998
11 *Eastern Province Herald*, 3 Mar. 1996
12 Mark Gevisser, in *Vogue*, Aug. 1997
13 Mandela, TV interview with Allister Sparks, SABC, 8 Feb. 1998
14 Andrew Young, talk at Johannesburg City Hall, 19 Feb. 1998
15 Graca Machel, interview with author, 22 Feb. 1998
16 Ibid.
17 Ibid.
18 [Johannesburg] *Sunday Times*, 19 Jul. 1998
19 Kathrada, in *Star*, 17 Jul. 1998; Kathrada, comments on text
20 Graca Machel, interview with author, 22 Feb. 1998

CHAPTER 39 Mandela's World

1 Wole Soyinka, *Times Higher Education Supplement*, 2 Dec. 1994
2 *Mail & Guardian*, 16 Oct. 1998
3 Mandela, interview with author, 8 Aug. 1997
4 *Foreign Affairs*, Nov. 1993
5 Mandela, interview with John Carlin, *Sunday Independent*, 6 Dec. 1998
6 *Star & S.A. Times*, 21 May 1997
7 *Cape Times*, 24 Feb. 1997
8 Mandela, interview with author, 21 Jan. 1999
9 *Independent*, 21 Nov. 1995
10 Mandela, interview with author, 27 Nov. 1995
11 *Observer*, 26 Nov. 1995
12 Duodo, *Mail & Guardian*, 13 Nov. 1998
13 *Sunday Independent*, 20 Sept. 1997
14 Mandela, interview with author, 21 Jan. 1999
15 T. Mbeki, *Africa: The Time has Come*, p.292
16 *Star & S.A. Times*, 16 Sept. 1998

17 *Sunday Independent*, 6 Sept. 1998; *Star & S.A. Times*, 16 Sept. 98
18 *Mail & Guardian*, 8 Sept. 1995
19 Mandela, lecture to Institute of Southeast Asian Studies, Singapore, 12 May 1887
20 Mandela, speech to Oxford Centre for Islamic Studies, 11 Jul. 1997
21 *Sunday Independent*, 3 Aug. 1997
22 Jonathan Hyslop, 'The African Renaissance Meets the Asian Renaissance? The Malaysian Impact on Contemporary South Africa'
23 Barbara Masakela, interview with author, 26 Oct. 1996
24 *Sunday Independent*, 24 Nov. 1996
25 *International Herald Tribune*, 16 Jan. 1997
26 Mandela, speech on Robben Island, 11 Feb. 1996
27 *Star*, 5, 6 Sept. 1996
28 *Cape Times*, 23 Jan. 1992
29 *Daily Telegraph*, 23 Oct. 1997; *The Times*, 23 Oct. 1997; *International Herald Tribune*, 24 Oct. 1997
30 *Guardian*, 30 Oct. 1997
31 *Guardian*, 28 Oct. 1997
32 *New Republic*, 17 Nov. 1997
33 Mandela, interview with author, 21 Jan. 1999
34 *Daily Telegraph*, 20 Mar. 1999; private information
35 Bill Clinton, transcript of speech at White House, 22 Sept. 1998
36 Mandela, interview with author, 21 Jan. 1999
37 *International Herald Tribune*, 27 Mar. 1997
38 Mandela, interview with author, 21 Jan. 1999
39 *International Herald Tribune*, 30 Mar. 1998; private information
40 Mandela and Clinton, speeches at White House, 22 Sept. 1998; *Sunday Independent*, 27 Sept. 1998
41 *The Times*, 10 Jul. 1996
42 *Financial Times*, 9 Nov. 1998; Glenys Kinnock, 24 Nov. 1998; *Financial Times*, 26 Mar. 1999
43 Mandela, interview with author, 21 Jan. 1999
44 Clinton, transcript of speech at White House, 22 Sept. 1998

CHAPTER 40 Mandela's Country

1 Mandela, speech to Parliament, 5 Feb. 1999
2 Mandela, interview with author, 21 Jan. 1999
3 Adam et. al., *Comrades in Business*, pp.165–6
4 Ibid., p.201; see also Stanley Uys, in *Times Literary Supplement*, 14 Nov. 1997
5 Tom Lodge, in *Indicator*, Johannesburg, Autumn 1995
6 *Guardian*, 30 Jan. 1998
7 Mandela, interview with author, 24 Feb. 1997
8 Mandela, interview with author, 21 Jan. 1999
9 Ibid.
10 Mandela, speech to Parliament, 5 Feb. 1999
11 *Mail & Guardian*, 30 Apr. 1998
12 *Financial Times*, 27 Jun. 1998
13 See *International Herald Tribune*, 15 Jul. 1998
14 Mandela, speech to Parliament, 5 Feb. 1999
15 *Mail & Guardian*, 3 Jul. 1998; *Sunday Independent*, 5 Jul. 1998
16 Mandela, speech to Johannesburg Press Club, 22 Feb. 1991; *Nelson Mandela Speaks*, p.83
17 Interview with Robert Gephard of US State Department, *Star*, 7 Aug. 1998
18 *International Herald Tribune*, 17 Jul. 1998
19 Dullah Omar, interview with author, 12 Feb. 1997
20 *Star & S.A. Times*, 24 Sept. 1997
21 *Sunday Independent*, 13 Sept. 1998
22 *Star & S.A. Times*, 21 Oct., 25 Nov. 1998
23 *Sunday Independent*, 6 Dec. 1998
24 Ibid., 13 Sept. 1998
25 Mandela, speech to Parliament, 5 Feb. 1999
26 *Economist*, 6 Jun. 1996; *Sunday Independent*, 20 Sept. 1998

27 *Star & S.A. Times*, 23 Sept. 1998
28 *The Times*, 14 Sept. 1998
29 *Sunday Independent*, 20 Sept. 1998
30 *Sunday Times*, 22 Nov. 1998; David Paton's letter appeared in the Johannesburg *Sunday Independent*, 21 Mar. 1999, but was not accepted by the *Sunday Times*
31 Mandela, interview with author, 21 Jan. 1999
32 Mandela, interview with author, 11 Feb. 1998
33 *Mail & Guardian*, 30 Apr. 1998
34 *Sunday Independent*, 29 Mar., 9 Apr. 1998; Mail & Guardian, 12 Apr. 1998
35 *Mail & Guardian*, 27 Mar. 1998
36 Ibid., 9 Apr. 1998
37 *Guardian*, 7 Apr. 1997
38 South African Institute of Race Relations, South *African Survey 1997–1998*
39 *Guardian*, 15 Mar. 1999
40 Mandela, speech to Parliament, 26 Mar. 1999

CHAPTER 41 Image and Reality

1 *Long Walk*, p.385
2 Brian Walden, BBC TV, 3 Feb. 1998; for S.A. reactions see *Cape Argus*, 5 Feb. 1998
3 Mandela, interview with author, 21 Jan. 1999
4 Slovo, interview for Menell and Gibson, *Mandela* (film)

AFTERWORD Living Legend, Living Statue

1 'Mandela', interview with John Battersby, published in *Christian Science Monitor*, 10 Feb. 2000. http://www.csmonitor.com/2000/0210/p15s1.html
2 In mid-2004 Anthony Sampson began drafting an additional chapter to *Mandela: The Authorised Biography*. It was never published in the book
3 Foreword by Verne Harris, in Mandela, *Conversations with Myself*, Macmillan, London, 2010, pp. xx, xxi
4 *Mandela: The Living Legend*, two-part BBC television documentary broadcast 5 and 12 Mar. 2003
5 Ibid.
6 Interview with Graca Machel, published in *The Sunday Times*, 2 Mar. 2003
7 BBC, *Mandela: The Living Legend*
8 Mandela, interview with Mike Hannah and broadcast in two parts on *Al Jazeera*, 17 Jul. 2008
9 'Mandela Attacks Mbeki's Aids Policy', Chris McGreal in *Guardian*, 18 Feb. 2002. http://www.guardian.co.uk/world/2002/feb/18/aids.nelsonmandela
10 BBC, *Mandela The Living Legend*
11 Ibid.
12 'Mandela: US Wants Holocaust', CNN World report on speech made by Mandela to the International Women's Forum, 29 Jan. 2003
13 Ibid.
14 'The United States of America is a Threat to World Peace', Mandela interview with Tom Masland, *Newsweek*, 19 Sep. 2002. http://www.msnbc.com/news/806174.asp?cp1=1
15 Sampson, *Observer*, 6 Jul. 2003
16 BBC, *Mandela: The Living Legend*
17 BBC documentary, *The 90th Year*, 31 Jan. 2009
18 Sampson, unpublished chapter, 2004
19 Ibid.
20 Ibid.
21 *Daily Telegraph*, 11 Jun. 2002
22 Private conversations with sources in SADC and sources close to Mandela and Mbeki
23 'Mandela speaks out on his mission in the ANC', interview with Mandela in the *Star* and the *Independent* group newspapers, 11 Mar. 2002. http://www.iol.co.za/news/politics/mandela-speaks-out-on-his-mission-in-the-anc-1.83126
24 *Sunday Times*, South Africa, 28 Oct. 2009
25 'Obituary tribute to Walter Sisulu by Nelson Mandela', ANC, 3 May 2003
26 Mandela/Battersby interview, *Christian Science Monitor*, 10 Feb. 2000

27 John Carlin, *Playing the Enemy: Nelson Mandela and the Game that Made a Nation*, Penguin, London, 2008, p.252. The book was the basis for the film *Invictus*, directed by Clint Eastwood, and was republished as *Invictus: Nelson Mandela and the Game that Made a Nation*. *The 16th Man*, a documentary narrated by Morgan Freeman, directed by Clifford Bestall and based on Carlin's book, was broadcast in the United States on ESPN on 4 May 2010

28 'Conversation with Nelson Mandela', interview with Tim Couzens, Verne Harris and Mac Maharaj, 13 Aug. 2005 in Mike Nicol and Tim Couzens, *Mandela: The Authorised Portrait*, Wild Dog Press, 2006. Mandela's close associates in jail, Mac Maharaj and Ahmed Kathrada, were the editorial consultants on the project

29 *Guardian*, 11 Feb. 2011

30 Mandela/Battersby interview, *Christian Science Monitor*, 10 Feb. 2000

31 Ibid.

32 Mandela/Verne Harris interview, ABC television, 21 Oct. 2010

SELECT BIBLIOGRAPHY

BY NELSON MANDELA

Long Walk to Freedom (revised edition), Abacus, London, 1995
No Easy Walk to Freedom (ed. Ruth First), Heinemann, London, 1965
The Struggle is my Life, International Defence and Aid Fund for Southern Africa, London, 1978
Nelson Mandela Speaks: Forging a Democratic, Nonracial South Africa, David Philip, Johannesburg, 1994
'We Defy', *Drum*, Aug. 1952
Articles in *Liberation* and *Fighting Talk*, Johannesburg, 1953–59
Africa Diary (unpublished, Brenthurst Library), 1962
Trial speech, first draft, 1962 (Cullen Library, University of the Witwatersrand, Johannesburg)
Brief Notes in the Event of a Death Sentence, 1964 (Institute of Commonwealth Studies, University of London)
Jail Memoir (unpublished), 1975–76
'National Liberation' (unpublished essay), 1977
'Black Consciousness Movement' (unpublished essay), 1978
Conversations with Richard Stengel for *Long Walk to Freedom*, 1994
Interviews for Joe Menell and Angus Gibson for *Mandela* (film), 1994
Speeches and interviews, 1990–99, ANC, Johannesburg, and Office of the President, Pretoria

BY ANTHONY SAMPSON

Drum: An African Adventure and Afterwards, Hodder & Stoughton, London, 1983 (originally published by Collins, London, 1956)
The Treason Cage, Heinemann, London, 1958
(with S. Pienaar) *South Africa: Two Views of Separate Development*, Oxford University Press, 1960
Macmillan: A Study in Ambiguity, Allen Lane, The Penguin Press, London, 1967
Black and Gold, Hodder & Stoughton, London, 1987
Diaries (unpublished), 1955–99
The Sampson Letter (fortnightly newsletter), Sept. 1984–Jul. 1986

* * *

Peter Abrahams, *Return to Goli*, Faber & Faber, London, 1953
Heribert Adam and Kogila Moodley, *South Africa Without Apartheid*, University of California Press, Berkeley, 1986
Heribert Adam, Frederik van Zyl Slabbert and Kogila Moodley, *Comrades in Business: Post-Liberation Politics in South Africa*, Tafelberg Publishers, Cape Town, 1997
Chris Alden, *Apartheid's Last Stand: The Rise and Fall of the South African Security State*, Macmillan, London, 1996
Neville Alexander, *Robben Island Dossier 1964–1974*, UCT Press, Cape Town, 1994
Amnesty International, *Political Imprisonment in South Africa*, Amnesty International, London, 1978
Kader Asmal, Louise Asmal and Ronald Suresh Roberts, *Reconciliation Through Truth*, David Philip, Johannesburg, 1996
Natoo Babenia, *Memoirs of a Saboteur*, Mayibuye, Cape Town, 1985
Martin Bailey, *Oilgate: The Sanctions Scandal*, Coronet, London, 1979
Pauline H. Baker, *The United States and South Africa: The Reagan Years*, Ford Foundation and Foreign Policy Association, New York, 1989
'Banned Leader', 'Problems of Organisation in the ANC', *Liberation*, Nov. 1955
Anthony Barber, *Taking the Tide*, Michael Russell, Norwich, 1996
Howard Barrell, *MK: The ANC's Armed Struggle*, Penguin, Harmondsworth, 1990
Howard Barrell, 'Conscripts to Their Age: ANC Operational Strategy, 1976–1986' (unpublished D.Phil thesis), University of Oxford, 1993
Mary Benson, *South Africa: The Struggle for a Birthright*, Penguin Africa Library, 1966
Mary Benson, *Nelson Mandela: The Man and the Movement*, Penguin, London, 1994
Mary Benson, *A Far Cry: The Making of a South African*, Viking, London, 1989
Mary Benson, Athol Fugard and Barney Simon, *Bare Stage, a Few Props, Great Theatre*, Ravan Press, Randburg, 1997
Hilda Bernstein, *The World that was Ours: The Story of the Rivonia Trials*, SA Writers, Robert Vicat, London, 1989
Rusty Bernstein, 'Memory Against Forgetting' (to be published in 1999)
Nicholas Bethell, *Spies and Other Secrets*, Viking, London, 1994
George Bizos, Notes for a Memoir (unpublished), 1996
Arthur Blaxall, *Suspended Sentence*, Hodder & Stoughton, London, 1965
Harry Bloom, *King Kong: An African Jazz Opera*, Collins, London, 1961
P.W. Botha, *Fighter and Reformer: Extracts from the Speeches of P.W. Botha* (compiled by J.J.J. Scholtz), Bureau of Information, Pretoria, 1989
Graham Boynton, *Last Days in Cloud Cuckoo Land*, Random House, New York, 1998

Fred Bridgland, *Katiza's Journey: Beneath the Surface of South Africa's Shame*, Sidgwick & Jackson, London, 1997
André Brink (ed.), *27 April: One Year Later*, Queillerie, Pretoria, 1995
André Brink, *Reinventing a Continent*, Secker & Warburg, London, 1996
Victoria Brittain, *Hidden Lives, Hidden Deaths*, Faber & Faber, London, 1988
Ralph J. Bunche (ed. Robert R. Edgar), *An African-American in South Africa: The Travel Notes of Ralph J. Bunche, 28 September 1937–1 January 1938*, Ohio University Press, Athens and Witwatersrand University Press, Johannesburg, 1992
Brian Bunting, *Moses Kotane*, Inkululeko Publications, London, 1975
Fran Lisa Buntman, 'The Politics of Conviction: Political Prisoner Resistance on Robben Island, 1962–1991' (unpublished PhD thesis), University of Texas at Austin, 1997
Alex Callinicos and John Rogers, *Southern Africa After Soweto*, Pluto Press, London, 1977
Luli Callinicos, 'Oliver Tambo and the Politics of Class, Race and Ethnicity in the ANC' (unpublished seminar paper), History Workshop, University of the Witwatersrand, 1997
Luli Callinicos, Notes for a Biography of Oliver Tambo (unpublished)
Joel Carlson, *No Neutral Ground*, Davis-Poynter Ltd, London, 1973
Stephen Clingman, *Bram Fischer: Afrikaner Revolutionary*, David Philip Publishers and Mayibuye Books, Belville, 1998
Richard Cockett, *David Astor and the Observer*, André Deutsch, London, 1991
Samuel Taylor Coleridge, *Biographia Literaria*, Cambridge University Press, 1920
Diana Collins, *Partners in Protest: My Life with Canon Collins*, Gollancz, London, 1992
John Collins, *Faith Under Fire*, Leslie Frewin, London, 1966
The Commonwealth Eminent Persons Group on Southern Africa, *Mission to South Africa: The Commonwealth Report*, Penguin, Middlesex, 1986
Tim Couzens, *The New African: A Study of the Life and Work of H.I.E. Dhlomo*, Ravan Press, Johannesburg, 1985
Chester Crocker, *High Noon in Southern Africa: Making Peace in a Rough Neighbourhood*, Jonathan Ball, Johannesburg, 1993
Jennifer Crwys-Williams (ed.), *In the Words of Nelson Mandela*, Penguin, London, 1997
Eddie Daniels, *There and Back: Robben Island, 1964–1979*, Mayibuye Books, University of the Western Cape, Belville, 1998
A.K. Datta, *South Africa*, Indian Council for Africa, New Delhi, 1960
Basil Davidson, *Report on Southern Africa*, Jonathan Cape, London, 1952
Peter Davis, *In Darkest Hollywood: Exploring the Jungle of Cinema's South Africa*, Ravan Press and Ohio University Press, Randburg and Athens, 1996

C.W. de Kiewiet, *The Anatomy of South African Misery*, Oxford University Press, 1957

F.W. de Klerk, *The Last Trek: A New Beginning – The Autobiography*, Macmillan, London, 1998

Marike de Klerk, *Marike: A Journey Through Summer and Winter* (as told by Maretha Maartens), Cape Diem Books, Vanderbijlpark, 1997

Willem de Klerk, *F.W. de Klerk: The Man in his Time*, Jonathan Ball, Johannesburg, 1991

Jacques Derrida and Mustapha Tlili (eds), *For Nelson Mandela*, Seaver Books, New York, 1987

H.H.W. de Villiers, *Rivonia: Operation Mayibuye*, Afrikaanse Pers-Boekhandel, Johannesburg, 1964

Hans d'Orville (ed.), *Leadership for Africa: In Honour of Olusegun Obasanjo on the Occasion of his 60th Birthday*, African Leadership Foundation, New York, 1995

Frank Diamond, *Portrait of Mandela* (film for IDAF, 1980)

Michael Dingake, *My Fight Against Apartheid*, Kliptown Books, London, 1987

Moses Dlamini, *Hell Hole, Robben Island: Reminiscences of a Political Prisoner*, Spokesman Books, Nottingham, 1984

Charles Douglas-Home, *Evelyn Baring: The Last Proconsul*, Collins, London, 1978

Peter Dreyer, *Martyrs and Fanatics*, Simon & Schuster, New York, 1980

C.J. Driver, *Patrick Duncan: South African and Pan-African*, Heinemann, London, 1980

Shirley Du Boulay, *Tutu: Voice of the Voiceless*, Hodder & Stoughton, London, 1988

Jack Dugard, 'Fragments of my Fleece' (unpublished), 1985

John Dugard (ed.), *The Last Years of Apartheid: Civil Liberties in South Africa*, Ford Foundation, New York, 1992

Stephen Ellis and Tsepo Sechaba, *Comrades Against Apartheid: The ANC and the South African Communist Party in Exile*, James Currey, London and Indiana University Press, Bloomington and Indianapolis, 1992

Stephen Ellis, 'South Africa's Third Force: Where did it come from? Where did it go?' (unpublished seminar paper), Institute of Commonwealth Studies, University of London, 1996

Stephen Ellis, 'The Historical Significance of South Africa's Third Force', *Journal of Southern African Studies*, Vol.24, No.2, Jun. 1998

Harold Evans, *Downing Street Diary: The Macmillan Years 1957–1963*, Hodder & Stoughton, London, 1981

Orlando Figes, *A People's Tragedy: The Russian Revolution 1891–1924*, Jonathan Cape, London, 1998

William Finnegan, *Dateline Soweto*, Harper & Row, New York, 1988

Foreign Policy Study Foundation, *South Africa: Time Running Out*, University of California Press, Berkeley and Los Angeles, 1981

Lionel Forman and E.S. Sachs, *The South African Treason Trial*, John Calder, London, 1957

Sadie Forman and André Odendaal (eds), *Lionel Forman: A Trumpet from the Housetops*, Zed Books, London, 1992

Julie Frederikse, *The Unbreakable Thread*, Zed Books, London, 1990

Bill Freund, *Insiders and Outsiders: The Indian Working Class of Durban, 1910–1990*, Heinemann, James Currey Ltd and University of Natal Press, Portsmouth, New Hampshire, London and Pietermaritzburg, 1995

J.A Froude, *Lord Beaconsfield*, Sampson Low, London, 1890

Athol Fugard, *Statements: Two Workshop Productions Devised by Athol Fugard, John Kani and Winston Ntshona*, Oxford University Press, 1974

M.K. Gandhi, *An Autobiography, or The Story of my Experiments with Truth*, Penguin, London, 1982

Gail M. Gerhart, *Black Power in South Africa: The Evolution of an Ideology*, University of California Press, Berkeley, 1979

Mark Gevisser, *Portraits of Power*, David Philip Publishers, Cape Town, 1996

Martin Gilbert, *Finest Hour: Winston Churchill, 1939–1941*, Heinemann, London, 1983

Emma Gilbey, *The Lady: The Life and Times of Winnie Mandela*, Jonathan Cape, London, 1983

Nadine Gordimer, *Six Feet of the Country*, Gollancz, London, 1958

Sir de Villiers Graaff, *Div Looks Back: The Memoirs of Sir de Villiers Graaff*, Human & Rousseau, Cape Town, 1993

James Gregory, *Goodbye, Bafana: Nelson Mandela, My Prisoner, My Friend*, Headline, London, 1995

Albrecht Hagemann, *Nelson Mandela*, Fontein Books, Johannesburg, 1996

Peter Hain, *Sing the Beloved Country*, Pluto Press, London, 1996

W.K. Hancock, *Smuts: The Fields of Force, 1919–1950*, Cambridge University Press, 1968

Nancy Harrison, *Winnie Mandela: Mother of a Nation*, Gollancz, London, 1985

Robert Harvey, 'The Great White Trek: A History of the Afrikaner Tribe from van Riebeeck to the Fall of Apartheid' (unpublished manuscript), 1996

Healdtown, 1855–1955: Centenary Brochure, Lovedale Press, Lovedale, 1955

Denis Healey, *The Time of my Life*, Michael Joseph, London, 1989

Tony Heard, *The Cape of Storms: A Personal History of the Crisis in South Africa*, Ravan Press, Johannesburg, 1990

Edward Heath, *The Course of my Life: My Autobiography*, Hodder & Stoughton, London, 1998

Denis Herbstein, *White Man, We Want to Talk to You*, Penguin, London, 1978

Denis Herbstein, 'IDAF: The History' (unpublished manuscript), 1998
Leslie Arthur Hewson, 'Healdtown: A Study of a Methodist Experiment in African Education' (unpublished thesis), Rhodes University, Grahamstown, 1959
Baruch Hirson, *Revolutions in my Life*, Witwatersrand University Press, Johannesburg, 1995
Jim Hoagland, *South Africa: Civilizations in Conflict*, George Allen & Unwin, London, 1973
Heidi Holland, *The Struggle: A History of the African National Congress*, Grafton, London, 1989
Alistair Horne, *Macmillan, 1957–1986: Volume II of the Official Biography*, Macmillan, London, 1989
Geoffrey Howe, *Conflict of Loyalty*, Pan, London, 1995
Trevor Huddleston, *Naught for Your Comfort*, Collins, London, 1956
Trevor Huddleston, *Return to South Africa*, Fount, London, 1991
Sir David Hunt, *On the Spot*, Peter Davis, London, 1975
Jonathan Hyslop, 'The African Renaissance Meets the Asian Renaissance? The Malaysian Impact on Contemporary South Africa' (unpublished seminar paper), Institute of Commonwealth Studies, University of London, 1998
Duncan Innes, *Anglo: Anglo-American and the Rise of Modern South Africa*, Ravan Press, Johannesburg, 1984
Noni Jabavu, *The Ochre People*, John Murray, London, 1963
Tim Jenkin, 'Talking to Vula: The Story of the Secret Underground Communications Network of Operation Vula', *Mayibuye*, May–Oct. 1995
Sheridan Johns and R. Hunt Davis Jr (eds), *Mandela, Tambo and the African National Congress: The Struggle Against Apartheid, 1948–1990 – A Documentary Survey*, Oxford University Press, New York, 1991
Paul Johnson, *Gold Fields: A Centenary Portrait*, Weidenfeld & Nicolson, London, 1987
Phyllis Johnson and David Martin (eds), *Destructive Engagement: Southern Africa at War*, Zimbabwe Publishing House, Harare, 1986
R.W. Johnson, *How Long will South Africa Survive?*, Macmillan, London, 1977
R.W. Johnson and Lawrence Schlemmer (eds), *Launching Democracy in South Africa: The First Open Election, April 1994*, Yale University Press, New Haven and London, 1996
Shaun Johnson, *Strange Days Indeed: South Africa from Insurrection to Post-Election*, Bantam Press, Johannesburg, 1994
Joel Joffe, *The Rivonia Story*, Mayibuye Books, Cape Town, 1995
Helen Joseph, *If this be Treason*, André Deutsch, London, 1963
Helen Joseph, *Side by Side*, Zed Books, London, 1986
John Kane-Berman, *South Africa: The Method in the Madness*, Pluto Press, London, 1979

John Kane-Berman, *Political Violence in South Africa*, SAIIR, Johannesburg, 1993
James Kantor, *A Healthy Grave*, Hamish Hamilton, London, 1967
Thomas Karis and Gwendolen M. Carter, *From Protest to Challenge: A Documentary History of African Politics in South Africa, 1882–1964. Vol.2: Hope and Challenge, 1935–1982*, Hoover Institution Press, Stanford, 1977
Thomas Karis and Gwendolen M. Carter, *From Protest to Challenge: A Documentary History of African Politics in South Africa, 1882–1964. Vol.3: Challenge and Violence, 1953–1964*, Hoover Institution Press, Stanford, 1977
Thomas G. Karis and Gail M. Gerhart, *From Protest to Challenge: A Documentary History of African Politics in South Africa, 1882–1990. Vol.5: Nadir and Resurgence, 1964–1979*, Indiana University Press, Indianapolis, 1997
Thomas G. Karis, 'Revolution in the Making: Black Politics in South Africa', *Foreign Affairs*, Winter 1983–84
Ronnie Kasrils, *'Armed and Dangerous': My Undercover Struggle Against Apartheid*, Heinemann, London, 1993 (second edn, Mayibuye Books, Belville and Jonathan Ball, Johannesburg, 1998)
Ahmed Kathrada, 'Summary of Different Viewpoints' (unpublished), 1977
Fergal Keane, *The Bondage of Fear: A Journey Through the Last White Empire*, Viking, London, 1994
Alexander Kerr, *Fort Hare 1915–1948*, Shuter & Shooter, Pietermaritzburg, 1968
The Kissinger Study on Southern Africa, Spokesman Books, Nottingham, 1975
Moses Kotane, *The Great Crisis Ahead*, New Age Publications, Johannesburg, 1957
Alf Kumalo and Es'kia Mphahlele, *Mandela: Echoes of an Era*, Penguin, London, 1990
Ellen Kuzwayo, *Call me Woman*, Ravan Press, Johannesburg, 1985
Anthony Lake, *The 'Tar Baby' Option: American Policy Toward Southern Rhodesia*, Columbia University Press, New York, 1976
David Lamb, *The Africans*, Vintage, New York, 1985
Brian Lapping, *Apartheid: A History* (television documentary, 1986, directed by John Blake)
Brian Lapping, *Apartheid: A History*, Grafton, London, 1986
Graham Leach, *South Africa*, Routledge & Kegan Paul, London, 1986
Mosiuoa Patrick (Terror) Lekota, *Prison Letters to a Daughter*, Taurus, Pretoria, 1991
Joseph Lelyveld, *Move Your Shadow*, Times Books, New York, 1985
Rev. Arthur J. Leonard, *A Brief History of Clarkebury*, Cory Library, Rhodes University
'A. Lerumo' (Michael Harmel), *Fifty Fighting Years: The Communist Party of South Africa, 1921–1971*, Inkululeko Publications, London, 1971

Doris Lessing, *Under my Skin*, HarperCollins, London, 1994
Julius Lewin, *The Rise of Congress in South Africa*, Indian Opinion, Phoenix, 1953
Merle Lipton, *Capitalism and Apartheid*, Gower, Aldershot, 1985
Tom Lodge, *Black Politics in South Africa Since 1945*, Longman, London, 1983
Tom Lodge, Bill Nasson, Steven Mufson, Khehla Shubane and Nokwanda Sithole, *All, Here and Now: Black Politics in South Africa in the 1980s*, Ford Foundation, New York, 1991
Albert Luthuli, *Let my People Go: An Autobiography*, Collins, London, 1962
Dale T. McKinley, *The ANC and the Liberation Struggle: A Critical Political Biography*, Pluto Press, London, 1997
Nosipho Majeke, *The Role of the Missionaries in Conquest*, Society of Young Africa, Johannesburg, 1952
Miriam Makeba, *Makeba: My Story*, Bloomsbury, London, 1988
Sebastian Mallaby, *After Apartheid*, Faber & Faber, London, 1992
Winnie Mandela, *Part of my Soul*, Penguin, London, 1985
Zindzi Mandela, *Black as I am*, Sereti Sa Sechaba & Madiba, Durban, 1989
Irwin Manoim, '*You Have Been Warned*': *The First Ten Years of the Mail & Guardian*, Viking Penguin, London, 1996
Shula Marks and Stanley Trapido (eds), *The Politics of Race, Class and Nationalism in Twentieth-Century South Africa*, Longman, London, 1987
Todd Matshikiza, *Chocolates for my Wife*, Hodder & Stoughton, London, 1961
Don Mattera, *Memory is the Weapon*, Ravan Press, Johannesburg, 1987
Frieda Matthews, *Remembrances*, Mayibuye Books, Cape Town, 1995
Z.K. Matthews, *Freedom for my People*, David Philip, Cape Town, 1981
Govan Mbeki, *Learning from Robben Island: The Prison Writings*, David Philip, Cape Town, Ohio University Press, Athens, Ohio and James Currey, London, 1991
Govan Mbeki, *Sunset at Midday: Latshon'ilang'emni*, Nolwazi Educational Publishers, Braamfontein, 1996
Thabo Mbeki, *Africa: The Time has Come*, Tafelberg Publishers, Cape Town and Mafube Publishing, Johannesburg, 1998
Fatima Meer, *Higher than Hope*, Hamish Hamilton, London, 1990
Fatima Meer, 'Past-Postscript' to *Higher than Hope* (for Dutch edition; unpublished in English)
Fatima Meer (ed.), *The CODESA File: An Institute for Black Research Project*, Madiba Publishers, Durban, 1993
Francis Meli, *South Africa Belongs to us: A History of the ANC*, Zimbabwe Publishing House, Harare, 1988
Clive Menell, Memoir on Mandela (unpublished), 1995
Joe Menell and Angus Gibson, *Mandela* (film), 1995. Research interviews:

Mabel Mandela, Godfrey Pitje, Ismail Meer, Joe Slovo, Albertina Sisulu, Leabie Piliso, Joe Matthews, Nthato Motlana, Winnie Mandela, Eddie Daniels, Sonny Venkatrathnam, Ahmed Kathrada

Martin Meredith, *The First Dance of Freedom: Black Africa in the Post-War Era*, Hamish Hamilton, London, 1984

Martin Meredith, *Nelson Mandela: A Biography*, Hamish Hamilton, London, 1997

Christopher Merrett, *A Culture of Censorship*, David Philip Publishers, Cape Town, 1994

William Minter, *King Solomon's Mines Revisited*, Basic Books, New York, 1986

Rich Mkhondo, *Reporting South Africa*, James Currey, London, 1993

Bloke Modisane, *Blame me on History*, Thames & Hudson, London, 1963

Naboth Mokgatle, *The Autobiography of an Unknown South African*, University of California Press, Berkeley, 1971

Kenneth Mokoena (ed.), *South Africa and the United States: The Declassified History*, A National Security Archive Documents Reader, The New Press, New York, 1993

T. Dunbar Moodie, 'The Moral Economy of the Black Miners' Strike of 1946', *Journal of Southern African Studies*, Vol.13, No.1, Oct. 1986

Noel Mostert, *Frontiers*, Jonathan Cape, London, 1992

Casey 'Kid' Motsisi (ed. Mothobi Mutloatse), *Casey and Company: Selected Writings*, Ravan, Johannesburg, 1980

Ezekiel Mphahlele, *Down Second Avenue*, Faber & Faber, London, 1959

Mqhayi (trans. Robert Kavanagh), *The Making of a Servant and Other Poems*, Ophir, Pretoria, 1972

Bruno Mtolo, *The Road to the Left*, Drakensberg Press, Durban, 1966

Bruce Murray, *Wits: The Open Years*, Witwatersrand University Press, Johannesburg, 1997

James Mutambirwa, *South Africa: The Sanctions Mission*, Zed Books, London, 1989

Indres Naidoo and Albie Sachs, *Prisoner 885/63: Island in Chains: Ten Years on Robben Island*, Penguin, London, 1982

Nat Nakasa (ed. Essop Patel), *The World of Nat Nakasa*, Ravan Press, Johannesburg, 1975

Jawaharlal Nehru, *Mahatma Gandhi*, Asia Publishing House, Bombay, 1960

Bernard Newman, *South African Journey*, Herbert Jenkins, London, 1965

Matthew Nkoana, *Crisis in the Revolution: A Special Report on the Pan-Africanist Congress of South Africa*, Mufabe, London, 1969

Lewis Nkosi, *Home and Exile*, Longmans, Green & Co., London, 1975

Rob Nixon, *Homelands, Harlem and Hollywood: South African Culture and Beyond*, Routledge, New York, 1994

Phyllis Ntantala, *A Life's Mosaic*, David Philip (for Mayibuye Centre), Cape Town, 1992

Olusegan Obasanjo and Felix Mosha (eds), *Africa: Rise to Challenge*, Africa Leadership Forum, New York, 1993

Dan O'Meara, *Forty Lost Years: The Apartheid State and the Politics of the National Party 1948–1994*, Ravan Press, Randburg and Ohio University Press, Athens, 1996

David Ottaway, *Chained Together: Mandela, de Klerk and the Struggle to Remake South Africa*, Times Books, New York, 1993

David Owen, *Face the Future*, Oxford University Press, 1981

George Padmore, *Pan-Africanism or Communism? The Coming Struggle for Africa*, Dennis Dobson, London, 1956

Alan Paton, *Cry, the Beloved Country*, Jonathan Cape, London, 1948

Alan Paton, *Hope for South Africa*, Pall Mall Press, London, 1958

Alan Paton, *Journey Continued*, Oxford University Press, 1988

J.B. Peires, *The House of Phalo*, Ravan Press, Johannesburg, 1981

Joseph A.M. Peppeta, 'A Portrait of a School: Healdtown Missionary Institution Through the Eyes of Some of its Ex-Pupils' (unpublished MA thesis), Cory Library, Rhodes University, 1998

Margery Perham, *African Apprenticeship*, Faber & Faber, London, 1974

Ben Pimlott, *The Queen*, HarperCollins, London, 1996

William Plomer, *The South African Autobiography*, David Philip, Johannesburg, 1984

Benjamin Pogrund, *How can Man Die Better: Sobukwe and Apartheid*, Peter Halban, London, 1990

Benjamin Pogrund, 'Killing the Messenger: A History of the *Rand Daily Mail*' (unpublished), 1996

Dr Daan Prinsloo, *Stem uit die Wilderness: 'n Biografie oor oud-pres. P.W. Botha*, Vaandel-Uitgewers, Mosselbaai, 1997

Progressive Forum, *The Defiance Campaign: A Study in Opportunism*, Progressive Forum, Johannesburg, 1953

Mamphela Ramphele, *A Life*, David Philip, Johannesburg, 1995

Enuga Reddy and Fatima Meer (eds), *Passive Resistance 1946: A Selection of Documents*, Madiba Publishers/Institute for Black Research, Durban, 1996

Robin Renwick, *Unconventional Diplomacy in Southern Africa*, Macmillan, London, 1997

Maggie Resha, *My Life in the Struggle: 'Mangoana Tsoara Thipa Ka Bohaleng*, Congress of South African Writers, Johannesburg, 1991

Edward Roux, *S.P. Bunting: A Political Biography*, published by the author and distributed by the *African Bookman*, Cape Town, 1944

James Sanders, 'A Struggle for Representation: The International Media Treatment of South Africa, 1972–1979' (unpublished PhD thesis), University of London, 1997 (to be published in 1999)

Claudia Schadeberg, *Voices from Robben Island* (film, 1994, directed by Adam Low)

Jurgen Schadeberg, *Voices from Robben Island*, Ravan, Johannesburg, 1994

Arthur Schlesinger Jr, *Robert Kennedy and his Times*, André Deutsch, London, 1978

Martin Schneider (ed.), *Madiba: Nelson Rolihlahla Mandela: A Celebration*, Martin Schneider & Co. and Twidale Publishing, Johannesburg, 1997

David Scott, *Ambassador in Black and White: Thirty Years of Changing Africa*, Weidenfeld & Nicolson, London, 1981

Jeremy Seekings, 'The Fragile Front: The United Democratic Front and the Referendum Issue, 1983–84' (unpublished seminar paper), University of Cape Town, 1993

Jeremy Seekings, 'What was the United Democratic Front?' (unpublished seminar paper), Yale University, 1994

Ronald Segal, *Political Africa*, Stevens, London, 1961

Ronald Segal, *Into Exile*, Jonathan Cape, London, 1963

Anthony Seldon, *Major: A Political Life*, Phoenix, London, 1997

Mark Hugh Shaw, 'South Africa's Other War: Understanding and Resolving Political Violence in Kwazulu-Natal (1985 –) and the PWV (1990 –) ' (unpublished PhD thesis), University of the Witwatersrand, 1997

A Short Pictorial History of the University College of Fort Hare, 1916–1959, Lovedale Press, Lovedale, 1961

Vladimir Shubin, 'The Soviet Union/Russian Federation's Relations with South Africa, with Special Reference to the Period Since 1980', *African Affairs*, Vol.95, 1996

George P. Shultz, *Turmoil and Triumph: My Years as Secretary of State*, Scribners, New York, 1993

Jack and Ray Simons, *Class and Colour in South Africa 1850–1950*, International Defence and Aid Fund for Southern Africa, London, 1983

Anant Singh, *Countdown to Freedom: Ten Days that Changed South Africa* (video, 1994, directed by Danny Schechter)

Anant Singh, *Prisoners of Hope: Robben Island Reunion* (video, 1995, directed by Danny Schechter)

Walter Sisulu, 'National Liberation' (unpublished essay), 1977

Walter Sisulu, interview with George Houser and Herbert Shore, Sept.–Oct. 1995

Gillian Slovo, *Every Secret Thing*, Little, Brown, London, 1997

Joe Slovo, *The Unfinished Autobiography*, Ravan Press, Randburg and Hodder & Stoughton, London, 1995

South African Institute of Race Relations (SAIIR), *Surveys, 1957–1998*, SAIIR, Johannesburg

Wole Soyinka, *Mandela's Earth and Other Poems*, Random House, New York, 1988

Allister Sparks, *The Mind of South Africa*, Heinemann, London, 1990

Allister Sparks, *Tomorrow is Another Country: The Inside Story of South Africa's Negotiated Revolution*, Heinemann, London, 1995

Allister Sparks, *The Death of Apartheid* (film, 1994, directed by Mick Gold)

Mark Stuart, *Douglas Hurd: The Public Servant – An Authorised Biography*, Mainstream Publishing, Edinburgh, 1998

Aelred Stubbs (ed.), *Steve Biko: I Write What I Like*, Heinemann, London, 1978

Helen Suzman, *Memoirs: In no Uncertain Terms*, Sinclair-Stevenson, London, 1993

Les Switzer (ed.), *South Africa's Alternative Press: Voices of Protest and Resistance, 1880–1960*, Cambridge University Press, 1997

I.B. Tabata, *The All African Convention*, Johannesburg People's Press, Johannesburg, 1950

I.B. Tabata, *The Boycott as Weapon of Struggle*, All African Convention Committee, Cape Town, 1952

Oliver Tambo, *Preparing for Power: Oliver Tambo Speaks* (compiled by Adelaide Tambo), Heinemann Educational Books, London, 1987

Margaret Thatcher, *The Downing Street Years*, HarperCollins, London, 1993

Can Themba (ed. Essop Patel), *The World of Can Themba*, Ravan Press, Johannesburg, 1985

Leonard Thompson, *The Political Mythology of Apartheid*, Yale University Press, New Haven, 1985

Leonard Thompson, *A History of South Africa*, Yale University Press, New Haven and London, 1995

Truth and Reconciliation Commission, *Truth and Reconciliation Commission of South Africa Report*, Vols 1–5, TRC, Cape Town, 1998

Desmond Tutu (ed. John Allen), *The Rainbow People of God*, Doubleday, London, 1994

Humphrey Tyler, *Life in the Time of Sharpeville*, Kwela Books, Cape Town, 1995

United Nations Centre Against Apartheid Notes and Documents, 'Observance of Mr Nelson R. Mandela's Sixtieth Birthday', Aug. 1978

United Nations Department of Public Information, *The United Nations and Apartheid, 1948–1994*, New York, 1994

United States Senate Hearings Before the Subcommittee on African Affairs of the Committee on Foreign Relations, 94th Congress, Second Session on South Africa, *South Africa: US Policy and the Role of US Corporations*, US Government Printing Office, Washington DC, 1977

W.P. van Schoor, *The Origin and Development of Segregation in South Africa*, Teachers' League of South Africa, Cape Town, 1951

Frederik van Zyl Slabbert, *The Last White Parliament*, Sidgwick & Jackson, London, 1985

Randolph Vigne, *Liberals Against Apartheid: A History of the Liberal Party of South Africa, 1953–68*, Macmillan Press Ltd, Basingstoke, 1997

Patti Waldmeir, *Anatomy of a Miracle: The End of Apartheid and the Birth of the New South Africa*, Viking, London, 1997

Frank Welsh, *A History of South Africa*, HarperCollins, London, 1998

T.R.H. White, 'Z.K. Matthews and the Formation of the ANC Youth League', *Kleio*, No.XXVII, 1995

Quintin Whyte, *Behind the Racial Tensions in South Africa*, South African Institute of Race Relations, Johannesburg, 1953

Brian Willan (ed.), *Sol Plaatje: Selected Writings*, Witwatersrand University Press, Johannesburg, 1996

Gordon Winter, *Inside BOSS: South Africa's Secret Police*, Penguin, Middlesex, 1981

Gordon Winter, 'Inside BOSS and After', *Lobster*, No.18, 1989

Donald Woods, *Biko*, Paddington Press, New York and London, 1978

Bob Woodward, *Veil: The Secret Wars of the CIA 1981–1987*, Simon & Schuster, London, 1987

Woodrow Wyatt (ed. Sarah Curtis), *The Journals of Woodrow Wyatt, Vol.1*, Macmillan, London, 1998

D.M. Zwelonke (pseudonym), *Robben Island*, Heinemann African Writers Series, London, 1973

INDEX